Constructivist Methods for Teaching in Diverse Middle-Level Classrooms

Constructivist Methods for Teaching in Diverse Middle-Level Classrooms

Kenneth T. Henson
The Citadel

Boston   New York   San Francisco
Mexico City   Montreal   Toronto   London   Madrid   Munich   Paris
Hong Kong   Singapore   Tokyo   Cape Town   Sydney

Series Editor: Traci Mueller
Editorial Assistant: Krista Price
Marketing Manager: Elizabeth Fogarty
Editorial-Production Service: Omegatype Typography, Inc.
Manufacturing Buyer: Andrew Turso
Composition and Prepress Buyer: Linda Cox
Cover Administrator: Kristina Mose-Libon
Interior Design: Studio Montage
Photo Research: Katharine S. Cook
Electronic Composition: Omegatype Typography, Inc.

For related titles and support materials, visit our online catalog at www.ablongman.com.

Copyright © 2004 Pearson Education, Inc.

All rights reserved. No part of the material protected by this copyright notice may be reproduced or utilized in any form or by any means, electronic or mechanical, including photocopying, recording, or by any information storage and retrieval system, without written permission from the copyright owner.

To obtain permission(s) to use material from this work, please submit a written request to Allyn and Bacon, Permissions Department, 75 Arlington Street, Boston, MA 02116 or fax your request to 617-848-7320.

Between the time Website information is gathered and published, some sites may have closed. Also, the transcription of URLs can result in typographical errors. The publisher would appreciate notification where these errors occur so that they may be corrected in subsequent editions.

Library of Congress Cataloging-in-Publication Data

Henson, Kenneth T.
    Constructivist methods for teaching in diverse middle-level classrooms / Kenneth T. Henson.
      p. cm.
    Includes bibliographical references and index.
    ISBN 0-205-39181-8 (alk. paper)
     1. Middle school teaching—United States.   2. Constructivism (Education)—United States.
I. Title.
LB1623.5.H46 2004
373.1102—dc21

2003049608

Printed in the United States of America

10 9 8 7 6 5 4 3 2 1   08 07 06 05 04 03

Photo Credits: p. 1: Comstock Royalty Free Division; pp. 30, 173, 225, 290, 321, 351: Will Hart; p. 57: provided by the author; p. 85: Brian Smith; pp. 116, 250: Tom Lindfors Photography; p. 137: Bill Aron/PhotoEdit.

Brief Contents

PART 1 — TEACHING AND YOU 1
Chapter 1 Teaching and You 1

PART 2 — PLANNING 30
Chapter 2 Using Performance Objectives 30
Chapter 3 Long-Range Planning 57
Chapter 4 Planning Daily Lessons 85

PART 3 — ASSESSMENT 116
Chapter 5 Evaluation 116
Chapter 6 Test Construction, Administration, and Scoring 137

PART 4 — PROVIDING FOR INDIVIDUAL DIFFERENCES 173
Chapter 7 Individualizing Instruction 173
Chapter 8 Teaching in Multicultural Settings 225

PART 5 — TEACHING STRATEGIES AND COMMUNICATIONS 250
Chapter 9 Teaching Strategies 250
Chapter 10 Communications 290

PART 6 — CLASSROOM MOTIVATION AND DISCIPLINE 321
Chapter 11 Motivation 321
Chapter 12 From Discipline to Self-Discipline 351

Contents

Foreword   xiii
Preface   xv

PART 1
TEACHING AND YOU   1

Chapter 1
Teaching and You   1

Objectives   1

Connecting Statements   2

The Teaching Profession   3

The Teacher's Attitude   4

Constructivism   11

The Role of Constructivist Teachers   15

The Case: Substituting Involvement for Apathy   17

Cooperative Learning Programs   20

Preparing Students to Participate in Cooperative Learning   23

Conducting Research   24

Using Research to Improve Teaching   25

Benefits of Conducting Research   25

Vignettes   26

Summary   27

Recap of Major Ideas   27

Activity   27

Looking Ahead   27

References   27

PART 2
PLANNING   30

Chapter 2
Using Performance Objectives   30

Objectives   30

Connecting Statements   31

Which Comes First, Content or Objectives?   32

National Standards   33

Outcome-Based Education   34

Education Expectations: Aims, Goals, and Objectives   34

Performance Objectives in the Three Domains   37

The Case: Professional Learning Communities   47

Vignettes   52

Summary   54

Recap of Major Ideas   54

Activities   54

Looking Ahead   55

References   55

Chapter 3
Long-Range Planning 57

   Objectives *57*
   Connecting Statements *58*
   Curriculum Determiners 59
   Poverty and Schooling 61
   Concept Development 62
   Concept Mapping/Cognitive Mapping 64
   The Question of Content 64
   The Case: Planning for Student Engagement 66
   Reaching Higher Levels of Thinking 73
   The Unit Plan 75
   Vignettes *81*
   Summary *82*
   Recap of Major Ideas *82*
   Activities *82*
   Looking Ahead *83*
   References *83*

Chapter 4
Planning Daily Lessons 85

   Objectives *85*
   Connecting Statements *86*
   Creating Daily Lesson Plans 87
   The Daily Lesson Plan 87
   Applying Constructivism to Daily Planning 89
   The Curriculum 92
   Implementing Daily Lesson Plans 93
   Learning Cycle Theory 95
   Planning Ways to Involve Students 95
   Homework 100
   The Case: Sic Semper "Huh?" 101
   Parent Involvement 108
   Sample Daily Lesson Plans 109
   Vignettes *111*
   Summary *112*
   Recap of Major Ideas *113*
   Activities *113*
   Looking Ahead *113*
   References *113*

PART 3
ASSESSMENT 116

Chapter 5
Evaluation 116

   Objectives *116*
   Connecting Statements *117*
   Past Use of Evaluation in Schools 118
   Formative Evaluation 119
   Summative Evaluation 121
   Competitive Evaluation 121
   The Case: Classroom Microsociety 124
   Noncompetitive Evaluation 129
   Grading 130
   Vignettes *133*
   Summary *134*
   Recap of Major Ideas *134*

Activities 135
Looking Ahead 135
References 135

Chapter 6
Test Construction, Administration, and Scoring 137

Objectives 137
Connecting Statements 138
The Teacher's Responsibility 139
Curriculum Alignment and Authentic Tests 139
Types of Tests 143
The Purpose of Testing 145
Test Construction 146
Writing Test Questions 148
Higher-Level Questions: Cognitive Domain 154
The Case: Assessment and Teaming: Meeting Everyone's Expectations 155
Affective Domain 163
Questioning Techniques 164
Test Administration 165
Accountability: Standardized and Alternative Tests 166
Giving the Test 166
Test Scoring 167
Returning Tests 168
Vignettes 168
Summary 170
Recap of Major Ideas 170
Activities 170
Looking Ahead 171
References 171

PART 4
PROVIDING FOR INDIVIDUAL DIFFERENCES 173

Chapter 7
Individualizing Instruction 173

Objectives 173
Connecting Statements 175
The Need to Individualize 175
In-Class Ability Grouping 180
Interclass Ability Grouping 182
Grade Contracts 183
Using Instructional Models 183
Matching Students' Learning Styles and Teachers' Teaching Styles 187
Using Computers to Individualize Instruction 192
Programs for At-Risk Students 192
Special Education 195
The Case: Doing What Makes Sense 198
Gifted and Talented Students 211
Underachievers 215
Vignettes 218
Summary 219
Recap of Major Ideas 220
Activities 220
Looking Ahead 221
References 221

Chapter 8
Teaching in Multicultural Settings 225

Objectives 225
Connecting Statements 226

Diverse Classrooms: Opportunity for All 227
Taking a Positive Approach 228
Personalizing Teaching 228
A Reason for Optimism 230
The Teacher's Decision 231
The Case: A Constructivist Approach to Teaching How Polls Work 233

The Teacher's Role 238
Selecting Ethnic Materials 241
Academic Achievement by Everyone 243
The Teacher's Wider Role 243
Using Process to Praise Diversity 243

Vignettes 245
Summary 247
Recap of Major Ideas 247
Activities 247
Looking Ahead 247
References 247

PART 5
TEACHING STRATEGIES AND COMMUNICATIONS 250

Chapter 9
Teaching Strategies 250

Objectives 250
Connecting Statements 251

Developing Lessons 252
The Lecture 253
The Case Study Method 258
Tutoring 260
Inquiry Learning 262
The Case: Making Connections 265
Questioning 268
Discovery Learning 273
Simulation Games 276
Story Telling 280
Cooperative Learning 280

Vignettes 284

Summary 285
Recap of Major Ideas 286
Activities 286
Looking Ahead 286
References 286

Chapter 10
Communications 290

Objectives 290
Connecting Statements 291

The Need for Communication Skills 292
Messages to Communicate 295
Verbal Communication Skills 297
Classifying Questions 301
The Case: From Empowerment to Leadership: Transforming a Problem into an Opportunity 303

Activities   135
Looking Ahead   135
References   135

Chapter 6
Test Construction, Administration, and Scoring   137

Objectives   137

Connecting Statements   138

The Teacher's Responsibility   139

Curriculum Alignment and Authentic Tests   139

Types of Tests   143

The Purpose of Testing   145

Test Construction   146

Writing Test Questions   148

Higher-Level Questions: Cognitive Domain   154

The Case: Assessment and Teaming: Meeting Everyone's Expectations   155

Affective Domain   163

Questioning Techniques   164

Test Administration   165

Accountability: Standardized and Alternative Tests   166

Giving the Test   166

Test Scoring   167

Returning Tests   168

Vignettes   168
Summary   170
Recap of Major Ideas   170
Activities   170
Looking Ahead   171
References   171

PART 4
PROVIDING FOR INDIVIDUAL DIFFERENCES   173

Chapter 7
Individualizing Instruction   173

Objectives   173

Connecting Statements   175

The Need to Individualize   175

In-Class Ability Grouping   180

Interclass Ability Grouping   182

Grade Contracts   183

Using Instructional Models   183

Matching Students' Learning Styles and Teachers' Teaching Styles   187

Using Computers to Individualize Instruction   192

Programs for At-Risk Students   192

Special Education   195

The Case: Doing What Makes Sense   198

Gifted and Talented Students   211

Underachievers   215

Vignettes   218
Summary   219
Recap of Major Ideas   220
Activities   220
Looking Ahead   221
References   221

Chapter 8
Teaching in Multicultural Settings 225

Objectives 225
Connecting Statements 226
Diverse Classrooms: Opportunity for All 227
Taking a Positive Approach 228
Personalizing Teaching 228
A Reason for Optimism 230
The Teacher's Decision 231
The Case: A Constructivist Approach to Teaching How Polls Work 233

The Teacher's Role 238
Selecting Ethnic Materials 241
Academic Achievement by Everyone 243
The Teacher's Wider Role 243
Using Process to Praise Diversity 243

Vignettes 245
Summary 247
Recap of Major Ideas 247
Activities 247
Looking Ahead 247
References 247

PART 5
TEACHING STRATEGIES AND COMMUNICATIONS 250

Chapter 9
Teaching Strategies 250

Objectives 250
Connecting Statements 251
Developing Lessons 252
The Lecture 253
The Case Study Method 258
Tutoring 260
Inquiry Learning 262
The Case: Making Connections 265
Questioning 268
Discovery Learning 273
Simulation Games 276
Story Telling 280
Cooperative Learning 280
Vignettes 284

Summary 285
Recap of Major Ideas 286
Activities 286
Looking Ahead 286
References 286

Chapter 10
Communications 290

Objectives 290
Connecting Statements 291
The Need for Communication Skills 292
Messages to Communicate 295
Verbal Communication Skills 297
Classifying Questions 301
The Case: From Empowerment to Leadership: Transforming a Problem into an Opportunity 303

The Questioning Grid 309
Reinforcement 310
Review 310
Nonverbal Communication Skills 311
Beyond the Curriculum 315
Effective Schools Research 315

Vignettes 316
Summary 317
Recap of Major Ideas 317
Activities 318
Looking Ahead 318
References 318

PART 6
CLASSROOM MOTIVATION AND DISCIPLINE 321

Chapter 11
Motivation 321

Objectives 321
Connecting Statements 322

Importance of Motivating 323
Extrinsic versus Intrinsic Motivation 323
Motivating Students in Multicultural Classrooms 324
Student Attitudes toward the Subject 325
Student Attitudes toward Themselves 326
Student Attitudes toward the Teacher 329
The Role of Humor 331
Enthusiasm 332
The Case: The Role of Dispositions in Becoming an Effective Teacher 333
Using Technology 336
Using Space 336
Keeping Students Challenged 337
Clarifying Goals and Procedures 339
Using Students' Opinions 339
Student Contracts as Motivators 339
Grades, Tests, Projects 340

Other Strategies 341

Vignettes 345
Summary 347
Recap of Major Ideas 347
Activities 348
Looking Ahead 348
References 348

Chapter 12
From Discipline to Self-Discipline 351

Objectives 351
Connecting Statements 352

A Preview of Discipline 353
Discipline: A Definition 356
Desirable Teacher Attitudes toward Discipline 357
Teacher Efficacy 358
A Focus on Learning 361
Using Theories 362
The Case: Abandoned Adolescence and a Cry for Help 369

The Case: Expecting the Unexpected   374
Classroom Management (Discipline) Models   376
Models Developed Specifically for Education   377
Trends in Discipline Today   379
The Cascade Model for Classroom Discipline   380
Avoiding Discipline Problems   382
Dealing with Problems   384
Vignettes   388
Summary   389
Recap of Major Ideas   389
Activities   390
References   390

Name Index   393

Subject Index   399

Foreword

Throughout most of the twentieth century, two very different worldviews have struggled for hegemony in American life. The terms *conservative* and *liberal* are the words most often used to describe these very different perspectives, although those labels have lost some of their usefulness in recent years. Those who hold to each view, however labeled, tend to have very different ideas about such heady topics as human nature, the role of government in human life, and most certainly, about the process of education. Over the last two decades, the conservative worldview, or paradigm, has attracted more and more adherents, and American education is currently very much under the influence of a conservative way of thinking about curriculum, teaching, and learning.

Advocates of a conservative perspective in education are perhaps best known for their enthusiastically fervent embrace of standards-based reform. Those who subscribe to this currently dominant conservative paradigm often seem to have more than a little pessimism about human nature and mistrust of both students and teachers at the heart of their ideas about how education ought to be conducted. I am persuaded that this is a group of people who honestly believe the following:

- Most students, and certainly most educators, cannot be trusted.
- Most students do not want to learn.
- The ability to pass examinations is the best criterion for selecting and grouping students for learning.
- Lecture equals teaching.
- Valued knowledge comes from the accumulation of brick upon brick of facts,
- Externally derived standards, objective examinations, and harsh accountability programs are the key to current reform.
- A free public education is truly inconsistent with the triumph of capitalism and private enterprise and, therefore, public education must be dismantled.

There are many of us in middle school education today, who hold tightly to a very different set of assumptions, to a dramatically different worldview than the dominant Washington and state capitol model. I am bold enough to hope that many of the readers of Professor Henson's book will subscribe to very different ideas about learners and learning than those put forward by many advocates of standards-based reform. Middle school educators are, together, representatives of a different point of view, one that is 500 years old, a view outlined well in this textbook. Today's middle school educators carry a banner first unfurled in the eighteenth century Enlightenment in Europe, following five centuries of intellectual and religious darkness. We carry a banner first held high by Jean Jacques Rousseau, and carried forward by Johann Pestalozzi, Friedrich Froebel, then Maria Montessori, Horace Mann, and into the twentieth century by Jean Piaget, John Dewey, A. S. Neill, Paolo Friere, John Holt, Jonathan Kozol, and Carl Rogers, More recently, we recognize the leadership of middle school educators such as Bill Alexander, Don Eichhorn, Conrad Toepfer, Jim Beane, Gordon Vars, and John Lounsbury.

Each of these leaders has believed and acted on the assumption that human beings are basically good and, given a proper education and appropriate developmental experiences and a real chance to do the right thing, can grow to become adults who are wise and good, loving, and kind. Those leaders, and now we, believe that education is a relationship process, a process based on trust and caring for the persons involved. We believe that economic hardship and isolation, the dramatic increase in persistent poverty, the destruction of American family life, and the harsh impact of violence, divorce, homelessness, forced mobility, hopelessness, and alcohol and drug abuse are the root causes of school failure. We assert that the so-called failure of school reform is the fault, not of learners, teachers, and principals, or even education professors, but of selfish politicians, bureaucrats, and corporate CEO's who do not have the courage to speak the truth or provide the real leadership and resources required for permanent improvement.

Most important, middle school education is firmly rooted in an irrevocable commitment to the characteristics and needs of American young adolescents. We have faith in them; we think that young adolescents are basically good human beings who are experiencing an incredibly important developmental period in their lives. We accept the thesis that education should therefore be developmentally appropriate. We believe that such a developmentally appropriate education, so crucial to the future lives of today's young adolescents, can only begin with a sharp focus on the authentic needs of those learners, not with a curriculum designed by the state government or national associations. We believe, as Ken Henson does, that young adolescents are naturally motivated and capable to constructing their own learning experiences, based on what they already know and what they perceive a real need to know. We are convinced that a truly vital education for today's youth is constructivist, democratic, student-focused, interdisciplinary, and cooperative and, once again, originates with the characteristics and needs of the learner.

In times like these, it may be helpful to recall the words of old Sam Houston. Most students of American history seem to believe that Houston was right when he urged his fellow Texas pioneers to "Do right, and damn the consequences." In the context of the particular challenges in middle school teacher education today, Houston's words mean that middle school teacher educators must speak out loudly about what we believe, not because our careers are in jeopardy, but because the education of millions of young adolescents depends on what we say and do in the years ahead. We are called to act because the whole paradigm of public life as we have known it, far beyond public education, is threatened as never before.

Ken Henson's *Constructivist Methods for Teaching in Diverse Middle-Level Classrooms* is a timely and practical guide for implementing classroom experiences that are congruent with the best thinking about young adolescents and their educational needs. Teachers who work hard at mastering and implementing the strategies outlined in Henson's text will, at the day's end, know that what they did was effective and, most important, what was right.

Paul S. George
Distinguished Professor of Education
University of Florida

Preface

Effective teaching in the middle grades requires the teacher to have a repertoire of strategies and know when to use each. Guskey (1990, p. 12) explains, "It is only when several strategies are carefully and systematically integrated that substantial improvements in learning become possible." *Constructive Methods for Teaching in Diverse Middle-Level Classrooms* is designed to prepare prospective middle-level teachers for their first classroom experience and to help in-service teachers improve their teaching skills. Each of the themes addresses a major goal set by the Carnegie Council on Academic Development or by the National Middle School Association particularly selected for middle-level programs. In particular, the Carnegie goals are (1) ensuring success for all early adolescents, (2) involving the family in their children's education, (3) improving academic performance through better health practices, (4) empowering teachers, and (5) connecting the learning program with the community. The National Middle School Association goals are listed in Chapter 1 on page 7.

Themes and Pedagogy

Proactive Teacher Theme

Proactive teachers anticipate coming events and prepare for them. The National Middle School Association (NMSA) recommends the empowering of teachers. Empowered teachers are proactive. They do not expect things not to work and then blame the administration, the students, the lack of family involvement, and other forces in the community and world. Instead, they expect success and they work in advance to ensure that it happens. There are many reasons why middle-level teachers should be proactive. First, the rapid change that is always associated with preadolescents brings with it an almost daily series of crises, and when a crisis develops, often our first thought is, "I wish I had prepared for this." Sometimes teachers who anticipate crises can prevent them, or at least adjust to minimize the damage. A second reason for being proactive is that, by anticipating events, teachers can often derive benefits from these events that otherwise would be missed. Put another way, sometimes an unwanted interruption can be turned into a welcomed opportunity. Perhaps an even greater need for anticipating and planning for the future is the value such activities offer the developing teacher. John Dewey (1938) believed that projecting into the future and adjusting the present accordingly was essential for cognitive growth: "Growth in judgment and understanding is essentially growth in ability to form purposes and select and arrange means for their realization" (p. 104). And one might also note that forming purposes and selecting and arranging means for their realization is what middle-level teachers do every hour of every day.

Too often the practitioner looks for a technique to cope with a challenging situation, without taking time to question its causes. This is tantamount to asking for a bucket of water without exploring the cause of the fire. Reflection is a valued skill for teachers and is encouraged throughout this book, but those teachers who live only in the present, reacting to the past, find fires breaking out all around them; they seem to live in a continuous state of crisis. Experienced middle-level teachers—even those with only one year of practice—are able to predict many future events. For example, middle-level teachers know that, sooner or later, a student will transfer to their school who speaks little or no English. Without proper preparation, students will have no option but to ignore their new classmate. New students need help, and those who are fortunate to be more stable can benefit from learning to reach out to others. All teachers have a choice. They can either perceive such situations as unfortunate and unavoidable, and wait helplessly for them to occur, or they can anticipate and prepare students for these events. By being proactive, teachers can actually help *shape* the future for themselves and their students.

Each chapter in this book includes two types of activities designed to help future teachers learn how to project and plan for future classroom events. Boxes titled *Teacher as Proactive Decision Maker* appear in each chapter. Each box describes a common situation with a parallel column of proactive alternatives. Teachers will need these skills to keep their classrooms running smoothly.

Effective teachers aim higher than at just keeping the status quo. John Dewey (1938) said, "In a certain sense every experience should do something to prepare a person for later experiences of a deeper and more expansive quality. That is the very meaning of growth, continuity, reconstruction of experience" (p. 47). Each chapter also has one or more boxes titled Proactive Exercise. Like the Teacher as Proactive Decision Maker boxes, these boxes describe situations to be resolved, but they go further, asking teachers to use their imaginations to create growth experiences and improved classrooms. These exercises can turn otherwise frustrating and fruitless events into growth opportunities.

Constructivist Theme

Constructivist teachers recognize that the only way to really learn is by connecting new information with prior knowledge, thus creating new knowledge. Constructivism is an excellent way to reach at least two goals set for middle-level teachers. First, it is an ideal way to personalize learning. Second, constructivism is an effective method for reaching *all* students. In constructivist-based cooperative learning groups, success for some requires the success of all. Constructivism is both old and new. Parts of the constructivist theory have been developing for centuries. John Dewey did a good job pulling them together over a half-century ago, and therefore he will be quoted repeatedly. However, two points should be made here. First, although these quotations are some sixty years old, the effective schools studies of the 1990s and early 2000s are validating these practices. Second, constructivism is still developing and should never be considered complete.

According to the constructivists, creating new knowledge requires at least two types of necessary connections: cognitive and personal. Each chapter is prefaced by a "graphic organizer," a visual drawing that shows the major ideas in the chapter and how these ideas relate to each other. Visual learners will find these drawings helpful in providing them an advanced feel (or articulation) for the nature of the chapter. John Dewey (1938) said, "It is also essential that there be some advance made in conscious articulation of facts and ideas." David Ausubel (1980) called for advance organizers to focus students' attention on important ideas as they are being introduced. Following each graphic organizer is a list of approximately ten objectives to extend students' focus on the chapter. Students often perceive a finite quality to each chapter, as though it were an entity, disjointed from the rest of the book. Included in the material at the end of each chapter is a short statement titled Looking Ahead. These statements connect all chapters, forming a whole. Each chapter also has a Recap of Major Ideas section, which you should find useful to preview and review or summarize the chapter and which students may find useful in preparing for exams.

All of the pedagogical features mentioned thus far (graphic organizers, Looking Ahead, and Recap of Major Ideas) are aimed at making cognitive connections. Such cognitive connections are essential to learning, but constructivists understand that even when important ideas are pulled together, they still will not be learned unless the information has personal meaning to the students. To invite students to become personally engaged with information, several pedagogical constructs have been designed. Immediately following the Objectives in each chapter is a list of Connecting Statements. Each of these statements asks students to tell whether they agree or disagree with the statement. Some of these statements are true; others are not.

At some time or another all of us have caught ourselves just reading words, without extracting any meaning at all. This occurs when we fail to relate the words to our prior personal experiences. John Dewey (1938) said: "To reflect is to look back over what has been done so as to extract the net meanings which are the capital stock for intelligent dealing with further experiences. It [reflection] is the heart of intellectual organization and of the disciplined mind" (p. 110). Throughout the chapters are boxes titled Reflection. These boxes are saying: "Wake up and tie this information to previous knowledge."

Some students will want to get more deeply involved with the chapter content than others. Each chapter includes one or more Case Studies. The Case Studies are followed by a few questions, which further challenge students to get involved. All case studies describe real school experiences and most were written collaboratively by educators who work in these schools and educators at nearby universities.

Some students will want to pursue some of the topics even beyond the chapter. To assist them with this goal, a list of References and a list of Suggested Readings are provided.

Current education reformers endorse authentic assessment and authentic experiences. When used in education circles, authentic means real or lifelike situations. The importance of authentic experiences can be seen in an expression that John Dewey (1938) made more than sixty years ago: "Perhaps the greatest of all pedagogical fallacies is the notion that a person learns only the particular thing he is studying at the time. Collateral learning is the way of formation of enduring attitudes, of likes and dislikes, may be and often is much more important than the spelling lesson or lesson in geography or history that is learned. For these attitudes are fundamentally what count in the future" (p. 49).

Such collateral learning occurs only in a context that permits people to experience feelings. Textbook information and direct instruction rarely provide such a context. Therefore, this book includes Teacher of the Year boxes, which enable readers to visit outstanding teachers in their classrooms. These teachers have been recognized as the best teachers in their respective states. That many of their messages are profoundly insightful should come as no surprise. Furthermore, many of these statements are rich with feelings.

Multicultural Theme

A common axiom heard among educational reformers today is "All students can and will learn." This is also a national goal for all middle-level students. This mandate makes many contemporary and prospective middle-school teachers nervous. Frankly, many beginning middle-level teachers are afraid they will not be able to meet the various needs in their multicultural classrooms. The rapidly growing minority student body and the much slower growth in the number of minority teachers intensify this problem.

To strengthen the practical dimension of the multicultural theme, for each chapter, a separate team of university/public middle school teachers was invited to write a case study revealing a success story describing a unique approach they are now using that is working effectively to meet the needs of one or more minority students. Some of these case studies involve African American students, some Native Americans, and some Mexican American students.

Both the constructivist theme and the multicultural theme are woven tightly into the major parts of each chapter of this book; both themes are included in the Objectives, Connecting Statements, Recap of Major Ideas, and Activities. The following tables show the extent to which these themes are covered.

Constructivism

Chapters	Objectives	Connecting Statements	Activities
1	5, 7, 8, 9		
2	9	4, 6, 8, 9	4, 5
3	2	7, 10	5
4	8	3, 4, 5, 6	1, 3
5	9	2, 3, 4, 6, 7	3, 4
6	8	2, 5, 8, 12	1, 5
7	3, 8, 9, 10	1, 2, 3, 4, 5, 7, 8, 9	1, 3, 4, 5
8	9	1, 2, 3, 4	3
9	6, 7, 9	1, 2, 6, 9, 10	1, 2
10	4, 5, 6	4, 5, 7, 8, 9, 10, 11, 12	3
11	4, 9, 12	3, 5, 6, 8	2
12	1, 9	5, 7	5

Multiculturalism

Chapters	Objectives	Connecting Statements	Recap of Major Ideas	Activities
1	4, 7			
2	2, 4, 7	2, 5, 6, 7, 9	1, 2, 3, 4, 7, 8, 10	4, 5
3	9	4, 5, 6, 7, 8	4, 6, 7, 8, 9	2, 5
4	7, 8	2	10	5
5	11	11, 12	11	2
6	10	13, 14	12, 13, 14	5
7	1, 2, 3	11, 12	15, 16	6
8	1, 2, 3, 4, 5, 6, 7, 8	1, 2, 3, 4, 5, 6	1, 2, 3, 4, 5, 6, 7, 8, 9, 10, 11	1, 2, 3
9	11	10	11	4, 5
10	10, 11	11	10, 11	4
11	9	8, 9	4, 8, 9	5
12	12	2, 13	10	5

Style

This book uses a straightforward writing style. The intent is not to impress but to communicate, clearly and easily. No one should have to read a paragraph a second time to understand it. Jargon is avoided, and new terms are set in boldface and defined.

Objectives

John Dewey (1938) said, "It is also essential that there be some advance made in conscious articulation of facts and ideas" (p. 90). David Ausubel (1980) called for advance organizers to focus students' attention on important ideas. Each chapter begins with a set of objectives. These objectives focus the reader's attention on the most important concepts.

Connecting Statements

Because middle-level students are at the stage in their lives during which change occurs most rapidly, these students often feel disconnected to the world around them. Each chapter in this book contains connecting statements designed to help you help your students make a variety of necessary connections, including connections among subjects; connections among levels of content within the same discipline, the school, and the home; and connections between students' personal lives and the content they are studying. These statements are not presented as facts to be accepted but as ideas to be pondered.

Case Studies

Each chapter includes one or two case studies to enable the readers to see the theory of the chapter in action. Each case study is written by a middle school teacher who has received the Teacher of the Year award for his or her state. Each case study describes a program that has been highly effective in meeting the needs of all students in modern middle-level multicultural classrooms. These programs have a wide geographic (coast-to-coast) representation and include rural, urban, and suburban settings. Each is followed by a few questions to prompt readers to sift out relevant information and issues and make decisions. The cases give support to two major themes of this book: teachers as proactive decision makers and meeting the needs of all students.

Teacher of the Year

Although this book is grounded in research and theory, it is also grounded in practice. Throughout the chapters, some of the best middle school teachers of all times share their tips on how to be a more effective middle-level teacher.

Activities

This book does not pretend to have all the information that future teachers will need to be effective in the classroom. On the contrary, hopefully it will raise many questions and will stimulate the reader to investigate further the issues it raises. The section titled Activities is included to achieve this goal.

Looking Ahead

John Dewey (1938) said, "The principle of continuity in its educational application means, nevertheless, that the future has to be taken into account at every stage of the educational process" (p. 47). Dewey was referring to both the long-term future and the immediate or short-term future. Students often view textbooks as a collection of independent chapters. The textbook should be more. Each chapter is written and placed to build on previous chapters. At the end of each chapter, a short section titled Looking Ahead is included to make this connection with the following chapter.

Tips for Teachers

Occasional practical suggestions will appear throughout the text in boxes titled *Tips for Teachers*. These will offer you opportunities to connect your own thoughts to the respective chapters in which they appear.

References

This book is rich in documentation, and each chapter contains many references to recent literature. The Reference section gives the readers a way to access the rich body of knowledge that is available to today's teachers.

Organization

Part One: Teaching and You

Part One has only one chapter, yet it is perhaps the most powerful part in the book because it forms the framework or the support structure for the book. Effective teachers—those whose students learn to their maximum potential—harbor several beliefs that shape their behavior, beliefs about their students and their students' potential as well as their own potential, beliefs about their roles as teacher and life-long learner, and what is possible when they take a proactive, decision-making posture, confident and determined to shape both the present and future to ensure that all of their students learn to their maximum potential. The first half of this chapter identifies these essential attitudes. Uneven growth rates among middle-level students accentuate the need for middle-level teachers to develop those skills that will make them confident in their students' ability to succeed and their own ability to ensure that this happens.

Constructivism is a theory that describes the teacher beliefs and teacher behaviors needed to guide students in activities what will ensure their cognitive growth. The second half of this chapter defines and discusses constructivism. A major part of this theory is *cooperative learning*, a program designed for teachers to use to help students learn to help each other learn. Cooperative learning is defined and discussed. Three sample cooperative programs are described in this first chapter. Because constructivism requires teachers and students to negotiate (collaboratively create) meaning, and action research is an excellent means for creating learning, the last part of this chapter discusses the constructivist teacher's role in action research.

Constructivists view all learning as temporary. Teachers must be in a continuous state of reshaping their understandings. This calls for reading professional literature, conducting action research, and collaborating, as when involved with students in writing and dialogueing. These are the topics that conclude Part One.

Part Two: Planning

Successful teaching results from effective planning. Good planning requires a working knowledge of behavioral objectives. Chapter 2 prepares you to write good objectives at all levels of all three domains of the educational taxonomies.

Although school systems and state departments of education frequently give to teachers curriculum guides and courses of study, teaching is a highly autonomous profession. Although national standards are to be met, ultimately you determine what to teach and what objective to pursue. Chapter 3 helps you examine the curriculum and design units to achieve the year's goals. Chapter 4 shows you how to reach each day's objectives by selecting appropriate content and activities and by sequencing them to facilitate students' mastery of the material.

Part Three: Assessment

Every teacher is responsible for testing and evaluation, terms that are frequently confused and misunderstood. Chapter 5 helps you understand the many uses of tests and evaluations in the classroom and alerts you to the changing role that national standards and standardized exams are playing as the new millennium begins. Most U.S. secondary and middle schools require grades, so you must learn all you can about constructing, administering, and scoring tests and about converting these results, along with other criteria, into grades. Because most teachers underuse formative evaluation and criterion-based evaluation, Chapter 5 explains their advantages for secondary and middle school teachers. Chapter 6 helps you construct, administer, and score tests for use in your classroom.

Part Four: Providing for Individual Differences

Early in their programs, most prospective teachers learn that, to be successful and enable students to attain a high level of achievement, they must meet all students' needs and interests. They quickly ask how this can be done in a class of thirty or so students whose needs and interests are so different. All teachers face this dilemma. Chapter 7 provides general information to help you develop an individualized approach to instruction. Chapter 8 acquaints you with the responsibilities and roles of teachers whose students come from different ethnic and cultural backgrounds.

Part Five: Teaching Strategies and Communications

Effective teachers take a definite approach to teaching each lesson. They select specific methods and develop them into more general and complex strategies. To do this well, a teacher must have a repertoire of methods from which to choose. Chapter 9 presents a variety of teaching methods. To help you select the most appropriate method for each lesson, the strengths and limitations of each method are discussed. To be effective, you must make strategies and methods come to life in the classroom. You do this by communicating effectively. Chapter 10 presents several verbal and nonverbal techniques to prepare you to communicate effectively.

Part Six: Classroom Motivation and Discipline

By this time you are probably wondering when we are going to get to the heart of the matter and discuss the teacher's role in the classroom. After all, such topics as discipline, classroom management, and motivation are the survival skills—without them, everything else you might learn about teaching becomes insignificant. Without good discipline, management, and motivation skills, today's teacher will have a short career. These skills are not merely desirable or important—they are indispensable.

As you read, think beyond the survival point. Effective instruction demands interaction with students. The higher levels of thinking are best achieved through dialectic teaching, in which the teacher and students share ideas. You must establish a climate in which student–student and teacher–student interactions occur freely.

Motivation is the key to effective classroom management. Put simply, students who are actively engaged in learning require less discipline effort from their teachers. Chapter 11 will strengthen your power to motivate your students.

The purpose of discipline and management is not to subdue students, but to align student behavior in positive directions. The ultimate goal is to move from a state of teacher-regulated discipline to student self-regulated discipline. This is the goal of Chapter 12.

Acknowledgments

Special thanks are given to those Teachers of the Year who contributed their tips to this text. I also want to thank all of the dedicated middle-level teachers and those educators who told their stories through the case studies in this book. Perhaps, like these dynamic educators, we all will learn to share the enthusiasm that comes from collaboratively reinventing our middle schools each day. Lastly, I would like to thank the following reviewers: Katharine G. Fralick, Plymouth State College; Mary Lynn Hamilton, University of Kansas; David C. Little, Samford University; Debra Pitton, Gustavus Adolphus College; Tracy W. Smith, Appalachian State University; Margie Stone, University of Wisconsin, Eau Claire; and Thomas Worley, Armstrong Atlantic State University.

References

Ausubel, D. P. (1980, Fall). Schemata, cognitive structure, and advance organizers: A reply to Anderson, Spire, and Anderson. *American Educational Research Journal,* 17, 400–404.

Dewey, J. (1938). Experience and education. 60th anniversary edition (1998). West Lafayette, IN. Kappa Delta Pi.

Guskey, T. R. (1990). Integrating innovations. *Educational Leadership,* 47(5), 11–15.

Constructivist Methods for Teaching in Diverse Middle-Level Classrooms

1

Teaching and You

If a teacher is indeed wise he does not bid you enter the house of his wisdom, but rather leads you to the threshold of your own mind.

Khalil Gibran (1965)

Objectives

- Describe the middle-level teacher's role in classroom success.
- Name two common teacher attitudes that promote learning.
- Name two common teacher attitudes that inhibit learning.
- Define constructivism.
- Explain the relationship between constructivism and cooperative learning.
- Name and describe three contributions that Lev Vygotsky made to constructivism.
- Name and describe three contributions that John Dewey made to constructivism.
- Describe recent changes in teacher behavior that improve classroom learning.
- Define and discuss the term *negotiating meaning*.
- Relate the goal, all students can and will learn, to the ever-increasing classroom diversity.
- Explain the middle-level teacher's responsibility for conducting research.
- Name and describe three programs that use constructivist theory.
- Explain how technology can and should be used to empower students.

TEACHING AND YOU

The Teaching Profession

Attitudes of Effective Teachers
- Positive View of Self
- Positive View of Students
- Life-Long Love of Learning
- Proactive Teacher
- Willingness to Share Power

Constructivism
- History & Development
- Philosophical Beliefs
- Psychological Beliefs
- Motivation Theory
- Nature & Organization of Knowledge

Role of Constructive Teachers
- Personal Approach
- Student Centered
- Problem Centered
- Major Concepts & Themes
- Small Groups

Cooperative Learning Programs
- History of
- Sample Programs
  - Jigsaw I
  - Jigsaw II
  - Service Learning

Vygotsky's Contributions
- Zone of Proximal Development
- Scaffolding
- Negotiate Learning
- Inner Speech
- Dialogueing
- Connections

U.S. Contributions
- Col. Francis Parker
- John Dewey
  — Learning by Doing
  — Cognitive Connections
  — Experience Connections
  — Personal Connections
  — Advance Organizers
  — Reflection
  — Collateral

Conducting Research
- Using Research to Improve Teaching
- Benefits to Teachers

Connecting Statements

	Agree	Disagree	Uncertain
1. Teachers' proper role with research is that of helping by collecting data for researchers to use.			
2. In the absence of creating new knowledge, learning is impossible.			
3. Parents should be involved more in the designing of curriculum and instruction.			
4. Constructivist teachers are more likely to introduce intellectual conflicts than answers.			
5. Constructivist teachers use students to help them teach.			
6. Intelligence quotients (IQs) remain relatively stable throughout life.			
7. Teachers' attitudes significantly affect the levels of achievement in their classrooms.			

The Teaching Profession

Congratulations! Of all the professions you might have chosen, none is more important than teaching, and no level is more exciting, challenging, or rewarding than the middle school. Whether you are just joining the profession or have been a teacher for years, this is an exciting, reforming profession that requires good teachers. The success of students in classrooms throughout the country hinges on the competency levels of their teachers. Teachers have always been known for their high level of dedication, an attitude that has brought a high level of satisfaction. Meek (1998), reporting on both the preparation and attitude of contemporary teachers, said: "Overall, this profile of U.S. teachers reveals a work force of committed and well-qualified U.S. teachers who find their work very satisfying." Ninety percent of all new teachers say that teaching requires more talent and harder work than many other professions, yet 96 percent say that it is work they love to do (Wadsworth, 2001). Furthermore, 98 percent of all administrators see the new teaching corps as highly motivated and energetic.

Clearly, teachers are the key to what happens in the classroom. A vast difference in academic attainment will be determined by whether teachers see their jobs as delivering services or as educating their students (Raywid, 1998). Nelson (1999) echoed this tribute to our teachers, saying: "In each classroom in this country there is a highly educated adult with the potential for creating meaningful learning environments that address the needs of all students" (p. 392).

U.S. schools are improving, and the public recognizes that progress. For the first time in the thirty-three year history of the Annual Phi Delta Kappa/Gallup Poll of the Public's Attitudes Toward the Public Schools (Rose & Gallup, 2001), the majority of Americans (51 percent) gave the schools an A or B rating. Recognizing that successful classrooms depend on two essential variables, what teachers know and how they use that knowledge, Linda Darling-Hammond (1998) said, "What teachers know and do is one of the most important influences on what students learn" (p. 6). After studying the research on the characteristics of **effective schools,** that is, schools with high academic success, Reynolds and Teddlie (2000, p. 136) reported that teachers in effective schools have a higher level of commitment than teachers in schools with less academic achievement.

John Steinbeck was insightful enough to realize that good teachers provide students with the motivation and skills needed to excel in all other professions. When invited to speak to the Kansas State Teachers Association, Steinbeck explained the importance of teachers:

My eleven-year-old son came to me recently and, in a tone of patient suffering, asked, "How much longer do I have to go to school?"

"About fifteen years," I said.

"Oh! Lord," he said despondently. "Do I have to?"

"I'm afraid so. It's terrible and I'm not going to try to tell you it isn't. But I can tell you this—if you are very lucky, you may find a teacher and this is a wonderful thing."

"Did you find one?"

"I found three," I said. . . .

My three had these things in common—they all loved what they were doing. They did not tell—they catalyzed a burning desire to know. . . . I shall speak only of my first teacher because, in addition to other things, she was very precious. She aroused us to shouting, book waving discussions. She had the noisiest class in school and didn't even seem to know it. We could never stick to the subject, geometry or the chanted recitation of the memorized phyla.

> Our speculation ranged the world. She breathed curiosity into us so that we brought in facts or truths shielded in our hands like captured fireflies. . . .
>
> She left her signature on us, the signature of the teacher who writes on minds. I suppose that, to a large extent, I am the unsigned manuscript of that high school teacher. What deathless power lies in the hands of such a person.
>
> I can tell my son who looks forward with horror to fifteen years of drudgery that somewhere in the dusty dark a magic may happen that will light up the years . . . if he is very lucky. . . .
>
> I have come to believe that a great teacher is a great artist and there are as few as there are any other great artists. It might even be the greatest of the arts, since the medium is the human mind and spirit. (National Education Association, 1959, 71)

Ironically, though he was not an educator, John Steinbeck recognized the importance of good teachers and identified several essential qualities for effective teaching. **Effective teaching** is teaching that leads all students to learn to their maximum potential. Effective teachers share certain attitudes and behaviors. This chapter examines some of these attitudes; the rest of the book is aimed at helping you put these attitudes into action.

Multiculturalism/Diversity

Multiculturalism is defined in many ways. To some, it refers to the physical presence of members of more than one culture assembled into one classroom. In this book, multiculturalism is used to refer to teacher attitudes and teaching practices that support the academic and social success of members from all cultures. A major goal set by the Carnegie Council on Adolescent Development for all middle-level schools is ensuring the academic success of all adolescents. This is the mission of all middle schools of the twenty-first century and therefore is the responsibility of all middle-level teachers. Multiculturalism recognizes that each student has his or her own heritage and has a right to that heritage. Multiculturalism further recognizes that each culture brings strengths to society. A common strength is a sense of belonging, a sense of pride in one's culture. Multiculturalism also recognizes that because of cultural and language differences, to have an equal opportunity to succeed in the classroom, teachers must make special efforts to accommodate members of various cultures.

Coupled closely with multiculturalism is the concept of **diversity.** Diversity is a set of beliefs in the worth and capability of all students and the practices teachers use to ensure that all individuals succeed. Following is a discussion of teacher attitudes that promote multiculturalism and diversity.

The Teacher's Attitude

A Positive View of Self

As John Steinbeck so clearly stated, good teachers make a difference. Effective middle-level teachers are dedicated to their job, and they respect and believe in themselves. This positive view of self includes a sense of **efficacy,** a belief in one's ability to do whatever must be done. Effective middle-level teachers believe in themselves and their ability to lead their students to succeed. Effective middle-level teachers know that they are ahead of their game; they are on the cutting edge of knowledge in their subject field and in their profession.

A Positive View of Students

John Steinbeck said something that suggests his teacher viewed her students positively: "In addition to other things, she was very precious." This sounds like a teacher who cared intensely for the academic and personal well-being of her students. Effective teachers care for and respect their students.

> **Teacher of the Year**
>
> I believe in treating students like fellow human beings who have feelings just like I do. They don't appreciate being embarrassed or humiliated or confronted with problems in front of their peers. But they do respond to kindness, encouragement, a friendly tease, and a smile. I try to teach manners in my classroom by being mannerly to my students.
>
> Former Nebraska Teacher of the Year Duane Obermier

Former Arizona Teacher of the Year Rachel Moreno (1999, p. 111) put it simply: "I touch kids' hearts." Effective schools research has shown that schools with consistently high academic success are characterized by a feeling of warmth toward students (Reynolds & Teddlie, 2000, p. 136). Another part of having a positive attitude toward students is having confidence in students' abilities. Effective teachers believe in the potential of their students, and they learn how to pass this sense of confidence on to their students, letting all students know they are valued. Students respond, in-kind. Parsley and Cocoran (2003) agree, "When students feel valued by their teachers, they are more willing to work harder at their assignments and comply with classroom rules." (p. 85)

John Steinbeck was right; good teachers can and do make a difference—but only if they possess the right skills and attitudes. You may be surprised when you read in Chapter 11 just how much a teacher's attitude can affect students' achievement. You must communicate to your students your belief that you can make a positive difference. Even the sequence of your actions on the first day of school communicates your competence (Slavin, 1998). Evidence that our teachers are getting better is found in the national test scores of minority students over the past several years. The inequity gap between African American and white students has been dropping. Differences in Scholastic Assessment Test (SAT) scores have declined and the National Assessment of Educational Progress (NAEP) difference between African American and white student scores has been cut in half.

Have you ever considered that students' perspectives differ greatly from those of their teachers? "They view learning only as the acquisition of knowledge" (Stefanich, 1990, p. 50). Students do not think of themselves as mastering knowledge, but as working to pass a test or please a teacher. We must teach them that knowledge is powerful, and we must help them learn to achieve, not for their parents or teachers but for themselves, and to demand the best from themselves and for themselves.

Teaching at the middle level is special: it is both especially challenging and especially rewarding, and it requires special attitudes and skills. Examine the priority events the National Middle School Association (NMSA) has set for middle-level education, shown in Figure 1.1 First, the existence of such a list is evidence that educators recognize that adolescents require a special kind of education, one especially tailored for them. A closer look at this list tells even more—much more, about the life and role of the middle-level teacher.

Folk singer Burl Ives sang a song titled "Mr. In-Between," which expressed the awkward nature of early adolescence. In that song, he used the lyric "nothing seems to fit," and he told how, at this awkward stage individuals are so concerned with how their peers see them that their primary goal in life is to be accepted by their peers. However, peer values and expectations often clash with home values and school values. The list of priorities in Figure 1.1 reflects these special qualities of preadolescence and adolescence.

A closer look at the list in Figure 1.1 shows that a special type of education is required if, indeed, a school is to be successful with this age group. Several priorities show that teachers of this level cannot be successful working alone in a traditional, self-contained classroom, focusing on one subject at a time. On the contrary, an interdisciplinary, cooperative, team approach is essential. The partners on this team must include all middle-level teachers of all subjects and other support personnel including school counselors and administrators, parents, and the students themselves. Above all, if this interdisciplinary curriculum is to be effective and, in Steinbeck's vernacular, is to "light up the world" for these students, it must be built not of teacher words but of student activities. Pennsylvania middle school teacher and Teacher of the Year Howard Selekman (1999, p. 59) said, "My best teaching occurs when my students are lighting the way through their cooperative discussion and problem solving, and I am a learner." Now let's examine other essential qualities of effective middle-level teachers.

Teacher as Proactive Decision Maker

Twenty-first century teachers work in complex, fast-paced, environments. Daily, literally hundreds of decisions must be made. Some of the events are spontaneous and unpredictable, but others are highly predictable. The section titled Teacher as Proactive Decision Maker will help you learn to anticipate situations that are predictable and, indeed, will go further and suggest some proactive alternatives—some actions you can take now that will help you prepare for these upcoming challenges. In many instances these suggestions will help you shape the future.

Classroom Situation

1. Your new teaching assignment may be in a school that is governed by a site-based council and you may be asked to serve on it.

2. Parents want to be involved more in their children's education.

3. Parents, teachers, and administrators may put the need to cover content above all other concerns.

4. You know that student involvement enhances learning.

Proactive Alternatives

Make a list of questions to ask a teacher who has served on a site-based council.

Practice your listening skills by refraining from speaking until the person you are talking to finishes.

List some meaningful ways you can let parents get involved in your classrooms.

Develop a survey to learn when parents would be available to participate in school activities.

Pull together some research to convince others that developing understanding occurs best in problem-solving classes and in student-active environments.

List five activities your students can use to develop important concepts.

Priority 1	Middle-level schools are recognized as a legitimate level of education, along with elementary and secondary schools.
Priority 2	Both curriculum and instruction become more relevant to the developmental characteristics of middle-level students.
Priority 3	Teams are organized or reorganized into interdisciplinary teams with shared responsibility for the same group of students.
Priority 4	Universities and colleges (nationwide) offer state-approved middle-level certification programs.
Priority 5	Public acceptance of the middle-school philosophy leads to a vision that supports the growth and development of middle-level schools.
Priority 6	Inservice/reeducation of existing middle-level and non-middle-level certified faculty is increased to implement and maintain knowledge of the middle-level child.
Priority 7	Cooperative learning and other heterogeneous strategies will replace current grouping and tracking strategies.
Priority 8	A majority of middle-level schools adopt interdisciplinary teaming and advisor-advisee programs.
Priority 9	State/local policy makers recognize the need for adequate funding of middle-level education.
Priority 10	Curriculum will be more integrated and interdisciplinary throughout the middle-school program.
Priority 11	Programs to develop skills in resisting peer pressures, to help form values, and to teach the causes and effects of substance abuse are increased.
Priority 12	Parents and schools form partnerships to meet the needs of the whole child.
Priority 13	Middle-level professionals are major student advocates, serving as connectors for students from elementary to middle school and from middle school to high school.
Priority 14	Collaboration and cooperative problem solving replace competition as the driving philosophy of middle-level instruction.
Priority 15	The "integrity" of the middle-school program is preserved.
Priority 16	Leaders are faced with developing plans that allow for continued growth and development of middle-level schools and the middle-school movement.

FIGURE 1.1 NMSA DELPHI REPORT—PRIORITY EVENTS

Source: From "The NMSA Delphi Report: Roadmap to the Future" by D. M. Jenkins and K. D. Jenkins, March 1991. *Middle School Journal, 82*(4), 29. Reprinted by permission.

Reflection

Examine the goals listed in Figure 1.1 and then respond to the following questions:

1. Which goals are most feasible? Which are least feasible?
2. Which two goals do you believe are most important?
3. Which goals can you help facilitate?

A Lifelong Love for Learning

Priority 6 of the NMSA (see Figure 1.1) is, "Inservice/reeducation of existing middle-level and non-middle-level certificated faculty is increased to implement and maintain knowledge of the middle-level child." Effective middle-level teachers know that they must stay abreast of developments in their disciplines. They also know that they must continue to find new ways to make content exciting for their students. Sixth-grade teacher and former Alabama Teacher of the Year Susan Cameron (1999, p. 225) gives excellent advice when she advises beginning teachers to "get out there and experience life—have an adventure, and then translate that into your teaching."

There is only one way to have the level of mastery in your field and in your profession that is essential for effective teaching: you must develop a lifestyle that includes reading professional journals, conducting action research, and writing. Former Alabama Teacher of the Year Susan Cameron (1999) says that most of her time is spent learning, attending lectures, reading current literature, and discussing issues.

Teacher of the Year

> I try to be a living example of the characteristics of a life-long, successful learner. Students are hopefully inspired to always want to know more.
>
> Former Alabama Teacher of the Year Susan Cameron (1999, p. 225)

John Steinbeck said that his teacher "breathed curiosity into us so that we brought in truths shielded in our hands like captured fireflies." Do such activities as attending lectures, reading current literature, conducting investigations in your own classroom, and engaging your students in writing require additional time and energy from teachers, most of whom are already physically and emotionally stretched? You bet they do, but the payoff is tremendous for both you and your students. These activities involve creativity, and because they do, they are energizing. Effective middle-level teachers also reflect on their behavior and the results of their behavior on student performance.

A Willingness to Self-Analyze

Effective teachers are critical of themselves. This means that they are reflective practitioners with several methods of analyzing their own behavior. Daniels (2002) discusses several of these methods, including journal keeping, peer coaching (asking fellow teachers to critique your teaching), and action research. Interestingly, the act of conducting action research makes teachers more open and willing to see their own shortcomings.

A Willingness to Share Power

Effective middle school teachers are more than just experts in their own right; they share their expertise and power with their students. Former Pennsylvania Teacher of the Year Howard Selekman is a life-long learner who shares the payoff of his life-long learning lifestyle with his class through intensive, ongoing writing projects.

Teacher of the Year

> I work hard at validating the "voice" of each student as an individual. We keep journals, and we write freely in them. We write at the beginning of class, in the middle of class, at the end of class. Sometimes we write with complete sentences; sometimes we don't. When appropriate we write over an extended

> period of time, revising, listing, and conferencing with one another, editing, sharing, even publishing. We write what we have learned, what our opinions are, what our questions are, what our predictions are. We write about what we know, and what we don't know. We reflect on our many experiences in our writing. We write about connections among the various subjects we are learning. These will be the moments when we discover our own voice, learning to develop and enrich it by sharing, taking risks, and experimenting with words, points of view, styles, and idiosyncrasies. These are, in fact, the defining features of the artist.
>
> Former Pennsylvania Teacher of the Year Howard Selekman

As Selekman notes, he and his students reflect on their work each day. Effective teachers reflect on their behavior and on their learning (Janas, 2001). And they ensure that their students reflect on their own behavior. As Weasmer and Woods (2001, p. 41) have said, "It is essential for them [students] to reflect on what they have learned in order to synthesize and articulate that knowledge."

Incidentally, it is important to know that while his students are writing, Mr. Selekman is also writing, and, like his students, he shares his writings, including his mistakes, with his class. And, like his students, he does not wait until he considers his writing to be a finished product to share it. This sends some important messages: Mistakes are to be expected but not feared. Knowledge is never complete or perfect; but it keeps getting better if we have the commitment to continue pursuing it and if we have the grit to share it and have it scrutinized by others.

A Proactive Attitude

More than four hundred studies were used in writing this book, and each can make you a better teacher, but only if you use this research base and resist the common temptation to overestimate the value of personal experience. The value of experience is proportional to one's knowledge base, and the knowledge base is dramatically increased when teachers conduct research and use research conducted by others. In contrast, when teachers ignore research, they forfeit the opportunity to bring maximum improvement to their teaching (Nelson, 1999). The result is that the ordinary classroom limits what students can do.

It has been said, but bears repeating, that teachers are the main force that determines the amount of learning that occurs in their classrooms. Because teaching is an art, the combination of ingredients needed to produce an optimal learning environment varies with the socioculture of each school, with each group of students, and even with the same group from day to day. Teachers can improve their students' ability to learn by improving their own ability to make decisions. Teachers whose students are consistently successful at learning are good decision makers.

Teachers must make two types of decisions: proactive and reflective. As mentioned previously, proactive decisions are needed for planning, and reflective decisions are needed to reflect on teachers' and students' behavior. All teachers must continually ask themselves why one method worked and another failed and why a method that succeeded yesterday failed today. Such answers are not found in their pure form; they are not found in books, nor from redesigning schools' organizational structure, nor from research, nor from using any particular method or strategy. In fact, no source can guarantee that one method will be best for any lesson. However, teachers who keep up with research findings, learn to theorize and reflect, and conduct their own classroom investigations tend to stay abreast of the most current best practices. As Bernauer (1999, p. 69) reminds future teachers, "to disregard existing knowledge is to ignore one of the most important features of human growth—learning from others."

To remain on the cutting edge, you must combine facts, intellect, and judgment to achieve academic success in your classroom. Do not think of these recommended behaviors (reading professional materials, dialogueing with colleagues, and conducting research) as just new responsibilities that increase teachers' workloads, for they provide unprecedented opportunities to improve teaching in your school. Take the time to make a difference by mastering your discipline and the pedagogy required to enable you to work effectively with colleagues, parents, and students to help all of your students reach their maximum level of potential. Describing the relationship between power and the school reform that is occurring throughout the country, Cook (1994, p. 48) says that "this reform movement is all about power and who has it; those inside the schools or those outside." If you learn to share your power, another surprising thing happens: your own power is increased. You can begin by sharing with your students and then extend this sharing to include your fellow teachers.

Top teachers recognize the importance of sharing power, and also that sharing is not always easy because it requires a lot of self-confidence.

Teacher of the Year

I can, however, empower my students and help them determine their own questions; and I can help guide them in gaining the skills necessary for solving questions. This requires a tremendous leap of faith on the teacher's part because it involves giving up a position of ultimate authority and assuming the position of facilitator of learning.

Former North Carolina Teacher of the Year Renee Coward (1999, p. 175)

It is also important to share power with parents. By the end of the 1990s most teachers were convinced of the value of involving parents on their school council. A national survey reported that minority teachers more than whites (55 percent versus 40 percent), and females more than males (46 percent versus 38 percent), believe that parent involvement on local councils is very important (MLS, 1998).

Modern technology has enabled teachers to empower their students to unprecedented levels. Teachers who use computers to full advantage are not threatened by their students' reaching this goal. As Eller (1999) explains, the Internet puts the world in the hands of today's students: "The technology is now available to teach 'interactively' in the remotest rural or inner-city classroom anywhere on the planet" (p. 114). It is worth noting that Eller stressed both the global nature of the Internet and its interactive nature; middle-level cur-

> **Proactive Exercise**
>
> **Anticipated Situation**
> - You know that:
>
>   Parent involvement in school matters develops a sense of ownership and commitment to improve, yet some of your future colleagues will be very reluctant to have parents involved in changing the curriculum.
>
> **Proactive Alternative**
> - You can:
>
>   Collect some data showing that parent involvement increases parent support. Also, collect data showing that parent involvement correlates positively with academic achievement. Be prepared to discuss these data when the issue of parent involvement arises.

ricula are built on activities, and the Internet has tremendous potential for letting students interact with the world at large. In the words of Weasmer and Woods (2001, p. 41), "When students are invited to pursue fields of individual interests online, they become resourceful." Resourcefulness is itself power, and it should be a goal in all contemporary middle school classrooms.

Constructivism

Constructivism is a theory about how learning occurs. Put crudely, it holds that individuals make sense of new information by connecting it to previously acquired understanding. In this sense, constructivism is a set of psychological beliefs. Constructivism is also a set of philosophical beliefs that separate it from traditional, teacher-centered education.

Background

Constructivism has developed over a period of centuries. Some insist that its roots go back at least to the 1660s, when English philosopher John Locke said that at birth the mind is a *tabula rasa,* or blank slate, and the only way to fill it is with experience. This recognition of the role that experience plays in learning opened the door for the development of *experiential* (experienced-based) education. Others argue that constructivism was born much later, in 1762, when the Swiss naturalist philosopher Rousseau wrote his book *Emile* describing the type of education that he recommended. Rousseau believed that children are good until they are corrupted by society, and that they should be educated *naturally,* with much attention given to the students' interests. He introduced the idea of developmental stages. Although he was tutor to a little boy and his sister (Emile and Sophie), Rousseau was not a classroom teacher. Swiss educator Johann Pestalozzi (1746–1827) was a classroom teacher, and he applied some of his own ideas along with some of Rousseau's ideas. He believed that the *whole* child should be educated (physically, mentally, and emotionally), and that children should be *nourished* like a plant while they *learned by doing.* Pestalozzi believed that the teacher must *respect* children and base discipline on love. He said that the school should be like a good home and the teacher should be like a good parent.

Almost two centuries ago, German philosopher Johann Herbart (1782–1852) got the idea that student learning requires motivation that comes from previous experiences. This need to connect current experiences with prior experiences is a fundamental belief of constructivists today. By the mid-nineteenth century, German educator Friedrich Froebel (1782–1927) used these ideas (learning by doing, teaching the whole child, and activities-based education) to develop the first kindergarten. Shortly after the U.S. Civil War (1861–1865), a New Hampshire native, Col. Francis Parker (1837–1902), went to Europe to study the child-centered approach to education, bringing it back to this country and earning the title, the father of child-centered education in the United States.

John Dewey (1859–1952) initiated this child-centered approach on a grand scale from the mid-1920s to the mid-1940s. Because this type of education differed so much from the traditional, teacher-centered approach, this period in the history of U.S. education is known as the Progressive Education Era. Meanwhile, a young Russian sociologist, Lev Vygotsky (1896–1934) was experimenting with small-group learning. Vygotsky said that children learn best when they are expected to teach others in their group and when they are asked to solve problems in a threat-free environment. He said that children will talk things through until they understand them. He called this process **negotiating meaning.** He believed that teachers should start where the children are and help them, step by step, using a process he called **scaffolding.** He believed that because each child brings a different set of past experiences, each student has a range within which he or she can develop. He called this range the **zone of proximal development.** Above all, Vygotsky thought that cooperation, not competition, was the major cause of learning. These activities led to the development of **constructivism,** the theory that individuals create their own understanding.

Philosophical Beliefs of Constructivists

Constructivists hold a unique set of philosophical beliefs that must be understood before one can grasp the concept of constructivism. Perhaps the most basic of these beliefs is the purpose of schools. Traditionally, Americans have viewed schools primarily as places to prepare youths for a vocation. The earliest U.S. schools were created to prepare students for a particular profession, the ministry. Within 16 years after the pilgrims landed, in 1636, an institution of higher education (Harvard College) had been created to further this mission.

The number and diversity of professions rapidly expanded, and Benjamin Franklin's Academy, forerunner to our secondary schools, which opened in 1749 in Philadelphia, quickly became the most popular type of American school because it offered such practical subjects as mathematics, engineering, and surveying. During their almost four hundred years of existence, American schools have retained their focus on preparing students for a vocation.

Constructivists do not question the value of preparing youths for better adult lives, but they believe that schools should do more. For example, they believe that schooling is about the present as well as about the future, and that students' quality of life in school is also important. They also believe that merely preparing students for work is an unacceptably narrow view of a school's purposes. They believe that schools should do more (e.g., help students develop their creative potential and an unquenchable thirst for knowledge). Constructivists also believe that schools should help students acquire as much understanding as possible, not just enough to get and keep a job (Table 1.1).

Constructivists are concerned with making school and information important to students. Constructivists' ultimate goal is not simply learning, but enjoying learning. John Dewey (1938, p. 49) said, "The most important attitude that can be formed is that of desire to go on learning." Constructivists argue that maximum learning can occur only when students are intrigued by what they study. Unlike traditional teachers, who are committed to covering the broad amount of material designated for each grade level, constructivists are committed to helping students learn less information but learn it more thoroughly. Tradi-

TABLE 1.1 Constructivist versus Preconstructivist Beliefs about the Purpose of Schools and Learning

Preconstructivist Beliefs	Constructivist Beliefs
School should prepare world-class workers	School should promote creativity
School should improve the quality of adult life	School should improve students' present and adult lives.
School should produce more knowledgeable adults	School should produce better thinkers
Breadth of content coverage is most important	Depth of understanding is most important

From Kenneth T. Henson, *Methods and Strategies for Teaching in Secondary and Middle Schools,* third edition. Published by Allyn and Bacon, Boston, MA. Copyright © 1996 by Pearson Education. Reprinted by permission of the publisher.

tional schools have sought to produce more knowledgeable students. Constructivists seek to produce more creative graduates.

Teacher of the Year

Students hopefully are inspired to always want to know more. In fact, the most significant evaluation of student achievement should be the extent to which they want to know more and their ability to do so.

Former Alabama Teacher of the Year Susan Cameron (1999, p. 225)

Psychological Beliefs of Constructivists

Traditionally, U.S. educators have equated learning with acquiring information. More has been viewed as better. The classic question, "What did you learn in school today?" reflects the idea that a successful education means an abundance of acquired knowledge. Constructivists, on the other hand, view learning as a process not just of acquiring information but of creating new understanding. They regard learning as a *personal* process that requires each individual to use newly acquired information to shape existing understanding, thus producing new insights.

John Dewey (1938, p. 46) said, "There is no such thing as educational value in the abstract." In other words, unless a personal connection is made with each student, the content being studied remains worthless. Although students may memorize it, they will not understand it. Constructivists believe that there is a preferred way to learn each discipline. Once the structure is unlocked, learning becomes possible (Table 1.2). Successful teachers have learned how to help their students unlock this hidden structure.

Since constructivism portrays learning as creating new insights and new understanding, knowledge itself is viewed as temporary. All knowledge is subject to error. For decades physicists believed that light traveled in waves (wave theory), but then it was discovered that light travels in particles (corpuscular theory). In fact, under certain conditions light appears to travel in particles and under other conditions light seems to travel in waves. Physicists continue to use both theories without trying to reject either; they do not see all things as having single, correct answers. They do not worry that they must adjust their current thinking to accommodate new discoveries.

TABLE 1.2 Constructivist versus Preconstructivist Beliefs about Learning

Preconstructivist Beliefs	Constructivist Beliefs
Quality of learning is reflected in the amount of knowledge accumulated	Quality of learning is characterized by the learner's level of creativity
Learning is remembering existing knowledge	Learning is creating new understanding
Learning is understanding of permanent information	Learning involves shaping information
The topic of study has little effect on the way it is learned	Success in learning any discipline requires discovering that discipline's unique structure

From Kenneth T. Henson, *Methods and Strategies for Teaching in Secondary and Middle Schools,* third edition. Published by Allyn and Bacon, Boston, MA. Copyright © 1996 by Pearson Education. Reprinted by permission of the publisher.

Motivation Theory Held by Constructivists

Constructivists also differ from traditionalists in what they believe motivates students to learn. For example, Americans have always valued competition, believing that competition among all students fosters learning. Constructivists accept the postulate that competition among classmates can be motivating and helpful when all students are of similar ability, but in most classes students vary greatly in ability. The rapid rate of development during the middle years accentuates the diversity among middle-level students. Constructivists maintain that competition is destructive to students of lower ability. Teachers can derive the motivational advantage of competition without damaging students simply by grouping students of similar ability or by establishing groups of similar students and then having the groups compete (Table 1.3), or they can use the constructivist method of grouping students of unequal ability in small groups and arranging for the more advanced students to help the slower students.

Constructivists believe that intrinsic or internal motivation is more powerful than extrinsic or external motivation. They therefore believe that learning should be made personal to each student and that students should be helped to find ways that make material important to them.

Constructivist Views of the Nature and Organization of Knowledge

Constructivists believe that all curricula should be designed around major content generalizations such as concepts and interdisciplinary themes. These generalizations are the key to understanding. Instead of worrying about covering the material designated for a particular grade level, the teacher should ensure that students learn the major concepts. This does not mean the teacher "teaches" the concepts. On the contrary, students themselves should develop these concepts. Recent research shows that teachers are often unaware of the concepts their students hold, and that students often hold very different understandings than

TABLE 1.3 Constructivist versus Preconstructivist Beliefs about Motivation

Preconstructivist Beliefs	Constructivist Beliefs
Competition is the main driving force of motivation	Cooperation is a major motivating force
Information and the learner may be unrelated	Students learn information that has personal value to them
Rewards and punishments are the main motivating forces	Discovering new relationships among concepts and developing new concepts are motivating
Good teachers are good motivators	The motivation required for learning is internal; therefore good teachers arrange conditions to invite learning
Intraclass competition is important	Interclass competition is important

From Kenneth T. Henson, *Methods and Strategies for Teaching in Secondary and Middle Schools,* third edition. Published by Allyn and Bacon, Boston, MA. Copyright © 1996 by Pearson Education. Reprinted by permission of the publisher.

TABLE 1.4 Constructivist versus Preconstructivist Beliefs about the Nature and Organization of Knowledge for Curriculum Content

Preconstructivist Beliefs	Constructivist Beliefs
Content is often assembled into seemingly unrelated bits of information	Content is built out of large understandings called content generalizations or concepts
Knowledge is permanent	Knowledge is temporary
Like any muscle, the brain needs rigorous exercise offered only by difficult-to-learn information	Information should be organized to simplify and expedite its learning
The textbook should shape the curriculum	Student interests, current events, and case of association should shape the curriculum

From Kenneth T. Henson, *Methods and Strategies for Teaching in Secondary and Middle Schools,* third edition. Published by Allyn and Bacon, Boston, MA. Copyright © 1996 by Pearson Education. Reprinted by permission of the publisher.

those their teachers think they hold (Heckman, Confer, & Hakim, 1994) (Table 1.4). Constructivist teachers use group-based problem solving.

Constructivists view all knowledge as temporary. They are less interested in students' acquiring a textbook's or teacher's knowledge and more interested in students' questioning their own understanding and discovering new understanding. All curricula should be organized so that major concepts are easily learned and new information can easily be tied to previously held information. Student interests, current events, and ease of connecting information should shape the curriculum. When students are connected to or engaged with problems that they find interesting, they develop insights that last a lifetime. Dewey (1938) referred to such meaningful, lasting, and often unplanned learning as collateral learning: "Collateral learning in the way of forming enduring attitudes, of likes and dislikes, may be and often is much more important than the spelling lesson or lesson in geography or history that is learned. For these attitudes are fundamentally what count in the future" (p. 49). Collateral learning is especially essential to middle-level students, who need all types of connections to gain stability in their rapidly changing and often disordered lives.

Teacher of the Year

Learning is not simply a matter of transferring information from the outside world to some sort of in-head storehouse. Instead, learners must actively construct knowledge for themselves; meaning generation is the essence of learning.

Former Minnesota Fourth Grade Teacher of the Year James Ellington (1999, p. 245)

The Role of Constructivist Teachers

Constructivist teachers' beliefs about school's purpose and about how students learn require them to behave differently than traditional teachers. Constructivist teachers must use a personal approach, focusing attention on each student to make the curriculum interesting to that student. Constructivist teachers recognize that some, most, or even all students may not be interested in the curriculum. These teachers believe they must find ways to involve students with the curriculum. This may require the teacher to keep up with news and sports events. It may require the teacher to attend school sports events, clubs, and fairs. Such attendance has two major benefits: It provides opportunities to learn more about students' interests, and it shows students that you are interested in them as people.

Constructivist teachers must identify and understand the major concepts in their subjects. They must then find ways to lead their students to discover and develop these concepts. Instead of teaching concepts to their students directly, constructivist teachers believe that they must introduce information that will conflict with students' present understanding, creating a state of **psychological disequilibrium** (a conflict among their understandings). This requires teachers to resist the common urge to point out correct answers (see Table 1.5).

How badly is this constructivist curriculum needed in today's schools? According to Gardner and Boix-Mansilla (1994, p. 14), "While students may succeed in 'parroting back' phrases from lectures and texts, they often falter when asked to apply their understandings to new situations." The news that today's students often do not clearly understand the discipline's major concepts comes as no surprise. Perkins and Blythe (1994) say:

Teachers were all too aware that their students often did not understand the key concepts nearly as well as they might. Research affirms this perception. (p. 4)

Constructivism offers much promise because it focuses on students' learning the major concepts in each discipline and because it personalizes learning. Vygotsky said that this happens best when students are working together, cooperating, and helping each other learn. A strategy has been designed and has since proven highly effective in ensuring that small-group work results in learning the lesson's major concepts. This part or subset of constructivism is called **cooperative learning**. Now, let's examine the particulars that make this system work.

Both the philosophy and practices of constructivists parallel those of today's middle schools, where depth of understanding is valued more than the covering of more topics. In

TABLE 1.5 The Roles of Constructivist and Preconstructivist Teachers

Preconstructivist Teaching Roles	**Constructivist Teaching Roles**
The teacher:	The teacher:
Provides information	Invites students to discover information
Preidentifies important information	Invites students to identify additional content that interests them
Helps students remember information by giving clear explanations and examples	Helps students discover information
Continuously strives for clarity	Arranges for discontinuity
Keeps students quiet and on task	Encourages students to create learning; considers a reasonable amount of noise and movement necessary and acceptable
Strives to convey all information designated for the particular grade level	Strives to help students reach a deeper understanding of fewer topics
Uses threats and other punishments to motivate	Uses students' personal interests to motivate
Uses intraclass competition to motivate	Uses interclass competition to motivate

From Kenneth T. Henson, *Methods and Strategies for Teaching in Secondary and Middle Schools,* third edition. Published by Allyn and Bacon, Boston, MA. Copyright © 1996 by Pearson Education. Reprinted by permission of the publisher.

THE CASE

Substituting Involvement for Apathy

Lienne F. Medford, Clemson University

Lienne Medford received her doctorate in Educational Leadership from East Carolina University in Greenville, North Carolina, in 1996. She presently teaches Reading for Early Childhood, Elementary, and Middle Grades majors at Clemson University in Clemson, South Carolina, where she is an assistant professor in the Department of Curriculum and Instruction.

The following case study examines an initiative designed for one purpose that had unexpected results in other areas. Although the emphasis is on communication, the discerning reader will see that a number of other pertinent issues are addressed.

Beach Middle School in Shoreville, North Carolina, is one of only a handful of middle schools that qualifies as a School of Distinction under the state's ABC (Accountability Basics Control) Program. To qualify as a School of Distinction, 90 percent of all students must score 90 percent or better in all subject areas at all grade levels that have state required end-of-course tests.

Beach Middle School (BMS) is located in Beachfront County, a rural, economically disadvantaged county on the coast of North Carolina. Its racial makeup is 61.3 percent white, 36 percent black, and 2.7 percent "other," mainly Hispanic and Native American. The school district has a little over 6,000 students, and 68% of these who graduate from its three high schools pursue postsecondary degrees. Much of the undeveloped portions of Beachfront County are owned by a large paper company, and sections of the county are cut off from one another by large tracts of forest that cannot be traversed. Beach Middle School serves the small town of Shoreville and the beach communities of Barrier Island, which have many year-round residents. Tourism and fishing provide the majority of its income. Its students come from a variety of socioeconomic backgrounds. There are many trailer parks, modest subdivisions, and luxury homes that comprise Shoreville's several golf course communities. There is also a large retirement-aged population. Many of the professionals living in Shoreville commute to Smithtown or Jonestown, the two closest cities, each in another, neighboring county. Except for the few dentists and doctors who hang out their shingles in Shoreville, and the teachers and administrators of its schools, few professionals actually work in the part of Beachfront County served by BMS.

> *Middle grades students still need structure; the more organized your classroom schedule, the fewer classroom management problems you will have.*

Many of Beachfront County's administrators, including BMS's principal, were brought to the county by the present superintendent when he was hired five years ago. The board of education was looking for an innovative leader who could bring the schools' communities together and produce results. Although there are many ways to measure success, schools that score well on state end-of-course exams and receive recognition through ABC Honors are very visible and provide much positive publicity. It is worth noting that the high school for which BMS is the only feeder school has been a top-ten high school in North Carolina for the past three years. BMS's excellent preparation has obviously contributed to the success of Beach High Schools (BHS).

So, how did BMS and BHS become so successful? Where did they start, and how did they end up at the front of the pack? What were the special challenges and innovative solutions that allowed for such growth and success? Interestingly, a problem that not all schools face led to a practice that all schools can adopt and a success that all schools can appreciate.

We all know that there is a teacher shortage. This has led to many creative solutions: alternative certification programs, Troops to Teachers, teaching fellows programs, and lateral entry. It stands to reason, then, that there is also a substitute teacher shortage. There seem to be few creative solutions in this area, however.

Consider, too, a large rural county and a school that serves bedroom communities for its two closest urban areas. There were virtually *no* substitute teachers available when the present principal of BMS was hired. The few who were listed at the central office were often members of the previously mentioned retirement community, who had little investment or interest in their service beyond supplementing their income. This was not good for the school or the students. In addition to the obvious problem of covering for sick teachers, it was difficult to provide coverage for teachers to go to workshops and other professional development activities that would improve staff performance and morale. The coverage that was available provided poor classroom management and little in the way of actual instruction.

A seemingly unrelated problem was that there was a lack of community and parent involvement in the school's parent–teacher organization (PTO). The school was there, the children went, and except for major events such as the holiday concert and the spring graduation, few parents appeared. Even Parent–Teacher Nights and Open Houses were poorly attended. And, of the parents who did attend, the minority community was greatly underrepresented. Under new management, the faculty members were working hard, innovative programs were being introduced, progress was being made, but no one knew!

The principals of BMS and BHS got together to brainstorm. How could they get more and better-qualified substitutes and increased support for their PTOs? How could they increase minority parent involvement?

In North Carolina, the minimum qualifications to substitute are as follows: you must be a high school graduate and you must attend a short training program provided by the school district in which you wish to substitute. So, the Beach school principals put out the word: we need substitutes and we would like any *parent* who is interested and qualified to apply. They put an ad in the community newspaper, they put up posters in local businesses, and they sent home newsletters with students. The replies trickled in. Midway through the fall semester, the list of substitutes reached the point where, at least in terms of numbers, the principals could breathe more easily. This solution, however, had some very interesting and perhaps unexpected results. The next portion of the study is a firsthand account of how it worked in my classroom.

I teach language arts. I like to use cooperative learning and keep my students busy and active. My favorite strategy is to use station work, in which groups of students rotate through different activities set up in different parts of the classroom. Each station's task must be accomplished in a certain amount of time; this keeps students on task and involved in their work. This type of classroom organization, however, is difficult for a substitute to set up and monitor. I was unhappy at having to leave films and worksheets for my students if I knew I would be absent, and I also knew that my students did not enjoy my class nor behave particularly well during the days I was gone. I found myself turning down opportunities because I felt I couldn't, in good conscience, leave my classes. Any number of times when I was ill I dragged myself to school, making myself worse, rather than leave my students with what I could pretty much count on being an unqualified sub.

My gifted class could be especially hard on substitutes. It was a large class that was very bright and very talkative. They were a joy to teach, but the energy and focus required to maintain a positive learning environment was far beyond what I could expect from any of the "old" substitutes. If I told my students that I would be absent the next day because of a scheduled meeting or workshop, they would groan and look extremely put upon. They knew what type of boring fare was likely coming.

There was an extremely social group of girls in this class, too. They could be quite a handful even under the best of circumstances. These girls were involved in many extracurricular activities, and most had siblings in the school system. Perhaps the most social, "Heather," had a stay-at-home Mom. She was one of the first parents to volunteer and take the required training. She substituted for me and it changed everything.

First of all, "Mrs. H" was an excellent classroom manager. She knew most of the students, their parents, and their siblings. As an experienced parent, she understood applying rules consistently and fairly. She also had a vested interest in her daughter's education and happiness. Therefore, she wanted lesson plans she could see promoted learning and that engaged students. The first time she was scheduled to sub for me she showed up the afternoon before to ask me about what she would be doing the next day. This was a first! She expressed worry that she would not be up to the task and wanted to be absolutely sure she understood my classroom's rules and what was expected of the students. I was somewhat ashamed of my usual substitute lesson plans and asked her if she would be interested in expanding them some and presiding over more challenging and engaging activities. We sat together and worked out some very nice plans indeed.

When I returned after her substitution I found detailed accounts of everything that had happened in my absence, and the good far outweighed the bad. Students commented that it was neat having Heather's Mom as a sub and that they liked her. Wow! What a difference! I sat down right away and wrote out a thank you note to let Mrs. H know what a great job she had done and how much I appreciated her efforts. But the greatest surprise and benefit was yet to come.

A few days later Mrs. H showed up at my classroom door after school and asked if she could come in for a chat. All was going well with Heather, so I was curious as to what she wanted to discuss. She started out by saying what a good time she had had substituting for me. Then she said, "You know, I never realized how much energy it takes to teach. I went home and took a nap for the first time in maybe twenty years!" She went on to say that as a parent, she would like to know if there was anything she could do to make my life as a teacher easier. It seems that Mrs. H had developed a new respect for teachers and how hard they work! And Mrs. H was not the only one. Almost every parent who came in to sub joined the PTO and canvassed among his or her neighbors and friends to recruit more subs and more members. The change in parent involvement and support was truly amazing. By the time Christmas arrived, it was a new school.

For example, the PTO gave the faculty a big holiday appreciation breakfast. They decorated the tables in the cafeteria and provided a wonderful meal of hearty casseroles and delicious home-baked goods. What was perhaps most amazing was that every teacher in the school received something on his or her "wish list" that we had been asked to put together. There was a roll of stamps for the yearbook adviser, dictionaries for one of the language arts teachers, supplies for the art teacher—everyone got something he or she would have had to pay for on his or her own or do without. We were overwhelmed.

The transformation was complete and continues to this day. Both BMS and BHS have large, strong PTOs that provide outstanding support and service to their respective schools. We have never been short of qualified, dedicated subs who have the best interests of our students at heart. Teachers feel good about the respect and understanding they have from the community. In addition, this support has certainly been a factor in BMS's academic success. Teachers no longer forfeit a day of instruction if they are absent. Parents who substitute in their child's class or at his grade level understand the types of high-stakes testing that is involved and share the school's concern about making sure students are prepared. Parents then actively share in the pride of accomplishment at the school's success. It is a true team effort—with the team extending to the whole community. Remember those wish-list goodies? Many of them came from community businesses and private donations of individuals who did not have children in the schools. Smallville's schools had become a true source of community pride.

It goes without saying that several of the most successful and active subs were minority parents. Those first volunteers were welcomed with such open arms that they returned to their community with the best PR money can't buy—word of mouth. When the "sub shortage" ended, so did the lack of minority parent involvement.

And there you have it. BMS has indeed distinguished itself among the schools of North Carolina and, more important, among the citizens of the community it serves.

Further Reflection

1. Do you think the size of the community that BMS serves had anything to do with the success of the initiative? Could it work in a city? How, if at all, would the plan have to be modified?
2. Describe the chain reaction of the events in the case study. How did one event lead to the next and the ultimate outcome of total community involvement?
3. Are there other ways an increase in parent understanding of a teacher's true workload benefits the school community?
4. Do you think there is a direct correlation between parental involvement and a school's academic

success? Why or why not? Are there different types and levels of parental involvement? Do you feel that BMS's experience is typical or not?
5. Consider the role of the substitute teacher. How do substitutes influence the success or failure of a school? Do you consider them much of a factor? What are the stereotypes of the substitute teacher's experience? Do you think that BMS's students feel different about substitutes than the average student? Why or why not?
6. Are there special considerations in substituting at the middle school level? If so, what might they be?

middle schools, teachers team with teachers in other disciplines, and often with students, to plan units that the teachers team-teach. The resulting interdisciplinary learning units are planned around themes, as opposed to teaching unrelated facts. The open-ended nature of inquiry learning, which is valued highly in middle schools, is seldom understood by today's education reformers, who wish to use common standards to measure the cognitive attainment (content learning) of students. Reformers at both state and national levels say that such standards are essential to hold schools accountable. The assumption is that they can cause schools to reach the desired levels of performance simply by raising the standards. However, this assumption is flawed. For over two decades, legislators have been dissatisfied with the level of achievement in the nation's schools. If, then, students are not meeting the current expectations, there is no logic in assuming that raising expectations will correct the problem.

Middle school educators understand that teaching and learning are complex activities that cannot be significantly improved by such quick-fix solutions as raising standards. Teachers must work together across disciplines, involving students in the planning of activities that will lead to deeper understanding. As Dugger (2001, p. 516) says, "Adolescents should be encouraged to consult with adults." While academic achievement is an indispensable goal for middle schools, it must not replace or overshadow concern for the personal well-being of students who are experiencing rapid and powerful physiological changes in their lives. Perhaps the popular phrase, "No child left behind," should be replaced by "No child overlooked."

For a discussion of the history of constructivism and learner-centered education, see Henson (at press).

Cooperative Learning Programs

Cooperative learning is a term used to describe a small-group strategy in which students help each other learn. In fact, the success of each member requires the success of the other group members. In this country, a large number of separate programs have been developed to capitalize on the benefits of cooperative learning. Most school faculties have always had members who are experimenters and developers. Because the individual teachers are unique and because the culture in each school is equally unique, it is easy to understand that while programs with certain common features may carry the same label, each program must be adjusted if it is, indeed, to work effectively in its school. Such is the case with cooperative learning. Some of these programs are relatively unknown outside the sites where they were developed. Other programs have been touted at professional conferences and in professional books and journals. Because many educators are experimenters, new programs are being developed. Some programs are tested only in the most informal sense; others are carefully tested (some at universities) to determine their effect on learning and social development. Some of these programs include (1) the Jigsaw method, (2) Jigsaw II, and (3) service learning.

Jigsaw

One of the more enduring examples of programs that use the cooperative learning strategies is the Jigsaw method. This program has been used for over two decades. It gets its name from the approach used to assemble jigsaw puzzles. Imagine that a classroom full of students is given an assignment. The class is then dividend into small groups and each group is given a subassignment. For example, a social studies class in Pittsburgh might be given the assignment to research and explain the history of this city. One group might be asked to determine why the city was developed. This group would identify its early products.

Another group might be asked to identify major shifts in the local products and the causes for those shifts. Another group could be asked to focus on the city's location. This group would discuss the effects of such physical characteristics as the mountains, rivers, and quality of soil (including its natural minerals). Another group might focus on conservation issues: how particular changes have affected the local wildlife, the air quality, and the water quality. Like many cities in every state, Pittsburgh has a fascinating history. Its residents are hard workers. Many are entrepreneurs. The city has remained strong because its planners have foreseen coming changes and its residents have adjusted to those changes. Its most recent major shift has been from steel manufacturing to technology. One group could investigate this shift, while another group could be assigned to study the role the schools have played in the city's development.

Each of these assignments would require visits to the library, Web searches, and perhaps even interviews with city planners and senior citizens. In-class time would be given for groups to plan, research, and write their reports. Members of each group might be sent to other groups for information needed in their report, and then bring this back to the group for a decision to select information to include in the report. Each group would be required to plan a presentation to give to the rest of the class. Students might be encouraged to use software such as PowerPoint in delivering their presentation.

Jigsaw II

Jigsaw II is a modified version of the original Jigsaw. Like its forerunners, Jigsaw II requires members of subgroups to meet with other subgroups to gather and share information. Both approaches require groups to give a report to their classmates. (Remember that intragroup dependency, cooperation, assisted learning, and shared learning are characteristics of all cooperative learning programs. A feature that distinguishes between Jigsaw and Jigsaw II is in the method used to introduce the assignment. Unlike Jigsaw, which requires the teacher to give the students materials needed in the investigation, in Jigsaw II students read a common narrative and each group member is given a separate topic on which to develop expertise (Good and Brophy, 2000).

Service Learning

As mentioned earlier, because of the creative nature of many educators in levels K–graduate level, new programs designed to capitalize on the strengths of cooperative learning are being developed every day. An example of a contemporary program is service learning. **Service learning** consists of experiential programs designed to promote learning and promote a sense of community citizenship. Paradoxically, each service learning program is unique, yet all share a common philosophy in that they are intended to develop citizenship while serving as learning vehicles. Most service learning programs involve the entire school student body by selecting a school-wide project and then using class, small group, and individual assignments to achieve the school-wide goals. For example, one school service learning project might focus on senior citizens. Visits might be made to senior citizens' housing, where some students might be assigned to read to seniors, and some might tape stories told by seniors and later put these into writing.

Another school might adopt a wildlife conservation service learning project. One such project involved building a natural garden designed to attract and serve a variety of birds. Located on the school grounds, this sanctuary was to become a living laboratory for studying the behavior of birds. After carefully researching the local birds and the migratory paths of birds that passed though the area, the students at this school designed gardens and physically built the sanctuary. Some trees were selected to provide seeds to attract local birds; other plants were selected to feed migratory birds. Once the sanctuary was built, students at all grade levels began observing and recording the visits to this garden. Other students were responsible for keeping feeders and water basins filled. Everything was recorded.

At certain intervals throughout the year, records were collected and collective reports were made. The students at this school chose to make video tapes chronicling the development and progress of the project. The tapes served several important functions, both within and outside the school. In the school, they built a sense of ownership and they celebrated the project, which, in effect, celebrated the learning community—the school itself. The tapes were also used to pull parents and other citizens into the projects.

This project was typical of service learning projects in that it was comprehensive and lent itself to being broken down into small-group assignments, providing students excellent opportunities to cooperate with and assist their classmates in learning, a characteristic of all cooperative learning programs.

Teachers interested in initiating service learning programs can ask their administrators or counselor(s) whether such a program would be feasible at their school. If so, the counselors can assist with the initiation of such a program. Local universities may have faculty members who would be interested in co-authoring a grant proposal to initiate a service learning program. Another possibility is simply to create an unofficial service learning program for your classroom, subject, or grade level, and invite other teachers to join you. Parents, too, should be involved (Phelps, 2003).

To varying degrees, these projects are cooperative learning programs, depending on the extent to which the teacher(s) in charge use cooperative learning strategies to ensure academic and social growth of all participants. The direct, hands-on, active involvement of students in all cooperative learning programs invites participants to create learning, building on previously acquired understandings. This is constructivism at its best.

The school classroom has been described as a microcosm of society at large. It is important to realize that Vygotsky was deeply interested in the welfare of the individual learner in the classroom society. He focused not just on the learning process, but on the student as a whole person and how that student felt about the class and about himself or herself. Vygotsky believed that maximum academic and social growth occur in a climate of respect, in which members respect each other and themselves. Thus, the teacher is responsible for establishing and promoting such a climate. Remember, earlier in this chapter former Nebraska

Teacher of the Year Duane Obermier said that students respond favorably to kindness. Vygotsky understood that the way students are treated in the classroom profoundly affects their learning. He would have agreed with contemporary educator M. E. Martinez (1998, p. 609), who said, "Anxiety is a spoiler in the problem-solving process." Vygotsky's need to keep the climate positive can be better understood if we consider the major role that classmates play in a student's learning. Vygotsky explained the interactive process among students as negotiation, saying that, through dialoguing, students *negotiate meaning.* **Dialogue** is defined as "a reflective learning process in which group members seek to understand one another's viewpoints and deeply held assumptions" (Garmston & Wellman, 1998, p. 31).

So, we see two additional qualities that play important roles in learning as viewed by constructivists. These are a *positive, risk-taking* environment and an environment that encourages students to *dialogue.* Notice that both of the Jigsaw programs and the service learning program had activities designed to engage students in dialogue about the topics under study.

Some Europeans had begun successful student-centered programs before either Vygotsky or any U.S. educators began studying this approach. When Vygotsky began his research on group learning, a similar student-centered approach had already been underway in this country. The approach was so different from the traditional, teacher-centered approach that it was labeled Progressivism. Col. Francis Parker from New Hampshire has been called the father of child-centered education in the United States. Professor John Dewey is known as the father of progressive education. Because of his progressive ideas, his inclination to test his ideas, and his longevity, perhaps John Dewey has contributed more to the shaping of U.S. education than anyone else, and especially to student-centered education. It is important to remember that although most of these practices are well over a half-century old, contemporary research studies find them unparalleled in their ability to promote academic achievement.

Preparing Students to Participate in Cooperative Learning

Success with cooperative learning programs can be affected by the extent to which the teacher prepares students for their role in the program (Good & Brophy, 2000). Many students need help with even the common process of dialogueing. For example, one essential property of successful dialogue is the ability of all participants to suspend judgment. By learning to suspend judgment, we set aside for a time our perceptions, feelings, and impulses and monitor our informal experiences (Garmston & Wellman 1998, p. 31).

Another skill that is prerequisite to successful dialogueing is empathizing. Unlike sympathy, which many know how to show freely, empathizing requires the ability to communicate to others that you actually *feel* what they are feeling. One way to teach students how to empathize is to have them repeat those parts of their classmate's comments that express feelings. "So, John, are you saying that you were really disappointed by Sam's behavior?" or "I can see that you are actually hurting when you discuss this issue."

An equally important skill needed in dialogueing and yet one that is also rather uncommon is the ability to listen to others. One way to improve this skill while simultaneously letting others know that you are, indeed, listening is to repeat what others have said: "Pat, if I recall correctly, you said that. . . ."

Frankly, many people lack this ability. The natural tendency for many, if not most, people is to ignore the other party's message and use their speaking time to concentrate not on the other party's message but to mentally assemble their own message. The self-centered nature of adolescence makes acquiring dialogueing skills especially critical in middle-level classrooms. Referring to adolescents, Hilliard (1999, p. 54) has said, "[They] are egocentric and they have difficulty seeing events and intentions from another's viewpoint." The same is true for people at all ages, but it is exaggerated in early adolescents.

Listening is a behavior that can be developed through practice. Before implementing cooperative learning in you classroom, you may wish to help you students improve their ability to listen. Such improvement begins at the awareness level, because most of us would argue that we are already good listeners.

Consider playing a short (5–10 minute) audiotaped conversation on speech, or another message. Prepare twenty short-answer questions over this material. Ask everyone to respond to these questions and submit their answers anonymously. Redistribute the papers and have each student grade a classmate's paper anonymously. Average the scores.

Next, hold a discussion on listening. Ask students to share some of their own listening techniques that they have found useful in class. Incidentally, Hilliard (1999) continues, saying, "Early adolescents have increasing abilities in metacognition. [**Metacognition** is the act of thinking about your own thinking]. They are beginning to understand learning style preferences and recognize that they have multiple intelligences" (p. 54).

This exercise offers several advantages. First, it calls attention to the inextricable role that listing plays in dialogueing. Second, it starts students to thinking about their own listening behaviors. Third, it invites students to begin developing intentional listening strategies and to begin thinking about their own thinking.

Conducting Research

The National Middle School Association recognized the need for middle level teachers to continue learning. One of the priority goals set for all middle schools is to see that "Inservice/reeducation of existing middle-level certified faculty is increased to implement and maintain knowledge of the middle-level child" (Jenkins & Jenkins, 1991).

For many years teachers have conducted research in their classrooms. Most did so as a service to researchers (Peik, 1938). As early as 1908, however, an effort was made to involve teachers in research for another purpose—to have teachers identify educational problems and investigate possible solutions (Lowery, 1908).

By the 1950s, Corey (1953) and Shumsky (1958) had begun encouraging teachers to conduct studies in their classrooms. The literature shows teachers performing the role of researchers (Allen, Combs, Hendricks, Nash, & Wilson, 1988; Busching & Rowls, 1987; Copenhaver, Byrd, McIntyre, & Norris, 1982; Fischer, 1988–1989; McDaniel, 1988–1989). Many teachers, however, have not conducted research (Olson, 1990), partially because preservice teacher education programs have not prepared or required them to do so. Although many teachers' schedules are already full without research (Darling-Hammond, 1993), and you will probably have to use your regular planning meetings and outside time to write up the research (McLaughlin, Hall, Earle, Miller, & Wheeler, 1995), twenty-first century teachers must consider conducting some research in the classroom.

Many more teachers say that they would conduct research were it not for their perception of research. Some see research as too theoretical (Chattin-McNichols & Loeffler, 1989), which may be a result of their concrete, applied world (Cuban, 1992). As busy as they are, teachers may need a little nudge, perhaps a forum to remind them to get involved with or even stay alert to research findings. O'Bryan (1999, p. 27) suggests that you consider asking your principal, department chair, or curriculum director to publish a newsletter that summarizes research articles for teachers.

Using Research to Improve Teaching

Action research offers still another advantage for middle-level teachers. More than any other group of educators, middle-level teachers must collaborate across the disciplines Gilbert and Smith (2003, p. 81) explain: "Teachers as a group haven't thought very much about their responsibility to improve their own practice, to constantly work with colleagues to improve the quality of teaching throughout the school." These authors offer action research as a tool that teachers can use to accomplish this goal.

Because the teacher is a strong determiner of achievement (Bellon, Bellon, & Blank, 1992; Chimes & Schmidt, 1990; Darling-Hammond, 1998; Good & Brophy, 2000), teachers must develop a high level of mastery both in their teaching fields and in pedagogy (Mertens, & Muthall, 2002). Conducting classroom research is one route teachers can use to increase their level of mastery in these areas (Stevens, Slanton, & Bunny, 1992). Teachers who conduct research increase the variety of methods they use in the classroom (Dicker, 1990; Santa, 1990).

Such teacher-conducted research is often called **action research.** As defined by McLaughlin et al. (1995, p. 7), "action research is a way for teachers to gather information about what is happening in their classrooms and throughout their school, and then to take action based on their analysis of that information." Action research encourages a mix of theory and practice (Gilbert & Smith, 2003).

Don't overlook qualitative research, such as story writing, case studies, and journal keeping. These methods for gathering information can become tools for penetrating the emotions and values of students. They are also forms of qualitative research.

Benefits of Conducting Research

Research should and must play an important role in reforming our schools. Bernauer (1999, p. 69) says, "Initiatives supported by research offer the most promising ways to develop school-improvement programs." Involvement in research also benefits individual teachers. Beyond finding answers to nagging questions and discovering more effective ways to teach, conducting research offers teachers many additional benefits. For example, research projects are mentally refreshing (Chattin-McNichols & Loeffler, 1989); teachers find them invigorating (Sucher, 1990). Perhaps the most important mental change that involvement with research brings to teachers is to make them more open and less defensive. Conducting research helps teachers realize that they do not have all the answers; they become lifelong learners (Boyer, 1990; Brownlie, 1990). Increased openness leads to increased confidence (Neilsen, 1990). As noted by Gilbert & Smith (2003, p. 81) "Because action research is pragmatic and goal oriented, it encourages a mix of theory and practice (praxis)."

The next time you are in a school, compare how the teachers act. Some teachers are forever negative about everything and everyone. They will be the first to speak out against anything that leads to change. Bennett (1993) reported on graduate students who were required to complete an action research project, saying that they entered the project feeling anxious and hostile but finished it feeling positive.

Much is heard today about the need to empower teachers. Indeed, teacher empowerment is a topic discussed earlier in this chapter. Involvement with research gives teachers a sense of mission or purpose (Marriott, 1990) and a feeling of expertness (Allan & Miller, 1990; Bennett, 1993). These are characteristics that empower teachers (Fullan, 1998). The Consortium on Chicago School Research (1993) reported that increased student learning depends on increased teacher expertise. Nelson (1999, p. 390) summed it up by saying, "As in other professions, teachers should be prepared to be researchers into the practice they control."

Involvement in research makes teachers more objective and reflective (Cardelle-Elawar, 1993). They become more critical of their own and others' beliefs (Neilsen, 1990).

Vignettes

Each chapter in this book has one or more short vignettes. These vignettes are based on true experiences and are included to help the readers see some of the principles introduced in each chapter at work in actual school situations. Each vignette is followed by a few questions to cause you to focus on the major issues and to give you an opportunity to resolve the conflict. As in real life, sometimes you will find that you don't have all the information you need, and sometimes you will find that you have to sift through some somewhat useless and unnecessary information that is superfluous to the situation. In fact, in most of the vignettes you will find that the information given is somewhat incomplete; given more information, you could make a better, more confident decision. Although you may find this frustrating, it realistically reflects teachers' dilemmas. Sometimes you will find the author's responses, telling what actions the teacher took and the results of those actions. Some of the vignettes give no follow-up, leaving the decisions as to what actions should be taken wide open.

Vignette One: Who Should Be Involved in Curriculum Development?

Demelza King had arrived at Warren Middle School enthusiastic to begin her first year of teaching, enthusiastic over the privilege of joining a school with a reputation as a leader in education reform. Two weeks had passed, and Demelza was even more pleased, for she had already been involved in several reform practices. If asked, she would tell you that the best part of all was the teachers and their attitudes—always positive toward experimentation, always willing to involve all of their colleagues, and always putting the students' welfare ahead of all else. Tonight would be a special opportunity, her first teachers' meeting.

Demelza noticed that, even after a long day at school, her new colleagues were as exuberant as always. Several topics that could be described as maintenance issues were addressed before reaching the main agenda. The first topic on this agenda was increased parent involvement. More accurately, the stated topic was "Ways to Enhance Parent Involvement." Everyone seemed to believe in this goal until the discussion progressed to include curriculum improvement. A few of the teachers supported the idea of encouraging parents to become involved in curriculum decisions, but others objected strenuously, saying that parents lack the professional expertise to make such decisions.

Demelza wondered about her own view of this concept. Before the evening was over, she would probably have an opportunity to vote on whether parents should be involved in curriculum decisions.

DISCUSSION

1. What advantages could occur from increased parent involvement in curriculum issues?
2. What dangers could be involved in increased parent involvement in curriculum issues?
3. How would you vote on this issue?

Summary

At no previous time in history have teachers been held so accountable for the success of all students in their classes. As classrooms become increasingly diverse, teachers must continue to learn more about those factors that affect the success of all students. Furthermore, the indispensable role of teachers in the success of all students is clearly recognized. Teachers are becoming increasingly effective because certain attitudes and behaviors are changing. As teachers master more pedagogy, their sense of efficacy grows, enhancing both their own self-confidence in their teaching abilities and their confidence in their students.

Middle-level teaching requires teachers to partner with teachers in other disciplines, with counselors and administrators, with parents, and even with students. Effective middle-level teachers must plan many activities that meet the special needs and interests of early adolescents. Effective teaching at the middle level requires certain attitudes, including confidence in student abilities, a positive view of self, and a dedication to lifelong learning. To remain effective, middle school teachers must be good consumers and conductors of research.

Constructivism is a set of theories and practices that can introduce teachers to effective attitudes and behaviors and can also make teachers aware of many commonly held attitudes and behaviors that inhibit learning. Constructivism is neither new, nor is it uniquely American. Rather, it has developed over a period of several decades, with strong contributions being made, first in Europe and later in Russia and the United States. Like other teaching and learning models, a constructivist program in one school differs from constructivist programs in other schools because, to be successful, each program must be adjusted to the climate or culture of its particular school.

A major U.S. contribution to constructivism has been the development of cooperative learning, an essential subset of constructivism. Constructivist teachers recognize that they must engage in research, however limited in size and however informal. When teachers do engage in research, they become empowered, more collaborative, less defensive (sharing their power with students, colleagues, and parents), more objective and reflective, and perhaps most important, they become lifelong learners.

Recap of Major Ideas

1. Some education reform reports of the 1980s and 1990s are too narrow in their perceived role of the school.
2. Most teachers are not effective utilizers of research.
3. The gap between mainstream and African American standardized test scores has been narrowing in recent years.
4. Constructivists believe it better to understand in depth, even at the expense of covering fewer topics.
5. Constructivists believe that learning can occur only by tying new information to already learned knowledge.
6. Cooperative learning bases individuals' success on group success.
7. As classrooms become more diverse, teachers must continue studying factors that inhibit learning for members of various cultures.
8. Constructivist teachers personalize teaching.
9. Parent involvement increases learning.
10. Teachers support increased parent involvement in most areas except curriculum improvement.

Activity

Interview three teachers, asking each teacher the three questions from Vignette One. Does this alter your original perspective?

Looking Ahead

This chapter has provided a theoretical framework for the remainder of this book. The next chapter will prepare you to write performance objectives, which you will need to ensure that each lesson leads your students to achieve the important concepts and skills they will need throughout their school years and beyond.

References

Allan, K. K., & Miller, M. S. (1990). Teacher-researcher collaborative: Cooperative professional development. *Theory into Practice, 29*(3), 196–202.

Allen, J., Combs, J., Hendricks, M., Nash, P., & Wilson, S. (1988). Studying change: Teachers who become researchers. *Language Arts, 65*(4), 379–387.

Bellon, J. J., Bellon, E. C., & Blank, M. A. (1992). *Teaching from a research knowledge base.* New York: Merrill.

Bennett, C. K. (1993). Teacher-researchers: All dressed up and no place to go. *Educational Leadership, 51*(2), 69–70.

Bernauer, J. A. (1999). "Emerging standards: Empowerment with purpose." *Kappa Delta Pi Record, 35*(2), 68–70 and 74.

Boyer, E. (1990). *Scholarship reconsidered: Priorities of the professorate.* Princeton, NJ: Carnegie Foundation for the Advancement of Teaching.

Brownlie, F. (1990). The door is open. Won't you come in? In M. W. Olson (Ed.), *Opening the door to educational research* (pp. 21–31). Newark, DE: International Reading Association.

Busching, B., & Rowls, M. (1987). Teachers: Professional partners in school reform. *Action in Teacher Education,* 9(3), 13–23.

Cameron, S. (1999). In K. T. Henson & B. F. Eller, *Educational psychology for effective teaching.* Belmont, CA: Wadsworth.

Cardelle-Elawar, M. (1993). The teacher as researcher in the classroom. *Action in Teacher Education,* 15(1), 49–57.

Chattin-McNichols, J., & Loeffler, M. H. (1989). Teachers as researchers: The first cycle of the teachers' research network. *Young Children,* 44(5), 20–27.

Chimes, M., & Schmidt, P. (1990). What I read over my summer vacation: Readings on cultural diversity. *The Clearing House,* 64(1), 44–46.

Consortium on Chicago School Research. (1993). Chicago elementary school reform: A mid-term exam. *The Education Digest,* 59(3), 4–8.

Cook, A. (1994). Whose story gets told? Rethinking research on schools. *Education Week,* 13(17), 48.

Copenhaver, R. W., Byrd, D. M., McIntyre, D. J., & Norris, W. R. (1982). Synergistic public school and university research. *Action in Teacher Education,* 4(1), 41–44.

Corey, S. M. (1953). *Action research to improve school practices.* New York: Teachers College Bureau of Publications, Columbia University.

Coward, R. (1999). A teacher's class. In K. T. Henson & Eller, B. F. *Educational psychology for effective teaching.* Belmont, CA: Wadsworth.

Cuban, L. (1992). Managing dilemmas while building professional communities. *Educational Researcher,* 21(1), 4–11.

Daniels, D. C. (2002). "What research says: Becoming a reflective practitioner." *Middle School Journal,* 33(5), 52–56.

Darling-Hammond, L. (1993). Reframing the school reform agenda. *Phi Delta Kappan,* 74(10), 753–761.

Darling-Hammond, L. (1998). Teachers and teaching: Testing policy hypotheses from a national commission report. *Educational Researcher,* 27(1), 5–15.

Dewey, J. (1938). *Experience and education.* Republished in 1998. West Lafayette, IN: Kappa Delta Pi.

Dicker, M. (1990). Using action research to navigate an unfamiliar teaching assignment. *Theory into Practice,* 29(3), 203–208.

Dugger, W. E., Jr., (2001). Standards for technological literacy. *Phi Delta Kappan,* 82(7), 513–517.

Eller, B. F. (1999). In K. T. Henson and B. F. Eller, *Educational psychology for effective teaching.* Belmont, CA: Wadsworth.

Fischer, R. L. (1988–1989). When schools and colleges work together. *Action in Teacher Education,* 10(4), 63–66.

Flowers, N., Mertens, S. B, & Mulhall, P. F. (2002). Research on middle school renewal. *Middle School Journal,* 33(5), 57–61.

Fullan, M. G. (1998). Breaking the bonds of dependency. *Educational Leadership,* 55(7), 6–11.

Gardner, H., & Boix-Mansilla, V. (1994). Teaching understanding: Within and across the disciplines. *Educational Leadership,* 51(5), 14–18.

Garmston, R., & Wellman, B. (1998). Teacher talk that makes a difference. *Educational Leadership,* 55(7), 30–34.

Gilbert, S. L. & Smith, L. C. (2003). A bumpy read to action research. *Kappa Delta Pi Record,* 39(2), 80–83.

Gibran, K. (1965). *The prophet.* New York: Alfred A. Knopf.

Good, T. L., & Brophy, J. E. (2000). *Looking in classrooms.* (8th ed.) New York: Harper & Row.

Heckman, P. E., Confer, C. B., & Hakim, D. (1994). Planting seeds: Understanding through investigation. *Educational Leadership,* 51(5), 36–39.

Henson, K. T., (2003). Foundations for learner-centered education: A knowledge base. *Education,* 124(1).

Hilliard, R. D. (1999). All I ever needed to know about teaching I learned in the middle school. *SRATE Journal,* 8(1), 50–56.

Janas, M. (2001). Striking a balance. *Kappa Delta Pi Record,* 38(1), 24–27.

Lowery, C. D. (1908). The relation of superintendents and principals to the training and professional improvement of their teachers. In M. J. Holmes (Ed.), *Seventh yearbook of the National Society for the Scientific Study of Education, Part One*. Chicago: University of Chicago Press.

Marriott, V. (1990). Transition. Unpublished paper. Nova Scotia, Canada: Mount Saint Vincent University.

Martinez, M. E. (1998). What is problem solving? *Phi Delta Kappan, 79*(8), 605–609.

McDaniel, E. (1988–1989). Collaboration for what? Sharpening the focus. *Action in Teacher Education, 10*(4), 1–8.

McLaughlin, H. J., Hall, M., Earle, K., Miller, V., & Wheeler, M. (1995). Hearing our students: Team action research in a middle school. *Middle School Journal, 26*(3), 7–12.

Meek, A. (1998). America's teachers: Much to celebrate: *Educational Leadership, 55*(5), 12–16.

MLS (Metropolitan Life Insurance Company Survey) (1998). *The American teacher*. New York: Louis Harris and Associates.

Moreno, R. (1999). A teacher's class. In K. T. Henson & B. F. Eller, *Educational psychology for effective teaching*. Belmont, CA: Wadsworth.

National Education Association. (1959). *The Education of Teachers—Curricular Programs*, Report of the Kansas TEPS Conference. Washington, DC: Author.

Neilsen, L. (1990). Research comes home. *Reading Teacher, 44*(1), 248–250.

Nelson, W. W. (1999). The emperor redux. *Phi Delta Kappan, 80*(5), 387–392.

O'Bryan, S. (1999). A view from the field. In K. T. Henson & B. F. Eller, *Educational psychology for effective teaching*. Belmont, CA: Wadsworth.

Olson, M. W. (1990). The teacher as researcher: A historical perspective. In M. W. Olson (Ed.), *Opening the door to classroom research* (pp. 1–20). Newark, IN: International Reading Association.

Parsley, K., & Cocoran, C. A. (2003). The classroom teacher's role in preventing school failure. *Kappa Delta Pi, 39*(2), 84–87.

Patterson, W. (2003). Breaking out of our boxes. *Phi Delta Kappan, 84*(8), 569–574.

Peik, W. E. (1938). A generation of research on the curriculum. In G. M. Whipple (Ed.), *The scientific movement in education. Thirty-seventh yearbook of the National Society for the Study of Education, Part 2* (pp. 53–66). Bloomington, IL: Public School Publishing.

Perkins, D., & Blythe, T. (1994). Putting understanding upfront. *Educational Leadership, 51*(5), 4–7.

Phelps, P. H. (2003, p. 56). For the record. *Kappa Delta Pi Record, 39*(2), 56–57.

Raywid, M. A. (1998). Small schools: A reform that works. *Educational Leadership, 55*(4), 34–39.

Reynolds, D., & Teddlie, C. (2000). The processes of school effectiveness (pp. 134–159). In Teddlie, C., & Reynolds, D. (Eds.), *The international handbook of school effectiveness research*. New York: Fulmer Press.

Rose, L. C., & Gallup, A. M. (2001). The 33rd annual Phi Delta Kappa/Gallup Poll of the public's attitudes toward the public schools. *Phi Delta Kappan, 83*(1), 41–48 and 53–58.

Santa, C. M. (1990). Teaching as research. In M. W. Olson (Ed.), *Opening the door to classroom research* (pp. 64–76). Newark, DE: International Reading Association.

Selekman, H. R. (1999). A teacher's class. In K. T. Henson & B. F. Eller, *Educational psychology for effective teaching*. Belmont, CA: Wadsworth.

Shumsky, A. (1958). *The action research way of learning*. New York: Teachers College Press.

Slavin, R. E. (1998). Can education reduce social inequity? *Educational Leadership, 55*(4), 6–10.

Stefanich, G. P. (1990). Cycles of cognition. *Middle School Journal, 22*(2), 47–52.

Stevens, K. B., Slanton, D. B., & Bunny, S. (1992). A collaborative research effort between public school and university faculty members. *Teacher Education and Special Education, 15*(1), 1–8.

Sucher, F. (1990). Involving school administrators in classroom research. In M. W. Olson (Ed.), *Opening the door to classroom research* (pp. 112–125). Newark, DE: International Reading Association.

Vygotsky, L. S. (1962. *Thought and language*. Cambridge, MA: MIT Press.

Wadsworth, D. (2001). Why teachers choose to teach. *Educational Leadership, 58*(8), 24–28.

Weasmer, J., & Woods, A. (2001) Encouraging student decision making. *Kappa Delta Pi Record, 38*(1), 40–42.

2
Using Performance Objectives

The more we proceed by plan the more effectively we may hit by accident.

Friedrich Dürrenmatt

Objectives

- Explain three advantages of using objectives in daily planning.
- Differentiate among educational aims, goals, and objectives.
- Discuss the three domains of educational objectives.
- Write an objective for each level of each domain.
- List three criteria essential to all performance objectives.
- Explain how performance objectives and daily lessons fit into the total curriculum.
- Give an example of a well-known educational aim, and explain why aims are needed.
- Write one goal appropriate for the subject and grade level you plan to teach.
- List three ways to involve students in curriculum planning.
- Give an example of how technology can be used to raise the level of expectations teachers hold for their students.

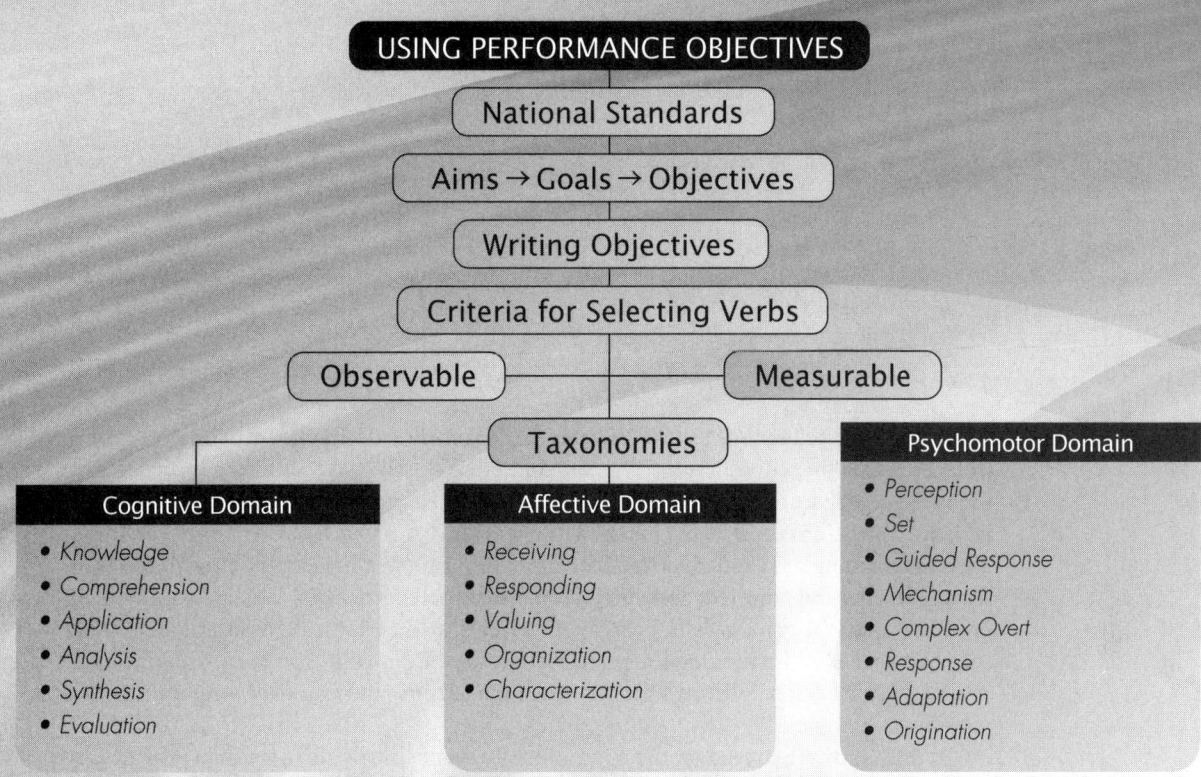

Connecting Statements | Agree | Disagree | Uncertain

1. Generally, teachers have both the freedom and the responsibility to plan their own lessons.

2. The terms aims, goals, and objectives mean the same thing when used in education, as they do elsewhere.

3. The more concise and precise an objective, the better it will be.

4. Every lesson should include some written objectives that involve students' attitudes.

5. Every lesson should contain objectives written at all levels of the taxonomy.

6. An objective should help you communicate to students exactly what you expect of them.

7. At the end of any lesson, students should be able to do some things they could not do at the beginning of the lesson.

> **Reflection**
>
> Middle-level students enjoy discussion because discussion allows them to be active; these students need opportunities to work off their energy, and because discussion gives them room to express their opinions. However, middle-level students should use discussion to absorb more information, not merely to express their own opinions. What implications does this knowledge have for you when you are conducting student discussions? Press students to give examples to support their conclusions. Because some middle-level students tend to dominate a discussion and others remain passive, try to involve every student in the discussion.

Which Comes First, Content or Objectives?

One of your first decisions as a classroom teacher involves deciding what content to cover in each class. Some school systems regulate content so closely that they virtually dictate what each teacher will teach. By providing externally designed curriculum plans, guides, and syllabi, they may even specify what material teachers must cover each day. In recent years, state and national standards and objectives have been implemented in teachers' classrooms. Written reports may be required, and curriculum directors, supervisors, assistant superintendents, and assistant principals in charge of curricula may periodically visit classes to make sure that each class is studying the prescribed lessons. Even within such closely supervised systems, you have flexibility in how you teach the lessons, and you have a right to include your own objectives.

At the opposite extreme are the many school systems that do no more than provide general guidelines. In fact, some teachers are not given anything more than a textbook from which to design their curricula. Fortunately, most school systems operate somewhere between these two extremes. They realize that teachers need suggestions and guidelines, but they also realize that teachers must be free to select content and plan their curricula according to their students' needs and interests and the community's desires and resources.

The question "How do teachers plan?" is quite different from the question "How *should* teachers plan?" Most education programs and professional literature advise teachers to use the curriculum planning model introduced by Ralph Tyler (1949). Tyler's model is often called the ends–means model because it encourages teachers to identify desired learning outcomes (objectives) before selecting instructional methods or activities.

Unfortunately, according to Walter (1984), "most teachers [ignore this model and] begin the planning process by determining the content to be covered and then design or select learning activities for students" (p. 55). Some educators say that the current education system actually encourages teachers simply to teach what they like to teach (Schmoker & Marzano, 1999). Walter adds, "Once teachers begin lessons for groups of students, they are very reluctant to change those lessons, even when things are going poorly" (p. 60). Too often, too many faculties find a level of comfort and security that they are unwilling to leave even to move forward with improving their lessons. Garmston and Wellman (1998, p. 31) were referring to this comfort zone when they said, "When a group confuses safety and comfort, it sacrifices productive tension for the ease of conviviality." But middle-level teachers must put aside concern for their own comfort level, because the rapid rate of development of early adolescents demands special consideration. Concern for the well-being and growth of the whole learner, as opposed to the traditional focus on content to be covered, requires teachers to collaborate and team plan as well as team-teach. The traditional focus and the traditional goal of "covering" a particular subject must be replaced with activities that let these fast-developing students explore as individuals and as groups because teachers' excessive efforts to cover content cause students to lose academic interest (Patterson, 2003).

Cooperative planning and team teaching accentuate the need for teachers to have a firm grasp on the intended outcomes. Perhaps this is why the National Middle School Association's priority events list (see Figure 1.1) contain both a priority addressing the need for continuing education for middle-level teachers and a priority calling for middle-level teachers to organized interdisciplinary teams. Each activity in today's highly active middle-level classroom should be selected because it leads to a desired skill, understanding, or attitude, or, even better, to the acquisition of a combination of desired skills, understandings, and attitudes. Cooperative planning is required because it enables teachers to pool their own talents. The nature of team planning demands excellent communications, and thus the importance of clear expectations is accentuated.

Constructivist teachers realize that the role of identifying clear outcomes is never-ending. As they work with their students to personalize their classrooms, middle-level teachers must continually adjust their curriculum to respond to the students' needs, which change daily as these students develop rapidly. Beginning teachers should be assisted in developing high-quality tasks for their initial lessons. Teachers need help to develop a repertoire of learning activities, so if one technique is ineffective in a particular class, they have other options.

National Standards

As mentioned in Chapter 1, the decision to set standards for the nation's schools has its roots in the belief that lawmakers need a way to compare the performance of one school to the average performance of all other schools. The push for a set of national standards began in 1989, when President George Bush called all governors together for the first National Education Summit. This summit produced the first set of national goals for education. The public favors such standards as national proficiency tests for graduation, a required national standardized curriculum for all schools, and, in general, increased federal government involvement in local schools ((Rose & Gallup, 2002). The goals sound good to laypersons, but even at the time they were written educators knew that they were foolishly optimistic. Consequently, they were never met: for example, "By the year 2000, all children will start school ready to learn," or "We will be first in the world in math and science by the year 2000."

The first national goals led to the creation of national standards, and the standards have led to high-stakes testing. John Merrow (2001, p. 658) warned that "Emphasizing testing may eventually drive parents away from public schools, particularly from high quality schools." Setting national goals also leads to such popular clichés as "All can learn" and "No child left behind." These ideals sound good, but they lead to such unintended consequences as establishing accountability based on state-developed tests, downplaying the need for early intervention for children who live in poverty, and using punishment as a motivator to improve schools (Thomas & Bainbridge, 2001). More will be said about national standards in Chapter 7.

Other Sources of National Standards

Whatever the content area you choose to teach, each area has a professional society. For example, English has the National Council of Teachers of English (NCTE); social studies has the National Council for Social Studies (NCSS); mathematics has the National Council of Teachers of Mathematics (NCTM); and science has the National Science Teachers Association (NSTA). In recent years, each of these societies has worked hard to develop minimum standards for its teachers to meet. Most states expect their teachers to meet the goals set by their respective national societies (Armstrong, Henson, & Savage, 2004). In addition, many states have established their own standards based on these professional society standards, which they require all of their teachers to meet.

National Certification

The National Board for Professional Teaching Standards (NBTPS) was created in 1987 to raise the level of teacher preparation. This organization sets high standards for teachers and issues certificates to those teachers who meet their high standards. This certification does not replace state teaching credentials or licenses (Armstrong et al., 2004). Over 10,000 teachers have met the NBPTS, and this number is expected to increase to more than 100,000 by the year 2006 (Harman, 2001). Getting certification by this board is optional. The benefits of certification include increased professional confidence, enhanced instructional skills (especially reflective skills), a clearer focus on student outcomes, and a greater commitment to professional growth (Bohen, 2001).

Outcome-Based Education

This chapter is about the expectations that teachers hold for their students. A popular term today is *outcome-based education* (OBE). Buschee and Baron (1994, p. 193) say that "outcome-based education is a student-centered, results-oriented design based on the belief that all individuals can learn." Objectives can give students direction and add meaning to education. Clarifying expected outcomes for students also allows students to be more involved with their assignments (Unger, 1994). If teachers choose the activities wisely, students' involvement can give them a better understanding of their own reasoning. Woods (1994) explains that "helping [students] understand the basis of their own reasoning and test it against the real world has become for many a fundamental curriculum practice" (p. 35).

As with most practices, OBE has not been universally accepted. Not all educators agree with stating anticipated outcomes. Some believe that setting outcomes may not help all students and may even hinder some. For example, Towers (1994) says that "to a degree OBE may be allowing our best and brightest future teachers to go unchallenged, drifting aimlessly from one undemanding task to the next. In short, minimum competency levels are stressed—not maximum learning expectations" (p. 627).

Connecticut, the first state to adopt statewide goals, has had an increase in graduate rate, percentage of students going to college, and average reading and math scores. However, even Connecticut has been criticized for using OBE. Zlatos (1994) summarized the effects of OBE in Connecticut: "Up until now, the consensus is that opponents have been winning the skirmish on OBE" (p. 28).

Aware that the practice of using objectives to design educational experiences is approved by some and disapproved by others, let us examine how objectives fit with other stated educational outcomes, including educational aims and educational goals.

Educational Expectations: Aims, Goals, and Objectives

Because you will be teaching at the middle level, you will be responsible for developing much of the curriculum. Because the curriculum should address what the state, the school, the community, and you the teacher want to achieve, you should examine these expectations at various levels. These will include the expectations set by professional learned societies representing the various disciplines (e.g., the National Science Teachers Association [NSTA], the National Council for the Teaching of English [NCTE], the National Council for the Social Studies [NCSS], the National Council for the Teaching of Mathematics [NCTM], the Interstate New Teacher Assessment and Support Consortium [INTASK], and local and state expectations. Expectations are written in different ways—aims, goals, and objectives—and all have different degrees of immediacy and specificity. The following discussion begins with educational aims, the broadest and most general expectations, and progresses toward objectives, the most immediate and specific expectations.

Aims

Educational aims are the most general expectations of all. In fact, they are so distant and so general that they can never be fully achieved. A good example of educational aims is the list of the *"Seven Cardinal Principles of Secondary Education"*:

1. Health
2. Development of good moral character
3. Worthy home membership
4. Citizenship
5. Worthy use of leisure time
6. Vocational efficiency
7. Development of the fundamental processes

Each of these expectations can never be completely fulfilled or attained (e.g., people must work all their lives to preserve their health, develop their morality, and be good citizens), and the same is true of all educational aims. They provide long-term direction, but no one can attain them completely.

Goals

Educational goals are expectations that take weeks, months, or even years to attain. A particular middle school may have as one of its goals that all students will be literate by the time they graduate. Every student may not attain this goal, but probably most will achieve it. Goals can spark a class's interest. Unger (1994), reporting on a class that had been introduced to a unit's goals, said: "Because they know the goals, Kendall's students became more involved in their projects and felt more at ease in exploring and assessing their achievement of the goals" (p. 9). Goals can be used to motivate and challenge students. High expectations are desirable in all classes; in planning, however, it is imperative that teachers involve students and keep their best interests at heart.

Teacher of the Year

It is vital to create an academic environment that is highly challenging. . . . I always try to combine this challenging environment with lots of positive reinforcement for students whose attention and effort are appropriately focused.

New Jersey Teacher of the Year Constance Cloonan (1999, p. 374)

A goal need not take six or twelve years to reach. For example, a science teacher may set a goal that all students will appreciate all forms of life by the end of the school year (a year-long goal). Or the teacher whose students spend six weeks studying endocrines may set the following goal: Students will understand reproduction, transportation, and respiration. Students thus can attain an educational goal, although some may not. The goal can require several days to several years to attain. Students usually have a set time to reach a goal, such as a semester or a six-week grading period.

Several factors facilitate goal attainment. Students are more likely to attain clearly stated, challenging yet attainable, and meaningful goals (Leithwood, Menzies, & Jantzi, 1994, pp. 43–44).

Objectives

This book uses the term **educational objectives** to refer precisely to what is expected of students daily. We might think of these as *performance objectives,* because each refers to students' ability to perform selected tasks in one or more specific ways. As Wulf and Schane (1994) notes, when objectives are used, "there are no unexpected or surprise results, since both parties have agreed upon the end product" (p. 117). Because performance objectives are the most specific of all educational expectations, they must be written in great detail. The following section explains how to write performance objectives.

There are many possible criteria for writing performance objectives, and professors of education endorse various ways of teaching students to write them. Most authorities agree, however, that all statements of performance objectives must meet at least four criteria:

1. Objectives must be stated in terms of expected student (not teacher) behavior.
2. Objectives must specify the conditions under which students are expected to perform.
3. Objectives must specify the minimum acceptable level of performance.
4. The student should be the subject of each objective.

Look again at the first of these criteria for writing objectives. Stating objectives in terms of expected student behavior is important, because all teaching is directed toward students. The lesson's success is defined by the students' response. To be more precise, school exists to improve students' mental, physical, social, emotional, and moral behavior. When you state objectives in terms of desired student performance and use observable and measurable specifics, you and your students will better understand what you expect of them and if they are meeting these expectations. Figure 2.1 shows verbs that describe specific, observable, and measurable actions (see the Yes column) and verbs that are too vague to be accurately observed and measured (see the No column).

Because students can grasp only a limited number of major ideas in a class period of 45 or 50 minutes, the daily lesson plan should contain only four or five major ideas. Suppose you are an English teacher who wants to teach composition writing. You select four or five of the most important ideas about capturing and holding readers' attention. These become the content for the first day's lesson in a unit titled "Composition Writing." You may determine that five ideas are essential to capturing the readers' attention and that four ideas are essential to holding it, once captured. If so, you might plan one lesson on how to capture the reader's attention and a subsequent lesson on how to hold the reader's attention.

Write your objectives in terms of desired student behavior. Emphasize not "Today I'll teach" but "As a result of the lesson, each student will be able to. . . ." Second, state the conditions under which students are expected to perform ("When given a list containing vertebrates and invertebrates. . . ."). Third, state the expected level of performance ("with 80 percent accuracy" or "without error"). Finally, avoid using verbs that cannot be observed or measured, such as *learn, know,* and *understand.* Instead, use specific, action-oriented verbs such as *identify, list, explain, name, describe,* and *compare.*

Effective teachers use **mnemonics,** which are mental devices or strategies designed to help students remember important concepts. Teachers also use mnemonics to enhance their own remembering. A good mnemonic for remembering the four essential characteristics of a performance object is ABCD, where A represents the audience (Students will . . .), B describes the expected behavior (what you expect students to be able to do as a consequence of the lesson), C describes the conditions under which you expect them to be able to perform this act (e.g., "Given a U.S. map, students will . . .), and D stands for the degree (how well you expect students to be able to perform this act, for example, "In eight tries out of ten").

Yes	No
Build	Appreciate
Classify	Consider
Contrast	Desire
Demonstrate	Feel
Distinguish	Find interesting
Evaluate	Have insight into
Identify	Know
Interpret	Learn
Label	Like to
List	Love to
Match	Really like to
Measure	Recognize
Name	Remember
Remove	See that
Select	Think
State	Understand
Write	Want to

FIGURE 2.1 PERFORMANCE TERMS: Specific and measurable (yes); vague, not measurable (no)

Adapted from Kenneth T. Henson, *Methods and Strategies for Teaching in Secondary and Middle Schools,* third edition. Published by Allyn and Bacon, Boston, MA. Copyright © 1996 by Pearson Education. Reprinted by permission of the publisher.

Reflection

Each performance objective should contain four parts. Check the above objectives against these criteria. It is as simple as A, B, C, D.

Audience: The student should be the subject of each objective.
Behavior: The student's behavior should be the verb of each objective.
Conditions: The objective should describe the conditions under which students are expected to perform this behavior.
Degree: The degree or level of performance required of the students should be specified.

1. Why is it necessary to focus each objective on student behavior as opposed to describing desired teacher behavior?
2. What assumption can be made if an objective has no statement of minimum level of performance?

Performance Objectives in the Three Domains

Some of education's aims and goals deal with thinking (e.g., command of fundamental processes), others involve attitude (e.g., development of moral character), and still others focus on physical skills (e.g., physical education). You should establish performance objectives in each of these domains (cognitive, affective, and psychomotor) for each class.

Writing Objectives in the Cognitive Domain

The first real systematic approach to helping teachers write objectives at specified levels came in 1956, when Benjamin S. Bloom and a group of students at the University of Chicago developed a taxonomy of educational objectives in the cognitive domain that includes six levels (Bloom, 1956):

Level 1: Knowledge
Level 2: Comprehension
Level 3: Application
Level 4: Analysis
Level 5: Synthesis
Level 6: Evaluation

To involve students in tasks that require them to function at these six levels, you must be able to write objectives for each level.

Level 1: Knowledge

The simplest and least demanding objectives are those that require students merely to memorize facts. Before students can move on to more advanced tasks, they must first know basic facts. For example, many middle-level mathematics problems require students to multiply. The multiplication tables are probably best learned by memorization. Unfortunately, many secondary classes fail to go beyond this most basic level. There is nothing dishonorable about introducing assignments or tasks at the knowledge level, as long as such assignments have a purpose and do not dominate the curriculum.

An example of an objective written at the knowledge level is "When given a list of 10 elements and a list of atomic weights, the student will be able to match 8 of the 10 elements correctly with their atomic weights." Another example is "When given a list containing 10 vertebrates and 10 invertebrates, the student will correctly identify 8 of the 10 invertebrates."

Notice that both objectives begin with a statement of the conditions under which students should perform the task ("When given . . . ") and define the desired student performance ("the student will . . . "). In addition, both objectives contain measurable, action-oriented verbs (*match, identify*) and state the minimum acceptable level of performance ("8 of the 10").

Level 2: Comprehension

Objectives at the comprehension level require students to do more than memorize. Students must translate, interpret, or predict a continuation of trends (Bloom, 1956). For example, two middle-level teachers team-teaching an interdisciplinary language arts/social studies class, who want students to learn the difference between phrases and clauses, may set the following objective: "When given a paragraph containing two clauses and three phrases, the student will correctly underscore the phrases using a single line and underscore the clauses using double lines." What is the minimum acceptable level of performance for this objective? Because no acceptable level is stated, assume that students are expected to perform with 100 percent accuracy.

See if you can write one objective in your teaching field at the comprehension level that requires students to translate, one objective that requires them to interpret, and one that requires them to predict. (Hint: You may want to use charts, maps, graphs, or tables.)

Level 3: Application

Objectives written at the application level require students to use principles or generalizations to solve a concrete problem. For example, a mathematics teacher might write the following objective for geometry students: "Given the lengths of both legs of a right triangle, the student will use the Pythagorean theorem to solve the length of the hypotenuse." Or the language arts teacher on this team might write the following objective: "Given the beats and measures in iambic pentameter, the student will write a five-verse poem in iambic pentameter without missing more than one beat per verse." The advantage of writing objectives at this level is that once students learn to apply a principle to one situation, they can apply it to multiple situations to solve many other problems.

Level 4: Analysis

Like the application-level objectives, analysis-level objectives require students to work with principles, concepts, and broad generalizations—but students must do this themselves. Students are required to break down the concepts and principles to understand them better, and to do this they must understand not only the content but also its structural form.

For example, a social studies teacher who is teaming with a science teacher might write the following objective for a class studying how a bill becomes a law: "Given a particular law, students will trace its development from its introduction as a bill, listing every major step without missing any." The science teacher on this team might write the following objective for a group of students studying the automotive electrical system: "Starting with the positive battery terminal, the student will trace the current throughout the automobile until it returns to the negative battery terminal, stating what happens in the coil, alternator, distributor, and condenser, without getting more than one of these steps out of sequence." The science teacher might also ask students to trace the circulatory system.

Suppose you are teaching the circulatory system to a science class. See if you can write an objective that will enable students to understand the sequence in which the blood travels throughout the body. (Hint: You may want to designate one of the heart's chambers as a beginning point.)

Check your objective to see whether it includes the designated criteria. Is it written in terms of expected student performance? If so, underline the part of the objective that identifies both the performer and the performance. Does the verb you used express action? Can it be observed or measured? Is your statement of conditions clear? Circle it. Does it accurately describe the conditions under which you expect students to perform? Did you begin the objective with a statement such as "Given . . . " or "When given . . . " (this is an easy way to be sure you have included a statement of conditions in each objective). Is your statement very general, such as "When given a test" or "following a lesson"? Can you make it more specific? Can you think of a way to alter the task, making it easier to perform, simply by changing the conditions? Finally, examine your objective to see whether it states a minimum acceptable level of performance. Draw a box around this statement. Does it tell the student exactly how accurately the task must be performed for it to be acceptable? Does it contain a percentage or fraction, such as "with 80 percent accuracy" or "four out of five times"? Can you express your concept of minimum acceptable level of performance without using percentages or fractions?

By now you probably would like to start over and rewrite your original objective, improving each part.

Level 5: Synthesis

In a way, the synthesis-level objective is the opposite of the analysis-level objective, because it requires the student to take several parts and put them together. The synthesis-level objective is more demanding, however, because it requires students to form a new whole. Unlike analysis-level objectives, synthesis-level objectives require students to use divergent thinking and creativity.

The student's attitude is especially important at the synthesis level. Synthesis requires experimentation—investigating the new. Furthermore, students must understand that there is not a definite solution or preconceived notion to reach.

For example, suppose our hypothetical social studies teacher, who wants students to understand problems the early settlers experienced, prefaces the unit with the following objective: "Suppose you are on a team of explorers that is going to another inhabited planet to start a new colony. List at least 10 rules you would propose to guide the new nationals, making sure that at least 5 of the rules would serve to protect the interests of all the native inhabitants."

Because they require creative thinking, synthesis-level questions are difficult to write. You may need practice before you feel comfortable writing objectives at this level.

Suppose you are an art teacher. In your class, you have studied such concepts as cubism (using cubes to form objects) and pointillism (using points to form shapes). Can you write an objective at the synthesis level? (Hint: Begin by identifying a particular effect you want your students to achieve using cubism and pointillism; this might be a specific feeling or mood.)

One example of such an objective is as follows: "While looking at cubism in Picasso's paintings and at pointillism in Seurat's paintings, the student will combine these two techniques and a new technique to create at least three of the following feelings: happiness, surprise, sadness, anger, love." At the synthesis level, be sure to provide enough structure to make the assignment meaningful and yet allow students enough freedom to put themselves into the work.

Obviously, the Internet can play an important part, enabling teachers to raise the level of thinking among their students by exposing them to the world. For example, students could be expected to track down a number of paintings that use cubism or pointillism and compare and contrast the ways the painters have employed each.

Level 6: Evaluation

The highest level in Bloom's cognitive domain is the evaluation level. Here the student is required to make judgments based on definite criteria, not just on opinions. Evaluation-level objectives contain various combinations of elements in the first five levels.

A teacher of gifted students might use the following objective with students who are studying diplomatic and persuasive techniques: "While viewing a video recording of a President's two most recent public addresses, each student will rate the speeches in terms of tact and persuasion, pinpointing in each address at least three areas of strength and three areas of weakness."

A physical education teacher who is teaching bowling may want to write an objective that involves the starting position, delivery, and follow-through. Can you help this teacher by writing an objective at the evaluation level? If you do not bowl, you may substitute another activity that involves the same three steps, such as golf or diving.

Now examine your evaluation-level objective. Must judgment be based on supportive data or on internal or external standards?

The ability to write objectives at each cognitive level is crucial, because this is the only way to ensure that your students will learn to develop intellectual skills at each level. Because teaching students to make judgments is vital, you must be able to state objectives clearly. You may want a classmate to critique a few of your objectives for clarity.

Not all educators agree that such distinct steps represent students' actual development. One skeptic is Donald Orlich (1991), who says:

> *For over a quarter of a century, I have assumed and taught my students that the four upper levels of the taxonomy had to be taught in a sequence. But the more that I observed young students in hands-on classes . . . the less support I found for the linear assumption. . . . I can no longer assume a linear connection to the four upper levels of the cognitive taxonomy. Nor can I support the idea of hierarchical arrangement of the entire model! (p. 160)*

Orlich uses the following selection from John Goodlad's 1984 book, *A Place Called School* (Goodlad, 1984), to alert readers that other educators also have concerns over the levels of objectives represented in high-school curricula:

> *Only rarely did we find evidence to suggest instruction [in reading and math] likely to go much beyond merely possession of information to a level of understanding its implications and either applying it or exploring its possible applications. Nor did we see activities likely to arouse students' curiosity or to involve them in seeking a solution to some problem not already laid bare by teachers or textbook. . . . And it appears that this preoccupation with the lower intellectual processes pervades social studies and science as well. An analysis of topics studied and materials used gives not an impression of students studying human adaptations and exploration, but of facts to be learned. (p. 236)*

When you accept your first teaching position, one of the first challenges you will face is to raise the thinking levels of your students. Good planning on your part will enable students to reach higher levels of the taxonomy, because students cannot function beyond their level of development.

Perhaps you have noticed that this book presents perspectives of critics as well as proponents of controversial topics. As a middle-level teacher, you will always want to examine both sides of issues, even those issues that you strongly favor or strongly oppose. Your success in using objectives and all other methods will depend on your understanding of each method's strengths and limitations.

Reflection
Verb choice is important in writing good objectives. All verbs should be both observable and measurable.

1. Which verb tense would be least desirable?
2. Why is *understand* a poor verb?

Writing Objectives in the Affective Domain

Educators have recently become more concerned with the effect of schooling on the attitudes of students. This concern has been stimulated in part by the students' own acknowledgment of the difference between their attitudes and values and those of "the system." Such differences began to show up in the 1950s with the beatniks, who were rebelling against the material-wealth syndrome that was sweeping the nation. Everyone seemed determined to get ahead of the Joneses by building a larger house and owning a larger car or boat. The youth of the 1960s expressed their dissatisfaction about U.S. involvement in Vietnam by burning draft cards and holding moratoriums and demonstrations. Further dissent was expressed in civil rights marches.

> ### Proactive Exercise
>
> **Anticipated Situation**
>
> - You know that:
>   It is more important that students understand fewer topics at greater depth, yet many parents and some teachers and administrators will press to have you "cover the book."
>
> - You know that:
>   Many students believe that their IQ is set at birth and never changes. Indeed, some will publicly announce, "I'm just not smart."
>
> **Proactive Alternative**
>
> - You can:
>   Prepare a brief presentation for parents' night or a teachers' meeting to show the advantages of pursuing topics in depth. You might include such advantages as increased motivation and even diminished discipline problems; two results associated with student-initiated learning.
>
> - You can:
>   Prepare visuals for your classroom that dispel this myth. Such evidence could include stories about slow starters (e.g., Einstein and Edison were considered to be too slow to master the content in their classes).

For a number of reasons, including the increase in drug abuse and a diminishing of the family, many of today's students are without a clear sense of purpose. This displacement is especially acute in middle schools because the rapid changes in the world are paralleled by the rapid interpersonal changes during adolescence. These combined conditions have led the Carnegie Council on Adolescent Development Staff (1995) to set as a goal for all middle-level teachers the making of their classes more personal.

In recent years the community at large has begun to blame schools for everything from pollution to destruction of natural resources to economic recession. The greatest accusation currently aimed at schools is that they are failing to prepare students to succeed on state and national exams (cognitive domain) as well as failing to *discipline* students (affective domain).

Society's interest in having schools address the affective domain is shown by a 1994 Gallup Poll (Elam, Rose, & Gallup, 1994, p. 50), which found that over 90 percent of Americans favor teaching respect for others, hard work, fairness, compassion, and politeness. Furthermore, two-thirds of Americans favor nondevotional instruction about various world religions in their local public schools. By 1998, 67 percent of Americans favored amending the U.S. Constitution to permit prayers in school (Rose & Gallup, 1998). Although schools will never rid society of all ills, they must play a major role in shaping students' views on such important issues as equality, world peace, honesty, integrity, and the value of life itself.

But what exactly *is* the school's role in shaping students' values? Does a teacher have the right to influence students' values? Patterson (2003) acknowledges, "Values are taught in our schools whether we mean to or not." (p. 570). First, you cannot avoid influencing your students' values. Second, all teachers should stress such values as honesty, fairness, and good citizenship. On the other hand, do not try to persuade students to accept your religious, political, or cultural beliefs.

Schools should help students become aware of their own values, question these values, and discover whether their values are factual and logical or prejudiced and illogical. David

R. Krathwohl helped develop a system to categorize values. The outcome was a hierarchy of objectives in the affective domain (Krathwohl, Bloom, & Masia, 1964):

Level 1:   Receiving
Level 2:   Responding
Level 3:   Valuing
Level 4:   Organization
Level 5:   Characterization

Level 1: Receiving

Receiving refers to students' being aware or alert to new information or experiences. Students receive information in varying degrees. In a given class, some may not receive the information at all, while others attend or receive at a low level of awareness. Still others may be very selective, attending only to what they find meaningful. Of course, teachers can help students develop attention skills.

All teachers want their students to listen carefully to their lessons and to be aware of their peers' feelings. Can you write an objective that enables you to measure how well students pay attention to a lesson? Now examine your objective. Does it include a statement of the conditions under which you want the students to perform? Does it specify a minimum acceptable level of performance? Is it observable and measurable? An example might be: "When participating in a group discussion, the student will ask every other student at least one question."

Can you write an objective at the receiving level for a ninth-grade art class taking a field trip to a local art museum?

Level 2: Responding

At the *responding* level, students react to whatever has attracted their attention. This requires physical behavior. Responses may be overt or purposeful or simple and automatic. A student who becomes involved at the responding level might, at the teacher's request or even voluntarily, go to the library and research an issue further. Or the student might obey the rules set forth in the class.

Can you write an objective at the responding level? Try a responding objective for a homework assignment. You choose the subject and grade level.

Examine your objective to determine whether it involves active student participation. Does it reflect the student's attitude(s)? It should. Specifically, a student who performs this objective shows a commitment to the homework assignment that a student who does not complete the objective might not have.

Level 3: Valuing

A *value* is demonstrated when someone prizes a behavior enough to perform it even in the face of alternatives. (A person who reacts without having had time to think does not necessarily demonstrate a value.) If people really value a behavior, they are likely to perform it even though they know the results it may bring, and they will do so repeatedly.

For example, a mathematics teacher whose students are learning to use simulation games might write the following valuing objective: "When given free time next week at the end of each period to read, play simulation games, talk to friends, or sleep, each student will choose to play simulation games at least two out of the five days." Note that the objective asks students to choose individually of their own free will and to repeat that choice. Also note that students can choose alternatives.

One of the most valued qualities of U.S. life is our freedom to be unique, and a basic strength of the United States results from its tradition of welcoming peoples of all cultures. Ironically, this orientation toward embracing all people makes the teacher's role in working with values, morals, and religions challenging. Teachers must make a special effort in multicultural classrooms to ensure that all students and the teacher understand values and morals that differ from their own. Unfortunately, there is no one way to do this. In fact, no one process ensures any success at all. Perhaps the best approach any teacher can take is a heart-centered one that begins by establishing and maintaining a classroom climate of mutual respect by all and for all class members and the teacher.

Teachers of multicultural classes should learn more about their students' cultures and encourage all students to do likewise. Including affective objectives in each lesson is a good start toward achieving this goal.

Level 4: Organization

The *organization* level of behavior requires individuals to join different values to build a value system. Whenever two or more of their values conflict, they must resolve the conflict. For example, secondary and middle school students constantly encounter friends' and parents' conflicting expectations. As students mature, it is hoped that they will not always react to peer pressure but will learn to listen to their own beliefs and values. At this level, students may change their behavior or defend it.

For example, a teacher might assign students to defend opposing positions on a controversial issue. By defending both sides, each student will compare the two points of view and may even learn to compromise between the two extremes.

A teacher of a class in U.S. government might introduce a hypothetical bill and have students form two teams, one composed of those who favor the bill and one of those who oppose it. The objective might read: "After having had the opportunity to support the bill, and the opportunity to try to defeat it, students will combine all the information and write a statement that expresses their feelings for and against the bill. Given the opportunity, the students will choose to modify the bill to make it fit better with their own value systems."

Level 5: Characterization by a Value or a Value Complex

At the *characterization* level, students have already developed their own value systems. They are so consistent in the way they behave that they are predictable. At this level, students also demonstrate a degree of individuality and self-reliance.

An example of an objective written at the characterization level is: "Each student will bring one newspaper article or news report to class and explain at least two ways in which the article caused the student to change his or her mind from a previously held position on a controversial issue." Does this objective prove that the student really has changed values? What if the student just says so? Right now the student may believe this, but what about a week from now or a year from now? Can you rewrite this objective to remove or reduce this doubt?

Writing Objectives in the Psychomotor Domain

The psychomotor domain involves developing physical skills that require coordination of mind and body. It is especially relevant to physical education, art, drama, music, and voca-

> ### Proactive Exercise
>
> **Anticipated Situation**
>
> - You know that:
>   Students learn and achieve in those classrooms for which they feel a strong sense of belonging.
>
> - You know that:
>   Contemporary teachers are strapped for time.
>
> **Proactive Alternative**
>
> - You can:
>   Begin collecting ideas of ways to personalize your classroom. Begin with a few simple practices such as using good manners. Make a list of ways you can make all students feel welcome, wanted, and liked.
>
> - You can:
>   Hold a discussion with your students to discover ways the class can use the computer to save time.

tional courses, but all subjects provide many opportunities to develop psychomotor skills. Although this domain was the last for which a taxonomy was developed, at least two scales have now been developed. The following taxonomy is based on a scale developed by E. J. Simpson (1972):

Level 1:	Perception
Level 2:	Set
Level 3:	Guided response
Level 4:	Mechanism
Level 5:	Complex overt response
Level 6:	Adaptation
Level 7:	Origination

Level 1: Perception

Purposeful motor activity begins in the brain, where phenomena received act as guides to motor activity. The performer must first become aware of a stimulus, pick up on cues for action, and then act on these cues. For example, a writer discovers that she is separating her subjects and verbs, thus diluting the impact of her themes. A baseball batter notices himself flinching and taking short steps away from the plate when swinging, causing him to miss the ball. A piano student becomes aware of failing to reduce the interval between double notes.

A sample objective at the perception level is: "Following a demonstration, a student who has been confusing x and y axes in plotting graphs will notice that the x axis always runs horizontally and the y axis always runs vertically."

Level 2: Set

In the psychomotor domain, *set* refers to an individual's readiness to act. It includes both mental readiness and physical and emotional readiness. For example, a diver always pauses before a dive to establish a psychological, emotional, and physical set. Emotionally, she must feel confident about her ability to make a safe and accurate dive. Psychologically, although she may have performed the same dive hundreds of times, she still takes the time to think through the sequence of steps before each dive. Physically, she must ready her muscles to respond quickly and accurately. On a less dramatic scale, students preparing to take notes or do a writing assignment may be seen flexing their fingers or rubbing their eyes—in short, getting set to perform at their best.

An example of a psychomotor objective at this level for piano students is: "At the signal 'ready,' each student will assume proper posture and place all fingers in correct keyboard position." Is there a minimum level of performance specified in this objective? Can you rewrite this objective to assign a more meaningful type of behavior? Take a minute to think about this objective. List two ways you can establish minimum levels of performance. Does either of your objectives explain what is meant by "correct posture" or "correct keyboard position"? Do both of your suggested changes help make the act measurable?

Level 3: Guided Response

Once students see the need to act and ready themselves to act, they may find that they need guidance for acts involving complex skills. For example, students in the photography club may need verbal guidance as they process their first negatives. An example of an objective to enhance the development of these skills is "When given step-by-step directions in the darkroom, each student will open the film cylinder, remove the film, and, without touching the surface of the film, wind it on a spool so that the surface of each round does not touch previous rounds."

Level 4: Mechanism

The *mechanism* level involves performing an act somewhat automatically, without having to pause to think through each separate step. For example, the photography teacher might want students to be able to perform the entire sequence of development operations while simultaneously counting the number of seconds required to wait between each step. A teacher might write the following objective at the mechanism level: "Given a series of compounds to analyze, the student will operate the electron microscope without having to pause even once to think about the sequence involved in mounting the slide, focusing the projector, and changing the lens size."

Level 5: Complex Overt Response

The level of *complex overt response* is an extension of the previous level, but it involves more complicated tasks. For example, in a first-aid unit a teacher might write an objective at this level such as: "When given an announcement that someone is choking, the student will immediately respond by applying the Heimlich maneuver, using proper grasp and pressure."

Level 6: Adaptation

At the *adaptation* level the student is required to adjust performance as different situations dictate. For example, when taken to the bowling lanes a physical education student will move to the left after throwing a ball in the left gutter.

Level 7: Origination

At the *origination* level, the highest level of the psychomotor domain, the student creates new movement patterns to fit the particular situation. For example, chefs add their own touch of genius, and pianists alter their style or the music itself. An art teacher might write the following objective: "Given a mixture of powders and compounds of varying textures, the student will use these to accentuate the feeling being communicated in an oil painting."

THE CASE

Professional Learning Communities

Karen Embry Mayo, Stephen F. Austin State University
Claudia Whitley, Thomas J. Rusk Middle School

Dr. Karen Embry Mayo is Associate Professor of Secondary Education and Educational Leadership at Stephen F. Austin State University. She received her B.S. from East Texas Baptist University, her M.Ed. from the University of Texas, and her Ed.D. From Texas A&M University.

Claudia Whitley is the Principal of Thomas J. Rusk Middle School in the Nacogdoches Independent School District in East Texas. She received her B.S., M.Ed., and Mid-management certification from Stephen F. Austin State University.

Background

Designing instruction that responds to the ever-changing needs of diverse schools is closely related to educating teachers through ongoing, long-term professional development. One context to sustain teacher learning occurs within constructivist professional development opportunities that encourage classroom practitioners to collaborate and talk in learning communities. The demands on school personnel, scheduling constraints of teachers, and teacher turnover contribute to the problem of achieving sustained, continuous professional development.

By setting goals and engaging in long-range planning, schools attempt to respond to student needs by promoting changes in teacher practice. A growing number of studies on educational reform clearly show that school improvement does not occur without concurrent change in the knowledge and skills of teachers (Wilson and Berne, 1999) Typically, the most common format for educating teachers occurs through single-day workshops, yet the influence of this type of professional development in actually changing teacher practice in classrooms has proven minimal. Ball and Cohen (2001) compare the effects of "one-shot" approaches to professional development to a patchwork quilt, an array of pieced-together school initiatives focused on the acquisition of isolated strategies, not based on teacher interest or need.

Today, however, professional development in schools is undergoing dramatic change (Willis, 2002). The traditional framework for educating teachers in a single-day workshop approach is being challenged by research into the nature of professional development in schools that are successful in serving diverse student populations Teachers need professional development

> *As you enter the teaching profession, consider carefully the school where you first decide to teach. Will this school nurture your professional skills and promote your individual growth? Will your voice be heard? If you do not think so, keep looking. Teachers, like students, need a positive learning environment in order to grow.*

that enables them to engage in long- and short-range planning while interacting with and assessing diverse students.

In a meta-analysis of the research related to professional development, Abdul-Haqq (1995) defined critical attributes necessary for meaningful professional development. Examining the effectiveness of changes in professional development over the past decade, Dr. James Stiglar (in Willis, 2002), reinforces and elaborates on the work of Abdul-Haqq. Together Abdul-Haqq (1995) and Stiglar (Wilson, 2002) agree on several core principles for promoting responsive professional development. These principles, which focus on building a professional learning community, are characterized by a learner-centered, or constructivist, approach to professional development. First, professional development must be school-based and related directly to teacher practice. Second, professional development should occur collaboratively. Third, professional development should be ongoing. Fourth, the activities of professional development should provide feedback and allow teachers to analyze their own practice. And finally, professional development activities need to allow opportunity for individual reflection and group inquiry, and include coaching with follow-up support.

Similar studies have underscored these principles, and as a result, professional development is shifting from a traditional top-down framework to an approach that is site-specific, contextualized within the community of teachers and students in a particular school (Ball, 1996; Little, 1994; Putnam & Borko, 1997). This type of professional development focuses on student learning, relates directly to both curriculum and practice, and targets ways to help teachers help students (Wilson, 2002). Stiglar (in Wilson, 2002) contends that professional development must utilize systematic feedback to guide its procedures.

The constructivist nature of this professional development embraces a Vygotskian, or social, perspective, which encourages learning in communities (see Chapter 1). Alternative professional learning formats, such as book clubs and teacher study groups, allow teachers to examine and investigate their personal assumptions and practices within a professional learning community. This case study describes one principal's efforts to redesign the delivery of professional development on a large, diverse middle school campus and to build professional learning communities of teachers who structure their own learning to facilitate their students' understanding.

Thomas J. Rusk Middle School

Thomas J. Rusk Middle School (TJR) is located in a small historic town in deep East Texas. The white limestone school building was constructed in 1939 by the Works Progress Administration (WPA) and sits squarely in the middle of a large sprawling city block located in the center of town near an area known as Washington Square, a historic district. From the blue hand-painted tiles of the built-in drinking fountains to its wrought-iron handrails and crown molding, TJR stands as a reminder of art deco style and post-Depression architecture found in many public buildings of this period.

TJR was originally built as a high school during a time when schools in the United States were racially segregated. A cornerstone in the boys' gym reads, "Washington Square Donated 1859 For the Education of White Children." A bronze plaque above explains that the cornerstone was preserved from the first brick school building in Nacogdoches, Texas, a grammar school built in 1904. Today however, TJR stands as a school with a very diverse campus population of nearly 1,000 students in grades 7 and 8. The current student body is approximately 48 percent Caucasian, 38 African American, and 22 percent Hispanic. These numbers are changing rapidly. The fastest-growing sector of the student population at TJR is the Hispanic population. From 1999 to 2001, the number of students identified as Limited English Proficient (LEP) increased by 62 percent at TJR. This rapid growth reflects the influx of Hispanics attracted to work opportunities on nearby poultry farms. Over half of the total student population (53.7 percent) is economically disadvantaged.

The staff at TJR is made up of about eighty teachers and twenty paraprofessionals and staff. There are three assistant principals. One assistant principal deals with curriculum and instruction, and two assistant principals, one for each grade level, oversee discipline. TJR also has two full-time counselors, one social worker, and several additional social workers on call. There is a diagnostic nurse, on campus full-time, and a juvenile probation officer. The campus police for the school district is also located on the TJR campus. Despite the large, open spaces, and traffic moving around the campus, there is a feeling of safety on the school grounds, as uniformed officers are visible and move easily about the campus.

The faculty and students at TJR are organized into seven academic teams. There are three seventh-grade teams, three eighth-grade teams and a team consisting of a combined seventh- and eighth-grade unit. Seven teachers serve each team. On each team, there are two language arts teachers, two math teachers, a science teacher, a social studies teacher, and the seventh teacher is either an English as a second language (ESL) teacher or a special education teacher who co-teaches with a teacher on the academic team. In order to meet the dual language needs of the LEP students, the cross-age team of seventh and eighth graders, referred to as the ESL team, was created. With the exception of the ESL team, the students on the other teams are mixed heterogeneously according to ethnicity, socioeconomic status, and academic achievement.

Currently, TJR is the only middle school in the town, but that will change in the near future. The local school district recently passed a $41 million bond issue for campus improvement. Part of the money will be spent on building a new middle school. The new campus is expected to open in the fall of 2003 and will serve 750 students in the sixth, seventh, and eighth grades. TJR will then become one of two middle schools in the town.

The Principal

The principal of TJR, Ms. Claudia Whitley, is an instructional leader who knows and understands the culture of TJR from a long history with the school. Ms. Whitley, a native of the local area, received her bachelor's degree in elementary education from Stephen F. Austin State University in 1977 and began her teaching career as a sixth-grade math teacher at TJR when it was located on another site. Two years later, she switched to teaching language arts when the school moved to the present location. Ms. Whitley described some of the changes:

> I was very fortunate to come to the district during that time when we made those critical decisions toward the forming of this school. We moved into this building in the fall of 1979 with sixth, seventh, and eighth grade. We used the middle school concept. We worked with Dr. Paul George from the University of Florida. He was one of the foremost gurus on middle school education. And we got a really good background on what middle school should be about. We began in 1979, which was kind of forward for the time. It was really neat to be a part of that.

In the new building, Ms. Whitley taught seventh-grade language arts and reading for seventeen years. She earned a reading specialist certification in 1987. Over the years, Ms. Whitley experienced a great deal of change in the school as curriculum and schedules were designed and implemented. These changes led her to question many practices. While working on her administrative certification, Ms. Whitley accepted an assistant principal position in 1995. She completed mid-management certification in 1996 and was appointed principal in 1998.

Ms. Whitley became principal during a time when TJR was undergoing drastic program and administrative changes under the supervision of a new superintendent. Ms. Whitley implemented quality school management and choice theory (Glasser, 1998), new district initiatives, in her building, but when she looked into what was happening in the classrooms, she wasn't seeing implementation. So she began to look for a model of professional development that would help teachers meet student needs. Ms. Whitley also knew that she needed to rebuild a sense of community among the teachers, who had been reassigned to newly formed academic teams.

> My biggest concern was a lack of evidence that what was being learned in professional development was actually applied in classrooms. We had good professional development. I thought we should grow, but I wasn't seeing the change that I wanted to see in the group. I attributed that to the approach. We would come in, and we would have an area of concern. We would work on that topic for one day and then there was not the follow-up to sustain change.

Examining professional development models in other schools, Ms. Whitley found a school district near Dallas that designed professional development based on individual teachers' needs. The principal worked with each teacher to determine what that individual teacher felt she or he needed to do to improve, and then an individualized learning plan was created for the teacher. In addition, the teachers assessed the areas where they felt the school, as a whole, needed growth. Using the individual plans and school goals, the principal created strands for year-long professional development.

Redesigning Professional Development

Adapting the model described, Ms. Whitley began implementation by refocusing the duties of the assistant principals around the subject areas. Ms. Whitley selected the reading/language arts teachers. The three assistant principals chose to work with teachers in one of the other content areas, math, science, and elective programs.

> *It was the most logical model of staff development that I had ever seen, and so I went to my principal and I said look it makes so much more sense to try this. And so we gave it a shot and came up with a proposal to offer staff development in strands and each teacher would select the strand they felt we needed. . . . What we [the principals] try to do is to take our strength and build on all our strengths. And we work very closely with that department. We evaluate the teachers in that department and we attend department meetings for those departments, so we become an expert and we truly know what's going on in that area that we are assigned.*

In the department meetings, the principals listened to what the teachers were saying. They learned why teachers were bored or resistant to professional development.

> *The other thing that I found as I talked with my teachers is that a lot of times people felt like not attending professional development because it was repetitive. With a staff as large as mine you have a lot of turn-over, and if you want to keep people on the same page you have to repeat the staff development that you are offering for the new people coming in.*

Before the end of the school year, Ms. Whitley and the teachers met and examined the goals described in the campus plan. Ms. Whitley then asked the teachers to identify the areas of professional development they needed in order to help students meet the objectives in the campus plan. Ms. Whitley then worked over the summer redesigning professional development for the following year. She described these as strands:

> *Our campus selected the strands we thought we needed based on our campus plan. . . . When the teachers came, we presented both of those strands to them and they each selected two strands they wanted to work on throughout the coming year. What happened then is rather than going through a full staff development where we spent one day on a certain topic, we designed it to where each strand would be in hourly sessions throughout the school year. So you would meet for one hour in September and an hour in October and so on. And we had a common strand over that year-long period and teachers were able to come in and be introduced to a small concept and go out and try it in a classroom for a month and come back and discuss what they did. . . . It worked very well for us because it gave teachers a chance to study the same topic for a period of time rather than that isolated "one shot" thing where you never dealt with it again.*

Some of the strands were led by principals, others by teachers. Facilitation came from a variety of sources, including teachers, administrators, university professors, and educational consultants. Finding personnel to facilitate the topics was also a shared responsibility among Ms. Whitley and the teachers:

> *As we went through the campus plan, we identified a strand and then I found someone who would facilitate that strand. It might be an administrator, it might be a teacher. So that someone was responsible for facilitating, not necessarily conveying all their knowledge to the group but was in charge of organizing and developing that strand and talking about what the group needs. We have had guests come in and talk about a specific topic, and we have done group book study, and we have had people trained in new programs. We have been able to look at content areas or come together and work on curricula on their department or their grade level.*

When the teachers returned in August, they were given the option of signing up for two strands of professional development for the year. The teachers decided when their strands would meet. Since this schedule for professional development varied from the district calendar (prescribing two whole days of professional development), Ms. Whitley submitted a proposal for two days of release time as compensation for attending the strands throughout the year:

> *That really sold the deal to the teachers. Once they were compensated for their time, they really got into the idea of doing staff development that way and we*

have had excellent feedback over time. This is the fourth year we have done our strands and I am very pleased with the results. We addressed individual needs, such as technology or classroom management, or individual areas they felt they needed to grow. Then we had strands to address our school community.

Assessing the Changes in Professional Development

Ms. Whitley, the principals, and the teachers agree that the year-long "strand" system is better than the old "shotgun" approach to professional development. Teachers have time to practice methods. Strands provide continuity for instruction all year long. Teachers serve as facilitators and peer coaches to support each others' learning. They meet in groups to discuss their learning and how it is influencing their teaching.

Standardized test data attest to positive responses in the classrooms at TJR. Test scores demonstrate steady increases in student achievement since moving to the strands for professional development. Comparing the 2000–2001 results of the Texas Assessment of Academic Skills (TAAS) scores, the seventh graders showed a 6.4 percent overall increase and the eighth grade gained 7 percent on all tests. Ms. Whitley is seeing the changes in teachers and students that she hoped for when she implemented the strand approach.

One day during their planning period, some of the teachers discussed their response to the ongoing professional development. Ms. Pam Buckner, a seventh-grade reading resource teacher, described the benefits of the strands:

> I like the strands better. They seem to key in on a specific area and we're given a choice. By having a choice of two strands, we can pick what's important to us and interesting to us. With strands we get a little bit every so often. I like the fact that we do it once or twice a month. I can take that information and do something. I can think about it and come up with more questions and then ask the questions when we come together . . . it's more relevant and we're more apt to implement.

Betsy Tucker, a language arts teacher with 19 years experience at TJR, said:

> One strand I did was really teacher-driven. We looked at different areas, conducted surveys, and made an action plan for the school environment.

Donna Heeney, a social studies teacher with 23 years experience at TJR, commented:

> I liked getting together with the same group of people.

Ms. Whitley added:

> What I think has happened is that my teachers' opinions about professional development have changed to something that they have ownership in. . . . They are better able to help a new teacher and carry out a new program in the classroom. And I see evidence of what we do in the classroom. Strands are designed according to what they want. Each group makes its own decisions. It is really interesting. We have been able to have groups meet before school and after school. Sometimes they go for two hours instead of one hour. Each strand is important.

One strand engaged in a book study of high-poverty schools. As they read, the teachers initiated dialogue on issues they needed to understand about diversity in relation to their belief that every child at TJR can be a success. They examined school culture. At the end of the book study, one of the recommendations this strand made was to charter a bus during staff development and tour the local community where their students live. They also proposed ways to get better family involvement and to reach out to the community.

Ms. Whitley summarized the process of building a professional learning culture and implementing a more constructivist-oriented approach to professional development at TJR:

> When you start thinking about it, staff development is the future. We have learned at the middle school level that students perform better when they have a relationship with their teachers. We've learned that they feel better if we have a relationship with them. We have learned that personalized is better to fit their own special needs. So that is exactly what we have done with professional development. With those strands, teachers get to build a relationship with those teachers in the same strand, and that facilitates their learning in that area. Also, we learn better if we have choices in what we learn. So what we have done here is take what we know about teachers and apply it to kids, and what we know about kids and apply it to teachers and the way that they learn.

Conclusion

Using an inquiry approach, the principal in this case study applied choice theory and the principles of quality schools management (Glasser, 1998) to identify and provide year-long strands of professional development based on teacher and campus needs. The value of this constructivist approach to professional development is unequaled. By listening to one's staff and focusing on the results from student data, school leaders can build ongoing professional development systems that are long-term and respond to the diversity and complexity within the school.

The constructivist orientation and professional learning community format described in this case study offers an array of research opportunities to explore how teachers learn, allowing us to examine the outcomes of teacher learning as they are translated into classroom practice. Research studies that inquire into the nature of professional development activity and its relationship to student learning are needed to increase our understanding of how successful change can occur within the context of the larger social and political agendas of educational reform.

Further Reflection

1. Compare and contrast traditional and contemporary methods of professional development. In what ways is professional development changing? Do you think professional development needs to change? Why? How?
2. Describe Ms. Whitley's leadership qualities. Do you think her experiences at TJR assisted or inhibited her in leading change in professional development and building a community of learners? Why or why not?
3. Discuss the nature of change in professional development in this case study. What do you foresee will be long-range outcomes of the new approach?
4. Do you think all schools should move toward this or a similar system for professional development? Why or why not?
5. How were the teachers affected by the changes in professional development that were described in this case study? How were the students affected? Do you think these influences were positive, negative, or mixed? Why?
6. What kind of professional development do you believe will nurture you as a life-long learner and help you succeed as a teacher?

Vignettes

This chapter covers techniques for writing behavioral objectives. As you read the following vignettes, consider how often you will use objectives in your future lesson planning.

Vignette One: A Principal Misuses Objectives

Lincoln Middle School had the reputation of being one of the most innovative, experimental, and advanced schools in the district. The large number of oil wells in the area made financing one of the least of the principal's worries. When Sondra Bell became principal last year, she promised the board that, with their support, she would lead the school to even greater heights.

As the principal planned her annual report, she realized that the board had delivered their part of the bargain, but she wondered whether they felt as positive about her. The report contained two parts, "In Retrospect" and "In Prospect." Because she thought that the first part looked a little weak, Sondra decided to compensate by planning an impressive "In Prospect" section.

She began spelling out her objectives for the coming year. Could she impress the board by planning everything for the coming year around those performance objectives that she would set for the students? It seemed logical, so she pulled out a taxonomy of educational objectives from the notes in her methods course. For each daily lesson, she wrote an objective at each level of the cognitive domain. But when she began writing objectives for all levels of the affective domain, her task became more difficult. Although she had initially planned to write objectives that represented all levels of all three domains, Sondra gave up in despair long before the task was completed.

Rather than admit failure, Sondra appointed a committee consisting of the department heads and one or two members of each department. She assigned them exactly the same task—to write sample objectives at all levels in all domains for each subject in the entire school curriculum. The faculty was not at all happy with this request. Most teachers were already using objectives in planning their lessons, but they thought this was going too far.

DISCUSSION

1. Was this principal wrong to require her faculty to use objectives in their planning? The mistake she made was more in the degree of the requirement than in the decision to require the use of objectives. Certainly all teachers should use objectives to help clarify their expectations of students and to organize their lessons better, but taken to this extreme, the objectives could become a nightmare for teachers and for students.

2. Why did Sondra have trouble writing objectives at all levels in all domains? It is almost impossible to write so many objectives in all levels for all subjects. The goal itself is admirable, because sample objectives can be very helpful to teachers who do not have extensive experience writing objectives.

3. If you were a teacher at Lincoln Middle School, how would you respond to this requirement?

Vignette Two: Marshall Middle School Faces No Child Left Behind Act

Marshall Middle School has earned a reputation as a school for the children of yuppies. Located in an upper-class suburban district of a major city, this school has received support that is unequaled in many districts. At a time when other schools are working to devise ways to increase attendance to benefit from the additional revenue, this fortunate school's principal, Ms. Ann Grimes, convinced the Parent–Teacher Association leaders to support the hiring of an assistant principal for instruction. Soon afterward, Mr. James Upchurch, a Phi Beta Phi graduate from one of the nation's most prestigious universities, was hired to help. Marshall retained its position as one of the nation's most innovative and academically elite schools.

During his interview, Mr. Upchurch was given a clear charge. Told that the mission of Marshall was to remain the state's premier middle-level academic institution, he was further notified that he was to make Marshall the state's leader in education reform. This was no minor task, because this state led the nation in education reform.

Mr. Upchurch knew that the demands were great, and that to succeed he must arrive at his new position with a plan in hand. After giving this task his total attention during the two months between his interview and his first day on the job, Mr. Upchurch arrived with his plan complete. He wasted no time introducing his new strategy. At the first chairs' meeting, he revealed the following plan. Marshall's curriculum included grades 6 through 8. Each grade had a designated department chair. Mr. Upchurch explained the following assignment to the three department chairs:

I am pleased and honored to receive this academic post at such a distinguished institution as Marshall Middle School, and I accept the responsibility for keeping this school's reputation. I'm sure that all of you know that the nation is headed toward a national curriculum. In opposition to the No Child Left Behind Act, which stresses stronger accountability and school choice, the National Forum to Accelerate Middle Grades Reform stresses: (1) challenging all teachers, to arrange for all students to use their minds, energy, and curiosity, (2) create small learning communities involving families as partners, and (3) promote social equity by acknowledging and honoring their students' cultures. Each grade-level chair is to develop a plan of action to ensure that these three goals are met. Begin by writing two objectives for each of these goals.

At the beginning of the first designated in-service planning day, each department chair recounted the instructions given at the chairs' meeting. Like all faculties, the Marshall Middle School faculty had some natural leaders who were eager to take charge of the job at hand.

As the chairs began discussing these goals with the teachers in their departments, everyone began to realize that these were important expectations that they could embrace. They wanted their students to benefit from these directions.

DISCUSSION

1. In which domain of the educational taxonomies would most of these performance objectives be written? Why?
2. What is one affective objective that could be written for one of these goals?

Summary

The current trend for holding schools and teachers accountable for student performance on standardized tests accentuates teachers' needs to be acquainted with national and state expectations. To increase the performance levels of their students, classroom teachers must set objectives activities that lead to the attainment of these expectations. This requires breaking down often general and ambiguous standards into clearly understood expectations.

Maximum academic success requires the ability to communicate to all students clear expectations. Otherwise general and vague teacher expectation can be changed into clearly understood expectations through the use of performance objectives. Each objective should meet four criteria: A, B, C, and D. A represents the audience, which must be the student. Instead of, the teacher will . . . , always state your expectations in terms of desired student behavior—The student will. . . . B stands for behavior. The objective must tell the student what behavior is expected or what skill the student will be expected to perform. Good verb choice is a must; each verb should be observable and measurable. Verbs such as *understand* and *know* address behaviors that cannot be seen or measured, but verbs such as *write, list, draw,* and *measure* can be seen and measured. D stand for degree, meaning how accurately must this behavior be performed to please the teacher. For example, the objective might require correct performance 8 times out of 10 or may specify a tolerance of 10 percent error.

Good objectives must be clear. To achieve clarity, teachers avoid jargon and other unfamiliar language and they keep the objectives short.

Recap of Major Ideas

1. Well-written objectives will help clarify the teacher's expectations.
2. Objectives should be precise and concise.
3. Verbs used in objectives should express action that can be observed and measured.
4. Objectives can be used to raise the level of thinking in the classroom.
5. Use textbooks as one of several sources of information.
6. In planning, first determine the desired ends (aims, goals, and objectives) and then choose the means (content and activities) accordingly.
7. Each objective should be stated in terms of student (not teacher) behavior, describe the conditions under which students are expected to perform, and specify the minimum acceptable level of performance.
8. For each lesson plan, identify objectives at varying levels of all three domains. However, a lesson probably will not have objectives at all levels of all domains.
9. Use a multitude of planning strategies in lessons, including discussion, field trips, oral reports, projects, and homework assignments.

Activities

Most teachers today recognize that carefully written, specific behavioral objectives will help them reach their broader goals.

1. Each teacher has different aspirations for students. Consider your subject and write one broad goal that you believe is essential for students to understand. Write several specific behavioral objectives to help your students reach this goal.
2. Think about the problems that characterize modern urban society. Write a general attitudinal goal to eliminate or minimize one of these problems. Now write a few specific behavioral objectives to help students attain this goal.
3. Have you any opinion(s) about the use of objectives that you are willing to share with your classmates? If

so, write these down and get another student to listen to your opinion(s). Of course, do the same for your partner.
4. Choose a topic for class discussion. Write five objectives for the discussion and select a reading for all members. Now identify at least one or two related sources that give information not contained in the student assignment.
5. Plan a field trip for a learning unit in your major field. Start by listing five objectives. Now construct a short questionnaire to evaluate the trip's degree of success.

Looking Ahead

This chapter has prepared you to write performance objectives. The next chapter will prepare you to use these objectives to plan for your classes.

References

Abdul-Haqq, I. (1995). Making time for teacher professional development (Digest 95-4). Washington, DC: ERIC Clearinghouse on Teaching and Teacher Education.

Armstrong, D. G., Henson, K. T., & Savage, T. V. (2004). *Teaching today*, 7th ed. New York: Prentice-Hall.

Ball, D. L., & Cohen, D. K. (2001). Developing practice, developing practitioners: Toward a practice-based theory of professional education. In Hammond, L. D., & Sykes, G. (Eds.), *Teaching as the learning profession: Handbook of policy and practice*. San Francisco: Jossey-Bass.

Bloom, B. S. (1956). *Taxonomy of educational objectives: The classification of educational goals, Handbook I: Cognitive domain*. New York: McKay.

Bohen, D. B. (2001). Strengthening teaching through national certification. *Educational Leadership, 58*(8), 50–53.

Buschee, F., & Baron, M. A. (1994). OBE: Some answers for the uninitiated. *The Clearing House, 67*(4), 193–196.

Carnegie Council on Adolescent Development Staff (1995). *Great transitions: Preparing adolescents for a new century*. New York: Carnegie Foundation.

Cloonan, C. E., (1999). A teacher's class. In K. T. Henson & B. F. Eller (1999). *Educational psychology for effective teaching*, Belmont, CA: Wadsworth.

Elam, S. M., Rose, L. C., & Gallup, A. M. (1994). The 26th Annual Phi Delta Kappan/Gallup Poll of the public's attitudes toward the public school. *Phi Delta Kappan, 76*(1), 41–56.

Garmston, R., & Wellman, B. (1998). Teacher talk that makes a difference. *Educational Leadership, 55*(7), 30–34.

Glasser, W. (1998). *The quality school teacher*. New York: Harper Perennial.

Goodlad, J. J. (1984). *A place called school*. New York: McGraw-Hill.

Harman, A. E. (2001). A wider role for the National Board. *Educational Leadership, 58*(8), 54–55.

Krathwohl, D. R., Bloom, B. S., & Masia, B. B. (1964). *Taxonomy of educational objectives: The classification of educational goals, Handbook II: Affective domain*. New York: McKay.

Leithwood, K., Menzies, T., & Jantzi, D. (1994). Earning teachers' commitment to curriculum reform. *Peabody Journal of Education, 69*(4), 38–61.

Little, J. W. (1994). Teachers' professional development in a climate of educational reform. *Educational Evaluation and Policy Analysis, 15*, 129–151.

Merrow, T. (2001). Teaching to the test. *Phi Delta Kappan, 82*(9), 653–659.

Orlich, D. C. (1991, January/February). A new analogue for the cognitive taxonomy. *The Clearing House, 64*(3), 159–161.

Patterson, W. (2003). Breaking out of our boxes. *Phi Delta Kappan, 84*(8), 569–574.

Putnam, R. T., & Borko, H. (1997). Teacher learning: Implications of the new view of cognition. In Biddle, B. J., Good, T. L., & Goodson, I. F. (Eds.), *The international handbook of teachers and teaching*. Dedrecht, The Netherlands: Kluwer.

Rose, L. C., & Gallup, A. M. (1998). The 30th Annual Phi Delta Kappa/Gallup Poll of the public's attitudes toward the public schools. *Phi Delta Kappan, 80*(1), 41–56.

Rose, L. C., & Gallup, A. M. (2002). The 34th Annual Phi Delta Kappa/Gallup Poll of the public's attitudes toward the public school. *Phi Delta Kappan, 84*(1), 41–58.

Schmoker, M., & Marzano, R. J. (1999). Realizing the promise of standards-based education. *Educational Leadership, 56*(6), 17–21.

Simpson, E. J. (1972). *The classification of educational objectives in the psychomotor domain. The psychomotor domain.* Vol. 3. Washington, DC: Gryphon House.

Thomas, M. D., & Bainbridge, W. H. (2002). No child left behind: Facts and fallacies. *Phi Delta Kappan, 83*(10), 781–787.

Towers, J. M. (1994). The perils of outcome-based teacher education. *Phi Delta Kappan, 75*(8), 624–627.

Tyler, R. W. (1949). *Basic principles of curriculum and instruction.* Chicago: University of Chicago Press.

Unger, C. (1994). What teaching for understanding looks like. *Educational Leadership, 51*(5), 8–10.

Walter, L. J. (1984, March). A synthesis of research findings on teacher planning and decision making. In Egbert, R. L., & Kluender, M. M. (Eds.), *Using research to improve teacher education.* Lincoln, NE: Clearinghouse on Teacher Education.

Willis, S. (2002). Creating a knowledge base for teaching: A conversation with James Stiglar. *Educational Leadership, 59*(6), 6–11.

Wilson, S., & Berne, J. (1999). Teacher learning and the acquisition of professional knowledge: An examination of research on contemporary professional development. In Iran-Nejad, A., & Pearson, P. D. (Eds.), *Review of research in education.* Washington, DC: American Educational Research Association.

Woods, R. K. (1994). A close-up look at how children learn science. *Educational Leadership, 51*(5), 33–35.

Wulf, K. M., & Schane, B. (1994). *Curriculum design.* Glenview, IL: Scott, Foresman.

Zlatos, B. (1994). Outcomes-based outrage runs both ways. *Education Digest, 59*(5), 26–29.

3

Long-Range Planning

Long-range planning does not deal with future decisions, but with the future of present decisions.

Peter Drucker

Objectives

- List several sources for selecting curriculum content.
- Give three reasons that teachers should plan their own curricula and explain the students' role in curriculum development.
- Describe how the teacher's philosophy affects curriculum planning.
- Explain the relationship between curriculum objectives and content and between curriculum content and student activities.
- List three unique characteristics of Taba's inverted curriculum model.
- Develop a learning-teaching unit for a subject and grade level that you plan to teach.
- Suggest some ways that teachers can help students focus on major concepts.
- Explain how today's teachers can use technology to keep their curricula current.

LONG-RANGE PLANNING

Curriculum Determiners
- Textbooks & Other Materials
- Vision, Goals, & Objectives
- Parent Involvement
- Concept Development
- Concept Mapping
- Curriculum Reformers
- Curriculum Guides

→

The Unit Plan
- Involving Students
- Involving Parents
- Curriculum Components
  - *Philosophy*
  - ↓
  - *Purposes*
  - ↓
  - *Content*
  - ↓
  - *Activities*
  - ↓
  - *Evaluation*
- Sample Plans

Connecting Statements	Agree	Disagree	Uncertain
1. All teachers are responsible for determining their classes' curricula.			
2. The textbook is the major source for curricula in secondary school classes.			
3. Teachers should not plan more than a few days (or at most a few weeks) in advance.			
4. Teachers should not use textbooks to select content for courses.			
5. Principles and concepts are more important than facts in selecting curriculum content.			
6. Students do not have the expertise to become involved in curriculum planning.			

> ## Tips for Teachers
>
> Middle-level teachers often have heavier and more diversified teaching assignments than high school teachers. The increased amount of preparation required, coupled with the diversity of assignments, makes it necessary for middle-level teachers to have expertise in a range of subjects. Sometimes this leaves middle-level teachers feeling frustrated and hopeless.
>
> One way to meet the need for expertise in a number of disciplines is to continue your formal and informal education. A 1986 survey of middle-level teachers showed that they benefit from a variety of educational experiences (Henson, Chissom, & Buttery, 1986). Middle-level teachers reported significant advantages from attending for-credit college courses and not-for-credit workshops. They also reported that they learned much about curriculum development from participating on school committees.
>
> This chapter gives you the opportunity to learn about curriculum development. Relate each principle and each example to the grade levels and subjects you plan to teach.

Curriculum Determiners

"Could it be that most of our schools are directing their efforts toward objectives that are less relevant than they once were? Are we focusing on the wrong things in thinking about education? Do we need to rethink the whole purpose of education?" These questions, raised by Eric Oddleifson (1994, p. 447), are just a few of many questions that current and future teachers must ask themselves whenever they work on their long-term plans. The curriculum is the school engine that drives learning. Its significance must not be overlooked or underestimated. As noted in Chapter 2, Thompson & Gregg (1997, p. 28) have observed that "the curriculum is the primary vehicle for changing the goals and objectives of the school." This makes long-term planning very important.

Have you ever wondered who decides what each course will cover? What will be the general goals? What experiences will be part of the course? Will there be field trips, guest speakers, or other special events? Who determines if there will be one or two units of composition in an English class? Is the decision based on the number of chapters devoted to each topic in the textbook? If so, who chooses the textbook? Surely not the principal or the superintendent. As you might suspect, teachers play a significant role in making all these important decisions. And this is as it should be. A current Carnegie Council on Adolescent Development Staff (1995) goal for middle school teachers is empowerment, and teachers become empowered when they are given the latitude and responsibility for making decisions about their classes. Most of the important decisions that teachers make are long-term ones. This means that the quality of education each of your future students (and these may number in the thousands) receives will depend on your long-term planning ability. How teachers should approach planning is a topic of continuing debate, but the importance of planning is not: "even the most inexperienced teachers recognize the correlation between careful planning and effective instruction" (Tannebaum & Faison, 1999, p. 36).

Involvement in curriculum development is teachers' ultimate opportunity to make large-scale impact. You don't have to plan for your classes in isolation from other teachers and your school's principal. According to Clark, Clark, and Irvin (1997), "Evidence also exists of instructional improvement and gains in student outcomes as a result of highly participative decision making that shares leadership among teachers and administrators and focuses on school mission and vision, curriculum and instruction, and teacher professional development" (p. 55).

Some teachers are willing to follow their textbooks, chapter by chapter, and bring little or no supplementary material to class. However, allowing textbooks to be the sole determiners of curricula is unwise. The authors of those books know nothing about your particular students' aspirations, strengths, and weaknesses. Furthermore, they do not know your community. Are there facilities for good field trips? Are there community members who can give excellent talks? Is there a good zoo, a museum, a park, an industry that can offer valuable learning experiences? And does the textbook content correspond to your background, so that you can use your own expertise? Or perhaps your own preparation has gaps that will prevent you from teaching textbook content that you do not understand.

Some teachers overuse textbooks because they feel safe following them; they believe that as long as they cover the text, they will cover the appropriate course content. This is a false sense of security. Textbooks do not always cover a discipline's important concepts. Textbooks also fail to cover content in depth because each year new material is added to each textbook to keep it "up to date" but material is seldom deleted. Tyson and Woodward (1989) explain the results: "It is not surprising then, that American textbooks have become compendiums of topics, none of which are treated in depth" (p. 15). For example, U.S. mathematics textbooks attempt to address 175 percent more topics than do German textbooks and 350 percent more topics than Japanese textbooks (Schmoker & Marzano, 1999).

Other teachers feel obligated to teach every chapter in the book, even though this leaves no time to pursue topics in depth or to involve students in activities needed to help students understand the content. Patterson (2003, p. 571) shares this concern, "The obsession with coverage leads to bored students who are rarely engaged in their own learning." Unfortunately, little attempt has been made through the years to balance the use of textbooks with other resources; the textbook has dominated all other resources. Applebee, Langer, and Mullis (1987) reported that numerous studies show that textbooks structure from 75 to 90 percent of classroom instruction. Hubbuch (1989) testifies to the importance of knowing how to use textbook structure: "A reader's assumption that a text has a structure, and his or her ability to recognize and use the cues to this structure, are central to successful reading. This frame is reflected in various units of the text, from chapters and sections to paragraphs and sentences" (p. 204). Yet successful teachers do much more than follow a prescribed textbook. They can be successful only if they articulate a vision of the higher levels of understanding that the course can lead students to reach. Articulating a vision is not easy. Weller, Hartley, and Brown (1994) explain the difficulty and the significance of obtaining such a vision: "Developing vision, that seemingly mystical and sometimes elusive concept, is the most important element in making any organization highly effective in promoting quality products" (p. 298).

Teachers, either alone or together (remember that the National Middle School Association encourages interdisciplinary team planning), begin long-range planning by translating educational aims and goals into objectives. They then use these objectives to select major concepts and activities students need to attain these objectives. After they have determined the major concepts, teachers must enable students to learn these concepts. However, things are changing. Teachers are coming out of their classrooms to dialogue and plan a unified curriculum in their school. Hall (1998) observed: "There is more discussion about curriculum than ever before, and teachers are coming together across grade levels and buildings to talk about what students should know and be able to do." (p. 383) This transition in middle schools is important because it defines the modern middle school in which interdisciplinary planning results in interdisciplinary curricula.

Poverty and Schooling

Reengaging families in the education of youths is a major goal set by the Carnegie Council on Adolescent Development Staff (1995). Increasing the level of parent involvement is essential because parent involvement can have major positive influence on academic success. Reinstein (1998) found that an assignment requiring students to locate and interview someone in their community who uses high-level math skills did more to motivate students than any action the school could take. While community involvement is important, some communities lack those elements that promote student success. For example, consider the effect that poverty has on literacy. Perhaps the reason that poverty correlates highly with illiteracy is explained by another negative correlation: between poverty and the number of books found in the home. Krashen (1998) notes, "Recent research also demonstrates a clear negative relationship between poverty and the amount of print at home and the amount of reading children do" (pp. 19–20).

We must not assume, however, that all types of parent involvement are good. Ironically, sometimes the wrong kind of parent involvement can be detrimental. Reinstein (1998) makes an interesting observation: "While problems in the inner city often stem from parents lacking power and high expectations, problems in the suburbs stem from parents with an unreasonable sense of entitlement" (p. 29). Reinstein offers as an example a parent who sued a school for giving his daughter a D, saying that she was not below average. Of all the proposed methods for involving parents with schools, the idea of including parents on committees that decide the curriculum of the school was deemed the least valuable ten years ago and continues to hold this position today. A decade ago, only one in five teachers (19 percent) thought that it would be somewhat valuable. Parents should be considered when deciding whom to involve in curriculum planning, but this is one area in which teachers are still unwilling to welcome parents' input. Again, only one teacher in five today believes that parents should serve on curriculum planning committees (MLS, 1998, p. 124).

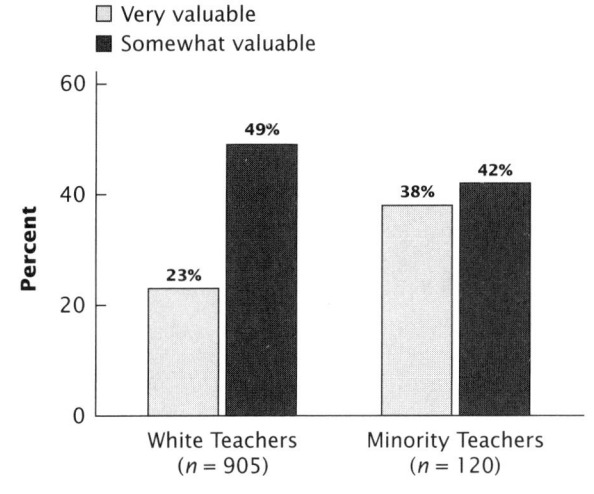

FIGURE 3.1 PLACING PARENTS ON COMMITTEES THAT DECIDE THE CURRICULUM OF THE SCHOOL

From *The MetLife Survey of the American Teacher, 2002: Student Life—School, Home, and Community,* conducted for MetLife® by Harris Interactive Inc.

As shown in Figure 3.1, minority teachers support the involvement of parents on curriculum planning committees more than white parents support it (MLS, 1998, p. 126).

Concept Development

Initially, all curricula in schools throughout the country were **subject-centered**. This means that the primary focus was on students learning a prescribed set of content. Until the mid-twentieth century, little difference was made between focusing on minute facts and on major ideas. The advent of space exploration caused Americans to focus on the *concepts* or major ideas being taught. Some educators associate the teaching of concept development with traditional teacher-centered teaching. Some perceive a conflict between the use of concept development and the student-centered, problem-solving, interdisciplinary approach that most contemporary educators believe appropriate for today's middle schools, but other educators point to the flaw in this association. Middle-level teachers can and must help their students master those concepts that hold together the disciplines and also tie together otherwise separate disciplines, whether the teaching method of the moment is **didactic** (teacher-centered) or **dialectic** (student-centered).

Sometimes students need help focusing on the major concepts in a lesson; they often fail to identify and understand important concepts. Perkins and Blythe (1994) report that "our early research was energized by the fact that most teachers could testify to the importance of teaching for understanding—and to the difficulty of the enterprise. Teachers were all too aware that their students often did not understand important concepts" (p. 4). Before beginning a lesson, teachers should ask questions, present a simple outline, or give students a few key words to help them focus on the major concepts. Such strategies are called *advance organizers*. Snapp and Glover (1990, p. 270) found that middle-school students who read and paraphrased an advance organizer before study answered more lower-order and higher-order study questions correctly than did students not given the organizer. This study's educational implications are straightforward. If a reasonable academic goal is to improve students' answers to study questions, advance organizers help accomplish that goal.

Harrison (1990) offers teachers the following ten steps to help students identify and become familiar with each lesson's (or unit's) major concepts:

1. Present a nominal definition of a concept and give examples.
2. Emphasize the common attributes and ask students to name further attributes.
3. Ask students to give examples.
4. Have students give totally opposite examples.
5. Have students name metaphors to compare with and contrast to the original idea.
6. Have students review contexts in which the concept takes place.
7. Describe the concept's overt application.
8. Identify environmental factors that facilitate or hinder concept application.
9. Formulate an operational definition involving the last steps of this process.
10. Discuss consequences in terms of viable solutions to a given problem.

Harrison (1990) reminded teachers that to understand concepts is not enough, stating that "instruction must focus on the use of the concepts and the context in which they occur in order to ascertain their practical connotations" (p. 203). Teachers can use the case study method to help students apply concepts (Kowalski, Weaver, & Henson, 1994). This method enables students to separate relevant from irrelevant information. Doing so will enable them to understand concepts.

Teacher as Proactive Decision Maker

Classroom Situation

1. You anticipate that many of your students will be totally unfamiliar with the idea of *concepts*.

2. You anticipate that some of your students will find the topic "philosophy" less than motivating.

Proactive Alternatives

Choose from this book or prepare your own written definition of concept. Present this definition and give some examples of concepts.

Ask your students to hold a short small-group discussion and identify other examples of concepts.

Give your students a written statement and ask them to identify its major concepts.

Make a transparency of the John Steinbeck quote in Chapter 1. Invite your students to revisit this quote as you show it on the overhead projector. Ask them what this quote tells them about Steinbeck's philosophy toward teaching.

Ask small groups of students to make a list of important parts of Steinbeck's philosophy of teaching.

Ask students to write their own philosophy of teaching, including their belief's about learners and learning.

Some educators are concerned that education reform programs have emphasized pedagogical techniques rather than mastery of content. Regnier (1994) refers to such errors as "the illusion of technique" and states that "the denigration of intellectual life has also led to a proliferation of 'interdisciplinary approaches' to instruction that blur important destinations, such as the different criteria of evidence and argument in, say, history and physics" (p. 82). Van Gulick (1990) believes that students' performance on standardized tests has declined because of how students store information. To be able to use new information, students must see how it relates to a larger whole. Markle, Johnston, Geer, and Meichtry (1990) say that constructivists (discussed in Chapter 1) subscribe to this belief: "Constructivists describe learning in terms of building connections between prior knowledge and new ideas and claim that effective teachers help students construct an organized set of concepts that relates new and old ideas" (p. 53).

The implications for middle-level teachers are great. The teachers' role will no longer be to dispense "truth," but rather to help and guide the student in the conceptual organization of certain areas of expertise (Hilliard, 1999). Such guidance is best achieved through group assignments that require students to describe the process they use to explore new material as it relates to existing knowledge (Markle et al., 1990, p. 54). This process will be discussed further in Chapter 5, under the heading "Student-Initiated Questions."

Because of these limitations, most teachers choose to become involved in the long-term planning of each course they teach. Yet most teachers know how important it is to have continuity throughout the year. "More recent research has shown the increased effectiveness in learning when experiences are organized to enable students to progress from unit to unit, in which each subsequent unit builds on the preceding ones" (Tyler, 1984, p. 36). Although most teachers are not free to make all these decisions alone, they have considerable influence. Through experience, teachers can learn how to plan a greater part of their courses.

Concept Mapping/Cognitive Mapping

Concept mapping, also called **cognitive mapping,** is a method that was designed to help students focus on the lesson's major concepts. The process involves having students identify main ideas and then diagram connections between them. Slavin (1995, p. 243) explains: "In networking and mapping, students identify main ideas and then diagram connections between them." An effective use of mapping is to let groups of students make cognitive maps to show how they perceive relationships among related concepts and use the overhead projector or chalkboard to show and control these maps.

Concept mapping should always begin with goals. For example, in small groups, students might be asked to write all the words studied in class that relate to diversity or multiculturalism, first on a piece of paper, and later on the board, draw lines connecting these words, and explain these connections. Do not miss the opportunity to have students add their own words to this map, connecting the lesson's concepts with their previously acquired concepts.

The Question of Content

At the beginning of the year you must decide what content to cover. Teachers often let their own likes and dislikes serve as the sole basis for selecting content (Armstrong, Henson, & Savage, 2004). For example, Scheville et al. (see Berliner, 1984, p. 53) report that an elementary school teacher who enjoyed teaching science taught 28 times more science than one who said she did not enjoy teaching science. Like most teachers, you will probably feel obliged to cover material that students will need as background for the next grade. Eisner (2001) has pointed out that many of today's education reformers are obsessed with measuring what students do in schools when what they can and will do outside the schools is of far more significance. More important, you must also ensure that students gain the understanding and skills they will need throughout their lives.

How do teachers determine what students should learn in each class? Make a list of ten ways you can determine what students must learn in a particular class. You might title it "Ways to Identify Content." No two teachers will have identical lists. Any new material cho-

---

Proactive Exercise

Anticipated Situation

- You know that:

    Students find media far more stimulating than traditional didactic teaching. Cognitive mapping can add more interest, while also introducing students to metacognition, i.e., thinking about their own thinking.

Proactive Alternative

- You can:

    Prepare a media fair for your own classroom. Begin with an important interdisciplinary theme. Using groups of two to four students, challenge each group to design a cognitive map to teach this topic. Let each group use a unique type of medium to share this map with classmates.

sen should relate to the existing curriculum. The curriculum components (philosophy, content, activities, aims, goals, objectives, and evaluation) should all mesh. The results of this meshing is called *curriculum coherence.*

One logical place to begin selecting content is to check the state curriculum guide's objectives and concepts. Each state produces its own guides. These guides are important because they consider a course's content in relation to the previous year and the following years. In other words, the developers of state curriculum guides consider the total content needed by students throughout the entire K–12 school program. Another important feature of state curriculum guides is their focal points. They begin with broad goals and identify general understandings that students are expected to acquire and develop at each grade level.

A second source of information is the syllabi that local teachers of the next grade up use to teach your subject. By paying special attention to the beginning of each unit of study, you can see what students are expected to know when they leave your class. One popular source of information is textbooks. Do not let a single textbook dictate your total curriculum, but do look at several texts to remind you to incorporate important material from each. Start by examining several current texts at your own grade level and make a content-comparison chart to determine any deficiencies in your own text and to compensate for them. Mather (2001) suggests that, when selecting texts or any other instructional materials, you always compare three materials. Examining three sources provides the opportunity to choose and yet is few enough to be manageable. Trying to compare more than three at once can be confusing. Table 3.1 provides an example of chapter comparison of middle-level methods texts.

Students learn best when they are involved with activities, but sometimes it is difficult to provide hands-on activities. Media offer a viable alternative. Stefanich (1990) explains:

> *Teaching must occur in an arena of active manipulation of concrete hands-on experiences. When a concrete experience is impossible, semi-concrete opportunities (i.e., films, simulations, games, illustrations) must be utilized. . . . There has never been an outstanding teacher. Learning requires active participation on the part of the learner; therefore, there have only been outstanding facilitators of learning. (p. 50)*

TABLE 3.1 Content Comparison

Chapter Topics	Book A	Book B	Book C	Book D	Book E	Book F	Book G	Book H
Adolescence and learning	X	X	X	X	X			X
Planning	X	X	X	X	X	X	X	X
Classroom management	X	X	X	X	X	X	X	X
Evaluation	X	X	X	X	X	X	X	X
Teaching styles	X	X	X	X	X			X
Motivation	X	X						X
Multicultural or disadvantaged students		X		X	X			X
History and aims		X						X
Audiovisual aids		X		X				X
Teaching special pupils		X	X					X
Communications			X					X

> THE CASE

Planning for Student Engagement

Holly Johnson, Texas Tech University
Vicki Sellers, Llano Estacado Middle School

Holly Johnson is an Assistant Professor in the Language Literacy Education Program at Texas Tech University. She received her Ph.D. at the University of Arizona in Tucson, where she also taught middle school language arts and reading. She believes that understanding adolescents and their humor will help establish student–teacher relationships that benefit the entire learning community.

Vicki Sellers is finishing her Masters in Language Literacy Education at Texas Tech University. She teaches eighth-grade language arts and reading in a small town outside Lubbock, Texas, and she suggests that continuing her education in adolescent literacy education has helped her be a better teacher.

Background

Television newscasts and political agendas often refer to teacher shortages and student literacy problems in urban schools. Little is said about the difficulties and successes that small rural school districts face as their numbers slowly diminish in size and number. Small rural districts face some of the same problems as their larger, urban counterparts, but they also have problems uniquely their own. Just like their urban counterparts, rural educators face challenges associated with their particular locations. These issues include poverty, lack of job opportunities, geographic isolation, and lower parental educational attainment (Maynard & Howley, 1997). Other concerns include issues of diversity and professional development (Murry & Herrera, 1998). Although there are positive aspects to rural schools, such as smaller class size, the challenge of geographic isolation greatly limits the resources available to rural areas (Alspaugh, 1998; Cotton, 1996). Because of their geographic isolation, rural schools with diverse populations may not possess the resources to inform teachers on how cultural and language differences affect student learning, or create opportunities to coordinate continuing education programs (Murry & Herrers, 1998).

Because resources are sometimes unavailable for the technology and readily available material and professional assets of larger cities, students and teachers in rural districts miss out on the opportunities to learn in ways that would benefit them and keep them abreast of current trends in education. To overcome this lack of resources, teachers in rural districts must find the time and the initiative themselves to help their students find fulfillment in these smaller and more isolated educational contexts. Working with young adolescents is especially important, since it is during the middle years that young people are most at risk of dropping out of school and society (Jackson & Davis, 2000). In Texas, over one-third of students drop out before completing high school. Planning for student engagement and educational longevity is an essential element of a rural teacher's job in the Lone Star State.

The Changing Landscape

Located in the agricultural South Plains region of Texas is such a rural school system, the Llano Estacado Independent School District (LEISD). One of only three county school districts, this 1A school district's total enrollment nears 450 students. The small town of 1,500 serves proudly as the county seat, and presiding over the town square is the staunch courthouse surrounded by the area's few trees. Only a few miles from the city limits, beautiful canyons contrast dramatically with the somewhat flat surrounding fields, which are in constant mechanical manipulation by area farmers and ranchers.

Once a thriving agricultural center with one of the world's largest and most modern cotton gins, the county seat now suffers the plight of other agricultural towns across the United States—a struggling economy. The region once abounded with numerous family farms, but now a growing number of these farms have become part of bigger business operations. Although the area struggles financially, LEISD School Board and Administration have managed to provide students with comfortable facilities, modern equipment, and enriching activities through effective grant resources and conscientious management.

Over the past thirty years, the town's cultural diversity has undergone changes due to the decreasing number of job opportunities in the area. In the past, cultural populations split the middle school population into near even thirds of Hispanic American, African American, and Anglo American cultural categories. Now, however, those statistics have changed, as indicated by the following statistics: Hispanic American 66 percent, African American 9 percent, and Anglo American 25 percent. Similar figures demonstrate the economically disadvantaged situation at Llano Estacado Middle School, where 65 percent receive free lunch fare, 8 percent pay a reduced lunch fare, and 27 percent pay a full lunch fare. The administration and faculty of LEISD struggle with economic challenges facing many school districts across the country, particularly in areas of severe economic decline.

Llano Estacado Middle School

Just one block from a major highway, and 40 miles from a small city on the southern plains, Llano Estacado Middle School (LEMS) shares a picturesque campus on the edge of town with the district's elementary, high school, and administrative buildings. At night and on weekends, students and parents shuttle between buildings for academic and parental functions, while younger children play on the green areas in front of each building. Towering above the sprawling campus is the town's water tower, adorned with an image of the school's mascot. Located across from a small neighborhood and down the street from a local convenience store and gas station, LEMS is a small hub of activity that feels welcoming to friends and visitors alike.

Well maintained but far from new, LEMS structures house 110 sixth-, seventh-, and eighth-grade students in a brick single-level building and a separate modular science building. The main building, with its tile floors and light green walls, offers teachers and students light, airy classrooms with ample room for creating life-size projects and small-group learning. On warm, often windy days, teachers may also take their students outside to work on descriptive writing or plains geography and geology. Students work with technology in computer lab classes, as well as spend time in a second computer lab equipped with eighteen networked and Internet-accessible computers for special projects. Keeping up with the newest technology, however, is still critical to student learning, and LEMS attempts to provide the labs with new software each year. The campus also houses dusty athletic fields that produce enthusiastic track, football, and baseball teams each year. Other sports include basketball and soccer, while the school system also encourages student participation in band and student clubs.

In this setting, LEMS students share elective art, athletic, and music classes with nearby high school classroom facilities taught by both middle and high school faculty members. The close proximity of the school district's buildings allows some faculty members to teach at both middle school and high school levels, as well as bonding the school district's administration, faculty, and students together.

The Teacher

An area resident for thirty years, Vicki Sellers earned her Bachelor of Arts degree in 1998 from a major nearby university as a nontraditional student. A native Texan, Ms. Sellers first attended college in the early 1970s but withdrew for over twenty years while she worked as a clerk/secretary in local cotton gin and tax offices. Always regretting that she had not completed her bachelor's degree, Ms. Sellers continued to plan to become a teacher one day and to fulfill her purpose as a human being, helping to prepare students for productive and happy futures.

Although Ms. Sellers has lived in the Llano Estacado area for thirty years, she spent her public school years in California, Tennessee, Virginia, and Texas as a military family member. Ms. Sellers often played school as a child and recalls being impressed and interested by her older brothers' textbooks, her family's home encyclopedias and *National Geographic* magazines, and television's *Jack Paar Show* and Peace Corps advertisements. As a self-proclaimed "child of the sixties," Ms. Sellers broadened her view of the world and its inhabitants, desiring to rise to President Kennedy's challenges to make a difference in the world and to contribute to peace. Through daily and global planning, Ms. Sellers brings the concepts of understanding across differences and community building to her classroom.

Having taught middle school students now for three years, Ms. Sellers enthusiastically embraces the challenges that she and her students daily face. Because she enjoys interacting with people, Ms. Sellers passionately shares her personal excitement with LEMS students and attempts to affect them on an emotional level. Motivated to be an active part of literacy education, Ms. Sellers maintains membership in several professional organizations, such as the National Council for Teachers of English and the International Reading Association, and subscribes to several journals published by the organizations. Ms. Sellers continues her life-long education, pursuing her Master's Degree in Education at an area university while serving LEMS as the eighth-grade language arts teacher. In 2002, Ms. Sellers was honored with the Outstanding Master's Student Award at the university's college of education.

Because of her desire for a passionate teaching and learning experience, Ms. Sellers believes that students will not learn effectively unless engaged with the learning experience. While some teachers complain of classrooms of young faces filled with boredom, Ms. Sellers explains that she has no bored students. Energetic and somewhat noisy students pour into her classroom and anxiously inquire, "Where're we going today?" As a team, Ms. Sellers and her students explore and interact with a variety of texts, actively engaged and learning. Before teaching the content, Ms. Sellers plans for student engagement, mulling over various texts and activities and immersing herself in a variety of topics to determine what will be most likely to activate interest in her eighth graders.

The Importance of Planning

Regardless of teaching style, planning is necessary and important. In Ms. Seller's case, before actual plans begin, she considers what purpose the unit or lessons will serve. After determining the purpose(s) of the unit, she maps out the unit's description and examines specific topics, skills, texts, and activities to be implemented throughout the unit. Always interested in smooth transitions from topic to topic or unit to unit, Ms. Sellers seeks connections between the last unit and the next one to be taught while spending time browsing the Internet and other print sources for inspiration and ideas.

Recently, Ms. Sellers planned to share the conflicts and changes of the 1960s with her students, exposing them to nonfiction, fiction, video, music, speeches, poetry, and other available resources. Such a unit offers an overabundance of material from which to choose, and planning readings and writings based on such a broad realm of information proved almost overwhelming to Ms. Sellers. Having planned a previous Inquiry unit based on African and African American history and readings, Ms. Sellers decided to approach her Sixties unit in much the same fashion—with enthusiasm and a belief that her students will learn more about themselves and the world simply by participating.

Establishing Purpose

First, Ms. Sellers considered the purpose of the unit. Certainly the language arts content ranked highly, but Ms. Sellers initially addressed her desire to ignite the interests of her students. Once engaged, students enjoyed various experiences while involved in learning. Considering her students' interests, Ms. Sellers shared her respect for the past with stories of real people, some local, who encountered adversity, some surviving it and some not. Studies that reflect experiences of ordinary as well as extraordinary people stirred the LEMS eighth graders at an emotional level. Once the emotional connections were present, students then willingly interacted and fully engaged with learning content from various texts.

Throughout the unit, Ms. Sellers continued to address student engagement through her planning. When students discovered particular information or interests, they were encouraged to share it with the class so others could benefit. Ms. Sellers knew that by keeping her teaching flexible, yet with established goals for all her students, language arts would become a place where students wanted to go each day.

Describing the Unit

To maintain student engagement, Ms. Sellers planned lessons that offered students opportunities for active learning. Using multidisciplinary texts, Ms. Sellers presented various perspectives through nonfiction articles, essays, films, and narratives—true stories told by voices from the sixties. Noting that her students want to know the truth and that they resist filtered information, Ms. S. sought to provide multiple experiences and viewpoints through Internet webquests, print texts, newspaper archives, government documents, and even picture books. These true accounts reached LEMS eighth graders, helping them to acknowledge contributions and sacrifices made by many people during the sixties.

Because she and her students love music, Ms. Sellers used samples from both current and sixties repertoires. This combination worked to create a connection for students and helped them see the roots of some of their own favorites. Besides music, similarities between current and past fashion trends interested some of Ms. Sellers students, and the Internet offered many suitable sites for exploration. Examining music lyrics as a form of poetry encouraged students to open their minds to poetry, a literary genre many dreaded.

Exploring Differing Perspectives through Multicultural Texts

In planning, Ms. Sellers addressed her students' largely Hispanic American culture by incorporating newspaper articles, essays, poetry, short stories, and music written by or about Hispanic Americans, as well as Anglo Americans and African Americans. One such activity began with reading a recent newspaper article entitled "Dress Blues for Arturo," a story of a local veteran who was killed in action in Vietnam. Written by a comrade veteran, the article pays tribute to this fallen young man, with whom several students were familiar.

After reading the article, students visited the local war veteran's burial site, divided into teams, and used butcher paper and charcoal to make "rubbings" of the veteran's name. As students reflected on the graveside experience, Ms. Sellers shared the children's book, *The Wall* (Bunting, 1992), followed by discussion and a personal reflection. This activity met students at a personal and emotional level, making the veteran's sacrifice tangible and comprehensible for eighth graders while providing a connection to their local history's past.

In order to offer students such a variety of texts and successful learning experiences, planning is a must. Ms. Sellers often compares her array of texts and activities to a buffet that allows everyone to enjoy at least some of the material:

> *I compare my selection of materials, along with the activities I plan, to two things: a buffet and a quilt. Those two metaphors may not seem comparable, but they are. For those who are cold and hungry, which I sometimes see the entire world being, these two things can bring comfort. I see multicultural literature and the ability to look at diverse and varied perspectives as something we should feel comfortable doing. A buffet lets you choose from the variety that is there, but like most people, if I am going to eat from a buffet, I want to try something I've never had before.*
>
> *That's how I teach reading and literature. I encourage my students to try something new. Maybe it has to be a little bit at a time, but "Hey! Go ahead and try it." In terms of the quilt, by allowing students to engage in the world with all its diversity is like having or creating a quilt with multiple threads, fabrics, and colors. Part of my job as a teacher is to show how the differences on the quilt—the multiple perspectives on the world—are still part of the whole, part of being human. I also want to point out to them that, just like quilts, these differences create something beautiful to look at and to utilize for various purposes. The quilt is also united, an aspect of the world that I hope students will begin to see and produce for themselves in their own lives.*

Challenging Students to Learn

Sometimes, teachers notice that students may complete assignments with a minimum of commitment.

To encourage active participation in learning, teachers must stir up interest or encourage students to become more involved in their educational experiences. This can be difficult, especially with middle-level students, who often find the world outside the window much more engaging than the instruction inside it.

While this sounds difficult, Ms. Sellers believes that sharing her passion with students instills interest and curiosity within them. For example, Ms. Sellers has described herself as an adult with an enthusiastic eighth-grade heart, a person who embraces life. Sharing her own curiosity or emotional reactions with students, Ms. Sellers brings her *self* (her personality, likes, dislikes, embarrassing moments, etc.) into the classroom and gets involved in relationships with her students. She says:

> *Although I do use textbooks, I notice that my students' attention levels increase when I share a personal experience with them. Just as they enjoyed storytelling as small children, they continue the desire for a good story told firsthand. I believe my students view our class as a team and me as only part of it—maybe as the driver or transporter for a variety of adventures we share together—and I am certain that they enter my classroom curious about what is in store for us as a class each day.*
>
> *When I share a personal experience with my students and listen as they share theirs, we unite as a whole "classroom family" and recognize the advantages in working together for a common good. We experience field trips, read articles and stories, create papier-mâché projects, and even dance to musical selections together, not alone but in our classroom cocoon, an experience which can often arouse the emotions of my students and myself. I recall many times while I read or related a story or an event, and as I either die with laughter or fill with tears, my students awaken and connect with me. They NEVER forget those moments, and they often bring them to my attention. These experiences arouse their passions and encourage them to get involved as learners.*

While onlookers might assume that Ms. Sellers's teaching style neglects structure and significance, in reality such an atmosphere requires a great deal of organization and planning. Ms. Sellers shared that one of her colleagues compared their teaching styles by commenting, "Ms. S, you're the flower and I'm the roots," implying that Ms. Sellers's active lessons were less meaningful than structured "in the box" textbook and worksheet lessons. According to Ms. Sellers, the same teacher often complained about difficulty getting her students motivated and interested in the, as she put it, "boring short stories" the textbook offered. In justification or support of active learning, Ms. Sellers believes that a student will resist the challenge to learn if the challenge does not excite his or her emotions, curiosity, or enjoyment.

Assessing Engagement

Ms. Sellers believes that students learn best when engaged, thus, she looks for signs of student enjoyment, some obvious and other less noticeable ones. Clearly, visual observations provide simple clues to student engagement. For example, students who are "into" an assignment are active participants in the task to be done. However, accounting for other signs of involvement and enjoyment can require other means of assessment. Because the classroom offers little time for pondering individual degrees of each student's involvement in learning, Ms. Sellers relies on video cameras, digital photographs, or battery-powered tape recorders to capture learning moments and comments made by students or those she makes of her own teaching.

She notices that if students are focused on their assignment, whatever it may be, they react to her wandering photography or videotaping very minimally. If they are not engaged with the content, students will usually notice the camera, posing or clowning for the camera, rather than remaining intent on the assignment. If they are engaged with the content, they may notice the camera, but they show no concern. Later, when viewing the photos, Ms. Sellers searches for visual clues to her students' engagement, such as facial expression and body language. Also, the pictures help her retain her memory of particular moments and student actions or comments during the lesson.

As for tape recording, when working in groups, her students seem to enjoy the opportunity to be in control of the technical device placed on their table or desk. She believes that her students realize that what they have to say really matters, and they of course enjoy the fun of hearing their voices recorded, something people never seem to outgrow. In addition, the tapes provide artifacts documenting a student's understanding of the lesson and his or her level of engagement.

Using these tools, Ms. Sellers can modify the strategies she uses to better suit the needs of her students. Students who are interested and engaged discover other questions or areas to investigate, the opposite of disruptive, bored, disengaged students. Although students who are "into" their learning experiences tend to be vocal and somewhat noisy during the lessons, the "noise" is all about the lesson, not about off-task topics and behaviors.

Suggestions for Improving Student Engagement

To reach high levels of student interest, teachers should not underestimate the benefit of the time factor. Taking time to plan for student motivation is extremely important, and Ms. Sellers feels that she needs to explore potential topics from her students' perspectives. She also finds that having her students complete an interest survey at the beginning of the year is one way to tap into what motivates her students to learn and to care about their learning. As the year continues, she "kidwatches" to ascertain new interests that she might encourage.

Further, using multicultural texts sends positive messages to students from various cultures, showing them contributions made by people from their cultural background. Not only do multicultural texts include multiple perspectives, teachers who use such texts frequently acknowledge the importance of their students and their cultures. When viewing a film or reading a text with her students, Ms. Sellers may mention people not represented in the texts. For example, films made during the 1940s and even some films today address mainly one culture, that of the Anglo American. When discussing the film, Ms. Sellers asks her students to find what perspectives or information is absent in the film or the text. In questioning the text, Ms. Sellers strives to lead her students to analyze and make their own discoveries about their assignments.

While Ms. Sellers confirms that school schedules and agendas sometimes make rushing through a unit seem necessary, she advises that hurrying through a unit's setup will result in a lack of student engagement with the topic. Ms. Sellers feels that a rushed unit or planning for the unit leaves her students with few memorable moments, ones that demonstrate a shallow level of learning rather than deeply engaged educational experience.

The Teacher's Leadership

Ms. Sellers most importantly wants to lead her students to embrace their own learning experiences. Sharing her enthusiasm with teens, she can positively affect their school experience, especially inside their language arts classroom. Because she is herself a student of higher education, Ms. Sellers shares some of her writing samples and assignments with her students, who view her as a life-long learner. At times, Ms. Sellers will seek opinions or editing from her students, who appreciate being considered a worthy source of help. The school superintendent refers to Ms. Sellers's enthusiastic demeanor, expressing that such a trait is contagious and needed among students and teachers.

Overall, Ms. Sellers enjoys the relationships and connections with students, and she hopes to improve as a facilitator in her classroom. While Ms. Sellers would like to affect her colleagues' teaching experiences positively, she tries to effect change by modeling and by examples of engaged student results in the classroom. Relating to parents, Ms. Sellers often sees her students' parents in the small town's only grocery store and other locations, where she makes a point to connect with them outside the school environment. Wherever she finds herself, Ms. Sellers places engagement at the top of her list of preferences, where she and her students can enjoy themselves while learning or completing any task. Like many of her students, in order to learn successfully, Ms. Sellers needs to transform even the most mundane tasks into personally engaging and fun experiences.

Student Transformation

Three years ago, Ms. Sellers taught sixth-grade language arts at LEMS, where one of her students entered the classroom obviously opposed to any educational experiences. An African American female student, L had gained a strongly defiant reputation, and few students or teachers dared tangle or interact with her in a personal way. Creating disturbances and disrupting her sixth-grade class with Ms. Sellers, L sought power in the classroom and continued to turn away from lessons that a majority of students enjoyed, activities such as group research projects, artistic collages, and other active experiences.

Finally, Ms. Sellers prepared for a large study based on readings about Africa, the Middle Passage, the Underground Railroad, and the Civil Rights movement.

During the unit, L awakened to reading for enjoyment and read every biography of African American figures that the school library had to offer. With the class, L participated in discussions about the novel, *Roll of Thunder, Hear My Cry* (Taylor, 1997), and she positioned herself as the classroom expert on Sojourner Truth, Harriett Tubman, Rosa Parks, and Martin Luther King, Jr. Not only did she provide information about historical African American leaders, L voluntarily shared her church's Kwanzaa celebration with the class.

While studying the unit's texts, LEMS sixth graders attended a nearby university program that musically shared the role of the African storyteller. Following the lengthy unit, Ms. Sellers noticed L's interest in the program and clicking songs and gave her a tape of the program. Ms. Sellers and L then began to relate to each other, and L put aside her defiance, engaging with Ms. Sellers and the lessons she planned.

Since that turning point, L and Ms. Sellers have established a positive relationship, and now Ms. Sellers, who teaches L again, this time as an eighth grader, happily reports that L engages with learning experiences in language arts and most other classes. Ms. Sellers believes that addressing L's culture, contributions, and interests helped to engage her with learning. Establishing a foundation on which to begin positive experiences with texts, teachers, and classroom activities, the engaging African heritage unit served as a bridge toward L's future experiences with education.

Conclusion

While all students may not engage their learning with the same defiance, or the same turnabout as L, the reality is that teachers must plan ways in which students can become more actively engaged in their educational experiences. Through knowing her students, and by consciously establishing relationships with them, Ms. Sellers is an effective and well-respected teacher. Her classroom is a hum of activity where students feel not only welcome, but needed to make the classroom community more complete, more real, more diverse. Despite, or perhaps because of, its rural location, Ms. Sellers is able to bring to life the world of the Southern Plains for her students, creating lesson plans and thematic units that address their interests, their questions, and their concerns as middle-level readers and learners. As Ms. Sellers emphasizes through her planning and her teaching, "People just have to get out more in order to really understand that the world is not just like them. And while we might not be able to get to the 'big city' every time we want, I can attempt to do that through the resources LEMS has and through the diversity of materials I have for my students' learning."

Further Reflection

1. Discuss the limitations and the potential of multicultural literature for rural schools or schools where the population is of one culture or ethnicity. What issues would you encounter as a teacher using multicultural literature in your classroom?
2. What problems persist for you in terms of global planning? What are the benefits and hazards of planning for middle-level students?
3. Discuss the idea of motivation. Can students be motivated by outside sources, or is motivation intrinsic? How can teachers motivate or encourage students to motivate themselves?
4. Evidence points to the idea that rural schools may not be able to offer students the same type of education as their suburban or urban counterparts. How do you feel about this belief? What problems result because of either this idea or its reality? What benefits would you argue come with rural schooling?
5. How can teachers both plan and respond to the needs and interests of their students? What tools can teachers utilize to bring these two factors together so that middle-level students can benefit academically and socially from teacher planning?
6. Respond to Ms. Sellers's metaphors about teaching and multicultural literature. What metaphor describes your teaching and planning?

Suggested Reading

Beach, R., & Myers, J. (2001). *Inquiry-based English instruction: Engaging students in life and literature.* New York: Teachers College Press.

Buehl, D. 2001). *Classroom strategies for interactive learning.* Newark, DE: International Reading Association.

Krogness, M. (1995). *Just teach me, Mrs. K: Talking, reading, and writing with resistant adolescent learners.* Portsmouth, NH: Heinemann.

Lindley, D. (1993). *This rough magic: The life of teaching.* Westport, CT: Bergin & Garvey.

Liston, D., & Zeichner, K. (1996). *Culture and teaching.* Mahwah, NJ: Lawrence Erlbaum Associates, Publishers.

McCabe, A. (1996). *Chameleon readers: Teaching children to appreciate all kinds of good stories.* New York: McGraw-Hill.

Reaching Higher Levels of Thinking

Although making chapter comparisons is a broad and therefore crude assessment of textbook content, it is a step in the right direction. A close examination of the texts in your field can help you identify the major concepts or principles in each content area. For example, a middle-level earth science textbook should cover the following major areas of study: astronomy, geology, meteorology, oceanography, and physical geography. You may be surprised that Figure 3.2, which compares four popular texts, shows that each book contains only a small percentage of pertinent principles. Such poor coverage is not at all uncommon, however. In fact, these texts cover between 8 and 33 percent of pertinent material. (Figure 3.3).

Because textbooks fail to cover all important principles and concepts, do not rely on them as your sole source to determine course content. Use them as one of many curriculum determiners. As Stefanich (1990) said: "A strong basis of research supports the notion that the thinking of individuals from ages 10 to 14 is distinctly different from adults, yet schools generally do not respond to these unique elements of thought when planning curriculum or guiding student decisions" (p. 47).

Another common weakness of textbooks is that they are geared to the lowest cognitive level. Studies by Davis and Hunkins showed that more than 85 percent of textbook content is written on the recall level (Orlich, 1980). An analysis of more than 61,000 questions in workbooks, texts, and teachers' manuals accompanying nine world history textbooks showed that more than 95 percent of those questions were lower-order (Trachtenberg, 1974, pp. 55–57).

Chapter 2 opened with a quotation that said, "The more we proceed by plan the more effectively we may hit by accident." If your students are to reach higher levels of thinking it will be not be by accident but rather the result of your purposeful planning, not by your

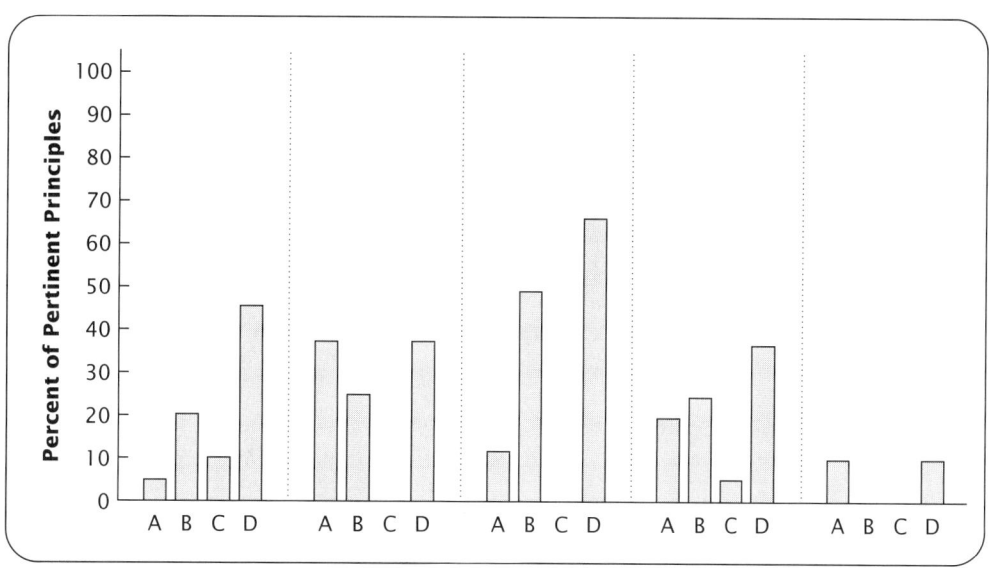

FIGURE 3.2 VARIANCE IN REPRESENTATION OF PRINCIPLES AMONG FOUR BASIC SCIENCE TEXTBOOKS

From Kenneth T. Henson, *Methods and Strategies for Teaching in Secondary and Middle Schools,* third edition. Published by Allyn and Bacon, Boston, MA. Copyright © 1996 by Pearson Education. Reprinted by permission of the publisher.

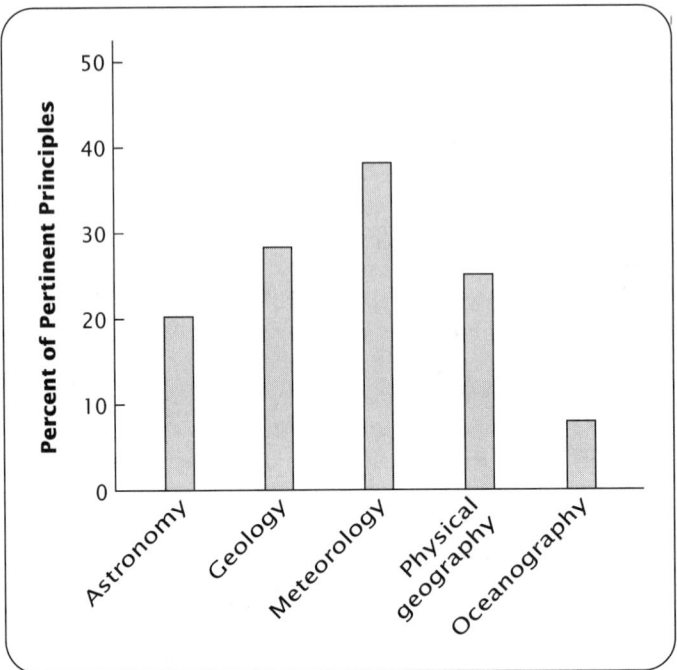

FIGURE 3.3 MEAN REPRESENTATION OF PERTINENT PRINCIPLES FOR EACH SUBJECT

From Kenneth T. Henson, *Methods and Strategies for Teaching in Secondary and Middle Schools,* third edition. Published by Allyn and Bacon, Boston, MA. Copyright © 1996 by Pearson Education. Reprinted by permission of the publisher.

demanding it but by your leading your students through carefully designed tasks. Stefanich (1990) explains, "Higher level thinking cannot be demanded. We must earn it through nurturing a series of successively more advanced learning tasks until the student reaches the desired level of performance" (p. 49). Students themselves must discover and develop some content generalizations; they must be given ample opportunities for direct experience with content in order to derive generalizations and invent [learning] algorithms on their own. . . . Gaps are left which students, themselves, must fill. This means that whatever sources you use, do not select material without considering your students and your intended teaching method.

Researchers at Michigan State University found more factors that influence selection of content: the effort teachers perceive as needed to teach a subject, how students perceive a subject, and whether the teacher enjoys teaching a subject (Scheville et al., 1981). To prevent your own likes and dislikes from dominating your selection of content, you should involve all your students in curriculum planning. Taba (1962) developed a way to do this in the 1950s. Models are recognized as useful tools in planning. "Models typically add the dimension of a philosophical or theoretical viewpoint of planning (LeBlanc & Lacey, 1999, p. 25). In contrast to the other curriculum planning models, which are developed outside the school, Taba's model is developed by teachers and their students. It is different in that it starts at the bottom—in the classroom—and moves upward, and it has come to be known as Taba's inverted curriculum model. Taba's model takes into consideration students' desires

> **Teacher as Proactive Decision Maker**
>
> **Classroom Situation**
> - You know that the school where you will teach will likely encourage you to work to raise the thinking level in your classes. You also know that when students don't know the meaning of words, they tend to gloss over (ignore) those words.
>
> **Proactive Alternatives**
> - Examine your lesson for words that your students may find unfamiliar. Introduce these words.
> - Engage students in defining these words. Pair students and have each pair write a definition for each word.
> - Compare all definitions including your own.

and abilities, and because you develop it, you are more likely to use it and to use it more effectively than an externally developed unit.

Another unique feature of Taba's model is that it connects curriculum with instruction. Taba achieved this by making the learning unit the center of her model. In other words, you and your students will choose major topics of study, such as astronomy or geology. Then you will develop for each topic a unit lasting from a few days to several weeks. For convenience, most units are designed to be the same length as a grading period. Since most secondary and middle-school systems report grades every six weeks, most units are six weeks long, but there is nothing wrong with having two three-week units in a grading period.

The Unit Plan

You should have a specific plan for each major objective you hope to accomplish during the year. This is the *unit plan*. For example, a teacher of middle-level earth science would probably want each student to acquire some understanding of astronomy, ecology, geology, meteorology, oceanography, paleontology, mineralogy, and physical geography. For each of these areas, the teacher would plan a unit of study lasting from a few days to a few weeks and containing the topics the teacher wants the students to learn. Because middle-level teachers realize that writing is an effective means for learning concepts in all disciplines, and because students grasp concepts at a deeper level when they write—a goal of the National Middle School Association—writing assignments are used to enable students to better grasp the major concepts in this unit.

> **Teacher of the Year**
>
> I have developed units and activities to improve the learning process, to increase motivation of students, and to allow students to enjoy success at their own academic level. I believe curriculum goes beyond the basic program offered in the textbook. To be meaningful, students need to see how the curriculum fits in with their everyday experiences and interests.
>
> Former Utah Teacher of the Year Marilyn Grondel
> (Henson & Eller, 1999, p. 316)

Planning

Once you have selected your unit topics, you can plan each unit. Students should help plan each unit. Vars (1997) explains the need to involve students from the onset. "Involving students in goal setting should begin on the very first day of class, as students and teachers get acquainted and share their hopes for the coming year (p. 45). It seems much more honest for teachers to present mandates 'up front' and invite students to help plan how to meet them, rather than to conceal mandates in thematic units presumably planned around student concerns." (p. 45) Yet, even experts on educational measurement continue to wrestle with how to make performance assessment valid and reliable, not to mention 'honest' and 'fair'; but first you must determine your role and their role in the planning process.

Your extensive study of the subject gives you insight into what students must learn—insights your students do not have. Therefore, you must identify important ideas or concepts to develop in the unit and explain their importance to your students. Students may want to omit certain ideas or sections because they dislike them, but you must include these concepts if you deem them essential.

Give students an opportunity to include material in the unit that they want to study. Even though you may consider certain topics less important than others, remember that when students find a topic interesting, it becomes relevant to them. Merely giving students more control of their education is an important, positive step (Des Dixon, 1994). Involving students in planning has another important advantage: it helps avoid the sequential approach that often limits learning. Students preferred participating in open discussions and brain-storming on topics of their choice. According to Hart (1983) "Because the ordinary classroom does not provide this richness in learning and, in most instances, limits what the brain can do, students become addicted or habituated to this limited, sequential approach" (p. 77). Involving students can make them more interested in a subject, which enhances their ability to learn that material. According to Levy (1983), "If students are engaged [in learning activities, as opposed to remaining passive], both sides of the brain will participate in the educational process regardless of subject matter." Students learn more when they participate in lessons (Finn, 1993).

You must also help the class select activities they need to understand a unit. With the Internet at their disposal, today's teachers and students have an unlimited supply of information. One effective approach that teachers are taking is using more questions and challenging their students to discover the answers by using the Internet. This approach supports the National Middle School Association goal of connecting the disciplines with authentic, interdisciplinary assignments. Activities are the vehicles through which students learn content, and students should participate in the selection of classroom activities. This does not mean that the teacher selects some of the activities and the students independently select others. When you broach the topic of selecting class activities, have a list of activities from which the class can choose. If the students want to add other feasible activities, let them. Ask yourself about each proposed activity: Is it contrary to school policy? Is it dangerous or harmful to me, to the students, or to others? Is it something I should first check with the principal? Is it worthwhile? And finally: Is it something we could try? If so, it may prove worthwhile because the students are interested in that particular activity.

Involving Parents

Another group you must not ignore when planning your curriculum is parents. Remember that reengaging families in youths' education is a major Carnegie goal for middle schools. Because of their vested interest in the schools and because they can influence students positively, effective curriculum planning includes parents. Fried (1998) has noted that some parents use the schools to serve their own purposes. Because some parents may have their own private agendas to serve, Armstrong et al. (2004) caution teachers to remain on guard. Other parents, especially poor and poorly educated parents, will need encouragement to become involved in school decisions (Kohn, 1998). The recent popularity of school-based decision making has intensified the need to include parents in all parts of schools, especially academics (LeBlanc & Lacey, 1999). O'Neal, Earley, and Snider (1991, p. 123) stress this need: "Research has constantly indicated that parent and family involvement is critical to the academic success of many children."

Components

The learning unit (or unit plan) outlines subject material on a given topic, but it also does more. Although they vary, most unit plans contain the following parts: (1) a title; (2) a statement of philosophy, goals, objectives, and content to be covered; (3) teacher and student activities to attain the objectives; and (4) a method to evaluate students' degrees of understanding of the unit. The unit plan may also include a list of resource people (consultants) and resource materials (bibliography). Figure 3.4 illustrates a learning unit.

The statement of philosophy contains the teacher's beliefs about the school's purposes, the nature of adolescence, how adolescents learn, and the purpose of life in general. Because teachers do not reflect enough on their beliefs about these all-important issues, the statement of philosophy is the most neglected part of learning units. Yet the first question teachers often hear when beginning a new unit is "Why do we have to study this stuff?" Only by thinking through these broad issues can you answer this question intelligently.

The statement of purposes is a list of general expectations that you want the unit to achieve. For example, a social studies teacher may expect students to understand how a bill is introduced, to become more tolerant of others' opinions, and to appreciate democracy as a type of government. Unlike the performance objectives teachers use in daily planning, which are stated in specific, observable, and measurable terms, a unit's statement of purposes should be much more general.

Base your selection of content for any unit on three broad considerations:

1. Must students master this content to reach the general objectives?
2. Is this content important?
3. What are your students' needs and interests?

Choose activities on the same basis: select experiences that will enable students to learn content. Do not feel obligated to select one activity for each objective; some of the best activities serve multiple purposes and allow students to attain several objectives. For example, one activity for a language arts lesson might be to write a composition contrasting Shelley's and Byron's poetry. This activity will allow students to gain writing skills and sharpen their concept of writing style.

Philosophy ⟶ Purposes ⟶ Content ⟶ Activities ⟶ Evaluation

FIGURE 3.4 ANATOMY OF A LEARNING UNIT

From Kenneth T. Henson, *Methods and Strategies for Teaching in Secondary and Middle Schools,* third edition. Published by Allyn and Bacon, Boston, MA. Copyright © 1996 by Pearson Education. Reprinted by permission of the publisher.

Some teachers do not believe their classes have time to achieve multiple objectives, but several objectives can be met simultaneously. Activities with multiple objectives are not necessarily inefficient. Each learning unit should contain different types of student performance and different types of measurement, such as written tests, oral tests, debates, term projects, homework assignments, classwork, and perhaps performance in class or group discussions. This type of evaluation, which examines the quality of a product, is called **product evaluation.**

Another type of evaluation you should apply to each learning unit is called **process evaluation.** This merely describes the effectiveness of the teaching of the unit. Process evaluation analyzes the various unit parts to determine whether the entire unit needs improvement. It also involves examining the unit as a whole to see how its parts relate. Ask yourself: Is my philosophy sound? Does it convince students that the unit is important? Are the purposes important? Is it realistic to expect these students to achieve them in the allotted time? Is the unit's content correct for the stated purposes? Will these activities help attain these objectives? Is the evaluation fair to everyone? Does it discriminate between those who have met the objectives and those who have not?

Learning units should also include certain practical information. In addition to title, subject, and grade level, they should contain a list of resources—consultants, equipment, facilities, supplies, and especially audiovisual aids—needed to teach the unit. They should also include references that students can use to pursue the topic further. Finally, each unit should contain performance objectives that (1) are stated in terms of student behavior, (2) describe the conditions, and (3) specify the minimum acceptable level of performance.

Sample Unit Plans

Examine the following unit plan. Notice that the title describes the unit; the statement of purpose or objectives describes what students should accomplish; and the evaluation is stated in terms of the objectives.

Reflection

Read the following statements and respond to the questions below.

Don't Fix It If It Ain't Broke

Teacher A

Too much attention is given to instructional planning, evaluating lessons, and replanning. Some of the most effective lessons occur as spur-of-the-moment insights that teachers have on the way to class. But this can occur only when teachers are mentally free from overly structured lesson plans. In fact, the cookbook approach to teaching often results in boring the students. Anyway, aren't lessons supposed to serve the students' needs rather than the teacher's needs?

Teacher B

Don't listen to that gibberish. Those words probably come from a teacher who is too lazy to plan lessons adequately. Granted, spur-of-the-moment insights may occur, but how often does that really happen? No sensible teacher will sit around and wait for an inspiration. It's far better to overplan than underplan—if indeed one can overplan at all.

1. List some benefits of instructional planning.
2. Think about a former teacher who did little or no planning. Was this teacher able to relate to students better? Describe the amount of learning that occurred in this teacher's class.
3. Can instructional planning serve students' needs? How?
4. In Chapter 4 we will see that effective teachers can be flexible and yet return to the lesson's focus. How does planning affect teacher flexibility?

Sample Lesson Plan

Meteorology/Language Arts Unit Plan:
What Meteorology Means to You

I. Purpose
  A. Knowledge: to understand—
    1. The different types of weather
    2. The principles of weather formation
    3. The role of the weatherperson
    4. The names and principles of commonly used weather instruments
    5. Weather vocabulary
    6. Sentence definition
    7. The effects of jargon on sentence clarity
    8. The relation between simplicity and clarity
  B. Attitudes: to appreciate—
    1. The damage weather can do
    2. The advantage of good weather
    3. How weather affects our daily behavior
    4. The rate of accuracy of weather predictions
    5. The precision use of weather instruments
    6. The fallacies of superstitions about the weather
    7. The importance of clarity
  C. Skills: To develop the ability to—
    1. Read and interpret weather instruments
    2. Read and interpret weather maps
    3. Predict future weather
    4. Write simple, clear sentences
II. Daily lessons
  A. Definition of weather
  B. Precipitation
    1. Different types of precipitation
    2. How each type of precipitation is formed
  C. Reading the weather map
  D. Reading weather instruments
  E. Predicting weather
  F. Effects of geographic location on weather
  G. Effects of the earth's rotation on weather
  H. Effects of the earth's tilting on weather
  I. How to change weather that can hurt you
III. Materials
  A. Weather reports from newspapers
  B. Weather maps
  C. Equipment for making fog: air pump, water, jar
  D. Barometer, thermometer, anemometer, wind vane
  E. Graph paper for each student
IV. Evaluation
  A. Tests for each section of the unit: approximately one test per week's study of the topic

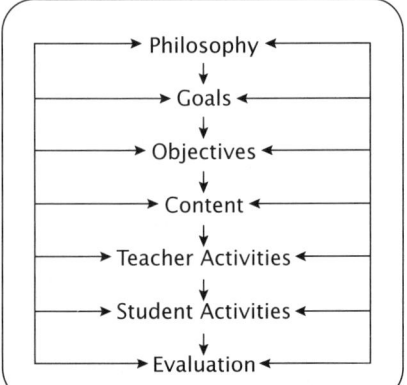

FIGURE 3.5 DIAGRAM OF A LEARNING–TEACHING UNIT

Let's Talk

Now that we have identified a purpose for the unit, set down the objectives for the lesson, and selected the major concepts and content generalizations needed to achieve those objectives, it is time to plan the daily activities. These should include the teacher's activities and the activities in which the students will be involved. Chapter 4, on planning daily lessons, will cover how to involve students in meaningful ways.

The above unit plan was chosen for its brevity and simplicity. This does not make it a superior plan, but such brief units are often used. Do you think the unit plan is too skimpy? What do you think about this format? Is the outline adequate? Figure 3.4 shows the parts commonly found in a unit plan. Which of the parts in Figure 3.5 are missing from the sample unit plan above?

Did you notice that the meteorology unit has neither a statement of philosophy nor a statement of rationale to show the unit's significance? Many educators feel that a statement of philosophy helps you clarify your own beliefs about life, school, and adolescents and how they learn. Goals and objectives should coincide and should reflect your basic beliefs. Other educators prefer to have a statement of rationale instead of a statement of philosophy. When you write a statement of rationale, you justify the unit to yourself; then you can use the rationale to convince students that the unit is worth their time and energy.

The meteorology unit has no sections titled "Teacher Activities" or "Student Activities." This is unfortunate, because at this time the teacher should be thinking about taking the class to a weather station or showing a film on meteorology. The weather station may need advance notice, and for field trips students must identify in advance what information they will gain from the trip. Films must be scheduled and ordered in advance, and you will need time to preview them. Students might do a writing assignment before the field trip, writing simple statements of what each student hopes to gain from the trip. Following the field trip, students could be asked to write statements expressing what they achieved, including both planned and unexpected outcomes. These were missed opportunities. You can probably identify other weaknesses in this unit plan.

Perhaps the most important part of planning is how the plan is implemented, particularly the degree of teacher flexibility.

Teacher of the Year

The students we recruit to our profession should be confident enough to withstand the assault of text makers, politicians, and apathetic students and vulnerable enough to share their fears and frustrations, accepting responsibility when things don't go as planned.

Former Idaho Teacher of the Year Shirley Rau
(Henson & Eller, 1999, p. 13)

Vignettes

This chapter focuses on the teacher's role in long-term planning. The chapter offers guidelines and suggestions for planning learning units for periods that may range from a few days to a few weeks. There are no blanket statements that dictate step-by-step planning. These guidelines and your own experience will enable you to develop a system with which you are comfortable one that will allow you to teach effectively.

You will have problems and struggles, however. The following vignettes are examples of the dilemmas teachers can encounter as they plan teaching units.

Vignette One: Should Lesson Planning Be Sequential?

Bongo Nagatah was realizing his dream of attending a U.S. university, where he could learn to become a master teacher and return to his native land for a lifetime of service. Bongo applied himself totally. He had indeed mastered his chosen teaching field, mathematics, which he enjoyed for its preciseness and structure, and he had done equally well in his professional education courses. Despite all this, however, he ran into problems. Ironically, much of his frustration resulted from his love of structure.

When his methods course began developing learning units, Bongo looked for guidelines or rules that would help him develop a learning unit. First, he wrote a brief statement of philosophy for the unit, but he was not sure about the next step. The professor had instructed the class to follow the statement with a list of general goals for the unit, but Bongo felt that he was leaving out some important content and that perhaps he should make a content outline before identifying the goals. Later, when he began identifying content and activities, the same dilemma emerged: if he selected the activities first, how could he be sure that content was being covered adequately; if he selected the content first, how could he take advantage of opportunities that he wanted to offer his students—field trips, speakers, and civic activities? He especially wanted to encourage his students to enter projects in the regional science and mathematics fair.

Bongo's level of frustration peaked when he was told that each student must pair up with a classmate with a different major. How would he ever have time to teach all the important math concepts if students would also be learning concepts from another discipline?

DISCUSSION

1. Is there a definite sequence for developing a unit? In a general sense there is. Write your statement of philosophy first. The goals should precede the behavioral objectives, and the objectives should precede the selection of content and activities. Most teachers find this sequence helpful, but many believe that following it in all situations is restrictive and could even damage their units.

2. How can you ensure complete content coverage and also take advantage of opportunities to involve students in valuable learning experiences? Because a general sequence of design can be helpful, you may prefer to follow the accepted sequence until you have a specific reason for changing it. Many teachers find that skipping a step and going back to it later can be useful in some situations.

3. When planning an integrated unit, is some breadth of coverage sacrificed? If so, what is gained from joining the disciplines?

> **Vignette Two: A Principal Requires Six Months' Advance Planning**
>
> When Hilda moved from teaching in a rural school to her first urban school, she learned the true meaning of planning. In the smaller, rural school, lesson planning had never been a topic of faculty discussion, but during her first faculty meeting at the urban school the principal handed each teacher a 300-page spiral book in which to enter lesson plans for the following six months. Because she had never planned for more than a week or two in advance, Hilda was overwhelmed; yet her colleagues accepted the principal's request without question.
>
> After the faculty meeting, Hilda asked whether the principal ever actually checked the plans to see if they were completed so far in advance and was told that there probably would be a surprise check once or twice a year. In addition, her lesson plan book would have to be left in the office in case she were absent, so a substitute teacher could use it.
>
> At this school, each teacher teamed with a teacher in another discipline. Because Hilda's field is language arts, she was paired with a social studies teacher, Ms. Campbell, who assured her that there was no required length for each lesson and suggested that they list only the name or title of each lesson, without attempting to describe it. However, even the co-planning of a skeleton integrated lesson plan consumed several hours of both teachers' time, hours that no middle-level teacher could find without giving up other important responsibilities. Hilda wondered whether such advance planning was really necessary.
>
> **DISCUSSION**
>
> 1. How far in advance should teachers plan?
> 2. What are some reasons for requiring teachers to plan months in advance?
> 3. What advantages can be derived from such integrated planning?

Summary

Teachers have both the latitude and responsibility for planning the curriculum for each of their classes. Historically, textbooks have had a strong influence on the curriculum. Middle-level teachers should collaborate across disciplines, involving students, parents, and other teachers, guarding against letting the textbook dominate the selection of curriculum content. Few textbooks cover a majority of the important concepts in their discipline.

To ensure that students understand the major concepts in each lesson, teachers should begin the planning of each unit by identifying the major goals and objectives and should then assign activities that enable students to discover these major ideas. By involving students and parents in curriculum development, teachers can form partnerships that focus on positive goals, and when students succeed, everyone can feel good about the success. Periodic re-evaluation of the curriculum is needed to prevent the curriculum from becoming dated.

Recap of Major Ideas

1. In selecting content, seek out generalizations that students need to understand the subject.
2. Use your own expertise, but also involve students in selecting content and activities.
3. Taba's inverted curriculum model is considered superior because teachers construct it in the classroom around teaching units.
4. Learning activities are the vehicle through which students develop the generalizations they need to understand a subject.
5. Add consistency to your lesson planning by beginning each unit with a written statement of your philosophy about life, school, and learning.
6. Each part of a learning unit should relate to the other parts. This is called *coherence*.
7. When beginning a unit, consider consulting teachers at the next grade level, textbooks, curriculum guides, and students.
8. Textbooks alone are an inadequate source of information for curriculum planning.
9. Long-term planning is essential for maximum learning opportunities.
10. Maximum learning requires students to relate new concepts to existing knowledge.

Activities

The objectives at the beginning of this chapter promised that you would learn how to develop a complete learning unit. If you are ready for this challenge, select a topic in one of your teaching fields and apply your skills as follows.

1. Write a brief statement of your philosophy of education. Include your beliefs about the general purpose of secondary schools, the nature of adolescence, and the nature of learning.
2. Write at least three broad goals for a unit of three to six weeks. Make certain that these goals represent at least two disciplines.
3. For each goal, write a few behavioral objectives.
4. Outline the major content generalizations for the unit.
5. Select some teacher activities and student activities to facilitate attainment of these objectives.
6. Design a grading system and a system for evaluating unit effectiveness. Consider whether it has all the essential parts; also check the sequence of these parts.

Looking Ahead

This chapter has focused on long-range planning, requiring you to look ahead for several weeks and months. The following chapter will prepare you to plan daily lessons.

References

Alspaugh, J. W. (1998). The relationship of school and community characteristics to high school drop-out rates. *The Clearing House, 71*(3), 184–188.

Applebee, A. N., Langer, J. A., & Mullis, I. V. S. (1987). *The nation's report card: Literature and U.S. history.* Princeton, NJ: Educational Testing Service.

Armstrong, D. G., Henson, K. T., & Savage, T. V. (2004). *Teaching today.* 7th ed. New York: Macmillan.

Berliner, D. C. (1984). The half-full glass: A review of research on teaching. In P. A. Hosford (Ed.), *Using what we know about teaching.* Alexandria, VA: Association for Supervision and Curriculum Development.

Carnegie Council on Adolescent Development Staff (1995). *Great transitions: Preparing adolescents for a new century.* New York: Carnegie Foundation.

Clark, S. N., Clark, D. C., & Irvin, J. I. (1997). Collaborative decision making. *Middle School Journal, 28*(5), 54–56.

Cotton, K. (1996). Affective and social benefits of small-scale schooling. ERIC Digest Report EDO-RC-96-5.

Des Dixon, R. G. (1994). Future schools and how to get there from here. *Phi Delta Kappan, 75*(5), 360–365.

Doyle, W. (1979). Making managerial decisions in classrooms. In D. L. Duke (Ed.), *Classroom management, 78th yearbook of the National Association for the Study of Education, part II.* Chicago: University of Chicago Press.

Eisner, E. (2001). What does it mean to say a school is doing well? *Phi Delta Kappan, 82*(5), 367–372.

Finn, J. D. (1993). *School engagement and students at risk.* Washington, DC: National Center for Education Statistics, U.S. Department of Education.

Fried, R. L. (1998). Parent anxiety and school reform. *Phi Delta Kappan, 80*(4), 264–271.

Hall, H. (1998). In Pitton, D. E., An interview with Howard Hall, Director of Curriculum, District 191, 5 June.

Harrison, C. J. (1990). Concepts, operational definitions, and case studies in instruction. *Education, 110*(4), 502–505.

Hart, L. A. (1983). *How the brain works.* New York: Basic Books.

Henson, K. T., Buttery, T. J., & Chissom, B. (1986). Improving instruction in middle schools by attending to teachers' needs. *American Middle School Education, 9*(2), 2–7.

Henson, K. T., & Eller, B. F. (1999). *Educational psychology for effective teaching.* Belmont, CA: Wadsworth.

Hilliard, R. D. (1999). All I ever needed to know about teaching I learned in the middle school. *SRATE Journal, 8*(1), 50–56.

Hubbuch, S. M. (1989, April–May). The trouble with textbooks. *The High School Journal, 72*(4), 203–209.

Jackson, A., & Davis, G. (2000). *Turning points 2000: Educating adolescents in the 21st Century.* Columbus, OH: National Middle School Association.

Kohn, A. L. (1998). Only for my kid: How privileged parents undermine school reform. *Phi Delta Kappan, 79*(8), 568–577.

Kowalski, T. J., Weaver, R. A., & Henson, K. T. (1994). *Case studies on beginning teachers.* White Plains, NY: Longman.

Krashen, S. (1998). Crossing the economic divide. *Educational Leadership, 55*(4), 28–29.

LeBlanc, P. R., & Lacey, C. (1999). The reflective model for staff development: Identifying best practice. *SRATE Journal, 8*(1), 24–32.

Levy, J. (1983). Research synthesis on right and left hemispheres: We think with both sides of the brain. *Educational Leadership, 40,* 66–71.

Markle, G., Johnston, J. H., Geer, C., & Meichtry, Y. (1990, November). Teaching for understanding. *Middle School Journal, 22*(2), 53–57.

Mather, C. (2001). In K. T. Henson *Curriculum Development,* 2nd ed. New York: McGraw-Hill.

Maynard, S., & Howley, A. (1997). Parent and community involvement in rural schools. ERIC Digest Report EDO-RC-97-3.

MLS (Metropolitan Life Insurance Company Survey) (1998). *The American teacher.* New York: Louis Harris and Associates.

Murry, K., & Herrera, S. (1998). Crisis in the heartland: Addressing unexpected challenges in rural education. *Journal of Research in Rural Education, 14*(1), 1–5.

Oddleifson, E. (1994). What do we want our schools to do? *Phi Delta Kappan, 75*(6), 446–453.

O'Neal, M., Earley, B., & Snider, M. (1991). Addressing the needs of at-risk students: A local school program that works. In R. C. Morris (Ed.), *Youth at risk* (pp. 122–125). Lancaster, PA: Tecnomic.

Orlich, D. C. (1980). *Teaching strategies: A guide to better instruction.* Lexington, MA: Heath.

Patterson, W. (2003). "Breaking out of our boxes." *Phi Delta Kappan, 84*(8), 569–574.

Perkins, D., & Blythe, T. (1994). Putting understanding up front. *Educational Leadership, 51*(5), 4–7.

Pitton, D. E. (1999). Interview with Howard Hall, director of curriculum, District 191, June 5th. *Phi Delta Kappan, 80*(5), 383–386.

Regnier, P. (1994). The illusion of technique and the intellectual life of schools. *Phi Delta Kappan, 76*(1), 82–83.

Reinstein, D. (1998). Crossing the economic divide. *Educational Leadership, 55*(4), 28–29.

Scheville, J., Porter, A., Billi, G., Flooden, R., Freeman, D., Knappan, L., Kuhs, F., & Schmidt, W. (1981). Teachers as policy brokers in the content of elementary school mathematics. National Institute of Education Contract P-80-0127. East Lansing, MI: Institute for Research on Teaching, Michigan State University.

Schmoker, M., & Marzano, R. J. (1999). Realizing the promise of standards-based education. *Educational Leadership, 56*(6), 17–21.

Slavin, R. E. (1995). *Cooperative learning,* 2nd ed. Boston: Allyn & Bacon.

Snapp, J. C., & Glover, J. A. (1990). Advance organizers and study questions. *The Journal of Educational Research, 83*(5), 266–271.

Stefanich, G. P. (1990, November). Cycles of cognition. *Middle School Journal, 22*(2), 47–52.

Taba, H. (1962). *Curriculum development: Theory and practice.* Orlando, FL: Harcourt Brace Jovanovich.

Tannebaum, M. D., & Faison, C. L. (1999). Strategies for planned curriculum change: Collaborative teaching. *SRATE Journal, 8*(1), 33–40.

Taylor, M. (1976). *Role of thunder: Hear my cry.* New York: Dial Press.

Thompson, S., & Gregg, L. (1997). Reculturing middle schools for meaningful change. *Middle School Journal, 28*(5), 27–31.

Trachtenberg, D. (1974). Student tasks in text material: What cognitive skills do they tap? *Peabody Journal of Education, 52,* 54–57.

Tyler, R. W. (1984). Curriculum development and research. In P. A. Hosford (Ed.), *Using what we know about teaching.* Alexandria, VA: Association for Supervision and Curriculum Development.

Tyson, H., & Woodward, A. (1989, November). Why students aren't learning very much from textbooks. *Educational Leadership,* 14–17.

Van Gulick, R. (1990). Functionalism, information, and content. In W. G. Lylcan (Ed.), *Mind and cognition.* Cambridge, MA: Basil Blackwell.

Vars, G. F. (1997). Student concerns and standards too. *Middle School Journal, 28*(4), 44–49.

Weller, L. D., Jr., Hartley, S. H., & Brown, C. L. (1994). Principles and TMQ: Developing vision. *The Clearing House, 67*(5), 298–301.

4

Planning Daily Lessons

A journey of a thousand miles must begin with a single step.

Lao Tzu

Objectives

- Define and differentiate between a daily lesson plan and a unit plan.
- List four essential qualities of a behavioral objective and write five behavioral objectives.
- List in order six pertinent parts of a daily lesson plan.
- Write a plan for each of two daily lessons.
- Develop a strategy for more efficient use of classroom time.
- Explain how teachers can use technology to help students connect new information with existing knowledge.

THE DAILY LESSON PLAN

Creating
- Traditional Strategies
- Factors Affecting Achievement
  — Engaged Time
  — Class Size
  — Personalizing
- Applying Constuctivism
- Multiculturalism
- Team Teaching
- Lesson Plan Qualities
  — Objectives
  — Organization
  — Curriculum

Implementing
- Time Management
- Summarizing Daily Lessons
- Learning Cycle Theory
- Textbooks
- Discussions
- Field Trips
- Oral Report
- Project
- Place-Based Education
- Homework
- Parental Involvement
- Sample Plans

Connecting Statements

	Agree	Disagree	Uncertain
1. All lesson plans should begin with a list of the subject content to be learned.			
2. A lesson plan that works well with one group may not work well with another group.			
3. The best lesson plans are those drawn up by outside experts (as opposed to teacher-made plans).			
4. To be effective, a lesson must cause students to change their behavior.			
5. A lesson is a failure unless it gives students new skills.			
6. Student activities are essential to all lesson plans.			

> ### Tips for Teachers
>
> This chapter shows that the amount of time teachers allocate to a subject does not mean students will learn it; however, the amount of time students are engaged with a subject does. This can hinder middle-level classes because their energy level is so high that keeping them on task is difficult. You must use their high energy level as a positive learning force, since the time they spend developing concepts (instead of just studying concepts) correlates positively with their achievement.
>
> Remember, do *not* try to suppress these students' high activity level; rather, channel their energy toward developing the concepts that comprise their chosen disciplines.

Creating Daily Lesson Plans

Chapters 2 and 3 emphasized the importance of planning to teaching, with Thompson & Gregg (1997, p. 28) saying that the curriculum is the primary vehicle for changing the goals and objectives of the school. Yet, for whatever reasons, middle school curricula are not being fully used to meet students' needs. The Carnegie Council on Adolescent Development reported that "a volatile mismatch exists between the organization in middle grade schools and the intellectual, emotional, and personal needs of young adolescents (Felner, Kasak, Mulhall, & Flowers, 1997, p. 521). You learned to begin each year by identifying the goals you hope to achieve and to select content accordingly. In Chapter 3 you learned how to design learning units through which your students and you could achieve these goals. As essential as they are, however, if they are left alone, goals will remain no more than elusive generalities. To enable students to attain them, you must design daily lesson plans. These plans include goals, but the goals are translated into more specific terms. Each daily lesson plan should cover a particular part of the unit; in fact, most units contain a series of daily lesson plans.

The Daily Lesson Plan

Traditional Planning Strategies

Because the teaching unit is usually content-oriented, you and the other teachers on your team must develop daily strategies to help students move nearer to the unit goals. For most teachers, this is the daily lesson plan. A teacher who attempts to teach without a lesson plan is like a pilot taking off for an unknown destination without a map. Like a map, a lesson plan provides direction toward the lesson objectives. If the lesson begins to stray, the lesson plan brings it back on course. Teaching can be difficult without a lesson plan. According to Walter (1984), however, despite the emphasis teacher education places on the "ends–means" approach, data now show that most experienced teachers do not begin the planning process by determining objectives. They begin by determining what content to cover and then design or select learning activities for students. One study, which examined planning in middle-level laboratories, found that teachers spend most of their planning time on content, a moderate amount of time selecting strategies, and the smallest amount of time on objectives (Peterson, Marx, & Clark, 1978). Furthermore, even when teachers modify their teaching approach, they seldom consider the lesson objectives (Clark & Peterson, 1986). You should choose strategies that work with the content (Acheson & Gall, 1992) and—because you alone know what is best for your particular students—strategies that feel right for you (Walker & Chance, 1994–1995).

Factors Affecting Achievement

Other data provide a framework for developing daily lesson plans. Romberg and Carpenter (1986) reviewed studies of mathematics classes and discovered three significant variables associated with student achievement. First, instead of just covering topics, students need to understand a subject. Teachers of the same subject and grade level may feel responsible for covering all the material in their textbooks (Patterson, 2003), yet the topics among textbooks vary greatly. Attempting to cover all the material reduces the time students spend studying important concepts and, as pointed out by Romberg (1983), "classes in which less time is allocated to mathematics instruction (or instruction in any subject) are likely to have relatively poorer achievement in the subject" (p. 60). Yet, as we saw in Chapter 3, the most frequent determiner of content—the textbook—usually does a poor job covering concepts that students need to understand a discipline. In a similar study of content coverage by textbooks, Schville et al. (1983) examined the three most commonly used fifth grade math textbooks and learned that there was very little content that all the authors considered significant; more than half the 290 topics common to one or more books were unique to a single book.

Engaged Time

A second factor in daily lesson planning is the amount of **engaged time,** that is, the time that is actually spent on a topic or concept compared with the time allocated for the subject. For example, during a 50-minute period, one class may spend 20 minutes on the day's lesson (engaged time), while another class may spend 40 minutes on the lesson and is likely to achieve more. The difference of engaged time can vary greatly from school to school. Reinstein (1998) reported that one school where he had taught provided 300 minutes of classroom instruction a week and another school where he had taught provided only 200 minutes of instruction a week. Plan each lesson so that it engages students with that subject's important concepts and skills.

A third factor that affects achievement is the **developmental time,** the time students spend *developing* particular concepts, as opposed to the time they spend just studying the concepts. In the developmental portion of a lesson, students spend time discussing such issues as why the concept is true, how skills or concepts are interrelated, and how to use these broader relationships to estimate answers to problems. In other words, developmental time puts the important concepts and skills in a broader and deeper context to help students understand those ideas.

Class Size

Class size has been studied for more than fifty years to determine its effect on student achievement. The results have been mixed (Gilman & Kiger, 2003). Carson and Badarack (1989), reported that "studies of the achievement effects of substantial reductions in class size indicate that smaller classes do have more positive effects than large ones, but the effects are small to moderate" (p. 9). Although data show smaller classes' positive effects on learning to be minimal, Carson and Badarack (1989) argue that, over time, the cumulative effect may be significant. Johnston (1990) reported that one advantage of smaller classes is improved teacher morale. Nye, Achilles, Boyd, Zaharias, Fulton, and Wallenhorst (1994) who have been conducting research on class size for several years at the Tennessee Center for Excellence: Basic Skills, reported that "small is far better" (p. 9). While there is disagreement over class size, Gilman and Kigers (2003) reported that "a growing body of anecdotal and qualitative evidence supports reducing class size" (p. 83).

The current practice of including challenged students in regular classrooms has increased the need for small classes. Waldron and Allen (1999) list small class size as an essential condition for successful inclusion. A statewide project in Wisconsin found that, when teaching smaller classes, teachers can expect fewer discipline problems, more time for instruction, and more time for individualization, varied instructional strategies, and more content and depth (Halbach, Ehrle, Zahorik, and Molnar, 2001). The degree to which smaller classes are better depends on the teacher's willingness to capitalize on these advantages.

Personalizing Lessons

Finally, make your lessons meaningful to all students. Miserando (1996) advises teachers to help students find personal meaning in each lesson. This advice parallels and reinforces the Carnegie Council on Academic Development's goal of personalizing learning experiences for adolescents.

Computers offer a means of personalizing lessons, which addresses the National Middle Schools Association (see Jenkins & Jenkins, 1991) (NMSA) goal of knowing and focusing on the middle-level child, while also increasing engaged time. By giving in-class and homework computer assignments, teachers can invite students to continuously share their opinions and insights. Such assignments also help meet the constructivist goal of enabling students to tie new information to existing understanding.

Applying Constructivism to Daily Planning

A continuing decline in student performance on the Scholastic Aptitude Test (SAT) is evidence that U.S. students are not learning how information fits together. Van Gulick (1990) believes that the lower scores on the SATs result from how students store information. To be

---

Teacher as Proactive Decision Maker

Classroom Situation

- Schools are getting more technologically advanced. Your new school will probably have more technology than you expect. You want your students to benefit from this technology.

Proactive Alternatives

- Just blindly participating with technology may not enhance student learning; you must want to change student behaviors in certain ways. Make a list of the behaviors that you will use technology to change.
- Introduce your students to PowerPoint. Prepare your own PowerPoint presentation to demonstrate some key features in this program.
- In small groups, have students prepare their own PowerPoint presentations of their assigned class projects.

able to use new information, students must see how it relates to a larger whole as they learn it. Markle, Johnston, Geer, and Meichtry (1990) say that constructivism subscribes to this belief: "Constructivists describe learning in terms of building connections between prior knowledge and new ideas and claim that effective teaching helps students construct an organized set of concepts that relates new and old ideas" (p. 53). The implications for teachers are great. Markle et al. quote Von Glaserfeld (1988) as saying: "The teachers' role will no longer be to dispense 'truth' but rather to help and guide students in the conceptual organization of certain areas of expertise" (p. 53). Certainly, this has always been the ideal role of middle-level teachers and will continue to be as they work together on interdisciplinary teams.

Such guidance is best achieved through group assignments that require students to describe the process they use to connect new information to existing knowledge (Markle et al., 1990). Incidentally, as we shall see in Chapter 8, personal connections between school and home play an equally important role in learning. Former Pennsylvania Teacher of the Year Howard Selekman (1999) speaks to the important role that personal connections have in learning. "At the root of the teaching profession are the basic human needs to make a bond, a link with others. . . . In my work as an English teacher of middle level students, I use literature as a grand opportunity to learn about the human condition and learn how critical it is to be able to make connections in the global community in which we all will live" (p. 59). Selekman uses writing assignments to make these connections. Incidentally, he writes along with his students, and to show his own limitations he shares his mistakes.

Traditionally, some teachers have not taken full advantage of opportunities to base their planning on factors that affect student achievement. Furthermore, clear concepts in each discipline, and effective models and strategies for teaching them, have not been available because they were not identified. As Armento (1986) stated, "Methodological advances have outpaced conceptual advances in the last 10 years" (pp. 948–949). Although Armento was referring to the field of social studies, the same is true of all disciplines. This expresses a most unfortunate state of affairs. It means that through the years the bulk of teacher activities have been without reason. But in recent years this condition has improved substantially, and the improvement continues.

More studies are identifying important concepts, and meta-cognitive studies have increased, which will help determine more effective ways to teach students to analyze how they process new information. For now, you should seek out the concepts and skills your students need to achieve each lesson's objectives and plan to use them as focal points for studying. Make these concepts and principles the content portion of each lesson plan. Concepts cannot be learned by definition, only by experience. The life-long challenge for teachers is to find more and better ways to help students discover the major concepts that give their discipline meaning.

Planning Lessons for Multicultural Classes

Teachers with diverse ethnic backgrounds and teachers in inner-city schools often plan fewer concepts into each lesson, providing more engaged time and more opportunities (activities) for students to be involved with these concepts. Constructivist teachers support the use of fewer concepts because they perceive it as a trade-off; covering fewer concepts allows students to understand these concepts more deeply. In other words, they believe that students should learn a few concepts in depth rather than have a shallow understanding of many concepts. Another reason that constructivist teachers cover fewer concepts is because they believe that students should discover these concepts; therefore, problem solving is the main strategy in constructivist classrooms.

Team Planning for Team Teaching

Middle-level teachers must be prepared to team plan and team teach interdisciplinary lessons. A survey sent to forty-one middle-level teachers (Stokes, 2000) found the ability to team in the top three areas considered most important for inclusion in effectively preparing middle-level teachers. Teaming was also the answer in which National Board Certified Early Adolescence/Generalist Teachers gave in a survey (McEwin, Dickinson, & Hamilton, 2000) were asked to tell how preparation for middle-level teachers should be different.

Effective teaming requires members to be cooperative, flexible, and patient. Risk taking is way of life for team teachers at the middle-level. A most important and sometimes difficult challenge for middle-level team members is to develop a spirit of community and to learn to embrace the objectives of the other team members and their disciplines. Failure to reach this goal results in turn teaching, which misses all the benefits of collaborative team teaching.

Hopping (2000) says that the primary challenge to members of a middle-level team is to search out the needs of the middle-level students, which are as varied as the students themselves. The social needs of these students must be met before their intellectual needs can be met. At times, team teachers should be willing to teach in stations, permitting students to rotate among learning centers (McQueen, 2001).

What Makes a Lesson Plan Good?

Lesson plans come in many sizes and varieties. Length or style does not make one plan better than another. A good lesson plan can be a formally worded, comprehensive outline, neatly typed on bond paper and enclosed in a plastic binder, or it can be a brief outline written in pencil on 3-inch by 5-inch cards. The styles of good lesson plans vary as much as their length. A good lesson plan contains material that will challenge students throughout the class period and activities that will involve every student. The format should be easy to follow with only a glance; you should not have to stop the lesson to read the lesson plan.

Arguing about types of lesson plans is a waste of time. Think of the lesson plan as a tool; like any tool, it is only as effective as the person using it. However, a worker who has good machinery has an advantage over a worker who has faulty equipment. You and your team-teaching partner(s) must develop and use lesson plans that work for your students.

Setting Objectives

Research on schools in which achievement is high has shown that when the teacher sets clear expectations for the class, students achieve more (Walker & Chance, 1994–1995; Good & Brophy, 2000). High expectations are needed for all students, including those who have special needs (Christie, 2002). Begin planning a daily lesson by thinking: How do I want this lesson to change my students? Or, what will this lesson enable them to do? State these proposals at the beginning, to give direction to daily activities.

Organizing Materials

Now that you have decided what material to include in the lesson, you must decide on a sequence in which to present the material. Sometimes a subject dictates its own sequence, so look at the major ideas you want to cover to see if there is a natural sequence.

For example, a physical education teacher who wants to teach students to drive a golf ball will think, "What ideas are important to understanding this process?" The answer is: "Addressing the ball, the back swing, the downswing, and the follow-through." The sequence is obvious because a natural process is involved. Another example is a home economics teacher planning a lesson on how to bake a chiffon cake. Again, the process dictates the sequence. A history teacher preparing lessons would follow events' chronological order.

If the four or five objectives of the day's lesson have no natural order, try to determine whether a particular sequence will help students understand the lesson. For instance, a science teacher will probably not teach students a compound's formula until they have learned to recognize the symbols for the elements.

The Curriculum

The word *curriculum* comes from a Latin word meaning "race course," but the concept of curriculum has changed considerably. At first, curriculum meant "program of studies." It was merely a list of the courses offered. Later the meaning of the word changed to denote course content. Today many educators define the word in terms of learning experiences. One earlier definition is: "the formal and informal content and process by which learners gain knowledge and understanding, develop skills and alter attitudes, appreciations, and values under the auspices of the school" (Doll, 1978, p. 6). To see a discussion of how the concept of curriculum has changed through the years, see Henson (2001).

Most contemporary educators view the curriculum as the content and experiences the school plans for students. This can mean either the plan (the document) itself or the actual functioning curriculum. This text regards the curriculum as the purposefully planned content and experiences you select to help students achieve goals and objectives.

Generally, experience is now emphasized more than content, because today's educators recognize that experiences are major avenues for learning (Finn, 1993). This is especially true in middle schools. A lesson plan must therefore describe what experiences you expect to use to teach the content. Students often complain (and rightfully so) that their lessons have no relevance, so educators tell us that we must provide meaningful experiences. How can you make experiences meaningful, so that your classes will be relevant? And because students should not engage in an activity without knowing what they are trying to accomplish, how will you plan their involvement?

Review your partially completed lesson plan. You have stated how you wanted the lesson to change the students (i.e., the lesson's objectives). Little (1985) found that objectives can be used as advance organizers to improve student achievement. You have also selected and organized some major ideas you want to develop. Now you are ready to plan involvement by assigning a task that will require students to use each of the major ideas in the lesson.

The language arts or English teacher who is planning a lesson on "How to Capture the Reader's Attention" will assign tasks that make students use what they have just learned. Presented with several compositions, students could be asked to identify the principles of capturing the reader's attention each time they occur. Later in the hour, each student will write the lead paragraph of a composition, employing the five techniques of capturing the reader's attention introduced earlier in the hour.

The physical education teacher who wants to teach the correct procedure for driving a golf ball may demonstrate each step and ask students to identify mistakes that the teacher deliberately makes in each phase. Eventually, students go through the process themselves while other students critique them.

Note that each experience is an assigned task. Students must have mastered the content to carry out the procedure correctly.

> ## Reflection
>
> It is time to begin building your own lesson plan. Choose a subject you plan to teach. Use the following template to assemble the essential parts of your plan.
>
> Objectives
> 1.
> 2.
> 3.
>
> Teacher Activities
> 1.
> 2.
>
> Student Activities
> 1.
> 2.
>
> Major concepts or essential ideas to develop
> 1.
> 2.
> 3.
> 4.

Implementing Daily Lesson Plans

A lesson will probably be no better than the daily lesson plan, yet a lesson plan does not guarantee that students will learn. Even the best plans may need modification as students interact with the materials and activities. Even the most prolific planning may be counterproductive if you become single minded and do not adapt the lesson to your students' needs. As you develop planning skills, consider ways to alter your plans if they are not effective with a particular group at a particular time. Keep in mind that the more thoroughly your lesson plan is developed, the more easily you can permit students to get off course with their discussions and then return them to the objectives.

Managing Your Time

Gallagher (1998, p. 741) has said that the biggest enemy of the teacher is time. Gallagher was referring to the variance among students' knowledge on almost any topic. How much time should the teacher spend on each topic? One response is to learn to use your time more effectively. Ciscell (1990) explains why teachers must manage their time effectively:

> Teachers' inefficient use of their professional time recently has become the focus of much attention within the educational community. What started out as simple efforts to measure the amount of on task behavior have resulted in somewhat alarming reports concerning the ways elementary and secondary teachers manage the school day. In the last decade, educational time has taken on a vocabulary all its own: Researchers now talk in terms of allotted time, engaged time, and academic learning time. Almost inevitably, teachers' use of classroom time has been blamed for declining achievement in America's schools. (p. 217)

Ciscell goes on to suggest that teachers can better use their time by delegating some responsibilities and by letting others know that you are time conscious. He suggests the following steps to achieve this goal:

- Keep an appointment calendar.
- Always be on time for meetings and appointments.
- Start and end meetings on time and follow an agenda.
- Limit time spent on idle teacher-lounge chitchat.
- Keep your classroom door closed to avoid spontaneous walk-ins by colleagues.
- Organize and manage your classroom efficiently.
- Forget trying to work in the teacher's workroom—find a place to hide. (p. 218)

A final way to manage time is to learn to say *no*. When you are asked to fill in for a friend on a committee or assignment, say, "I'm sorry but I'm tied up at that time," or negotiate—"I'll be happy to if you will take my place selling football tickets Friday night." With practice, these strategies will become natural and easy, and your colleagues will learn to find an easy target elsewhere. "Benefits accrue not only for teachers themselves but also for students as they take on the responsibility and challenge of a well-planned assignment" (Ciscell, 1990, p. 218).

Effective teachers separate important information and salient information and simplify these major concepts for their own students; less effective teachers attempt to deal with more issues. Because beginning teachers often cannot simplify and make sense of classroom events, make a wise investment by identifying your discipline's major principles and concepts. Simplifying the concept does not equate with spoon feeding; constructive teachers allow students to discover the concepts and solutions. The teacher is responsible for ensuring that students do, indeed, understand these important concepts.

Summarizing the Daily Lesson

End your lesson plan with a review of the main ideas you have covered. Do not review every detail in the lesson or merely list the lesson's main parts. Harrison (1990) makes an excellent suggestion for ending a lesson summary or review: "Have students name analogies and metaphors, and compare and contrast these with the original idea" (p. 503). The review should show the relationships among the major ideas and tie together the lesson's parts.

For example, the physical education teacher planning a lesson on how to drive a golf ball would include in the review each of the major ideas—the address, the back swing, the downswing, and the follow-through—and review the major issues related to each. The review would begin with the first idea, how to address the golf ball, and include the major points involved in the proper address as they were mentioned in the lesson. Likewise, the English lesson on "How to Capture the Reader's Attention" would include each point and its development.

Constructivists perceive learning as an ongoing process of finding connections between what has been learned and what is to be learned. Teachers who share this view will wish to consider establishing a routine of reviewing each chapter, each lesson, or each unit as an introduction to the following chapter, lesson, or unit. This practice will facilitate learning of the new material by helping students make connections between the material to be learned and insight gained from the previous study.

Learning Cycle Theory

Another instructional theory is called the **learning cycle theory.** Lawson, Abraham, and Renner (1989) introduced a learning cycle approach to instruction to help students move through the levels of understanding. The program has three parts: *exploration, concept introduction,* and *application.* The hands-on introduction enables students to develop descriptive and qualitative understandings. The concept introduction lets them talk about their experiences, either with the teacher or in cooperative learning groups. The teacher guides the discussion. During the application phase, students are given assignments to apply the concepts in different ways.

Markle et al. (1990) caution teachers against making unwarranted assumptions about what students know. They advise teachers to provide procedural structure that tells students in advance what they are going to do, what the key points are, and what they should know when the lesson is completed. Brown (at press) recommends story telling as a means of testing teaching theories to improve learning for diverse classrooms, "The frequencies of teachers telling stories and collectively testing theories for diverse populations will create learning environments where learners experience success."

Planning Ways to Involve Students

In addition to varying your lesson plans, you also must use a variety of learning avenues, such as textbooks, discussions, field trips, oral reports, term projects, and homework. We now turn to the use of these and your role in each.

Textbooks

Throughout the history of education in the United States, one type of textbook or another has dominated the curriculum. At first, the textbook determined the content to be studied. There were virtually no experiences other than rote memorization and recitation, which often resulted in a boring, irrelevant curriculum. To a large extent, this is still true: "Teachers consider the textbook as the major (and usually only) source of content" (Walter, 1984, p. 58). Although the twentieth century is changing the textbook's role as sole determiner of content, the textbook can still play an effective role in today's planning.

One common way to use a textbook is to build the curriculum around it. The textbook may be the center of the curriculum, but it is supported by other textbooks, journals,

---

Proactive Exercise

Anticipated Situation

- You know that:

  Students who are involved in planning are more committed to achieving the goals and objectives that they help set.

Proactive Alternative

- You can:

  For each of your classes, identify those objectives that you believe are *indispensable*. Be up front with your students. Let them know that you consider these essential. Prepare another list of *desirable* goals and objectives. Hold a discussion and let each class select those that the group wishes to adopt.

magazines, and newspapers. This approach is probably a good choice in communities or school systems that press for traditional education and in schools with very limited resources. But it is much more likely to succeed if you include some contemporary problems and help students apply their acquired knowledge toward solving them. Teachers must work with their students to form a cooperative social environment to develop meaningful learning activities for all students (Keefe and Jenkins, 2002).

Another approach is to use the textbook along with other materials. Instead of letting the textbook lead your students and you in the selection of content and experiences, take the lead in designing the curriculum. For example, determine the sequence of topics, instead of following the textbook organization from Chapter 1 to Chapter 2. Perhaps some chapters are not worth including in your curriculum. Teachers are becoming increasingly competent in curriculum development, and more and more teachers insist on having the freedom to shape the curricula in their classes as they see fit.

Not all school systems provide teachers with such freedom to develop their own curricula. Concern that students may not "cover" all the content needed for the following year or for college has been and, even in the presence of a more visible concern for preparing students for standardized tests, remains a concern. Such concern over content coverage is legitimate. School administrators know that they are responsible for seeing that the total school curriculum does not have major content gaps. Many larger schools hire a curriculum director, a curriculum supervisor, or an assistant principal who is directly responsible for curriculum. You should work with the curriculum leader and other teachers to avoid curriculum redundancy and gaps.

Other teachers make very little use of the textbook, almost totally avoiding it. They substitute current problems, learning activity packages, or learning units they develop themselves. Of course, these teachers are in school systems that permit an unusually high degree of teacher freedom.

Some school districts take money designated for buying textbooks and spend it on computers and other information technology. Many districts are using these funds to help students learn how to use the Internet. Whatever freedom your system permits you in using the textbook, be sure you do not spend most of the class period reading the text or requiring the students to read it. It is much better to assign a chapter as homework, giving students specific concepts to search for, the evening before a lesson, and use class time to discuss what students have read.

Discussions

Today's students want to be involved. They feel that their own opinions and judgments are worthwhile, and they want to share them. For this reason, discussion has increased in popularity. A good discussion involves all participants. Everyone has an opportunity to relate the topic to his or her own experiences. This sharing of various perspectives can enrich individual participants' knowledge and understanding. Avoid discussions that are merely rambling gossip sessions and that do no more than share ignorance.

Plan discussions carefully. First, to encourage total participation, group students according to their interest in the topic. Achieve this by letting students choose discussion topics. Second, avoid assigning both very passive students and aggressive students to the same groups. By putting the reserved students together, you will force one or more to assume leadership, and by placing aggressive students in the same group, some will be forced to learn to yield the floor to others. By assigning roles, such as "discussion moderator" and "recorder," and then varying these roles, you will prompt all group members to participate even more.

Select topics that have answers, although there may be multiple answers depending on individual perspective. Letting students know that you expect a definite outcome gives them a sense of purpose and responsibility.

If the moderator fails to keep group discussion progressing and on target, you may want to intervene, but too much interference will cause a group to become dependent on your leadership. Take care, also, to ensure that the group moderator does not dominate the discussion. In addition, the discussion must reflect the belief that all serious comments are worth hearing, regardless of how inaccurate or insignificant others may consider them.

A free-flowing discussion provides a valuable opportunity to develop social skills, which is in itself an important goal for secondary and middle-level students. It also helps students identify with their peers. All adolescents need to belong, and all need positive recognition and approval from peers. Group discussions should help fill these needs.

Participants must know that each person has a definite role in every discussion. First, each participant is obligated to read the assignment, so the discussion will begin from a common base. Second, each person is responsible for contributing additional information to the discussion. Opinions and contributions of knowledge are prized only when the participants can present evidence or knowledge to support them. Third, each participant is responsible for listening to others and, when possible, for referring to others' specific comments. This assures all participants that their comments are being considered.

You and your team partners are responsible for seeing that the environment remains informal, pleasant, and nonthreatening. You must also be a facilitator, helping students to locate adequate resources and to plan their discussion. When the discussion is over, you can help them evaluate discussion techniques and redesign their strategies for future discussions. When interdisciplinary teaming, it is imperative that you are committed to the objectives set for the other subjects represented on your team.

Field Trips

Like many fine inventions of the past, the field trip has become almost prematurely moribund (dead and gone before its time), even though it still has many unique advantages. The reasons for its loss of popularity are many. First, there has been a growing trend toward more lawsuits against schools, and the courts have begun to find more schools liable as charged. Because administrators and teachers can also be found liable, many of them are reluctant to encourage field trips, which are perceived as unnecessary risks.

This is unfortunate, because field trips still have unique potential. There is no better way for a social studies class to study the habits of an ethnic group than to visit a local community. A group of students interested in aerodynamics could find nothing more meaningful than a visit to a wind tunnel. A science class may benefit tremendously from a visit to an agriculture education agency, an experimental station, or a local farm.

Before you arrange a field trip, first check school policy, because many schools now forbid field trips of any type. Even if you are teaching at such a school, however, you might try to bring the "field" to the school. For example, a middle school earth science teacher might arrange for a few truckloads of several types of soil and rocks to be dumped on the school grounds so that students can take an on-campus geology field trip.

If your school does permit field trips, you might let your students suggest the need for one—assuming that they are mature enough and self-disciplined enough to be trusted. Some groups of students simply present too great a risk, and a teacher would be foolish to pursue a trip with such students. If the idea comes from the students, they may be willing to work harder and organize better.

Next, make sure that the trip is indeed necessary and purposeful. Each student should be assigned, or should assume, definite responsibilities for gathering specific data. Students may also share responsibility for organizing the trip, clearing it with the principal's office, arranging the visits, filling out the necessary insurance forms, and securing the necessary permissions and finances. Lotan (2003, p. 72) reminds teachers that any group-worthy task must have five characteristics. It must: (1) be open-ended and require complex problem solving, (2) provide students with multiple entry points to the task and multiple opportunities to show intellectual competence, (3) deal with discipline-based, intellectually important content, (4) require positive interdependence as well as individual accountability, and (5) include clear criteria for the evaluation of the group's product. Each of these criteria can easily be applied to the planning of each field trip by the students under your supervision to make it a meaningful learning experience.

After the field trip, a follow-up lesson in which students report their data and discuss implications will accentuate what the trip accomplished. As with all other instructional approaches, evaluation of each trip will improve the quality of future trips. Evaluations are more effective when done immediately after the trip, while the teacher and students still remember specifics.

Oral Reports

For several decades, oral reports have been popular in middle level schools, but this technique's success depends on how it is used. When you are considering using oral reports, first decide each report's purpose. Teachers often give assignments without really thinking through the report's purpose. Oral reports can have several purposes that may be considered important goals.

For example, you might assign a report to an advanced student who is delving into one aspect of a topic. The report would give that student an opportunity to share what he or she has learned while at the same time enabling the rest of the class to benefit from the study. Or you might assign a report to a group of students to give them an opportunity to learn to work together cooperatively. Another teacher might assign reports to give students experience in public speaking.

Each of these purposes is legitimate and worthwhile, as long as you communicate the main purpose(s) of the reports to the students. However, assigning a report to punish misbehavior or to substitute for effective planning is not wise. Students will quickly connect the report with those purposes, and probably no significant learning will result. This occurs when reports are used at the end of a grading period to give students an opportunity to improve their grades.

Whatever your reason for assigning oral reports, you must communicate to the reporter(s) the assignment's primary purposes. Tell other class members what you expect of them during the report. Should they take notes? Ask questions? Take issue with the speaker? Should they ask for clarification when they do not understand? Should they interrupt the speaker with comments, or wait until the end of the presentation? Will they be held accountable on the next test for the information their peers present orally? By answering these questions before the report is delivered, you can draw other students into their peers' oral presentations and thereby maximize interest and involvement.

As a precaution against students' taking reports too lightly, you might have a policy of always assigning credit for oral reports—and perhaps to the rest of the students for their responses. You can do this without presenting a threat to the students. Consider a positive reward system that lets students earn credit for participation in the discussion without penalizing those whose contributions are minimal.

The timing of oral reports can be critical. Avoid scheduling too many reports in succession. The student who is giving the twelfth consecutive report in class is at a definite disadvantage. To avoid the repetition and the boredom that students experience when too many reports are given, spread the reporting out so that no more than two are given in any week.

Students need ample time to prepare reports. Depending on the subject's level of sophistication, students will need between one and several weeks of lead time. Because some middle school students hold part-time jobs, and extracurricular activities consume some of their out-of-class time, you might allot some class time for preparing oral presentations. This is needed especially when students are planning group presentations.

Never make assignments without giving students an opportunity to present the results. This would be especially destructive if oral presentations are involved. Of course, a teacher would never be so callous intentionally, but sometimes teachers forget to save enough time in the term for the reports. Avoid this by scheduling the reporting dates when you make the assignments. Then students will not be disappointed, and they will see oral presentations as worthwhile.

Projects

Whatever subject you teach, you will find that assigning projects is valuable. You can choose among many types of projects: long-term projects, which may last for a grading period or even a semester; short-term projects; and individual projects. As Vars (1997, p. 46) cautions, "Both teachers and students must be encouraged to look for the real 'meat' of students' presentations." You have probably considered several types of projects as assignments for oral presentations, but not all projects should end with an oral presentation. Some may conclude with written reports or with presentations of concrete products that have resulted from the assignment. Whatever the product, give students an opportunity to show their creations. For example, a science teacher may want to arrange a local science fair to display students' insect collections, or a music teacher may want to set up a student recital.

Teachers who offer projects as options (i.e., not required of all students) may use a liberal grading system. One great advantage of projects is that they permit students who for one reason or another do not benefit from didactic forms of instruction to become totally involved. Many teachers take advantage of the opportunity to grade these activities in a way that rewards student effort. Many students who appear to be failures on tests can produce excellent projects. Perhaps it is because they want to do the projects, or perhaps they feel more competent doing something with their hands, or it may be a combination. Therefore, many teachers view projects as an opportunity to provide successful experiences for everyone. You might want to experiment by assigning all A's and B's to the projects for one term. Of course, you are free to let it count for as much or as little of the total term grade as you prefer.

Gallagher (1998, p. 742) suggests the following questions for evaluating projects. What were the most important ideas you learned from this project? Were the activities interesting and challenging or mainly routine? Do you now have some new skills that will improve your ability to do such tasks better in the future? Describe them. Would you like to do some other activities like this later on? Such as? What was the hardest part of the project or problem to do?

Place-Based Education

Place-based education refers to planned activities that connect students to their communities. Smith (2002, p. 594) says, "The primary value of place-based education lies in the way that it serves to strengthen children's connections to others and to the region in which they live." Although the term itself is new, the practice is not, at least not at the lower levels. For decades kindergarten teachers have taken their students to fire stations, police stations, stores, banks, and car washes to acquaint them with their community. These are examples of place-based education. The many service learning programs that currently involve students in everything from painting over graffiti to picking up litter, to planting gardens and wildlife sanctuaries, to visiting senior citizens in nursing homes, are engaging in place-based education.

The significance of such activities is great. All students in an entire classroom or even all students in a school can become involved in the same comprehensive problem. This builds a sense of community in the school, giving all students a feeling of belonging. The social benefits from place-based program are as important as the learning opportunities.

Homework

About every 15 years, homework becomes a controversial topic, with parents changing their minds over the amount they believe the schools should assign (Cooper, 2001). A recent poll of public attitudes (Public Agenda, 2000) found that, at least for now, parents are generally satisfied with the amount of homework their children are receiving. Some two-thirds (64 percent) of parents surveyed say that their children are getting about the right amount of homework assignments, and only 10 percent say they are getting too much.

While the findings of research on the effects of homework on learning vary drastically from one study to the next, the one characteristic that correlates highest is the student's grade level. Generally, homework does not enhance learning significantly for elementary school children, but it has a major positive effect on high school students (Cooper, 2001). Middle-level students gain academically from having homework if they don't have too much. A good rule of thumb is to ensure that your students' total homework assignments for any night do not exceed 10 minutes of homework multiplied by the student's grade level.

Homework can be used for different purposes, and one of these purposes is to develop higher-order skills. The purpose of the homework should determine the teacher's instructional behavior (Cooper, 2001). You should always base a decision to use homework (or not) on a purpose for which it is suited and introduce it accordingly. Far too often, homework is used only for practice. Because many states now require all teachers to give homework (many districts specify the number of hours a night), you must become familiar with the variety of uses for which homework is suited.

THE CASE

Sic Semper "Huh?"

Michael F. Hawke, Tarleton State University
Laurie M. Hawke, Tarleton State University
Kyle Boles, Cleburne Middle School

Michael Hawke is an Associate Professor teaching methods and educational foundations classes to undergraduates in the Tarleton State University Teacher Preparation Program. He earned his B.S., M.Ed., and Ph.D. in education from the University of Arizona in Tucson, Arizona. Dr. Hawke is a past president of the Middle School Educator Preparation Association in Texas, the Consortium of State Organizations for Texas Teacher Education, and the Texas Directors of Field Experiences. He is a member of the Texas Middle School Association, the National Middle School Association, and the Texas Directors of Field Experiences.

Laurie Hawke is currently an Associate Professor working with interns and teaching curriculum design and implementation at the graduate level at Tarleton State University. She is a past president of the Tarleton State University Chapter of the Texas Association of College Teachers and was Treasurer of the Middle School Educator Preparation Association. Dr. Hawke is the faculty advisor for Kappa Delta Pi, an international honor society for education, and Middle School Educators of Tarleton.

Kyle Boles is an English teacher at Cleburne Middle School and is the leader of the eighth-grade Energizers Team. He received his B.A. degree in history from the University of Texas at Austin. He taught special education for one year and then taught eighth-grade English for six years at Cleburne Middle School in Cleburne, Texas, where he currently serves as vice principal.

Community

Cleburne Independent School District is located in Cleburne, Texas, a community of 26,569 located approximately 25 miles due south of Fort Worth, Texas, which is the county seat of Johnson County. The ethnic mix is approximately 74 percent white, 20 percent Hispanic, and 5 percent African American. The median age of the Cleburne population is 33 years. The main sources of employment are: management, professional, and related occupations (25 percent); sales and office occupations (25.5 percent); production, transportation, and material moving occupations (22 percent); and service occupations (14 percent). The four primary industries are: education, health, and social services (20 percent); manufacturing (20 percent); retail trade (15 percent); and construction (10 percent). Median household income is $35,500. Because of its proximity to Fort Worth, Cleburne is a community on the move. (Source: U.S. Census Bureau, Census 2000)

The School

Cleburne Independent School District includes seven elementary schools, one intermediate school, one middle school, and one high school accommodating approximately 6,200 students. The district covers 206 square miles and is the largest employer in Johnson County, with more than 700 employees.

Cleburne Middle School has approximately 967 students in the seventh and eighth grades. Each grade level is divided into teams. The seventh-grade teams have been named the "Challengers," "Right Stuff," and "The Stingin' Stars." The eighth-grade teams are called the "Champions," "Energizers," and the "Swarm." There are between eight and ten teachers on each team. Cleburne Middle School is in a new building, the cornerstone of which was laid on Friday, August 10, 2001. The campus is beautiful and very well taken care of. You may take your own campus tour by visiting their website at http://www.cleburne.k12.tx.us/Campuses/CMS/JFlynn/virtualtour.htm. You will enjoy your visit.

The Teacher

Kyle Boles is an eighth-grade English teacher. He is the team leader of the Energizers. We have the distinct honor of knowing Mr. Boles both personally and professionally. Kyle was a student in our professional development classes at Tarleton State University in Stephenville, Texas. One of the first things you notice about Kyle is his inquisitiveness. He always wants to know "why." As a student he was always trying to find ways to do "it" better—it didn't matter what "it" was, there just had to be a way to improve "it." As you will see later in this case study, Kyle has not changed his way of thinking. He is an excellent communicator and has a driving desire to learn. He has a wonderfully diverse background of life experiences, which he uses to his students' advantage in the classroom.

In fact, it is because of his background that he is able to relate so well to his students. As most of us who have taught for any length of time know, lessons seldom work precisely as planned. Top-notch teachers with diverse experiential backgrounds have the innate ability to take a student's seemingly off-the-wall comment or question and turn it to their advantage in a learning situation. These same teachers can take an event that happened the night before or just that morning and tie it effectively to the lesson about to be taught. They make the event relevant to the students' learning. Kyle Boles is one of these teachers. As is common among exceptional teachers, sometimes they have a difficult time explaining why they are successful and often question their effectiveness. The following will give you a glimpse into an excellent teacher's thought processes and reveal why having a broad, diverse experiential and knowledge background as well as the ability to monitor and adjust is crucial to being an excellent, effective teacher.

The Situation

Students are naturally inquisitive—all the more so in the middle school years. However they do not always put a voice to their inquisitiveness. Many times you have to deduce students' questions or concerns by observing their body language. If you are not focused on your students, you will not notice their unspoken questions or concerns. When reading about the assassination of President Lincoln and the Latin words John Wilkes Booth shouted as he jumped to the stage, Kyle noticed a change in the students' facial expressions. He describes the expression as the "Huh?" look. What follows is Kyle's story of that incident and others.

It is difficult for me to believe, but four years have now passed since I decided to take on the task of attempting to educate the "youth of America." One of my college professors many years ago used that phrase all the time, and it always seems to stick in my mind. For some unknown reason, the phrase "youth of America" places a real sense of responsibility on my shoulders and what I imagine to be the shoulders of the thousands of educators in our nation grappling over the scientifically tested methods of classroom instruction. It's the type of phrase that really makes a teacher wonder. At times, it makes me want to reexamine what is going on in my classroom from day to day.

From time to time, whenever I think of that awesome phrase, I stop and wonder if what I am doing is really having any impact on my students' education. It's something I guess all teachers do. But there are also times when I think I'm analyzing my methods and lessons too much. It is as if I am attempting to fix something that isn't broken. Have I reached this particular level of Blooms' taxonomy? Is this a student-centered activity? Do I have enough activities for my hands-on learners? If you have ever taught in a public school classroom, then you know exactly what I mean. Teachers are trained to be planners. However, it may be that learning comes from spontaneous curiosity as well. Sometimes plans don't always unfold as expected and lessons simply evolve from unanticipated questions.

For example, I have constantly been amazed at how a simple, very direct lesson can turn into a completely different lesson in a span of fifty minutes. One minute you'll be talking about Mark Twain and within the next two minutes the entire class is involved in a discussion about the important role of parents in society. It sounds crazy, but once again, if you have ever taught school you know the experience. That experience led me to a very important question early in my career. Is this changing of direction in a lesson a good thing, or is it a bad thing? There were times, when I first began teaching, when I thought that leaving the main focus of my lesson to answer questions related to what I was doing was a really bad thing to do. It's no secret. If a student wants to find a way to waste class time and his goal is to waste class time, then he will waste your class time by asking all types of questions. But in some cases, the change in direction is legitimate. Over time I have discovered just when those legitimate moments take shape. I believe it has something to do with experience and knowing your students. There are spontaneous moments when questions turn into whole new lessons.

The key, in my opinion, is whether or not the pending discussion is truly a subject worthy of making a student more knowledgeable, even though it seems to be straying away from the main lesson. Furthermore, another key factor is whether or not the change in direction is helpful in giving students knowledge that they can use at a later date. If these points of criteria are met, then you just might have a situation where you're about to put on the brakes in your main lesson and throw everything into reverse to cover a new point.

Many times this appears to be a fiasco to those I work with and even know fairly well. I cannot tell you how many times I have felt the need to close my room door, fearing that another teacher will casually walk by and discover that my discussion for that particular day may be about supply and demand, and its influence in different countries. To a new teacher the word fiasco, or a more colorful word, may come to mind. But it is my thought that as long as the teacher can take the situation at hand and turn into an opportunity for learning, then a new goal for the day has been achieved. Is this direction change always successful? As anyone knows, education deals with a large amount of experimentation. What may be good for one class may not be good for another. However, sometimes an educational redirection in your lesson may be the right catalyst to lead your students into an important subject worthy of attention. It just might not be following your rigid lesson plan timeline.

For weeks in one of my English classes, I had been trying to address how prefixes play a part in how basic root words can gain new and different meanings. I listed prefixes on the board with their meanings. I used examples of one root word with different prefixes connected to it and showed how the word changed meaning. I had students working in groups with root words and prefixes creating their own new words. To make a long story short, we did just about everything I could honestly think of. I was beginning to think that I didn't know what I was doing. It all seemed so simple, yet the students were not getting the idea. It was getting to the point where even mentioning the word "prefix" would cause many of my students to cringe and just look at me with a stare. I have come to call this stare the "I don't care" stare. My first thought was to just start all over; however, it was time for a change and I thought that possibly I might catch them at a weak moment in the future and lull them into the whole lesson once again. Little did I know that my chance for a reteach would come much sooner than I thought.

In the following weeks, my classes began a unit on historical literature. This unit dealt with short stories, articles on U.S. history, speeches, and anything else I could find that might be interesting that pertained to the history of the United States. Being a history major in my college days, I was really looking forward to this unit. It was to be part of my interdisciplinary work for the year. We read all types of work in class aloud. We read the Gettysburg Address, we discussed and read a story about the journey of the *Mayflower*, and then we read an account covering the events that surrounded the assassination of President Lincoln. My goal for the day was to explain and show the students how eyewitness accounts can play a powerful role in reporting a story. The gentleman who wrote this particular account of the death of Lincoln used actual eyewitness testimonies in explaining how the assassination occurred. At least, that's what I thought we would be discussing.

About halfway through the story, we began reading about John Wilkes Booth slowly moving toward the Presidential box in Ford's Theater. Then we came to that fateful moment when Booth fires his weapon and, as reported, yells to the crowd, "Sic semper tyrannis!" As I recall, the student who was reading began fumbling through the words in an honest attempt to try to pronounce the words correctly, and before I could even explain anything about those words, every student in the class said, "Huh?" It is no stretch of the imagination. Every student looked at me with the old "What kind of English is this?" stare. It is completely different from the "I don't care" stare. I call it the "what, where" stare. What happened then was a change in educational direction. For some reason, I saw an opportunity to make a point.

The first thing we did was to talk about what they were reading. My students received a mini lesson in Latin. The words "Sic semper tyrannis!" are Latin words that when translated mean, "Thus always to tyrants!" I explained that the words shouted by Booth were the same words used in the state motto of Virginia, and we briefly discussed why a Southern gentleman might make this bold statement. We then began a discussion about the language of Latin itself. Some students made a connection between Latin and "pig Latin," asking if they were one and the same. After dispensing with that idea, I attempted to explain the origins of the language. We talked about the Roman Republic, the Roman Empire, and how this Roman influence changed the very voice of Europe in creating the various Romance languages. Though my students didn't know it, I was leading them into a kind of educational trap.

To my surprise they really didn't catch on until I stated the obvious: prefixes. First, of course, there was a moan. After the initial panic, we then discussed Latin's influence on the English language in words such as *coexist, supersensitive, transatlantic, exclude, postindustrial,* and even *AD* (Anno Domini—in the year of our Lord). To my surprise the interest level in prefixes began to rise because a connection was made. Slowly students began to realize that some of the prefixes were coming from Latin. To understand the prefixes, a simple translation from Latin into English was all that was needed to understand how the prefix changed the root word. It was definitely one of those rare moments when everything slowly began to click. The strange part was that we worked from John Wilkes Booth into how Latin has a connection with English I prefixes. Try to explain that in your lesson plans or to your principal when he wants to know what's going on in your class.

Further Reflection

1. When is it appropriate to deviate from your lesson's objectives?
2. Why do you think it is important for teachers to be able to "seize the moment" in a lesson?
3. What are the benefits for a teacher being able to make connections across the curriculum?
4. Mr. Boles talks about looking at students' facial expressions to determine student understanding. Talk about other methods that teachers can use to check for understanding.
5. In what ways does an environment in which the students feel safe contribute to their desire to respond as Mr. Boles's students did or to ask questions?
6. How does the lesson illustrated above develop the students' ability to think critically?
7. What conditions are necessary for students to think critically?

Parent Involvement with Homework

We have already seen that increasing the level of parent involvement in adolescents' academics is a major goal of the Carnegie Council on Adolescent Development. The Majority of seventh- though twelfth-grade students believe that parents should be involved with homework assignment. As shown in Figure 4.1, more seventh- and eighth-graders believe that the involvement should be at a high level (MLS, 1998, p. 97).

Lack of parent involvement is perceived as the major obstacle facing students when doing schoolwork, yet many other obstacles also impede students' getting their homework. As shown in Figure 4.2, the obstacles students face when doing schoolwork at home vary among types of community.

Homework Guidelines

The following suggestions will help you design and implement a system for assigning homework that will work well for your students.

Clarify the Assignment

Homework assignments must be clear. If they involve problem solving, you may want to give students an opportunity to work at least one problem of each type in class before you ask them to do problems at home. Simply giving verbal instructions and explanations may not be enough. Perhaps you can remember a time when, as a student, you thought you understood how the teacher wanted you to complete an assignment, but when you got home you found that you could not start the problem because you did not know how to begin. If you had been given an opportunity to work just one problem in class, you could have raised questions at that time.

QB8.2: How much of a say should parents have in decisions your school makes in the following areas: Homework assignments–how much and how often?

Base: All students

	TOTAL	GRADES 7–8
Base:	1301	557
	%	%
A lot	19	26
Some	41	45
None	35	24
Don't know	5	5

FIGURE 4.1 STUDENTS' OPINIONS ON THE SAY PARENTS SHOULD HAVE ON HOMEWORK ASSIGNMENTS

The MetLife Survey of The American Teacher conducted by Louis Harris & Associates, NY: NY.

Q105: In your opinion, what is the main obstacle facing students when it comes to doing schoolwork at home?
Base: All teachers

	Total	Size of Place				
		Inner City	Other Urban	Suburban	Small Town	Rural
Base:	1035	132	126	284	280	210
	%	%	%	%	%	%
Uninvolved parents/lack of parental support	20	19	28	18	20	21
Students lack motivation	14	6	11	12	17	18
Television, computer	12	15	10	15	11	10
Not quiet enough, too many distractions	9	10	7	8	9	10
After school employment	8	9	8	11	5	10
Students spend too little time doing schoolwork	6	5	7	7	5	5
Not enough discipline on part of student	4	2	5	4	6	5
Not enough structure in the home	4	6	5	2	3	7
Not enough discipline on part of parent	4	5	2	5	4	4
Extra-curricular activity	4	1	3	6	5	4
Students are disorganized or unorganized	2	—	3	3	1	1
Time management	1	2	—	*	2	1
Lack of parental supervision	1	2	1	*	2	*
Peer pressure	*	1	—	*	1	—
Other (specify)	9	17	11	8	9	5
Don't know	*	1	—	—	—	—

FIGURE 4.2 MAIN OBSTACLES FACING STUDENTS WHEN DOING SCHOOLWORK AT HOME

Individualize Homework Assignments

Students who cannot understand how to do their classwork even with your help will benefit little from a homework assignment of more of the same type of problem. You must consider each student's abilities and needs. Certain homework assignments for slower students will help them catch up with the rest of the class, while the more advanced students can explore areas of special interest in depth. Such an individualistic approach to homework assignments can relieve the ever present dilemma of teachers—how to challenge the brightest students without losing the slower students.

Make Homework Creative

Teachers today realize that the old practice of assigning students to "read the next chapter and work the problems at the end of the chapter" is not challenging or stimulating. Homework assignments are more interesting when they include variety. Students could be asked to respond to something that is on the evening news, in the newspaper, or on an educational television program. Multisensory activities can replace written assignments. Creativity cannot be forced, but you can establish a climate that stimulates and nourishes creativity. Let your students use all their senses and manipulate objects; have them investigate problems that have no fixed answer.

Parents should be informed of the school's homework policy. Many teachers believe the level of parent involvement should go further. Over two-thirds (71 percent) of seventh and eight graders say that they believe they should have either some or a lot of involvement (see Figure 4.1).

Be Reasonable

Avoid making too many demands on students' time at home. Many students come from homes that have no books or any place that is well lit or quiet enough for studying. Disruptions by brothers and sisters make homework difficult for many students. Then, too, many

---

Proactive Exercise

Anticipated Situation

- You know that:

    Your classes will be comprised of students from various ethnic and socioeconomic backgrounds. Included will be many students who live in poverty, students with part-time and even full-time jobs, whose homes have crowded space, noisy environments, and even abusive parents or guardians. These conditions make doing homework assignments impossible for many of these students.

Proactive Alternative

- You can:

    Consider the type of assignments you give. Although a written paper may be impossible, such assignments as interviews or discussions with neighbors and family members offer possibilities. Consider providing opportunities in class for some of these events to occur.

    Provide opportunities for students to share job experiences. You should be able to use these students as consultants, tying their job experiences to topics that in more traditional classes may have been the focus of homework assignments.

older middle school students work after school at part-time jobs on which their families depend for some essentials. For such students, homework assignments that require a few hours each evening to complete are impossible. Remember that it is the total number of hours that all teachers assign your students that must be limited.

When you evaluate homework, take into account the conditions under which students must perform. As with classroom or term projects, grade homework leniently enough so that students who are faced with the most adverse environments will not become discouraged.

Follow-up

Nothing can be more disheartening than spending time and energy on an assignment, only to have the teacher forget about it or push it aside for more critical matters. If you schedule a follow-up time at the time of the assignment, you can prevent these annoying situations. Follow-up also lets students know that they are expected to complete each assignment. According to Phelps (1991), regular follow-up results in improved results: "When students are held responsible for assigned work, they are more likely to do the work than when their efforts go unnoticed" (p. 242).

Returning homework promptly tells students that it is important and enables students to learn from it. Williams, Alley, and Henson (1999) say, "It is extremely important that teachers check assignments by collecting and grading them immediately" (p. 104).

Overview of Steps for Assigning Homework

The following steps for assigning homework can be used as a summary of this discussion and as a guideline for making homework assignments.

1. As an alternative, plan for assignments to be completed at some time during the school day in a supervised area.
2. Be sure the purpose of every homework assignment is clear in your mind and you have made it clear to the students.
3. Try to match assignments with students, making sure each student is treated fairly and equally.
4. Be sure every student knows exactly what is required.
5. Check the assignment when it is due.
6. Don't expect homework to teach a student who is not learning properly in the classroom.
7. Remember that assignments that use a multisensory approach are most effective in teaching. (Berry, 1977, p. 52)

These seven steps are now over a quarter of a century old, and they were actually designed for elementary school teachers. Do you think any (or all) of them are adequate guidelines for today's middle school teacher?

We have now discussed the uses of textbooks, discussions, field trips, oral reports, term projects, and homework. When making any of these assignments, perhaps the most important question a teacher can ask is: What will this homework assignment permit students to do that they cannot do in class? And how can I (we) design the assignment to benefit the student and perhaps the rest of the class?

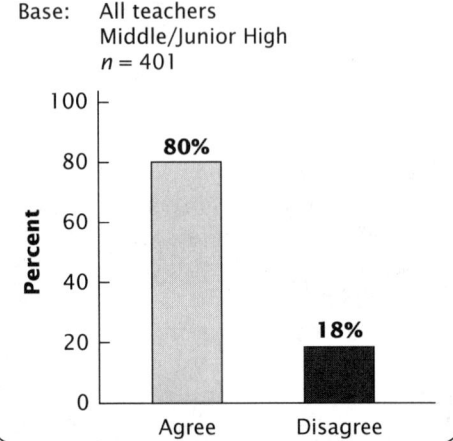

FIGURE 4.3 TEACHERS' PERCEPTIONS OF SCHOOL-ENCOURAGED PARENTAL INVOLVEMENT IN NON-SUBJECT AREAS

From *The MetLife Survey of the American Teacher, 2002: Student Life—School, Home, and Community,* conducted for MetLife® by Harris Interactive Inc.

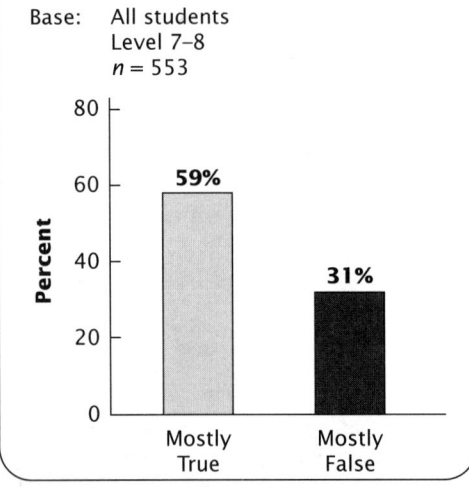

FIGURE 4.4 STUDENTS' PERCEPTIONS OF SCHOOL-INITIATED PARENTAL CONTACT

From *The MetLife Survey of the American Teacher, 2002: Student Life—School, Home, and Community,* conducted for MetLife® by Harris Interactive Inc.

Parent Involvement

The 1994 Gallup Poll showed that over the last decade the frequency of many forms of parental contact with their schools has practically doubled (Elam, Rose, & Gallup, 1994, p. 54). Teachers feel positive about the efforts made in their schools to engage parents in school activities. Indeed, four-fifths of middle school teachers say that their school does a good job of encouraging parental involvement (see Figure 4.3), yet, as shown in Figure 4.4, two-thirds of middle-level students say that their school contacts their parents only when there is a problem with their child.

The 1998 Gallup Poll (Rose & Gallup, 1998) showed that an average of half of the public wants more involvement with all the seven areas included in the Poll, including shaping the curriculum, selecting books, and hiring administrators. Parents' responsibility for helping their children succeed with homework has been recognized for many years, yet their exact role in this matter has not been clear. Solomon (1989) offers the following suggestions for teachers to help guide parents who wish to help their children achieve in their homework assignments:

> *Teachers should encourage parents to: (1) set a definite time for study each day with a beginning and ending time and no interruptions; (2) provide the proper environment; (3) provide the materials needed, (4) require the student to organize school materials including books, notes, assignments, and papers, (5) require a daily list of homework assignments; and (6) provide support and guidance if the child becomes discouraged or frustrated. (p. 63)*

During the last few decades, teacher–parent relations have remained strong. For example, in 1987 over two-thirds (68 percent) of teachers rated teacher relations with parents as either good or excellent. In 1997, 71 percent rated teacher–parent relations as either good or excellent (MLS, 1998). When parent involvement includes the academics, it can enrich the quality of their children's education. Former Pennsylvania Teacher of the Year Howard Selekman says, "My best teaching occurs when my students' parents are engaged in the issues and themes their children are working with." As shown in Figure 4.5, over half of our schools are providing parents with help on how to help with homework. The National Middle School Association recommended as a priority goal of all middleschools that "Parents and schools form partnerships to meet the needs of the whole child" (Jenkins & Jenkins, 1991).

Q100A: Has your school provided parents with information on how to: Help the children with homework assignments, or not?
Base: All teachers

	Total	Size of Place				
		Inner City	Other Urban	Suburban	Small Town	Rural
Base:	1035	132	126	284	280	210
	%	%	%	%	%	%
Has provided	66	70	66	73	65	59
Has not provided	29	27	27	23	33	37
Don't know	5	3	7	5	5	5

FIGURE 4.5 SCHOOL-PROVIDED INFORMATION FOR PARENTS ON HOW TO HELP WITH HOMEWORK

Sample Daily Lesson Plans

Stallworth (1998, p. 78) said that "teachers need samples of successful lesson plans and time to practice them." Following are some sample daily lesson plans. They differ in style, but each contains a few major ideas and is arranged in a sequence that facilitates learning. Note that each major idea is followed by an assigned task that requires students to use the idea. Note also that each sample lesson ends with a review that ties together the lesson's major ideas.

The parts of a plan (statement of purpose, introduction, student activities, and summary) vary among plans. Make a list of all the parts you find in these plans. Put an asterisk next to the parts you believe will be helpful when you teach. Use the results as an outline to make a lesson plan in your subject area.

Sample Lesson Plan

Lesson Plan 1: *Physical Education, Grade 9*
  I. Purpose: To develop the ability to score a complete bowling game
  II. Materials: Score sheet and lead pencil with eraser for each student
  III. Equipment: Overhead projector
  IV. Main ideas
     A. How to score and add an open frame
     B. How to score and add a spare
     C. How to score and add a strike
     D. How to score and add the last frame
  V. Procedure
     A. Five-minute explanation of each concept
     B. Demonstration of scoring a game
  VI. Assignment: Students are to score and add the following games at their desks.
  VII. Summary: The teacher will show a transparency of the game on the overhead screen and use questions to lead the class in filling out each step in the game.

Discussion of Lesson Plan 1

Do you like the lesson plan? Is it clear? Among its strongest assets are its initial statement of purpose, telling immediately what the lesson should do for the student, its clear statement of the ideas being taught, and its summary. The task is also stated clearly. Notice that the teacher selected as an example a game that starts with the simplest ideas and moves to progressively more complex ideas until it covers everything one must know to score a bowling game. Note also that because the game contains all the essential ideas of scoring, it provides a satisfactory review of the whole lesson.

How could you improve this plan? Note the procedures. Would the plan be easier to follow if time limits were stated alongside the activities? Can you think of other ways to improve it?

Sample Lesson Plan

Lesson Plan 2: *English, Grade 9*

I. Objective: The student should understand the importance of using proper grammar.
II. Objective: Teach students to identify nouns and know their classes.
    A. Introduce subject: Grammar. (5 min.)
        1. Give a brief outline of the plan of study.
        2. Announce the noun as the first part of speech you will study.
    B. Present the idea that proper use of grammar is important. (10 min.)
        1. Give one example.
        2. Ask students for other examples.
    C. Give the definition of nouns and explain classes. (15 min.)
        1. Common.
        2. Proper.
        3. Abstract.
        4. Concrete.
    Give an example of each on the board.
    Ask students to give other examples and add to list.
    D. Have each student make a list of 15 nouns, naming objects seen in the classroom (3 min.). (15 min.)
        1. List the four classes on the board.
        2. Call on students for nouns and have them designate the proper list of each case.
    E. Summary (5 min.)
        1. Conduct a brief questioning period reviewing the definition and classes of nouns.
        2. Evaluate the effectiveness of the lesson by the response of the students. Did they understand the various classes? Could they easily choose the appropriate list for each noun?

Discussion of Lesson Plan 2

What is your reaction to the time indicators in this plan? Would they help you teach this lesson, or would they make you uncomfortable? Perhaps they are too restrictive. The teacher's activities and the students' activities are listed in steps. Do you like this? Notice the objective stated in the beginning. How could it be improved? There is no written evaluation at the end. Would this make it difficult to evaluate accomplishment of the stated objective, "To understand the importance of using proper grammar?" Can you rewrite the objective, stating it in performance terms?

Vignettes

The quality of planning is as important as the act of planning. Poor planning, overstructuring, and lessons that are too short or too long can lead to serious problems. The following vignettes are examples of problems caused by inadequate planning.

Vignette One: A Teacher Uses Note Cards for Planning

Every student in the school liked Mr. Little, the teacher who supervised my student teaching experience. Mr. Little's classes were both entertaining and successful. Students seemed to learn automatically in his classes. During the three months I spent in his classes, I never once saw a detailed lesson plan.

During class, Mr. Little—who coincidentally was small in stature—always sat in front of the room perched on a high stool. As he talked, joked, and laughed with his students, he continually shuffled a few three-by-five cards, glancing at them while carrying on a dialogue with the students. After his introductory lesson on rocks and minerals, I examined Mr. Little's note cards (Figure 4.6).

Although the cards were not detailed or impressive, they did structure the lesson. Each item was mentioned briefly. The cards contained key words and phrases rather than complete sentences. This system enabled Mr. Little to glance at his notes without taking his attention away from the students, and I believe it contributed significantly to his unusually effective teaching.

DISCUSSION

1. What are some advantages of brief lesson plans? When lesson plans are brief, you are less likely to "read" the lesson to the class. Brief plans also leave room for flexibility: you have time to let students pursue both planned topics and any related topics and materials that interest them. A brief plan also leaves time for students to become involved.

2. What are some dangers in too-brief lesson plans? If a lesson plan is too brief, you may run short of material and have time left with nothing planned. In addition, a brief lesson may be "shallow"; it may not challenge students to think.

2. Can a lesson be too highly structured? Yes, if you mean too detailed. When a lesson is too detailed, you are likely to dominate the class, leaving students no opportunity to ask questions and to comment on the lesson. If you interpret this question literally and answer no, I agree with you. The more structure (not detail) a lesson has, the more likely students will reach set goals. Although educators often stress the value of pupil-centered discovery approaches, this method cannot succeed without much planning and hidden structure. Although pupil-centered classes may appear to have little structure, the successful ones are usually more highly structured in terms of objectives and activities than are traditional classes.

```
          Rocks & Minerals

    1. Why study rocks
    2. Joke about igneous
       rocks
    3. Basic types of rocks
       a. Sedimentary
       b. Igneous
       c. Metamorphic
    4. Rock collecting
```

FIGURE 4.6 THREE-INCH BY FIVE-INCH CARD USED FOR PLANNING

Vignette Two: A Teacher Fails to Use Objectives

Our college biology teacher had a style of her own. Each hour Mrs. Woods promptly opened her notebook and began the lesson. She wrote everything she said on the board in perfect outline form. Her speaking speed was equaled only by her writing speed; she did not waste a minute during the hour. Students were amazed by how neat, organized, and professional her approach to every lesson was.

Mrs. Woods always kept to the day's objectives. Once when she was absent, her husband, who was also a biology teacher, took over for the day. Having specified no objectives, he kept students wondering when he was going to get into the lesson. They complained that his remarks had nothing to do with the topic being studied. Mr. Woods understood biology, but his lecture seemed to confuse students.

Some of the best students in school got their lowest marks in Mrs. Woods' classes. Furthermore, they said they learned very little about biology. Students were surprised that they had benefited so little in the class of a teacher who was not only brilliant in her subject but also extremely well prepared for every lesson.

DISCUSSION

1. Did Mrs. Woods's lessons lack structure?
2. Why did the students feel so lost in Mr. Woods's class?

Vignette Three: A Teacher Gets Lost in His Own Lessons

Each day, when students came to my class after their music class, they complained to me about their music homework assignments. I heard complaints like "This assignment has nothing to do with what we studied in class today," "I don't see the value in this," and "Why does Mr. Marshall make us do this?" I reminded them that they should not direct their criticisms to me, because it would be unprofessional and unethical for me to discuss the issue with them. I refused to comment, but I continued to hear complaints: "Mr. Marshall rambles," "He skips around with the material so much that it doesn't make sense."

Finally, the complaints reached administrators, who spoke with Mr. Marshall about the issue. I do not know what was said during the meeting, but it apparently produced a change in Mr. Marshall's teaching, because the complaints became fewer and fewer. I always wondered how Mr. Marshall managed to change so quickly and to improve his teaching so effectively.

DISCUSSION

1. Teachers of special subjects, such as music, art, and physical education, are usually assigned to teach several sections of the same class. This often contributes to a teacher's forgetting just what was covered with each group, which was apparently what happened to Mr. Marshall. What would you do if you ever found yourself forgetting where you ended the previous class and exactly what you had covered in it?
2. When teaching multiple sections of the same class, should you make separate lesson plans for each section?
3. Should you ever stray from the planned lesson?
4. Does a teacher's ability to plan improve with experience?

Summary

Lesson plans are good only if they are useful. You can increase the utility of your lesson plans by beginning each plan with objectives and keeping each plan succinct. When planning, attention should be paid to time. Research shows that the amount of time assigned to a topic does not affect achievement as much as the time students spend on the topic (engaged time) and the time they spend actually developing the concepts (developmental time). Effective teachers plan ample time for students to be engaged with the topic making sure that students spend most of that time developing major concepts. Another factor that affects learning is the degree to which teachers personalize their lessons. Through the use of computer assignments and homework assignments, teachers can offer students opportunities to express their own insights and opinions. Using constructive strategies, students should be encouraged to tie class content to their personal lives outside of school.

You can help all students, and especially minority students, by: (1) introducing fewer topics and (2) providing more opportunity to explore these topics in depth. Constructivists encourage teachers to use problem solving to let students discover the major concepts.

Because individuals learn differently, variety should be purposefully planned into each unit and lesson. Field trips, oral reports, and projects can capture student interests and exercise their unique skills. Place-based assignments can strengthen students' connections with their local communities.

Special attention should be paid to assigning homework. Begin by knowing what purpose each assignment should achieve. Middle-level students can benefit from good homework assignments if they are not too long. The total homework assigned on any day should not require the student to spend more than 10 minutes times the grade level of that student. Most middle-level students believe that parents and guardians should be involved with the homework assignments of their children.

Recap of Major Ideas

1. Daily lesson plans are essential for students to attain the expectations set forth in units.
2. Do not become so enslaved to lesson plans that you read them step by step to students. On the other hand, do not ignore the value that planning offers in giving necessary direction as each lesson progresses.
3. Like any other tool, the value of a lesson plan depends on how it is used.
4. Begin lesson plan design by identifying desirable changes in student behavior.
5. All lesson plans should contain activities to involve students.
6. Organize content according to natural sequences, simple to complex, or sequences that facilitate students' understanding of the material.
7. End each lesson plan with a review of the lesson's major concepts.
8. Teachers seldom use objectives when beginning lesson planning and when changing their approaches.
9. Constructivists advise teachers to tie newly introduced concepts to students' existing knowledge.
10. Through inquiry training, teachers can broaden their perspectives and use this knowledge to teach diverse students.

Activities

1. Develop a daily plan in your own major teaching field. Specify the subject and grade level and include performance objectives, content generalizations, activities to help students attain the objectives, and a summary of the most significant ideas in the lesson.
2. Write a unit plan in your area of specialty. Begin by writing a brief statement of your philosophy of education. For each curriculum component, write one sentence to explain how your particular philosophy should affect each component.
3. Identify a topic you might select for a lesson. Now write several student activities to use during the hour. Finally, order these in the best sequence possible. Explain why you put each activity in its selected sequence.
4. Examine all the sample lesson plans in this chapter. For each plan, select one or more features you would change if you were using the plan in your classes. Explain your reason for making each change.

Looking Ahead

This chapter has prepared you to plan daily lessons. However, as you should remember from Chapter 1, you will not teach in a vacuum. Rather, you will be evaluated through your students' scores on standardized examinations. The following chapter will help you better understand the various roles that evaluation plays in your classes and beyond.

References

Acheson, K. A., & Gall, M. (1992). *Techniques in the clinical supervision of teachers*. White Plains, NY: Longman.

Armento, B. J. (1986). Research on teaching social studies. In M. C. Wittrock (Ed.), *Handbook of research on teaching* (3rd ed.). New York: Macmillan.

Berry, K. (1977). Homework: Is it for elementary kids? *Instructor, 86*, p. 52.

Brown, K. L. (2003). "From teacher-centered to learner-centered curriculum: Transition or paradigm shift? *Education, 124*, (1).

Calderhead, J. (1981). *Research into teachers' and student teachers' cognitions: Exploring the nature of classroom practice.* Paper presented at the annual meeting of the American Educational Research Association, Montreal, Canada.

Carson, M. D., & Badarack, G. (1989). *How changing class size affects classrooms and students.* Riverside, CA: University of California at Riverside, California Educational Research Cooperative.

Christie, K. (2002). Expectations for students with special needs. *Phi Delta Kappan, 83*(9), 650–651.

Ciscell, R. E. (1990). A matter of minutes: Making better use of teacher time. *The Clearing House, 63*(5), 217–218.

Clark, C. M., & Peterson, P. L. (1986). Teachers' thought processes. In M. C. Whittrock (Ed.), *Handbook of research on teaching* (3rd ed.). New York: Macmillan.

Cooper, H. (2001). Homework for all—in moderation. *Educational Leadership, 58*(7), 34–38.

Doll, R. C. (1978). *Curriculum improvement: Decision making and process* (4th ed.). Boston: Allyn & Bacon.

Elam, S. M., Rose, L. C., & Gallup, A. M. (1994). The 26th annual Phi Delta Kappa/Gallup Poll of the public's attitudes toward the public schools. *Phi Delta Kappan, 76*(1), 41–56.

Felner, R. D., Kasak, D., Mulhall, P., & Flowers, N. (1997). The project on high performance learning communities. *Phi Delta Kappan, 78*(7), 520–527.

Finn, J. D. (1993). *School engagement and students at risk.* Washington, DC: National Center for Education Statistics, U.S. Department of Education.

Gallagher, J. J. (1998). Accountability too gifted students. *Phi Delta Kappan, 79*(10), 739–742.

Gilman, D. A., & Kiger, S. Should we try to keep class sizes small. *Educational Leadership, 60*(7), 80–85.

Good, T. L., & Brophy, J. E. (2000). *Looking in classrooms* (8th ed.). New York: Harper & Row.

Halbach, A., Ehrle, K., Zahorik, J., & Molnar, A. (2001). Class size reduction: From promise to practice. *Educational Leadership, 58*(6), 32–35.

Harrison, C. J. (1990). Concepts, operational definitions, and case studies in instruction. *Education, 110*(4), 502–505.

Henson, K. T. (2001). *Curriculum planning: Integrating multiculturalism, constructivism, and education reform* (2nd ed.). New York: McGraw-Hill.

Hopping, L. (2000). Multi-age teaming: A real life approach to the middle school. *Phi Delta Kappan, 82*(4), 270–272 and 292.

Jenkins, D. M., & Jenkins, K. D. (1991). The NMSA Delphi Report: Roadmap to the future. *Middle School Journal, 2281*(4), 29.

Johnston, J. M. (1990, April). *What are teachers' perceptions of teaching in different classroom contexts?* Paper presented at the annual convention of the American Educational Research Association, Boston, MA.

Keefe, J. W., & Jenkins, J. M. (2002). Personalized instruction. *Phi Delta Kappan, 83*(6), 440–448.

Lawson, A. E., Abraham, M. R., & Renner, J. W. (1989). A theory of instruction: Using the learning cycle to teach science concepts and thinking skills (NARST Monograph No. 1). Cincinnati, OH: University of Cincinnati, National Association for Research in Science Teaching.

Little, D. (1985). An investigation of cooperative small group instruction and the use of advance organizers on the self concept and social studies achievement of third grade students. Doctoral dissertation, University of Alabama.

Lotan, R. A. (2003). "Group-worthy tasks." *Educational Leadership, 60*(6), 72–75.

Markle, G., Johnston, J. H., Geer, C., & Meichtry, Y. (1990, November). Teaching for understanding. *Middle School Journal, 22*(2), 53–57.

McEwin, C. K., Dickinson, T. S., & Hamilton, H. (2000). National board certified teachers' views regarding specialized middle level teachers' preparation. *The Clearing House, 73*(4), 211–213.

McQueen, C. (2001). Teaching to win. *Kappa Delta Pi Record, 38*(1), 12–15.

Miserando, M. (1996). Children who do well in school: Individual differences in perceived confidence and autonomy in above average children. *Journal of Educational Psychology, 88*(2), 203–214.

MLS (Metropolitan Life Insurance Company Survey) (1998). *The American teacher.* New York: Louis Harris and Associates.

NMSA (National Middle School Association) Delphi report: Roadmap to the future (1991). Westerville, OH.

Nye, B. A., Achilles, C. M., Boyd Zaharias, J., Fulton, B. D., & Wallenhorst, M. P. (1994). Small is far better. *Research in the Schools,* 1(1), 9–20.

Patterson, W. (2003). Breaking out of our boxes. *Phi Delta Kappa,* 84(8), 569–574.

Peterson, P. L., Marx, R. W., & Clark, C. M. (1978). Teacher planning, teacher behavior, and student achievement. *American Educational Research Journal,* 15, 555–565.

Phelps, P. H. (1991, March-April). Helping teachers excel as classroom managers. *The Clearing House,* 64(3), 241–242.

Public Agenda (2000). Playing their parts: What parents and teachers really mean by parental involvement. www.publicagenda.org/specials/parent/parent.htm

Reinstein, D. (1998). Crossing the economic divide. *Educational Leadership,* 55(4), 28–29.

Romberg, T. A. (1983). *Allocated time and content covered in mathematics.* Paper presented at the annual meeting of the American Educational Research Association, Montreal, Canada.

Romberg, T. A., & Carpenter, T. P. (1986). Research on teaching mathematics: Two disciplines of scientific inquiry. In M. C. Wittrock (Ed.), *Handbook of research on teaching* (3rd ed.). New York: Macmillan.

Rose, L. C., & Gallup, A. M., (1998). The 30th annual Phi Delta Kappa/Gallup poll of the public's attitudes toward public schools. *Phi Delta Kappa,* 80(1), 41–56.

Schville, J., Porter, A., Billi, G., Floden, R., Freeman, D., Knappan, L., Kuhs, T., & Schmidt, W. (1983). Teachers as policy brokers in the content of elementary school mathematics. In L. S. Schulman & E. G. Sykes (Eds.), *Handbook of teaching and policy.* New York: Longman.

Selekman, H. (1999, p. 245). A teacher's class. In Henson, K. T., & Eller, B. F., *Educational psychology for effective teaching.* Belmont, CA: Wadsworth.

Smith, G. A. (2002). Place-based: Learning to be where we are. *Phi Delta Kappan,* 83(8), 584–594.

Solomon, S. (1989). Homework: The great inforcer. *The Clearing House,* 63(2), 63.

Stallworth, B. J. (1998). Practicing what we teach. *Educational Leadership,* 55(5), 77–79.

Stokes, L. C. (2000). What middle school teachers perceive to be essential elements in preservice middle school teacher programs. *SRATE Journal,* 10(1), 28–32.

Thompson, S., & Gregg, L. (1997). Reculturing middle schools for meaningful change. *Middle School Journal,* 28(5), 27–31.

Van Gulick, R. (1990). Functionalism, information, and content. In W. G. Lylcan (Ed.), *Mind and cognition.* Cambridge, MA: Basil Blackwell.

Von Glaserfeld, E. (1988). *Environment and communication.* Paper presented at the Sixth International Congress on Mathematics Education, Budapest. As cited in Tobin, K., Bugler, K., & Fraser, B. (1990). *Windows into science classrooms: Problems with higher level cognitive learning.* New York: Falmer.

Waldron, K. A., & Allen, L. V. Z. (1999). Successful strategies for inclusion at the middle level. *Middle School Journal,* 30(4), 18–27.

Walker, V. N., & Chance, E. W. (1994–1995). National award winning teachers' exemplary instructional techniques and activities. *National Forum of Teacher Education Journal,* 5(1), 11–24.

Walter, L. J. (1984). A synthesis of research findings on teaching, planning, and decision making. In Egbert, R. L., & Kluender, M. M., (Eds.), *Using research to improve teacher education.* Lincoln, NE: American Association of Colleges for Teacher Education/Teachers College, University of Nebraska—Lincoln.

Williams, P. A., Alley, R. D., & Henson, K. T. (1999). *Managing secondary classrooms.* Boston: Allyn & Bacon.

5
Evaluation

Objectives
- Define evaluation.
- Differentiate between testing and evaluation.
- List three factors a term grade should reflect.
- Justify using assignments for extra credit and justify rejecting the practice.
- Describe one major limitation of using the bell curve in assigning high school grades.
- Determine the stanine scores for a class of students, and transfer stanines into percentages.
- Differentiate between formative and summative evaluation.
- Design an evaluation system to replace some classroom competition with cooperation.
- Explain how criterion-referenced tests support the use of a basic constructivist concept (cooperation).
- Describe a technique using computers to enhance formative evaluation.
- Explain two ways in which criterion-referenced tests help minority group members.

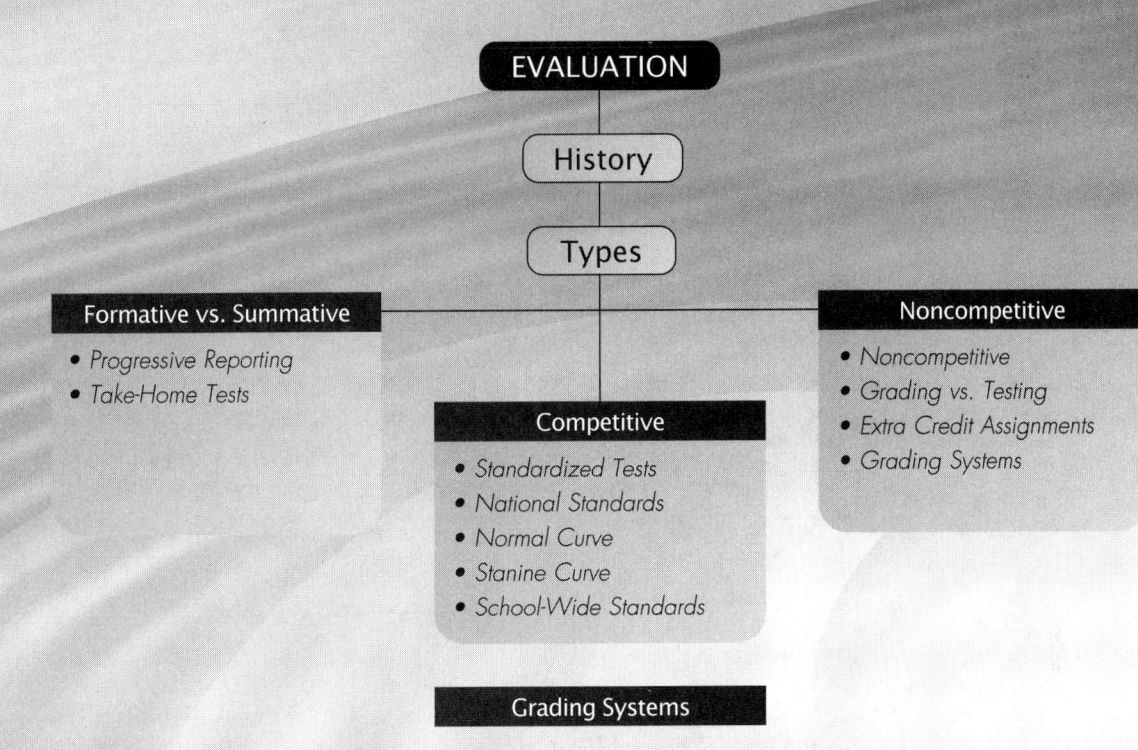

Connecting Statements	Agree	Disagree	Uncertain
1. Evaluation is the same as the sum of a student's test scores.			
2. The bell curve is appropriate for assigning letter grades in most secondary and middle-level classes.			
3. For a group of middle school students, final course grades should parallel their respective intelligence quotients (IQs).			
4. The teacher's judgment should not enter into the grading process.			
5. Evaluation is frequently used in secondary and middle schools to promote learning.			
6. A student's effort should determine that student's success in class.			
7. Criterion-referenced tests help teachers meet minority student needs for self-competition as opposed to competition with other students.			
8. Standardized tests are especially well suited for meeting the needs of minority students.			

> ### Tips for Teachers
>
> Testing is one thing, evaluation is another. Be careful if you do not know the difference. You may be like the dog that chased the skunk—when he caught it, he didn't know what to do with it. Before giving your first tests, consider what you will do with the results. This process of deciding what to do with the results is called evaluation. Middle-level learners need organization in their lives. You can help provide organization for your students by mastering the concepts in this chapter and coordinating your tests with your more comprehensive evaluation program. Most teachers fail to use the most valuable type of evaluation—formative evaluation. Formative evaluation can help you promote learning. A second important type of evaluation is criterion-referenced evaluation. Most teachers fail to use this type of evaluation too.
>
> Begin thinking of evaluation as an important instructional tool. You can even use it to diagnose your own teaching weaknesses. Use this chapter to learn how to use evaluation positively to raise your students' achievement levels.

Past Use of Evaluation in Schools

Research has provided much information that can help teachers use evaluation effectively, but as Parsons and Jones (1990, p. 17) explain: "Unfortunately, the litany of our knowledge about classroom evaluation does not match our usual practices as teachers."

For decades teachers have misused evaluation. Winton (1991) warns teachers against the temptation of using grades for the wrong ends:

> *Teachers sometimes use grading to motivate, punish, or control. In this they frequently have parents as allies. It is assumed that students with poor grades will naturally work harder to achieve better grades. Good marks become the objective of learning. Grades become the currency which students, teachers, and parents may use for different purposes. (p. 40)*

Evaluation differs from testing. Testing should be conducted objectively and apart from the teacher's own values. Evaluation demands that you make a qualitative judgment, or set values, on what you measure (Armstrong, Henson, & Savage, 2004). There is no statistical or completely objective method that can be used to assign grades to a student's score or a student's product. Ultimately, a judgment of the worth or value of that score or product must be made by the teacher. Evaluation is also much broader than testing. Testing requires such tasks as selecting or constructing appropriate examinations, administering them, and scoring the responses, but all this is merely a prerequisite to evaluation.

Evaluation begins where testing ends. Once the results are determined and the tests have been returned, you must use these results to make the testing worthwhile. How you use test results is evaluation. The following list shows the relationship between measurement and evaluation and their parts.

Measurement
1. Deciding on type of test
2. Selecting a ready-made test or constructing a teacher-made test
3. Administering the test
4. Scoring the test

Evaluation
1. Formative: using the test to promote learning
2. Summative: using the test (and possibly other criteria) to grade the student, teacher, or program

Note that evaluation is divided into two main categories, formative and summative. As you read the following paragraphs, note the sharp distinction between the two. Your effective use of evaluation depends on your ability to separate the two basic types.

Formative Evaluation

Comparatively little use has been made of formative evaluation. **Formative evaluation** can be defined as the designing and use of tests for only one specific purpose—to promote learning. Formative evaluation enables teachers to monitor their instruction so they can keep it on course (Oliva, 1997). The middle school of ensuring success for all students makes the use of formative evaluation indispensable for middle-level teachers.

Dagley and Orso (1991) note the purpose of formative evaluation: "Formative evaluation is an ongoing process, designed to improve the teacher's performance" (p. 73). Also, "If any student cannot learn excellently from the original instruction, the student can learn excellently from one or more correctives" (Block & Henson, 1986, p. 24). Put simply, students often need a chance to test their knowledge without penalty, so they will know how to adjust their study techniques. According to Markle, Johnston, Geer, and Meichtry (1990), tests can become strong clarifiers of teacher expectations, thereby guiding students toward expected outcomes. Although most teachers agree that going over test answers in class can help some students learn more about the material, they are aware that this is not likely to result in students' total mastery of the material.

Students usually do not see how tests can promote learning. "After a test is finished, it is time to shut down the schema. Teachers are sometimes frustrated because students do not exhibit any interest in reviewing their tests" (Stefanich, 1990, p. 50). There must be a much more systematic use of evaluation, separate from grading and aimed only at promoting

---

Proactive Exercise

Anticipated Situation

- You know that:
  Formative evaluation is a virtually untapped source for promoting classroom learning.

- You know that:
  Grades should reflect more than test scores. The two purposes of school are learning and social growth, the latter of which is often overlooked.

Proactive Alternative

- You can:
  Make a list of ways you can use formative evaluation in your classes. This list should include weekly quizzes that don't count in the grading system. It should also include returning tests and reviewing them to learn those concepts that were missed.

- You can:
  Develop a grading system for each class. Be sure to include some activities that promote socialization (e.g. cooperation in group projects).

learning. Successful use of formative evaluation requires both teachers and students to change their attitude of equating tests with grades. When using tests for formative purposes, you should:

1. Avoid recording individual scores.
2. Be concerned only with whether the student has mastered the material at an acceptable level.
3. Involve each student in keeping a continuing record of individual progress.
4. Avoid mentioning grades.
5. Assume that, when properly motivated, all students can master the material.
6. Avoid pushing students so fast that they become confused and discouraged.
7. Reassure students that these test results will not count toward their grades.

These guidelines provide the student support that all students need, especially minority students. Because students and teachers usually never perceive evaluation in this way, you must be patient and reassuring if you elect to use tests to help students learn.

Progressive Reporting

Schools are replacing letter grades with progress reports, which can be both more personal and more insightful than traditional grades. Winton (1991) explains:

The use of progress reporting is a viable alternative since it imparts information—information about what is being taught, alternative activities the student has completed, and how he or she is coping with the course. No individual letter grade can do this. Direct conferences supplement narrative reports and a portfolio of student work is much more revealing and reliable. (p. 40)

The 26th Gallup Poll (Elam, Rose, & Gallup, 1994, p. 55) found that U.S. parents find written descriptions the most useful of the ways schools inform them of their child's progress. A full 95 percent of parents rate written progress reports as either quite useful or very useful. Thus, progress reporting is a direct route to reaching the Carnegie goal of increasing the level of parent involvement in adolescents' education (Carnegie Council on Adolescent Development Staff, 1995).

Teacher as Proactive Decision Maker

Classroom Situation

1. You know that some of your students' parents, and perhaps some of your students, will believe that competition is desirable.
2. When you give test results, you know that many of your students will fail to appreciate the power of using the results to promote further learning.

Proactive Alternatives

1. Make a list of the negative repercussions of classroom competition. Be prepared to share these with parents and teachers.
2. Prepare definitions of formative evaluation and summative evaluation. Have students identify contrasting features that separate these concepts.
3. Prepare a list of the advantages of formative evaluation. Ask small groups of students to make their own lists of advantages.
4. Compare your lists with students' lists.

TABLE 5.1 A Comparison of Progressive Reporting and Traditional Evaluation

Traditional Evaluation	Progressive Evaluation
Spot-checks understanding	Measures comprehensive understanding
Detached from student	Involves student
Nondescriptive	Descriptive
One-time evaluation	Ongoing evaluation

Compared with traditional grading practices, progressive reporting is more comprehensive, more specific, more descriptive, and more personal for the student (Table 5.1). Perrone (1994, p. 13) says that "on-going assessment is critical." Gifford (2002) reminds teachers that a test is not the most appropriate instrument for evaluation because when teachers use tests, students usually are not involved in establishing goals for their own growth. By 1998, the Gallup Poll found that the public rated open houses and newsletters to be the most effective communication devices.

Take-Home Tests

An example of formative evaluation is the use of take-home tests. These tests give students access to more information sources and more time to internalize that information. According to Parsons and Jones (1990, p. 17), "Take-home tests can provide an answer for teachers who wish to evaluate student progress with longer and more complex problem situations."

Computers offer multiple ways to enhance formative evaluation. For example, when returning an essay test, the teacher can require students to rewrite their responses until a satisfactory level is reached.

Summative Evaluation

Dagley and Orso (1991, p. 73) present one use of summative evaluation: "The purpose of summative evaluation is to decide if the teacher meets minimal accountability standards." Summative evaluation is also used to measure student performance to determine such major decisions as grades, passing, and failing. Lindblad (1994, p. 292) reminds us that in most communities parents insist on the use of letter grades. "Although many teachers will indeed use a variety of instructional methods, the vast majority of schools systems still require that grades be assigned to each student." Parents insist on having grades (Louisell & Descamps, 1997).

Because teachers have used tests almost exclusively to determine student grades, you might assume that with all that practice, teachers are systematic in the way they convert raw scores into letter grades. But this is not so. Each teacher seems to have an individual system, and many teachers use a different system each grading period. Why? Because most teachers never find a system that satisfies them. No single system is right for all classes. When you become aware of the strengths and weaknesses of various grading systems, you will be in a better position to choose wisely. To compare summative and formative evaluation, see Table 5.2.

Competitive Evaluation

All evaluation systems can be grouped into two categories: those that force a student to compete with other students (norm-referenced), and those that do not require competition

TABLE 5.2 A Comparison of Summative and Formative Evaluation

Summative Evaluation	Formative Evaluation
Purpose: issue grades	Improve teaching
Time given: following instruction	Before and during instruction
Basis: norm-referenced	Criterion-referenced
Follow-up: seldom	Always

among students but instead are based on a set of standards of mastery (criterion-referenced). As Clark and Astuto (1994) explain:

> The argument in support of competition is based on the belief that an individual can push beyond current levels of skill and achieve at the highest possible levels when pressed to do so in the heat of competition. . . . The counter-argument is that self-motivation is sustained when individuals maintain a sense of their own efficacy and work in a context in which people help one another develop skills, take risks, and challenge standard operating procedures. (p. 516)

Traditionally, U.S. schools have required competition among students, and many teachers believe that competition motivates students. Many also believe that competition prepares students for adulthood in a competitive world, especially for getting ahead in their future employment. However, middle-level educators often disagree. For example, Winton (1991) expresses concern over excessive use of competition: "Over and over again in homes and in schools we set up situations which guarantee that children will feel defeated and inept" (pp. 40–41). He continues: "Evaluation should be for the purpose of promoting further learning. It should be a positive, supportive experience." Because middle-level students need encouragement and opportunities to build their self-confidence, criterion-referenced evaluation is especially well suited for middle school curricula. The need to put cooperation ahead of competition was also expressed in one of the goals of the National Middle School Association priority goals list (see Jenkins & Jenkins, 1991): "Collaboration and cooperative problem solving replace competition as the driving philosophy of middle level instruction."

Standardized Tests

One test that forces students to compete among themselves is the standardized test, which is very popular in U.S. schools today. Standardized tests have several features in common. First, they are based on norms derived from the average scores of thousands of students who have taken the test. Usually these scores come from students nationwide, so each student's performance is compared with that of thousands of other students.

Standardized tests are usually used to measure or grade a school's curriculum. Seeking to make teachers more accountable, state officials have forced schools to use standardized tests, given to students to measure teacher success—and yes, they are even used to measure student success. For example, for decades the state of New York has administered its Regents examinations to determine student success. In 2003, New York City's mayor took over the responsibility for managing the nation's largest school district, confident that he could save money and raise student performance. By the early 1980s almost all states had legislated minimal learning standards, and tests are presently being developed to determine each student's and each school's level of attainment. States throughout the nation are using standardized tests to make their students, teachers, and colleges of education accountable.

Critics say that standardized tests pose special problems for members of minority ethnic and cultural groups by denying many the opportunity to pursue postsecondary education (Armstrong et al., 2004). They also say that a system is needed that will provide developmental opportunities for the fastest-growing school-age population. Nelson (1999) has accurately cautioned that "When assessment is used to control outcomes rather than to identify needs, and when test results rather than learning become the goal, the education system serves the controller, not the student" (p. 392). Middle-level teachers can become self-empowereed by gaining understanding about standardized testing.

National Standards

The current press for national standards is causing a lot of controversy. Some people believe that it is long overdue, while others worry that it will do more harm than good. Those who support national standards believe they are necessary to prompt all states to provide adequate education for their youth (Noddings, 1997). Opponents of the national standards movement argue that the type of education Americans want for their youth cannot be legislated or imposed by the state (Pitton, 1999). Opponents fear that nationally imposed standards will set a ceiling that will actually lower academic gains for the better students (Ostrom, 1997), and that they will stifle creativity.

The success or failure of the national standards movement will hinge on the types of standards set and the way these standards are administered. If, indeed, the standards are to be helpful, they must be broad enough to be articulated with benchmarks (Marzano & Kendall, 1996), and teachers must be involved in their development (Pitton, 1999). Precautions should be taken to ensure that the new standards do not serve as barriers to some students (Sweeny, 1999).

Like the swing toward national standards, there is also a swing toward national testing. The public generally supports this trend as long as schools are not forced to administer the tests. The 1998 Gallup Poll (Rose & Gallup, 1998) found that 71 percent of the public favor a voluntary national testing program.

The Normal Curve

A second use of tests that requires students to compete with others is the normal curve (also called the normal probability curve or the probability curve). This curve could equally well be called the natural curve or chance curve, because it reflects the distribution of all sorts of things in nature. This distribution is shown in Figure 5.1.

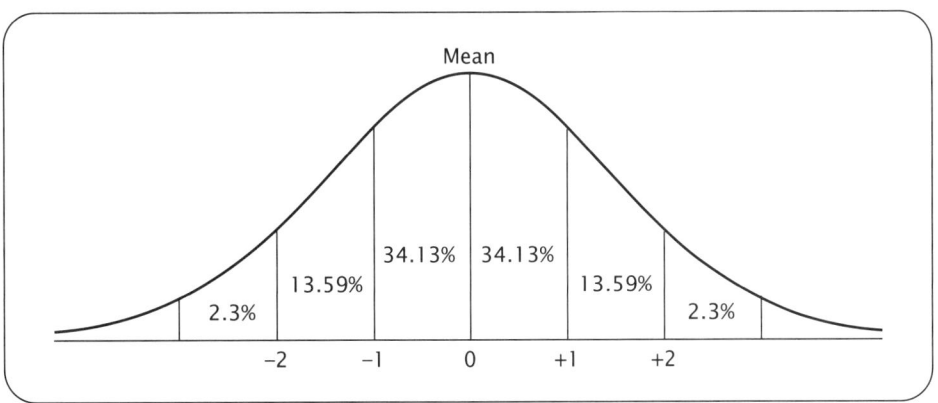

FIGURE 5.1 NORMAL PROBABILITY CURVE

THE CASE

Classroom Microsociety

Lynda Paznokas, Washington State University

Lynda Paznokas *received her doctorate from Oregon State University in Corvallis, Oregon. She teaches in the Department of Teaching and Learning at Washington State University where she holds the title, Boeing Distinguished Professor of Science Education.*

Background

Many schools throughout the United States have implemented programs simulating adult economic, governmental, and societal issues, to make education more relevant for students. Through classroom simulations, students become personally involved in a microsociety in which they have active learning experiences with politics, law, government, and economics. These experiences bring to life the role of social studies education. The National Council for the Social Studies states, "Social studies educators teach students the content knowledge, intellectual skills, and civic values necessary for fulfilling the duties of citizenship in a participatory democracy." In addition to these social studies concepts and skills, a microsociety is an excellent vehicle for subject integration, showing students a "real-life" reason for their school assignments. All aspects of societal issues emerge during the development of a class town, providing for extensive debate and deep thought. Elementary and middle school students are able to develop awareness for these political, social, and economic concepts. They learn that they are currently contributing members of their community; this is not something that happens after they become adults.

The Community

The microsociety program began in a small town in the Pacific Northwest about 20 miles west of a major metropolitan area. The community was founded on agriculture but had begun attracting leading electronics manufacturers. The district had six elementary schools. After six years, the teacher moved to the other side of the state, where the program was used only in her classroom, in one of the three middle schools. The community is the retail center for this rural part of the state. It borders alpine forests and high desert. The economy of this community is founded on the wood products industry, but tourism is becoming the leading industry.

The School

The first school where the microsociety program was used was a K–6 school located in a middle-class suburban neighborhood. The second school served grades 6–8 and was also located in a mostly middle-class suburban neighborhood. Both schools encouraged innovative programs from their teachers.

The Leader

Jessica Kincaid started this classroom microsociety program after her first year of teaching. During the ten years the program was used most extensively, she taught sixth-grade students in elementary and middle school classrooms in the Pacific Northwest. She started the program when she taught a "low group" in a school in which students were ability-grouped for math instruction. Although she was not comfortable with ability grouping, she felt she had little choice as a new teacher in a new school. The economics aspect of the program began on a small scale with the use of a stock market to teach some math concepts. The "low students" were able to "shine," by learning sophisticated stock market skills the "top students" did not understand. The confidence of the "low students" grew enormously.

In future years, she did not participate in ability-grouped math instruction, so the economic system could be used with all students in the classroom. The economics program expanded throughout the ten years it was used, growing far beyond just a stock market. During this time, Jessica completed her master's degree with an emphasis in mathematics education, partly to learn techniques to enhance this program.

Issues in Implementation

After many years of teaching sixth grade, it became apparent to Jessica that her students needed a better connection to the "real world." They were at an awkward transition age, exploring the world beyond their school and families, wondering how they fit into community life and how school related to future jobs. Their schoolwork needed to help bridge these transitions, giving them personal reasons for completing assignments and a greater desire for life-long learning.

To help with these transitions, Jessica developed a program in which her sixth graders built a "refrigerator box" town as a year-long economics and microsociety project. The students designed and constructed their buildings around a theme, worked each day as employees and customers in their businesses, and solved problems through their city council and court system. There were many purposes for the project, including:

- An economic system within the classroom
- A springboard for a study of the community and related social issues
- A reason for studying architecture
- A problem-solving exercise in construction, group process, and cooperation
- A classroom management system within the classroom

Over the ten years of developing and refining this project, Jessica learned which parts of the town should be predetermined, which would be the choice of the students, and which could evolve over time as situations arose. For example, she learned that the town functioned best if five basic buildings were constructed at the beginning of the school year: bank, post office, insurance company, government office, and store. A small jail was also built, which was used only on limited occasions. Other buildings might arise through need, but it was best to start with these five.

The establishment and construction of the town provided an excellent way to start the school year. Students needed to work together for the planning and construction of the buildings, as well as developing each business. They knew they were creating an atmosphere that would last throughout the year, so they took their work seriously. Although the process was similar each year, the following is a description of how Jessica worked with the students one year to establish the town.

Students voted on the theme of the town, such as a jungle setting, Western-style buildings, or an outer space design. For this example, during the year being discussed, the students used architectural ideas from the Middle Ages, so the town was named Medieval Manor. The medieval theme dealt only with the architecture, not with the type of businesses that were common in Europe from A.D. 500 to about A.D. 1400. Medieval architecture was researched and each student made a sketch of a favorite building. The class decided which of the town businesses should have which style of architecture. For example, they decided the most important building in their class town was the bank, so that would be constructed in cathedral style because they felt the cathedral was the most important medieval building. Insurance protected them, so the architecture for that building would be a sturdy castle. The government office was modeled after the Brussels Town Hall. The jail, post office, and store were a simple "village style," which was their description of half-timbered construction. The students phoned businesses in town to locate empty refrigerator boxes and organized parents to bring these large boxes to Juniper Heights Middle School.

The sixth graders were divided into business groups and chose a temporary boss for the construction phase of their business. Each group looked at the collection of student sketches for their type of building. For example, the insurance group looked at all the castles the students had drawn, to determine the "look" of their business. The students sketched what the four sides of the business would look like. Some years, including the "Medieval year," an architect worked with the students. He reviewed their plans and helped them transfer their sketches to the four sides of the refrigerator boxes.

One-and-a-half class days were usually set aside to construct the businesses. To help control the mess, students wore old clothes and covered the floor with newspapers and tarps. The refrigerator boxes were spread throughout the room after desks were pushed to the sides. Designs were drawn on the boxes with pencil or chalk, to make sure they were the correct size and design. Students used X-acto® knives to cut the doors and windows. Using rollers, boxes were painted with water-based house paint remnants, to save the cost of school tempera paints. Small brushes and tempera paints were used for the name of the business and other details. Finishing touches were added, such as turrets for the castle. The boxes were then lined up along one side of the classroom, where they stayed throughout the year.

After the outsides of the boxes were done, the inside work began. Some boxes had carpeting, desks, and posters on the walls. Jessica gave each business a list of jobs to complete before it was ready to open, such as printing currency, making checks, writing tax-collection forms, making postage stamps and postcards, and sending letters to the parents about donating "junk" for the store. Jessica gave them these required tasks, but the students also determined some of their own needs.

The town was then ready to open for business each day. Before an individual student could participate in the town, though, both a check-writing and check ledger packet had to be completed. Also, a check balancing unit, provided by a community bank, had to be completed correctly. This was also an excellent review of addition and subtraction at the beginning of the school year.

"Town time" was held for about 20 minutes at the beginning of each day. This time provided a natural way to ease into the school day because students had a chance to talk to their friends as they carried out the business of the town as employees and customers. In order to get money for their town business, Jessica paid the students 5 cents a point for grades from their class assignments in their "fake money." Payment checks were issued approximately every two weeks. No payments were given for late assignments. This money provided an incentive to do their work well, but Jessica found it important to continually stress the importance of intrinsic motivation for good work so students didn't view payments as "bribes." Students were also paid for the work they did in their businesses. Each business had a boss, and the workers had contracts telling them which days to work and explaining conditions of their pay. Students decided individually how to spend their money. For example, the money could go in a checking or savings account in the bank. Items could be purchased at the store ("junk" students brought from home). Notes could be sent to friends through the post office, with proper postage.

A fine or taxes might need to be paid to the government. Insurance could be purchased to guard against having to pay fines for misdemeanors under the legal system set up by the city council and mayor. This approach greatly helped with classroom management. Students set the laws (behavior rules), and the government workers helped Jessica enforce them. An interesting phenomenon occurred each year: students always got carried away with writing and enforcing laws, creating a near-police state. Abuse of power on the part of government workers became a hot topic of debate. When she felt they were ready to deal with this problem, she invited someone from the community's police or court system to talk to them about responsible law making and law enforcing. The students then had to work through their justice structure to change the atmosphere of the classroom.

Court cases occurred on Fridays for students who were charged with felonies. Defendants and plaintiffs had to hire attorneys, develop their cases, and present them to the class court. Each week a judge, clerk, bailiff, court reporter, and court artist were drawn from a hat. Except for witnesses, the rest of the class was the jury. Court cases provided classroom management consequences and learning about "real-life" justice. The judge could levy fines and/or short "jail time" in a small "washer/dryer box building," keeping in mind how the severity of the current case fit with previous cases. Court cases also provided a format for practicing skills in writing, speaking, listening, and drawing.

City council members were elected. Their meetings were held at least once a week during the noon hour. This group had to decide on the class laws and whether each law should be a felony or a misdemeanor. The class elected a mayor each month to lead city council meetings.

As the year went on and more advanced skills were learned in math, new aspects were added to the town structure, such as income and property taxes. A stock market was introduced in January, after students had completed a stock market unit. Following an English unit in journalism, a newspaper was started. After several months, credit cards were made from railroad board and lettering was done with a label-maker. Crayon rubbings were used for making credit card receipts. Of course, Jessica always looked for creative additions students wished to add to the town structure.

Eventually, Jessica added competition from new businesses, and permission for students to go on strike and to hire and fire employees. These aspects caused great debate among the students. They struggled with the necessity of providing unemployment to classmates who had not done their jobs well and had, thus, been fired. This led to excellent discussions about social issues and provided an opportunity for guest speakers. One of the most interesting speakers was an elderly gentleman representing Meals-on-Wheels, a program that provides noon meals to senior citizens who are home-bound. The students gained empathy for those who needed extra support from society. An unexpected bonus was this man saying he "might consider" voting for a school levy now that he knew such good things were happening in schools!

As the year progressed and they learned more about the structure of a town, they began to study their community. They visited some of the businesses that corresponded to those found in their class town, which sometimes led to school/business partnerships. The class mayor usually visited the community's mayor to learn about the job. The students studied about architecture, city government, urban planning and growth issues, employment/unemployment laws, and the history of their community.

One year the students presented a written and photographic summary of the building and carrying out of their class town to a statewide Built-Environment Education contest sponsored by the American Institute of Architects. Their entry won first place for the state, in recognition of creative ideas about improving the quality of the environment in which we live.

Further Reflection

Jessica's biggest concern was making sure that students understood that they completed their assignments in a way that made them proud for intrinsic reasons, not because they were going to be paid in the class economic system. She was also concerned that some issues were sometimes "too close to home" for some students. If their parents were on welfare or facing court hearings, for example, they might be uncomfortable when these topics came up for debate during class. Overall, however, she felt it was important that students had these "real-life" experiences so they would be better able to understand where they fit into the community and learn how their actions resulted in real consequences.

The normal curve is divided into equal segments. The vertical line through the center (the mean) represents the average of a whole population. Each mark to the right of the mean represents one average, or standard deviation, above the average. Each vertical line to the left of the center represents one standard unit of deviation below the mean. As the figure shows, about 34 percent of the population is within the one standard deviation unit above the mean, and about 34 percent of the population is within the one standard deviation below the mean. Only about 14 percent of the population is in the second deviation range above the mean, and about 14 percent is in the second deviation range below the mean. A very small portion of the population (approximately 2.3 percent) deviates enough from the mean to fall within the third unit of deviation above the mean; an equal portion deviates three standard units below the mean.

To give another example, if the temperature is taken every day at 3 p.m. from June 15 until August 15 for ten years, and if a mean or average is taken, the individual temperatures are listed vertically from hottest to coldest, and the line is divided into six equal parts, then 34 percent of the temperatures will fall in the section just above the middle, 34 percent will fall within the section just below the middle, 14 percent will fall in the second section above the mean, and 14 percent will fall in the second section below the mean. Only 2.3 percent of the temperature readings will fall in the third section above the mean, and 2.3 percent will fall in the lowest section below the mean.

Some of the many things subject to this type of distribution are the weight and height of animals and plants, the margin of error of both humans and machines, and, of course, the IQs of human beings. Not all phenomena are distributed in the ratios represented by the normal curve. For example, the chronological ages of the human population do not follow this pattern.

The normal curve, as it is often applied to the assigning of grades in a school classroom, makes several bold assumptions. First, like other evaluation schemes based on competition among students, it assumes that the level of a particular student's performance compared with the average of a group of students (usually the student's classmates) is important. Second, it assumes that all students have an equal opportunity to succeed—as though all have equal potential, which is extremely unlikely unless the class has been grouped homogeneously. Third, it assumes that the number of students used as a norm is large enough to reflect the characteristics of all students at the particular grade level. Unless the class size exceeds 100 students, this is a bold assumption indeed. The use of the normal curve assumes that 68 percent of the students will earn C's, 13.5 percent will earn B's and another 13.5 percent D's, 2.5 percent will earn A's, and 2.5 percent will fail.

Stanine Scores

Many schools use stanine ("standard nine") scores to determine student performance. This method uses the normal distribution curve to group test scores into nine categories (Figure 5.2). This modification of the bell-curve evaluation gets rid of the A's, B's, C's, D's, and F's. Many educators feel that the psychological advantage of escaping the letter-grade stigma is important. Also, having nine categories gives the teacher more groups in which to place projects that must be evaluated arbitrarily.

School-wide Standards

Even more popular than the standard curve is the practice of schools' setting their own standards. You are undoubtedly familiar with the following system:

90 percent and above = A
80–89 percent = B
70–79 percent = C
60–69 percent = D
Below 60 percent = F

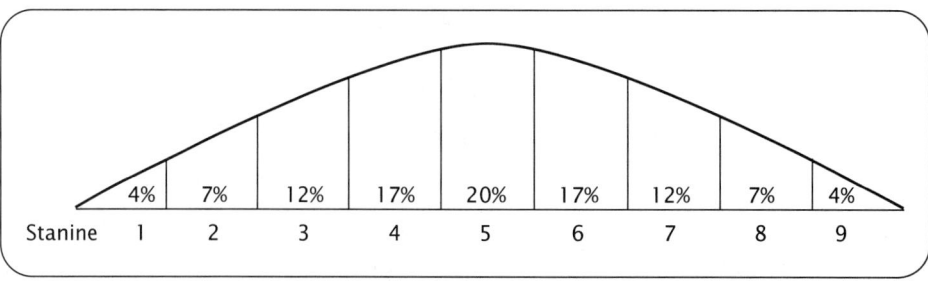

FIGURE 5.2 NORMAL DISTRIBUTION CURVE TO DETERMINE STANINE SCORES

This type of evaluation makes an important, and often false, assumption. It assumes that the test's level of difficulty fits students' abilities exactly. Student teachers usually realize this error as they begin marking their first set of papers and find that almost everyone failed the test. Although the exact percentage requirements may vary among schools, the system remains a common method of evaluation.

> ### Reflection
>
> The following passage illustrates the magnitude of the standard of error in geology and demonstrates why standardized test scores often have an equally alarming high standard error.* Read the passage, then think about this as you respond to the questions below.
>
> **A Very Standard Error**
>
> My friend was a geologist. We were in his backyard, awed by the majesty of the Rocky Mountains. The monstrous flat sloping rocks that are the hallmark of Boulder, Colorado, were the subject of our conversation.
>
> "Do you know how old those rocks are?" my friend inquired.
> "I have no idea at all," I replied.
> "They are about four hundred million years old," he said, "give or take a hundred million years."
>
> 1. Do you think the general public is aware of the large standard of error common to many standardized test scores? What evidence can you offer to support your answer?
> 2. What do educators do that suggests that they do not consider the fallibility of standardized test scores?
> 3. Realizing that standardized tests frequently have large standards of error, how do you think this should affect your use of standardized test scores? Why?
>
> *This passage is from J. Frymier. (1979). "On the way to the Forum: It's a very standard error." *Educational Forum*, 36, 388–391. Published by Kappa Delta Pi, International Honor Society in Education. Reprinted by permission.

Noncompetitive Evaluation

Researchers and educators have recently discovered much evidence to show that grading in the middle school should be strictly an individual concern—involving the teacher and the student. Criterion-referenced evaluation bases a student's grade on the student's level of performance in terms of a preset standard (Gallager, 1998). Criterion-referenced tests, which do not force competition among students (Louisell & Descamps, 1997) contribute more to student progress than do norm-referenced tests. Once it was thought that competition for grades was necessary to motivate students to do their best. This may be true for the more capable students, but forcing less capable students to compete with their classmates can discourage them and lead them to concentrate on their inadequacies. Competition can also be bad for the more capable student. You can reduce this damage by not making test scores and grades public.

Many contemporary educators feel that grades should reflect the student's effort, that no one should receive an A without really trying, and that no students exerting themselves to their full potential should receive an F (Williams, Alley, & Henson, 1999). This reflects the contemporary goal of personalizing learning in middle-level classes. These teachers believe that grades should not acknowledge high IQs and punish those who do not have high ability, but that each grade should reflect a student's degree of progress relative to his or her ability. In other words, our schools should reward those behaviors that we want to encourage students to develop (Haberman & Bracey, 1997).

You can improve performance evaluation by using complementary grading systems. Epstein and MacIver (1990) recommend blending performance evaluation and progress grades: "A school that officially rewards improvement by using progress grades along with performance grades can expect at least 1.7 percent fewer of its male students to eventually drop out" (p. 39).

Another method for personalizing learning is requiring students to keep a record of their progress in class. Many schools allow students to write their own self-appraisal. This encourages students to reflect on their own learning. Seek and use students' judgment in determining their grades. A relevant question may be "How do you believe the quality of your work now compares with your previous work? Do you believe this is the best you can do?" Of course, this approach requires that the teacher know each student—and not as a face but as a developing, growing person.

Grading

Although the terms *grading* and *testing* are often used synonymously, to do so is a mistake. A student's grade should reflect more than test scores, because no test reveals all there is to know about a learner, and no test should be used as an exclusive measure of any student's capacity. Neither can a single test measure all a student knows about any topic. Some things other than the acquisition of knowledge are important in school. For example, teachers must ensure that each student develops certain behavioral patterns and attitudes, such as honesty, promptness in completing assignments, the ability to work with others, and respect for others. Therefore a student's grade should reflect each of these traits. Evaluation of these qualities is essentially subjective, and to avoid becoming prejudiced you should decide at the beginning of the year just how much weight this part of the total evaluation will carry and take care not to exceed the limits.

Guidelines for Grading

Grades should represent all the major activities in which a student engages while in your classroom. Daily work and term projects may, and perhaps should, carry as much weight toward the final grade as tests. If you use several tests (weekly or biweekly), daily assignments, term projects, and daily discussions, you will have more satisfactory material on which to base the final grade. Winton (1991, p. 40) says, "Good middle school philosophy limits competition and substitutes direct conferences and written evaluations for formal grading systems." Grading practices should be based on a philosophy of teaching and learning that respects student differences and reflects individual growth (Tomlinson, 2001). Grades should reflect the degree to which students are achieving educational outcomes, and one of those outcomes that should not be overlooked is students' attitude toward learning.

Teacher of the Year

In fact, the most significant evaluation of student achievement should be the extent to which they want to know more and their ability to do so.

Former Alabama Teacher of the Year Susan Lloyd
(Henson & Eller, 1999, p. 225)

These same outcomes should also be considered among the major criteria for evaluating teachers.

Begin with Much Understanding

Having been recently exposed to rigorous tests, many beginning teachers grade too firmly. To avoid alienating and discouraging your students, be a little lenient at first. This does not mean you should always change a grade when a student is unhappy with it, because this often reinforces complaints. Being lenient at first means you should not expect only one particular answer on most types of questions, and you should not expect everyone to score 70 and above. It means that if you believe Jimmy is trying, even though he scores 55 instead of the 60 set as passing, he may receive a C or D rather than an F. Waldon and Allen (1999) say, "The consensus in the literature is that students should be graded on effort and progress, rather that solely on final product" (p. 24). Discussions with Jimmy throughout the year will let you assess the degree to which he is applying himself.

Assignments for Extra Credit

To challenge the most capable students, some teachers include a bonus question on every major test. This is fine if those who do not answer it correctly are not penalized. Some teachers offer extra credit to students who come to special sessions and complete extra assignments on problems with which they are having difficulties. This procedure also can be helpful in motivating students.

When a student asks for an assignment for extra credit at the end of the grading period, however, the student may be less interested in learning than in raising a grade. The student may really be asking, "Will you assign me some extra punishment so that my grade can be elevated?" The teacher may respond by assigning the student forty problems the student already knows how to work, or by assigning the task of copying 2,000 words from an encyclopedia, library book, or magazine without having to learn the content. This practice is most undesirable, because it encourages some students to procrastinate until the last minute and then subject themselves to X amount of punishment rather than attaining X amount of understanding. Most students find such assignments boring, consequently, they learn to dislike the subject that produces the pain.

When students ask to do extra work for credit, base your decision on whether you believe they will learn from the task. You may ask the students what type of assignment they propose to do and what they expect to learn from it. If they can convince you that they can and will learn from the task, the assignment may be warranted.

Grading Systems

The decision on a specific grade is essentially a subjective one. One question may help you each time you assign a grade: What grade will be the best for this student? The student's ability and application will determine your answer. To assign a grade that is higher than deserved is certainly not good for the student, and neither is assigning a grade lower than what the student has earned.

Having a philosophy of grading is not enough, however. As a teacher, you will make decisions based on available information. And the task is a serious and often thankless one. In the past, too often teachers have relied on test scores alone to determine student grades. As Parsons and Jones (1990) explain, teachers should use a variety of criteria to assign grades: "In fact, the more diverse and imaginative the evaluation activities used by the teacher, the more all-encompassing and valid the evaluation is likely to be" (p. 20). The use of a variety of grading criteria personalizes learning by recognizing and rewarding students' individual strengths.

So let us begin by examining a typical situation at the end of a grading period. Ideally, you will have a variety of feedback on which to base each grade—for example, some class projects, presentations, class work, homework, and tests. Following is a list of such feedback that you might have on each of your students at the end of a six-week grading period:

6 weekly tests
1 final examination
1 term paper
1 oral presentation or term project
1 group project
30 homework assignments
20 classroom assignments

To arrive at a grade for the six-week period, assign relative values to each item on your list. Be sure to consider the amount of time the student has spent on each activity. You may want to begin by ranking these elements according to the time invested in each, for example:

Activity	Time Required (Hours)
Homework 30 × 40 minutes	20
Class work 20 × 30 minutes	10
Group project	6
6 weekly tests at 50 minutes	5
1 term paper	4
1 presentation of project (including preparation)	3
1 final examination	1

These activities required 49 hours of student time. To simplify the process, you might simply assign an additional hour's credit to class participation. With a new total of 50 points, you may choose to assign 2 percent of the total grade to each hour spent in each activity. Thus the following system would emerge:

Activity	Percentage of Grade
Homework	40
Class work	20
Group project	12
Weekly tests	10
Term paper	8
Oral presentation	6
Final exam	2
Classroom participation	20

But suppose you as the teacher of this class are not happy to have the final examination count only 2 percent against 10 percent for classroom participation. This is no problem, because you can now distribute 6 percent to the final examination and 6 percent to participation, or 7 percent and 5 percent, and so on. Suppose you discover an error in addition;

if these percentages total more than 100 percent, you could reduce the other percentages in proportion to their size, taking off about 10 percent of each of the eight items.

The distribution in your particular system will not be identical to this one. That does not matter, as long as you assign each grade based on your chosen system. But on what criteria other than the time spent on each activity could you base your grading system? How about the emphasis given each topic in class? What about students' cooperation with other students, and so on?

Your school may require a certain percentage for an A, B, C, or D, but if you are free to design your own requirements, do not forget to ask yourself what grade will be most appropriate for and most helpful to each student. The familiar evaluation practices will not meet the needs of future citizens. Smith (1991) criticizes traditional evaluation, expressing this concern: "Traditional evaluation, on the other hand, is not likely to provide the clarity and focus students need" (p. 21).

Vignettes

As in other aspects of teaching, you will daily encounter new challenges related to evaluation. No list of principles can be comprehensive enough to guide your behavior in all circumstances. The following vignettes show the complexity of such a seemingly simple task as assigning a student a grade or convincing others of grades' limitations and functions.

Vignette One: A Parent Confuses Grades with Success

Susie Bates was in the eighth grade when her schoolwork took a rapid decline. From one six-week grading period to the next, her grades fell from B to F. Susie's father, a high school principal, telephoned Susie's principal to discuss the matter—after report cards were passed out. Susie's principal called Susie's homeroom teacher to the telephone. Mr. Bates began with the usual question: "Can you tell me why Susie's grades have fallen so much?" The teacher responded "No." Mr. Bates mentioned that Susie had started playing in a pop band a couple of nights a week and had suddenly become especially interested in boys. Did the teacher think this could have any connection with her low grades? As difficult as it may be to believe, this was how a high school principal responded to the failure of his own child.

The Bates case was typical in that the parent called after the grading period was over to ask what could be done about Susie's low grade. He was really asking, "What are you going to do about it?" but the teacher can do very little after the fact, except help Susie and her father realize that Susie's problem is not that she received an F but that she did not learn enough in a given time and that little can be done to correct the past. We can only try to avoid repeating the mistake. Teachers who are serious about helping students learn to be suspicious of a Bates-type call, much as they learn to appreciate a sign of parent interest that comes early enough to help a child.

The teacher explained to Mr. Bates that he wanted to help Susie achieve and learn, not just get higher grades, and that perhaps together they could do this by encouraging Susie and then rewarding her achievements by letting her know how proud they were of her.

DISCUSSION

1. **Should a teacher change a grade at a parent's request? Generally not, unless there has been a mistake. To yield to parental pressure will teach the student that force is a satisfactory method for achieving success.**

2. **Students often come to teachers near the end of a grading period and ask for an extra assignment to pull up a grade. Should this be permitted? Only if the student can learn from the assignment—and even then the teacher should avoid allowing this too often. Extra assignments to increase a grade can teach students to procrastinate during the term because they expect they will be allowed to increase their grade at the last moment.**

Vignette Two: A Student Is Given a Break

Linda Eliot was in Mrs. Rolando's ninth-grade math class. She was a delightful girl, always bubbling and happy. Perhaps her lack of seriousness explained the D's and F's in all her subjects, or perhaps her D's and F's had caused her to become less serious about her schoolwork. At the end of the school year Linda had a D+ average. The fact that she had performed higher than usual tempted Mrs. Rolando to give her a C rather than the earned D+, but she decided to talk with Linda before assigning a grade.

Mrs. Rolando began by asking if Linda was aware that she was on the C and D border. Linda responded with enthusiasm. Mrs. Rolando told Linda that the grade was unclear but that she believed Linda was a C student rather than a D student and that if she really wanted to know which she was, there was a plan for finding this out. Linda listened eagerly while her teacher explained that she would assign her a C for the semester if Linda agreed to bring her report card at the end of the first grading period of the next year. At that point they would check her math grade to see if the assumption was correct. Linda happily agreed to these terms. Mrs. Rolando thought the possibility of Linda's remembering the plan throughout the summer vacation and into another school year was remote, but no harm could come of the ploy.

Following a pleasant summer, a new school year began. Mrs. Rolando had a total of 180 new faces to remember and get to know. At the end of the first grading period she was handing out report cards when two girls came rushing through the doorway. Without saying a word, Linda handed over her report card. Mrs. Rolando recalled the agreement they had and scanned the card. She found not only that Linda had a B– in math but also that in all her subjects the lowest grade was a C–. Linda explained that she was now eligible to try out to be a cheerleader. This was obviously an important moment and a triumph for Linda.

DISCUSSION

1. Was the teacher justified in giving Linda a higher grade than she earned?
2. What potential damage is there in telling a student you are assigning a grade that is above his or her average earned grade?

Summary

Traditionally, quantitative evaluation has been used almost exclusively in the schools because of the common belief that the use of numerical data to force students to compete with each other is an effective way to increase learning. State and national, so-called "high-stakes" testing programs operate under this same assumption. Such evaluation is called summative evaluation because it is given at the end of learning units. But not all comtemporary educators believe that competition is effective or good for students. Contemporary educational researchers encourage the use of another type of evaluation called formative evaluation. Formative evaluation is not associated with reported grades, and its purpose is to promote improvement of instruction and learning.

Traditional evaluation has mainly been quantitative. However, researchers are finding that many qualitative evaluation methods have strong potential for enhancing learning. Portfolios, class work, homework, projects, and presentations are a few of many examples of opportunities to use qualitative evaluation. Grading should include a variety of types of feedback, including daily assignments.

Recap of Major Ideas

1. Report card grades should reflect a variety of types of student performance, including class work, homework, reports, projects, and tests.
2. Few middle-level classes are large enough to support using the bell curve to determine grade distribution.
3. Middle-level teachers can use formative evaluation to promote learning.
4. Criterion-referenced tests let students compete only with themselves and clearly inform students what is expected of them before they take each test.
5. Competition among students of varying capabilities can damage both less capable and more capable students.

6. Consider what is best for each student when you assign a final grade.
7. Unlike the act of measurement, you cannot perform grading and evaluation without reference to your own values.
8. Standardized tests deny many members of cultural and ethnic minority groups opportunity to pursue postsecondary education.
9. Criterion-referenced evaluation, when used properly, can meet minority students' need for self-competition versus competition with other students.

Activities

As you read this chapter, your mind probably leaped forward to the time when you will be teaching and grading your own middle-level classes and the types of activities that would become your criteria for grading. You had an opportunity to examine a grading system for a hypothetical class. Here you have an opportunity to design a system of your own.

1. Suppose you have complete autonomy with regard to grading. (This is very rare in contemporary middle schools.) Decide whether you would use a norm-referenced or criterion-referenced system, and defend your choice.
2. Suppose you are forced to use the ABCD system with 90, 80, 70, and 60 percent intervals. List the criteria you would use for grading, and assign a relative value (percentage) to each.
3. Because formative evaluation is seldom used in secondary and middle schools, research the literature and prepare a report on formative evaluation. Discuss with your professor or classmates the relevance of each characteristic to secondary and middle school classes.
4. Arrange a debate between one team that defends grade competition among classmates and a team that opposes such competition. Ask both teams to limit their remarks to those they can substantiate with a written article. During the debate, have a judge (perhaps the professor) throw out any comments that students cannot defend with written support. Make a list for each point earned by each team. Then, with all the points listed on the board, hold a general discussion (not a debate) on whether and when to hold student competition.
5. Make a list of the opportunities that formative evaluation affords minority students and a corresponding list for criterion-referenced evaluation.

Looking Ahead

This chapter has introduced the many roles that evaluation plays in modern education. The following chapter will prepare you to construct, administer, and score tests for your own classroom.

References

Armstrong, D. G., Henson, K. T., & Savage, T. V. (2004). *Teaching today* (7th ed.). New York: Prentice-Hall.

Block, J. H., & Henson, K. T. (1986). Mastery learning and middle school instruction. *American Middle School Education, 9,* 21–29.

Carnegie Council on Adolescent Development Staff (1995). *Great transitions: Preparing adolescents for a new century.* New York: Carnegie Foundation.

Clark, D. L., & Astuto, T. A. (1994). Redirecting reform: Challenges to popular assumptions about teachers and students. *Phi Delta Kappan, 75*(7), 513–520.

Dagley, D. L., & Orso, J. K. (1991, September). Integrating summative and formative modes evaluation. *NASSP Bulletin, 75,* 72–82.

Elam, S. M., Rose, L. C., & Gallup, A. M. (1994). The 26th annual Phi Delta Kappa/Gallup Poll of the public's attitudes toward the public schools. *Phi Delta Kappan, 76*(1), 41–64.

Epstein, J. L., & MacIver, D. J. (1990, November). National practices and trends in the middle grades. *Middle School Journal, 22*(2), 36–40.

Gallager, J. (1998). *Classroom assessment for teachers.* Columbus, OH: Merrill.

Gifford, S. P., (1999). See Henson, K. T., and Eller, B. F. *Educational Psychology for Effective Teaching.* Belmont, CA: Wadsworth.

Haberman, M., & Bracey, G. W. (1997). The antilearning curriculum of urban schools: Part 1: The problem. *Kappa Delta Pi Record, 33*(3), 88–89.

Henson, K. T., & Eller, B. F. (1999). Educational psychology for effective teaching. Belmont, CA: Wadsworth.

Jenkins, D. M., & Jenkins, K. D. (1991). The NMSA Delphi report: Roadmap to the future. *Middle School Journal, 22*(4), 27–36.

Lindblad, A. H., Jr. (1994). You can avoid the traps of cooperative learning. *The Clearing House, 67*(5), 291–293.

Louisell, R. D., & Descamps, J. (1997). *Developing a teaching style.* Prospect Heights, IL: Waveland.

Markle, G., Johnston, J. H., Geer, C., & Meichtry, Y. (1990, November). Teaching for understanding. *Middle School Journal*, 53–57.

Marzano, R. J., & Kendall, J. S. (1996). *A comprehensive guide to designing standards-based districts, schools, and classrooms.* Aurora, CO: McReel.

Nelson, W. W. (1999). The emperor redux. *Phi Delta Kappan*, 80(5), 387–392.

Noddings, N. (1997). Thinking about standards. *Phi Delta Kappan*, 79(3), 184–189.

Oliva, P. F. (1997). *Developing the curriculum* (3rd ed.). New York: HarperCollins.

Ostrom, C. (1997). *Graduation standards facilitator's manual.* St. Paul, MN: Department of Children, Families, and Learning.

Parsons, J., & Jones, C. (1990, September–October). Not another test. *The Clearing House*, 64(1), 17–20.

Perrone, V. (1994). How to engage students in learning. *Educational Leadership*, 51(5), 11–13.

Pitton, D. E. (1999). The naked truth isn't very revealing. *Phi Delta Kappan*, 80(5), 383–386.

Rose, L. C., & Gallup, A. M. (1998). The 30th Phi Delta Kappa/Gallup Poll of the public's attitudes toward the public schools. *Phi Delta Kappan*, 80(1), 41–56.

Smith, M. W. (1991, January). Evaluation as instruction: Using analytic scales to increase composing ability. *Middle School Journal*, 22(3), 21–25.

Stefanich, G. P. (1990). Cycles of cognition. *Middle School Journal*, 22(2), 47–52.

Sweeny, B. (1999). Content standards: Gate of bridge. *Kappa Delta Pi Record*, 35(2), 64–67.

Tomlinson, C. A. (2001). Grading for success. *Educational Leadership*, 58(6), 12–15.

Waldon, K. A., & Allen, L. V. Z. (1999). Successful strategies for inclusion at the middle level. *Middle School Journal*, 30(4), 18–27.

Williams, P. A., Alley, R. D., & Henson, K. T. (1999). *Managing secondary classrooms.* Boston: Allyn & Bacon.

Winton, J. J. (1991, January). You can win without competing. *Middle School Journal*, 22(3), 40.

6

Test Construction, Administration, and Scoring

The bottom line in teaching is always assessment.

Dale R. Phillips and Darrell G. Phillips
(Phillips, Phillips, Melton, & Moore, 1994, p. 52)

Objectives

- List two advantages of objective test questions and two of essay questions.
- Develop an objective test that measures different levels of the cognitive domain.
- Describe a minimum and a maximum standard that teachers can use to determine the appropriate level of difficulty for writing test questions.
- List five guidelines for administering a test.
- Construct a discussion-type test that will measure students' ability to judge or evaluate.
- State two practices that ensure fairness on a discussion-type examination.
- Design a system for scoring an essay examination that will justify assigning more value to some questions than to others.
- Write a general essay-type question that promotes divergent thinking. Then rewrite the same question, making it more specific.
- Write a multiple-choice question with five choices, two of which are viable distracters.
- Write a question for each level of the affective and cognitive domains.
- Write a simple recall-level test question and rewrite it twice, each time raising the level of behavior required to answer the questions.
- Explain the advantage that essay tests offer to minority students that objective tests do not offer.
- Name one precaution that teachers should take when using technology in testing.

TEST CONSTRUCTION, ADMINISTRATION, AND SCORING

The Teacher' Responsibility

Curriculum Alignment and Authentic Tests

Types of Tests
- Objective
- Essay

Purpose of Testing

Portfolios

Oral Tests

Reflections

Construction

- General Suggestions
  - State directions
  - State value of questions
  - Select a variety of questions
  - Include easy and difficult questions
  - Test the test
  - Preferred number of alternatives
  - Phrasing the stem
  - Selecting alternatives
  - Avoiding common errors
- Types
- Writing Essay Items
- Writing Multiple Choice Questions
- Writing Fill-in-the-Blank Questions
- Writing Higher-Level Questions
- Achieving Balance
- Writing Affective Questions
- Questioning Techniques

Administration

- Preliminary Arrangements
- Accountability and Standardized Tests

Connecting Statements

	Agree	Disagree	Uncertain
1. Objective questions test only the student's ability to retain facts.			
2. Competition among all students is good.			
3. Teachers must score essay questions subjectively.			
4. Essay questions tend to measure what students know, whereas objective questions measure what they do not know—that is, their learning gaps.			
5. Beginning teachers tend to make tests too difficult.			
6. Tests should contain both objective and essay questions.			
7. Essay tests reveal students' thought processes.			
8. Essay tests and objective tests have similar capacities for meeting the needs of minority students			

> ### Tips for Teachers
>
> Teachers often view testing as their most unpleasant responsibility. This occurs when they fail to understand how to use tests appropriately. Middle-level teachers often express a need to know more about classroom management and motivation strategies. Perhaps this accounts for much of their misuse of tests. Middle-level and high school teachers must learn more about the use of tests and their effects on students. In this chapter you will learn how you can use a variety of tests to assess student performance. You will also learn each type of test's major advantages and limitations and how to construct, administer, and score tests to increase student achievement. Help your students realize that test scores are not important terminal goals but important indicators of success.

The Teacher's Responsibility

As a middle-level teacher, you are responsible for the testing program in your classes. You will have to help construct, administer, and score the tests. Therefore, the bulk of this chapter focuses on helping prospective and experienced teachers improve their skills in these areas.

Your responsibility for testing can be the most unpleasant role you will have, or it can be an important, meaningful part of your teaching, depending on your level of expertise in this area. Frankly, few teachers take full advantage of how a good testing program can help their teaching. Fielding and Shaughnessy (1990, p. 90) say, "The gap between the potential of testing as a teaching-learning tool and the reality of current practice is wide." This chapter is concerned with teacher-made tests.

Curriculum Alignment and Authentic Tests

Increased pressures on teachers to have their students score well on standardized tests cause teachers to think about how and what they teach. Accountability for their students' performance on these tests motivates teachers to explore ways of helping students perform better. Paradoxically, those who hold teachers accountable for students' performance are often the same critics who accuse teachers of teaching to the test. What do they expect teachers to do, teach one set of content and activities and test for another? Such behavior is completely illogical.

Faced with the choice between (1) ignoring the tests, thereby risking poor student performance, and (2) feeling guilty about teaching to the test, middle-level teachers have another alternative, a very good one. They can plan their curriculum so that it fits the evaluation and then design their learning activities accordingly. Fenwick English (1992) calls this process curriculum alignment. Popham (2001) distinguishes between the reprehensive practice of using test items (either the exact or similar items to those on the test), a practice he has labeled *item-teaching*, and the appropriate, acceptable practice of directing teaching to the curriculum, which he has labeled *curriculum-teaching*. The big difference is that the former focuses on words used on the test, which the students can memorize without understanding, and the latter aims at getting the students to understand the major concepts in the lessons.

Education reformers frequently use the word *alignment* to pressure teachers to direct their curriculum toward national or state standards. Kohn (2001) warns teachers to be aware of this tactic: "That's why we should react with caution, if not alarm to the word alignment. The dictates to which we are supposed to be aligning the curriculum are often pedagogically suspect, and the motive for doing so may have more to do with compliance than with what is in the best interests of children" (p. 352).

Portfolios

Wiggins (1989) cautions that schools must adjust their graduation requirements to require the same skills that state tests require. Wiggins offers an example of a final exhibition of mastery required of seniors at a high school in Racine, Wisconsin (Figure 6.1). Note that these students are required to complete a portfolio. A **portfolio** is a combination of tangible products that provides evidence of the student's skills. Portfolios involve the students by having them select pieces of their work that they consider important and often requiring them to write about this work, explaining why it was worthy of selection (Keefe, 2002). It can serve the prospective teacher much as a commercial artist's portfolio shows the artist's skills in several related areas. Note that this portfolio requires a variety of products, such as writing, artwork, and oral performance. Such variety is a common strength of most portfolios. This portfolio requires the same skills as the goals required for high school graduation in Wisconsin. Because a portfolio is part of a student's curriculum, this quality makes this portfolio a good example of curriculum alignment. However, teachers should not assume that a portfolio is evidence that a high-quality assessment program is intact (Stiggins, 1997). There are good portfolios and bad portfolios. You must decide whether you want a working portfolio, a showcase portfolio, or a record-keeping portfolio (Gallagher, 1998).

Former Texas Teacher of the Year Sandra Parks Gifford says, "Evaluation is necessary for growth of both students and educators, but a test is not the most important instrument for evaluation. A portfolio of student work or teacher accomplishments has more validity" (quoted in Henson & Eller, 1999). Portfolios can serve several functions, but only if their purposes are clear to the teacher and students (Wilcox & Tomei, 1999). Barton and Collins (1993) explain the importance of clear portfolio objectives. The first characteristic of portfolio development is explicitness of purpose. Teachers by themselves and teachers and learn-

---

All seniors must complete a portfolio, a study project on U.S. history, and 15 oral and written presentations before a R.O.P.E. committee composed of staff, students, and an outside adult. Nine of the presentations are based on the materials in the portfolio and the project; the remaining six are developed for presentation before the committee. All seniors must enroll in a year long course designed to help them meet these requirements. The eight-part portfolio, developed in the first semester, is intended to be "a reflection and analysis of the senior's own life and times." The requirements include:
- A written autobiography,
- A reflection on work (including a resume)
- An essay on ethics
- A written summary of coursework in science
- An artistic product or a written report on art (including an essay on artistic standards used in judging artwork)

FIGURE 6.1 THE RITE OF PASSAGE EXPERIENCE (R.O.P.E.) AT WALDEN III, RACINE, WISCONSIN

From Wiggins, G. (1989, April). Teaching to the authentic test. *Educational Leadership*, 46(7), 4–47. Used by permission of the Association for Supervision and Curriculum Development. Copyright © 1989 by ASCO. All rights reserved.

ers together must explicitly define purposes of the portfolio so that learners know what is expected of them before they begin developing their evidence file (p. 202).

The project in Figure 6.1 is a research paper on a topic of the student's choosing in U.S. history. The student is questioned orally about the paper in the presentations before the committee during the second semester. The presentations include oral tests on previous work as well as six additional presentations on the essential subject areas and "personal proficiency" (e.g., life skills, setting and realizing personal goals). The presentations before the committee usually last an hour, with most students averaging about six separate appearances to complete all fifteen. A diploma is awarded to those students who pass twelve of the fifteen presentations and meet district requirements in math, government, reading, and English.*

This sample portfolio program emphasizes writing: writing about science, writing about history, writing about ethics, and writing about art. Perrone (1994) considers the role of writing across the curriculum so important to portfolios that he says, "If students are not regularly writing across a variety of topics and in a variety of styles for diverse purposes, then promoting self-evaluation has limited value" (p. 13).

The same can be said of having students reflect on the content in the portfolio. Effectiveness with portfolios requires continuous reflection by their owners (Van Wagenen & Hibbard, 1998; Wilcox, 1998). Portfolio builders should include samples of their good work, but they must also include samples of their owner's "bad" and "ugly" work, so the students can see the progress they have made (Van Wagenen & Hibbard, 1998). Improvement, then, is enhanced by continuous reflection and self-assessment.

Another example of curriculum alignment is an oral history project for ninth graders designed by Albin Moser at Hope High School, Providence, Rhode Island (Figure 6.2). This project has two outstanding strengths: It requires the student to reflect and to be creative.

Tests designed to help students to develop those skills measured by standardized tests are called **authentic tests**. "Authentic assessment seeks to engage students by situating problems and tasks in real-world contexts" (Postner & Rudnitsky, 1994, p. 96). Keefe and Jenkins (2002) say that "Assessment is authentic when it focuses on real performance and mastery of a field of knowledge. . . . Tests are only one form of assessment. Assessment goes beyond testing and includes such activities as demonstration, oral and written presentations, performances, contests, projects, and problem-solving activities" (p. 447). As shown in Chapter 1, the National Middle School Association (See Jenkins & Jenkins, 1991) included in their priority goals list the need to engage in cooperative problem solving: "Collaboration and cooperative problem solving [should] replace competition as the driving philosophy of middle level instruction" (NMSA, 1990). This means asking some new types of questions: Are my students' educational needs being met? What information and information-gathering skills will they need to excel when they leave school? How can I put my students in charge of gathering this new information and developing these much-needed information-gathering skills? How can I help them plan their learning and then supervise the process so that they understand the major concepts throughout and across the disciplines? How can I assess their learning when many of each student's educational goals may be unique? How can I shift much of the responsibility to the students and then shape my new role to let me become a learner again? What are their social and emotional needs? Erb (1997) reminds us that, "While the public and legislators may be mandating evaluation only

---

*This summary is paraphrased from both the R.O.P.E. Student Handbook and an earlier draft of Archbald and Newmann's *Beyond Standardized Testing* (1988).

> To the student:
> You must complete an oral history based on interviews and written sources and then present your findings orally in class. The choice of subject matter is up to you. Some examples of possible topics include: your family, running a small business, substance abuse, a labor union, teenage parents, and recent immigrants. Create three workable hypotheses based on your preliminary investigations and four questions you will ask to test out each hypothesis.
>
> **Criteria for Evaluation of Oral History Project**
>
> *To the teacher:*
> Did student investigate three hypotheses?
> Did student describe at least one change over time?
> Did student demonstrate that he or she had done background research?
> Were the four people selected for the interviews appropriate sources?
> Did student prepare at least four questions in advance, related to each hypothesis?
> Were those questions leading or biased?
> Were follow-up questions asked where possible, based on answers?
> Did student note important differences between "fact" and "opinion" in answers?
> Did student use evidence to prove the ultimate best hypothesis?
> Did student exhibit organization in writing and presentation to class?
>
> Note: This example is courtesy of Albin Moser, Hope High School, Providence, Rhode Island. To obtain a thorough account of a performance-based history course, including the lessons used and pitfalls encountered, write to Dave Kobrin, Brown University, Education Department, Providence, RI 02912.

FIGURE 6.2 AN ORAL HISTORY PROJECT FOR NINTH GRADERS

From Wiggins, G. (1989, April). Teaching to the authentic test. *Educational Leadership, 47*(7), 44. Used by permission of the Association of Supervision and Curriculum Development. Copyright © 1989 by ASCD. All rights reserved.

in academic areas, success there can only come if the young adolescents we teach are socially and emotionally healthy as well" (p. 2).

> **Reflection**
>
> Examine the history portfolio project in Figure 6.1 and the oral history project in Figure 6.2. Make a list of the qualities you like in these projects. Using the qualities, create a project in your discipline. Design some goals and write some test items that are aligned with this project.

Students remain the central foundation for building a curriculum model. Paramount middle school concerns include students' abilities, how they learn, and how they are motivated. Concern for content is as important as ever, but students must learn how to evaluate the information and identify what they must know. These human and subject matter issues must be at least partially resolved before students and teachers can move to the next step and determine how modern technology can help meet these needs. All this is a prerequisite to the selection of hardware and software. This holistic view focused on students' various needs is a Carnegie goal for middle-level education.

Assessment refers to the purposeful collection of data from a variety of sources (Gallagher, 1998) or to the process of gathering information about students (Keefe & Jenkins, 2002). Through continuous self-assessment or keeping an ongoing record of their own progress, students can fill the gaps in their own learning. Furthermore, by including a variety of self-assessment techniques such as drawings, charts, and diagrams, students can move from concrete to symbolic or abstract thinking (Phillips, et al., 1994). Some students find assessing their own performance difficult, yet with their teacher's help, students can learn to evaluate their performance and often enjoy it. Simmons (1994) explains:

> Some students are reluctant to engage in peer and self-assessment because they feel that such activities are the teacher's—the expert's—job and that their own work will ultimately suffer from their own or their peers' assessment. Yet, we have seen in our work that when students and teachers set forth criteria and use them as a basis for reflection on student work, both groups are often surprised at the positive outcomes. (p. 23)

Types of Tests

Before you begin constructing tests, remember that there are many types of tests and you have many options. For many years, U.S. educators have been predisposed to written tests. The practice of using written tests may have been so strongly embedded in your own teachers that when you hear the word "test" you think of a pencil-and-paper exercise.

However, there are alternatives. Teachers can choose simply to ask questions orally to solicit oral responses, or they can give a performance test that requires students to perform exercises, such as role playing in a drama class, assembling an engine in an auto mechanics class, or responding in dialogue in a foreign language class. Concern that written tests too frequently measure only the recall of knowledge, ignoring the student's ability to apply it, has prompted greater use of oral and performance options. Most teacher-made tests are of the pencil-and-paper variety. As we examine several types of written tests, keep in mind their potentials and limitations for measuring different student competencies.

Essay versus Objective Tests

When choosing to use a written test, decide whether it will be an objective test or an essay-type test, or possibly a combination. The two types differ drastically in many ways. First, the essay test measures what students know, whereas the objective test is often accused of measuring what students do not know. The essay test does permit students to select from and use their own knowledge in the response. By contrast, the objective test (true–false, matching, and multiple-choice) does not provide this freedom. In fact, the objective test can leave students thinking that they understand the lesson but the test questions just happened to be from less familiar areas.

Most important, the essay test is flexible enough to give students opportunities to express their own views—to reach beyond the recall level into the application, analysis, synthesis, and evaluation levels and even into the affective domain. In addition, essay questions enable teachers to determine a student's thought processes. The essay format is especially useful for assessing how students reach and explain their conclusions. Armstrong, Henson, and Savage (2004) remind teachers to consider students' background characteristics and use essay items to meet them: "Ideally, assessment procedures should take into account background characteristics that typify many minority group members."

Essay Tests

Of all types of test items, the essay question is perhaps the most misused. When questions are stated broadly, such as "Discuss Shakespeare's work" or "Discuss the Industrial Revolution," students wonder, "Where should I begin?" and "What issues am I supposed to address?" By carefully restricting the question, you can reduce the ambiguity—for example, "Discuss the types of humor in Shakespeare's *Twelfth Night*," or "Discuss the role of Eli Whitney's cotton gin in the Industrial Revolution." By sharpening essay questions' focus, you also simplify your scoring. The more exactly you state your expectations, the more accountable your students become for including expected content in their answers. By giving an example, you further clarify your expectations—for example, the question, "Discuss the role of Eli Whitney's cotton gin in the Industrial Revolution" could be followed by "Address its effect on the labor market."

Explanation Tests

Good questions on explanation tests focus on a certain process—for example, "Explain the water cycle." Because the water cycle involves a definite sequence of activities (e.g., rain—runoff—evaporation—condensation), students can be held accountable for a specific body of knowledge, plus the sequences involved in the process. When using explanation questions, avoid general questions such as "Explain the civil rights movement of the 1960s." Stated that way, the question is at best just a discussion and would be better worded as such.

Situation Tests

Situation test items measure a student's response to a certain situation. Students are asked to apply their knowledge, values, and judgment to decide how they would respond to a given set of circumstances. For example, the teacher of a first-aid course might ask, "If you were driving down the road and came to an accident that had left a person lying in the road unconscious and breathing heavily, what would you do?" Like other types of essay questions, situation questions are best when they request a definite body of knowledge. They also require students to apply that knowledge. Can you explain why the use of situation test items is a constructivist practice?

Compare and Contrast

Questions that ask students to compare or contrast force them to sharpen their understanding about similar or dissimilar concepts. In other words, they require students to differentiate between two or more concepts by focusing on particular similar or dissimilar qualities—for example, "Compare and contrast World War I with World War II." You can get more specific answers by adding limits to the question: "Compare and contrast World War I with World War II according to their ground strategies, air strategies, number of casualties, and number of countries involved."

Objective Tests

Some popular types of questions found on objective tests include true–false, multiple-choice, and matching. Less common is the fill-in-the-blank question. Each type calls for a specific, predetermined answer. Objective test items are often criticized for testing what students do not know rather than what they do know. Furthermore, they tend to encourage guessing. In addition, the advantage of their objectivity and easily accomplished scoring leads to one of their major limitations, namely, the trivialization of the knowledge tested. The concise, clearly delimited response is emphasized; critical thinking, analytical skills, and conceptualization are all but ignored. Multiple-choice and fill-in responses are preferred; exposition and creativity are penalized.

A study for the National Center for Education Statistics—Special Study Panel on Education Indicators for the National Center for Education Statistics (1991)—identifies some weaknesses of traditional tests used to measure schools' success, noting the limitations of multiple-choice tests. Note the differences in trends of future testing:

> *The panel wants to point out that most national assessments rely heavily on multiple-choice formats. Obviously, such tests have their uses. However, education and learning are complicated endeavors, and the panel believes the effort to assess the results must be equal to the task. "Authentic," "alternative," and "performance" are all terms applied to emerging assessment techniques.*
>
> *Whatever name they go by, their common denominator is that they call on students to apply their thinking and reasoning skills to generate often-elaborate responses to the problems put before them. In many of these testing situations, there are multiple "correct" answers; in almost none of them is the student forced to select from a list of prespecified multiple-choice alternatives. Extended writing assignments, hands-on science assessments, student portfolios, and group projects over time are the next generation of tests that will assess a new generation of Americans." (pp. 69–70)*

Objective tests do have certain advantages over essay tests. First, they are more quickly scored. This is important to today's teachers, who would better invest time in preparing lessons than in scoring tests. Furthermore, objective questions are likely to be more fairly scored because there is no doubt about whether an answer is correct. This too is an important advantage, since most teachers want their students to perceive them as fair and impartial.

The Purpose of Testing

Is testing necessary? What are its advantages? Could these advantages be achieved some other way? How does testing assist the instructional program? How can I improve my own testing program? When we think of testing, we think of grades. But if we say that the purpose of testing is to determine grades, another good question is, "Why do we need grades?" Justifying tests merely as grade determiners is not sufficient; many educators are not convinced that grades are necessary.

Testing helps your students determine their general rate of progress in a specific subject. DeRoma et al. (at press) reported on three studies that found that teachers who give regular quizzes have higher academic performance in their classes. This information is important to both the student and you. And to report a grade—which most school systems require and most parents expect if not demand—you must know the student's general rate of progress. When students know their rate of achievement, they can be motivated or encouraged to achieve even more (Stiggins, 1997).

Testing also helps you determine the class's progress as a whole. The rate of progress in teaching is always proportional to the class's learning rate. In other words, your teaching cannot be better than your students' learning. Test results can help you identify areas where you must improve your methodology and clarify misunderstandings in the classroom—that is, where to slow down, where to repeat more, or where to use different methods. Testing also provides a way to diagnose teacher and student strengths and weaknesses. Through testing, you can help students identify areas that need more effort. Weekly quizzes have been found to have more power to increase learning than homework assignments (Tuckman, 1996).

Recognize the test as a tool for helping you improve your methodology and for helping your students improve listening and study habits. Then construct, administer, and evaluate tests with these purposes in mind.

Recognize also that your use of tests should not be piecemeal but should be a continuous, connected program to help your students develop to their maximum knowledge, attitudinal, and performance potential. This program should be flexible enough to be altered to meet our students' needs, which themselves will change as the students grow intellectually, emotionally, socially, and physically. You, like your students, should view your students on a point in their developmental paths. You should build your curriculum and thus your assessment program on the previous curriculum and experience of your students.

As your students grow, their capacities for performing activities should also grow and, therefore, the quality of their performance should grow. Thus, you should keep in mind that your students should be given repeated opportunities to perform activities and tests. Use your school's terminal expectations for your students to guide your development of tests. In other words, each test and each test item should be aligned to your course objectives and ultimately to your school's expectations of its graduates.

Finally, your testing should also be aligned with your teaching. The following is a discussion to help guide your construction of tests. As you read it, remember that your tests should be a natural outgrowth of your teaching. As you will see, the results of your testing must also reshape your planning, which in turn will continuously reshape your teaching.

Test Construction

If you experience mild shock when grading your first set of test papers, do not immediately question your teaching ability. Many teachers argue that the topic of test construction has not been addressed sufficiently in undergraduate teacher training programs and that they need programs to help them develop, manage, and provide practice for evaluation. Many teachers are unable to recognize what skill a particular test item was testing. Preservice teacher training often fails to include a course on testing, and assessment is rarely a topic for inservice training (Stiggins, 1985). Realizing that most of the fault is not in the teaching but in the testing, you may ask: How can I construct good tests?

The Directions

Begin each test with a written statement explaining how to complete the test. Like all assignments, make the directions specific. For example:

> Each item on this test is worth one point. Select the single choice you believe is best. Do not leave questions blank, and do not mark more than one choice. If you have questions, please raise your hand and I will come to your desk. When you finish, please turn your paper face down on your desk and begin working quietly on the assignment now written on the board.

Once you have written the test, check it for any ambiguity or possible misinterpretation, making changes and clarifying accordingly. Include in the directions the maximum time allotted students for taking the test. Clear directions will prevent unnecessary interruptions during the testing period and will prevent the discomfort students feel when they are not sure what is being asked of them.

State the Value of Each Question

Most teachers find it convenient to specify or assign values to questions in terms of percentages. Assign relative values, asking yourself how much each question is worth in relation to the other questions. Make the value of each question proportional to the amount of class time spent on that topic and the amount of test time required to answer that question.

Often a test will consist of several short-answer questions or short problems that carry equal value. On such tests, do not specify separate values; merely state in the directions that each question has equal value. On tests with questions of varying values, specify the value of each question in the margin alongside the question.

Select a Variety of Questions

Which type of question is best—objective or subjective? Actually, each type offers advantages that the other does not, so most tests should contain both objective and subjective questions. Objective questions require more time to construct, but they require less time to answer and to score, so many objective questions can be included on each test. Subjective questions can measure creativity and allow students to express their feelings and attitudes; they also show how well students can organize their thoughts.

Many testing experts believe that multiple-choice questions are the best type of objective questions. True–false questions are seen to be of average value, and fill-in-the-blank questions are the least valuable. Do use several types of objective questions, however, because students who find one type of question especially difficult to answer will not be penalized by having an entire test of that type. Multiple-choice and other types of test questions are discussed later in this chapter.

Include Both Easy and Difficult Questions

Remember that a goal of middle-level education is to ensure success for all students. Every test should have some questions so easy that almost every student can answer them correctly. Begin the test with the less difficult questions to encourage each student to go on to the following questions. Placing easy questions at the beginning of multiple-choice examinations has increased test scores significantly. Remember that tests should measure ability, not tolerance. Avoid placing a 40-point question at the end of the test. Slower students will think it is unfair if they fail the test because time ran out just as they began answering a last question that is worth that many points.

If every question on a test were so easy that every student could answer it correctly, the test would be of little use. Include some questions that challenge even the most capable students. Make each question a little more difficult than the preceding question, but never try to make the question difficult by wording it so it is vague, too general, or tricky. The difficult questions should be difficult because they are especially challenging and involve a complex process, and they should measure students' attainment of important concepts.

Cover Important Material

Most teachers believe it is necessary to test at least once every two weeks. From the large volume of material covered in this time span, what should you include on the test? A good rule is that any test should contain questions about information covered each day of the testing period. In other words, it should begin testing where the previous test stopped and should test right up through the day preceding the test date.

Ideally, the time spent studying various areas of content should be in proportion to the material's importance. Therefore, the percentage of time studying an area should be proportional to the percentage of the test that the particular area comprises. For example, if, in a unit on astronomy, the class spent a week studying the sun and only one day studying the moon, the total value of test questions about the sun should be about five times as great as the total value of questions about the moon.

Testing the Test

Many teachers insist on taking a test themselves before administering it (Mather, 2000). In addition to catching typographical errors and ambiguously worded questions, the teacher can at the same time develop a master answer sheet. Without a list of answers when beginning to score a test, a teacher tends to accept the first students' answers and to use these as a standard for judging the accuracy of the answers on the other students' papers.

Writing Test Questions

Selecting the Type of Test

Upon completing a unit of study—or, as we shall see, even during a unit—the teacher must decide when to give an examination and then either design the right type of questions or select the right type of ready-made examination. Base both decisions—when to measure and what type of test to use—on the test's purpose. Essay questions measure some skills best, whereas objective questions are more suitable for measuring other skills. Let us look at the more commonly used types of test questions and some advantages and limitations of each. The suggestions for improving the questions should be of particular interest.

Essay Questions

Although all test questions fall into two categories—subjective or objective—the subjective, or essay, question is a type of its own. Essay questions have some important limitations. First, they are difficult to control. Actually, they require the teacher to relinquish some control, because students are free to answer (and actually must do so) in terms of their own perspectives. Teacher empowerment is an important Carnegie goal for middle-level teachers. Ironically, by shifting responsibility to students, teachers empower both their students and themselves. This leads to another problem—scoring. You must decide whether to count such variables as

- Ability to focus on the teacher's perspective
- Writing and spelling skills
- General neatness
- Comprehensiveness
- Specific facts and concepts
- Broad generalizations
- Creativity
- Attitudes
- Logical reasoning
- Other skills outside the knowledge category, such as the ability to synthesize or evaluate

Resolve these uncertainties before giving the test to avoid potential disagreements between you and your students. To avoid this risk, you may want to avoid essay or discussion tests in favor of more specific, objective tests. But first consider the advantages of essay questions.

Essay-type questions excel in their ability to let students express themselves. In responding to an essay question, students can be as creative, imaginative, and expressive as they wish; furthermore, they can state and evaluate their own beliefs and values. This is especially important for two reasons. First, evaluation is the highest known level of thinking (according to Bloom's taxonomy of educational objectives, as seen in Chapter 4). Second, when responding to test questions, students often want to express their own beliefs and justify their responses. Members of some minority cultures have an exaggerated need to express themselves, a need that is seldom met by schools.

Writing Essay Questions

Structure each essay question to emphasize the ideas the student should address. This will minimize the difference between teacher and student perceptions of expectations. Following are examples of good and bad essay test items.

    A. Discuss the causes of the Revolutionary War.

How would you respond to this question? What is wrong with it? You probably would not know where to begin, because the question is far too general. Suppose it were rewritten to read:

    B. Name and discuss three main causes of the Revolutionary War.

Now the question lets you know you are expected to cover three main causes, but it is still a monumental and time-consuming task. You could not ask more than two or three questions of this type on any test. A test should reflect the complete range of material covered in class since the previous test. Suppose the question is altered further, as seen in sample C:

    C. Name and discuss three economic factors that contributed to the development of the Revolutionary War.

Now the scope of the question has been limited drastically. The student can immediately eliminate the many political and social factors. By making the question more specific, you reduce its ambiguity and limit the scope of responses the question will elicit. But because discussion questions offer the teacher a unique opportunity to stimulate students to think independently and creatively, you probably will want to include at least one question designed for that purpose. An example of such a question is sample D:

    D. Suppose England had won the war. What changes would have occurred in the U.S. lifestyle?

This question gives students the opportunity to use divergent thinking—that is, it requires them to expand their thoughts by using their imaginations. Therefore it is of a higher order than the previous questions. Note, though, that it requires you as teacher to give up much of your ability to regulate or restrict student responses. In a class of thirty students, this question would probably elicit thirty different responses and create problems in scoring the answer. For this reason, before asking such a question, be sure that the question will measure imagination and creativity; these two considerations would count heavily in determining a grade for this question.

Take the time to word questions very carefully so they will achieve their objectives. You will save time in scoring essay answers if you structure questions unambiguously. To be sure, wording and scoring good essay questions are not easy; they require time and thought. The quality of the responses you get will probably correlate highly with the amount of time you spend on the questions.

Scoring Essay Questions

A good approach to assigning values to each part of a response is to take the test yourself before administering it. Then you can assign credit for each part of the expected response according to the respective values. For example, consider sample question D:

D. Suppose England had won the war. What changes would have occurred in the U.S. lifestyle?

Assume that the classroom discussion or textbooks and other materials included such concepts as more rigid tariffs, lower prices, and worsening labor conditions. Each concept could receive 2 points' credit. Other reasonable responses could receive 1 point each, making the question's total value 9 or 10 points.

Consider at least two important considerations in determining how much value to assign to each test item. First, consider the amount of time and emphasis given to this item in class and in homework. Does this item reflect one or more class objectives? "The items on the test should be similar to the instructional objectives" (Griswold, 1990, p. 19). Simply stated, test items should be weighted (or assigned a value) according to the importance of the content being measured.

Second, consider the amount of time required to respond to items. The grade value that items are assigned should approximate the percentage of time required to answer the question. Once you have decided how many points to assign each question, sequence the items so that the ones that count the most are at the beginning of the test. Should you place these items near the end of the test, some students might run out of time before getting to them by spending too much time on questions of lesser grade value.

Multiple-Choice Questions

Multiple-choice questions are popular today, partly because machine scoring is increasingly available, but also because the questions themselves have merit. Like true–false and fill-in-the-blank tests, a multiple-choice test enables the teacher to ask many questions and thus cover many topics on the same test. Unlike true–false and fill-in-the-blank tests, however, the multiple-choice test restricts the amount of success derived by guessing. Multiple-choice items seem best suited to bringing out the finer distinctions between what is good, what is best, and what represents loose thinking, if not downright error. However, this advantage is realized only when the teacher designs each test question appropriately. Keep in mind also that tests should be used to help students learn. When correctly written, the multiple-choice test can become an excellent learning device.

Like all other types of tests, select the multiple-choice test on its merits—that is, on its ability to achieve specific goals. Then design it to achieve those goals. If its purpose is formative (to promote learning), design it one way; if its purpose is to determine student success (summative), design it differently. We shall look at specific designs for specific purposes, but first let us answer some general questions that you might have about developing multiple-choice tests.

How Many Alternatives Should I Include?

It is wise to include at least four choices, and five may be desirable if the test is intended to promote learning. Should I include among the alternatives "all of the above" and "none of the above"? Because "all of the above" enables one to measure knowledge about the question, it is a legitimate option. Because "none of the above" does not enable the student to relate specifically to the question, avoid it (Ellsworth, Donnell, & Duell, 1990). The last alternative could be more wisely used to include a concept related to the material being tested.

How Should I Phrase the Stem of a Multiple-Choice Question?

First, keep it brief. Avoid using more than one sentence, lest a student trip on the question itself. Second, avoid negatives in the stem. Both unnecessary length and negatives tend to confuse and interrupt the thought process. Write a test question so that it communicates as clearly as possible; see the following examples.

E. All isosceles triangles
   a. Have at least two equal sides
   b. Have at least two unequal angles
   c. Have at least three equal sides
   d. Have at least three equal angles

Item E could be simplified as follows:

E. All isosceles triangles have at least
   a. Two equal sides
   b. Two unequal angles
   c. Three equal sides
   d. Three equal angles

Now consider item F:

F. Which of the following is not an example of sedimentary rock?
   a. Limestone
   b. Sandstone
   c. Chert
   d. All of the above

Item F should be changed to read as follows:

F. An example of igneous rock is
   a. Limestone
   b. Sandstone
   c. Chert
   d. All of the above

How Should I Select the Alternatives?

If you are designing the test to promote learning, purposely include several closely related alternatives. If the purpose of the test is grading, reduce the number of near-correct answers to only one or two. For all answers to be almost acceptable is unduly taxing and might result in teacher preference as opposed to student preference. A question with only one attractive answer is equally poor design. It does not promote learning or thinking and therefore does not discriminate between those who have mastered the material and those who have not. Examine items G, H, and I and for each question identify at least one major flaw. Then rewrite each to eliminate those flaws.

G. Alexander Graham Bell invented the
   a. Cotton gin
   b. Telegraph
   c. Radio
   d. All of the above
   e. None of the above

H. Water is not an example of a
   a. Liquid
   b. Solution
   c. Fluid
   d. Compound
   e. Base

I. The Pilgrims began arriving in America in the early 1630s. Some came by way of Holland; others came directly from the port of Southampton in England. The real reason for their coming was to
   a. Escape persecution
   b. Seek freedom of religion for all
   c. Form a new denomination
   d. All of the above

The obvious error in item G is the alternative "none of the above." Correct the question simply by eliminating the fifth choice. The stem of question H contains a negative. Correct the question by deleting the "not" and changing the choices. The stem of item I is unnecessarily long. Correct it by eliminating the first two sentences.

What Other Common Errors Can I Avoid?

Some multiple-choice questions give the correct answer unintentionally. Items J and K make this mistake. See if you can identify which part leads the student to the correct answer. Then rewrite the question to avoid the error.

J. A well-known French psychologist is
   a. Wilburn Smith
   b. Robert O. Williams
   c. Jean Piaget
   d. Warner Hayes
   e. Sam Jones

K. The nickel is an example of an
   a. Alloy
   b. Solution
   c. Compound
   d. Metal

L. The speed of light is
   a. 100 feet/sec
   b. 100 miles/hr
   c. 120 miles/hr
   d. 186,000 miles/sec

Item J leads the student to select an alternative based on grounds other than knowledge about psychologists. In item K, the use of the word "an" suggests the correct answer; incidentally, the alternative being sought in item K is not the only correct alternative provided. In summative tests, take care not to include more than one correct answer. Test item L is poor because it fails to include a strong distracter (a plausible or near-correct choice).

Fill-in-the-Blank Questions

Although the fill-in-the-blank question can boast no real strengths, it has managed to survive throughout the history of U.S. schools. Not only does this type of question limit the teacher to measuring only knowledge (or recall)-level information, it seldom achieves this with any degree of accuracy. The fill-in-the-blank question often puts the student in the impossible position of trying to guess what the teacher wants. Mastering the material does not guarantee success on this type of test.

Nevertheless, the fill-in-the-blank test appeals to many teachers because it can be developed quickly and effortlessly. (This does not reflect the way it should be developed, but merely the way it often is developed.) Some teachers lift sentences right out of the text and print them verbatim on the test, substituting a blank for one or more words. Item M is an example of a typical fill-in-the-blank question. How would you answer it? Can you modify it to eliminate its ambiguity?

M. The Battle of New Orleans was fought in _____.

This type of question unintentionally invites the imagination to run wild. A creative student might respond with New Orleans, the rain, winter, anger, or mud, blood, and beer. An infinite number of correct answers is possible and should be given full credit, but the student need not know anything about the Battle of New Orleans to respond correctly. Other students may become discouraged over the ambiguity and leave the space blank, thereby getting penalized for the teacher's failure to communicate clearly.

Although you would usually be wise to choose another type of question, suppose you want to test for highly technical or specific factual information. When written properly, the fill-in-the-blank question can achieve this. A teacher writing item M to test for the date of the beginning of the battle need only insert "the year _____" that is, "The Battle of New Orleans was fought in the year _____."

N. Tests are more _____ than are _____ tests.

This kind of question can be even more frustrating to students than single-completion items.

In conclusion, avoid fill-in-the-blank tests when other types of tests will achieve your objectives. If you do use them, remember that being specific is the key to designing good questions.

Matching Test Items

Most teachers use matching tests at some time or another. This type of test enables you to measure students' ability to make important associations. Its value is apparent from the number of national standardized tests that test for the examinee's ability to make associations, ranging from the picture association game on *Sesame Street* to the Miller Analogy Test (MAT) that many college graduate programs use.

Matching tests are not easy to construct. Take care to avoid using a stimulus that matches more than one response. An examiner wishing to have students use a stimulus more than once should inform them that they may use the same number or letter in their answers repeatedly. For example, in item O, stimulus number 1 would fit in both responses A and D.

O. Stimulus   Response
   1. Noun   _____A. Water   _____E. Slowly
   2. Verb   _____B. Blue   _____F. Her
   3. Adjective   _____C. Fishing   _____G. Into
   4. Pronoun   _____D. Moon
   5. Adverb

Note also that in item O the number of responses exceeds the number of stimuli. This is to discourage guessing. Another important precaution in writing matching items is to avoid giving hints. Item P illustrates such carelessness in item writing.

P. Match the dates with the corresponding events.
   1. 1861   A. Signing of the Magna Charta
   2. 1812   B. Beginning of the Civil War
   3. 1776   C. Storming of the Bastille
   4. 1215   D. Signing of the Declaration of Independence
   5. 1918   E. War of 1812
                    F. Cardinal Principles of Secondary Education

Obviously, "War of 1812" is a dead giveaway. Avoid such matches on matching tests because they fail to measure any level of understanding.

Higher-Level Questions: Cognitive Domain

Returning to Bloom's taxonomy of educational *objectives,* discussed in Chapter 2, we find that the major areas in the cognitive domain are

Level 1:   Knowledge
Level 2:   Comprehension
Level 3:   Application
Level 4:   Analysis
Level 5:   Synthesis
Level 6:   Evaluation

Most types of objective questions discussed so far have been limited to measuring the retention of information, but this does not mean such test items as multiple-choice and matching cannot be designed to test for higher levels of understanding. Do not conclude that only discussion-type questions can measure higher levels of understanding. Each type of question can be used to measure different levels of all three learning domains. The following examples show prospective teachers, student teachers, and experienced teachers at least one way of designing questions to measure understanding at each level.

THE CASE

Assessment and Teaming: Meeting Everyone's Expectations

Chuck Watson, James Madison University

Jacqueline Beliveau

Mary Nelsen

Charles Watson has been involved in teaching, education, and school improvement for over thirty years. He has been a middle school math and science teacher, an administrator, and is currently an associate professor of education at James Madison University (JMU) and Director of the JMU School of Education. He teaches courses in science education and methods, teacher leadership, and assessment. His areas of expertise and research are middle-level education, science education, curriculum alignment and integration, educational reform and improvement, parent involvement in schools, rural education, and school leadership. He has worked with schools and teams of teachers and administrators in the areas of middle-level education and school improvement in many states, especially throughout the Appalachian area and the eastern United States. He has published in the area of instructional practice, curriculum models, and curriculum alignment and improvement. He holds degrees in business administration, school counseling, and a doctorate in educational leadership.

Jacqueline Beliveau graduated from James Madison University with a B.S. in psychology and a M.Ed. in middle education. Jackie is currently in her fourth year of teaching at Glasgow Middle School in Fairfax County, Virginia. She teaches sixth grade math and reading. Jackie has presented at the local, state, and national levels on the topics of diversity, beginning teaching, technology, and language arts and math integration.

Mary Nelsen is a sixth-grade language arts teacher at Glasgow Middle School in Fairfax County, Virginia. Mary has been teaching for four years. Mary attended James Madison University, where she received a B.S. in psychology and a M.Ed. in middle education. Mary has presented at various state and national conferences on the topics of beginning teaching, diversity in the classroom, technology, and language arts and math integration.

Introduction

Middle school teachers and interdisciplinary teams in schools blessed with very diverse student bodies face both common and unique problems and challenges when trying to integrate curriculum. In an age of high-stakes testing, multiple sets of standards, curriculum mandates, and public scrutiny, it is often hard for middle school teachers to advocate for and use multidisciplinary approaches. Middle school teachers of diverse students find the challenges even more daunting when students have difficulty with the English language, come from poor or low-income homes, face daily social and environmental challenges, or have other learning difficulties. And in many states, these students are also required to pass state-mandated tests.

This case study presents a situation in which middle school teachers and administrators face all of these problems and yet are having notable, and in some cases astonishing, results, both in terms of student achievement and in terms of using multidisciplinary approaches.

The School

Glasgow Middle School is located in the suburbs of Washington, D.C.; students attending Glasgow come from a wide variety of households, families, and communities. Students represent sixty-seven different countries and speak thirty-three different languages; about 30 percent of the nearly 1,200 students are classified as white, 37 percent as Hispanic, 12 percent as African American, and the remainder as either Native American or multiracial. It is indeed a diverse school culture, and there is no majority group. Over a hundred teachers are organized into interdisciplinary teams, and the school is fortunate to have a number of co-curricular programs to address the many needs of its students. The school has an active Gifted program that enrolls over a hundred students, an English as a Second Language (ESL) program, and a number of Special Education Resource Centers and programs. The interdisciplinary teams are further supported by teacher advisories, peer helping, peer mediation, and conflict resolution programs. The school has also implemented the International Baccalaureate Middle Years Program. Over 60 percent of Glasgow's students qualify for free or reduced-cost lunches.

Adding yet another level of difficulty for the teachers at Glasgow is the way in which the Commonwealth of Virginia ties school accreditation to test scores. To be accredited, 70 percent of the eighth-grade students must pass tests in the core subjects; to address this requirement, the school has implemented a revised set of mathematics curricula that prepares eighth-grade students for Algebra One—not an uncommon strategy in a high-stakes testing environment, but one that can place barriers to curriculum integration and thematic instruction. In addition, the school requires all eighth-grade students to take a foreign language. These factors place additional curricular burdens on the sixth- and seventh-grade teams, essentially driving some aspects of the curriculum downward through the grades.

The Team

The sixth-grade Galaxy team consists of four core subject teachers and three specialists who work with ESL and special needs students. The team consists of ninety heterogeneously grouped students who come to Glasgow with a wide range of reading, math, and language skills. The team is housed in what is fondly called "temporary-permanent" buildings connected to the older main structure. The four rooms are internally connected, and both teacher and student movement among the rooms is frequent, although at times distracting.

Even with these complicating factors, the notion of integrated curriculum and topics into large complex units of instruction is very attractive to the team, and is particularly attractive to Mary Nelson, the language arts teacher, and Jackie Beliveau the mathematics teacher, who have several years experience teaching together. These two teachers are skilled in working with students from diverse cultures and languages, and are also quite skilled at creating differentiated instructional activities to tailor learning outcomes to individual students and small groups of students. One of the more challenging aspects of their work, of course, is the difficulty their students face with speaking, reading, and using English properly.

The Unit

The instructional unit created by this team is simply called "Word Problems"—an intentional double entendre that is perhaps lost on the students, but clear to the teachers—that is, lost to the students because of the difficulties they face with the English language, they often struggle with comprehending mathematics instructions, word problems, standardized tests, and terminology. Mathematics is difficult content area material to read; it presents more concepts per word, sentence, and paragraph than other subjects; yet, research suggests that the mathematical achievement of children correlates highly with their ability to read mathematics (Siegel, 1989), and that reading skills are essential to mathematical problem solving (Tanner & Casados, 1998). Making this even more difficult is the reality that in English, many commonly used words have very different meanings in mathematics (sum, difference, dividend, side, product, sine, factor, mean, origin, etc.) than in common usage. Jackie had observed that the vast majority of her students often skipped over any reading in a mathematics textbook and immediately began trying to solve problems.

Jackie and Mary felt that an effective way to address this dual problem of limited English and reading in mathematics was to create an integrated unit that combined writing, vocabulary development, assessment, and mathematical terms. Specifically, their goals were to help their students understand mathematical concepts, ideas, and terms written in English, and to help students verbalize mathematical concepts in English.

The Approaches

The team used multiple approaches over a period of eight weeks. The primary approaches used were vocabulary units and games, math journals, and exit passes. Jackie and Mary met for several weeks planning and developing a workable, realistic unit that was both relevant to their students' needs and the need for their students to be prepared for the high-stakes tests they would be facing in the eighth grade.

Jackie and Mary created sets of vocabulary lists of words that have both a mathematics definition and "real-life" definition, and then created memory games to match the words and symbols—key to the success of the memory games was the use of the words both as pronounced and written. The games were used for short periods in both math classes and language arts classes, and the words were also used in conjunction with other language arts lessons and activities. Another method the team used to easily review terminology was through "zip-around cards." Zip-around is an oral activity in which one student describes a term or problem and the answer is found on another student's card. For example, student A says, "What is the sum of x plus 7, if x equals 2." Student B replies, "I have 9," and then proceeds with the question found on his card. The beauty of this game is that all students must be listening (especially if they are holding several cards), and they are practicing their oral language.

The math journals proved to be one of the most successful aspects of the unit. Daily "warm-up" activities are a normal part of each day's math class, and are recorded in students' math journals; these activities generally consist of a few problems to help "spiral" the curriculum—that is, the purpose is to help students see the connections and how mathematics concepts build on each other. Likewise, Mary, the language arts teacher, uses a similar process of journaling, incorporating most of the same words into these activities. During the unit, students are asked to create meaningful paragraphs in their journals, using as many of the vocabulary words as possible. For instance, if given words such as *analyze, statistics, tally, collect, title, data, display, frequency*, and the like, students can create a paragraph or short story about a student conducting a study of the various plants found around the school yard.

Mary uses the paragraphs in her class for such activities as peer editing, punctuation, and usage. Both teachers read the math journals and short paragraphs each day, and each teacher also writes short responses to the paragraphs. In another use of written work in journals, the teachers ask students to create "flip books" that describe mathematical procedures in words and then provide a numerical example. Flip books are shared with other students, thus reinforcing the proper use of mathematical terms. By using these approaches, the teachers are able to assess proper word usage and they are able to quickly ascertain certain understanding of mathematics concepts as well as any misuse of terms.

Exit passes, a commonly used form of short and direct classroom assessment and review, have also proved valuable. Exit passes often ask students to define a vocabulary word in the students' own words, alternating between common usage and mathematical usage. For example, one side of an exit pass might ask the student to write out the steps to be followed when solving an equation (without using any numbers), and the other side of the exit pass might have the same sort of problem or concept written out for students to solve. Other exit passes ask students for short responses to particular problems in which proper word usage is critical to solving the problem.

In order to more fully assess the degree of success of this type of unit and learning activities, the team conducted some additional evaluations. Using one of the district's instruments, the Entry Assessment Mathematics Evaluation for ESL Students (EAMES), the team found that at the end of the school year, nearly half of the students had gained up to two grade levels, with the remaining student group remaining at the same grade level. The team, however, felt that test scores did not reflect a true picture of the levels of understanding, especially regarding terminology. Therefore, they conducted additional assessments, using the math journals as well as anecdotal information from both math classes and language arts classes. The journal analyses revealed a significant improvement in the common and proper usage of mathematical terminology as a part of the continued journalizing done by students. That is, after the unit, the teachers found that students used mathematical and other terms properly as a matter of course; for example, Jackie found that there was significant improvement in the proper use of the words *product, numerator,* and *denominator,* and words used in the creation and usage of graphs and charts, such as *bar, display,* and *data* were more frequent. Mary found the same was true for the words and terms and their use in writing; that is, homophones, homonyms, and homographs were used properly and in contexts that made sense.

Finally, both Mary and Jackie found that many students who were previously embarrassed or afraid to respond to questions in class were now volunteering answers and asking many more questions, both orally and in written form. In one case, a shy and reserved Spanish-speaking student was asked the difference between a regular and an irregular polygon. He responded quickly and eagerly with "A regular polygon has equal sides and an irregular polygon has no equal sides." In another instance, a learning-disabled ESL student was asked if a circle was a polygon; the student replied, "No, because it doesn't have sides and no angle." For many teachers, these responses would not seem out of the ordinary, nor particularly eventful; however, in these cases, the students not only responded with correct answers, they responded with the proper terminology and using good English.

Expanding the Unit

Both Jackie and Mary are looking at ways to expand on this already successful unit and approach by incorporating graphic organizers, glossaries, and additional content reading into the unit. In addition, they are looking at better ways to assess and evaluate the effectiveness of the unit, both in mathematics and language arts.

The approach, however, again provides strong evidence that regardless of language ability, creating relevant, linked, and meaningful concepts and vocabulary, can lead to significant learning for all students.

Further Reflection

These teachers were able to address students' language needs by carefully planning games and activities into the curriculum. Their results were multiplied by using a team approach to develop integrated units.

Level 1: Knowledge

Since we are all familiar with questions that test only one's ability to recall facts, this first level need not be discussed.

Level 2: Comprehension

Charts, maps, graphs, and tables lend themselves well to measuring learning mastery at the comprehension level. Questions at this level should require the student to translate, interpret, or predict a continuation of trends. For example, Figure 6.3 shows the general sales ratio of a textbook during its first three years of publication. If a certain book has sold 10,000 copies in the first year and 30,000 copies by the end of a second year, how many copies can we estimate it will have sold by the end of a third year? Of course, a multiple-choice question could be written to use with this graph—for example:

Q. The total accumulated sales projected by the end of the third year are:
   a. 10,000
   b. 20,000
   c. 30,000
   d. 40,000

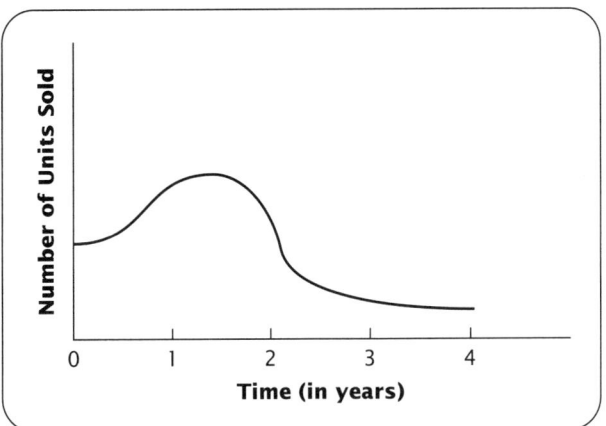

FIGURE 6.3 SALES RATIO OF TEXTBOOKS
From Kenneth T. Henson, *Methods and Strategies for Teaching in Secondary and Middle Schools*, third edition. Published by Allyn and Bacon, Boston, MA. Copyright © 1996 by Pearson Education. Reprinted by permission of the publisher.

Level 3: Application

Questions measuring the ability to think at the application level must require students to apply abstractions—such as general ideas, rules, and methods—to concrete situations. In other words, the student must use a principle or generalization to solve a new problem.

When students are taught concepts, they are seldom able to generalize from one situation to another. Stefanich (1990) addresses this concern:

Students tend to deal with concepts in isolation. They cannot effectively consider a number of isolated examples and apply these to general theory or principle. They cannot effectively apply a general principle to a number of instances or examples. They are unable to cognitively process variable time frames or situations which require simultaneous consideration of multiple characters or events. (p. 48)

The following example (Ward, 1969) is offered to clarify the process of generalizing:

You enter the old kitchen, in which there is a blazing hearth fire complete with bubbling, boiling teakettle. Oh, it's always there anyway; you've seen it before. Besides, your mind is on something else. Your quaint kitchen is pretty well tuned out by you, or you only perceive it at the (blob) level. Wait, something focuses your attention on the event system that is the boiling kettle. You've noticed. Now you're beginning to operate. You've noticed something, and something is happening. The lid jumps up and down. You wonder why. Ah, cause, the why sets you to scrutinizing relationships. First you attend, focus, observe, isolate. Next you want the cause of something. Establishing tentative cause gets you to infer a low-level generalization. 'That lid will move because steam is pushing it up and down. If that particular kettle is put on that fire and it boils, then its lid will jump up and down' a relatively low level of abstraction because the particulars of the scene are still involved. The next level of abstraction, of generalizations, will take you to a point of thinking, 'When a kettle is placed on a fire, the water will boil and cause a loose lid to move.' (p. 423)

You have gone from the particular to the general, although you are still involved with the category of tea kettles. Several levels of application are possible here. First, the student can match a principle with its correct corresponding situation, as in item Q.

R. Match each situation with the principle at play. Each stimulus may be used repeatedly.
   1. Radiation   A. A sea breeze
   2. Convection   B. An air conditioner
   3. Conduction   C. A kite
                      D. A heater
                      E. A hot coffee cup

A second level of application requires the student to restate a problem. For example, in the story of the tea kettle you might say that the problem at hand is to determine why the lid is moving. Given this situation and problem, ask students to state the problem without using the word *steam*. Still another level of application would require students to generalize to predict what will happen in a different situation involving the same principles. You might ask students a question, "Suppose the kettle lid were held fast and the spout were stopped up. What would happen when the kettle was placed on the stove?" (Caution: Do not try this experiment!)

There are other levels of application, but these examples show how you can arrange experiences or tasks that force students to perform at the application stage.

Level 4: Analysis

The analysis level requires breaking down generalizations, concepts, and principles to clarify ideas or understand them better. A common type of question for measuring at the analysis level gives the student one or more paragraphs to read and then a list of questions. These questions do not simply ask for retention (knowledge level) and the ability to predict patterns or trends (comprehension level); they require the student to identify the author's underlying assumptions.

For example, students might be asked to read the following parable on education taken from Plato's *Republic*. In the seventh book, which opens with a beautiful description of the nature of man confined in a dark cave, Plato proceeds to show the means and plan for learning true philosophy and how we may attain the serious and sober practice of social life and politics.

> *Behold men, as it were, in an underground cave-like dwelling, having its entrance open toward the light and extending through the whole cave, and within it persons, who from childhood upwards have had chains on their legs and their necks, so as, while abiding there, to have the power of looking forward only, but not to turn round their heads by reason of their chains, their light coming from a fire that burns above and afar.*
>
> *Let us inquire then, said I, as to their liberation from captivity . . . and their cure for insanity, such as it may be, and whether such will naturally fall to their lot; were a person let loose and obliged immediately to rise up, and turn round his neck and walk, and look upwards to the light, and doing all this still feel pained, and be disabled by the dazzling from seeing those things of which he formerly saw the shadows; what would he say, think you, if any one were to tell him that he formerly saw mere empty visions, but now saw more correctly, as being nearer to the real thing, and turned toward what was more real, and then, specially pointing out to him every individual passing thing, should question him and oblige him to answer respecting its nature; think you not he would be embarrassed, and consider that what he before saw was truer than what was just exhibited?*
>
> *But if, said I, a person should forcibly drag him thence through a rugged and steep ascent without stopping, till he dragged him to the light of the sun, would he not while thus drawn be in pain and indignation, and when he came to the light, having his eyes dazzled with the splendor, be unable to behold even any one thing of what he had just alleged as true?*
>
> *And consider this, said I, whether, in the case of such as one going down and again sitting in the same place, his eyes would not be blinded in consequence of coming so suddenly from the sun? Quite so, replied he . . . and as for any one that attempted to liberate him and lead him up, they ought to put him to death, if they could get him into their hands? Especially so, said he.* (Davis & Burgess, 1901, pp. 209–210)

This is a powerful story that can be used to spark student interest. It can turn otherwise dry words into a vital discussion of the role of philosophy in teaching. The teacher might follow this passage with a series of questions, such as the following:

1. Why does Plato select an underground cave for his location for "mankind"?
2. Why does Plato have his released prisoner look at the blinding firelight and then the blinding sun?

3. Why did Plato choose to have the released prisoner dragged to the outside rather than merely led?
4. On his return to the cave, why might the released prisoner be put to death for telling the truth?

Note that each question focuses on a specific part of the parable. This is important to the analytical process. Note also that the student is required to use the particular passage to solve a problem. If this assignment seems difficult or bizarre, remember the assignments you had in high school poetry class. You probably have had extensive contact with analysis assignments and analysis-level test questions. This is only one of several types of analysis questions, but it should help prepare you to introduce your students to analysis tasks.

Level 5: Synthesis

In recent years, middle-level students and teachers have come to hold in high esteem assignments that have no single, predetermined, "correct" answer, but that require students to apply their unique talents and perceptions to arrive at an acceptable answer. Unfortunately, today's teachers are pressured by community members who want the schools to reject these exercises in divergent thinking and return to the traditional approach to teaching the "three R's."

The value of such synthesis tasks is summed up in the concept of *gestalt*—that is, "The whole is greater than the sum of its parts." The student is given the task of putting together a number of concepts to communicate a uniquely different idea, one that is his or her own. This is the essence of creativity itself, which is known by the artist, painter, songwriter, movie producer, dancer, architect, and others who use their minds, bodies, and talents to express themselves. Rich in esthetic qualities, it also has practical value, because the synthesis process requires perceiving problems from different perspectives, leading to inventions and to "building a better mousetrap." Instead of trying to satisfy the demand for exercises that require "the" correct answer, students could better spend the time seeking out relationships that will guide their actions. If this sounds unscientific, today's scientists would not agree that such open-ended exercises requiring divergent, creative thinking are at all unscientific.

We should recognize the value of lower levels of thinking and their importance in the curriculum. What better way is there to master the multiplication tables than by rote memorization? Yet to limit classroom tasks only to those that require memorization would be to keep students from experiencing the types of problems they must be prepared to solve in adult life. Such a restriction also robs them of the ability to form new perceptions and express new conceptualizations.

In synthesis tasks, students are asked to take certain material, reorganize it, and assemble it in a new way to give it new meaning. The problem must be new to the students and, when possible, of special interest to them. For this reason, students should be involved in identifying the problem. This does not preclude assigning a particular problem to a group of students or to the entire class.

You are responsible for providing problems for students or for leading them in the selection process. Since there is no single, correct answer, be sure to stipulate exactly what criteria will be used in evaluating the work. For example, consider the following problem:

> In many U.S. communities, interest and participation in high school sports is so intense, and the financial support for athletics is so great, that many complain that academic subjects are neglected. Suppose you are captain of the football team at such a school. Furthermore, suppose the classrooms have deteriorated and the school does

not have the funds to restore the buildings. To make things worse, suppose your team has just ended another losing season. Prepare a statement to justify continuation of an interscholastic sports program in the face of these critical circumstances. Devise a plan that will enable the school to finance the necessary building restorations and still finance the team for coming years.

Or a science teacher may present a rock for students to examine, giving each student, or group of students, the materials needed to run tests for color, hardness, and acidity. The students are to tell where the rock originated and substantiate this conclusion with logic. The main objective is that the student design a plan for locating the derivation of particular rocks. The location itself is irrelevant. Another example of a synthesis task is to give each student a box of assorted materials with which to devise a container that will support the fall of a raw egg when it is dropped from a two-story window.

E. E. Thrower (1999, p. 358) says that teachers can use the following practices to promote creativity:

- Provide lessons that encourage students to take risks.
- Provide problems where creative answers are reinforced.
- Ask cooperative learning groups which answers were the most creative and why.
- Deviate from the lecture form of teaching.
- Model creative behavior. Be open to different types of answers.

Volkman (1999, pp. 359–360) agrees that teachers should remain flexible and open. When unexpected opportunities to learn outside the planned objectives occur, seize on those opportunities; you can return to the planned lesson after capitalizing on the moment.

When you develop tasks at the synthesis level, consider these conditions and try to provide an atmosphere that is most conducive to creative thinking.

Level 6: Evaluation

Tasks at the evaluation level require students to make judgments based on logical accuracy, consistency, and other given criteria in addition to remembered criteria. An example of a task at this level would be to present students with a politician's election platform and ask them to examine it for accuracy, logic, and consistency. Students would also be expected to compare it with the politician's previous political behavior or support or rejection of bills involving similar issues—in other words, does he practice what he preaches?

Other levels of evaluation tasks require students to identify values or assumptions on which judgments are made. For example, in your methods classes you may be asked to critique your peers while they teach a minilesson. Suppose you were asked to respond to the following questions:

1. The critic found the lesson organized so that the concepts
    a. Flowed smoothly
    b. Were presented illogically
    c. Were arranged in chronological order
    d. Both a and b
    e. Both b and c
2. According to the critic, the delivery of the lesson was
    a. Enhanced by the teacher's poise and self-confidence
    b. Strengthened by the use of good visual aids

TABLE 6.1 Sample Activities from the Levels of Bloom's Cognitive Taxonomy

Level	
6	Critique two per lesson and describe the qualities that make each lesson superior to the other lesson.
5	Reshape a piece of clay to increase its buoyancy. Explain why the newly formed shape is more buoyant.
4	After reading *The Republic* explain (interpret) Plato's use of the image of the "blinding light."
3	Examine a boiling tea kettle and explain why the lid is bobbing up and down.
2	Interpret the annual rainfall as shown on a chart.
1	Name three types of rocks.

    c. Augmented by the absence of unnecessary jargon and technical terms
    d. All of the above

Other types of evaluation questions require the student to judge a particular work based on similar works. Students may even be given an opportunity to form their own lists of criteria to use for evaluation. Table 6.1 shows a sample activity for each level of the cognitive domain. Space limitations do not allow discussion and samples of test items in all the sublevels of the six categories of Bloom's taxonomy, but you can explore further by examining the sources listed at the end of this chapter. Of special help are the Mager (1962) and Stiggins (1997).

Affective Domain

The attainment of knowledge and of skills needed to apply that knowledge are what school is all about, but unless students elect to use that knowledge and those skills, a great deal has been wasted. For example, although the ability to read has some intrinsic value, suppose students choose not to read because they do not like to read. Suppose other students master just enough skills in math to pass required courses, but in the meantime develop such fear or contempt toward mathematics that they refuse even to try to keep an accurate checkbook. In a sense the efforts of those students and their teachers have failed, because learning itself is defined as a long-term or even permanent change in behavior. Exactly what have these students failed to learn? They have failed to learn to appreciate what reading can enable them to accomplish; they have failed to realize their own potential in mathematics.

Experience with people who have chosen not to use the knowledge and skills they have shows how important attitude toward knowledge is. The proper attitudes are indispensable for successful, happy living, as the cases of learned people who have become destructive to society or to themselves demonstrate. The best lists of aims for U.S. education include aims that depend on certain attitudes. For example, examine:

The Seven Cardinal Principles of Secondary Education
1. Health
2. Command of the fundamental processes
3. Worthy home membership
4. Vocational efficiency
5. Civic participation
6. Worthy use of leisure time
7. Ethical character

Success in any of these areas depends on the development of certain attitudes. Even for the aim that may seem most separate from attitudes—vocational efficiency—certain attitudes are necessary for success. More than 85 percent of all jobs lost are lost because workers cannot get along with their supervisors and co-workers.

A national poll of attitudes toward education concluded that "Character education, which is uncommon as a formal subject in public high schools, has as much support as a required subject" (Elam, 1990, p. 49). Teachers must help students develop both necessary skills and certain attitudes. Twenty-first-century middle school educators hold character education as a major responsibility of middle schools.

Questioning Techniques

In their *Taxonomy of Educational Objectives: The Classification of Educational Goals, Handbook II: Affective Domain*, Krathwohl, Bloom, and Masia (1964) give five levels of internalization of values:

1. Receiving—a willingness to tolerate a phenomenon
2. Responding—voluntarily using the phenomenon
3. Valuing—prizing and acting on the phenomenon
4. Organizing—using values to determine interrelationships between the phenomena
5. Characterizing—organizing values, beliefs, ideas, and attitudes into an internally consistent system

As you consider your expectations of your future students, take time now to list two attitudes you want them to have toward the subject you will teach. Now, using the following examples as models, write a question that will measure student attitudes at each of the four levels: receiving, responding, valuing, and organizing.

Example 1: A math teacher uses the following questions to measure attitudes at each level.

1. Receiving: Would you like to join the math club?
2. Responding: When you play games that involve scorekeeping, do you ever volunteer to keep score?
3. Valuing: Do you plan to take math next year when it becomes an elective?
4. Organizing: Have you ever thought of math as an art?

Example 2: A history teacher covering the Civil War asks the following questions.

1. Receiving: Would you like to own Confederate relics?
2. Responding: If your family or friends planned a vacation that had Vicksburg, Mississippi, on its route, would you suggest visiting the battleground?
3. Valuing: Do you feel excited when seeing a movie on the Civil War?
4. Organizing: While studying this unit on the Civil War, have you ever tried to decide for yourself ways in which each side was wrong?

Using the definition of each level of internalization, and using these examples as models, write a question to test each level of your two statements about attitudes that you want your future students to have.

Your role in the development of students' attitudes will extend into other areas. First, you must help students learn to examine their current attitudes, particularly their values (values clarification), and to understand the basis for their values—that is, the process they use to develop values. To achieve this, you can give students tasks requiring them to analyze their values. Second, you can help students develop their moral values by assessing the level of their moral maturity and then giving them problem situations requiring them to perform at a level slightly above their current maturation level.

Lawrence Kohlberg (1976), formerly a professor at Harvard University, developed a hierarchy of three major stages through which each person must pass in the development of ethical awareness. These are:

Level 1. Preconventional—behavior is determined by rewards and punishment. (What is best for me?)
Level 2. Conventional—behavior is controlled by anticipation of praise or blame. (What will others think?)
Level 3. Postconventional—behavior is regulated by principles embodying generality and comprehensiveness. (What is the right thing to do?)

A familiar example is why a person obeys a stop sign:

- To avoid getting a fine (Level 1)
- To avoid criticism from others and to avoid breaking a law (Level 2)
- To avoid hurting others (Level 3)

A different version of the same problem might be as follows. In one of our major cities, the fine for violating a stop sign was increased overnight from about $20 to $87.50. Many police officers refused to enforce the law, which they perceived as unreasonable; others enforced it because they had taken an oath to enforce all the laws. At what level did each group of police officers behave?

Not all attitudes are limited to moral behavior. Other important behaviors that the school should foster include learning to appreciate, desire, find interesting, enjoy, and empathize.

Test Administration

For your test to be valid, you must make certain preliminary arrangements. First, see that all students are physically prepared—that they have the necessary materials, such as sharp pencils, paper, reference sources, and measuring instruments. If not, allot time before the test for each student to make these preparations.

Second, be sure everyone is comfortable. The room should not be hot or cold or noisy. Merely closing windows facing a noisy highway or closing the door to a noisy hall can help. Adjusting a room thermostat or radiator controls can help. Each student should have enough room to avoid being cramped. Remind everyone to remove unnecessary books and papers from desktops, lest some students try to balance their paper on top of a stack of books or support books or purses in their laps.

Finally, if test results are to reflect true abilities, students should be mentally relaxed. Many students become so tense during tests that they are unable to show that they know the material.

Accountability: Standardized and Alternative Tests

A key practice in the new education reform movement is accountability (Gallagher, 1998). Two-thirds of the public favor the use of national standardized tests for even the lower grades 3–8 (Gallup & Rose, 2002). Harris and Longstreet (1990) raise several critical questions about the standardized testing that has become so rampant in school districts throughout the nation.

> *Despite a growing interest in alternative forms of assessment, standardized measures of achievement are more extensively used than ever before. Why? One obvious response that comes quickly to mind is that of accountability. Has education achieved the goals established for it? Standardized tests would appear to offer an objective means for assessing how well teachers, individual schools, and the nation's schools as a whole are functioning. Seduced by the ease with which these tests are administered and the illusory importance of the numbers they yield, we have not sufficiently examined their adequacy as a measure of educational accountability.*
>
> *At best, they reflect only a small portion of what American education is about. What is omitted is everything not subject to the multiple-choice questions typically used in these tests. What kind of accountability is this? . . . The reality is that nothing substantive is gained from standardized testing other than the improvement of some students' test-taking skills. (p. 91)*

Too often the mention of tests conjures up the image of a room full of students taking the same pencil-and-paper test. Because today's middle schools have both academic goals and nonacademic goals, and because students' abilities to express themselves vary greatly at this age, middle school teachers should practice giving a variety of non-pencil-and-paper tests, including such self-assessments as journal writing, portfolios, and oral feedback. These methods can foster such skills as socialization, self-motivation, self-expression, and the promotion of life-long learning—skills that are just as important as measuring cognitive attainment (learning).

Increasingly, computer assignments are being used in testing. Pennypacker (cited in Henson & Eller, 1999, p. 143) cautions teachers to ensure that students have the computer skills needed to perform successfully on the test. In instances where these skills are lacking, Pennypacker reminds teachers that there is no shame in backing up and using pencil-and-paper tests. Will special students and minority students have any options or choices, such as being permitted to take the test orally? Such alternatives can be fair if other class members are afforded the same option.

Giving the Test

Anxiety toward taking a test can be reduced if you explain the test's purpose and permit students to practice taking tests (Griswold, 1990). You can help relieve tension by telling a joke, relating a humorous personal experience, or simply talking for a moment about a ball game, a party, the weather, or another activity unrelated to the test.

Before the test begins, specify how the students should ask questions, if they have any. Do you want them to raise their hands and direct their questions to you at once? Or do you want to go to the student to answer a question? Usually it is better if the students do not ask questions so the whole class can hear, because it disrupts others. Also, tell students in advance what to do when they finish the test. Should they bring it to you? Then should they study another subject, read a library book, or just relax?

> **Proactive Exercise**
>
> **Anticipated Situation**
> - You know that:
>
>   Above everything else, students want their teachers to be fair. A common complaint that teachers hear is that a test item was tricky, which at least borders on being unfair.
>
> **Proactive Alternative**
> - You can:
>
>   You can prepare a response to use when you are told that a test item was tricky. You will need separate responses for objective items and essay items. Introduce your students to item analysis. Show them how you compute discriminatory power and show them that you have discarded those items that have negative discriminatory powers because the negative discriminatory powers have let you identify those items that really are tricky. For essay items, show the students how you broke each item down and assigned weights to each part of the answers according to the time spent in class and the time required to answer each part.

Begin each test by reading the instructions aloud and allowing time for questions. All students should begin at the same time. This provides structure. Also, do not permit students to talk or otherwise disrupt others. Conduct test administration comfortably but uniformly.

Once the test has begun, do not interrupt. If students ask questions, answer them and make a note of each necessary clarification or correction. To avoid interruptions, near the end of the testing period you can inform the entire class of all these corrections at one time. Avoid making disturbing noises during the test, such as rattling papers, talking, or walking around the classroom. Remain in the room at all times during the test.

To end the test in an organized way, take up all remaining papers when time is called. Otherwise, students who feel pressured and do hand in their papers, and then see that a few persistent students are allowed additional time to finish, will feel cheated.

Test Scoring

Whether the test questions are objective, subjective, or both, scoring should always be as objective as possible. Otherwise your judgment will be affected by your likes and dislikes for the students, by the paper's general appearance, and by a force that all teachers experience—a tendency to equalize the scores by subconsciously accepting poor responses from the poorer papers and being overly critical and deducting credit from respectable responses on the better papers. Because this is common among beginning teachers, test scoring leaves them feeling guilty, and many develop a real dislike for testing.

Testing is as much a part of the teacher's role and responsibility as preparing and executing lessons. How, then, can you avoid developing the common distaste for testing? Learning and using the following principles should be of some help.

Teacher as Proactive Decision Maker

Classroom Situation

1. You know that most beginning teachers are shocked and disappointed when they grade their first test.
2. No teacher attribute is more important to students everywhere than fairness. Effective teachers know that they must do more than just be fair, they must devise strategies that demonstrate their fairness. You can be confident that almost without exception, when this test is over some students will say it included trick questions.

Proactive Alternatives

1. Stress the importance of students focusing on the major concepts, and when making your first test, include these concepts and weight them heavily.
2. Review the major concepts before administering this test.
3. Ask students to identify important content and include test items that measure the mastery of these concepts.
4. Prepare a chart to show the connection between each test item and major class objective(s) and/or concept(s).
5. Include one open-ended question, inviting students to write their own question and response to cover an important concept studied that was not covered by your questions.

Returning Tests

As mentioned in Chapter 5, when correctly constructed and administered, tests can play a powerful part in determining how much is learned in a teacher's classroom. As Merrow (2001, p. 657) has said, "Excellent teachers create good tests, grade them carefully, and get them back to their students in a matter of days." A challenging yet worthy goal is to plan to return each test on the following day. Many teachers choose to give all of their tests on Fridays so they can meet this goal.

Vignettes

All teachers must develop, administer, and score teacher-made tests. Failure to develop expertise in any of these dimensions of testing can lead to serious problems. The following vignette shows a common problem situation in which teachers find themselves.

Vignette One: A Ninth-Grade Class Wants Information about an Upcoming Test

Ms. Wheeler had been teaching physical education for about five years when she noticed a sudden change in student attitudes toward tests. Up until that time she had considered that discussing tests before giving them was unethical and absurd. If an examination was going to be a fair measure of students' knowledge about the subject, would not a previous discussion destroy the test's validity and purpose? The only information she ever gave about a test was when it would be given. Although previous classes had teased, asking questions about what would be on the test, Ms. Wheeler knew that they never expected her to answer their questions.

This ninth-grade class was different. When students asked for information about the upcoming test, they expected her to provide it. They never asked about specific content, but they did ask such questions as "How many questions will the test have?," "How much will each question count?," and "How many are true–false questions?" Taking these questions as good-natured teasing, Ms. Wheeler ignored them and went on with the lesson. However, it gradually became clear that the students were serious. They became upset when they had no advance notice about how long a test would be and the type of questions it would contain.

Soon after being confronted by these disgruntled students, Ms. Wheeler changed her policy and began holding a discussion about each test a few days before giving it. This practice was successful. First, the students no longer felt she was trying to trick them with an unfamiliar test, and they could study according to the type of test they were to take. Second, she came to see that answering certain questions about a test did not suggest what content to study as much as it suggested the correct method of study.

DISCUSSION

1. If you reveal the number and type of questions to be included on an upcoming test, will the test be less valid and less reliable? No, not if all the students in your class have this information. It may help them identify the important ideas in the unit. It may improve the scores of students who use the information to study for the test, but these students will probably learn more in accordance with their increased scores. If you are afraid to provide information about an objective, factual test you are planning to administer, you can increase the length of the test. It will then be so comprehensive that the student who scores high on it will have to know a majority of the content studied during the unit.

2. Do today's students view tests as less important than did the students of a few years ago? Today's students feel that tests are important. The main difference is that yesterday's students saw tests as important for one reason only—to determine grades. Today's students see an additional purpose in tests: they want to score well because they know that test scores reflect the quality of their learning. This is why they want to know how to study for each test. They realize that a test that tricks them is not an accurate instrument for measuring their learning progress.

3. How can you make testing more palatable? By removing fear from testing, you can make it less distasteful to you and your students. Develop a routine for test administration and return, and always be as pleasant as you can. Your manner will help the students relax, and if you follow the same routine each time you give a test, you can ease feelings of insecurity.

When returning tests, always go over each question and explain the correct answers. Give partial credit when it is earned.

Vignette Two: Education Reform Affects Assessment

Samuel Clemens Middle School is located in a state that takes pride as a national leader of education reform. Jimmy Smith, a May graduate of Regional State University, was delighted to have landed a teaching position at Clemens Middle School because he had heard of the school's reputation as a leader in education reform. After all, Regional State had adjusted its mission statement six years ago to include education reform as a major component, and, consequently, Jimmy had been well grounded in all the state's reform practices.

Jimmy's teacher education program had stressed the importance of ongoing self-evaluation. The use of portfolios throughout the program was consistent with this emphasis. To promote education reform, Clemens Middle School required each teacher to design an assessment system and present a rationale statement linking the system with education reform. Put simply, Jimmy's task was to write a convincing statement telling how his new assessment system promoted education reform.

Jimmy began by reviewing his college notes to reacquaint himself with the concepts on education reform that related to assessment. His review turned up such terms as self-assessment, continuous assessment, portfolios, objective-based education, curriculum alignment, alternative testing, authentic tests, and valued outcomes. The number of terms alone was a reminder of how much material he had covered on assessment related to education reform. Although he felt confident that he had mastered most or all of the topics on assessment and education reform that his college curriculum had covered, he mused silently, wondering where to begin the seemingly monumental assignment.

DISCUSSION

1. Which of these topics would be the most useful to an assessment system to promote education reform?
2. What major precautions should a teacher take to prepare students for a reform-oriented assessment program?
3. How should education reform change the role and nature of teacher-made tests?
4. How does and how should education reform alter a teacher's emphasis on the affective domain?

Summary

Traditionally, tests have been used to give parents a report on their children's progress in school, with the idea that grades are good tools for motivating students to do their best, and the assumption that *tests* mean written tests. The continuing increase in attempts to make schools and teachers accountable for student performance on standardized tests reinforces this narrow perception of tests. But, this chapter has pointed out that written tests are just one of many types of tests, and that portfolios and other types of tests can be powerful tools for helping students assess their own progress.

Traditionally, *tests* have meant summative tests, or tests given following instruction. But this chapter has pointed out another type of tests, *formative tests*, which are tests given during instruction to improve teaching and learning. Teachers are encouraged to use formative tests to improve their teaching and to help students improve their learning.

Objective tests have dominated throughout the decades. They are faster to develop, administer, and score than essay tests. Objective tests enable teachers to cover more content than essay tests. But essay tests should also be used because they enable students to express their ideas and their opinions. When developing essay tests, teachers should specify what they expect students to give in their responses, as opposed to just "talking about" the topics. When giving opinions, students should be encouraged to offer support for each opinion.

Tests can be powerful motivators when teachers return them promptly and take time to hold discussions on topics that received low scores. Tests can also be designed to cause students to use their higher level thinking skills. Items that answer the question, "Why?" cause students to think at higher levels.

Recap of Major Ideas

1. Because both objective-type and subjective-type questions have unique advantages and disadvantages, it is usually best to include questions of both types on a test.
2. Objective questions are easily scored and permit the teacher to cover much material by including many questions on a test, but they do not enable the student to be self-expressive or creative.
3. Subjective items permit students to show their knowledge and state their feelings, and they enhance writing and synthesizing skill development; however, they restrict the teacher's ability to test all material covered. Subjective questions are also difficult to score.
4. Grade all tests, including essay-type tests, as objectively as possible.
5. Each test should measure everything covered since the previous test.
6. Assign credit to each item according to the time and emphasis it received in class and the time required to answer it.
7. On discussion-type tests, give partial credit for accurate answers, even though they were unanticipated.
8. Multiple-choice items should contain four or five choices, one or two of which should be strong distracters.
9. To pilot the test, take it before administering it to students.
10. Essay tests provide minority students a much-neglected opportunity to fulfill the need of self-expression.

Activities

In this chapter you have read about good practices for constructing, administering, and scoring tests and have examined questions written at different levels of the cognitive and affective domains. Now you have an opportunity to assemble and apply your knowledge and skills in testing.

1. In your major teaching field, develop an objective test containing a combination of true–false, matching, and multiple-choice items. Include questions that measure the higher cognitive levels as well as some that measure in the affective domain.
2. Construct an essay test, then rewrite each question to make it more precise and manageable.
3. Decide exactly how you would prefer to administer a test. Then write a set of instructions to guide student behavior during and immediately following the test. Ask some of your classmates to interpret your instructions. Look for discrepancies in the interpretations and rewrite items that had multiple interpretations.
4. Write a subjective test item. Identify and list the most important points that students should include in their responses. Now identify and make a list of secondary points that are important but less so than the primary points. Assign 2 points each to the primary points and 1 point each to the secondary points.
5. For the preceding test item, develop three alternative ways of testing that do not use pencil and paper. Try to make each of these alternative tests discriminate between those who understand the primary and secondary points and those who do not.
6. Make a list of unique advantages offered by essay questions and a list of unique advantages offered by objective questions.

Looking Ahead

This chapter has prepared you to design, administer, and score tests for use in your classes. The earlier chapters prepared you to write objectives and write plans to help your students achieve your classes' expected outcomes. However, not all students are alike. On the contrary, each one is different and has individual needs. The following chapter will prepare you to help individuals fulfill their educational needs.

References

Archbald, D., & Newmann, F. (1988). *Beyond standardized testing: Authentic academic achievement in the secondary school.* Reston, VA: NASSP Publications.

Armstrong, D. G., Henson, K. T., and Savage, T. V. (2004). *Teaching today* (7th ed.). New York: Prentice-Hall.

Barton, J., & Collins, A. (1993). Portfolios in teacher education. *The Journal of Teacher Education, 44*(3), 200–210.

Davis, H., & Burgess, G. (Trans. 1901). *The republic: The statesman of Plato* (pp. 209–210). New York: Dunne.

DeRoma, V. M., Young A., Mabrouk, S. T., Brannan, K. P., Hilleke, R. O., & Johnson, K. Y. (at press).

Elam, S. M. (1990). The 22nd annual Gallup Poll of the public's attitudes toward the public schools. *Phi Delta Kappan, 72*(1), 41–55.

Ellsworth, R. A., Donnell, P., & Duell, O. K. (1990). Multiple-choice test item: What are textbook authors telling teachers? *Journal of Educational Research, 83*(5), 290–293.

English, F. (1992, March). *Curriculum alignment.* Paper presented at an Eastern Kentucky University/Phi Delta Kappa Conference, Richmond, KY.

Erb, T. (1997). Student-friendly classrooms in a not very child-friendly world. *Middle School Journal, 28*(5), 2.

Fielding, G., & Shaughnessy, J. (1990, November). Improving student assessment: Overcoming the obstacles. *NASSP Bulletin,* pp. 90–98.

Gallagher, J. (1998). *Classroom assessment for teachers.* Columbus, OH.: Merrill.

Griswold, P. A. (1990, February). Assessing relevance and reliability to improve the quality of teacher-made tests. *NASSP Bulletin,* pp. 18–23.

Harris, K. H., & Longstreet, W. S. (1990). Alternative testing and national agenda for control. *The Clearing House, 64,* 90–93.

Henson, K. T., & Eller, B. F. (1999). *Educational psychology for effective teaching.* Belmont, CA: Wadsworth.

Jenkins, D. M., & Jenkins, K. D. (1991). The NMSA Delphi report. Roadmap to the future. *Middle School Journal, 22*(4), 27–36.

Keefe, J. W., & Jenkins, J. M. (2002). Personalized instruction. *Phi Delta Kappan, 83*(6), 440–448.

Kohlberg, L. (1976). Moral stages and moralization: The cognitive developmental approach. In T. Lickona (Ed.), *Moral development and behavior: Theory, research, and social issues* (pp. 31–53). New York: Holt, Rinehart & Winston.

Kohn, A. (2001). Fighting the tests: A practical guide to rescuing our schools. *Phi Delta Kappan, 82*(5), 349–357.

Krathwohl, D. R., Bloom, B., & Masia, B. (1964). *Taxonomy of educational objectives: The classification of educational goals. Handbook II: Affective domain.* New York: McKay.

Mager, R. F. (1962). *Preparing instructional objectives.* Belmont, CA: Fearon.

Mather, C. (2000). Chapter 11: Current and future curriculum trends. In K. T. Henson. *Curriculum development* (2nd ed.). New York: McGraw-Hill.

Merrow, T. (2001). Teaching to the test. *Phi Delta Kappan, 82*(9), 653–659.

Perrone, V. (1994). How to engage students in learning. *Educational Leadership, 51*(5), 11–13.

Phillips, D. R., Phillips, D. G., Melton, G., & Moore, P. (1994). Beans, blocks, and buttons: Developing thinking. *Educational Leadership, 51*(5), 50–53.

Popham, J. (2001). Teaching to the test. *Educational Leadership, 58*(6), 16–20.

Postner, G. J., & Rudnitsky, A. N. (1994). *Course design: A guide to curriculum development for teachers* (4th ed.). New York: Longman.

Rose, L. C., & Gallup, A. M. (2001). The 33rd annual Phi Delta Kappa/Gallup Poll of the public's attitudes toward the public schools. *Phi Delta Kappan, 83*(1), 41–48, 53–58.

Schell, V. J. (1982). Learning partners: Reading and mathematics. *The Reading Teacher, 35,* 544–548.

Siegel, M., et al. (1989) A critical review of reading in mathematics instruction: The need for a new synthesis. *U.S. Department of Education* ED 301 863.

Simmons, R. (1994). The horse before the cart: Assessing for understanding. *Educational Leadership, 51*(5), 22–23.

Special Study Panel on Education Indicators for the National Center for Education Statistics (1991). *Education counts.* Washington, DC: U.S. Department of Education.

Stefanich, G. P. (1990, November). Cycles of cognition. *Middle School Journal, 22*(2), 47–52.

Stiggins, R. J. (1985). Improving assessment where it means the most: In the classroom. *Educational Leadership, 43,* 69–74.

Stiggins, R. J. (1997). *Student-centered classroom assessment* (2nd ed.). Columbus, OH: Merrill.

Tanner, M., & Casados, L. (1998). Promoting and studying discussion in math classes. *Journal of Adolescent and Adult Literacy, 41*(5), 342–350.

Thrower, E. E. (1999). A teacher's class. In Henson, K. T., & Eller, B. F. *Educational psychology for effective teaching.* Belmont, CA: Wadsworth.

Tuckman, B. W. (1996, April). *Using spot quizzes as an incentive to motivate procrastinators to study.* Paper presented at the American Educational Research Association, New York, NY.

Van Wagenen, L., & Hibbard, K. M. (1998). Building teacher portfolios. *Educational Leadership, 55*(5), 26–29.

Volkman, B. (1999). A teacher's class. In Henson, K. T., & Eller, B. F. *Educational psychology for effective teaching.* Belmont, CA: Wadsworth.

Ward, M. W. (1969). Learning to generalize. *Science Education, 53,* 423–424.

Wiggins, G. (1989, April). Teaching to the authentic test. *Educational Leadership, 46*(7), 41–47.

Wilcox, B. (1998). *Writing for publication workshop.* Pittsburg, PA: Duquesne University.

Wilcox, B., & Tomei, L. (1999). *Professional portfolios for teachers.* Norwood, MA: Christopher-Gordon.

7
Individualizing Instruction

*If students do not learn the way we teach them,
then we must teach them the way they learn.*

Carol Marshall

Objectives

- List at least four approaches commonly used to meet individual learning differences.
- Differentiate between two major categories of ability grouping.
- Describe ways to avoid common problems that result from ability grouping.
- Describe ways instruction for low-ability groups should differ from instruction for average groups.
- Name the elements on which mastery learning hinges.
- Design a contingency contract.
- Differentiate between teacher-paced and group-paced instruction and between group-based and individual-based instruction.
- List categories of learner preferences used to determine learning styles.
- Discuss strengths and weaknesses of matching learner and teacher styles.
- Describe one way that you can make your classroom environment more personal.
- Describe a method of using technology to reach challenged students.

INDIVIDUALIZED INSTRUCTION

Need
- Multiple Intelligences

Grouping
- In-Class
- Interclass

Instructional Models
- Information Processing
- Mystery Learning
- Matching Styles

At Risk Students
- Special Students
- IEPs
- Inclusion
- Disabilities

Grade Contracts

Computers

Other Ways to Involve Students
- Textbooks
- Fields Trips
- Oral Reports
- Projects
- Homework
- Parent Involvement

Connecting Statements

	Agree	Disagree	Uncertain
1. Individualizing instruction is contextual, which means that the success of a particular approach may vary as the situation changes.			
2. The simple act of grouping students according to ability usually increases learning.			
3. Ability grouping can be psychologically destructive to both high achievers and low achievers.			
4. Intraclass grouping produces more competition than interclass grouping.			
5. In many ways learning is an individual experience.			
6. As many as one-third of all students are at risk.			
7. Hispanic students tend to prefer cooperation over competition			

> ### Tips for Teachers
> One question prospective teachers usually have is how to plan and teach so that each lesson meets the needs of twenty to thirty students whose abilities range from educationally handicapped to gifted. By the time such a diverse class reaches the senior grades, many of the poor performers drop out of school, and some mediocre performers find themselves and become serious students. But at the middle level this narrowing process has not yet occurred. At this level the teacher must face the very difficult challenge of meeting a wide range of needs. Bradley and Fisher (1995, p. 13) have said that "students in middle school vary in as many ways as imaginable, including physically, emotionally, intellectually, and socially." This is true.
>
> Although there is no guaranteed solution to this problem, one approach to meeting individual needs is ability grouping. But sometimes this approach produces disastrous results because teachers mismanage the groups. Because adolescents' general lack of self-confidence makes them especially vulnerable to the psychological damage that ability grouping can produce, you must learn how to avoid these common effects of the approach.

The Need to Individualize

As prospective teachers begin their involvement in public school classrooms, they are quickly introduced to classes that contain students with a wide range of abilities. This is especially true of middle-level teachers, whose students' range of abilities is exaggerated because of rapid development. Beginning teachers can be overwhelmed by the challenge of designing instruction for students who have not only a broad range of abilities but also different levels of motivation (Bradley & Fisher, 1995).

This chapter looks at ways to meet the instructional needs of all students in secondary and middle school classrooms, but you can use many of the strategies presented in this chapter in special and multicultural classes. Chapter 8 discusses special techniques for teaching students of varying ethnic groups and cultures.

Recall that one of the Carnegie Council's goals for middle schools is ensuring academic success for all students (Carnegie Council on Adolescent Development, 1996). Individualized instruction can be defined as instruction that meets all students' needs. Its existence is based on the premise that students are different—indeed, that each student is different and therefore has unique learning needs that each teacher must make special efforts to meet. Parents believe that individual attention to their children's needs leads to academic growth (Gilman & Kiger, 2003). Pitton (1999) has noted that in each classroom of this country are young people with the potential for unique, individualized growth and development. When teachers do not consider the variety of student needs, at least two things happen: some students become bored because they are inadequately challenged, and others become discouraged because too much is expected of them.

Although middle-level educators recognize the need to individualize instruction, few agree on how to do so. This chapter looks at some common approaches that schools and teachers use to individualize instruction. The approaches discussed are far from all-inclusive, however. New approaches are being applied every day. Some of the more successful innovations may never get beyond the immediate classroom walls; others are studied and tested, and the results are disseminated through the professional literature. This is the case with the approaches described in this chapter.

As you read about each innovation, consider its potential for your future classes. Make a list of ways to improve each method, and think of ways to modify these approaches to make them more useful for you with your own future students. Remember that most of these approaches began in the minds of a few teachers who believed they needed a certain method to reach particular students. Explore your own mind, the minds of other educators with whom you come into contact, and the ideas of those who have done research and shared their findings in journals and books.

Multiple Intelligences

In the mid-1980s Howard Gardner introduced a program that today is referred to as *Multiple Intelligences.* Built on the earlier work of J. P. Guilford, Gardner challenged some well-accepted assumptions about individuals' abilities. Basic to these assumptions was the way educational psychologists viewed intelligence. Throughout the century, educators believed the theory that each individual is born with a single intelligence, that this intelligence can be accurately measured (reported as intelligence quotient or IQ), and that this level of intelligence changes little or none from the moment of birth until death. This system of beliefs is still very much alive and, indeed, is exerting tremendous influence in our higher education system today. For example, says Gardner (as cited in Checkley, 1997):

> We don't do much IQ testing anymore, but the shadow of IQ tests is still with us because the SAT—arguably the most potent combination in the world—is basically the same kind of disembodied language-logic instrument.
>
> The truth is, I don't believe there is such a thing as scholastic aptitude. (p. 10)

Instead of accepting the theory that each individual has a single intelligence, Gardner proposed that individuals have at least seven intelligences. These distinctly different intelligences are shown in Figure 7.1, along with an eighth intelligence that Gardner discovered in the mid-1990s.

A second accepted belief that Gardner challenged is that each of us is stuck with the level of intelligence we received at birth. Gardner believes we have the capacity to improve each of these intelligences and that an individual's capacity to increase one intelligence is greater than that same individual's ability to increase another intelligence. Further, Gardner believes that a student's success in improving an intelligence depends on the learning/teaching strategies.

Applying Multiple Intelligences Theory to Teaching

As with any educational theory, the theory of multiple intelligences has the potential for an unlimited variety of classroom applications, limited only by the teacher's own level of creativity. A popular approach is for teachers to begin by assessing their own intelligences. This assessment need not be formal; just ponder the list shown in Figure 7.1 and give yourself a 1–10 rating on each. This exercise will enable you to begin learning the various intelligences and will make you aware of how much individuals' intelligences vary.

Having assessed your own intelligences, now share this information with your students. (Remember Hilliard's comment, "Early adolescents have increasing abilities in metacognition," meaning that they are capable of thinking about how they learn and they have the capacity to improve their learning strategies). If teachers stopped at this point, their use of multiple intelligences would already have been significant, but why stop here. Let's revisit Gardner's beliefs about multiple intelligences. In a 1997 interview (Checkley, 1997, p. 11), Gardner made this comment: "We know people truly understand something when they can represent the knowledge in more than one way."

- Linguistic intelligence is the capacity to use language, your native language, and perhaps other languages, to express what's on your mind and to understand other people. Poets really specialize in linguistic intelligence, but any kind of writer, orator, speaker, lawyer, or a person for whom language is an important stock in trade highlights linguistic intelligence.
- People with a highly developed logical-mathematical intelligence understand the underlying principles of some kind of a causal system, the way a scientist or a logician does; or can manipulate numbers, quantities, and operations, the way a mathematician does.
- Spatial intelligence refers to the ability to represent the spatial world internally in your mind—the way a sailor or airplane pilot navigates the large spatial world, or the way a chess player or sculptor represents a more circumscribed spatial world. Spatial intelligence can be used in the arts or in the sciences. If you are spatially intelligent and oriented toward the arts, you are more likely to become a painter or a sculptor or an architect than, say, a musician or a writer. Similarly, certain sciences like anatomy or topology emphasize spatial intelligence.
- Bodily kinesthetic intelligence is the capacity to use your whole body or parts of your body—your hand, your fingers, your arms—to solve a problem, make something, or put on some kind of a production. The most evident examples are people in athletics or the performing arts, particularly dance or acting.
- Musical intelligence is the capacity to think in music, to be able to hear patterns, recognize them, remember them, and perhaps manipulate them. People who have a strong musical intelligence don't just remember music easily—they can't get it out of their minds, it's so omnipresent. Now, some people will say, "Yes, music is important, but it's a talent, not an intelligence." And I say, "Fine, let's call it a talent." But, then we have to leave the word *intelligent* out of *all* discussion of human abilities. You know, Mozart was damned smart!
- Interpersonal intelligence is understanding other people. It's an ability we all need, but is at a premium if you are a teacher, clinician, salesperson, or politician. Anybody who deals with other people has to be skilled in the interpersonal sphere.
- Intrapersonal intelligence refers to having an understanding of yourself, of knowing who you are, what you can do, what you want to do, how you react to things, which things to avoid, and which things to gravitate toward. We are drawn to people who have a good understanding of themselves because those people tend not to screw up. They tend to know what they can do. They tend to know what they can't do. And they tend to know where to go if they need help.
- Naturalist intelligence designates the human ability to discriminate among living things (plants, animals) as well as sensitivity to other features of the natural world (clouds, rock configurations). This ability was clearly of value in our evolutionary past as hunters, gatherers, and farmers; it continues to be central in such roles as botanist or chef. I also speculate that much of our consumer society exploits the naturalist intelligences, which can be mobilized in the discrimination among cars, sneakers, kinds of makeup, and the like. The kind of pattern recognition values in certain of the the sciences may also draw upon naturalist intelligence.

FIGURE 7.1 THE INTELLIGENCES, IN GARDNER'S WORDS

From Kathy Checkley, "The First Seven . . . and the Eighth: A Conversation with Howard Gardner," *Educational* Leadership 55(1), 1997, p. 12. Used by permission of the Association for Supervision and Curriculum Development. Copyright © 1997 by ASCD. All rights reserved.

Suppose you are teaching middle-level journalism and one of the course objectives is to enable students to prepare an article manuscript for submission to a magazine or journal for publication. You have been stressing to your students the need to know each journal's audience. Using Gardner's comment, "We know people truly understand something when they can represent the knowledge in more than one way," give your students a second assignment: "Now describe the audience of a second journal and rewrite this manuscript so that it will serve the needs of this second audience." Incidentally, this practice is tried and proven; Rita Dunn, whose work with learning styles is described later in this chapter, has given this assignment to her graduate students in a course she teaches on writing for publication at St. John's University. It can work equally well with middle-level students.

Another concern of Gardner (See Checkley, 1997) was that our prior conception of fixed intelligence gave no room in the curriculum for creativity, and little or no room for the arts. Most students have studied Maslow's Hierarchy of Needs (shown in Figure 7.2). In examining Figure 7.2 we are reminded that the arts are near the top of Maslow's needs triangle. Thus, they lend themselves to engaging students emotionally and intellectually.

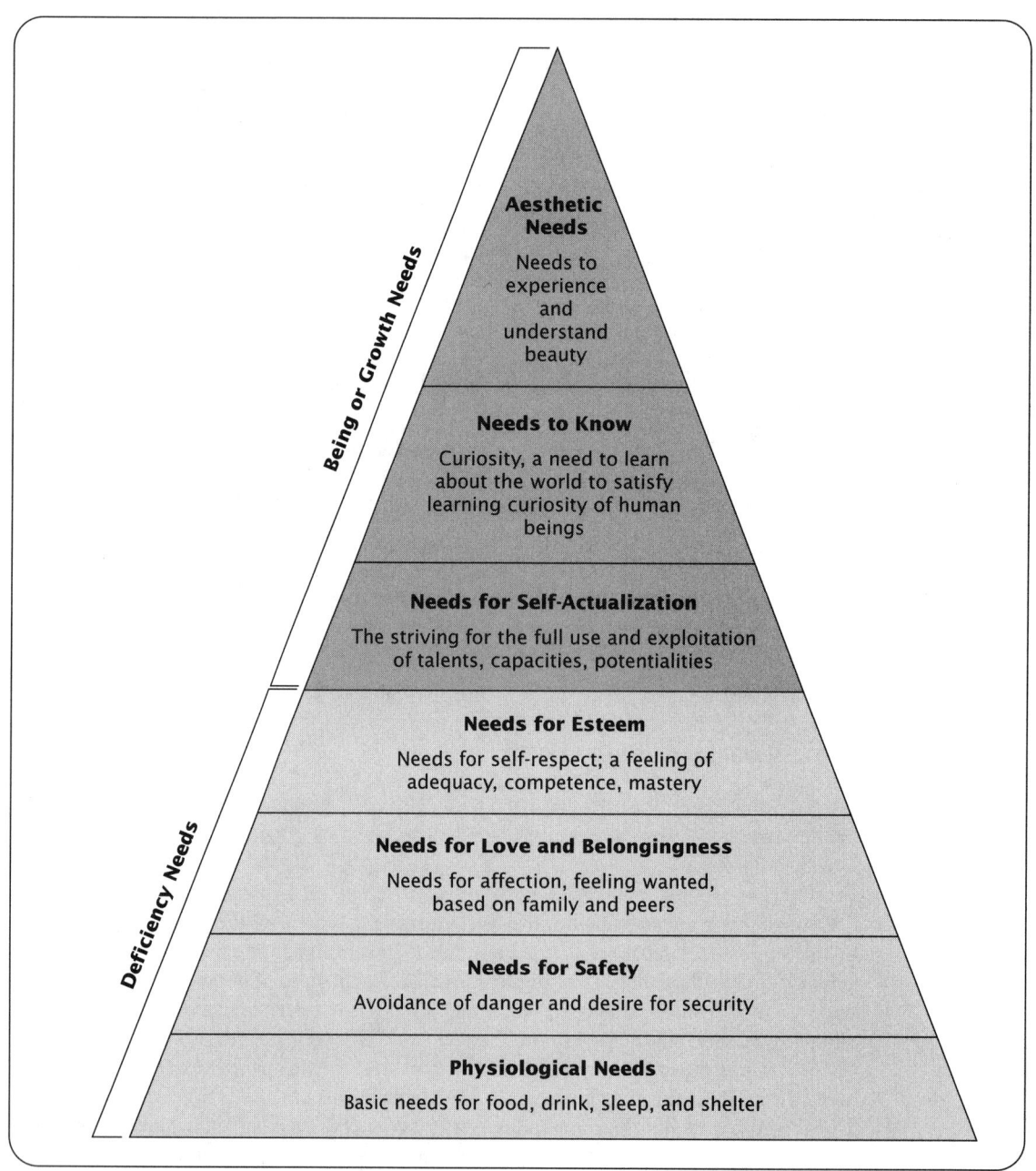

FIGURE 7.2 MASLOW'S HIERARCHY OF NEEDS

Adapted from Maslow (1970, p. 150).

> **Let's Talk**
>
> You can learn which intelligences you use the most by using the Yahoo search engine. Simply type in *Yahoo.com* and then type in *world wide brain club*. Next, click on *a user manual for your mind*. On the menu bar labeled Site Index, located on the left side of the screen, click on the first option, titled *Your Seven Intelligences*. Follow the directions.

Application of multiple intelligences theory to your lessons will become easier with practice. But, like any other innovation in busy classrooms led by teachers with heavy workloads, in time it can also easily fade away. One measure you can take to ensure that you continue to use multiple intelligences theory in your classes is to keep a record, an inventory. Pennsylvania high school teacher Veronica Emig designed the inventory shown in Figure 7.3 to track the intelligences used in five lessons. Emig (1997) admits that she does not believe it is necessary that every lesson use all intelligences, but she says that this tracking system makes lesson planning easier. She also reports that when students are using their intelligences more fully, they become engaged in class activities at a higher level and, because their higher level of participation enhances their ability to see connections, they retain the lesson's major concepts longer.

The act of keeping a reflective record or journal of your successes and failures is a powerful system for continuing improving. Debra Daniels (2002) says, "Writing reflective journals facilitates the writer in inquiring into his or her existing assumptions and beliefs by looking at them again, turning them around, and viewing from a different perspective"

Course: World Cultures   **Unit:** Introduction to Cultures

INTELLIGENCE	Lesson 1 Provides for This Intelligence	Lesson 1 No. of Students Using This Intelligence	Lesson 2 Provides for This Intelligence	Lesson 2 No. of Students Using This Intelligence
Linguistic	✓	37	✓	6
Logical–Mathematical			✓	4
Spatial	✓	9	✓	66
Bodily-Kinesthetic	✓	4		
Interpersonal	✓	6	✓	
Intrapersonal	✓	20		
Musical			✓	

Topic	**Cultural Relativism**	**Development of Cultural Leads**
OBJECTIVES	To understand meaning of culture through various lenses; to be aware of prejudice and stereotypes	To understand processes in human cultural development
FORMAT	Read about "Ritual of Nacirema"—an illustration of bias and ethnocentrism. Act out (charades), discuss, and write about	Readings, cartoons, individual presentations, short essay.
COMMENTS	Most preferred written reports; disliked charades. Many wrote diary entries.	Almost all chose cartoon over report; four liked computer presentations.

Unit Evaluation: These sophomores have strong cooperative learning skills. Many like art projects. Four or five are computer experts. Group needs specific rubrics—not terribly creative without suggestions. Students pretty balanced re multiple intelligences: 129 spatial, 73 linguistic, 7 musical.

FIGURE 7.3 TEACHER'S MULTIPLE INTELLIGENCE INVENTORY

Adapted from an assessment of student presentations for five lessons. From Kenneth T. Henson, *Methods and Strategies for Teaching in Secondary and Middle Schools,* third edition. Published by Allyn and Bacon, Boston, MA. Copyright © 1996 by Pearson Education. Reprinted by permission of the publisher.

(p. 54). Reflective journal keeping is an example of qualitative research that contemporary middle-level teachers use frequently.

In-Class Ability Grouping

A common approach to reducing the task of teaching thirty or so students of varying abilities and needs is to form subgroups of students who share abilities and interests. Simple arithmetic suggests that dividing a class of thirty students into five groups of six students each will reduce the range to which the instruction must be adapted to one-fifth the original range. However, to conclude that this maneuver will improve the level of performance by a similar margin is wrong. There are those who do not support even grade-level grouping. Patterson (2003) says, grouping students according to their grade level has little to do with the educational needs of students." (p. 571). The results of ability grouping are not usually so monumental, yet ability grouping does tend to improve student learning. An analysis of more than forty studies of ability grouping found that grouping improves students' ability to learn slightly and improves their motivation level greatly (Julik, 1981).

Effects of Grouping

Ability grouping may not be appropriate for all students. Lindblad (1994) explains that "students with poor self-images and those with over-inflated egos can create group conflict that is difficult to resolve" (p. 292). For example, Hispanic students tend to favor group work over individual assignment, but only if there is a sense of cooperation rather than competition (Henson & Eller, 1999). Native American students generally also prefer group work, but they are often sensitive to public criticism. As mentioned earlier, many educators are concerned that grouping lowers the expectations set for all students and is especially damaging to gifted students (Agne, 2001).

When students with extremely weak or extremely strong self-images are grouped, teachers may need to increase the level of supervision. Perhaps this is why the National Middle School Association (NMSA) recommends that middle-level teachers replace traditional grouping practices with cooperative learning and other heterogeneous strategies (NMSA, 1991).

Individualizing Instruction

How effectively ability grouping improves learning depends on how you adjust the instruction to each group. We do know that, in general, less capable students need more concrete material and examples of ways to apply newly learned concepts to real-world experiences, and that more capable students need greater challenges. But the challenges must be of different types. For example, a teacher of ability-grouped math students should not merely assign the upper group a much larger number of the same type of problems given to less capable groups. Instead, the upper group might receive more creative challenges that require divergent thinking. Advanced groups might even be assigned to develop problems instead of solutions, or to find a variety of solutions to a problem.

Expect to spend more time with the less capable students, especially after the more capable groups get on task, when you use ability grouping. Slower students may require more careful monitoring and guidance. Good, Reys, Grouws, and Molyran (1990–1991) say that when working in groups, higher-ability students tend to dominate the group or to work alone. Furthermore, low-ability students perform less well in school when placed with other low-ability students. This is probably partly because teachers usually spend less time with the lower groups. A review of the literature found that the amount of time teachers devote to direct instruction is directly related to student achievement (Centra & Potter, 1980); so, teachers often receive pressure to use more direct instruction. Middle-level teachers should strive to balance direct instruction with student-centered learning, because such goals as the development of positive attitudes, social skills, and a love for learning may be difficult or impossible to achieve through direct instruction.

Unintentional Differential Treatment

To be effective, ability grouping requires different treatment for different groups at different levels, but you must avoid unintentional differential treatment. For example, although it is realistic to expect high-ability students to cover more material faster than lower groups, teachers often make unrealistic demands. Shavelson (1983) found that high-ability groups were paced as much as fifteen times faster than lower-ability groups, increasing dramatically the difference in amount of material the two groups covered.

Teachers tend to treat students for whom they hold low expectations in several different ways. For example, Good and Brophy (1997) report that teachers treat these students in the following unique ways. The teacher will:

- Wait less time for lows to answer questions
- Give lows the answer or call on someone else
- Provide inappropriate reinforcement
- Criticize lows more than highs for failure
- Praise lows less than highs for success
- Fail to give lows feedback on their public responses
- Interact with lows less and pay less attention to them overall
- Call on lows less often in class
- Seat lows farther away from the teacher
- Ask for lower performance levels from lows
- Smile less, have less eye contact, have fewer attentive postures toward lows
- Give high performers (highs) but not lows the benefit of the doubt on answers on tests
- Give less smiling and other positive interactions
- Give briefer and less informative feedback
- Plan less use of effective but time-consuming instructional methods
- Give less eye contact and other nonverbal communication of attention
- Give less acceptance and use of lows' ideas
- Expose lows to an impoverished curriculum (pp. 90–91)

Some low performers are students who are physically or mentally challenged. Touch- and sight-sensitive adaptive technology is now available to serve these students.

Differences in Evaluation

You may want to devise nontraditional ways to evaluate advanced students. For example, objective tests may not be able to measure the kinds of growth anticipated for this group. You may choose oral discussions or one-on-one questioning to discover the depth of insight these students have developed. Term projects may be preferable to examinations. For example, the teacher of a student who writes a computer program to breed plants may find that the resulting product—that is, the computer program—is itself the best measure of success for this assignment.

Precautions

Whenever students are grouped by ability, you must take certain precautions. There is a certain prestige in being affiliated with the upper group(s), while a certain disgrace befalls students who are assigned to the lower group(s). Attempts to disguise the ranking or ordering of groups usually fail. Indeed, students often know the level to which they are assigned even before their teachers know it.

Do not make comments that allow comparisons among ability groups, and do not allow students to make judgmental or derogatory comments about any group. Sometimes teachers contribute to the caste problem without even realizing their error. Mrs. Bentley's keyboard class had about thirty girls and ten boys, none of whom had previously taken typing. She had a unique system for reporting individual grades. Along one wall she posted a white sheet of paper with a landscape scene. It had a fence in the foreground and a blue sky above the fence. Higher up were beautiful, fluffy cumulus clouds. On the fence sat about forty bluebirds. Each had the name of a student.

The namesake of the bird called "James" lived in one of the city's worst ghettos. As each student developed the ability to type 25 words a minute, the namesake bird would leave the fence and begin to ascend. Right away, several birds made their departures. These represented students who owned a computer and had been familiar with typing at the beginning of the class. This frustrated James because he was still learning the keys when others were typing more than 25 words per minute. Each day he found himself trying a little harder and making more mistakes (each mistake carried a 5-word penalty). By the end of the year, some of the bluebirds were flying into the clouds. James's bluebird was still sitting on the fence.

Peer approval is important to students in middle and high school, and its absence can reinforce the emotional damage resulting from ability grouping. Also, upper-level groups tend to become snobbish and condescending toward members of lower groups. Make a list of at least five ways teachers can limit the amount of psychological damage that ability grouping might cause.

Interclass Ability Grouping

In some schools, ability grouping is done independently of teachers—standardized intelligence tests determine student placement in groups. Under these circumstances, teachers are still responsible for protecting the lower groups from ridicule. **Interclass grouping** (grouping among classes) and **intraclass grouping** (grouping withing a class) produce different types of competition. When students are grouped within the same class, they are forced to compete with classmates, but when the grouping is done externally the competition is between two or more classes.

For several centuries schools in England have had "houses." A house is a group of students whose abilities are heterogeneous. In other words, each group (or house) contains students with a wide range of abilities. The houses frequently compete in oral debates. This encourages cooperation, not competition, among members of a group.

Other schools choose homogeneous ability grouping. For example, five groups of students with similar abilities may be formed, producing five "tracks," each track representing a different level of general ability. Here is an example.

> *Reflection*
>
> Read the following description and respond to the questions below.
>
> **A School District Uses Systematic Grouping**
>
> You walk into a seventh-grade classroom and see several groups of students throughout the room. On closer observation, you notice that Group A is collecting weather data, using a weather vane, thermometer, and hygrometer; Group B is constructing a U.S. map with a weather symbols key at the bottom, and Group C is shading the map to show general rainfalls, altitudes, and temperatures. Groups D and E are competing vigorously, developing new ways of forecasting the weather one year into the future. On the wall are color-coded charts that show at a glance the group level to which any student belongs.
>
> You notice that Bobby Burns belongs to Group A in English, Group B in social studies, and science, Group C in mathematics, and Group D in spelling. A small square is added above Bobby's name as he completes a unit in the appropriate subject. It doesn't seem to bother Bobby that he belongs to groups of different academic levels; his rate of performance in each group appears to be more important to him.
>
> If you were teaching in a school system that was contemplating using a similar approach, and if you had an opportunity to vote for or against a tracking program, how would you vote? Why?

This example is typical of a classroom in one of the nation's largest and most progressive school systems; all 185 schools use the approach found in this classroom. Several similar approaches to cooperative learning have been developed. One system, called Teams–Games–Tournaments (TGT), has heterogeneous groups competing for academic awards. It enables low-ability and high-ability students to contribute the same number of points to the team. TGT has been used in more than 2,000 schools. Group games arrange for each group member to have some of the information needed to solve a problem, ensuring that everyone is responsible for group success.

Grade Contracts

Grade contracting is a method that recognizes that students are more highly motivated by some topics than others. It permits a student to place more emphasis on certain topics. Here is how it works.

At the beginning of each unit of study, students are issued contracts. According to the student's ability and interest in the topic, the student agrees to perform a certain amount of work to earn a certain grade. A sample contract is shown in Figure 7.4. As shown in Chapter 11, grade contracts can be powerful motivators. In addition to contracting for specific grades, students can contract to earn free time and other rewards.

Using Instructional Models

Another way to organize lessons is to use the formats provided by instructional models. An advantage to using models is that models have been examined and tested and have been proven theoretically and practically sound. Lewellen (1990, p. 63) says that a model should be "systematic, descriptive, explanatory, and widely applicable." Some examples of instruc-

> Grade of B*
>
> The grade of B can be earned through attending the class meetings and contributing to class discussions—especially those that involve critiquing the manuscripts of other participants and preparing a folder containing the following:
>
> 1. One query letter with all required criteria clearly marked as such
> 2. One cover letter with all required criteria clearly marked as such
> 3. A list of at least three journals selected for this manuscript, with a description of the following characteristics of each journal:
>   a. audience
>   b. average reading level
>   c. average minimum-to-maximum manuscript pages, using an average of 300 words per manuscript page
>   d. guidelines for submitting manuscripts
>   e. name and address of editor
> 4. A list of idea for topics
> 5. A list of your personal writing requirements including preferred time of day, length of writing sessions, physical conditions, and materials and equipment
> 6. A description of at least two strategies that will help you deal with rejection.
>
> Grade of A*
>
> Complete all assignments for the grade of B and
>
> 1. Submit a second article on this topic rewritten to fit another type of journal, using the same cover-page format as on the first article.
> 2. Explain how this manuscript is more suited to this new audience in terms of the readership and the requirements of this journal.
> 3. Submit a system for tracking your manuscripts.
> 4. In one page, explain how this course has helped you to
>   a. improve your writing skills (style)
>   b. improve your chance of getting manuscripts accepted
>
> *All assignments are due and must be submitted on or before the last class session. All materials should be submitted typed and bound in a folder. Part I should contain the B-level assignments; Part II, the A-level assignments. Inexpensive cardboard folders with metal tabs inside are preferred.

FIGURE 7.4 TWELFTH-GRADE ENGLISH SIX-WEEK WRITING UNIT CONTRACT

From Kenneth T. Henson, *Methods and Strategies for Teaching in Secondary and Middle Schools*, third edition. Published by Allyn and Bacon, Boston, MA. Copyright © 1996 by Pearson Education. Reprinted by permission of the publisher.

tional models include direct instruction, scientific inquiry, concept attainment, and the Socratic questioning model. Reyes (1990) endorses the use of such models to plan lessons:

> *Models provide a convenient organizer for teaching the precepts of effective teaching or for teaching the steps of lesson planning. For the teacher in the classroom at any level, models of instruction can structure his or her decision making. For example, the teacher's choice of classroom questions, homework assignments, introductions to lessons, and so on are typically influenced by the instructional model being used as an organizer. (p. 214)*

Information Processing Model

A popular contemporary way to examine and describe learning is by viewing it mechanically, as you might describe the process that computers use to store and retrieve information. Using the five senses to gather information (Figure 7.5), humans immediately decide which infor-

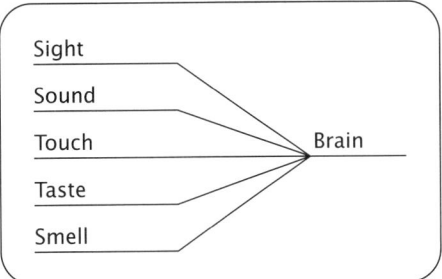

FIGURE 7.5 OUR FIVE SENSES ACT AS RECEPTORS

From Kenneth T. Henson, *Methods and Strategies for Teaching in Secondary and Middle Schools*, third edition. Published by Allyn and Bacon, Boston, MA. Copyright © 1996 by Pearson Education. Reprinted by permission of the publisher.

mation to store. A perceptual screen is used to filter out unwanted information (Figure 7.6).

Information selected for keeping is stored in one of two places. Information that is to be used immediately or in the near future is stored in the working memory; other information is stored in the long-term memory. Van Gulick (1990) believes that students cannot possess information unless it is stored in a manner that allows them to use it. He stresses the need for interconnections.

As you introduce new information to students you can use advance organizers to enhance retention. **Advance organizers** are strategies that point students toward the most important information, thus affecting the information they retain. Then, by helping them relate this new information to existing knowledge, you can help your students get meaning from otherwise meaningless information.

Historically, teachers have generally taught subject matter without emphasizing—indeed, often without even addressing—the question of how we know what we know. When the "how" has been addressed, our teachers have taught us that we learn through our senses and through applying logic. Notice that these channels are cognitive. In recent years, we have learned to study our minds directly (metacognition) to discover how they operate. Note, too, that this emphasis has also been restricted to cognition.

What our teachers have failed to teach us is that we also learn through our emotions. Since a major way that we express our emotions is through the arts, should we not also explore the role that the arts play in our learning? Are there not many other ways that our feelings and perceptions affect our learning? Should we also be studying how our feelings help us learn?

Oddliefson (1994) tells us that several prominent scientists, including Albert Einstein, have stressed the inextricable link between the sciences and the senses and that Einstein said that the aim of science is to comprehend the sense experiences in their full diversity. Through the arts, we can and do grasp meanings that we might otherwise never have. Unfortunately, those who hold the education pursestrings seem to lack an appreciation for the perceptual arts. Considering the arts as frills in education (Perrin, 1994), less than 1 percent of the U.S. Department of Education's budget is devoted to arts education, and when local school districts are forced to trim their budgets, the arts are usually first to go.

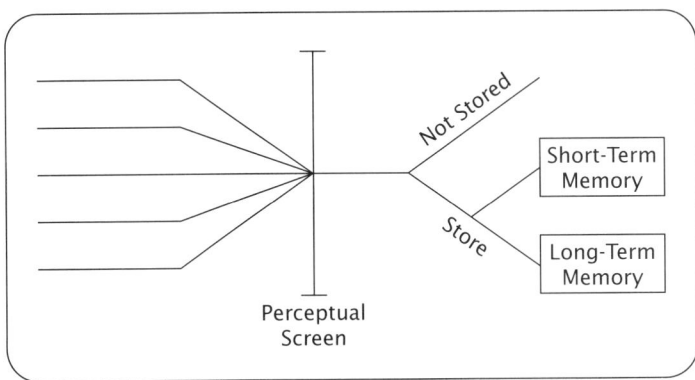

FIGURE 7.6 INFORMATION IS STORED IN EITHER SHORT-TERM OR LONG-TERM MEMORY

From Kenneth T. Henson, *Methods and Strategies for Teaching in Secondary and Middle Schools*, third edition. Published by Allyn and Bacon, Boston, MA. Copyright © 1996 by Pearson Education. Reprinted by permission of the publisher.

As you continue to study long-term curriculum planning, consider the need for balance among the arts and sciences. As you select activities, consider the power that each has for providing insights into our perceptions. In attempting to raise the rigor of the curriculum, education reformers have increased the sciences at the expense of snuffing out the arts, a process that Kohn (2001) has called cannibalization: "Across the nation, schools under intense pressure to show better test results have allowed those tests to cannibalize the curriculum. Administrators have even eliminated vital parts of schooling; programs in the arts . . . " (p. 350). The push for high test scores and standardization smothers the important advantage the arts offer students to expand their unique potentials, curiosities, and interests in learning.

Saying that the high-stakes testing and standards movement will replace many existing good practices, one educator described the movement as a virus: "At whatever point a high-stakes, standardized test is imposed as the sole basis for determining student success, the test will replace whatever content and performance standards were previously in place. It's something like a computer virus that erases and replaces everything that was stored on one's hard drive" (Thompson, 2001, p. 361).

As Eisner (2001, p. 370) said, we need to be concerned not only with what students can do, but also with what they will do. Because early adolescents are experiencing one of the fastest growth rates of their lives, middle-level teachers must find ways to integrate art into their classes and give students avenues in which to express and stretch their unique ideas and abilities.

Mastery Learning

In 1963 a professor at Harvard University wrote an article titled "A Model of School Learning," in which he challenged the then-accepted belief that students' intelligence quotients (IQs) are a major factor in determining academic success (Carroll, 1963). Carroll hypothesized that if three conditions were met, at least 90 to 95 percent of all high school students could master class objectives. The three conditions were (1) the student must be given all the time he or she needed, (2) each student must be properly motivated, and (3) the subject matter must be presented in a manner compatible with the individual student's learning style.

Using Carroll's model, Benjamin S. Bloom and his students at the University of Chicago developed an education system called Learning for Mastery (LFM) (Block & Henson, 1986). This is a teacher-paced and group-based system. In other words, the teacher leads the lessons and the class as a group follows. Most mastery learning programs, however, are student-paced (i.e., the students set the pace) and individually based. Each student pursues learning individually—at that student's own preferred pace (Guskey & Gates, 1986).

All mastery learning programs have several important characteristics in common. First, they provide students with different lengths of time to master each topic. Second, they give students opportunities to remediate or restudy material that proves difficult and then to retest without penalty. Third, all mastery learning programs use formative evaluations—evaluation designed to promote learning, not to be computed in the grading system. Short daily or weekly tests are given to diagnose learning weaknesses and teaching weaknesses; teachers and learners then adjust to improve the resulting learning. Finally, all mastery learning uses criterion-based evaluation. Criterion-based, or **criterion-referenced,** evaluation tells students what criteria their performance will be graded on before the study unit begins.

Finally, with mastery learning programs, as with all other programs, the success depends on how it is used. Cunningham (1991) explains:

> There are two essential elements of the mastery learning process. The first is an extremely close congruence between the material being taught, the teaching strategies employed, and the content measured. The second essential element is the provision of formative assessment, opportunities for students followed by feedback, corrective and enrichment activities. (p. 84)

How effective is mastery learning compared with traditional programs? Burns (1979) examined results from 157 mastery learning studies and discovered that 107 studies found that mastery learning students significantly outscored their traditionally taught counterparts, while 47 of the studies showed no significant differences. Only three of the 157 studies reported traditionally taught students outscoring mastery learning students. Burn's (1979) study of mastery learning over 15 years in 3,000 schools concluded that mastery learning was consistently more effective than traditional curriculums (Hyman & Cohen, 1979). Guskey and Gates (1986) reviewed 25 studies of group-based and teacher-paced mastery learning in elementary and secondary schools. In all 25 studies, the students in the mastery learning groups outlearned their counterpart control groups.

However, mastery learning is not without its critics and criticisms. In a 1984 review of studies on mastery learning, Arlin (1984) reported some of the more popular criticisms. According to this report, some critics claim that the ability of mastery learning to equalize students' learning abilities is an overstatement. Some critics describe mastery learning as a "psychological trap"; many claim that it does not have a proper conceptual base. Some even label mastery learning as a "Robin Hood" phenomenon that takes from the advanced students and gives to the poor students. Arlin himself argues that studies that find all students equally capable should be interpreted more cautiously. Slavin (1989) says that "if school districts expect that by introducing group-based mastery learning or Madeline Hunter's methods they can measurably increase their students' achievement, there is little evidence to support them" (p. 79).

When you read professional journal articles, remember that any innovation may experience either astounding success or total failure, depending on the conditions of the moment. The old adage, "Never believe anything you hear, and believe only half of what you see," is good advice as an admonition to proceed with caution as you continue to learn more about your chosen profession.

Matching Students' Learning Styles and Teachers' Teaching Styles

The first step in effective teaching is to learn how your students learn (Johnston, 1998), yet often schools ignore those factors that affect learning most. For example, the peak learning time for most high school students is afternoon, yet most high school classes are held in the mornings (Callan, 1998). How individuals concentrate on, process, internalize, and remember new and difficult academic information is called their learning style (Dunn & Dunn, 1992; Dunn, Dunn, & Perrin, 1994). Approximately three-fifths of learning style is biologically determined; the remaining two-fifths develops as an outgrowth of life experiences (Thies, 1979).

Dunn and Dunn (1992, 1993) describe several factors that determine individual learning styles:

1. *Environmental* (quiet versus sound, warm versus cool, bright versus soft illumination, and formal versus informal seating)
2. *Emotional* (motivation, persistence, responsibility, and internal versus external structure)
3. *Sociological* (learning alone, learning with peers, learning with adults present, learning in varied ways versus in patterns or routines; being motivated by a teacher; or being motivated by a parent)

4. *Physiological* (auditory, visual, tactual, or kinesthetic perceptual memory preferences, intake, energy highs and lows, and mobility versus passivity)
5. *Psychological* (global versus analytic and reflective versus impulsive) preferences (see Figure 7.7).

Research has demonstrated that teachers are able to identify only a few elements of their students' learning styles through observation; other elements are identifiable only through administration of reliable and valid tests (Beaty, 1986; Dunn, Dunn, & Price, 1977; Marcus, 1977). Keefe (1982) reported that the Learning Style Inventory (LSI) (Dunn & Dunn, 1978) is the most widely used instrument to identify the learning styles of K–12 students.

Although learning style changes with age and maturity, in every family: (1) mothers and fathers invariably have opposite styles; (2) siblings learn differently from each other; and (3) offspring tend to learn differently from at least one or both of their parents (Dunn, Beasley, & Buchanan, 1994). Some learning-style differences exist between students from different cultures, but more have been shown among students within the same culture (Milgram, Dunn, & Price, 1993; Dunn & Griggs, 1995).

Research conducted at more than a hundred institutions of higher education indicates widespread and growing interest in this construct (*Research on the Dunn and Dunn Learning*

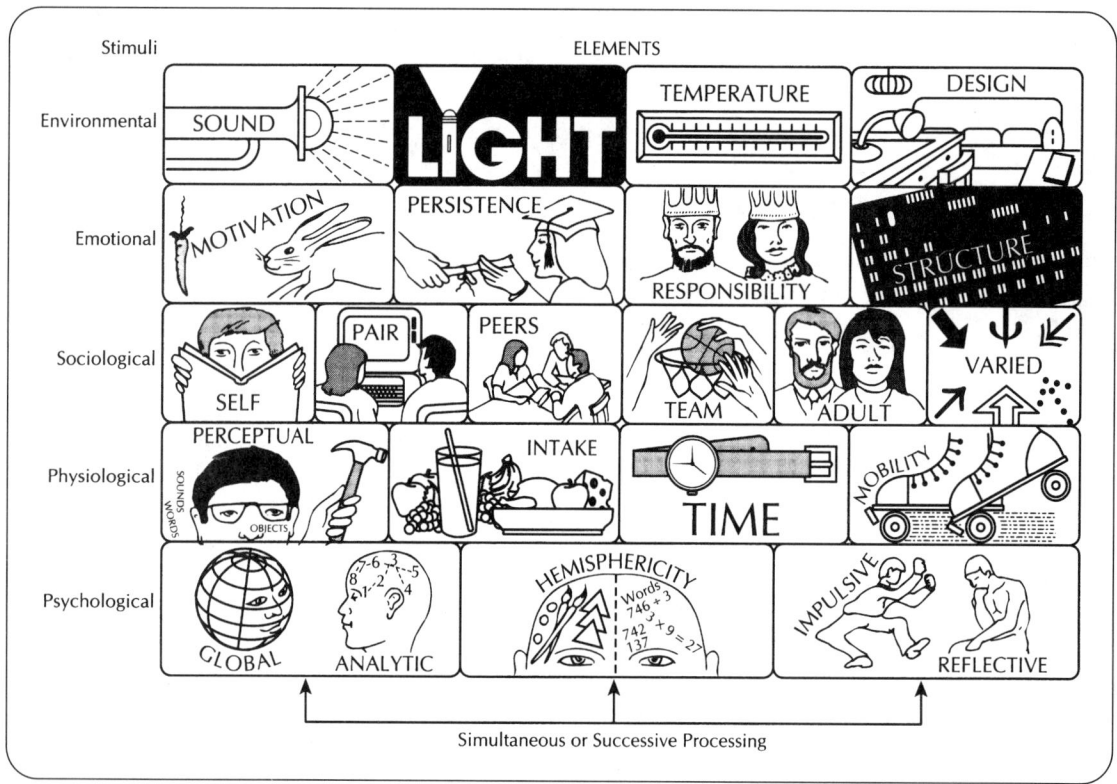

FIGURE 7.7 LEARNING STYLES MODEL
From *Teaching secondary students through their individual learning styles* (p. 4) by R. Dunn and K. Dunn, 1993. Boston: Allyn & Bacon. Reprinted by permission.
Designed by Dr. Rita Dunn and Dr. Kenneth Dunn.

Styles Model, 1994). No learning style appears to be better or worse than another. Crucial to academic success is the matching of each student's learning style with either a complementary teaching style or instructional approaches that match students' learning styles. Statistically higher standardized reading and mathematics achievement test scores were reported for elementary (Andrews, 1990, 1991; Lemmon, 1985; Stone, 1992) students and significantly higher grade-point averages were reported for secondary (Elliot, 1991) and college (Clark-Thayer, 1987) students. These data were confirmed in a meta-analysis of 42 experimental studies with the Dunn and Dunn Learning Styles Model conducted at many universities between 1980 and 1990 (Dunn, Griggs, Olson, Gorman, & Beasley, 1996). In addition, practitioners reported impressive standardized achievement test gains among average students and underachievers (Andrews, 1991) and for special education students (Quinn, 1993).

For example, under the supervision of a team of researchers from the State University of New York at Buffalo, classified learning-disabled (LD) and emotionally handicapped (EH) students (K–6) in the Buffalo city schools were randomly selected and randomly assigned to two groups. The learning styles of the students in the experimental group were identified, and complementary methods and resources were used to teach them through their learning-style strengths and to teach themselves and each other with tactual and kinesthetic resources. The control group was taught with conventional lectures, discussions, readings, and writing assignments by their experienced special education teachers. Results at the end of two years revealed that the experimental group achieved statistically higher test scores than the control group in both reading and mathematics on two different standardized achievement tests, the Woodcock-Johnson (WJ) and the California Tests of Basic Skills (CTBS). In contrast, the control group evidenced academic losses between the connecting statements and posttest (Quinn, 1993) (Figure 7.8).

Results of Standardized Achievement Test Scores in Reading and Mathematics for Students in the Buffalo City Schools' Learning Style Program (Experimental Group) in Contrast with the Results for Students in its Nonlearning Styles Program (Control Group) for the First Two Years of Program Implementation

Test Name	Group	Pretest	Posttest	Net Difference
WJ Reading	Exper.	72.38	79.1	+6.72
	Control	76.48	71.52	–4.96 (loss)
WJ Math	Exper.	69.67	84.2	+14.53
	Control	73.52	69.09	–4.43
CTBS Reading	Exper.	18.76	31.33	+12.57
	Control	24.83	21.25	–3.58
CTBS Math	Exper.	15.83	18.61	+2.78
	Control	23.44	16.95	–6.49

WJ: Woodcock-Johnson
CTBS: California Test of Basic Skills

FIGURE 7.8 REPORT FROM THE INDEPENDENT RESEARCH TEAM FROM THE UNIVERSITY OF BUFFALO

These findings revealed that LD and EH students whose instruction was not responsive to their learning styles achieved significantly less well than LD and EH students whose instruction was responsive to their learning styles. Buffalo's special education population was composed of multiculturally diverse students who had not been achieving well with conventional instruction. Improvement in the students' test scores suggested that their teachers' traditional teaching styles had been inappropriate for them. Significant improvement was also revealed in students' behavior and attitude test scores (Kryriacou & Dunn, 1994). Buffalo, which normally reported a minimum 3 percent suspension rate, reported no suspensions at all during the entire two-year period in which the LD and EH students were involved in learning-styles instruction.

The Learning Styles of Gifted and Talented Adolescents in Nine Diverse Cultures

The learning styles of gifted versus nongifted adolescents in nine different cultures were examined. The populations included Brazilian, Canadian, Egyptian, Greek, Guatemalan, Israeli, Korean, Mayan, Filipino, and U.S. adolescents diagnosed with the Learning Styles Inventory (Dunn, Dunn, & Price, 1977). The learning-style preferences of students with high versus low levels of creative accomplishment in eight domains assessed by the Tel Aviv Activities Inventory were examined. Those domains were athletics, art, dance, leadership skills, literature, mathematics, and music.

 I. Although significant differences existed among the nine culturally diverse groups, there were as many differences within each group as between groups. Despite some similarities among cultures, there were clear cross-cultural differences in both learning style and creative activity.
 II. Gifted and nongifted students revealed significantly different learning-style characteristics. Thus, instruction provided for one group is unlikely to be beneficial, and is likely to be detrimental, to other groups.
 III. Gifted adolescents who comprised the population for the Milgram, Dunn, and Price (1993) investigation were highly motivated, with strong preferences for kinesthetic or tactual—as opposed to visual and auditory—instruction. A meta-analysis of experimental research conducted in the United States between 1980 and 1990 revealed that students' learning-style preferences were the traits through which they most easily mastered new and difficult information (Dunn et al., 1996).
 IV. Although gifted students prefer kinesthetic (active) and tactual (hands-on) instruction, they are able to learn auditorily or visually, although less easily or enjoyably. On the other hand, underachieving students, who also prefer kinesthetic or tactual learning, can only master difficult information through those modalities. It is not unusual for slow learners to have either only one or no perceptual strength.
 V. Despite cultural background, students gifted in a particular domain had essentially similar learning styles, which differed significantly from the styles of the gifted in other talent domains. Thus, the gifted in each talent domain—art, dance, drama, leadership, literature, mathematics, music, or sports—reported learning through styles that were significantly different from the characteristics of the gifted in other talent domains and from those of nongifted.

VI. The gifted adolescents from nine diverse cultures preferred to learn either by themselves or with an authoritative teacher. Cooperative learning and small-group instructional strategies should not be imposed on gifted students, because few of them learn best with classmates. When permitted to learn alone, with peers, or with a teacher based on their identified learning-style preference, even highly achieving students in grades 1–12 consistently obtained significantly higher achievement and attitude test scores through their preferred—rather than their nonpreferred—sociological styles (Dunn, Dunn, & Perrin, 1994).

VII. Although some of the gifted adolescents in this study learned well in the morning, many more preferred late morning, afternoon, or evening as their best time for learning. Previous research documented the influence of time-of-day energy patterns on achievement (Dunn, Dunn, & Perrin, 1994). Conventional schooling practices that require early-morning testing appear to be unresponsive to the majority of gifted adolescents, whose best time of day frequently is not early morning. At best, conventional school schedules are responsive to only a minority of K–12 learners, because no single period during the day was preferred by more than 40 percent of school-age learners (Dunn, Dunn, & Perrin, 1994).

VIII. Of the gifted and talented in this population who were tested for processing style, 18.5 percent were analytic, 26 percent were global, and 55.5 percent were integrated processors who functioned in either processing style when interested in the content. These results demonstrate that both global and analytic students can be gifted students. However, instructional incongruence may be the rule in schools, because both textbooks and teacher training tend to promote analytic rather than global lesson planning and delivery. The revived emphasis on a thematic approach to curriculum (Dunn & Dunn, 1992) may be responsive to global students, but the handicap then may be transferred to those who are analytic. Until we either teach each group of processors differently, or teach students to teach themselves through their strengths, education will continue to help some and not help others.

Strategies for Matching Learning and Teaching Styles

Most educators recognize differences in how students learn but lack the knowledge about which methods are effective for which students and the skills for individualizing instruction. Teachers must experiment with:

1. Electroboards, learning circles, task cards (and other essentially tactual/visual resources that students can create themselves) for tactually strong learners
2. Floor games or experientially based activities for kinesthetic students
3. Contract activity packages, which permit choices of objectives, resources, activities, and student interactions, for motivated, perceptually strong, and/or nonconforming students
4. Programmed learning sequences, designed with global subtitles and introductions and many tactual resources built into the frames, for students who need structure
5. Multisensory instructional packages for unmotivated, perceptually poor, unconventional learners (Dunn, Dunn, & Perrin, 1994).

> **Reflection**
>
> Read the following description and respond to the questions below.
>
> **The Matching-Learning-and-Teaching-Styles Movement**
>
> The movement to match learning styles with teaching styles is a fluke that several educators dreamed up to get attention. Little quality research had been conducted in this area, and some of the limited studies on matching styles found little or no difference in learning. Some studies suggest that teachers should expose students to several styles, but teachers naturally tend to alter their approaches according to student responses. So matching teaching and learning styles is nothing new—it is the same old wine in a new bottle. To quote Shakespeare, it is "much ado about nothing."
>
> 1. How consistent must research findings be to be considered conclusive? In other words, must all studies produce the same answer before the answer can be considered factual?
> 2. Choose one of your favorite teachers. Does this teacher use different teaching styles? List three or four of this teacher's styles.
> 3. Do you have a single preferred style? To reach an intelligent answer to this question, draw a vertical line down the middle of a sheet of paper. On the left side list variables that enhance learning for you. On the right list variables that impede learning for you.

Using Computers to Individualize Instruction

Personal computers offer teachers unprecedented opportunities to individualize instruction. As Magney (1990) so aptly notes:

> Computer games can be a window [through] which students can enter many academic realities.... Prior to the microcomputer, computers were used primarily to give rules and other information to players but now the computer often makes decisions for the players. Unlike most of the older games, and simulations, which focus on group work, those computerized activities can be easily designed for individual use. (pp. 55–56)

Computers and other technology can also be used to empower students. Edinger (1994, p. 58) prepared fourth graders to use computers in a writing workshop to achieve this goal. As she explains, "The children decide what to write about, how much revision to do, and when and how to publish their work." Furthermore, computers can enable students to pursue topics at their own individual paces. Weasmer and Woods (2001, p. 41) explain, "Because computer use is self-paced, all students can proceed at a comfortable rate and can backtrack when needed." See also the subheading *Using Technology* later in this chapter for suggestions for using technology to teach gifted and talented students.

Programs for At-Risk Students

Much attention is being given to increasing the success of at-risk students. These are the millions of students with a greater-than-average likelihood of dropping out. These students often come from poor families or have no family at all. The characteristics that identify at-risk students are well documented. They include low achievement, retention in grade, behavior problems, poor attendance, low socioeconomic status, and attendance at schools with large numbers of poor students (Morris, 1991). These factors are stress-related; they ultimately affect classroom performance.

According to Levin (1987), approximately one-third of secondary school students are at risk of dropping out of school. Other reports estimate that the percentage of secondary students who are at risk is even higher, perhaps approaching 50 percent (Aksamit, 1990). Druian & Butler (2001) have identified several **risk factors** or characteristics of students whose academic performance is poor, including:

- Living with only one parent
- Being a child of a single parent
- Having parents who failed to complete high school
- Living in a low-income household
- Living in high-growth states
- Having poorly-developed academic skills
- Having low self-esteem
- Speaking English as a second language

Several societal conditions have contributed to the larger number of at-risk students. For example, one-half of U.S. families in all social groups will at some time become involved in dangerous behavior. The Carnegie Council on Adolescent Development (1996) reported that "At least one quarter of all adolescents are at high risk for engaging in dangerous behaviors that threaten their health and long-term prospects" (p. 4). The United States leads the entire industrialized world in its rate of adolescent pregnancy; 1 million children run away from home every year; adolescents are the only age group in the United States for which the statistics for suicide, obesity, sexually transmitted diseases, drug and alcohol abuse, and violent death keep increasing (Banks, Kopassi, & Wilson, 1991). Between 1980 and 1992, the suicide rate for 10- to 14-year-olds more than doubled (Hilliard, 1999).

A condition that contributes heavily to academic failure for millions of students is poverty. Emphasizing the role that poverty plays in school success and failure, Kohn (2001) says, "Don't let anyone tell you that standardized tests are not accurate measures. The truth of the matter is that they offer a remarkably precise method for gauging the size of the houses near the school where the test was administered" (p. 349). One reason that students from low-income families find school success difficult to achieve relates to reading. Success in all subjects correlates highly with success in reading. Krashen (1998) has noted that "Too many of our students, particularly those in high poverty schools, struggle to become fluent readers (p. 19)." One approach to helping students improve both their reading skills and their love for reading is called "free reading." **Free reading** is providing reading material to students, without charge. For example, some schools give subscriptions to magazines. Knowing that they will be having a quiz on material after it is presented, it causes students to focus on the lesson; therefore, teachers can help at-risk students by administering weekly quizzes immediately following lessons.

Even the schools conduct several activities that seem to work against students' best interests. For example, a *Phi Delta Kappan* study of at-risk students found that failure to promote students is clearly harmful because it increases the likelihood that students will drop out and diminishes the probability that they will raise their achievement levels (Frymier & Gansneder, 1989). Many at-risk students are vulnerable to failure of any kind because they do not have the assurance lent by academic success; therefore, their blossoming depends on a supportive, warm, confidence-building environment (Blumenthal, Holmes, & Pound, 1991). "In a changing America, the sense of community that once was common to small towns and even urban neighborhoods, has eroded. Stable, close-knit communities that once provided safety nets and support systems are much less common now than they were a generation or two ago" (Hilliard, 1999, p. 52).

A study at Florida State University found that arts education has considerable potential for helping at-risk students improve their levels of self-confidence. Sautter (1994) reported:

> *The Florida researchers also discovered that students in the arts learned to take criticism from peers, teachers, parents, and audiences. The constructive use of criticism, they said, built confidence in at-risk students. It helped the students come to value themselves and their achievements. (p. 436)*

As Perrin (1994, p. 453) has said, "Artists take risks and learn from their mistakes."

At-risk students have developed counterproductive behaviors. Wellington and Perlin (1991, p. 88) say, "We need innovations for 'unteaching' counterproductive behavior." Alternative learning styles also can contribute to programs for at-risk students. One program director (Friedman, 1991) says, "We respect the fact that individuals learn differently and we empower our students to accept responsibility for maximizing their learning potential" (p. 89). You may recall reading in Chapter 5 that one way to empower students is to use student-initiated questions.

Other appropriate qualities for at-risk curricula include high involvement, high reinforcement, and personalization. However, each program must be designed or altered to meet students' particular needs. Elkind (1991) cautions that making programs more rigorous is an overly simplistic view that is both mindless and destructive. At-risk students need clear objectives, a variety of instructional methods, frequent monitoring, and frequent evaluation of their progress toward the lesson objectives (Druian & Butler, 2001).

Today, educators realize that to meet the needs of at-risk students, schools must begin addressing them early in their school experiences, preferably even in preschool. Karweit (1987) found that full-day kindergarten programs, as opposed to half-day programs, improved the performance of at-risk students. The additional time is required for attitude changes. These children must develop self-confidence. But students don't outgrow this problem, and middle-level teachers have a big role to play in educating at-risk students.

Successful programs for at-risk students have several common characteristics. Most have close relationships among the schools, other community agencies, and the homes. Successful classrooms for at-risk students also have several common characteristics, including:

- Using a minimum of clearly stated classroom rules
- Setting clear expectations
- Monitoring student behavior

Early adolescence is a particularly confusing age. Hilliard (1999) explains: "In the process of moving their identity from being mom's and dad's little boy or girl, they develop a group identity centered largely around their peers. Both relationships are often in a state of flux as they are attempting to maintain both identities while moving to still a third, their own independent identity" (pp. 52–53). Because many at-risk students do not have anyone who can have a conversation with them, one program for at-risk students provided students at least 30 minutes each day to discuss whatever they wanted to talk about (Blumenthal et al., 1991).

In response to the isolation that at-risk students experience in our society, most programs for these students require them to work cooperatively with their classmates. For example, in a program called Writing Roulette, one participant identifies a problem in writing, another writer suggests ways for solving the problem, and a third concludes by solving the problem. This cooperative approach encourages persons who may be reluctant to express their ideas in writing (Lile, Lile, & Jefferies, 1991). Because at-risk students are often isolated and alienated from the mainstream in our society, successful at-risk programs tend to be personal, requiring one-on-one attention (Coleman, 1991). "The driving force in reaching and teaching at the middle level requires knowing your students as well as you know your subject matter. More than knowing, caring is crucial to the development of physically and emotionally healthy young adolescents" (Hilliard, 1999, p. 56).

The teacher's attitude toward at-risk students has a strong influence on the success level of these students. Slavin (1998) suggests that the first rule for helping at-risk students is to begin by thinking of all students as being not at risk but *at promise.*

Special Education

Special education is that part of the education process that attempts to meet the needs of youngsters who require modification of regularly accepted school practices to develop to their maximum potential. According to Potter, Carruthers, and Green (2002, p. 43), more than one student in ten (11 percent) need special help to achieve. The problem is not so much that the student is different, but that the educational process must be different. "But," you may say, "isn't this the job of specialists who have been trained to work with these students?" The answer is yes, there are specialists whose training enables them to work with these students, but the classroom teacher is the one who helps them move into the mainstream. Many contemporary educators believe that the mainstreaming approach to working with challenged children is the best approach because:

- Every child has a right to an equal education opportunity, even at the expense of having different education experiences.
- Most exceptional children need integration, not segregation.
- Labeling is an administrative crutch that says nothing about a student's assets and desires to be accepted as a normal person.

Once students are labeled, there is a tendency to stop expecting them to excel; therefore, this book will avoid such terms as *crippled* and *handicapped,* replacing them with *challenged,* which promises hope. Similarly, the term *disabled* will be replaced with *students with disabilities.* For many years U.S. society has recognized that a free or public education is all citizens' right. Although each state determines the methods of providing such education, federal legislation guarantees the right. On average, special education costs nearly twice as much as regular education. Because some states have been too casual about providing education for challenged youngsters, federal legislation now specifies exactly what services must be provided and supplies the funds needed to run these programs. You must become familiar with some of the more important laws that guarantee quality education for your challenged students. Professional journals can alert you to new legislation.

Public Law 94-142

The greatest single federal legislative action on behalf of challenged students is Public Law 94-142 (the Education for All Challenged Children Act, enacted in 1977). This law requires that each state provide special education services for its challenged students at public expense and under public supervision and direction. These special services must meet state education agency standards; include an appropriate preschool, elementary, and secondary school education; and conform with the individualized education program. The law required that by September 1, 1978, all students aged 3 to 19 (later extended to 21) were to be served, which includes receiving adequate classroom instruction. The impact of this law on schools continues to grow.

PL 94-142 is a complicated law. Nowhere in its many pages does it mention "mainstreaming." Instead it uses the words "least restrictive environment," which does allow for special students to be removed from special classes if those students are restricted when placed in special classrooms. The thrust of the law seems to be to keep challenged students in the classroom with nonchallenged students, as opposed to grouping challenged students together for instruction. *Although the term mainstreaming is not used, PL 94-142 requires the practice.*

The findings that led to enactment of PL 94-142 may help us understand the need for this legislation:

1. There are more than 8 million challenged children in the United States today.
2. Challenged children's educational needs are not being fully met.
3. More than half the challenged children do not receive appropriate educational services.
4. One million challenged children are excluded entirely from the public school system.
5. There are many students in regular programs whose challenges are undetected.
6. Because public school systems lack adequate services, families must find other services at their own expense.
7. With appropriate funding, state and local educational agencies have the knowledge and the methods to provide effective special education and related services.
8. State and local educational agencies have this responsibility, but they have inadequate financial resources.
9. It is in the national interest to help state and local educational agencies provide programs to meet challenged children's educational needs to ensure equal protection under the law.

One major provision of PL 94-142 is that before placement or denial of placement in educational programs, students and their parents must be offered (1) notice of the proposed action, (2) the right to a hearing before final action, (3) the right to counsel at that hearing, (4) the right to present evidence, (5) the right to full access to relevant school records, (6) the right to confront and cross-examine officials or employees who might have evidence of the basis for the proposed action, (7) the right to an independent evaluation, (8) the right to have the hearing open or closed to the public at the parent's option, and (9) the right to an impartial hearing officer. The hearings must be held at a place and time convenient for the parents. In other words, students and their parents have a right to question the appropriateness of individual educational plans or programs.

As a teacher, you will probably be directly involved in complying with the guidelines set forth in PL 94-142 and its successor, PL 101-476. This will include developing a program plan each year to show how your school is meeting the requirements. If your school fails to meet these requirements, it will lose its federal funding. One of your responsibilities as a teacher is to help challenged students get the support to which they are entitled.

Meeting Special Needs in the Regular Classroom

Regular classroom teachers have voiced strong concerns about having challenged students in their classes. One reason for these concerns is the additional responsibilities this law places on classroom teachers. (These responsibilities are discussed later in this chapter.) But basic to the worries and frustrations that PL 94-142 and the resultant mainstreaming have caused is teachers' lack of knowledge about their new role and responsibilities. Put simply, most teachers do not think they are adequately prepared to meet this challenge. Indeed, many insist that their preparatory programs contained little or no information about teaching challenged students.

Teachers need in-service education to prepare them for mainstreaming; however, some in-service programs have failed to improve teacher attitudes toward mainstreaming (Baines & Baines, 1994). Sometimes additional contact with mainstreamed students improves teachers' attitudes toward challenged students, but in other instances additional contact with challenged students fails to improve teachers' attitudes (Baines & Baines, 1994). Another factor affecting teachers' attitudes toward mainstreaming is the level of support services available to them.

The most important thing for preservice teachers to know is that the more information about mainstreaming teachers accumulate before actually becoming involved in the process, the more positive their attitude about mainstreaming will be. Accordingly, preservice teachers should seek out opportunities to learn more about challenged students and about the roles of regular teachers who have one or more challenged students in their classrooms. The remainder of this chapter is a good beginning point. The "Activities" section at the end of the chapter will facilitate your continuing this pursuit.

Inclusion

A similar concept to mainstreaming is inclusion, which has several definitions. One definition is: **inclusion** involves keeping special education students in regular classrooms and bringing support services to the child, rather than bringing the child to the support services (Smelter, Rasch, & Yudewitz, 1994). Another definition of inclusion is offered by Bradley and Fisher (1995): "**Inclusive education** is the formal name given to an educational arrangement in which all students are given the opportunity to participate in general education

---

Teacher as Proactive Decision Maker

Classroom Situation

1. You can expect to have one or more emotionally challenged students in your classes. Sometimes these students will startle their classmates and you with a sudden scream or outburst of laughter.

Proactive Alternatives

1. Plan a discussion that you can conduct with the entire class. Remind them that each of us is different. We must learn to adjust to the differences of others as we hope they can adjust to our uniqueness.

2. Relax. A study by Williams (1998) showed that classmates find it easier to adjust than teachers.

3. Before these students join the class, meet with a counselor and gather positive information about your challenged students. Share this good news with the class.

> **THE CASE**

Doing What Makes Sense

Marjorie Economopoulos, Kennesaw State University
Pam Cole, Kennesaw State University
Anne Bowen, Awtrey Middle School

Dr. Marjorie Economopoulos is Chair of the Department of Secondary and Middle Grades Education, and Associate Professor of Mathematics Education, Kennesaw State University, Georgia. She received her Ph.D. in mathematics education from Georgia State University.

"Learn to practice active listening. Your students have important ideas to share both academically and personally."

Dr. Pam Cole is Associate Professor of Middle Grades and Language Arts Education, Department of Secondary and Middle Grades Education, at Kennesaw State University. She received her Ph.D. in curriculum and instruction with a concentration in English education from Virginia Tech University.

"Relationships have the power to make or break you as a teacher. As you begin your career, seek out highly successful educators as mentors, participate in professional organizations, and establish teacher/student relationships that foster mutual respect."

Ms. Anne Bowen teaches sixth-grade mathematics at Awtrey Middle School. She received her M.Ed. in Middle Grades Education from Kennesaw State University with concentrations in mathematics and social studies.

"I want kids to enjoy math and see it as solving problems, not following rules."

Background Information

Today's beginning teachers find themselves in a Catch-22. Having completed teacher education programs that promote cutting-edge pedagogy (i.e., student-centered learning, cooperative learning, hands-on activities, discovery and inquiry teaching), new teachers are ready to set the world on fire. Their visions and dreams are crushed, however, in school cultures that advocate lecture and "drill and kill" worksheets, which place little value on social aspects of learning, prior knowledge, and relevancy. High-stakes testing and student and teacher accountability thwart teaching and learning theories that position students at the heart of learning, that challenge them to think critically, that teach them to collaborate. As a result, beginning teachers feel torn between best practices and traditional pedagogy very early, often at the initial job interview. Below are sample interview questions and student comments that illustrate this point:

"If we hire you, you will be expected to do sentence diagramming in your classroom. How do you feel about that?"

(New teacher thinks but doesn't say, "I suppose I feel okay since I want a job.")

"We know what your university teaches, but we use a scripted math program with plenty of practice exercises."

(New teacher again, "That's okay. I need the job, and I don't really know that much about this math program anyway.")

"In our classes, we respect silence and expect our teachers to keep their students in neat rows and columns in their desks."

(New teacher, "How can students work in cooperative groups? Well, I'm not too sure how to do that anyway.")

"You have to teach grammar here."

(New teacher thinks, "Oh, well, yeah, I knew I'd be made to do that, even though I know it's bogus. Dr. So-and-So warned me.")

"We don't believe in . . . you know . . . the fluff they teach out there in the ivory tower."

(New teacher again, "Is it really fluff? I don't think so . . . but, then . . . maybe . . . .")

So the transformation begins. Though beginning teachers admit students are often jaded and see little relevancy when taught traditionally, many routinely dismiss social learning and constructivist approaches out of fear. Jobs depend on it; so do test scores. Teachers are bored; students are bored; yet it's easier and safer to follow the status quo.

A myriad of reasons, often working together, determine whether teachers stay "true" to their training or yield to the status quo. Lacking the "experience" of their peers, not knowing the ropes, not feeling supported by peers or administration, not knowing whether they can maintain good classroom discipline or whether they have what it takes to "teach," beginning teachers find it easier to mold to their surroundings. They lack self-assurance; they lack support. Consequently, the strength to stand up for themselves wavers and the needs of their students take a backseat to mandates and tradition.

In the business world, novice employees prove themselves worthy of the most challenging, most demanding assignments; education works in reverse. New teachers are frequently placed in the most taxing classes with the most difficult students and most inadequate resources. They're expected to hit the ground running with a high level of expertise. Consequently, many spend the first year treading water and seldom catching their breaths. Following a textbook, using worksheets, and utilizing class lecture are lifesavers. Teaching is about survival.

Beginning teachers have more time during preservice experiences to prepare lessons; thus, they can focus more on creative, student-centered strategies because they are not really "responsible" for an entire group of students—their cooperating teacher helps deal with student/parent issues, and they don't have other administrative and/or extracurricular duties. Neither do they have peers, parents, or administrators pushing test scores, reminding them if scores don't improve, the school, and possibly their jobs, are in jeopardy.

Believing that preservice teachers can learn from reading about the experiences of highly successful first-year teachers, we share teaching experiences of Anne Bowen, a sixth-grade math teacher in a diverse middle school. Her story is significant, for it illustrates the beliefs, attitudes, skills, as well as experiences beginning teachers need in order to overcome the status quo.

Preservice Years

Anne was a conscientious, attentive, and cooperative nontraditional student who enrolled in a teacher education program in 1989, having worked in the business world and as a housewife and mother of three. At the urging of the assistant principal and encouraged by teachers at a school where Anne was working as an assistant, Anne enrolled in a middle-grades education program, concentrating in mathematics and social studies.

During student teaching, Anne was placed in a mathematics classroom with a very talented eighth-grade middle school teacher who was more comfortable

---

Having finished my student teaching, I was reconsidering whether I wanted to teach. There seemed such a chasm between the "ivory tower" and the actual world of teaching. In the real world I envisioned a teacher sitting at an overhead and students taking copious notes and memorizing them for the next test. The room would be dark and cool. Students would learn enough math to perform well on state and national tests, and I would be secure in my position as a teacher. However, a nightmare accompanied this vision: I asked students to analyze a mathematical real life situation. For example, how many miles could you go if you had "x" dollars and gasoline cost "x" per gallon. They were dumbfounded; they couldn't do it—better leave that problem to "Lady Luck." Consequences, I knew, were serious!

It was at this point I observed an extraordinary sixth grade math teacher. When I arrived that first morning, Mrs. Bowen was very gracious and welcoming. She waited at the door and welcomed each student. They filed in and seated themselves, and she began: "I'm looking for prepared students. . . ."

—Pat Churney, student teacher

and knowledgeable in a language arts setting. Anne and her cooperating teacher developed an open line of communication from the onset, and Anne was given free reign to explore and design whatever lessons she wished. She did not feel pressure to please or to design lessons that followed her cooperating teacher's practices.

Anne enjoyed the freedom and the open line of communication and began experimenting with student-centered pedagogy, even though her teacher was unable to assist her with anything other than traditional instruction. She had been convinced of standards-based teaching and best practices through her multiple mathematics classes and methods classes. Her vision of teaching included hands-on strategies, student-centered pedagogy, and group and problem-solving activities. She explored this vision with the support of her classroom teacher and university supervisor, who "expected" standards-based teaching and best practices.

The school in which Anne did her student teaching was quite diverse—approximately half the students were minorities and about half were eligible for free or reduced-cost lunches. Unlike many of her classmates, who felt fortunate to be placed in higher-income schools posing less challenge, Anne felt she was the lucky one for being allowed to work with a group of students who needed her. Rather than being intimidated by the students and the school culture, she believed she could make a difference in students' lives and proceeded to develop student-centered lessons with real-world relevance that encouraged high-level mathematical thinking. Anne was committed to making mathematics accessible to all her students, including those who had not been successful in more traditional settings. She believed that all students could learn mathematics at a high level; she believed no students should be relegated to only practicing multiplication, addition, and subtraction. She did not want to limit their access to higher thinking in mathematics, patterns, problem solving—the real "stuff" of mathematics.

Anne was committed to student success and had a belief that students can learn to love mathematics. Though Anne was placed in a traditional mathematics setting, what proved paramount was being supported by her cooperative teacher and being given the freedom to implement student-centered teaching. Anne was willing to take risks; she was willing to fail.

She was able to explore and implement ideas she encountered in her teacher education program, and she saw that they worked! Students succeeded; students gained confidence and developed a love for "mathematics." Anne gained confidence in her vision of teaching and began to soar.

In the Trenches

Anne accepted a teaching position in a middle school that currently enrolls approximately 1,300 students, located in a changing suburban area outside metropolitan Atlanta, Georgia. During the 2000–2001 school year, racial composition was 73 percent white, 16 percent black, 4 percent Hispanic, and 7 percent "other." The percentage of students eligible to receive free/reduced-price lunches was 15 percent.

Anne began teaching seventh-grade social studies and an occasional seventh-grade mathematics class. At that time, her school was over capacity, so she was assigned a "portable" classroom behind the school, an environment that isolated Anne and her students but proved an asset.

Capitalizing on her successful student teaching experience, Anne began designing hands-on, student-centered activities. Students worked on projects, discussed, cooperated, and conducted debates. Students described her as "creative" and having the ability to make "something out of nothing." She begged, borrowed, and pasted together units, capturing student interest. For example, for a math class, she made spinners from paperclips to illustrate probability concepts; she found unused geoboards, tangrams, calculators, and red and yellow counters in her school for hands-on activities to develop mathematical concepts and ideas. She asked open-ended questions to help students "figure it out" themselves; she trained their "habits of mind" in mathematical thinking.

Anne enjoyed the seclusion of the portable because her students could make noise without disrupting other classes or drawing attention from teachers or administrators who might think they were "off-task." She felt comfortable trying new ideas because she didn't feel "watched." When she did some lecture-teaching, she wondered if she could figure out a "constructivist" or inquiry manner of teaching the material. She kept notes and incrementally improved each lesson. After three years of teaching both social studies and mathematics, she began teaching sixth-grade mathematics full time.

Anne created a classroom of relevance, encouraging student input, and implementing strategies she had acquired in her teacher education program. She brought pertinent questions, concepts, and activities into their lives; she connected subjects to prior knowledge and interest. Confidence, commitment to student success, and a desire for students to love learning propelled Anne forward and prepared Anne to reach even higher levels as an educator.

Early in her teaching Anne understood the importance of bringing instructional technology into her classroom. At first, she invited college professors into her classroom, who taught students how to use graphing calculators. Anne then borrowed them to teach a "Cars and Ramps" unit about functions and slope. Students rolled cars down ramps, measured, conjectured, created scattergrams, and began to understand independent and dependent variables, equations of lines, and many other mathematical concepts.

As a fourth-year teacher, Anne was selected as the school's "Teacher of the Year," a remarkable honor for such a new teacher. Anne distinguished herself as a teacher who cares for students and colleagues, always being positive and helpful, always warm and personable, and volunteering to help others, always willing to shares ideas and materials. She earned respect. This recognition encouraged her and set her on the road to becoming a teacher leader.

Staying "Gold"

A cornerstone in Anne's maintaining a commitment to standards-based teaching and best practices in education has been her willingness to establish and maintain professional relationships and her personal desire to be a lifelong learner.

From her beginnings as a student teacher, through her early years as a classroom teacher, Anne bonded with proponents of best practices in middle-grades education. In her early years, she invited university professors into her classroom to teach, and she hosted preservice teachers in her classroom. Later, she pursued a master's degree and began serving on university/school partnership committees and mentoring new teachers, sharing her insights, yet learning from them as well. She became active in local, state, and national professional organizations, attending conferences, reading widely, and sharing her personal beliefs about how children best learn and teachers teach.

When asked why she never gave in to the status quo, Anne answers, "I just did what made sense." Anne observed student success and growth in their attitudes about "doing mathematics." She observed enthusiasm and student confidence. As a result of her observations, Anne remained committed to constructivist views of teaching and learning.

Anne, as is true of all teachers, has faced accountability issues. According to Georgia's 2000–2001 Public Education Report Card, approximately 20 percent of students in Anne's school do not meet the state's standards in sixth-grade mathematics as determined by the Criterion-Referenced Competency Tests (CRCTs). That percentage increases in the eighth grade to 31 percent. Though this school has a 0 percent dropout rate for this year, teachers and administration remain concerned that nearly one-third of students do not meet state standards on the CRCT. Pressure exists to raise test scores. In the beginning, Anne wasn't sure how well her students would perform but remained committed to constructivist approaches to teaching and learning. She taught multiplication and division in the context of problem solving. She used fractions while introducing probability. She created relevance and meaning for the operations rather than introducing context-free math problems. She shunned decontextualized "drill and kill" exercises.

Students at this school were grouped heterogeneously in sixth-grade math classes, so it's a fair assumption that all sixth-grade classes have similar ability levels. When Anne's class scores were compared with those of more traditional classrooms, her students did at least as well as the other classes. On indicators that were *not* measured (i.e., confidence, concept formulations, higher order skills), how might her students have scored? There's a good chance her students might have soared. That study is yet to occur. If the edict is "Do what makes sense," she is ahead of the curve.

In Summary

While we know that beginning teachers face tremendous pressures in today's public schools and many fall into the traditional mainstream, teachers like Anne remind us it is possible to stand apart from the status quo. While support from mentors is essential in the early going, the desire to be a life-long learner, a commitment to best practices in teaching, building of confidence, and a willingness to stay connected professionally play important roles in shaping teaching philosophies once mentor ties are severed.

Through her professional relationships, her desire to learn more, and her commitment to best practices in teaching, Anne empowers students to become confident in mathematics. She poses problems and questions that relate to them. She applies mathematics in meaningful ways; she involves students in decisions; she teaches them to think and ask questions; she creates an environment in which it is safe to ask questions and safe to be wrong.

Further Reflection

1. Discuss challenges a new teacher encounters in a first year.
2. What potential conflicts can you see in a new job setting that might not fit with your own "vision" of teaching? How might you address these?
3. What kinds of support systems should new teachers seek out in the early years and beyond?
4. How can teachers set up environments in which students are comfortable learning and not afraid of making mistakes?
5. How can teachers help build student confidence?

---

with their typical age peers to the greatest extent possible" (p. 13). A major distinguishing quality between mainstreaming and inclusion is the time students with disabilities spend in the regular classroom; mainstreamed students spend part of the day in regular classrooms, whereas students in inclusion curricula spend the entire day with all students.

Some of the advantages of inclusion classes include improved self-esteem, peer relationships, and mutual respect (Federico, Herrold, & Venn, 2000). The teacher's own behavior as a role model is an essential element for reaching these advantages, which often requires teachers to become more flexible. For example, teachers in included classrooms learn to be more tolerant toward frequent absences, and they must learn to plan redundancy into their lessons. Inclusion is not effective for meeting the needs of all students. Salend and Garrick-Duhaney (1999) said that inclusive programs effectively meet the needs of only some students with mild disabilities. Other students perform better academically when more traditional special education programs are used (Holloway, 2001).

A Special Curriculum

One approach to meeting the needs of special students is by modifying the curriculum. In traditional curricula, students with disabilities were perceived as problems for the teacher, but today the curriculum is considered the problem. In other words, if we accept the premise that all children can learn, then teachers and schools are responsible for ensuring this premise (Bradley and Fisher, 1995). Having determined that the existing curriculum is inappropriate for these students, the next step is to identify special elements that need modification (Hoover, 1990, pp. 410–411). The following checklist can be used:

1. Content: Does student possess sufficient reading level?
    a. Has student demonstrated mastery of prerequisite skills?
    b. Does student possess sufficient language abilities?
    c. Does student possess appropriate prior experience?
2. Instructional strategy: Is student motivated to learn through strategy?
    a. Does strategy facilitate active participation?
    b. Is strategy effectiveness relative to content to be learned?
    c. In what conditions is strategy effective/ineffective?

3. Instructional setting: Does setting facilitate active participation?
   a. Is student able to complete tasks in selected setting?
   b. Is student able to learn in selected setting?
   c. Is setting appropriate for learning selected?

4. Student behavior: What types of behaviors are exhibited by the learner?
   a. Time on task?
   b. Attention to task?
   c. Self-control abilities?
   d. Time-management skills?
   e. What are the most appropriate behaviors exhibited in selecting a strategy?

When changing the curriculum, pay careful attention to the materials you use, especially textbooks and other written materials. Cheyney (1989) suggests a nine-step process for adapting strategies to teach written materials to special learners:

1. Change the nature of the learning task from one that requires reading and written responses to one that requires listening with oral responses (e.g., use a cassette tape or peer tutor).
2. Allow the student to demonstrate understanding through group projects or oral reports.
3. Allow the student to complete smaller amounts of material in a given time.
4. Have the student circle or underline the correct responses rather than write them.
5. Fasten the student's materials to the desk to help with coordination problems.
6. Provide extra drill-and-practice for those students who understand the material but need more time to master it.
7. Present information using graphs, illustrations, or diagrams.
8. Incorporate rhyming, rhythm, music, or movement into lessons.
9. Lessen distractions from other sources within the learning environment.

Special education teachers, however, encounter additional organizational problems peculiar to an individualized learning environment. "Factors such as student expectations, instructional goals, record keeping strategies, and behavior or social patterns pose a unique managerial dilemma for the teacher of special needs students" (Guernsey, 1989, p. 55).

Categorizing Students with Disabilities

We can categorize all students with disabilities by type of impairment—physical, mental, emotional, sensory, and neurological—but we cannot assign a group of students to these subgroups without noticing much overlap. It is better to view the individual differences as lying on a continuum grouped around a norm. Furthermore, keep in mind the degree of involvement (mild, moderate, or severe), the length of time the student has had the condition, and the stability of the condition.

The following sections discuss categories of disabilities. As you read about each, remember to consider all the above criteria (degree of involvement, length of time the student has had the condition, and stability of the condition) when deciding how to serve these students best.

The Physically Impaired

Orthopedically challenged persons have crippling impairments that interfere with normal bone, joint, or muscle function, including impairment of internal organs and systemic malfunctions. These impairments range from congenital conditions and deformities—such as dwarfism, limb absence, heart defects, hemophilia, cerebral palsy, epilepsy, and spina bifida—to traumatic conditions, such as amputations or burns.

Students with physical impairments may have limited mobility and use of certain materials or equipment and may lack motor control. As is true of most categories, the degree of impairment among orthopedically challenged students varies greatly. If the cause was congenital (a birth defect), as with cerebral palsy, the student may not have had experiences needed for intellectual growth and may now suffer from secondary challenges, such as mental retardation. Visual and speech defects are common; poor facial muscle control may cause drooling, giving the false impression of mental retardation. Thus, view and treat each challenged student as an individual.

Be careful to avoid the common tendency of nonchallenged people to underestimate orthopedically challenged students' abilities, because these students are often able to succeed with extremely complicated tasks. Their ability to conceptualize, or "know how" to do things, yet not be able to do them because of physical challenges, may frustrate them. Orthopedically challenged students' frustrations often lead to verbal aggressiveness, blaming other people, repressing desires, withdrawing into fantasy, degrading the original goals, acting less mature, and compensating by shifting to different interests.

All students display these behaviors at times, but probably to a lesser degree because their successes minimize their frustrations. You can reduce frustration in orthopedically challenged students by providing a climate of success and by accepting and including them in the schools' social activities. Teacher pity, overprotection, and ignoring may perpetuate their condition. These students must become involved if they are to learn to function and become independent. Above all else, remember that physical impairment does not automatically mean lowered mental functioning.

The Mentally Retarded

Mentally retarded students have learning rates and potentials that are considerably lower than the average for other students. Depending on the degree of retardation, there are four classifications of mental retardation, based on intelligence test scores. (Score ranges may vary slightly among states.)

Mild: 55–59
Moderate: 40–54
Severe: 25–39
Profound: 24 and below

Mildly retarded students may appear similar to normal classmates in height and weight, but closer observation reveals that they lack strength, speed, and coordination. They also tend to have more general health problems. Students who are mentally retarded may experience frustration, especially when they have been expected to function at their chronological age with materials and methods geared above their ability. They often have short attention spans and are unable to concentrate. Antisocial or impersonal behavior can also be attributed to expectations of teachers and others that they perform beyond their abilities.

The Trainable Retarded

Trainable retarded students respond slowly to education and training because their intellectual development is only 25 to 50 percent of normal, yet many can be trained for jobs that require simple skills under adequate supervision.

Retarded mental development may include slow maturation of intellectual functions needed for schoolwork. Because the retarded may be significantly low in memory skills, ability to generalize, language skills, conceptual and perceptual abilities, and creative abilities, give them tasks that are simple, brief, relevant, sequential, and designed for success.

The Emotionally Disturbed

Emotionally disturbed children are most simply perceived as those who are confused or bewildered. They do not understand their own social stresses, and they feel unaccepted in their efforts to resolve them. "Aha," you say, "so that is the category used to describe the troublemakers." Often this is true. The emotionally disturbed do tend to be either hostile or apathetic. Seriously emotionally disturbed students require psychological services. Less seriously or socially maladjusted students do not.

Most students who exhibit apathy and hostility should not be classified as emotionally disturbed. The key element is how frequently they display such behavior. For example, the student who occasionally disrupts or hits a classmate is probably not disturbed, but the one who disrupts a lesson or bothers others several times during the hour may be emotionally disturbed. At the middle and secondary levels, emotionally disturbed students often show oversensitivity to criticism and unusual anxiety because of a weak self-concept. Some may show extreme depression. Again, the behavior's frequency, duration, and intensity indicate the condition's seriousness.

In dealing with emotionally disturbed students, you must arrange opportunities for them to succeed. You must also use a considerable amount of reinforcement and avoid creating a highly threatening climate in the classroom, such as overemphasizing the importance of examinations. Do not force students who appear unusually aggressive or timid to speak in front of classmates. Ensure that the classroom is free of threat, ridicule, and other abuses from peers.

The Sensory Deprived

Students who have visual and hearing impairments are among the sensory deprived. The visually challenged category includes the partially sighted and the blind, while the hearing impairment category includes the deaf and the hard of hearing.

Visually challenged students vary tremendously in the degrees to which they are challenged; only about 10 percent of the legally blind are actually totally blind. Therefore, the first thing to consider when working with visually challenged students is the degree of the challenge. Another thing to consider is the length of time the student has had the challenge. Those whose problems have been life-long will need help developing concepts of space and form, whereas those whose blindness is recent will need help adjusting to their challenge.

Students who have hearing problems range from those who can hear and understand speech with difficulty, using such supports as hearing aids, to the deaf, who at most are able to distinguish only amplified sounds. In considering the extent of the hearing challenge, try to determine how much and how clearly the student can hear. Again, determine how long the student has had the challenge, because whether it occurred before or after speech and language comprehension developed makes a difference. The major problem of students who have been deaf since birth is not that they are deaf but that they are unable to develop speech and language comprehension through hearing.

When working with visually and hearing-challenged students, begin by providing psychological support. You can do this by accepting the students in their condition and believing in their ability to adjust to their challenge and to become productive individuals. Indeed, students with sensory challenges can learn to do extremely complicated tasks. Your expression of confidence in students leads to increased self-confidence.

You must create this climate of acceptance among the student's peers. Because both blind students and deaf students are unable to pick up on all the stimuli that provide cues on how and when people respond, their timing may be off or they may not respond at all. Peers who are sensitive to these limitations may interpret their response (or absence of response) as unfriendly or antisocial. Challenged students' limited vocabulary may further limit their response. Above all else, do not show pity. On the contrary, provide a positive climate that focuses on these students' abilities and potentials rather than on their limitations.

The Learning Disabled

Students who are learning disabled have normal intelligence but are unable to process information. In other words, their problem involves a dysfunction or emotional disturbance, as opposed to mental retardation or sensory deprivation. Such students may be awkward, hyperkinetic, and impulsive; a few may appear slow. Because most school programs are not designed to accommodate this type of behavior, these students are frequently viewed as having behavior problems. Some students with learning disabilities tend to be aggressive, irritable, and highly emotional; others may be even-tempered and cooperative. They may have quick changes of behavior from high-tempered to remorseful. They may even feel panic in what others see as only mildly stressful situations.

The basis of the problem with learning-disabled students can lie in the psychomotor, visual, or auditory domain. Students who have psychomotor disabilities are likely to be in poor physical condition or may frequently bump into things, for example. Their written assignments can also give clues—handwriting may be unusually large or small and crammed into one corner of the paper.

Proactive Exercise

Anticipated Situation

- You know that:
  You will have physically, mentally, and emotionally challenged students in your classes.

  The severity of the limitations of some of your students will make them unable to compete with their classmates, yet we know a majority of students believe you should use the same grading standard that you use for their nondisabled classmates.

Proactive Alternative

- You can:
  Write a brief statement of your own beliefs about whether a separate grading system for these students is justified. Invite your students to write their own philosophy regarding this issue *before* sharing yours.

  As a class, discuss your statements. Be prepared to answer the ultimate question, So what will you do?

If the student's problem is visual, you may notice that the student cannot follow visual directions, may tend to forget things seen, and may be easily distracted by surrounding activities. Furthermore, students may tend to move their eyes excessively or inappropriately. Teachers can recognize auditory disabilities when students fail to follow oral directions, forget directions, are easily distracted by noise, and confuse similar sounds.

One method of getting information on students with learning disabilities is to use learning styles inventories. Once you determine learning styles, you can then choose and use instructional treatments that match those styles. When applying this process to learning disabled mathematics classes, Dunn et al. (1994–1995, p. 3) learned that the teachers were able to improve students' achievement and attitudes. Teachers who have disabled students should also make special efforts to combine technology and small group instruction (Bradley & Fisher, 1995).

The Individualized Educational Program

The current mode of working with challenged students is to move them from groups consisting of only challenged students and to put them back into the regular classroom, but this alone does not mean that their special needs will be met. To make certain that each student's needs are met—and the special needs of each differ from those of others who may share a general problem—PL 94-142 requires that a specific individualized program be provided for each challenged student from age 3 to age 21. This approach, called Individualized Educational Programming (IEP), calls for a written statement for each challenged child that identifies that child's particular needs and describes how those needs are being met. When each IEP is completed, it becomes a legally binding contract. Potter et al. (2002) caution teachers about the need to follow it precisely: "There is no leeway with the IEP; you must follow it as it is written, just as you would a formal contract" (p. 43).

There must be a special meeting to develop the program for each challenged student. The representative of the local education authority who will be assigned to supervise the student's program, the student's teacher(s), and parents will attend. When appropriate, the student will attend the meeting too. In effect, you will be held responsible for seeing that the services planned are actually rendered. Furthermore, you are required to see that the program of each challenged student in your class is constantly evaluated. Federal law requires at least one progress review each year, and the state may require more. If a parent does not request the review, you should.

The teacher of a challenged middle or secondary student should try to establish good communications and a good working relationship with the student and parents. Because many challenged students of this age can participate in developing their own program, you should try to create a team spirit. By uniting your efforts, you, the student, and the parents can provide a program that is superior to one you plan alone. During conferences with parents, avoid using educational jargon. Being clear, precise, and up-front with parents will pay high dividends.

Each IEP must contain, as a minimum, these statements and projections:

1. The child's present level of educational performance.
2. Annual goals and short-term instructional goals.
3. The specific educational services to be provided—by whom, when, and for how long.
4. To what extent the child will be able to participate in regular educational programs.

5. Appropriate, objective criteria for evaluation, and a schedule for determining (at least annually) whether instructional objectives are being achieved.
6. The program's beginning and ending dates.
7. A statement of the parents' roles in relation to the plan.
8. Changes needed in the school situation (staffing, in-service education, etc.).

Any member of the planning team, including the student, can make the initial draft of the IEP. The rest of the team can accept the plan, revise it, or develop another plan they consider more useful for teachers and other school personnel.

Since each IEP is a cooperative effort involving the parents, you should keep the parents informed at every stage and solicit the parents' ideas, suggestions, and reactions. Assure the parents that if part of the plan proves inoperative or ineffective you will recommend changes to serve their child better. Ask the parents to let you know how the plan is working at home. A "we" approach will help you minimize any parental resistance and maximize parental cooperation. Parental cooperation is especially important because this is a team project in which you will need parental suggestions.

To further enhance your relationship with the parents, remind them that they have complete access to their child's records. Give them copies of each report, and explain exactly how assessments are made. Whenever possible, make the parents team members in the diagnosis, treatment, and education processes. Have a positive attitude. Be sure the parents understand their child's abilities and assets. Emphasize the things their child can do rather than those he or she cannot do. Help the parents learn how they can influence their child to think positively about himself or herself. Parents can also help others who might be working with the child to focus on the child's strengths and assets.

For years educators have been aware of the value of involving parents of students at all stages, but recently we have discovered the advantages of allowing students to help plan their own educational experiences. Now we have the opportunity (and responsibility) to involve both parties in planning, administering, and evaluating these special programs. Although the paperwork may be a hassle, there is no doubt that we will learn a great deal about individualizing instruction as we participate in IEPs. Most teachers will want to do whatever is necessary to help challenged students profit from their instruction.

Teacher Reactions to Public Law 94-142

Although several years have passed since PL 94-142 was introduced, many teachers are uncomfortable with this additional responsibility. A major concern is teachers' lack of faith in their ability to help challenged students. Teachers' reluctance to integrate special students into regular classes may be caused by their lack of knowledge of special students. At Michigan State University, a 3-credit-hour course on mainstreaming was used to measure the effect that increased knowledge about challenged students has on teacher confidence about putting these students into regular classes (Pernell, McInytre, & Bader, 1985). The twenty-eight participants in the course had an average of six years' teaching experience. Initially, the attitudes toward mainstreaming were in the negative to neutral ranges, but at the last session the attitudes were all in the high-positive range. The conclusions were that "the results of the findings support the importance of increased experience, knowledge attainment, and skill acquisition as a catalyst in the formation of positive attitudes towards mainstreaming students" (Pernell et al., 1985, p. 136).

As a beginning teacher, you will have help from experienced personnel when you do your first IEPs. This book gives you a good introduction, but you must learn as much as you can about PL 94-142 during your clinical experiences and once you begin teaching. You must continue learning about this law and similar laws as they emerge and change.

Public Law 101-476

PL 94-142 (The Education for All Challenged Act) was amended on October 30, 1990, becoming Public Law 101-476. The title of the new law is "Individuals with Disabilities Education Act (IDEA)." This new law refers to challenged children as "children with disabilities." The law's definition of children with disabilities has expanded to include autistic children and children with traumatic brain injury. The act also adds "rehabilitation counseling" and "social work services."

PL 101-476 provides help for students in moving beyond high school. A category titled "Transition Services" provides for movement to college education, vocational training, integrated employment, continuing and adult education, adult services, independent living, or community participation.

PL 101-476 requires an IEP for all students with disabilities. Each IEP must include a statement of transition services needed. These services must begin no later than age 16 and must be reevaluated annually thereafter.

Summary of Major Changes in Parts A–H of Public Law 101-476

Part A contains the general provisions of the act. Part B addresses the assistance for education of all challenged individuals. Part C describes the centers and the services the public schools must provide to meet the needs of students with disabilities. For example, extended school-year demonstrations for infants, toddlers, and youths with severe disabilities are provided. Also, money is available to state education agencies and state vocational rehabilitation agencies to fund state grant proposals to increase the availability, access, and quality of transition services (NASDSE, 1990, p. 12). Such services include:

1. The system must include training of primary referred sources regarding the basic components of early intervention services available in the state.
3. Increasing the availability, access, and quality of transition assistance through the development/improvement of policies, procedures, systems, and other mechanisms for youth and their families
4. Improve the ability of professionals, parents, and advocates to work with such youth to make the transition from student to adult
5. Improve working relationships among educators, relevant state agencies, the private sector, employment agencies, PICS, families, and advocates to identify and achieve consensus on the general nature and application of transition services to meet the needs of youth with disabilities

Part C also provides for children and youth with serious emotional disturbance (NASDSE, 1990, p. 13). For example, money is provided for local education agencies in collaboration with mental health entities to:

6. Increase the availability, access, and quality of community services
7. Improve working relations among education, community mental health and other personnel, families, and their advocates

8. Target resources to school settings (e.g., providing access to school and/or community mental health and other resources to students who are in community school settings)
9. Address the needs of minority children

Part D provides training to educate students with disabilities. For example, grant proposals may be written for funds to recruit and train members of minority groups and groups with disabilities.

Part E supports research to advance and improve the knowledge base and practice of professionals, parents, and others who provide intervention, special education, and related services to improve learning and instruction (NASDSE, 1990, p. 15). These activities may include:

10. Organization, synthesis, and interpretation of current knowledge and identification of knowledge gaps
11. Identification of knowledge and skill competencies needed by personnel
12. Improvement of knowledge regarding the development and learning characteristics of children in order to improve the design and effectiveness of interventions and instruction
13. Evaluation of approaches and interventions
14. Development of instructional strategies, techniques, and activities
15. Improvement of curricula and instructional tools
16. Development of assessment techniques, instruments, and strategies for the identification, location, and evaluation of eligible students and for measurement of their progress
17. Testing of research findings in practice settings
18. Improvement of knowledge regarding families, minorities, LEP, and disabling conditions
19. Identification of environmental, organizational, resource, and other conditions necessary for effective professional practice

Activities to advance the use of knowledge by personnel providing services may include (NASDSE, 1990, p. 16):

20. Improvement of knowledge regarding how such individuals learn new knowledge and skills, and strategies for effectively facilitating such learning
21. Organization, integration, and presentation of knowledge so it can be incorporated into training programs
22. Expansion and improvement of networks that exchange knowledge and practice information

Part G supports the use of technology in the education of infants, children, and youth with disabilities (NASDSE, 1990, p. 17):

23. Funds may be used to increase access to and use of assistance technology devices and assistance technology services in the education of infants, toddlers, children, and youth with disabilities and other activities authorized under the Technology Related Assistance for Individuals with Disabilities Act (PL 100-407) as such Act relates to the education of students with disabilities.

24. Funds may be used to examine how program purposes can address the problem of illiteracy among individuals with disabilities.
25. With respect to new technology, media, and materials utilized with funds under this section, the Secretary is directed to make efforts to ensure that such instructional materials are closed captioned.
26. No funds may be awarded under Sec. 661(a)(1)–(4) unless the applicant agrees that activities carried out with the assistance will be coordinated, as appropriate, with the state entity receiving funds under the Title I State Grant Program of PL 100-407.

Part H provides guidelines for parents of infants and toddlers in need of early intervention services (NASDSE, 1990, p. 18):

27. Under the Public Awareness component of the statewide system, the lead agency must prepare and disseminate to all primary referral sources information materials for parents on the availability of early intervention services, and procedures for determining the extent to which primary referral sources disseminate information on the availability of early intervention services to parents.

> *Reflection*
> Three questions that should always be asked when evaluating a disability condition are: (1) The extent of the disability, (2) the stability, and (3) how long the subject has had the disability. Why are (2) and (3) important?

Gifted and Talented Students

Some of the most neglected students in U.S. schools today are students whose abilities are unusually high—gifted and talented students. According to the U.S. Commissioner of Education, "Gifted children are frequently overlooked in our schools" (Gallager, 1998). A review of current educational practices shows that the majority of public schools need to do more to meet the needs of this special group of children. When money is scarce, gifted programs and art programs are first to be eliminated. Furthermore, as pointed out by Agne (2001), "Gifted children are the only exceptional learners that are not protected under federal law for a free and appropriate education" (p. 168). Some teachers and administrators believe it is undemocratic to give bright students special attention; other teachers, resenting the superior student's competency, enforce egalitarianism as a sort of equalizer.

Teachers of gifted and talented students have more positive attitudes toward these students than do regular teachers, and schools that have gifted programs have less positive attitudes toward gifted students. The prevailing negative attitudes in schools with gifted programs can be attributed to the disruption of classes when these students are pulled out periodically to attend the special programs. Teachers are more willing to have this occur when they know more about gifted children. However, some educators are questioning purposeful neglect of this group of special students and point out that there is historical precedent in Thomas Jefferson's advocacy of special education provisions and settings for students of more able learning capacity (Durr, 1964). During the nineteenth century, private schools for the intellectually elite proliferated in New England and in the South. The first systematic provision of special programs for the gifted in the public school setting was in the St. Louis school system in 1868. The first federal legislation for the gifted student was the 1958 National Defense Education Act, which provided loans for the gifted to pursue higher education (Johnson, 1976). Only two years later the U.S. Office of Education began operating "Project Talent" programs to stimulate discovery and development of national human resources. In 1969, PL 91-230 mandated a report to Congress from the U.S. Office of Education on the education of the gifted and talented. During the mid-1980s many states created combinations of loans and grants to attract gifted students into math and science teacher-education programs.

Who Are the Gifted and Talented?

There has always been a tendency to use intelligence quotient (IQ) scores to identify the gifted. In the past, "talented" referred to those who do not have the aspiration or motivation needed to score highly on these tests. Unfortunately, there are few other measuring devices, so most schools and researchers continue to use standardized intelligence tests.

Some authors insist that the term *gifted* be reserved for students who are highly motivated as well as capable. Another author provides the following definition: "The gifted student is likely to have above-average language development, persistence in attacking difficult mental tasks, the ability to generalize and see relationships, unusual curiosity, and a wide variety of deep interests" (DeHann & Havinghurst, 1961). Other authors who accept a broad definition of gifted still consider only the high performers on intelligence tests in their programs for the gifted. Whatever the current status of the definition, the best method for identifying the gifted is, at least at this time, the individual intelligence test.

Teaching Gifted Students

In attempting to meet gifted students' needs, schools have made many adjustments in school curricula. One of the most common adjustments has been grouping these students for either part or all of the school day. This enables the teachers to present challenges to them. According to Feldhusen (1989), a grouping can enable teachers to enrich the curriculum, providing additional motivation, which he says gifted students need:

> Gifted and talented children complain a great deal about the boredom of their classroom experiences; they are forced to spend a lot of time being taught things they already know, doing repetitive drill sheets and activities, and receiving instructions on new material at too slow a pace. These experiences probably cause gifted youth to lose motivation to learn, to get by with minimum effort, or to reject school as a worthwhile experience.
>
> Grouping gifted and talented youth for all or part of the school day or week also serves as a stimulus or motivator. Interaction with other students who are enthusiastic about astronomy, robotics, Shakespeare, or algebra motivates gifted and talented students. (p. 9)

Once gifted students are grouped, a special curriculum is needed. Van Tassel-Baska et al. (1989) describe some components they say are needed in this new curriculum:

> An appropriate curriculum for gifted students has three equally important dimensions: (1) a content-based mastery dimension that allows gifted learners to move more rapidly through the curriculum; (2) a process/product/research dimension that encourages in-depth and independent learning; and (3) an epistemological concept dimension that allows for the exploration of issues, themes, and ideas across curriculum areas.

Van Tassel-Baska et al. (1989) also note:

> *Effective differentiation takes into account both the written and the delivered curriculum. Manipulation of the written curriculum alone will not bring about curriculum appropriateness for the gifted; but if it is accompanied by a shift in instructional techniques and a procedure for reviewing and adopting text materials, the results should be positive. (p. 9)*

Over the years the gifted have been victimized by such false stereotypes as "social misfits," "weird," or "mad scientists." Like all other people, the gifted feel a need to use their talents. A study of gifted programs in nine school districts reported that over half of gifted students in middle schools say that they are not challenged in arts, social studies, and science (Gallagher, 1998, p. 741). When a teacher does not challenge students or provide opportunities for them to use their abilities, like all other students they are apt to become frustrated.

As a teacher, you will want to find different materials and assign different tasks to challenge these students. Education programs for the gifted "must deal with their subject matter profoundly" (Bull, 1986, p. 42). The traditional practices of giving the gifted the same assignments—and, perhaps even worse, assigning more of the same problems—must be replaced by activities that will hold their interest and challenge their minds. Many school systems have specially trained professionals to work in programs for the gifted. Find out if your school or school system has such a person, and inquire about testing programs for identifying gifted students. The first responsibility you have to these students is to identify them. Then you must either try to provide adequate challenges or see that someone else does.

Using Technology

A major problem that teachers have faced throughout the years is how to challenge gifted and talented students. New technologies that were not available in the past provide unique opportunities to address this problem (Armstrong et al., 2004). A good example is the effect that using the World Wide Web can have in promoting higher level thinking. Through using this tool, gifted students can learn to develop their own sophisticated research skills, not only to solve problems but also to identify society's needs and ways to improve society.

Using Creative Projects

Another way that teachers can enrich the curriculum for gifted students is by providing more creative projects. According to Gallager (1998), "A wide variety of efforts have been made to enhance the creative and productive thinking abilities of gifted students" (p. 740). Burns (1990), who says that gifted students need more opportunities to use their creative abilities, tested 515 subjects to determine whether students who had prior experience with a creative project would be likely to choose to become involved in future creative projects. She reported:

> *This study indicates that there is value in teaching students how to manage, focus, and plan a project or investigation. . . . Along with the development of lessons to teach strategies for creative productivity, gifted education teachers might also become more aware of the importance of self-efficacy in increasing the likelihood that students will begin curative investigations. (pp. 35–36)*

Gifted students often feel isolated from their classmates. Although previous studies of gifted students' personality traits and emotional adjustment have generally concluded that the gifted are, at best, as well adjusted emotionally as the average student, a recent study by

Dauber and Benbow (1990) concluded that extremely precocious adolescents, especially the verbally precocious, may be at greater risk for developing problems in peer relations than modestly gifted youth.

Teachers should be sensitive to any feelings of isolation extremely gifted students may have and should realize that these students may need help in gaining peer acceptance. Many students face peer pressure to limit their level of academic performance. This is particularly true of high achievers. Brown and Steinberg (1990) explain why so many students try to limit their peers' achievements:

> *First, high achievers seem to be swimming against the development tide of adolescence. A second reason is that by doing well in school, high achievers help raise teachers' expectations, which forces other students to work harder just to get by. Third, even with extra effort, some students simply can't make the grades, and they blame high achievers for setting the standards that make them look bad. (p. 57)*
>
> *Research has shown that a focus on weaknesses at the expense of developing gifts can result in poor self-esteem, a lack of motivation, depression, and stress. What is needed in addition to remediation is attention focused on the development of strengths, interests, and superior intellectual capacities in their own right. (p. 55)*

Feldhusen (1989) presents a good summary for this section in the following highlights of research on gifted youth:

Highlights of Research on Gifted Youth
The voluminous research on gifted and talented students provides educators with guidelines for serving this special population.

Identification
Schools are often ineffective in identifying gifted students, especially in finding talent among children from poverty and minority backgrounds, among very young children, and among underachievers. Identification is most often based on intelligence tests; use of creativity tests or achievement tests is rare. Multiple data sources should be used to identify alternate types of giftedness and to specify appropriate program services.

Acceleration
Acceleration motivates gifted students by providing them with instruction that challenges them to realize their potential. Accelerated students show superior achievement in school and beyond. Despite the fears of some educators, acceleration does not damage the social-emotional adjustment of gifted youth.

Grouping
Grouping gifted and talented youth for all or part of the school day or week serves as a motivator. In special classes or cluster groups for the gifted, mutual reinforcement of enthusiasm for academic interests prevails. Removing gifted students from regular classrooms does not deprive other students of role models; instead, it allows them to be leaders and top performers.

Overall
To provide for the gifted, we must upgrade the level and pace of instruction to fit their abilities, achievement levels, and interests. The only suitable enrichment is instruction on special enriching topics at a high level and a fast pace. We must also provide them with highly competent teachers and with opportunities to work with other gifted and talented youth. (p. 10)

Matching Teaching Styles and Learning Styles for Gifted Students

Research conducted with the Dunn and Dunn model at more than 115 institutions of higher education has reported successful applications of their strategies for matching instructional approaches to students' learning-style strengths at the primary, elementary, secondary, and college levels (*Research on the Dunn and Dunn Learning Style Model,* 1994). For example, a meta-analysis of 42 experimental studies conducted with this model between 1980 and 1990 at thirteen different universities revealed that eight variables coded for each study produced 65 individual effect sizes (Dunn et al., 1995). The overall, unweighted group effect size value (r) was .384 and the weighted effect size value was .353, with a mean difference (d) of .755. Referring to the standard normal curve, this suggests that students whose learning styles are accommodated would be expected to achieve 75 percent of a standard deviation higher than students who have not had their learning styles accommodated. This indicates that matching students' learning style preferences with educational interventions compatible with those preferences is beneficial to their academic achievement.

According to the Center for Research in Education (CRE), the 20-year period of extensive federal funding (1970–1990) produced few programs that consistently resulted in statistically higher standardized achievement test scores for special education students (Alberg et al., 1992). Prominent among those programs was the Dunn and Dunn Learning Style Model. Interestingly, despite the Alberg et al. (1992), Andrews (1990), Perrin (1990), Stone (1992), and Quinn (1994) findings of widespread academic improvement among poorly achieving and special education populations, the sample of *average* students in the Dunn et al. (in press) meta-analysis revealed the largest effects. Dunn, Dunn, and Perrin (1994) perceive learning-style preferences as strengths teachers can use to design more effective instructional experiences.

Dunn and Dunn (1992, 1993) reported that difficult academic material needs to be introduced through each student's strongest perceptual modality, reinforced through his or her secondary or tertiary modality, and then *applied* by the student when *creating an original resource that includes the information,* such as a poem, a set of task cards or Flip-Chute cards, a time line, or a kinesthetic floor game. Using these procedures, the Dunns developed guidelines for having students do their homework through their learning-style strengths. At almost every grade level, students have achieved statistically higher achievement and attitude test scores by following those Homework Disc prescriptions. Studies show that such matching learning style and instructional approach consistently increases academic achievement, improves attitudes toward school, and reduces discipline problems. This last finding is consistent with the often heard expression: A well-planned lesson is the greatest deterrent to discipline problems.

Using the Arts Curriculum to Teach Gifted Students

The visual and performing arts are an excellent means of providing unique experiences for gifted and talented students. Unfortunately, these areas are often ignored in programs designed for gifted and talented students. Gifted students need curricula that will push them and challenge them to progress to higher levels. Because the arts are defined by creativity, they can be highly useful to meet this goal.

Underachievers

Underachievers are students with high intellectual or academic potential whose performance falls in the middle third in scholastic achievement—or worse, in the lowest third. Few educators realize how serious this problem is. First, the percentage of gifted students who are achieving far below their abilities is staggering. One study found that more than half the highly gifted students work well below their abilities. The tremendous waste in potential is enough to prompt serious concern.

A second reason for concern is that these gifted students who are achieving below their abilities academically are also contributing socially below their abilities. Thus, there is a further waste of human resources. Still another reason for concern about underachievers is that once gifted students begin to perform below their ability, the trend is difficult to reverse. It quickly becomes accepted as a way of life.

Identifying the Underachiever

Underachievers, like all special students, must first be identified by the teacher before they can get help. You may find it more difficult to recognize underachievers because they are frequently mistaken for low-ability students. One teacher in-service program lists the following characteristics of underachievers:

1. Belligerent toward classmates and others
2. Extremely defensive (given to rationalizing, ad-libbing, excusing failures, lying)
3. Fearful of failure and of attempting new tasks because of the likelihood of failure
4. Resentful of criticism, yet likely to be highly critical of others
5. Prone to habitual procrastination, dawdling, daydreaming, sulking, brooding
6. Frequently absent
7. Inattentive—wriggling, doodling, whispering
8. Suspicious, distrustful of overtures of affection
9. Rebellious
10. Negative about own abilities

No student would display all these characteristics simultaneously, but one who shows several at once should be investigated.

Some of the likely causes of underachievers are physical limitations (such as poor vision or hearing), learning disabilities, dysfunctional families, and even social maladjustments. Often low performance is a result of low expectations at home and school, which eventually lead to low expectations by the student. Students afflicted with learned helplessness are often unwilling to try because they expect to fail. However, to be sure that a particular student is indeed performing well below ability, you must check previous performance records or report cards and standardized tests. For example, a student who is making C's but has stanine scores of 8's and 9's is clearly performing far below ability.

Actually, a balance is required between expectations that are too low and those that are too high. Williams, Alley, and Henson (1999, p. 148) express concern that teachers and parents often set expectations at levels that are beyond students' reach. Some parents inhibit their children's academic growth by raising the bar too high. These parents want their children to be stars, and when they don't meet the parents' expectations, both the parents and the students see themselves as failures.

Learning Styles of Underachievers

Seven learning style traits significantly discriminate between high-risk or dropout students and students who perform well in school. Many—but not all—dropouts and underachievers need (1) frequent opportunities for mobility, (2) choices, (3) a variety of instructional resources, environments, and sociological groupings rather than routines and patterns, (4) to learn during late morning, afternoon, or evening hours—not in the early morning, (5) informal seating—not wooden, steel, or plastic chairs and desks, (6) soft lighting to concentrate (bright lights contribute to hyperactivity), and (7) to be introduced to a new topic with either tactual-visual instructional resources reinforced by kinesthetic-visual resources or kinesthetic-visual instructional resources reinforced by tactual-visual resources. Underachievers find it extremely difficult to remember what they have been taught through lectures. They tend to have poor auditory memory, although short verbal explanations can be used to reinforce learning after new material has been introduced through manipulatives or activities. When underachievers have visual preferences, they often learn through pictures, drawings, graphs, symbols, and cartoons rather than printed text. They also learn well with highly structured multisensory instructional resources. Although underachievers often *are* motivated, they cannot remember many facts taught through lectures, discussions, or readings.

Helping Underachievers

Once you have identified the underachievers in your classes, you may have many approaches to help them improve their performance, academically and socially. You may want to consider using some of the following:

- Special guidance to develop positive self-concept
- Extensive use of films and captioned filmstrips instead of textbooks; use of taped lessons to improve listening, thinking, reading skills
- First-hand experiences to stimulate and motivate, especially for students from disadvantaged backgrounds (remember, middle-class white students, as well as the poor and some minority students, may come from such backgrounds)
- Assignments and teaching methods adjusted to students' individual interests and abilities and relating to hoped-for or established goals, whether personal or academic
- Teacher–student sessions for planning work to be covered
- Tutoring by willing and able senior citizens who can provide the warmth and understanding, kind encouragement, and praise often missing at home
- A special opportunity class for underachievers of mixed ages with similar problems working out of the regular class, even out of the regular school where possible, for at least part of the day
- Group therapy with a warm, understanding counselor or teacher to discuss freely any fears, frustrations, angers
- A team approach to working with underachievers who are gifted and talented, including the teacher(s), parent(s), a counselor, and perhaps the student
- Use of grades and tests only as measures of progress and thus as indicators of areas needing additional work
- Instruction in how to learn—how to concentrate, remember, understand and follow directions, use key words, and so on.
- Instruction in problem-solving techniques and the inquiry method

Many contemporary programs for gifted and talented students include nontraditional content and skill. Research shows that basic research skills can be taught to gifted children of middle school level and even younger (Kent & Esgar, 1983). Scientific research methodology has been taught successfully in science classes. There are numerous reports of junior high students being employed by school districts to conduct workshops for teachers on the use of computers (Torrence, 1986). Other common trends include teaching gifted students inventing, debating, logical reasoning, creative writing, thinking, and forecasting. Whatever method(s) you choose, remember that no one type of program will meet all the needs of all gifted and talented students.

Vignettes

The two vignettes here show how matching learning styles and teaching styles can be used. Each incident actually occurred in the Wichita, Kansas, area and describes a real-life application of learning-styles theory.

Vignette One: An Individual Teacher's Efforts

Sometimes teachers must experiment with new educational theories in the isolation of their classrooms, with little support from anyone. However, teachers who accept the responsibility not only for what they teach but also for what is learned are eager to use any technique they believe will help them in diagnoses, prescription, and treatment of their students.

One such teacher in Wichita, Kansas, attended a district in-service meeting where he learned about learning styles theory and application. This middle-level teacher decided to experiment with the idea and invited a consultant from the teacher center to come to one of his classes and explain the concept to the students. The teacher and consultant spent a considerable amount of time making sure the students understood the implications of learning styles theory and the teacher's interest in using it.

The teacher administered a learning-styles preferences questionnaire, and the students scored the survey, developed their profiles, and shared the results within the class. Students were then encouraged to contribute ideas for classroom organization that would take advantage of the variety of preferred learning modalities within the class. They helped set up auditory areas where students could listen to tapes or form discussion groups. They also arranged visual corners, where other students could read or work on written assignments. Student enthusiasm was soon reflected at home, and parents became interested. The teacher decided to carry the program further and arranged a parent meeting. He explained the learning styles concept and how he was implementing it. He then administered the survey to the parents and helped them interpret the results regarding their own preferences. The teacher then began to use the parents' learning styles when he conducted parent–teacher conferences. The results of this experiment were very positive.

In this classroom, responsibilities shared by students and teacher in the planning of learning procedures and outcomes increased. Students' willingness to accept learning differences in others also increased. In addition, the parent–teacher conferences became more effective and mutually appreciated. The enthusiasm for the process in this particular classroom led this teacher to introduce the procedure in his other classes. Other teachers in the school also began experimenting with the concept in their classrooms.

DISCUSSION

When a teacher wants to initiate a new program or other innovation, is it necessary to sell others on the idea? If so, how can the teacher do this? Innovations often require additional facilities, materials, space, and program flexibility, so innovators' success depends on the cooperation received when administrators, teachers, and others understand the importance of the change. A simple approach is first to inform others about the process and then to involve them with the innovation.

> ### Vignette Two: A School-Wide Individualized Program
>
> Often middle school educators can learn from their counterparts at the elementary level. Cloud Elementary School in Wichita, Kansas, adopted the IGE (Individually Guided Education) program as its basic instructional process. The IGE approach to schooling provides a framework for individualized instruction and continuous progress. Instead of being organized into the usual self-contained classes in which all students of a single age are grouped together, students and teachers are organized into "learning communities." Each learning community is composed of students of several age groups and teachers of varying talents and backgrounds.
>
> This elementary school program had several goals, one of which was to determine students' learning styles. After experimenting with several assessment techniques, the teachers in the school decided that a locally developed learning styles inventory gave them usable and practical information that the faculty could easily manage. They arranged for the local district's computer department to put the student data from the instrument into a computer program. The computer-based analysis was designed to identify students who fell below a previously defined score.
>
> Style data were shared both with the students in the advisement programs and with the parents during conferences. A profile for each student was developed, and the results were used to determine the best way for each student to reach his or her learning objectives. In addition to developing learning objectives to complement each student's learning preference, the teacher identified students whose styles preference analysis revealed a possible inability to use a wide range of learning styles successfully. These students were then given help in expanding their styles. Thus, one major learning goal was to increase "style flex" among students.
>
> Results of the experiment were encouraging. There was increased student achievement and parental satisfaction. Teachers were pleased with the effort because they had acquired an additional tool for individualizing instruction. They also believed that student attitudes toward the classroom were enhanced.
>
> ### DISCUSSION
>
> If a student has a preferred learning style that works well for that student, why introduce that student to other styles? Students who have only one preferred learning style are in trouble when they are assigned to a teacher whose teaching style varies drastically from the student's style. By introducing students to a variety of styles, students have an opportunity to expand their "style flex."

Summary

Because each ethnic group and each student is unique, today's teachers need all the skills they can acquire to enable them to individualize education in their classrooms. The need is accentuated for middle-level teachers because the students in their classrooms are rapidly developing, and as they develop, their preferred ways of learning change. Chapter 1 made the point that effective teachers are lifelong learners. To promote learning among all of their students, contemporary middle school teachers must continue learning new teaching theories and methods and must use this knowledge to continue reinventing their teaching.

Howard Gardner's multiple intelligences theory made teachers aware that individuals are intelligent in many ways. Teachers must tap into the potentials of all students and promote student development in many directions. Traditionally, teachers have grouped students according to their age or their intelligence, as measured on a single written test. The National Middle School Association recommends that middle-level teachers replace these bases for grouping with cooperative learning groups, in which two to five students work together to help each other learn.

Mastery learning is another learning model that has been and continues to be used all over the world. This model recognizes that some students work faster than others and provides extra time for students who need it. It also provides students multiple opportunities to prove their mastery, without being punished for needing more than one try.

Another tool that teachers can use to individualize their instruction is matching their teaching styles with their students' learning preferences. Tools are available for teachers to use to detect the preferred learning styles of their students.

Some students are so different that they need their own special curricula. The current trend is to favor inclusion of these students in classrooms with regular students. Federal law requires teachers to design special curricula for these students. When working with students who have disabilities, always remember to consider how long the student has had the disability, the degree of seriousness of the disability, and the degree of stability of the disability (whether it is getting better, worse, or staying the same). An individualized education program (IEP) must be written and followed precisely for students who are severely challenged. Other students who are considered special are students who are especially gifted. Unfortunately, far less money has been available to teachers of gifted students.

Recap of Major Ideas

1. Students' instructional needs vary greatly.
2. Ability grouping is one common approach to meet individual students' needs.
3. In-class (intraclass) grouping often results in improved learning, but it does not enhance learning substantially; intraclass grouping usually improves motivation more than it improves learning.
4. Attempts to conceal the levels of ability groups almost always fail.
5. Interclass grouping produces group competition, whereas intraclass grouping produces competition between students.
6. Given adequate motivation, presentation style, and time, most middle school students can master the goals set for them.
7. Instruments are available to determine individuals' preferred learning and teaching styles.
8. Teachers should purposely master and use a variety of teaching styles.
9. Several instructional models such as grade contracts, mastery learning, and information processing can help teachers improve their instruction.
10. Mastery learning offers students flexible timing and opportunities to remediate without penalty, but traditional school schedules and parents who believe competition is essential make it difficult to implement.
11. Grade contracts can be highly successful when teacher and student expectations are clearly specified.
12. Homework assignments should have a stated purpose, be creative and reasonable, and reflect student interests.
13. Teachers should always follow up on assignments.
14. Homework serves two functions. It reinforces concepts learned in the previous lesson, and it prepares students for the coming lesson.
15. There are more differences among members of a culture than between cultures.
16. Hispanic students tend to favor cooperation over competition.
17. Native Americans and Hispanic students tend to prefer group work over individual assignments.
18. There is a strong trend toward keeping challenged students in classes with nonchallenged peers whenever possible.
19. Nonchallenged people tend to underestimate physically challenged students' mental ability.
20. Federal law requires teachers to design a special learning program for each challenged student.
21. In working with challenged students, always consider how severe the challenge is, how long the student has had it, and how stable the condition is.
22. Parents of challenged children have a right to help plan the program for their children and a right to evaluate it and even insist on changes to improve it.
23. The percentage of gifted students whose performance is substandard is very high.
24. There are ways to identify underachievers and help them.
25. PL 94-142 was amended in 1990 to become PL 101-476, Individuals with Learning Disabilities Act.

Activities

1. Because the success of any method selected to individualize instruction depends greatly on the enthusiasm of the teacher who applies it, you are encouraged to select one of the approaches discussed in this chapter—for example, contingency contracts, mastery learning, matching teacher and learner styles, or a type of ability grouping—and investigate it further. Go to the library, research the method, and determine how you would personalize it to fit your own preferences. An alternative would be to use your library's Educational Resources Information System (ERIC) (or similar reference guide) to discover other approaches to individualizing instruction. Make a list of these approaches and select one

to pursue further, then determine how you would adjust the approach to fit your own preferences.
2. Make an appointment to visit a school counselor. Ask the counselor to discuss some students who require special instruction. Do not expect the counselor to divulge a student's name, but ask for an explanation of how instruction was altered for that student. Make a list of learning activities that the counselor found successful.
3. Visit the reading center or a student assistance center on your campus or at a nearby university or public school. Volunteer your services for as many hours as you can spare. Keep a record of the techniques you observe in use at that center.
4. Because one of the most common problems teachers face is the need to teach students with a wide range of abilities simultaneously, spend a few hours preparing for this task. Visit with several secondary or middle school teachers and ask them how they teach a heterogeneous class of varying abilities. Make a list of the techniques they use. Choose one technique and research the literature to learn all you can about it.
5. Use the diagnostic learning styles model shown in Figure 7.7 to analyze your classmates' preferred learning styles. Ask your professor for permission to present the results to the class.
6. Ask your professor to hold a discussion about students' preferences for competition versus cooperation and group work versus individual assignments. Notice whether the preferences seem to be ethnic or gender related.

Looking Ahead

This chapter has helped you prepare to help individual students meet their unique needs. Because classrooms across the country are becoming more diverse, the following chapter will focus on helping students from diverse backgrounds.

References

Agne, K. J. (2001). Gifted: The lost minority. *Kappa Delta Pi Record, 37*(4), 168–172.

Aksamit, D. (1990). Mildly handicapped and at-risk students: The greying of the line. *Academic Therapy, 25*(3), 227–289.

Alberg, J., Cook, L., Fiore, T., Friend, M., & Sano, S., (1992). *Educational approaches and options for integrating students with disabilities: A decision tool.* Triangle Park, NC: Research Triangle Institute.

Andrews, R. H. (1990, July–September). The development of a learning styles program in a low socioeconomic, underachieving North Carolina elementary school. *Journal of Reading, Writing, and Learning Disabilities International, 6*(3), 307–314.

Andrews, R. H. (1991). Insights into education: An elementary principal's perspective. In Lewis A. Grell (Ed.), *Hands on approaches to learning styles: Practical approaches to successful school* (pp. 50–52). New Wilmington, PA: The Association for the Advancement of International Education.

Arlin, M. (1984, Spring). Time, equality, and mastery of learning. *Review of Educational Research, 54*, 71–72.

Armstrong, D. G., Henson, K. T., & Savage, T. V. (2004). *Teaching today.* 7th ed. New York: Prentice-Hall.

Baines, L., & Baines, C. (1994). Mainstreaming: One school's reality. *Phi Delta Kappan, 76*(1), 39–40 and 57–64.

Banks, R., Kopassi, R., & Wilson, A. M. (1991). Interagency networking and linking schools and agencies: A community based approach to at-risk students. In R. C. Morris (Ed.), *At-risk students* (pp. 106–107). Scranton, PA: Technomic.

Beaty, S. A. (1986). The effect of inservice training on the ability of teachers to observe learning styles of students. *Dissertation Abstracts International, 47*, 1998A.

Block, J. R., & Henson, K. T. (1986, Spring). Mastery learning and middle school instruction. *American Middle School Education, 9*(2), 21–29.

Blumenthal, C., Holmes, G. V., & Pound, L. (1991). Academic success for students' at-risk. In R. C. Morris (Ed.), *Youth at-risk.* Scranton, PA: Technomic.

Bradley, D. F., & Fisher, J. F. (1995). The inclusion process: Role changes at the middle level. *Middle School Journal, 26*(3), 13–17.

Brown, D. B., & Steinberg, L. (1990). Academic achievement and social acceptance. *Education Digest, 40*(7), 57–60.

Bull, B. L. (1986). Education for gifts and talents: A change in emphasis. *Education Digest, 51*(5), 40.

Burns, D. E. (1990). The effects of group training activities on students' initiation of creative investigations. *Gifted Child Quarterly, 34*(1), 31–36.

Burns, R. B. (1979). Mastery learning: Does it work? *Educational Leadership, 37*, 110–113.

Callan, R. J. (1998). Giving students the (right) time of day. *Educational Leadership, 55*(4), 84–87.

Carnegie Council on Adolescent Development (1996). *Great transitions: Preparing adolescents for a new century.* New York: Carnegie Corporation.

Carroll, J. B. (1963). A model of school learning. *Teachers College Record, 64,* 723–733.

Centra, J., & Potter, D. (1980). School and teacher effects: An interrelational model. *Review of Educational Research, 50,* 273–291.

Checkley, K. (1997). "The first seven . . . and the eighth." *Educational Leadership, 55*(1), 8–13.

Cheyney, C. D. (1989). The systematic adaptation of instructional materials and techniques for problem learners. *Academic Theory, 25*(1), 25–30.

Clark-Thayer, S. (1987). The relationship of the knowledge of student-perceived learning style preferences, and study habits and attitudes to achievement of college freshman in a small urban university. *Dissertation Abstracts International, 48,* 872A.

Coleman, J. G. (1991). Risky business: The library's role in dropout prevention. In R. C. Morris (Ed.), *Youth at-risk* (pp. 61–62). Scranton, PA: Technomic.

Cunningham, R. D., Jr., (1991, September). Modeling mastery teaching through classroom supervision. *NASSP Bulletin, 75*(536), 83–87.

Daniels, D. C. (2002). Becoming a reflective practitioner. *Middle School Journal, 33*(5), 52–56.

Dauber, S. L., & Benbow, C. P. (1990). Aspects of personality and peer relations of extremely talented adolescents. *Gifted Child Quarterly, 34*(1), 10–14.

DeHann, R., & Havinghurst, R. (1961). *Educating gifted children.* Chicago: University of Chicago Press.

Druian, G., & Butler, J. A. (2001). *Effective schooling practice and at-risk youth: What the research shows.* Portland, OR: Northwest Regional Educational Laboratory, School Improvement Research Series.

Dunn, R., Beasley, M., & Buchanan, K. (1994). What do you believe about how culturally-diverse students learn? *Emergency Librarian, 22*(1), 8–14.

Dunn, R., & Dunn, K. (1978). *Teaching students through their individual learning styles: A practical approach.* Reston, VA: Reston Publishing Division of Prentice-Hall.

Dunn, R., & Dunn, K. (1992). *Teaching elementary students through their individual learning styles.* Boston: Allyn & Bacon.

Dunn, R., & Dunn, K. (1993). *Teaching secondary students through their individual learning styles.* Boston: Allyn and Bacon.

Dunn, R., Dunn, K., & Perrin, J. (1994). *Teaching young children through their individual learning styles.* Boston: Allyn & Bacon.

Dunn, R., Dunn, K., & Price, G. E. (1977). Diagnosing learning styles: Avoiding malpractice suits against school systems. *Phi Delta Kappan, 58*(5), 418–420.

Dunn, R., & Griggs, S. A. (1995). *Multiculturalism and learning style: Teaching and counseling adolescents.* CT: Greenwood.

Dunn, R., Griggs, S. A., Olson, J., Gorman, B., & Beasley, M. (1996). A meta-analytic validation of the Dunn and Dunn learning styles model. *Journal of Educational Research.*

Durr, W. K. (1964). *The gifted student.* New York: Oxford University Press.

Edinger, M. (1994). Empowering young writers with technology. *Educational Leadership, 51*(7), 58–60.

Eisner, E. (2001). What does it mean to say a school is doing well? *Phi Delta Kappan, 82*(5), 367–372.

Elkind, R. (1991). Success in American education. In R. C. Morris (Ed.), *Youth at-risk.* Lancaster, PA: Technomic.

Elliot, I. (1991, November–December). The reading place. *Teaching K–8.* 21(3), 30–34.

Emig, V. B.(1997). A multiple intelligences inventory. *Educational Leadership, 55*(1), 47–50.

Federico, M. A., Herrold, B., and Venn, J. (2000). Inclusion reaches beyond the classroom. *Kappa Delta Pi Record, 36*(4), 178–180.

Feldhusen, J. F. (1989). Synthesis of research on gifted youth. *Educational Leadership, 46*(6), 6–11.

Firek, H. (2003). "One order of ed tech coming up . . . You want fries with that?" *Phi Delta Kappan, 84*(8), 596–597.

Friedman, R. S. (1991). Murray high school: A nontraditional approach to meeting the needs of an at-risk population. In R. C. Morris (Ed.), *Youth at-risk.* Lancaster, PA: Technomic.

Frymier, J., & Gansneder, B. (1989, October). The Phi Delta Kappa study of students at risk. *Phi Delta Kappan, 71,* 142–146.

Gallagher, J. J. (1998). Accountability for the gifted. *Phi Delta Kappan, 79*(10), 739–742.

Gardner, H. (1983). *Frames of the mind: The theory of multiple intelligences.* New York: Basic Books.

Gardner, H. (1999). *Intelligence reclaimed: Multiple intelligences for the 21st century.* New York: Basic Books.

Gilman, D. A., & Kiger, S. (2003). Should we try to keep class sizes small? *Educational Leadership, 60*(7), 80–85.

Good, T. L., & Brophy, J. E. (1997). *Looking in classrooms* (7th ed.). New York: Harper & Row

Good, T. L., Reys, B. J., Grouws, D. A., & Molyran, C. M. (1990–1991). Using work-groups in mathematics instruction. *Educational Leadership, 47*(4), 56–62.

Glazer, N. T., & Williams, S. (2001). Becoming a reflective practitioner. *Middle School Journal, 33*(5), 52–56.

Guernsey, M. A. (1989). Classroom organization: A key to successful management. *Academic Therapy, 25*(1), 55–58.

Guskey, T. R., & Gates, S. L. (1986). Synthesis of research on the effects of mastery learning in elementary and secondary classrooms. *Educational Leadership, 43*(8), 73–80.

Henson, K. T., & Eller, D. F. (1999). *Educational psychology for effective teaching.* Belmont, CA: Wadsworth.

Hilliard, R. D. (1999). "All I ever needed to know about teaching I learned in middle school." *SRATE Journal, 8*(1), 50–56.

Holloway, J. H. (2001). Inclusion and students with learning disabilities. *Educational Leadership, 58*(6), 86 and 88.

Hoover, J. J. (1990, March). Curriculum adaptation: A five step process for classroom implementation. *Academic Therapy, 25*(4), 407–416.

Hyman, J. S., & Cohen, A. (1979). Learning for mastery: Ten conclusions after fifteen years and 3,000 schools. *Educational Leadership, 37,* 104–109.

Johnson, B. (Ed.) (1976). *Federal legislative history on gifted and talented.* Bulletin 2. Washington, DC: U.S. Government Printing Office.

Johnston, C. A. (1998). "Using the learning combination inventory." *Educational Leadership, 55*(4), 78–82.

Julik, J. A. (1981, April). The effect of ability grouping on secondary school students. Paper presented at the American Educational Research Association, Los Angeles.

Karweit, N. (1987). Effective kindergarten programs and practices for students at-risk. Report No. 21. Baltimore: The Johns Hopkins University, Center for Research on Elementary and Middle Schools.

Kohn, A. (2001). Fighting the tests: A practical guide to rescuing our schools. *Phi Delta Kappan, 82*(5), 349–357.

Keefe, J. W. (1982). Assessing students learning styles: An overview of learning styles and cognitive style inquiry. In *Student Learning Styles and Brain Behavior.* Reston, VA: National Association of Secondary School Principals.

Kent, S., & Esgar, L. V. (1983, May–June). Research techniques for gifted primary students. *G/C/T, 28,* 28–29.

Krashen, S. (1998). Bridging inequity with books. *Educational Leadership, 55*(4), 18–21.

Kryriacou, M., & Dunn, R. (1994). Synthesis of research: Learning styles of students with learning disabilities. *Special Education Journal, 4*(1), 3–9.

Lemmon, P. (1985). A school where learning styles make a difference. *Principal, 64*(4), 26–29.

Levin, H. M. (1987). New schools for the disadvantaged. Unpublished manuscript, Stanford, CT.

Lewellen, J. R. (1990, October–November). Systematic and effective teaching. *The High School Journal, 63*(1), 57–63.

Lile, B., Lile, G., & Jefferies, B. (1991). Project rebound: Effective intervention for rural elementary at-risk students. In R. C. Morris (Ed.), *Youth at-risk* (pp. 40–41). Scranton, PA: Technomic.

Lindblad, A. H., Jr. (1994). You can avoid the traps of cooperative learning. *The Clearing House, 67*(5), 291–293.

Magney, J. (1990). Game-based teaching. *The Education Digest, 60*(5), 54–57.

Marcus, L. (1977). How teachers view learning styles. *NASSP Bulletin, 61*(408), 112–114.

Marshall, C. (1991, March/April). Teachers' learning styles: How they affect student learning. *The Clearing House, 64*(4), 225–227.

Maslow, A. H. (1970). *Motivation and personality* (2nd ed.). New York: Harper & Row.

Meek, A. (1998). America's teachers: Much to celebrate. *Educational Leadership, 55*(50), 12–16.

Milgram, R. M., Dunn, R., & Price, G. E. (Eds.). (1993). *Teaching and counseling gifted and talented adolescents: An international learning style perspective.* Westport, CT: Praeger.

Morris, R. C. (Ed.). (1991). *Youth at-risk.* Lancaster, PA: Technomic.

NASDSE. National Association of State Directors of Special Education. Education of the Handicapped Act amendments of 1990 (P.L. 101–476: Summary of major changes in Parts A through H of the act) (1990, October). Washington, DC: NASDSE.

NMSA (1991). *National Middle School Association Delphi report: Roadmap to the future* (1991).

Oddliefson, E. (1994). What do we want our schools to do? *Phi Delta Kappan, 75*(6), 446–453.

Patterson, W. (2003). Breaking out of our boxes. *Phi Delta Kappan, 84*(8), 569–574.

Pernell, E., McIntyre, L., & Bader, L. A. (1985, Winter). Mainstreaming: A continuing concern for teachers. *Education, 106,* 131–137.

Perrin, J. (1984). An experimental investigation of the relationships among the learning style sociological preferences of gifted and non-gifted primary children, selected instructional strategies, attitudes, and achievement in problem solving and rote memorization. *Dissertation Abstracts International, 46,* 342A.

Perrin, S. (1994). Education in the arts is an education for life. *Phi Delta Kappan, 75*(6), 452–453.

Pitton, D. E. (1999). The naked truth isn't very revealing. *Phi Delta Kappan, 80*(5), 383–386.

Potter, L., Carruthers, M., & Green, K. (2002). Special education challenges for the principal: Be prepared. *Middle Ground, 5*(5), 43–44.

Quinn, R. (1993). The New York State compact for learning and learning styles. *Learning Styles Network Newsletter, 15*(1), 1–2.

Research on the Dunn and Dunn learning style model (1994). Jamaica, NY: St. John's University's Center for the Study of Learning and Teaching Styles.

Reyes, D. J. (1990). Models of instruction: Some light on the model muddle. *The Clearing House, 63*(1), 214–216.

Salend, S., & Garrick-Duhaney, L. (1999). The impact of inclusion on students with and without disabilities and their educators. *Remedial and Special Education, 20*(2), 114–126.

Sautter, R. C. (1994). An arts education school reform strategy. *Phi Delta Kappan, 75*(6), 432–437.

Shavelson, R. J. (1983). Review of research on teachers' pedagogical judgments, plans, and decisions. *Elementary School Journal, 83,* 392–414.

Slavin, R. E. (1989, April). On mastery learning and mastery teaching. *Educational Leadership, 46*(7), 77–79.

Slavin, R. E. (1998). Can education reduce social inequity? *Educational Leadership, 55*(4), 6–10.

Smelter, R. W., Rasch, B. W., & Yudewitz, G. J. (1994). Thinking of inclusion for all special needs students? Better think again. *Phi Delta Kappan, 76*(1), 35–38.

Stone, P. (1992, November). How we turned around a problem school. *The Principal, 71*(2), 34–36.

Thies, A. P. (1979). A brain behavior analysis of learning style. In J. W. Keefe (Ed.), *Student learning styles; Diagnosing and prescribing programs.* Reston, VA: National Association of Secondary School Principals.

Thompson, S. (2001). The authentic standards movement and its evil twin. *Phi Delta Kappan, 82*(5), 358–362.

Torrence, E. P. (1986). Teaching creative and gifted learners. In M. C. Whittrock (Ed.), *Handbook of research on teaching* (3rd ed.). New York: Macmillan.

Van Gulick, R. C. (1990). Functionalism, information, and content. In W. G. Lylcan (Ed.), *Mind and cognition.* Cambridge, MA: Basil Blackwell.

Van Tassel-Baska, J., Feldhusen, J., Seeley, K., Wheatley, G., Silverman, L., & Foster, W. (1989). *Comprehensive curriculum for gifted learners.* Boston: Allyn & Bacon.

Weasmer, J., & Woods, A. (2001). Encouraging student decision making. *Kappa Delta Pi Record, 38*(1), 40–42.

Wellington, P., & Perlin, C. (1991). Palimpsest probability and the writing process: Mega-change for at-risk students. In R. C. Morris (Ed.), *Youth at risk.* Lancaster, PA: Technomic.

Williams, P. A., Alley, R. D., & Henson, K. T. (1999). *Managing secondary classrooms.* Boston: Allyn & Bacon.

8
Teaching in Multicultural Settings

In the larger society, tolerances for diversity, a measure of concern for fellow human beings, the responsible exercise of citizenship, and a sense of social responsibility are essential to the functioning of local communities and the nation itself.

        Special Study Panel on Education Indicators for the National Center for Education Statistics

Objectives

- Name three qualities of U.S. high schools that inhibit success for minority students.
- Give two approaches for helping students build a positive self-image.
- Write a daily lesson plan that exalts several cultures' unique characteristics.
- Explain the significance of the 1975 Lau v. Nichols decision by the U.S. Supreme Court.
- List ten things a teacher of a multicultural group should do to adjust to students, then list ten things the teacher should avoid doing.
- Create a one-hour simulation activity that will enable all students in a class to experience different cultural roles.
- Name five principles of multicultural education.
- Explain the significance of the following quotation in promoting healthy multicultural attitudes: "We must learn to listen and listen to learn."
- Explain the relationship between group work and meeting the needs of all students.
- Describe one way that computers can be used to meet a multicultural goal.

TEACHING IN MULTICULTURAL SETTINGS

Preliminary Considerations
- A Positive Approach
- Personalizing Teaching
- Reasons for Optimism

In the Classroom
- The Teacher's Decision
- The Teacher's Role
- Do's and Don'ts for Teachers
- Selecting Ethnic Materials
- The Teacher's Wider Role
- Using Process to Praise Diversity

Beyond the Classroom
- Director of Learning
- Counselor and Guidance Worker
- Mediator of Culture
- Link with Community
- School Staff Member
- Using Process to Praise Diversity

Connecting Statements

	Agree	Disagree	Uncertain
1. There is little a teacher can do to meet the needs of students from other cultures unless the teacher has special training.			
2. Teachers should not concern themselves with different cultures because all students are Americans and must learn the American way of life.			
3. Schools do not have to provide instruction in other languages just because some students speak first languages other than English.			
4. Students who belong to other cultures should be grouped with like students throughout the school day.			
5. To avoid embarrassment, teachers should not discuss the backgrounds of minority students.			
6. It is dangerous to generalize about cultures other than your own.			

> ### Tips for Teachers
>
> You have often heard of people with a reputation for turning liabilities into assets. Middle-level teachers who teach in multicultural settings have the opportunity to do this. They can view the situation either as a handicap or as a unique opportunity. The results usually parallel the teacher's view.
>
> If you choose to turn your pluralistic classes into an asset, you can do so by identifying the unique contributions each ethnic group has made to U.S. society. Then you should find ways to amplify these contributions. In this chapter you will learn how to make members of each ethnic group more aware of and proud of their heritage. You will also learn how to select textbooks and other materials to facilitate attainment of this goal.

Diverse Classrooms: Opportunity for All

Demographers tell us that U.S. classrooms in the twenty-first century are populated by a new majority—students of color, low-income students, and students of non-English-speaking backgrounds, the same learners currently failing in large numbers in U.S. schools (Gomez & Smith, 1991). Although over a third of the entire U.S. population is nonwhite (Chimes & Schmidt, 1990), U.S. teaching remains a white, middle-class occupation, with increasingly fewer teachers of color (Haberman, 1998).

As Alexander (1994) notes, demographic changes accentuate the need for teaching students to appreciate cultural diversity: "Developing an appreciation for many cultures is a national educational concern tied to the emerging demographics of our nation and the rapid disappearance of political boundaries that previously isolated many ethnic groups" (p. 266). Hilliard (1991–1992) says that if the curriculum is centered in truth, it will be pluralistic because human culture is the product of the struggles of all humanity, not a single racial or ethnic group's possession. By helping others develop and fulfill their need to appreciate their own heritage, we can bring enrichment to ourselves (Banks, 1999).

Interest in and commitment to multicultural education peaked in the 1960s and shaped the curricula throughout the 1970s; it was not emphasized during the 1980s but regained its position of major concern in the 1990s (Reed, 1994). Millions of dollars have been spent on programs to raise the academic performance of minority-group children, only recently have we begun to see positive results. Through learning about other cultures we grasp a clearer, more thorough understanding about our culture (Banks, 1999). Multilingual and multicultural educations are no longer frills but major necessities. The traditional approach to multicultural education has been simply to give students information. Clearly, this approach will not work by itself. Guyton and Fielstein (1991, p. 207) explain: "Although information is necessary, it cannot be expected by itself to modify learned attitudes." Future curricula must provide students with opportunities to express feelings, analyze attitudes, and participate in discussions.

How much, and exactly what, can you do? Teachers may be the only people who can significantly improve the education that minority students receive. Teacher education programs must prepare future teachers to teach in urban settings (Haberman, 1998). U.S. schools have several features that make it difficult for multicultural students to succeed. First, U.S. schools are so large that they appear impersonal to immigrants, and they are getting larger. As noticed by Patterson (2003), "High schools in the U.S. have grown larger and larger during the past 50 years." (p. 570) Second, teachers tend to be overly concerned with tests, grades, and competition. Furthermore, teachers tend to sell minority students short and underestimate their ability to succeed and to contribute. Third, and this is perhaps the greatest obstacle to improving education for all, "Because of lack of exposure to diverse settings, future teachers typically maintain the values and norms indicative of their own cultural and socioeconomic levels" (Nuby & Doebler, 1999, p. 41).

Taking a Positive Approach

To many students and teachers, the term *multicultural* has negative connotations. "Further, our economy is increasingly based on a global economic model, forcing us to become familiar with ways of life not long ago considered exotic and strange," write Chimes and Schmidt (1990, p. 44). To many, multicultural brings to mind problems, which is unfortunate because this in itself may cause problems. In other words, if teachers interpret multicultural settings as prone to problems, they may approach multicultural classes with skepticism. Students sense this and will not trust the teacher. However, if teachers view the multicultural setting as an opportunity to increase their own knowledge and enrich their own values, the classroom experience is more likely to prove rewarding for everyone. According to McCormick (1984, p. 94), "a cornerstone of multiculturalism in education is cultural pluralism, an ideology of cultural diversity, which celebrates the differences among groups of people." Teachers should remind students that diversity strengthens our country. As Nelson (1999, p. 391) says, "A truly democratic society values diversity."

Personalizing Teaching

The erosion of the family and of neighborhoods and the negative effects of these changes on youth are familiar to all teachers. In addition, the U.S. population has become very mobile. With one family in five moving each year, even many small schools have multicultural student populations. In every situation teachers must recognize and exalt cultural differences to make students feel proud of their cultures and capable of applying their uniqueness to strengthen the United States. The best way to begin planning for teaching multicultural classes is to learn about your students' cultures (Slavin, 1994). Sometimes we overlook the obvious. Voltz (1999, p. 29) says that one way to understand your diverse students' needs is to talk to them about their hopes, dreams, and wishes.

No matter where you teach, cultural differences will abound. This is true in affluent suburbs, working-class urban areas, and rural areas. Even when students have similar ethnic and economic backgrounds, pronounced differences in religious backgrounds will exist. As long as there is one student whose background is different, you need skills in working with culturally mixed classrooms, even in the smallest communities and schools.

The impersonalization is greater in larger schools, in which there are so many students that even getting to know them all is difficult. In this setting, however, the challenge and the need to personalize is even greater, because members of similar cultural backgrounds tend to form cliques. Cultural cliques can be hotbeds of prejudice. This, of course, refers not to organized clubs but to the informal gatherings in parking lots, hallways, and cafeterias with no constructive purpose. Every teacher can contribute to dissolving such groups by getting to know each student on a more personal level and by volunteering to sponsor clubs for students of similar cultural backgrounds. International clubs are excellent for acquainting students with other cultures.

Americans have been in awe of Asian education systems because of their students' performance on science and mathematics exams, often assuming that these students spend more time than U.S. students spend studying these subjects. In fact, Asian students spend less time than their U.S. counterparts studying science and mathematics. The big difference is that they study fewer topics, giving them time to study them in depth and time to pursue social and personal growth. When Japanese teachers were asked to rate the importance of eight educational goals, those teachers gave first and second priority to student's personal growth, fulfillment, and self-understanding and human relations skills (Lewis & Tsuchida, 1998, p. 32). You can attend to your student's personal growth by providing them opportunities to internalize the curriculum, relating it to their personal lives. As you plan each lesson, include a solid answer to that familiar question, "Why do we have to study this?" Invite your students to add to your response to this question their personal views and their personal goals.

Such techniques are applicable in all classes, multicultural or not. Most students, regardless of cultural background, would profit if more classes were personalized, if competition among students were reduced, and if realistic demands were made of everyone. All students' self-concepts are enhanced when teachers assign tasks that require students to work together toward common goals (Manning & Lucking, 1991), tasks that are within students' ability and provide encouragement and rewards. However, students from other cultures are different in several specific ways, and you must be aware of these differences when learning how to teach them.

A group of teachers interested in discovering the strengths of various minority and ethnic students surveyed teachers throughout much of southern Florida, identifying 2,000 such strengths (Cheyney, 1976, pp. 41–42). The survey showed that the children were generally:

Highly responsive to affection	Independent
Physically dexterous	Imitative
Protective of siblings	Uninhibited
Academically persevering	Emotionally cool
Musically oriented	Monetarily proficient
Artistic	Rich in humor
Authority minded	Competitive
Resourceful	Forgiving

Although awareness of these qualities can help you design learning experiences for multicultural classes, teachers must resist the temptation to build yet another stereotype for all multicultural children. Each student is an individual, and as such may possess all or none of these traits. This list is included because it provides teachers of multicultural classes with a point at which to begin analyzing their students. And this is how teachers should begin—by analyzing each student's strengths and needs.

Perhaps the greatest obstacle to teaching an appreciation for diversity is teachers' reluctance to teach about cultures that are not their own. Alexander (1994) explains: "But the greatest obstacle lurks in the basic human fear of change. Change is slow, awkward, and bumpy at first (Laud, 1998, p. 25; Fullan, 2002). Many teachers feel that their own mythology and values, noted in the Renaissance of Western Europe, are being challenged by multicultural texts" (Alexander, 1994, p. 267).

Can people be taught to accept change? According to Anderson, Rotheiser, and Gordon (1998), "Teaching about the issues and process of change strengthened the coherence between coursework and practical experience" (p. 61). Perhaps the most effective approach to changing is through self-reflection (Wilcox, 1998). Stallworth (1998) has said that "A teacher's greatest opportunity for growth is systematic inquiry into his or her own teaching and learning" (p. 77).

All teachers need:

- Fresh teaching ideas and management strategies
- Samples of successful lesson plans, and time to practice them
- Time to share resources and personal stories (for validation and rejuvenation)
- Time to read useful materials on issues directly affecting their teaching and learning, such as multiculturalism
- Time to reflect
- Opportunities to reinvent (Stallworth, 1998, p. 78)

While Stallworth recommends self-change, Fullan (2002) reminds us of the need for teachers to share their changes, "Knowledge creation and sharing fuel moral purpose in schools led by cultural change principals" (p. 18).

Schwahn and Spady (1998) say that most people will not change unless they see a compelling reason, and they offer five prerequisites for getting people to change:

- People don't change unless they share a compelling reason.
- People don't change unless they have ownership in the change.
- People don't change unless their leaders model that they are serious about change.
- People are unlikely to change unless they have a concrete picture of what the change will look like for them personally.
- People can't make a change—or make it last—unless they receive organizational support for the change. (p. 46)

A Reason for Optimism

In 1975, in *Lau v. Nichols* (U.S. 563, 18. Ct. 786), the U.S. Supreme Court mandated that all schools in the United States with twenty or more students who speak a common first language other than English are to provide systematic instruction in that language. This emphasis has had a great impact on many schools, but this or any other federal mandate alone is inadequate. Meeting minority students' needs will occur through teachers' concerns, skills, and efforts.

Another reason for optimism is professional associations' emphasis on multicultural education. For more than two decades the Association for Supervision and Curriculum

Development has given high priority to multicultural education in its publications and meetings. In 1979 the National Council for the Accreditation of Teacher Education (NCATE) added a multicultural standard that colleges of teacher education must meet if they are to attain and retain accreditation. This means that colleges of teacher education must provide students opportunities to enable them to "understand the unique contributions, needs, similarities, differences and interdependencies of students from varying racial, cultural, linguistic, religious and socio-economic backgrounds." The 1998 revision of NCATE standards (NCATE, 1998) continues to stress multicultural education.

Another major reason for optimism is that the public is embracing multiculturalism as part of the curriculum. The 26th Annual Phi Delta Kappa/Gallup Poll of the Public's Attitudes toward the Public Schools (Elam, Rose, & Gallup, 1994) found that three-fourths of the public think that the schools should promote both a common cultural tradition and the diverse cultural traditions of the different population groups in the United States. The 30th Annual Gallup Poll (Rose & Gallup, 1998) found that almost two-thirds of the respondents (62 percent) believe that schools in their communities are taking the necessary steps to promote understanding and tolerance among students of different racial and ethnic backgrounds.

Perhaps the best reason to celebrate relates to student performance. The inequity gap between African American and white students has been dropping. Differences in Scholastic Achievement Test (SAT) scores have declined, and since the National Assessment of Educational Progress (NAEP), differences between African American and white student scores have been cut in half (Slavin, 1998).

The Teacher's Decision

We are fortunate to have multicultural classes. Schooling involves learning about life, and life in the twenty-first century is multicultural. Although all multicultural classes have some unique problems, they also offer students a chance to learn about contemporary life. And to accept themselves and others, students must understand and appreciate cultural diversity (Fantini, 1986). Yet these advantages do not come to our attention as quickly as the problems do. To realize the advantages, teachers must commit themselves to enjoy and capitalize on cultural differences in their classes (Henson & Henry, 1976). It is a matter of teacher attitude. "It is easy for students and faculty to focus only on differences, rather than also paying attention to the issue of common humanity in cultural diversity," write Chimes and Schmidt (1990, p. 46). Former Pennsylvania Teacher of the Year Howard Selekman says, "At the root of the teaching profession are the basic human needs to make a bond, a link with others." In his middle-level English classes Selekman uses writing assignments. "Writing about human conflicts becomes the tool by which my students and I engage with the world in a socially conscious manner" (Henson & Eller, 1999, pp. 59–60).

In-service education and other information-gathering methods can help improve teacher attitudes toward multicultural education. Although some programs have not done this, other programs have left participants feeling more positive about multicultural education. Over two decades ago, Dandridge (1980) found that the more teachers know about multicultural education, and the more professional preparation they have, the more positive their attitudes will be. Knowledge and preparation can prevent resentful and negative attitudes toward multicultural education.

Glatthorn (1993, p. 38) says that we should be aware that minority students often must cope with an environment outside of school that differs from the school environment. He calls this dilemma **cultural dissonance.** This distance can be reduced by increasing the school's contact with parents, a goal of the National Middle School Association (Jenkins & Jenkins, 1991): "Parents and schools [should] form partnerships to meet the needs of the whole child." These students must learn how to live in the school environment while maintaining their cultural identity (Ross, Bundy, & Kyle, 1993). This cultural dissonance places these students at risk. For many of these students, academic success depends on teachers "who are prepared to understand and meet the needs of students who come to school with varying learning styles, and with differing beliefs about themselves and what school means for them" (Darling-Hammond, 1993, p. 775).

All students are members of some culture. We should not think of minority students as being culturally disadvantaged. Every group is rich in heritage. If a white person fails to understand the richness of a minority student's background, is not the white person culturally disadvantaged? I think so. The teacher who views a multicultural classroom as a positive climate for overall student learning will help erase some of each student's cultural ignorance. People tend to fear and distrust what they do not understand, and you can do much to alleviate this lack of understanding.

> ## Reflection
> After reading the following assumptions (Tesconi, 1984, p. 88), respond to the questions below.
>
> **Assumptions of Cultural Pluralism**
> 1. An individual's membership in . . . a cultural group life . . . promotes . . . self-esteem, sense of belonging, respect for others, purposefulness, and critical thinking.
> 2. The development of tolerance and openness to different others . . . is dependent upon the opportunity of individuals to encounter and interact with a variety of culturally different others.
> 3. No one way of life can be said to be better than any other, and to be humane, a society must afford room for many competing and oftentimes conflicting ways of life.
> 4. It is valuable to have many ways of life in competition. . . . Such competition leads to a balance or equilibrium in the social order.
> 5. Loyalty to a larger society—a nation—is a function of, and dependent on, socially sanctioned loyalties rooted in a multiplicity of diverse ethnic and cultural groups.
>
> **Questions**
> 1. With which of these assumptions do you agree? Disagree? What are the bases for your agreements? Disagreements?
> 2. Do you believe loyalty to a single ethnic group, as opposed to loyalty to a multiplicity of ethnic groups, facilitates or impedes loyalty to the nation?
> 3. Name some ethnic groups in the United States, and list at least one advantage of membership in each group. List one contribution each group has made to the United States.

In working with multicultural students, you cannot help but know that there are differences, but the effective teacher will also realize that, basically, children are children. If you question whether time spent preparing to teach minorities is time well spent, remember that lessons and methods that work effectively with these students will also work well with the other students.

THE CASE

A Constructivist Approach to Teaching How Polls Work

Jamie Curts, University of Texas Pan American

Dr. Jamie Curts *received his Ph.D. from the University of Wisconsin–Madison. He teaches in and coordinates the Middle and Secondary School Program at the University of Texas Pan American, in Edinburg, Texas. His special interests include statistics education, constructivism, electronic portfolios, and learning communities.*

Geographical and Demographic Background

The case study described here took place in a middle school at the Rio Grande Valley of Texas, located in the southern tip of the state and encompasses Cameron, Hidalgo, Starr, and Willacy counties, which combine to be a total of 2,7162160 acres or 4,244 square miles (http://www.valleychamber.com/map.html). It is bounded on the east by the Gulf of Mexico, on the south by the Rio Grande, which forms the international boundary between the United States and Mexico, on the west by Zapata County, and on the north by Jim Hogg, Brooks, and Kenedy counties.

The school where our case developed is South Middle School in the city of Edinburg, Hidalgo County, which is the most populous in South Texas, with 569,463 people according to the 2000 U.S. Census. The city of Edinburg (www.edinburg.com) is part of a large metropolitan area including the cities of McAllen and Mission.

It all started when a mathematics student teacher of mine (Rolando Casas), from the University of Texas Pan American (UPTA, www.panam.edu), was taking my instructional methodology class (EDCI 4307) during fall 2001 and reported a scene from his field-experience duties. An eighth-grade student from South Middle School, Xavier Ramos, addressed his math teacher, saying that he couldn't understand how polls worked. He added that he was very surprised with the results published in a local newspaper about the preference of the public for two public candidates running for county judge. Xavier went further to say that the poll predicted one week before election day that candidate A was preferred to candidate B on a 6:4 proportion. One week later he was surprised at the results, since they were close to those predicted by the poll.

"They must be *brujos* (witches)," he claimed and went further to say that Candidate B was his *tio* (uncle) and that probably the *brujos* did not like his uncle.

Rolando reported in his journal that his mentor teacher just upheld his shoulders and said first in Spanish, "Ni modo (can't help it)" and continued in English, "That's the way it is. Polls, by the way, are complicated to understand. But *brujos*! Come on! They don't have anything to do with polls. It's the other guys with nice suits and ties that do this type of study." He then continued to start his lesson in probability and statistics.

My reaction to Rolando's journal report was immediate, and I decided to call a conference between him, the mentor teacher, and me. I saw the perfect opportunity to help Rolando and the mentor teacher develop a constructivist approach to link students' interest to new knowledge and thus help them understand the basic principle of how polls work.

Before we continue the case, we should address how statistics became a rapidly growing area within the mathematics curriculum at the K–12 levels, point out some of the problems in teaching this subject area, and address how technology can help discover key ideas and statistics concepts with hands-on activities and computer simulation experiments.

The New Statistics in the K–12 Curriculum

The amount of probability and statistics in the secondary mathematics curriculum has increased dramatically over the last ten years. When the NCTM's *Curriculum and Evaluation Standards for School Mathematics* was published in 1989, probability and statistics were primarily relegated to end-of-the-book units in a few textbooks. However, soon after *Principles and Standards for School Mathematics* was published, the encouragement to increase the emphasis on the studies of chance, data collection, and analysis of data (http://standards.nctm.org/document/chapter3/data.htm) has affected curricula greatly, even though most mathematics teachers are not comfortable teaching statistics. Most believe that their backgrounds are inadequate to use materials in teaching statistics properly. Much of the fear is that the new standards do not allow teachers simply to teach algorithms that are easy to learn. Today's students are encouraged to discover key ideas and concepts with hands-on activities or simulations and to be able to communicate their ideas. This discovery is aided through computers or calculators—tools with which many in-service and prospective teachers feel inadequate (http://www.nctm.org/dialogues/2000-10/areyour.htm).

The increased emphasis on statistics is due to the way the world is moving toward electronic decision-making processes in business, politics, research, and everyday life. Consumer surveys guide the development and marketing of products, daily weather predictions, political polls, and experiments that are used to evaluate the safety and efficacy of new medical treatments. Students need to know about data analysis and related aspects of probability in order to reason statistically—skills necessary to becoming informed citizens and intelligent consumers.

To understand the fundamentals of statistical ideas, students must work directly with data and spend time planning data collection procedures and evaluating their methods. As students move through the elementary grades and move into middle and high school, they should work more with data that have been gathered by others (electronic public databases) or generated by simulations. The emphasis on working with data entails students' meeting new ideas and procedures. The next section advocates computer-generated data simulations and the advantage of using such procedures when teaching probability and statistics.

The Role of Computer Simulations in School Mathematics and Science

Computer simulation has changed the underlying strategy of science and mathematics and the way we teach these subjects. Computation is an integral part of contemporary basic and applied science. In school science and mathematics, computer simulation is widely recognized as an important tool for its unique teaching and learning capabilities. Computer simulation allows students to experience reality, which motivates their capacity, ability, and appreciation for real and complex systems. Simulation requires "hands-on" and "minds-on" activities, so students become participants, not just listeners or observers. Student involvement in computer-generated simulations is so great that interest in learning more about the activity or the subject matter increases.

Even though there is a wide world of instructional software that includes simulation routines for teaching and learning science and mathematics, school teachers can have their students use electronic spreadsheets to experience number randomness. This case study will illustrate some principles and procedures of how randomness can be taught in grade 8 and will use computer-generated data to show how a poll works.

A Rationale to Plan a Constructivist Lesson on Polls

Up to now we know that this case study describes an eighth grader, Xavier, from a Rio Grande Valley school, asking his teacher how a poll works and thinking that *brujos* might be responsible for recent election results published. Rolando, the student teacher assigned to a mentor teacher, is aware that the answer given by the teacher should be addressed in some other fashion and thinks about developing a student-centered activity in which students can actually discover by themselves how polls function. When Rolando came to me, we both immediately recognized that polls are part of our daily lives and students are aware of them. Xavier's main concern and obvious challenge (how do polls work and how do they know that?) set up an excellent opportunity for students to experience the connection between polls and randomness. They could be taught how to elaborate simple models (including graphs) to predict outcomes from random sampling.

We decided to meet Rolando's mentor teacher and planned how to answer Xavier's question. We knew that *random sampling* had to be taught—not an easy task because it required students' previous knowledge of the following concepts: population, sample, variance, standard deviation, and frequency distribution charts. On top of that, students would have to add to their knowledge new concepts: probability of an event, random variable, random sampling, and random sampling distribution.

From my experience, most students see these concepts as stand-alone concepts. However, the best way to learn these concepts is to relate them to familiar daily activities. I suggested to Rolando and his mentor that it is always important to start with good, simple definitions and that I had found a "statistical glossary" very helpful for such a purpose (http://www.stats.gla.ac.uk/steps/glossary/). The concepts of population and sample can be downloaded from that website and students can discuss their meaning:

Population
A population is any entire collection of people, animals, plants, or things from which we may collect data. It is the entire group we are interested in, which we wish to describe or draw conclusions about.

Sample
A sample is a group of units selected from a larger group (the population). By studying the sample it is hoped to draw valid conclusions about the larger group. A sample is generally selected for study because the population is too large to study in its entirety. The sample should be representative of the general population. This is often best achieved by random sampling. Also, before collecting the sample, it is important that the researcher carefully and completely define the population, including a description of the members to be included.

The above definitions are very important in understanding that a poll is a sample from a population. I suggested that they use the above definitions and design class activities that included ballots for the students to vote on some life aspects (like–dislike; yes–no; agree–disagree, etc.). The activity included coding the results using a discrete scale (0, 1), calculating manually statistical summaries (the mean of the proportion and the standard deviation), and plotting (frequency distribution chart) the results. A discussion was set to interpret their results. Rolando wrote in his journal that the lesson had been very successful and that students had decided to vote on three issues: between two female rock stars, two rock bands, and on the following question: "You're given the chance to decorate your bedroom. Choose between painting your room or using decorated wallpaper." Student participation was very high, and the results elaborated two bulletin boards showing female and male results. As Rolando noted, "boys' standard deviation on each of the three questions was smaller compared to the girls," . . . and now for the first time I clearly saw students understand the true meaning of a standard deviation: the average deviation of the results around the mean." He also wrote that a boy, "Enrique," shouted, "You see . . . the standard deviation really tells you how guys are . . . the great majority of us will paint our room with some few exceptions, only two guys don't like Cristina Aguilera, and most of us like Manu Chao." Rolando learned to appreciate gender differences in class and the importance of designing lessons around students' life interests.

I also suggested to Rolando and his mentor to use "live and delicious" examples of populations, like a big bag of M&Ms, and to follow several lesson plans published on the Web (go to any search engine and look for M&M lesson_plan; there are plenty of good ideas). Any of these lessons are targeted for students to learn (at least at the awareness level) how to estimate a population parameter through random sampling distribution and visualize results on a frequency distribution chart.

A Rationale on "Why a Lesson on Computer Data Simulation?"

Once these experiments were conducted it was time to have another lesson in which students are taught how to use the random generating function from a spreadsheet or a basic statistical package. The plan required the students to search the meaning of "simulation" and how it is used in reality to increase knowledge of some aspect of life. As Rolando recorded in his journal, "Most of the students had a pretty good idea what simulation was, specially 'cause they are experts in video games and most of them reported using the simulation game called *The Sims Family*."

Computer data simulation can be viewed as the "experimental" side of the science of data analysis. In the classroom, simulation experiments play the same role for statistics as laboratory experiments do in many sciences. The teacher can use data simulation to illustrate principles or procedures, to demonstrate facts and methods, and to provide a controlled body of experience for the student with computer software.

At this point, a lesson was planned for students to use a spreadsheet and simulate the experiment of rolling fair dice. This experimental approach allowed them to "experience randomness"* and, as Rolando recorded, "It improved their intuition and critical faculties." The class was divided into groups of three, and each group used an electronic spreadsheet to simulate ten experiments of rolling fair dice thirty times. When they looked at their results (means, standard deviation, and frequency charts), it was clear that there was "no mystery" and they "discovered" that each experiment is "independent" from another and no favorite numbers can be tracked down. However, I asked Rolando as part of his duties to discuss the following questions, since I believe student teachers should be prepared to be reflective practitioners using the action research paradigm: When students are first confronted with the concepts of chance or probability, what kinds of misconceptions do they commonly have? Are these misconceptions intimidating to them? In what manner has computer technology been used to assist students with their misconceptions concerning probability, and what does research say about the level of success of such uses? Later I will discuss his answers.

As part of the lesson plan described above, students are expected to understand the meaning of randomness and random number. A discussion was set with the students to explain to them that these concepts have traditionally been used for a variety of purposes, such as rolling dice, market surveys, and so on.

The underlying concept of this lesson is for students to formalize the concept of random variable—in this lesson, defining x as the random outcome of rolling fair dice n times—and have them look at their experiment results by plotting the frequency distribution of that random variable. Students plot the frequency of appearance (which can be defined as probability) against the possible values of the random outcome (in this case x can be 1, 2, 3, 4, 5, or 6) for each experiment. The pedagogical attractiveness of having students learn how to plot and visualize their results is of immense value, since it engages students in comprehending their results and discovering some aspects or patterns that were previously unknown.

Using Computer-Simulated Experiments to Teach about Polls

The next step was to engage the students in a "real" poll. This time Rolando took control of the whole lesson. In his plan he explained to the students that in order to conduct a poll they needed to start with a pilot study (selecting a sample from the population), and that the results obtained from the pilot study were going to be crucial to the study. In fact, he recorded in his journal, "The students asked me what was the purpose of the pilot study and I told them that it will allow us to sneak a quick look at the results and get a glimpse of what's going on." This lesson was to be an excellent opportunity for them to learn how a model works, and it started by having the students develop an opinion questionnaire to be administered at the school. Using guided practice, Rolando pushed students to think about modeling, and they defined the population as total number of students in the school, which "represented" the state of Texas, and each classroom as a specific county. The pilot sample consisted of going to each classroom and selecting one student at random. Students selected would be asked to cast a secret ballot containing the following question: "If you had the capability of voting today for the best pop star, whom would you vote for: Candidate A or Candidate B? Please mark an X on the ballot. Thank you, results will be posted soon on our bulletin board." At this point, students understood that the random variable of interest had two possible values: a vote for candidate A or one for B.

Rolando explained his plan to his colleagues a few days before the experiment started. They all agreed to

---

*Computer-generated "random" numbers are more properly referred to as *pseudo-random* numbers. They are computed from a mathematical formula or simply taken from a precalculated list. Algorithms for generating them are so good that the numbers *"look"* exactly like they were really random; however pseudo-random numbers have the characteristic that they are predictable.

pull one student at random and ask that student to step outside the classroom to participate in the poll.

Students from Rolando's class were organized in groups and were instructed to come back to class with the results and input the data as a single column into an electronic worksheet such as Excel. A vote for Candidate A would be entered as a "zero," and one for Candidate B as a "one." He reminded his students that the purpose of the pilot study was to collect data and obtain a "good guess on how people voted." This "guess," identified as p, is the average or mean proportion of the data entered, and it is critical for them to understand that it represents an estimate of the population parameter.

Once they "know" how the population might vote, you might want to ask the following question: "Do you think the results would be equal if two or three or more students were selected at random from each classroom?" You should do this if nobody has questioned the "quality" or how "certain" the estimated parameter is. These "what-if" types of questions are essential for knowledge construction and push students into high-order thinking. At this point we have determined that computer data simulation will allow students to "discover" and learn knowledge by themselves.

The Actual Lesson

Remember that this lesson is motivated by the question, "How do polls work?" Our objective is for students to learn basic aspects of how a poll is conducted and how results from such an exercise are used in real life. We will introduce them to computer data simulation and "create" several hypothetical polls.

Your class has mastered basic concepts and they have recently been exposed to the concept of estimating a population parameter (p) through sampling distribution. They have been challenged about how much confidence they have in the value of such a parameter, since it was estimated using "only one student at random from each classroom."

Obviously the students will suggest repeating the experiment and increasing the sample size. However, at this point it is essential to introduce them to the significance of simulation and its advantages. With the latter in mind, you should start the lesson, "How do polls work?" as follows:

1. Explain the objective to the class: students will learn by conducting a simulation of a poll how to elaborate and interpret a random sampling distribution process.
2. Review the definition of a simulation process. Identify previous knowledge that they can use to anchor this concept, for example, "flight simulator," etc. Look for simulation applets published on the Web.
3. Explain qualitatively the Bernoulli random process. Tell them that a computer has the capability of generating "random numbers." Use the estimated value of p and generate a column size 50 of random numbers (0, 1). Show them that the average or mean of the column is p. Calculate also the standard deviation.
4. Up to this point be sure that they understand that the Bernoulli process is defined by a random variable with possible outcomes of "zero" or "one" ($x = 0, 1$) and that given these values you can estimate a mean and a standard deviation.
5. Make a demo using the estimated value of p by generating a 50 × 2 matrix on a screen (fifty rows arranged in two columns). Explain to your students that the matrix being projected is a simulation using the information they gathered yesterday. Let them think that each row represents a random sample of two persons selected "from a classroom." From here they see "simulated" results when sampling two people at random from fifty classrooms.
6. Have your students or each team generate their own matrices using the p estimate or give them a copy from your file. Tell them to start with a 50 × 2 matrix.

The problem to be addressed now is what to do with the data that has been "gathered" through this simulation process. Continue with the following.

7. Instruct them that everybody or a team should use the spreadsheet capabilities to calculate the mean proportion of each sample, that is, the mean from each row. The result should go to a designated column called "sample mean distribution," and its size should be 50 × 1.
8. Ask students to construct a frequency plot distribution of the "sample mean distribution" column and to calculate the mean and the standard deviation of the sample mean distribution column. Repeat steps 7 and 8 using different size matrices.

Examples of Students' Experimental Results

The following table shows the results obtained by one student simulating several Bernoulli experiments with $p = 0.6$. The first experiment consists of sampling one student from each of the fifty classrooms. The second considers sampling "two students at random" and calculating the mean for each sample (students were instructed that the mean of each sample should be placed in a different column labeled "mean sample distribution"). The mean and the standard deviation of the mean sample distribution were calculated and some of the results are shown below. This mean is known as the grand mean, and the standard deviation of this distribution is known as the standard error of the mean.

Exp. No.	Matrix Size	Sample Distribution Mean	Mean Sample Distribution Standard Deviation
1	50 × 1	0.6000	0.4999
2	50 × 2	0.5800	0.3350
3	50 × 3	0.6109	0.2973
4	50 × 5	0.6063	0.1990
5	50 × 10	0.6259	0.1665
6	50 × 20	0.5987	0.0985

The results shown above allowed each student to discover the effect of sample size when predicting the mean proportion of votes that each candidate will obtain. In fact, through their simulation experiment, they will intuitively understand the importance of marginal errors of polls by comparing the standard deviation* of each sample mean frequency distribution. They can also see that the sample distribution mean is fairly consistent, but the variability around it depends on the sample size used.

Challenging students with new experimental situations will allow them to contrast quantity versus quality in sampling. For example, what if a new research team decided to randomly sample ten classrooms out of fifty and from these chooses ten students at random, or for the same situation but three students at random. Again, generating computer simulation data for these situations should be given to students as a challenge and an opportunity for high-order thinking. It is important to point out that you are not teaching the Bernoulli distribution, but using it to simulate a given situation. Your emphasis is on the effect of sample size when estimating an unknown parameter of a population.

Further Reflection

A Chinese proverb says, "I hear and I forget, I see and I remember, I do and I understand." This case study illustrates the need of having more mathematics teachers plan and teach probability and data analysis within a constructivist approach. Students need to listen, visualize, and experiment with basic concepts as an integrated activity in order for the following equation to be true:

$$\text{hear} + \text{see} + \text{do} = \text{anchored knowledge}$$

Exposing students to randomness through computer-generated data simulation experiments can ease construction of algebraic expressions, simulate probabilistic situations, search for patterns, justify conjectures, generalize concepts, and graph and chart data.

*The standard deviation of a sample mean distribution is called the "standard error of the mean."

The Teacher's Role

The history of U.S. treatment of minorities tells us that teachers' actions determine whether multicultural students receive a quality education. "The courts can grant equal opportunity, but cannot give equal chance" (Payne, 1984, p. 124). As Chimes and Schmidt (1990) explain, only teachers can provide all students equal opportunity: "If books and ensuing discussions become magnifiers of guilt, injustice, and shame, no good can come of it. The responsibility to keep discussions informative, challenging, and positive lies solely with the faculty" (p. 46).

As this millennium begins, teachers must consider themselves world citizens. Erasmus (1989) explains:

Teachers must be able to reach beyond their own world to touch that of their students and assist students to do the same. We can begin by learning to listen. We, as teachers, must confirm and validate the experience and knowledge [of our students] as well as the cultural context in which those experiences live and that knowledge is situated. To do this, we must listen to their stories, and hear who they are. We must learn to listen and listen to learn. (p. 274)

The good news is that teachers have tremendous power to influence members of minority cultures. Singham (2003) reported that teachers, whether mainstream or minority, have more influence over minority students than they have over mainstream students. For example, 81 percent of black females and 62 percent of black males want to please the teacher more than they want to please a parent; the comparable figures for whites are 28 percent for females and 32 percent for males.

Although this book makes a conscious attempt to avoid long lists, one list is essential at this point. Read and consider each of the following (Dawson, 1974, pp. 53–54). Collectively, these dos and don'ts provide an excellent guide for teachers in multicultural classrooms.

Dos for Teachers in Multicultural Classrooms

1. Do use the same scientific approach to gain background information on multicultural groups you would use to tackle a course in science, mathematics, or any subject area in which you might be deficient.
2. Do engage in systematic study of the disciplines that provide insight into the cultural heritage, political struggle, contributions, and present-day problems of minority groups.
3. Do try to develop sincere personal relationships with minorities. You can't teach strangers! Don't give up because one minority person rejects your efforts. All groups have sincere individuals who welcome honest, warm relationships with members of another race. Seek out those who will accept or at least tolerate you.
4. Do recognize that there are often more differences within one group than between two groups. If we recognize diversity among races, we must also recognize diversity within groups.
5. Do remember that there are many ways to gain insight into a group. Visit their churches, homes, communities; read widely and listen to various segments of the group.
6. Do remember that no one approach and no one answer will help you meet the educational needs of all children in a multicultural society.
7. Do select instructional materials that are accurate and free from stereotypes.
8. Do remember that there is a positive relationship between teacher expectation and academic progress.
9. Do provide an opportunity for minority students and students from the mainstream to interact in a positive intellectual setting on a continuous basis.

10. Do use a variety of materials, especially those that utilize positive, real-life experiences.
11. Do provide some structure and direction to children who have unstructured lives, primarily children of the poor.
12. Do expose all students to a wide variety of literature as a part of your cultural sensitivity program.
13. Do remember that even though ethnic groups often share many common problems their needs are diverse.
14. Do utilize the rich resources within your own classroom among various cultural groups.
15. Do remember that human understanding is a lifetime endeavor. You must continue to study and provide meaningful experiences for your students.
16. Do remember to be honest with yourself. If you can't adjust to children from multicultural homes, get out of the classroom.

Don'ts for Teachers in Multicultural Classrooms

1. Don't rely on textbooks, teachers guides, and brief essays to become informed about minorities. Research and resources will be needed.
2. Don't use ignorance as an excuse for not having any insight into the problems and culture of African Americans, Chicanos, Native Americans, Puerto Ricans, Asian Americans, and other minorities.
3. Don't rely on the "expert" judgment of one minority person for the answer to all the complicated racial and social problems of his or her people. For example, African Americans, Mexicans, Indians, and Puerto Ricans have various political views on all issues.
4. Don't be fooled by popular slogans and propaganda intended to raise the national consciousness of an oppressed people.
5. Don't get carried away with the "save the world concept." Most minorities have their own savior.
6. Don't be afraid to learn from those who are more familiar with the mores and cultures than you.
7. Don't assume that you have all the answers for solving the other person's problems. It is almost impossible for an outsider to be an expert on the culture of another group.
8. Don't assume that all minority group students are culturally deprived.
9. Don't develop a fatalistic attitude about the progress of minority students.
10. Don't resegregate students through tracking and ability-grouping gimmicks.
11. Don't give up when minority students seem to hate school.
12. Don't assume that minorities are the only students who should have multicultural instructional materials. Students in the mainstream can be culturally deprived in their lack of knowledge and understanding of other people and of their own heritage.
13. Don't ask parents and students personal questions in the name of research. Why should they divulge their suffering?
14. Don't get hung up on grade designations when sharing literature that provides insight into the cultural heritage of a people.

15. Don't try to be cool by using the vernacular of a particular racial group.
16. Don't make minority students feel ashamed of their language, dress, or traditions.

These dos and don'ts are presented as general guidelines for teachers who have members of one or more ethnic minority groups in their classes. Because all teachers have some representatives of other cultures in their classes from time to time, these guidelines should be appropriate for all of us. One additional suggestion, which is so obvious that you may overlook it: Do not give in to the temptation to make quick, automatic generalizations about any culture.

> ## Reflection
>
> The following statement was made by a minority ethnic group member who has become a recognized national leader in the study of multicultural education (Garcia, 1984, p. 104). Consider his comments as you respond to the questions below.
>
> ### Correcting Classroom Discrimination
>
> "I remember well my eighth-grade English teacher who made me write a letter to the school newspaper ten times before submission. The fact that my father was an unemployed coal miner, that my parents had seven years of schooling between them, and that English was spoken minimally in our house did not impede her from making a positive difference in my life. Not only did I learn to write a letter well, but I learned the importance of discipline, perseverance, and mentorship—all very important outcomes of schooling."
>
> 1. Some teachers overlook minority-group students whose level of success is minimal. Do you think the person who made this statement condones this practice? Can you give one reason teachers should or should not hold high expectations for members of minority groups?
> 2. As a teacher, what can you do to win minority students' confidence and respect?
> 3. Assuming that all people have some degree of prejudice toward members of certain minority groups, how can you elevate your appreciation for minorities?

These guidelines are based on volumes of data, but even when you use scientifically derived suggestions, remember that regardless of culture, all students are individuals. Respect their individuality.

Selecting Ethnic Materials

Because more than half the states in the nation require multiethnic programs and development of multiethnic materials, special materials for multiethnic groups should not be difficult to find. As Bishop noted (1986), "It is promising to realize that efforts to include books that reflect all ethnic backgrounds not only enable minority students to identify more closely with the school while improving their reading ability, but also enable nonminority students to broaden their understanding of other peoples and cultures" (p. 23). In selecting materials for teaching about ethnicity—and in selecting all materials to use in multicultural settings—do not automatically assume that different ethnic groups need elementary or remedial materials. The following classification system was designed to help teachers select multiethnic materials at the appropriate levels of complexity, depending on the units' objectives.

Level I materials are low in complexity and designed to highlight the achievements of all ethnic groups. Such material includes biographies and success stories of ethnic Americans. These materials are usually highly complimentary—so much that they often exaggerate. They are usually attractive and conspicuously displayed in the classroom by teachers. Use them sparingly and selectively.

Level II materials depict "true/real" experiences of ethnic groups. Problems of the group are shown in a way that suggests that members of other groups, such as the majority ethnic group, are responsible for bad experience, but without specifying who the others are. Limit the use of these materials.

Level III materials show the historical experiences of more than one ethnic group. Portrayals are limited to racial groups (blacks, Hispanics, Native Americans) or white groups (Irish Americans, Italian Americans, or Polish Americans), but not both. A common approach is to select a major theme, such as "metropolitan/urban life," and present each group's unique experiences. Such materials purposefully accentuate the differences between minority groups or white ethnic groups and fail to show the experiences and behaviors common to all groups. If misused, this material could widen existing gaps between classmates of differing ethnic groups.

Level IV materials, the most complex materials, are designed around broad content generalizations. They chronicle experiences common to all groups and identify common characteristics. They provide students with a multiethnic perspective on the American experience. Because these materials require critical analysis, use them with students who can conduct sophisticated discussion and critical, objective analysis.

Case Studies

Multicultural classes offer students an opportunity to learn how to get along with members of various ethnic groups; however, this can happen only in an environment that permits students to interact with their classmates. One method that invites students to interact and share opinions is the case study method (Kowalski, Weaver, & Henson, 1994).

The case study method is fun to use because it encourages the sharing of opinions and insights. Teachers enjoy using this method because is frees them to observe students interacting with each other. Learning how to use the case study is not difficult. One effective way to learn more about case studies is to write your own cases for your students to use (Barnes, Christensen, & Hansen, 1994).

As you approach your first teaching position, you may want to develop a portfolio of materials to use with multicultural groups. But whether you do this or not, you must view multicultural experiences as a challenge and an opportunity, not as an opportunity to "save" minority students from their own ethnic group. All students should learn to appreciate and respect cultures other than their own. A sensible, if not the best, approach to selecting materials for multicultural groups is to achieve some balance of materials from the varying levels of complexity. However, the most important criterion for selecting materials is how well a source will help you attain a lesson's objectives.

Because cultural diversity has made the United States strong, do not try to melt down the cultures into one. On the contrary, schools should help preserve many of the characteristics that make each culture unique. In the past, teachers have made some common mistakes in working with multicultural groups. Often they made such a fuss over the differences between and among groups that they exacerbated the gap in students' minds about groups' differing characteristics. On the opposite end of the continuum, teachers have tried to blend all cultures into one. For two hundred years the United States was considered a melting pot. The concept was first created by a French-born writer, Crevecoeur, in 1782 (Ramirez & Castaneda, 1974).

Academic Achievement by Everyone

Too often teachers accept low performance from minority students—"That's just the way they are"—but this is a cop-out. By making an exception for minority students and letting them go along without experiencing maximum success, teachers deny them their right to develop to their maximum potential—a goal that we should hold for all students. And this demand for quality work from everyone includes students who speak little or no English. Rich Miyagawa (1999), an English teacher in Pasadena, California, reported that he found the computer to be an excellent route to immediately engaging non-English-speaking students in academics. Each non-English-speaking student is hooked up with another student with the same language and background. Your attitudes and behaviors will have a significant impact on students' enthusiasm or reluctance toward technology. Remember that teachers are always role models, intended or not. Your influence as a role model is likely to be especially strong among the Hispanic students in your classes (Vasquez; see Henson & Eller, 1999). Parsley & Corcoran (2003, p. 87) concur: "Teachers who consistently communicate the belief that all students have the ability to learn and succeed make a difference to at-risk students."

The Teacher's Wider Role

We have been examining the teacher's role in working with multicultural classes with respect to instruction, but the teacher has a much broader role. Because teaching involves more than mere instruction, you should find opportunities to fulfill the goals of multicultural education.

A Teacher Corps/Association of Teacher Educators project resulted in a book titled *In Praise of Diversity: A Resource Book for Multicultural Education* (Grant, Meinich, & Riven, 1977). The book concludes with an article that identifies a number of implications for teachers of multicultural groups that extend beyond the classroom into all areas of the teacher's work.* Two avenues teachers can use to praise diversity are identified. These avenues are process and content. Now we turn to some ways to use process to praise diversity.

Using Process to Praise Diversity

Have you ever considered that as a teacher you will be positioned in a prominent (highly visible) position in the community? This will enable you to affect and shape significantly the community's atmosphere and the general attitudes toward different cultures. Your behavior both inside and outside the classroom is important. According to Grant, Meinich, and Riven (1977), teachers have at least the following functions:

1. Director of learning
2. Counselor and guidance worker
3. Mediator of culture
4. Link with the community
5. Member of the school staff
6. Member of the profession

---

*Appreciation is extended to Carl A. Grant, Susan L. Melnich, and H. N. Riven, to the Teacher Corps, and to the Association of Teacher Educators, for permission to adapt material from the article "In Praise of Diversity: Some Implications."

Director of Learning

Much of this chapter has focused on the teacher's instructional role. Because suggestions were provided to show how teachers should "gear up" their instruction to allow for, praise, and promote cultural differences in the classroom, we need not discuss this dimension again.

Counselor and Guidance Worker

Because this book's philosophy is personalizing education, each chapter emphasizes the need for you to work with each student in a way that extends beyond academics. Only one further comment seems warranted. Each teacher is responsible for vocational guidance. The best vocational guidance programs are interdisciplinary and run throughout the grades. Each teacher should help students become aware of vocational possibilities. Do not assume that members from all cultures feel an equal need for long-range planning; you must introduce some students to this concept and its advantages.

Mediator of Culture

Earlier in this chapter we discussed a need to stress the contributions of all cultures represented in the classroom to "our culture" and to humanity at large. This should not preclude emphasis on the democratic processes and U.S. citizens' rights and responsibilities; rather, it should complement this goal. One way to do this is to teach problem-solving skills for coping with potential conflict areas. Simulations can be used to develop these skills.

Link with the Community

The LINKS Project was established at Indiana State University in the 1970s. Written by a science educator, Chris Buethe, this project helped nonscience teachers develop science materials for use in their classes. For example, English teachers were able to link the high-interest area of science to their classes by assigning students essays or other projects that would link otherwise seemingly unrelated subjects. This strategy can also be used to link the multicultural class to the community. Cultural diversity should be exalted in the community at large. Since most teachers sooner or later accept leadership roles in the community, they can use these positions toward these ends. Perhaps most important of all, teachers can demonstrate their own commitment by praising diversity and affirming pluralism as they work and live in the community.

Teacher as Proactive Decision Maker

Classroom Situation

1. You will have classes with students from several ethnic backgrounds.

Proactive Alternatives

1. Locate role model members from various cultures in your school's community that you can call on as consultants to visit your classes.
2. Plan a class activity to identify commonalities among students of various ethnic backgrounds (preference for artichokes, o.k., then pizza; enjoy dancing; like '65 Mustangs).

Member of the School Staff

Since teachers' roles within the school extend beyond the classroom and involve other teachers, administrators, and auxiliary personnel, they can find many opportunities to influence their colleagues. In most schools an important location for informal influence is the teachers' lounge, but of course not all influence there is positive. In a supervision text, Henry and Beasley (1989) use the phrase "lounge lizards" to caution teachers of the potential damage that can inadvertently result from careless comments in informal settings. However, if such settings do affect participants' behavior, the lounge can also be an ideal place for teachers dedicated to multicultural education to demonstrate their concerns, not in negative ways but in positive, constructive behaviors.

Member of the Profession

As members of a profession, teachers must use their influence and skills to improve themselves and the profession. One major responsibility is to communicate education's positive dimensions to all members of society. The previous decade brought criticism and scorn to U.S. schools. Individual teachers can communicate their schools' roles and achievements through conversations, discussions, and the written word. Professional meetings offer excellent opportunities for communication, and professional journals offer similar opportunities. Teachers who are committed to furthering multicultural education will find that many education and teacher associations give top priority to these ends.

Vignettes

Vignette One: A Teacher Belittles a Slow Student

In terms of performance quality, Jerry Simms was one of the poorest students Shelly had ever had. At first she tried to encourage Jerry to listen, then she tried to force him to do his daily home assignments. Nothing seemed to help. Finally, Shelly made an inexcusable response to his indifferent behavior. She remarked in front of his peers, "Jerry, you don't have one iota of understanding about the subject we are studying, do you?"

Later, when relating the incident to some other teachers, she learned that Jerry had almost no home life. She began to regret what she had said and decided to drive by and see where he lived. The temperature was below freezing, and cracks in the walls let the lights show through. She learned later that the building had once been a storehouse for grain and had dirt floors. A student told her that there were only two chairs and a table inside.

Shelly's experience with Jerry began to haunt her. She began to ask herself, "How can I help him?"

DISCUSSION

1. How can a teacher learn about a student's home life? An experience like Shelly's makes the teacher want to see the student's home and family. But this is not always practical and is not necessarily a wise method. It is not practical because there are too many students in similar circumstances. It is not wise because the student may be embarrassed to have his family and home exposed for observation.

As a beginning teacher, you will be amazed at how much other teachers know about the students in your class—even the teachers who have never taught your students. Do not hesitate to ask other teachers about your students. It is perfectly professional so long as the discussion is directed to understanding the student better and does not degenerate into a gossip session. Your school will keep a cumulative record on each student. This record will contain comments made by the student's previous teachers. Here you can learn about a student's general behavior and academic potential.

2. Why might a dedicated teacher lose her temper with a low-performing student like Jerry? Most classes have students whose performance is low because they are too lazy to improve. The teacher cannot always know which students are lazy and which are handicapped by a disadvantaged home life. Therefore, instead of becoming irritated with students who are not attentive, try to determine the cause of their apathy.

3. To what ethnic group would you guess Jerry belongs? Shelly? Shelly and Jerry are both white Americans.

Vignette Two: A Poor School Has a Good Atmosphere

When Bob, a supervisor of student teachers, first saw Rio Grande, an inner-city school, his reaction was disbelief that such a school could exist in the twenty-first century—the buildings should have been condemned decades ago because they were firetraps. Placing two beginning teachers in this environment went against Bob's better judgment, but he took a deep breath and went in to meet the principal.

Mr. Lopez was a delightful middle-aged man, gregarious and energetic. He introduced Bob to his secretaries and to several members of his large faculty, which was 95 percent Hispanic. Each teacher had the same spark of enthusiasm and pleasantness.

Bob was still suspicious because he had been inside many dilapidated inner-city schools. He was keenly aware that in schools like this the students were often discourteous, rude, disrespectful, and difficult to control. Nevertheless, his responsibility was to assign two student teachers to this staff for the next term, so he promised himself he would visit frequently and provide encouragement and reassurance to make the experience tolerable for them.

When Bob visited, both student teachers assured him they were getting along well. There were apparently no major discipline problems in their classes. Both worked hard and enjoyed teaching in this school. From talking with the principal, some of the faculty members, and these two student teachers, Bob found three elements that seemed to be working together to produce the wholesome, optimistic atmosphere in a physical environment that had initially seemed so depressing. First, the principal stressed the importance of total involvement by all, including faculty and students, on both academic and extracurricular matters. These student teachers were immediately involved in evening and weekend school activities. The principal considered them important members of the faculty.

Second, the principal's enthusiasm was reflected in every faculty member and classroom. Most of the students were very poor readers, which severely limited the rate of learning, but the teachers were patient and continually encouraged their students.

Bob discovered the third element contributing to this school's wholesome atmosphere when he expressed his concern at the slow rate at which material was being covered. A faculty member responded that because many of the students were academically slow and had poor home lives that destroyed their concern and respect for others, one of the most important objectives was to teach the students to cooperate with others. The faculty members at Rio Grande certainly set good examples for their students.

DISCUSSION

1. Teaching respect for others should be an important objective in any deprived community, but exactly what can the teacher do to teach students to respect others?

2. Some student teachers never intend to teach in rundown buildings located in inner-city ghettos, so why do they need the experience of teaching in such schools?

3. Could the fact that this faculty was composed almost entirely of Hispanics explain the unexpected open climate in this school?

Summary

The nation's classrooms are becoming more diverse, offering teachers a mixture of challenges and opportunities. Members of minority cultures can benefit most from some of the same practices and conditions that favor learning for all students. Paramount among these is a personal approach.

Teachers can also serve minority students by teaching about the contributions that each group has made here in the U.S. They can further enhance the education of all students by focusing on individual strengths and interests, and by making all students aware that the differences among members of any culture are greater than the differences among cultures.

Problem solving and simulations (including computer-based simulations) can improve learning and motivation for all students, especially for members of some cultures who enjoy and derive more benefits from hands-on learning. Another practice that enhances learning for everyone is holding high expectations for all. But it is imperative that teachers match these high expectations with daily behavior that demonstrates the teachers' confidence in the ability of all students.

Recap of Major Ideas

1. Several qualities of U.S. schools militate against minority group students' efforts to succeed academically and socially.
2. Twenty-first-century classrooms are populated by a new majority.
3. Having students of several cultural backgrounds strengthens a class and a school.
4. By assigning tasks within students' ability range, by providing encouragement, and by giving rewards, teachers can help minority and other students build their self-concept.
5. Federal law requires schools to teach in the national language of students when twenty or more students share a common first language.
6. Discuss in class the contribution of minority groups to society.
7. Select and use textbooks that portray all cultures in positive and realistic ways.
8. There are more differences within than among cultures.
9. Some professional associations make concentrated efforts to ensure proper education for minority groups and the development of positive attitudes toward multicultural education.
10. Demand continuous academic growth from minority students.
11. Strive to build a positive attitude toward cultural diversity in your classroom.

Activities

At one time or another, all of us will teach classes that represent different cultures, so we will need strategies for working with cultural differences. In fact, even in a class whose ethnic composition is similar, there is often a diversity of cultural backgrounds. The following activities will help you work with multicultural groups.

1. Most of us are biased toward our own ethnic group. Make a list of your own biases.
2. All ethnic groups have some cultural qualities that can make a contribution to U.S. society. Name some ethnic groups, and identify one such quality of each.
3. Describe a strategy that would be appropriate in your subject and grade level for breaking down cultural prejudices. Consider including techniques for showing the attributes of different classes and groups.

Looking Ahead

This chapter has focused on helping you meet the needs of students from diverse ethnic backgrounds. The students who face the most daunting challenges of all are labeled "special." Because of recent laws, you can be certain that students with mild to severe emotional, physical, and mental challenges will enter your classrooms. The following chapter will introduce several teaching strategies and alert you to the major strengths and limitations of each.

References

Alexander, J. (1994). Multicultural literature: Overcoming the hurdles to successful study. *The Clearing House*, 67(5), 266–268.

Anderson, S., Rotheiser, C., & Gorden, K. (1998). Preparing teachers to be leaders. *Educational Leadership*, 55(5), 59–61.

Banks, J. A. (1999). *An introduction to multicultural education* (2nd ed.). Boston: Allyn & Bacon.

Barnes, L. B., Christensen, C. R., & Hansen, A. J. (1994). *Teaching and the case study method* (3rd ed.). Boston: Harvard Business School Press.

Bishop, G. R. (1986). The identification of multicultural materials for the middle school library: Annotations and sources. *American Middle School Education, 9,* 23–27.

Cheyney, A. B. (1976). *Teaching children of different cultures in the classroom* (2nd ed.). Columbus, OH: Merrill.

Chimes, M., & Schmidt, P. (1990, September–October). What I read over my summer vacation: Readings on cultural diversity. *The Clearing House, 64*(1), 44–46.

Dandridge, J. A. (1980). *The attitudes, knowledge of subject matter and classroom behaviors of teachers using multicultural/multiethnic programs.* Unpublished doctoral dissertation, University of Southern California, Los Angeles.

Darling-Hammond, L. (1993). Reforming the school reform agenda. *Phi Delta Kappan, 74*(10), 756–761.

Elam, S. M., Rose, L. C., & Gallup, G. (1994). The 26th annual Phi Delta Kappa/Gallup Poll of the public's attitudes toward the public schools. *Phi Delta Kappan, 76*(1), 41–56.

Erasmus, C. C. (1989). Ways with stories: Listening to the stories aboriginal people tell. *Language Arts, 66*(3), 267–275.

Fantini, M. D. (1986). *Regaining excellence in education.* Columbus, OH: Merrill.

Fullan, M. (2002). The change leader. *Educational Leadership, 59*(8), 16–20.

Garcia, J., & Garcia, R. (1980). Selecting ethnic materials. *Social Studies, 44,* 232–234.

Garcia, R. L. (1984). Countering classroom discrimination. *Theory into Practice, 23,* 104–108.

Glatthorn, A. A. (1993). *Learning twice.* New York: HarperCollins.

Gomez, M. L., & Smith, R. J. (1991, January–February). Building interactive reading and writing curricula with diverse learners. *The Clearing House, 64*(3), 147–151.

Grant, C. A., Meinich, S. L., & Riven, H. N. (1977). *In praise of diversity: A resource book for multicultural education.* Washington, DC: Association of Teacher Educators.

Guyton, J. M., & Fielstein, L. L. (1991, January–February). A classroom activity to increase student awareness of racial prejudice. *The Clearing House, 64*(3), 207–209.

Haberman, M. (1998). Teachers for multicultural schools and the power of selection. *Theory into Practice, 37*(2), 96–104.

Henry, M. A., & Beasley, W. W. (1989). *Supervising student teachers: The professional way* (4th ed.). Terre Haute, IN: Sycamore.

Henson, K. T., & Eller, B. F. (1999). *Educational psychology for effective teaching.* Belmont, CA: Wadsworth.

Henson, K. T., & Henry, M. A. (1976). *Becoming involved in teaching* (chap. 9). Terre Haute, IN: Sycamore.

Hilliard, J. (1991–1992). Why must we pluralize the curriculum? *Educational Leadership, 49*(4), 12–13.

Jenkins, D. M., & Jenkins, K. D. (1991). The NMSA Delphi report: Roadmap to the future. *Middle School Journal, 22*(4), 27–36.

Kowalski, T. J., Weaver, R. A., & Henson, K. T. (1994). *Case studies on beginning teachers.* White Plains, NY: Longman.

Laud, L. E. (1998). Changing the way we communicate. *Educational Leadership, 55*(7), 23–25.

Lewis, C., & Tsuchida, I. (1998). The basics in Japan: The three c's. *Educational Leadership, 55*(6), 32–37.

Manning, M. L., & Lucking, R. (1991, January–February). The what, why, and how of cooperative learning. *The Clearing House, 64*(3), 152–156.

McCormick, T. E. (1984). Multiculturalism: Some principles and issues. *Theory into Practice, 23,* 93–97.

Miyagawa, R. (1999). Technology in the classroom. In Henson, K. T., & Eller, B. F., *Educational psychology for effective teaching.* Belmont, CA: Wadsworth.

National Council for the Accreditation of Teacher Education (1998). *Standards for the accreditation of basic and advanced preparation programs for professional school personnel* (p. 5). Washington, DC: NCATE.

Nelson, W. W. (1999). The Emperor Redux. *Phi Delta Kappan, 80*(5), 387–392.

Nuby, J., & Doebler, L. K. (1999). The impact of inner-city high school placement on teacher trainees: A qualitive analysis. *SRATE Journal, 8*(1), 41–45.

Parsley, K., & Corcoran, C. A. (2003). The classroom teacher's role in preventing school failure. *Kappa Delta Pi Record, 39*(2), 84–87.

Patterson, W. (2003). Breaking out of our boxes. *Phi Delta Kappan, 84*(8), 569–574.

Payne, C. (1984). Multicultural education and racism in American schools. *Theory into Practice,* 23, 124.

Ramirez, M., & Castaneda, A. (1974). *Cultural democracy.* New York: Academic.

Reed, D. F. (1994). Multicultural education for preservice students. *Action in Teacher Education,* 15(3), 27–34.

Rose, L. C., & Gallup, A. M. (1998). The 30th annual Phi Delta Kappa/Gallup Poll of the public's attitudes toward the public schools. *Phi Delta Kappan,* 80(1), 41–56.

Ross, D. D., Bundy, E., & Kyle, D. W. (1993). *Reflective teaching for student empowerment.* New York: Macmillan.

Schwahn, C., & Spady, W. (1998). Why change doesn't happen and how to make sure it does. *Educational Leadership,* 55(7), 45–47.

Slavin, R. E. (1994). *Educational psychology: Theory and practice* (4th ed.). Boston: Allyn & Bacon.

Slavin, R. E. (1998). Can education reduce social inequity? *Educational Leadership,* 55(4), 6–10.

Stallworth, B. J. (1998). Practicing what we teach. *Educational Leadership,* 55(5), 77–79.

Tesconi, C. A. (1984). Multicultural education: A valued but problematic ideal. *Theory into Practice,* 23, 88.

Voltz, D. M. (1999). Empowering diverse learners at the middle level. *Middle School Journal,* 30(4), 29–36.

Wilcox, B. (1998, June 26–27). *Writing for publication workshop,* Duquesne University, Pittsburgh, PA.

9
Teaching Strategies

It is only when several strategies are carefully and systematically integrated that substantial improvements in learning become possible.

T. R. Guskey

Objectives

- Differentiate between questioning and the Socratic method.
- List three unique strengths of simulation gaming.
- List two teaching strategies that are good motivators.
- List two guidelines for teachers who use questions in classroom instruction.
- Give three suggestions to help teachers improve their lectures.
- Define inquiry learning.
- Name one major advantage and one major limitation of inquiry learning.
- List three advantages of the lecture.
- Explain how using case studies can help students develop important concepts.
- Justify the use of cooperative learning.
- Identify some teacher behaviors to which members of various ethnic groups respond favorably.
- Give one advantage that computer-assisted instruction offers.

TEACHING STRATEGIES

- Lecture
- Case Study
- Tutoring
- Inquiry Learning
- Questioning
- Discovery Learning
- Simulation Gaming
- Cooperative Learning
- Definition
- Strengths
- Limitations
- Teacher's Role

Connecting Statements   Agree   Disagree   Uncertain

1. Teaching methods are unimportant because good students learn in any setting and poor students do poorly regardless of the teaching method.

2. Some methods are best for some students; others are best for other students.

3. The way a teacher implements a teaching method is more important than which method is selected.

4. The lecture has no place in secondary schools because other methods are superior in every way.

5. Games the teacher and students develop are usually superior to commercial learning games.

6. Questions' effectiveness is enhanced when teachers give students more time to respond, help students reach acceptable answers, and encourage students to ask questions.

7. Most African American students respond favorably to public recognition of their academic achievements.

> **Tips for Teachers**
>
> The success of any lesson hinges on the teacher's ability to get the students' attention. At the middle level this can be a real challenge. This chapter introduces advance organizers that can help you get students' attention at the beginning of the period and hold it throughout the period as you introduce new concepts.
>
> This chapter also introduces a variety of teaching methods. All teachers need a repertoire of methods from which to choose. Because of the transescent's need for socialization opportunities, middle-level teachers should pay especially close attention to discussions, simulations, and games as teaching methods. Learn when to use each of these methods and how to use them to achieve each method's full potential.

Developing Lessons

Not long ago, teachers could be described according to their particular teaching style. Prospective teachers spent many hours wondering what their own teaching style would be. Would they use mainly expository teaching—something like the many lectures they had listened to in college? Or would they use an entirely different approach, which would lead students to discover for themselves the important truths of a discipline?

Today's education majors are asking different questions because they recognize that there are many teaching methods—expository, inquiry, questioning, discovery, and simulation gaming. The old question, "Which one should I use?," has given way to a new one: "Which ones should I use and for what purposes?" Education students know that certain methods work best with certain objectives.

This chapter looks at several teaching methods and helps you develop the skills you need to select and use each to achieve particular goals. "Particular" is emphasized because if the stated goals are too broad, any one method has no particular advantage over another. For example, suppose your goal is to select and use the method that will produce maximum learning or understanding. "Of eighty-eight comparisons between traditional lecture and traditional discussion methods, as reported in thirty-six experimental studies, 51 percent favored the lecture method and 49 percent favored the discussion method" (Berliner & Gage, 1975). In other words, 51 percent of the studies found that the lecture method was superior to the discussion method for effective learning; 49 percent found the discussion method superior to the lecture. By the turn of the twenty-first century, this had not changed; the research still did not support one method over another (LeFrancois, 1999).

This does not mean that teaching methods are unimportant; it does mean that they are contextual. A method's success depends on your ability to relate it to the overall instructional program in a particular classroom with a particular group of students. In fact, hundreds of studies show that, if used correctly, each method can produce certain specific results. The overriding message for future teachers is that by developing a repertoire of methods, teachers can empower themselves to make better instructional decisions (Good & Brophy, 2000) that will help them meet the needs of all students. Both of these goals—empowering teachers and meeting the needs of all adolescents—were selected as goals for all middle school classrooms by the Carnegie Council on Adolescent Development Needs (Jenkins & Jenkins, 1995).

Obviously, teachers with a variety of methods have the means to enrich their teaching and reach students with varied preferred styles.

> **Teacher of the Year**
>
> I use a smorgasbord of teaching techniques: lecture, participatory learning, games and simulations, and learning with technology. Very simply, I use whatever methods I feel will work best with the students in a particular class.
>
> Former South Carolina Teacher of the Year Nancy Townsend
> (Henson & Eller, 1999, p. 276),

As you study each method, keep these questions in mind: What are this method's unique potentials? How can I best implement this method? If I decide to experiment using this method, what precautions should I take? Can I learn to implement this method effectively, along with other approaches, to develop overall instructional strategies that will enable students to achieve my course objectives?

The Lecture

The lecture has been the teaching method used most frequently in U.S. classrooms and in most other countries. It has dominated North American classroom teaching for two centuries (Cienkus & Ornstein, 1997). Although contemporary educators have criticized the lecture, it has survived because it does have value as a teaching method. It is getting a resurge of popularity from recent research that indicates that academic attainment is higher in classes where more time is spent giving instruction (Good & Brophy, 2000). When used almost exclusively, the lecture fails to measure up against less didactic methodology, but this does not imply that it is worthless. Used sparingly, and for the purposes for which it is most suited, the lecture is an important tool for all teachers to have on hand. As you study it, try to grasp the goals for which it is effective and those for which it is not.

When to Use the Lecture

When deciding whether to use the lecture, keep your students in mind. If your classes are composed of students whose potential is limited, the lecture is a poor choice because it requires students to take notes; most students are not good note takers. In fact, under ideal conditions, even college students are able to capture only 52 percent of a lecture's important ideas (Maddox & Hoole, 1975). King (1990) says:

> *Researchers have found that when students take notes during a lecture they are far more likely to record bits and pieces of the lecture verbatim or simply paraphrase information rather than organize the lecture material into some sort of conceptual framework or relate the new information to what they already know. (p. 131)*

The lecture's success also depends on whether students are self-motivated, because the lecture itself is a poor motivator. So before you decide whether to use the lecture, consider your students' interest level. Many students prefer the lecture because it demands little direct participation and involvement. Less capable students tend to favor the lecture over other modes of instruction that place more responsibility on them. Teachers should not lecture frequently to groups of low performers.

Weaknesses

Although students may learn well with a well-planned and well-executed lecture, they often say that lectures are boring, do not involve them, are poorly organized, focus on the lowest level of cognition, and do not recognize individual differences. Lectures also make students anxious, more so than other teaching methods. Many teachers use the lecture to show off their own knowledge. Feeding their egos, these teachers tend to be too formal, too authoritative, and too structured. They often stress technical points instead of interpreting or relating information, and they may not be receptive to students' questions. Such domination of students is an example of gross misuse of the lecture.

The lecture, when properly planned and executed, works best for capable, motivated students. The lecture is most appropriate when all students have similar abilities and backgrounds (Rothstein, 1990). But is it best for teaching a certain subject? Is it best for communicating in general? No. In fact, a review of ninety-one surveys covering four decades of research on comparative teaching methods found no difference between the effectiveness of the lecture and other methods of teaching (Voth, 1975). The lecture is superior only for certain objectives; it is inferior for others. For example, the lecture generally does not stimulate interest, promote creativity, or help students develop responsibility or imagination, nor does it help students synthesize, internalize, or express themselves. Compared with educational games, the lecture is equally as effective for immediate cognitive gain and significantly less effective for retention over three weeks or longer. To be sure, there are times when having students use rote memory alone is appropriate, but beware that excessive linear thinking is dangerously limiting. Phillips (1998) is more emphatic: "Linear logic is the scourge of our society today."

Strengths

The lecture does have several unique attributes. It is an extremely effective way to introduce a unit or build a frame of reference. It is also a superior technique for demonstrating models and clarifying matters that may confuse students. A short lecture can effectively introduce and summarize a lesson's major concepts. It allows the teacher to collect related information and assemble it into a meaningful and intellectually manageable framework.

Developing a Lecture

There are limitless ways to develop a lecture. First you must determine your own philosophy. For example, suppose, like John Locke, Col. Francis Parker, and John Dewey, you believe that learning is the result of experience and that the only way students learn is by tying new information to existing knowledge. And suppose, like these constructivists, you believe that to understand any discipline you must develop the major concepts that hold that discipline together.

Given this constructivist view, a logical place to begin developing a lesson is to identify a few major concepts the class will learn during one class period. Don't get overzealous. A few means six or fewer, maybe only three or four. For each concept, you might develop a transparency. Each transparency might be a visual drawing. To add interest, you might make some or all of the concept transparencies humorous.

Next, build into each lesson one or more student activities. Vary the activities so that some are independent tasks, some pair students together, and some involve small groups (three to five students). If your class periods are an hour or less, do only one or two activities.

Next, reconsider your objectives for this lesson. In addition to wanting students to understand the lesson's major concepts, what else would you want them to learn from this lesson? Do not forget the affective and psychomotor domains. For each additional objective (e.g., attitude or psychomotor skill), develop at least one transparency.

You now have a stack of transparencies. Arrange them in the order that you believe easiest for your students to learn. Next, make a list of these concepts and make a transparency of the list. This list will become the first transparency on the stack. Use it to present an overview at the beginning of the lesson. You may wish to make a second copy to use near the end of the period to review the lesson. You may wish to embellish this lesson by planning questions throughout the lesson to focus students' attention and to involve students.

Do not forget that variety itself is motivating, and the number of ways a lecture can be developed is limitless. This is just one of many ways to develop a lecture.

Implementing the Lecture

Why are some lectures good and some bad? Why are some teachers stimulating and others boring? Not all lectures are the same. How do they differ, and how can you make them more interesting and informative?

Most successful lectures are relatively short. Few people can concentrate for a long time, so even the best lecturers should limit their lectures to short periods, occasionally changing to activities that involve students. The next section presents some effective ways to improve the lecture through correct planning and delivery and by combining the lecture with other instructional approaches.

Improving the Lecture

Instructional Objectives

Much attention has recently been given to instructional objectives. Do they really affect learning? If so, how? Should you introduce them before or after the lesson?

Instructional objectives do affect students' reactions to the lecture. Those introduced at the beginning of the lecture tend to increase intentional learning (i.e., the learning that teaching seeks to stimulate); those used after the lesson affect students' incidental learning. To ensure that students will learn a lesson's most important concepts, always introduce the objectives before the lecture. In this way the objectives become advance organizers, giving learners a basis for new concepts. In addition, many teachers lecture above their students' cognitive level. Such lessons fail. Stefanich (1990, p. 49) says that this practice leads to failure: "In order to be successful teachers, we must be prepared to lower the level of instruction to the point at which the student can become a successful learner."

Tempo

One important variable in any lecture is the tempo, or pace. When the pace of a lecture is too slow, students become bored; when it is too fast, their inability to keep up with and understand the lesson discourages them. Lemlech (1999, p. 23) says that "Timing is essential to effective teaching." Armstrong, Henson, and Savage (2001, p. 211) say that active teachers are very concerned about presenting lessons well and they "maintain an appropriate lesson pace. Knowing when to quicken the pace or to change activities to prevent restlessness, satiation, or misbehavior appears to be almost instinctive in some teachers, while others have to develop it." The pall level—a state of physical, program-related fatigue—is reached when students lose interest because the concept is too simple or too difficult or when the steps in its presentation are too short or too long. In both cases, students tend to respond by generating their own discussions. Lectures that move at a moderate pace produce less noise than those that move at a slow or fast pace. Studies show that most studio-recorded presentations are too slow and that students would learn more if the lecturer increased the speed by as much as three times. If the lecture is too fast, however, students feel rushed and begin to reject the speaker.

Stimulus Variation

Certain actions during a lecture help prevent student boredom, especially among secondary school students. Stimulus variation—such as your moving through the class or gesturing and pausing—correlates positively with student recall of lectures. At the elementary level, however, stimulus variation actually lowers student performance on lecture tests; excessive teacher movement distracts younger students from the lecture content.

With a little imagination and effort, teachers can vary their evaluation activities in much the same way as they vary their other classroom teaching activities (Parsons & Jones, 1990). Varying instructional methods can help teachers reach the underachievers in their classes. O'Neal, Earley, and Snider (1991) stress the need for instructional variety: "Research indicates that while many underachieving students have poorer auditory and visual skills, their kinesthetic and tactile capabilities are high. Implications are that teachers may need to use a greater variety of instructional methods" (p. 122).

Structure

Most lectures can be vastly improved and simplified by (1) organizing the content into only a few (three to five) major concepts, (2) ordering the concepts in a logical or natural sequence, (3) limiting the lecture to ten or fifteen minutes, (4) providing tasks that require all students to use the concepts, and (5) summarizing the major concepts. English teachers often outline the major concepts in a story and put them in a definite sequence; history teachers may use events and dates. Identification and ordering of concepts are equally important in math, science, and social studies.

The following list can lead the preparation of a good lecture:

1. Graphic organizer
2. Objectives
3. Limit number of concepts
4. Student activities, including problem solving
5. Review of major concepts

Vocabulary

Concern for language is especially warranted. Too many lectures are loaded with jargon, technical vocabulary, or other unfamiliar language that confuses students (Titus, 1974).

Audio-Visual Aids

Visual aids should accompany all lectures. The overhead projector seems to have replaced the chalkboard as the most popular visual aid in today's classroom. The most effective use of either tool occurs when the lesson is not predeveloped but built up in front of the students, who help develop the concepts by working the problems or by responding to the teacher's questions as the lesson develops. In other words, the most effective delivery depends on student participation in developing the ideas set out by the lesson plan.

Histrionics

The high anxiety level that is common among students during lectures can be reduced if the teacher tells jokes. It is interesting to note that students for whom a lecture is appropriate (high-ability, low-anxiety students) also benefit most from humor, whereas their counterparts—the slow, anxious students—retain less from humorous lectures. In some instances, humor does not affect students' immediate cognitive gains, but several weeks later students find that they have retained significantly more concepts from lectures containing humor. Humor also serves those students who are socially isolated from their classmates. It can become a method of reuniting these students with their peers. Barth (1990) addresses this potential of humor. He says that "humor can be the glue that binds an assorted group of individuals into a community" (p. 515).

Altering the Lecture Method

In addition to improving the lecture itself and its delivery, teachers can greatly improve lectures by combining them with tutorials and student discussions. When tutorials were added to lectures in an eleventh-grade class, the combination increased immediate cognitive gains and retention measured over an 11-week interval (Rowsey & Mason, 1975). The individualizing effect seems to be of special benefit to lower-ability and lower-achievement students, whereas increasing emphasis on recitation and problem solving benefits higher-ability and higher-achieving students. Adding modeling demonstrations to the lecture tends to increase both immediate and long-term learning and also improves student attitudes toward the lesson. Social learning theorists contend that social reinforcers, such as modeling, are critical to the learning process (Henson & Eller, 1999).

Teacher of the Year

> Teachers are more successful when we learn how powerful our own modeling is for our students, and when we brave the waters that show them that we too have our vulnerable spots.
>
> Former Pennsylvania Teacher of the Year Howard Selekman
> (Henson & Eller, 1999, p. 60).

For lecture blending to be effective with students, they must be exposed to nonlecture teaching styles at early ages. By seventh grade, many students are already conditioned to the lecture method, and alternatives should be used earlier. For students who are accustomed to the straight lecture, combining lectures with student discussion produces little difference in cognitive gain among seventh-graders and may actually damage their attitude toward the lesson. For this reason, teachers should balance their selection of learning methods to improve student achievement and attitude.

The Case Study Method

For several decades the case study method has been popular in schools of business and in law schools. For example, in the Harvard Business School curriculum, the case study method has been a prominent feature for over sixty years. The case study method refers to the use of cases as educational vehicles to enable students to put themselves in the decision maker's or problem solver's shoes. Most case studies focus on a single participant or event (LeFrancois, 2000).

Strengths

Case studies involve students in what they are studying (Kowalski, Weaver, & Henson, 1990) through repeated personal analysis, peer discussion, definition of problems, identification of alternatives, statement of objectives and decision criteria, choice of action, and plan for implementation; they also enable students to develop analytical planning skills in a laboratory setting.

Because good cases are realistic and because the case study method involves students, it is highly motivating. Increasingly, schools are providing students with opportunities for social and emotional learning (Cherniss, 1998, p. 28). Because it usually requires group work, the case study method fosters development of good social skills.

Limitations

Success with the case study method depends on the availability of quality cases. Armchair cases (contrived cases) can be as effective as real events, but students must perceive both types as plausible. Good cases must contain an ample amount of pertinent information, but, as in real life, the problem solver never has all the information needed. Good cases must also contain some irrelevant information. (The importance of this will become evident in the following section.) Paget (1988, p. 175) explains:

> *A case report is a description of a factual situation that must be realistic and not obviously contrived or artificial. It must reflect the kind of situation encountered naturally in the conduct of the discipline concerned. It must be of practical and immediate importance to have relevance as an illustrative example.*

Teachers must understand the case study method's potential and limitations. They must give students the time and guidance needed to explore alternatives and help them to accept the less-than-perfect conditions that always describe real problems.

Methodology

When using the case study method, remember that its purpose is not to enable students to find the one right choice, but to enhance their ability to make judicious decisions.

Using Case Studies to Develop Concepts

Case studies can be used to reinforce a lesson's major concepts. Case studies can complement on-site observation and hands-on experience to help students grasp the practical significance of concepts. However, simply understanding concepts is not enough. Instruction must also focus on the use of the concepts and the context in which they occur in order to ascertain their practice connotations.

Harrison (1990) uses ten steps to teach a concept:

1. Present a concept and give examples.
2. Emphasize the common attributes and ask students to identify further attributes.
3. Ask students to generate examples.
4. Have students give opposite examples or nonexamples.
5. Have students name analogies and metaphors and compare these with the original idea.
6. Have students review contexts in which the concept takes place.
7. Have students describe the overt behavior in identifying the concept.
8. Have students identify environmental factors that facilitate or hinder application of the concept.
9. Help students write an operational definition involving the elements of these last steps.
10. Discuss the consequences or how viable the definition really is. (pp. 503–504)

Developing a Case Study Lesson

From the discussion of ways to develop a lecture, we learned that one strategy to develop any type of lesson is to begin by examining your own philosophy. This enables you to build on your own strengths. Another strategy for developing any type of lesson is to begin by examining the strengths of the case study method. For example, one of the case study's major strengths is its power to motivate. Therefore, you might begin by writing a case that you believe your students will enjoy. Suppose you are a middle-level teacher. You know that students in this age group have vivid imaginations. When you studied poisonous snakes, several students became excited and offered stories that their parents, grandparents, or older siblings told them. You watched their eyes (and a few of their mouths) open wide as they embellished the tales they told. You will want to use this knowledge about your students in developing your case. Be sure to include some information that especially interests this age group.

Next, you also know that a good case study includes irrelevant information that students must sift through (Kowalski, Weaver, & Henson, 1994). So include such information; load your case with high-interest but irrelevant information.

Consider recording your case. A simple audio recording can add interest to the lesson and can enable you to monitor student reactions and learn what type of stimuli work best for your age group. Adding different sound effects can make the lesson more interesting. If you do not have time to develop a recording, you can use a written copy of the case.

The case study method invites creativity. Plan your lesson so that students can use their imaginations. Give them opportunities to explore their own ideas by asking questions that have no "correct" answers. For example, "What would have happened if. . . ."

Summarize the lesson by listing the major problem(s) in the case, the major issues in the case, and the major conclusions. List these items on the chalkboard or on an overhead transparency so that all students can see them and become involved in developing the summary.

An alternative method for using the case study is to have students role-play the characters in the case and following discussion questions. You may also want students to write their own cases to present to the class.

Tutoring

The act of tutoring dates back many centuries. It continues to be considered one of the most effective teaching methods (Shanahan, 1998). In England it has been a major, if not the major, teaching strategy for many years. It derives its strength from being a one-on-one process that gives the student personal, individual attention. The student receiving the help (the tutee) receives immediate feedback and has continuous opportunity to ask questions.

But tutoring has limitations. Tutoring does not always lead to academic gains. Farr (1998) reported that tutored science students showed little or no increased learning. It requires much time from the tutor, and because most teachers cannot give so much time to each student, students are often used as tutors. Students selected to tutor other students are usually the brightest and highest achievers in their classes. Some say these high-achieving students are giving up time they could spend pursuing their own learning. Others say that having high-achieving students tutor lower-achieving students lowers the self-esteem of the latter and makes the former arrogant.

After many years of experience directing the tutoring program at the University of Wisconsin in Madison, Herbert Klausmeier concluded that tutoring probably does little psychological damage to the tutors because they tutor for unselfish reasons. They want to help others, and tutoring makes them feel needed. Klausmeier suggests that, to be fair to the students, tutors should be volunteers who can stop whenever they wish.

Ross MacDonald (1991) states that:

> *Tutoring has four primary benefits.* First, *one-on-one instruction motivates students by demonstrating a personal interest in their learning.* A teacher who expresses interest in a child will be rewarded by a student more interested in the subject matter and more attentive to what the teacher has to say. Second, *tutoring is an effective intervention for a student struggling with a particular lesson, especially if it is begun before a student falls dangerously behind.* Third, *tutoring provides an effective means to fill gaps in students' knowledge.* . . . Finally, *our nation's agenda for social change can be advanced by one-on-one instruction.* A disproportionate number of students who fall behind are minorities. Extra efforts, such as tutoring, are sometimes necessary to prevent past educational inequities from being continued in current classrooms.
>
> Of particular importance to any instruction is a teacher's sensitivity to cultural differences between the expectations of students and their home environments and the expectations of the teacher and the school environment. (p. 25)

Limitations of Tutoring

Effective tutoring requires skills that often must be taught (Hock, Schumaker, & Deshner, 2001). You may wish to ask your team leader or principal to consider providing faculty development workshops on tutoring.

Combining Tutoring and Grouping

Research has focused on how tutoring affects student achievement. Studies have reported varying results. Tutoring alone does not always increase learning, so some educators have begun combining tutoring with other teaching strategies. Of notable repute is the work of Benjamin Bloom at the University of Chicago. According to Bloom (1984), the most striking finding was that with tutoring, the best possible learning condition, "the average student is two sigmas above the average control student taught under conventional group methods of instruction" (p. 6). This is powerful testimony for tutoring. First, it says that one-on-one tutoring is the very best learning condition we can devise. Second, it says that, on average, students who are tutored outscore their counterparts by two sigmas, or two standard deviations. Another way to express this is to say that the average tutored student outperformed 98 percent of the students in the control class. Bloom (1984) offers the following suggestions for all schools and teachers:

1. Improve how students process information by using the mastery learning feedback-corrective process or enhance the initial cognitive prerequisites for sequential courses.
2. Improve the tools of instruction by selecting a curriculum, textbook, or other instructional material that has proved effective.
3. Improve parental involvement in student learning by beginning a dialogue between the school and the home.
4. Improve instruction by providing favorable classroom conditions for all students and by emphasizing better learning skills for all students. (p. 17)

As you study instructional strategies and ways to individualize instruction, identify techniques that you can combine with tutoring to make tutoring more effective in your classroom.

Developing a Tutoring Lesson

Since tutoring does not always guarantee increased learning, design lessons that use tutoring to achieve multiple benefits. For example, tutoring can help at-risk students fill in educational gaps. One approach to developing tutoring lessons is to identify gaps that otherwise might go unnoticed. You might assign all students to write a brief essay, using the topic the next unit will cover. While tutors are tutoring, you can focus on those students who need the most help. Using their essay as a guide, you can clarify misunderstandings and fill in gaps. This approach also allows you to give students your individual attention. An effective tutoring model, reported by Hock et al. (2001, p. 50), uses metacognition, teaching students to examine and improve their thinking strategies. The teacher might model the strategy, using acronyms to help students memorize, or might underline important words.

Make sure the directions for writing the essay tell students to focus on the major concepts you want them to understand. In a multicultural class, include objectives to help students to learn to work harmoniously with members of other cultures.

Reflection

Read the following statement and respond to the questions below.

Another Bandwagon

Tutoring is not new. In fact, it's the most primitive type of education, even predating civilization. Today's educators seem to get excited over every bandwagon that comes along. Some of the bandwagons simply don't produce music worth the price of the players, and tutoring is an excellent example. The students who tutor don't need the ego trip they get from being the leader. The tutees already know that they are below-average students—they don't need the additional humiliation. Bright students should not waste their time helping slower students. Instead, the program should be challenging the bright students to achieve even higher goals, but in tutoring they give valuable learning time to do the teacher's job. And if this isn't enough, not all studies agree that the tutee achieves more with tutoring.

1. Do you think that tutees experience lower self-esteem? What evidence can you give to support your answer?
2. Do you think that receiving tutorial help exposes a student's performance level, or do students already know their peers' general achievement level? When you were in middle school, did you know your peers' performance level? Has this changed in recent years?

Inquiry Learning

Inquiry learning, a familiar and popular concept in education today, is student-centered instruction. The student's role is to question, explore, and discover. Moore (1999) says that the emphasis is placed on the process, and that is motivating. "Watching the chemicals bubble in the test tube and trying to figure out the causes. . . . Students love the method because it lets them get involved, invites them to discover, and lets them use their creative abilities (Williams, Alley, & Henson, 1999, p. 101). The teacher's role is to question and guide students toward understanding; therefore, inquiry learning is often called *guided discovery learning.*

At all levels and in all subjects, inquiry learning is recognized as a viable teaching strategy. Despite its popularity and prestige, however, confusion exists over exactly what inquiry learning is. When we consider that inquiry is itself a most complicated style of learning, this comes as no surprise. Furthermore, inquiry is closely related to other, similar learning approaches that are often confused with it.

Basic to the complexity of inquiry learning is its paradoxical nature. Inquiry learning is concerned with solving problems, but it does not require solutions. It involves a flexible yet systematic approach to solutions—systematic in that a set of activities is used, yet highly flexible in that the sequence of the activities, and other activities can be changed or substituted at any time. The success derived from inquiry learning does not necessarily depend on solving the problems at hand. In fact, identifying and defining problems may be as important as solving problems. Henson & Eller (1999) explain: "Problem finding is important in scientific discovery." Einstein and Infield (1938) comment:

> *Galileo formulated the problem of determining the velocity of light, but he did not solve it. The formulation of a problem is often more essential than its solution, which may be merely a matter of mathematical or experimental skill. To raise new questions, new possibilities, to regard old problems from new angles, requires creative imagination and marks real advance in science.*

A special panel for the National Center for Education Statistics (Special Study Panel on Education Indicators for the National Center for Education Statistics, 1991) says that students need the ability to integrate information from all disciplines and use integrative reasoning to solve problems:

> *Integrative reasoning is essential in modern life and today's workplace. It represents not the ability to recall bits and pieces of information but the "things" one can demonstrate one can do. These include communication, using technology and information effectively, and proficiency in working in a problem-solving capacity either alone or in teams.* (p. 65)

Advantages

Inquiry learning involves all those who participate in the process. This is by no means unique to inquiry learning, because many other teaching strategies (such as simulation gaming, individualized instruction, discovery learning, and problem solving) offer participants an equal amount of involvement. But inquiry offers involvement that is more meaningful. It is characterized by early and continuous involvement. In true inquiry learning, the student must be involved from the very beginning, even in setting up the problems.

Another major advantage of inquiry learning is its flexibility. In attempting to understand their environment, people have fallen into a trap of trying to systematize everything within human awareness. For example, for years U.S. schools required students to learn a certain set of behaviors and were led to believe that this was the "method" scientists used to discover, invent, and find solutions to all problems. Yet studies failed to show that any specific pattern of thought exists to any reliable degree in problem solving. Inquiry is somewhat systematic, without being as rigid as the "scientific method." Instead of just answering questions, students are also involved in asking questions. Instead of just verifying the truth, students are actually seeking the truth.

The absence of a single, predetermined correct answer in inquiry learning is another advantage, because it frees the investigator to explore diverse, multiple possibilities and because it frees the psyche from fear of failing to achieve what is expected. On the contrary, inquiry learners are motivated positively and by the strongest type of motivation—internal motivation. They learn to work for the joy of learning. Involvement in inquiry learning improves students' attitudes toward the subject and, more important, toward school in general. Students in inquiry learning often become so aroused that they return to class on other days eager to continue pursuing the concepts.

The nature of inquiry enhances the development of creative potential. True inquiry learning provides freedom and encouragement in using the imagination, and the learner is responsible for determining what information to gather and then determining how important it is. These are essential conditions for creative thinking.

The teacher–student relationship in inquiry classes must remain positive. Although you must give students the freedom to develop their own hypotheses or hunches, your role is nevertheless important. In fact, no learner can develop critical thoughts alone, but students can be taught in a way that develops critical and inquiry-oriented thinking. An interesting thing happens to the total perspective and behavior pattern of teachers who use the inquiry approach in their classes: They become student-oriented rather than subject-oriented. Students also become more cooperative, whereas students in textbook-oriented classes tend to be more competitive.

For those who are concerned primarily with cognitive gains, note that the relative retention rate of inquiry learning (as opposed to lecture, for example) is extremely high. The highly personal experience involved in inquiry adds meaning to the learning.

Disadvantages

Like all other teaching strategies, inquiry learning has its share of disadvantages. First, it is a slow process for exposing students to material. Teachers who feel obligated to cover certain amounts of content (e.g., to get through a textbook) may find the process inefficient for their goal. A more critical disadvantage of inquiry learning is that it requires teachers to have a unique type of expertise that most cannot acquire without special training. Today's teachers need more training in inquiry activity.

The Teacher's Role

Because inquiry learning is a flexible process, you may want to set the stage in different ways. Using heterogeneous subgroups within a classroom to capitalize on unique personalities, interests, and skills can enable each student to contribute to the task at hand. In inquiry learning lessons, your major role is that of a catalyst. You must give students the freedom to investigate in their own ways. Students must be allowed to develop their own ideas and to discover ways to explain what they observe. The questions and problems they form are theirs, not yours. You passively provide direction by selecting objectives, activities, events, problems, or questions. You can provide much closer direction by giving cues and supportive feedback. Don't be tempted to give information before it is necessary, and avoid making nonverbal communications, such as grimacing.

The student of inquiry should not have to worry about pleasing the teacher. In fact, learners must not be dominated by others. The most impressive precondition for inquiry undoubtedly is the learner's autonomy. Encourage students to form hypotheses and test them on their own initiative. Also encourage students to recognize that a problem can have many aspects and solutions. Students who participate in inquiry must not be afraid to make mistakes. You must encourage each student to make bold conjectures and then test them. Students should pursue any hypothesis that seems at all probable.

Participants in inquiry learning are self-motivated. They must learn to work for the joy of learning, even in the absence of feedback—which students in traditional classes get from test scores and grades. Inquiry is a cooperative process, not a competitive one. Even the teacher who becomes involved with inquiry soon becomes student-oriented rather than subject-oriented. Students' independence and separate responsibility, coupled with the opportunity to pursue learning for the joy of it, produce a high level of motivation. For this reason, inquiry learning's retention rate is superior to that of most other teaching strategies and offsets its disadvantage of being slow in content coverage.

Effective inquiry learning does, however, require certain special skills that some teachers simply do not have. You must be able to match personalities, interests, and skills to get the most out of each student. Perhaps most of all, you must learn to give students enough freedom to investigate in their own ways. Do not give information before it is necessary. The student of inquiry must treasure diversity, and the teacher must be able to encourage and reinforce students who take risks, make bold conjectures, and then explore a variety of aspects and solutions.

Developing Inquiry Lessons

Inquiry lessons are one of the most exciting types of lessons to plan because of the suspense that inquiry always involves. Providing just enough information to whet students' imaginations, a teacher can stimulate a line of inquiry. Like any type of lesson, successful inquiry requires some purposeful objectives. Your role is to intervene only enough to guide students to discover the concepts that you expect them to gain from the lesson.

THE CASE

Making Connections

Patricia M. Chandler, The Citadel
Stephanie M. Hewett, The Citadel
Carol Albrecht, Cario Middle School

Stephanie M. Hewett *received a B.S. in early childhood education from Clemson University, an M.Ed. in reading education from Clemson University, and a doctorate in C and I from New Mexico State University and has taught at all levels of education. She has presented at national and international conferences. She is currently an assistant professor in the School of Education at The Citadel.*

Carol Albrecht *received her B.S. in elementary education from Winthrop College and her M.Ed. in C and I from The Citadel. She is a 20-year veteran middle school teacher in the Charleston County School District, where she was named Teacher of the Year in 2002.*

Patricia M. Chandler *received her Ph.D. in C and I from Clemson Unviersity. She is a teacher specialist for the South Carolina State Department of Teacher Education.*

Background

Each day a middle school teacher may be in contact with over a hundred students. The current educational climate pulls teachers in many different directions, with standardized testing, noninstructional paperwork, increased requirements for professional development, and student issues of twenty-first century homes and communities. The ability to connect with these students, their parents, and fellow teachers is one of the most important challenges facing today's educator. Teachers are rightly concerned with their changing role and their ability to make the connections necessary for student academic success. This case study looks at the path that one middle school teacher has taken to make the connections with students, parents, and colleagues through her own professional growth.

The Community

Mount Pleasant is a suburban coastal community of 100,000 residents in the southern region of the Atlantic seaboard. The socioeconomic background of the student families is predominantly middle-class. Many of the parents are professionals in the tourism, business, and medical fields. Also, many parents are employed by the state port authority and work on the docks. There are three middle schools and one high school in the community.

The School

Cario Middle School is a three-year-old neighborhood school that serves over seven hundred students in grades 6 through 8. Twenty-eight percent of the students are minority, and 18 percent of the students receive free or reduced lunch. There are forty-five faculty members, four with National Board Teacher Certification, with an average teaching experience of 8 ½ years. Academic teachers use their two planning periods to collaborate within the grade levels and to meet with parents. A comprehensive academic program includes honors classes, on-grade-level classes, and special education programs for students with learning, speech, orthopedic, and emotional disabilities.

The Teacher

Carol Albrecht has taught all subject areas during her twenty years as a middle school educator. After seventeen years of teaching math at the same middle school, she moved three years ago to face the challenge of opening a brand new school, Cario Middle. She has a bachelor's degree in elementary education and a master's degree in curriculum and instruction. In the spring of her second year at Cario Middle School, she was nominated by her colleagues as Teacher of the Year. Subsequently, she was selected as the Teacher of the Year for the county school district. This year she is teaching four 75-minute periods of sixth-grade math and honors math.

Connections with Students and Parents

As Ms. Albrecht was interviewed during her planning period, her connections with students became evident. Students came by to say hello, request help on the computer, and ask for supplies. Each student received personal attention and a good-bye hug. When she describes her relationship with her students she says, "They are my babies. We are all family. They come to me. They confide in me. They share things with me." The relationships that she builds with the students do not end when they graduate from middle school. She tells the story of a former middle school student who came by to see her. His Navy ship was leaving the next day, and he just wanted to tell her good-bye. She said, "I don't know why he came. Other former students have told me that they felt like I was a teacher—that I *taught* them. I didn't just assign."

Her special relationship with her students is also demonstrated by her connections with their parents. When asked about her connections with her students' parents, she said, "I always try to think, if that was my child, how would I find out how he is doing?" At least four times in each 9-week grading period, she sends home a packet of student materials that includes student work, grades, teacher comments, and space for parent response. Although the portfolios require a lot of work, they are invaluable in keeping parents informed and involving them in the educational process of their child. This leads to academic success for her students.

Connections for Academic Success

Middle school students thrive in environments that make them feel safe, secure, and good about themselves. Ms. Albrecht's room offers that environment. The classroom is bright, with students' work predominantly displayed. A bulletin board entitled "Ponder These Perplexing Problems" provides practice on standardized test items. Students' desks are arranged in double rows to encourage pair/share activities. Several networked computers, used by students even during her planning period, provide a center for math exploration. "I like to have lots of things for them to touch. They still like to play." Along with a physical environment, Ms. Albrecht has an effective classroom management philosophy that encourages academic success.

"In my classroom, you will see discipline—but they are free to get up and get a tissue or get up and move around. They are always busy *doing* something." When asked about the role of discipline in her classroom, Ms. Albrecht said, "I use a lot of humor in discipline. Because I try to instill the idea of family . . usually they will 'fess up. They know that if there is a punishment, that it will be fair."

To link academically with other classes, she searches for connections between math and other content areas. "I try to plan activities, special activities. Creating learning activities is one part of my job that I absolutely love. I might teach Roman numerals when they are studying about Rome in their social studies classes." She also plans activities that have real-world value and meaning for the students. Ms. Albrecht developed an activity on perimeter that involves the students in calculating paper borders for the classroom bulletin boards. "While completing this math activity, they felt as though they were helping me, and they were learning about perimeter and applying previously learned skills." Another real-world activity that Ms. Albrecht designed involves the students in budgeting for a field trip. "Students complete an assignment that requires them to figure the total cost of the trip by calculating the total mileage that we travel, total cost of the bus mileage, the bus driver's fees, and the admission fee for the total number of students who participated. . . . Most students think that the school bus transportation for field trips is free, and they are amazed when they learn how much it costs just for transportation."

The students' math content is provided in a structured format that provides security for the students. Their student portfolios, which are kept in the classroom except for trips home for parent review, include samples of their daily work, quizzes, projects, cumulative grade reports, and teacher/parent comments.

This not only teaches organization to the students but also allows parents and students to see the students' academic progress. Ms. Albrecht believes that she academically connects with her students when she is one-on-one with a student. She focuses on each individual student for at least part of each class, using encouraging words and looks. She tells her students to put everything at home behind them and just focus on being successful in her classroom.

Connections with Colleagues and Administration

Ms. Albrecht has spent twenty years developing relationships with colleagues and administrators. She believes that their support has been vital to making her a successful teacher. The decision to change schools after seventeen years reflects her continuing enthusiasm for teaching. "I came here for a challenge and the kids." The majority of the staff for the new middle school came from two existing middle schools in the community. "I was the new kid on the block. [It] made me feel like a new teacher. I knew that I had to get myself in gear and work harder than ever before to show that I am a talented, good teacher. I had to prove myself." Ms. Albrecht immersed herself in collegial activities including department and school committees. Mentoring new teachers has been a special joy for Ms. Albrecht. She states, "I use a sense of humor—I provide therapy. 'Do you need to talk?' I just listen. . . . They get so wrapped up. . . . I will sit them down and tell them what is real. . . . I will tell them to stop worrying about this. . . . I offer them assurances, short cuts, and realities."

Connection to Professional Growth

What was the process that led her to become a Teacher of the Year? From the time that she was in high school, Ms. Albrecht knew that she wanted to be a teacher. While participating in a church-related mission trip, she had the opportunity to teach. "I found that I liked planning the lessons. I wanted to give back to all who wanted to help me. I did not want to get locked in to one thing. Teaching enabled me to use all of my talents." She majored in elementary education in college and began her professional career as a middle school teacher. She taught math, science, literature, health, and social studies. She served on school-based management teams, and textbook adoption committees, and these activities fostered professional growth. She is always open to professional development opportunities.

Even after twenty years of teaching, Ms. Albrecht continues to take classes. She has participated in special training including peer mediation, standards-based classroom proficiency, and Teacher Forum Leadership Council. She has been nominated by both schools as their Teacher of the Year. She also considers the nomination process for Teacher of the Year, even with its time-intensive paperwork, to be a professional development opportunity. Applying to become the district Teacher of the Year is a "self-cleansing thing to do." "I poured my heart into it. It just hit me in the interview that I was one of the top five teachers in the county, and I just broke into tears." In keeping with Ms. Albrechts's educational philosophy, she has even turned the Teacher of the Year process into a learning activity for her students. "When kids ask why I am going to be out [for Teacher of the Year activities], I tell my children, that this is a learning experience for me. I am a life-long learner, and I am demonstrating that."

Ms. Albrecht is obviously successful as a middle school teacher. The students, their parents, her peers, and the district administration recognize her as a model teacher. The connections that she has made come together to enhance her teaching for student success. Her enthusiasm is enhanced by her ability to reflect on the teaching process. From twenty years of teaching experience and professional growth, she has learned that certain things must be in place for her best teaching to occur. She states, "My best teaching occurs:

- When I am prepared.
- When I am rested.
- When I don't have a bunch of paperwork.
- When the children are actively involved—but I don't mean hands-on activities all of the time.
- When there is a rapport, and we are feeding off of each other, almost like a tennis match.

"Sharing, being involved and dedicated, demonstrating respect, creating things, having fun, setting goals, learning about new things, and striving to do my best—these are the characteristics I would use to personally describe myself. These are also the characteristics that carry over into my professional life to create my own personal style of teaching."

Further Reflection

1. The middle school teacher highlighted in this case study spoke often of "connections." Describe a teacher from your own experience who helped you see the connections often found in school and life.
2. You are a first-year social studies teacher in a middle school. What do you say to your students when they say that mathematics has nothing to do with social studies?
3. All too often parents have a negative view of parent–teacher interactions. What specific actions can you take to promote a sense of positive connections between yourself and your students' parents?
4. One of the common complaints of teachers is that they feel isolated in their classrooms. As you begin interviewing for a classroom teacher position, what would you ask about or look for that indicates a school climate that encourages collegiality?
5. What do you see as the role of the principal in establishing a school climate that encourages making connections? What specific steps could the principal take to encourage this?
6. Teachers are increasingly required to prepare students for content-specific state and national standardized tests. What would you say to someone who feels that no time should be taken away from the English class to study interdisciplinary materials?

Resources

Banaszak, R. A. (1998). Making connections: Interdisciplinary lessons to prepare tomorrow's citizens. ERIC Document ED429909.

> This paper describes an interdisciplinary civics curriculum designed to teach students how to look at problems, consequences, and decision making. Effective instructional strategies are included.

Manouchehri, A. (2001). Collegial interaction and reflective practice. *Action in Teacher Education, 22,* 86–97.

> Case study of middle-school teacher teams that look at efforts to increase collegial interaction. Findings indicate difficulty of breaking through the isolation among teachers.

Thomas, C. D. & Santiago, C. (2002). Building mathematically powerful students through connections. *Mathematics Teaching in the Middle School, 7,* 484–488.

> Connections in mathematics are illustrated using a project called "From Point to Polyhedron: The Icosahedron" for seventh-graders.

Van Voorhis, F. L. (2001). Interactive science homework: An experiment in home school connections. *NASSP Bulletin, 85,* 20–32.

> Discusses a study of interactive middle school science homework assignments. Designed to promote parent–child discussions at home.

Questioning

Chapter 10 examines in depth the role that questioning plays in communications. Here we will look at questioning in a more focussed context, that is, at the many ways teachers can use questions in various phases of their teaching methods.

When we think of using questions to teach, Socrates usually comes to mind. One of the greatest teachers of all time, Socrates used a variety of instructional techniques. A master of the art of questioning, he used questions to lead his students down a treacherous path of contradictions. Tricky? Of course. But his students respected and admired him. Socrates knew the importance of self-analysis and of discovering one's own errors.

The Socratic method—that is, teaching by asking questions and thus leading the audience into a logical contradiction—is one style of questioning. Many other questioning strategies are in use today. As a teaching style, questioning is second in popularity and in common use only to lecturing, but the technique of questioning is grossly misused. It is helpful to identify several valid uses of questioning and several ways that teachers can improve their questioning skills.

Another reason for using questions is to determine how well students are learning major concepts in the lesson. *Effective teachers,* i.e., teachers whose students succeed academically, ask many questions to check students' understanding (Rosenshine & Stevens, 1986).

How Teachers Should Use Questions

Although the textbook is the major curriculum determiner in most classes, most textbooks do not stimulate advanced levels of thinking. The Wisconsin School Improvement Program found that 90 percent of all textbooks are written at the knowledge (recall and memory) level. Therefore, if students' thinking is to climb to higher cognitive levels, you must find other ways to stimulate it. Studies that use interaction analysis show that most teachers never achieve this goal and most thinking in the classroom remains at the recall level. Of course, some knowledge-level questions can be desirable, as long as they are complemented with higher-level questions. Teachers who ask more higher-order questions have students who achieve considerably more.

To raise students up to higher levels of thinking, substitute for recall-level words such as *state, name, identify, list, describe, relate, tell, call, give,* and *locate* such evaluation-producing words as *judge, compare, analyze, contrast, measure, appraise, estimate,* and *differentiate,* and then move on to creative and stimulating words such as *make, design, create, construct, speculate, invent, devise, predict,* and *hypothesize.*

Teachers can use students' names to increase students' response; teachers should pause after each question to give students time to think about it. Studies by Santieslebau (1976) and Rowe (1974) show that there are a number of advantages to waiting at least three seconds after each question is asked. Sund (1971, p. XX) lists twelve:

1. The length of students' responses increases.
2. The number of unsolicited but appropriate responses increases.
3. Failure to respond decreases.
4. Students' confidence increases.
5. The incidence of speculative creative thinking increases.
6. Teacher-centered teaching decreases.
7. Pupils give more evidence before and after inference statements.
8. The number of questions pupils ask increases.
9. The number of activities students propose increases.
10. Slow students contribute more.
11. The variety of types of responses increases.
12. Students react more to each other.

Santieslebau (1976) found that as wait time increased to at least three seconds, the confidence of the slow students increased, speculative thinking increased, the number of experiments by students increased, and observation and classification skills improved. The price for these advantages appears to be cheap. Just by pausing and doing nothing, the teacher can stimulate these results. However, a study by Rowe (1974) found that the average wait time in the public school classroom is only one second.

Another common mistake teachers make is to overuse questions. Teachers begin many lessons with a series of cognitive questions, but research shows that it is far more effective to wait until a knowledge base has been established before initiating questioning (Armstrong et al., 2001; Good & Brophy, 2000). For example, a short lecture is far more efficient for

> ### Teacher as Proactive Decision Maker
>
> **Classroom Situation**
>
> 1. You anticipate that your new students will be accustomed to conducting conversations at the lower levels of the cognitive domain.
>
> 2. You know that your students will enjoy and benefit from helping plan the class curriculum.
>
> 3. You know that many of your students will have the ability to stay on task, yet you anticipate that others may wander from the assignment.
>
> **Proactive Alternatives**
>
> - For each lesson during the first week, make a list of "why" questions.
> - Practice the art of asking higher-order questions and helping students give correct responses.
> - Give your students a goal for the first six-week period. Ask them to assist you in writing some objectives to help them reach this goal.
> - Next, ask your students to assist you in planning some activities to help them reach this goal.
> - Write the assignment on a transparency or on the board, so that you can redirect the attention of students who stray from the assignment.
> - Discuss with students strategies they may use to remind their group members to stay on task.

building this necessary framework. Furthermore, too many questions turn students' attention from one subject to another.

Classroom questions that seek cognitive feedback often lack specificity. For example, the question, "What was the cause of the Civil War?," is impossible to answer. In posing such a question just to create an entry into the lesson, the teacher rejects some correct responses—and there are many for that question—in hopes that a student will finally guess the particular desired response. The session proceeds as follows:

> Q: What was the cause of the Civil War?
>   A: Slavery.
> Q: Okay, but that's not what I'm looking for.
>   A: Economics? [This time the student is less certain.]
> Q: What about economics? [Another broad question.]
>   A: The North's economics.
> Q: What about it?
>   A: It was different from the South's.
> Q: But what about the North's economy? [etc., etc.]

In addition to increasing the lesson's efficiency and preventing student embarrassment, the teacher's specificity will enhance student recall of related material. Shiman and Mash (1974) suggest that instead of using a series of fact-seeking questions, teachers should move back and forth among the factual, conceptual, and contextual modes. Factual questions elicit only recall-level information; conceptual questions probe, analyze, compare, and generalize; and contextual questions promote judgment. To help increase the number and quality of responses to each question in these categories, teachers should tape-record or write their questions, testing themselves for the answers. This will remove much ambiguity and generate more specific and precise questions.

Some educators believe that students are becoming less curious and less inquisitive—less eager to ask questions. Far too often a student attempts to answer a question only to hear the response "Yes, but" or a murmured "Uh-huh" as the teacher looks quickly to another student for the "correct" answer. To improve students' attitude toward answering questions, the teacher should help the faltering student with an "Oh, that's interesting. I hadn't thought of it that way" or "Oh, yes, I see what you mean" or "Are you saying . . . ?" Further reinforcement can be provided by returning later to quote the student. For example, "John, what you're saying now seems to agree (or disagree) with Debbie's earlier comment that. . . ." This tells John, Debbie, and everyone else in the class that you do listen to other people's comments.

This does not suggest that all teacher questions should seek to provoke student responses. Rhetorical questions increase motivation and enhance learning and recall of facts among audiences with low motivation. Yet teachers must resist the temptation to answer all their questions and should let students know, by calling on students by name, when they expect an answer.

Questions can also be used effectively before and after a lesson. Bull and Dizney (1973) found that asking questions before a reading assignment can stimulate students to remember relevant information. In a similar study, Sanders (1973) found that students questioned after they read a paragraph retained both relevant and irrelevant material, while students questioned before reading showed increased retention of relevant material only. Teachers can apply this knowledge about questioning to reading assignments, field trips, laboratory exercises, and such audio-visual materials as the tape recorder, filmstrips, and films. Students also must learn to ask productive questions.

Reciprocal Peer Questioning

King (1990) presents another questioning strategy, which she recommends using to enrich the lecture:

Reciprocal peer-questioning is a strategy that can be used with any lecture regardless of subject matter and is appropriate for fourth grade to university students. With this strategy, a form of guided group questioning in conjunction with classroom lecture is used. Students are given a set of generic questions and trained to use those questions as a guide for generating their own specific questions on the lecture content. During the self-questioning step of the procedure, students usually make up two or three thought-provoking questions. Those questions may or may not be ones that they themselves are able to answer.

Following the self-questioning, they engage in peer-questioning. Working in groups of three or four, students pose their questions to their group and then take turns answering each other's questions. . . .Students who were trained to use this strategy demonstrated lecture comprehension superior to students who used other comprehension strategies, such as group discussion or independent review. (p. 131)

Irving Sigel found that children's ability to move from the concrete to the symbolic level requires distancing themselves from the present (Ellsworth & Sindt, 1994). Combining higher-order questions with drawing can help students make this necessary time transit

(Phillips, Phillips, Melton, & Moore, 1994). Ramsey, Gabbard, Clawson, Lee, and Henson (1990) give the following guidelines to help teachers improve their use of questions:

- Ask knowledge-level questions when assessing students' ability to recall, recognize, or repeat information as it was learned.
- When assessing students' higher-level thinking, use terms such as *how, why,* and *what if* to encourage deeper thought.
- Prepare questions in advance.
- Ask questions in a logical sequence.
- Ask specific questions that students can answer silently.
- As direct questions are asked, sprinkle the questioning with direct statements.
- Request that students repeat the teacher's question before answering.
- When a specific student is asked a question, have another student repeat the question before allowing a response.
- Allow students to converse with each other in a directed manner after a question is asked or answered.
- Request that students express their own questions fully and specifically.
- Name specific students in a random order to respond to questions.
- Provide adequate waiting time after naming a respondent. Rowe (1974, pp. 421–422) found that waiting approximately three to five seconds after naming a respondent before eliciting a response brought better responses from more students.

Building Lessons around Questions

Perhaps the most common mistake teachers make when building a lesson around questions is starting the lesson with questions and continuing throughout the period with questions. A far better approach is to introduce some information to build a common knowledge base. Discussions can then draw on this well of knowledge, thus preventing a mere sharing of ignorance.

As with other methods, a lesson built on questions will likely be no more productive than the degree to which a teacher sets specific objectives and plans. So, as with other types of lessons, preface a lesson built on questions with a few clearly stated objectives.

The Socratic method is one of many effective strategies that use questions. Since it requires special skills and charisma, it is not the best type of lesson for a novice teacher. A better approach is to (1) write a few objectives (perhaps between three and six), (2) give the class a few basic concepts (by a short reading assignment, a short audio or video recording, or a short written assignment), (3) write a few questions for each group to answer, (4) have each group report its response to the group, and (5) summarize the lesson.

Student-Initiated Questions

As powerful as teacher-initiated questioning is, it may not be nearly as powerful as student-initiated questions because the act of posing questions is, itself, an essential part of learning. Elliot Eisner (2002) says, "The kind of school we need would be staffed by teachers who are as interested in the questions students ask after a unit of study as they are in the answers students give" (p. 579).

> ### Teacher of the Year
>
> The answers today may not solve the problems of tomorrow. I can, however, empower my students and help them determine their own questions; and I can help guide them in gaining the skills necessary for solving questions. This requires a tremendous leap of faith on the teacher's part because it involves giving up a posture of ultimate authority and assume the position of facilitator of learning.
>
> Former North Carolina Teacher of the Year Renee Coward
> (Henson & Eller, 1999, p. 175)

Discovery Learning

What is discovery learning? Chances are you have some understanding of, and faith in, the discovery process. Most contemporary students have experienced this approach. The following paragraphs define discovery learning, list its advantages and disadvantages, and provide suggestions for teachers who want to try discovery learning for the first time or improve their skills with planning and implementing discovery learning.

Definition

Most of the literature on discovery learning does not define it; this leaves the reader feeling embarrassed about not knowing exactly what it is and probably ashamed to ask. Discovery learning is not easy to define. There is no single clear-cut definition, just as there is no single process of discovery learning; in fact, there are many. Each experience is unique, ranging from guided to open discovery. Furthermore, each type of discovery has its own advantages, and the management of each is unique. Weimer (1975) lists six types of discovery learning: (1) discovery, (2) discovery teaching, (3) inductive discovery, (4) semi-inductive discovery, (5) unguided or pure discovery, and (6) guided discovery. Notice that these six types are actually degrees in which discovery is controlled.

The term discovery learning is frequently but erroneously used interchangeably with two other terms: *inquiry* and *problem solving*. Actually, each of these other terms is, or can refer to, a specific type of discovery learning. The educational process called inquiry is more accurately defined as **guided discovery**—that is, during an inquiry lesson the teacher carefully guides the student(s) toward a specific discovery or generalization. Discovery learning and problem solving are synonymous when a solution to the problem is discovered. In other words, by definition, problem solving must involve the solving of problems.

A good working definition of discovery learning is intentional learning through problem solving and under teacher supervision. In other words, individuals can sometimes solve problems without any leadership, guidance, or supervision: they can also make discoveries quite accidentally. Neither of these activities is discovery learning, which must be intentional and supervised. At one extreme, it may be carefully guided (inquiry learning); at the other extreme, it is very casually supervised (free discovery). In fact, your main function may be to supply a stimulus, or it may be to organize or arrange tasks (or problems) to make the result obvious. In inquiry learning, the students themselves are involved in setting up the problem as well as in seeking its solution.

Advantages

Discovery learning has advantages other instructional approaches share. For example, the high degree of student involvement is a strong motivator for most students, especially students who find it difficult to remain quiet and passive. Discovery learning appears to be appropriate for almost all students. Only about one-third of today's college students are able to reason in an abstract, logical way. An even smaller percentage of secondary and middle school students is able to profit from abstracting. Can most students benefit from discovery learning? Yes. Anyone can take part in and create experiences in generalizing, testing conjectures, discarding or modifying false hypotheses, and forming rules or theorems. A study involving junior-high math students (Vance, 1974) found the discovery approach to be a superior motivator in traditional math classes and inferior only to an experimental laboratory setting.

The high student activity level in discovery learning is internally motivating (Moore, 1999). When students are more motivated, they learn and retain knowledge more effectively. However, discovery learning has another advantage. The correlation between a student's knowledge and later success in life is constantly diminishing. Far more important are one's understanding of broad concepts and principles and one's ability to get along with other people. When discovery learning involves group work, the socialization is itself a worthy goal.

The discovery process is superior to lecture-type lessons because it offers students an opportunity to focus on major concepts and principles and to develop positive social skills. Discovery learning is a cooperative process. Vance (1974) found no significant difference in the ability of junior-high math students in discovery, laboratory, and traditional lessons to score on an examination administered just after learning. However, students in the discovery classes scored highest on a special examination designed to measure high-level thinking and problem solving. Another test designed to measure divergent thinking showed that the students in the discovery classes could better relate the new set of materials to their study of mathematics. Students also preferred a learning style that permitted them to work at their own rate and without a teacher always telling them what to do.

Disadvantages

It may be difficult to believe that a learning system with so many advantages also has inherent disadvantages, but it does. First, unlike the lecture (which requires little more of students than their attention and an ability to take notes), the discovery method demands more of students and teachers. Probably its greatest demand is that both teacher and students understand and adjust to the nature of discovery. At the beginning, teachers and students are uncomfortable because the discovery approach has no constant feedback to show them how well they are progressing. The lack of competition in discovery learning also upsets students. Discovery learning is ideally a cooperative process, not a competitive one. The competition is between the student and the task.

At its best, discovery learning is an inefficient system because it is not a good way to cover large amounts of material. Students and teachers are usually highly concerned about completing the amount of material they are expected to cover in a particular course. College preparatory classes are especially concerned with this limitation of the discovery learning approach.

> ### Reflection
> Jay Barker is known by football fans as the quarterback who has no special talent; he is said *not* to be a strong runner and he is said *not* to have a good throwing arm. But anyone who knows anything about him will tell you that he does one thing consistently well. That one thing is win. As a University of Alabama college quarterback, this athlete held the enviable record of 35 wins, 2 losses, and 1 tie. How can this incongruence be explained? To be candid, not very well. But failure to explain the phenomenon that surrounds such a leader does not negate its existence.
>
> On closer observation, Jay Barker has three strengths: an unwavering awareness at all times of what is happening on the playing field, an excellent sense of timing, and a coolness under pressure.
>
> 1. What similarities can you see between the roles of a quarterback and a teacher?
> 2. Each classroom seems to have its own character. How does this character affect the teacher's role?

Methodology

As with any instructional approach, the degree to which discovery learning is successful is determined by the teacher's ability to plan and execute effectively, that is, manage and supervise the lesson. The teacher's task is to organize or arrange tasks (or problems). The problem situation can be a dilemma, deliberately created by the teacher, which forces students to think, analyze, draw conclusions, and make generalizations. In other words, the teacher's role is to provide a situation that allows students to see a contradiction between what they already know and newly discovered knowledge. Sobel (1975) suggests the following guidelines:

- Make use of contemporary materials (e.g., daily newspaper, comic strips).
- Use topics from the history (of the subject).
- Introduce applications (of the subject).
- Provide opportunity for guessing.
- Provide for laboratory experiences.
- Introduce new topics with innovative teaching strategy.
- Make frequent use of visual aids.
- Set the stage for student discovery.
- Use motivation.
- Teach with enthusiasm.

Two suggestions can help the teacher in discovery learning. First, the teacher and the textbooks must use unambiguous terms. Second, the student must be allowed to discover generalizations. This suggests that teachers should learn to put more trust in their students and to refrain from interfering with students' work. The many interdisciplinary programs of the 1960s and 1970s stimulated by the Woods Hole Conference (1959) were based on generalizations, and a later study reported by Goodlad (1984) in *A Place Called School* reiterated the important role that principles and generalizations play in learning.

Because discovery learning naturally leads students to cross over subject boundaries, this approach is especially adept for using in interdisciplinary, theme-based programs. To be successful, discovery lessons must focus on topics and activities students enjoy. Bernstrom and

O'Brien (2001, p. 31) provide a useful list of questions that you can ask to make discovery learning appealing to your students' interests:

- What do you know a lot about?
- What kinds of people, animals, or places would you like to know more about? Why?
- In what places in the community do you like to do things? Why?
- What kinds of materials, equipment, experiences, or tools interest you?
- What is your favorite topic or theme to pursue out of school? Why?
- What could you bring to the program to make this theme more exciting?
- What types of posters, resources, and materials should we collect?

Overview

Like all teaching–learning approaches, the discovery method has advantages and disadvantages. Although discovery learning and traditional lessons both enable students to learn, discovery learning is better at motivating students toward learning broad concepts and principles and developing social skills. Its main disadvantages are that it is not a good way to cover large amounts of material and that it fails to provide constant feedback. Discovery learning is most effective when students are involved in planning the lesson and making their own discoveries, conclusions, and generalizations and when teachers combine it with visual aids and contemporary, easy-to-read materials.

When using discovery learning, avoid pressuring students unduly. Excessive pressure produces anxiety and anxiety inhibits learning. As Martinez (1998) has said, "Anxiety is a spoiler in the problem solving process" (p. 609). Martinez offers the following suggestions to guide teachers as they work in discovery lessons. "Errors are a part of the process of problem solving, which implies that both teachers and learners need to be more tolerant of them. If no mistakes are made, then almost certainly no problem solving is taking place. Unfortunately, one tradition of schooling is that perfect performance is often exalted as an ideal. Errors are seen as failures, as signs that the highest marks are not quite merited" (p. 609).

Simulation Games

Games have always played a significant role in children's learning; children are quick to mimic adults and to invent games that allow them to assume adult-like roles. The records credit a nineteenth-century schoolteacher, Maria Montessori, with being the first person to realize the potential of games for purposeful use in the school curriculum. By watching children play, Montessori learned to devise games based on children's natural behavior. Such natural curricula reflected the philosophy of John Locke, Jean Jacques Rousseau, and John Dewey, who believed that children should be actively involved in the curriculum. Today, simulations and games are used extensively in industry and in schools to train and educate. A simulation is a technique that teaches some aspect of the world or environment by imitation or replication (Alessi & Trollip, 1991).

The use of games in schools is actually worldwide. For example, more than one-third of all schools in England and Wales now include games in their syllabi, and the use of computer-based simulations is increasing (Moore, 1999). The most popular type of game used in educational settings is the simulation game, which allows players to experience a variety of roles that are common in life. By definition, a simulation game must imitate some reality and give players the opportunity to compete in a real-life role, yet the emphasis on competition must be kept in perspective. Winning is not the major object of a simulation game. On the contrary, because games offer great socializing potential, use them to help students learn to empathize with others. Every player should have a chance to win. Above all, the game should be fun. Games using machines tend to become dehumanizing and require special effort by the teacher to counterbalance this with a high level of personal contact with students.

This does not imply, however, that games are effective only for developing social skills. On the contrary, a good simulation-type game can provide a sound and interesting learning experience. Simulation games can:

1. Actively involve students
2. Create a high degree of interest and enthusiasm
3. Make abstract concepts meaningful for students
4. Provide immediate feedback to students
5. Allow students to experiment with concepts and new skills without feeling they must be correct at all times
6. Give students the opportunity to evaluate their mistakes
7. Allow students to practice communication skills

Basic to the learning potential for any strategy is motivation. When using simulation games and having students work together in small groups and allowing them to discover strategies for playing the game, low achievers and students with discipline problems become more motivated. Even shy students become involved, and all students are likely to consider the activity relevant.

Simulation games offer special opportunities to learners. Hostrop (1972) found that U.S. history students who used a simulation on the impeachment proceedings against President Andrew Johnson learned far more effectively than had they listened to a lecture. Simulation games enable students to interact at their own level and learn how to compete and cooperate with others. But exactly how effective are games compared with more traditional modes of instruction? Wylie (1974) reports on a study in which a simulation game is compared with a programmed text in social studies. After the material was introduced by these two methods, a test showed no significant difference between learning in the two groups. Two weeks later, however, the same two groups retook the test, and students who played the game outscored the control group.

Simulation gaming is apparently equal to traditional methods in producing learning and superior in producing retention. Lucas, Postma, and Thompson (1975) found that, compared with the lecture, simulation games used to teach mathematics had similar learning and retention results for up to five weeks, but after ten weeks students using the simulation had a significantly higher retention rate. Games are especially effective for use with slow learners. Learning itself can be increased during simulations when students work in small groups, when they are permitted to evaluate their own mistakes, and when the vocabulary level is kept simple.

However, the question, "Is simulation gaming more effective than a textbook?", may not be an appropriate question, because simulation games can be used to supplement the text.

> ### *Teacher as Proactive Decision Maker*
>
> **Classroom Situation**
>
> 1. You know that most if not all of your future students will enjoy those lessons that have a lot of student activity. You also know that your students will tend to ignore words they find unfamiliar.
>
> **Proactive Alternatives**
>
> 1. Develop your own version of a popular game show. Include a lot of familiar words along with these less familiar words.
> 2. At the beginning of the year, invite students to develop a notebook of new words they learn, organized by chapters in the sequence they are covered. Give extra credit each six weeks (ex. ½ point per word up to a maximum of 5 points each grading period).
> 3. Help students identify critical words that represent critical concepts covered each six weeks. Offer an extra 5 points credit for the grading period for students who write a theme using all of these key words.

Simulations can make the abstract material in a textbook more real and vivid. Taylor (1976) lists the advantages of developing your own simulation:

- You are able to pick the precise subject matter.
- You know best your students' ability level.
- Time constraints are not a problem.
- You can change or alter the game if necessary.

From studying the characteristics of effective schools, i.e., schools with a high rate of academic achievement, Reynolds and Teddle (2000) reported that group games produce more learning than individual games: "Higher achieving schools were more likely to use games that emphasized team, rather than individual learning" (p. 135).

Implementing Simulations

The success of any simulation depends on its design and implementation. To help teachers design their own simulation games, Taylor (1976) makes the following suggestions:

- Identify your objectives.
- Decide on a problem or simulation.
- Define the simulation's scope.
- Construct the rules.
- Identify the participants' goals.
- Write rules and teacher instructions.
- Design any additional parts.
- Develop a debriefing.

When designing simulation games, consider how to teach the simulation and your students' ability. Simulation games are valid only if they teach the desired ideas, values, and facts. The best game development involves students. Students who help develop a game are more involved in playing the game and have a more positive attitude.

How you use the simulation also determines its success. In fact, many teachers shun simulations because they are afraid they might not work. Heyman (1976) gives four rules for directing a simulation game:

1. Say no more than the few words necessary.
2. Run the simulation, not the students.
3. Run the game; do not teach.
4. Do not tell students how to behave.

Good classroom management and rapport with students are necessary for good gaming. Anyone adapting a game for classroom use should keep the rules simple, keep the game shorter than one class period, and attain a balance of risk, chance, skill, and knowledge in determining victory.

When designed and implemented properly, simulation games are an effective mode of instruction. Games enable students to develop generalizations, which take students to higher levels of the educational taxonomy. Parsons and Jones (1990) testify to this advantage: "Games in the classroom lend themselves easily to learning facts, generalizations, and concepts" (p. 18).

In addition to being a sound method for learning, simulation gaming is a good motivator and therefore can increase retention. Games can also promote development of social skills. Some of the best simulation games were designed by teachers, who themselves can select, relate, and adjust the game to their own students. When using a simulation game, be sure all students will enjoy it and resist the temptation to interfere with the students.

Developing a Simulation/Gaming Lesson

Simulations and games are among the most enjoyable lessons to develop. By joining the two and forming a simulation (or lifelike) game, you can give your lesson a sense of realism and a sense of competition. A simple yet remarkably stimulating simulation game—baseball—is appropriate for all levels of middle and high school. If you understand the real game of baseball, designing such a lesson is quite simple: Identify the concepts that you wish your students to understand. Then write questions to help students learn these concepts. Next, assign a value to each question ranging from 1 to 4 points, depending on the level of complexity of each question. You will need at least two or three dozen questions. Write each on a strip of paper, fold the strips, and put them in a hat or box.

Next, divide the class in half, assigning the most capable students equally between the two teams. Let each team choose a captain. Start by flipping a coin to see which team bats first. Give each team an alphabetized list of its members. This list determines the batting order. Let the person at the top of the list on the team that wins the toss pick a question. Unfold the question and announce whether the ball will be a single, double, triple, or home run (4-point question). Read the question or ask the captain of the opposing team to read it. The batter gets to continue until he or she misses a question. One missed question constitutes an out. Scores are kept, and when a team misses a total of three questions, it must retire to the field and let the opposing team bat. The game should continue until all questions are asked. Should time run out, the team captains should note who is up to bat when the next lesson resumes, how many outs there are, and the running score. Be sure to let the students resume the game during the first available period. If you do not understand the scoring of baseball, you may choose to develop a game based on a television quiz show.

Another popular type of simulations used in today's schools is computer-assisted instruction (CAI). In addition to providing a safe way to learning about dangerous subjects, CAI games provide students the opportunity to integrate previously learned factual knowledge with abstract concepts (Sawyer, 1992).

Story Telling

Perhaps the most underused teaching strategy is story telling; yet story telling is also one of the most powerful teaching tools. It is powerful because it connects the cognitive side of learning with the emotional side. This two-sided learning approach (called *confluency*) is the richest type of learning.

Teacher of the Year

The smartest students love story telling; the weakest ones worship it. You can be stiff as you teach about the Panama Canal or you can tell them a story they will never forget.

Former Virgina Teacher of the Year Mary Bicouvaris
(Henson & Eller, 1998, p. 124)

Cooperative Learning

Throughout the history of our schools, teachers have permitted students to work together in groups. By the turn of the twentieth century, Col. Francis Parker had introduced student-centered curricula in the Quincy, Massachusetts, school system (Campbell, 1967). Indiana (The Gary Plan) and Illinois (The Winnetka Plan) had begun experimenting with student-centered programs. By the mid-1920s the Progressive Education Era was underway, with John Dewey proclaiming that "learning is doing." By mid-century, an Illinois superintendent, Lloyd Trump, introduced the Trump Plan, which designated 20 percent of students' time to be spent in working in small groups and 40 percent to be spent in large groups.

Twenty-first-century U.S. education is characterized by student activities, and these activities have often been pursued by students working together. By the layperson's definition, students working together to pursue assignments is a type of cooperative learning. However, cooperative learning emphasized today is distinctly different from this loose definition. The following discussion focuses on this more modern view of cooperative learning.

Cooperative learning is a designed approach to enhance learning of all students by involving two or more students in working toward a common goal. It was the heart of two of the priority goals that the National Middle School Association set for all middle schools: "Cooperative learning and other heterogeneous strategies will replace grouping and tracking strategies," and "Collaboration and cooperative problem solving [should] replace competition as the driving philosophy of middle level education" (Jenkins & Jenkins, 1991).

Distinct goals are set for the group to reach. All students in the group help attain their group goal(s). Because students differ in their abilities, differentiated assignments may be required to allow all students to contribute to attaining the group goal. Unlike the group work used in student-centered curricula during the first half of the twentieth century, today's cooperative learning programs require all group members to succeed. Performance is based on total group success, because it prompts all group members to help their fellow group members and because the group's success depends on all its members' success.

Team performance in contemporary cooperative learning programs is generally evaluated differently than in the past. Then, the success of any group was determined by how well that team competed with other teams. Today, team success is often determined by comparing the team's performance with earlier performance of the team (Slavin, 1995). Today, cooperative learning groups compete with themselves. This self-competition has a distinct advantage. Cooperative learning definitions vary. Linblad (1994) says that:

> *In its purest form, cooperative learning is merely a few people getting together to study something and produce a single product. Thus, because self-reliance is every bit as important a skill to master as cooperative relationships, good teachers will continue to emphasize the importance of individual effort and accountability at the same time that they use cooperative learning techniques."*
> (pp. 291–292)

The future of the United States and of the world will require not so much a spirit of competition but a spirit of cooperation. Manning and Lucking (1991) explain:

> *The need for people to interact cooperatively and work toward group goals undoubtedly will increase during the 1990s. Yet, American education traditionally has emphasized individual competition and achievement, an approach that results in winners and losers and sometimes produces outright hostility among learners. (p. 152)*

Although cooperative learning programs seem especially suited for low achievers, most studies show that high, average, and low achievers gain equally from cooperative learning experiences (Manning & Lucking, 1991). Spencer Kagan (1989–1990), a former professor at the University of California—Riverside who has researched effective learning for twenty-five years, reports that "both behavioral and paper-and-pencil measures in over 20 published research studies document that cooperative learning leads to a more pro-social orientation among students" (p. 9).

Augustine, Gruber, and Hanson (1989–1990) reported on their collective twenty-three years of experience in using cooperative learning strategies. Their conclusion was "we are confident that cooperation works: it promotes higher achievement, develops social skills, and puts the responsibility for learning on the learner" (p. 4).

For cooperative learning to be effective, students must get to know one another, communicate accurately and unambiguously, accept and support one another, and resolve conflict. These skills should be taught just as systematically as subject content. Several research studies have concluded that cooperative learning teams increase students' self-esteem (Manning & Lucking, 1991). However, these authors quickly remind their readers that "emphasizing cooperation over competition requires teachers to change their teaching roles from a power figure or conveyor of knowledge to a guide of learning events or to a resource person" (p. 155).

Johnson and Johnson (1989) also view cooperative learning much more specifically than the loose definition given at the beginning of this section. They say that all real cooperative learning has five basic elements: (1) positive interdependence, (2) face-to-face interaction, (3) individual accountability, (4) collaborative skills, and (5) group processing. Positive interdependence means that each student's success (grade) depends on a group grade. The converse of this principle is also true; the group's success depends on each member's mastering the material being tested (individual accountability).

Not all students automatically know how to work together, or cooperate, so Johnson and Johnson (1989) provide an organized set of activities to help students develop the social and collaborative skills needed to contribute to and benefit from group learning. They refer to the group's discussing and assessing their progress as group processing.

Advantages

Traditionally, a distinguishing characteristic of graduate education has been the seminar. Educators have long recognized that graduate students can contribute to the class. Interestingly, even at this level of maturity, students are often extremely uncomfortable during the first few seminars. This level of discomfort is intensified when the professor pauses to think and to give students time to think about issues. Ironically, even in school—a place designated for learning—students are made uncomfortable by pauses, even though those pauses give them time to think.

Equally unusual is educators' failure from kindergarten through college to recognize that students of all levels can contribute to the learning process and can help others learn. Cooperative learning welcomes students to benefit from their classmates' knowledge and thoughts. Currently, U.S. schools are experiencing a paradigm shift in the way learning is perceived to occur. As discussed in Chapter 1, constructivism is a dominating learning theory that recognizes that knowledge is temporary and that each student can construct knowledge. Cooperative learning theory also recognizes that each student can not only learn but can help classmates learn.

Cooperative learning also removes competition between and among students. Some of the harmful effects of such competition are discussed in Chapter 5. Some teachers believe that competition with all classmates is necessary to motivate students to perform at their best. The assessment used with cooperative learning motivates students yet protects less capable students from impossible challenges.

A closely related strength of cooperative learning is that it teaches students to cooperate with others. Since the team's score is a sum of the team members' scores, each participant is encouraged to help fellow team members. Most adult jobs, like daily living, require cooperation.

Another advantage of cooperative learning is that this method is motivational. Unlike such traditional images as the "bookworm" and the "gentlemen's C," which have militated against academic success, cooperative learning encourages all students to do their best. It is uncertain whether these terms were purposefully developed to discourage maximum academic success, but the fact that they have this effect is certain. In contrast to traditional classrooms, in which each student knows that the teacher is likely to distribute an allotted number of A's and that any classmate's star performance reduces others' chance to earn an A, discovery learning students actually want their classmates to succeed (Hulten & DeVries, 1976; Madden & Slavin, 1983; Slavin, 1978). Furthermore, several studies have found that students in cooperative groups who improved academically gained in peer status (Slavin, 1975; Slavin, DeVries, & Hulten, 1975).

Developing a Cooperative Learning Lesson

As with all teaching strategies, how you use cooperative learning determines its success. Lindblad (1994) cautions teachers not to interfere with group work:

> *Too often the traditional teacher feels the need to be part of everything going on in the class. Let students handle their own team progress. When the teacher stays removed from minor discord, the team members are forced to deal with those problems themselves. (p. 293)*

Heckman, Confer, and Hakim (1994, p. 39) say that "children's own questions are the most powerful source of curriculum topics and investigation."

Alfke (1974) explains that such questions develop skills in learning how to learn, to inquire, and to conceptualize. Teachers can achieve this by asking fewer but better questions and by requiring students to pose more productive questions. Data suggest that all teachers should:

- Avoid using questions to introduce lessons.
- Delay questions about content until a knowledge base has been established.
- Use a combination of levels of questions, extending from recall to evaluation.
- Pause for at least three seconds following each question.
- Not expect students to be able to guess what you mean.
- Address questions to individual students, using students' names.
- Keep content-oriented questions specific.
- Help students by modifying their inaccurate answers until they become acceptable.
- Encourage students to ask questions.
- Help students develop skills in asking questions.
- Listen carefully to students' questions and respond using their content.
- Before assigning reading, showing a film, or taking a field trip, ask questions about that experience's major concepts or objectives.

Cooperative learning is more than just letting students work together. Begin developing your lesson by developing a short assignment. You can use the same variety of media as used to build a knowledge base in a questioning lesson (i.e., recordings, mini-lecture, introduction). Remember that in cooperative learning the competition is between or among groups, not individuals. Assign students to groups of about four members each. Designate membership so that each group has about the same potential as the other groups.

Advise all students that at a designated time you will administer a test on the lesson they are studying and that each member's success depends on the group's success. Explain that it is to each student's advantage to help the other group members understand the lesson's major concepts.

A strategy that can be combined with most of these methods is team teaching. Its primary benefit is its potential for letting teachers use their expertise more extensively than when teaching a self-contained class. Teaming is often effective when used with large groups of students. Alexander (1995) recommends this combination of team teaching and large groups in the new middle school, combining one or two science and math teachers with one or two language arts and social studies teachers and one fine arts or language teacher.

The number of teaching methods this chapter discusses may seem a little overwhelming. One way to understand these methods is to think about the sizes of groups in which they are used (Figure 9.1). For example, you will generally use a lecture, simulation game, and case study method with the entire class. Individual students generally pursue inquiry and discovery

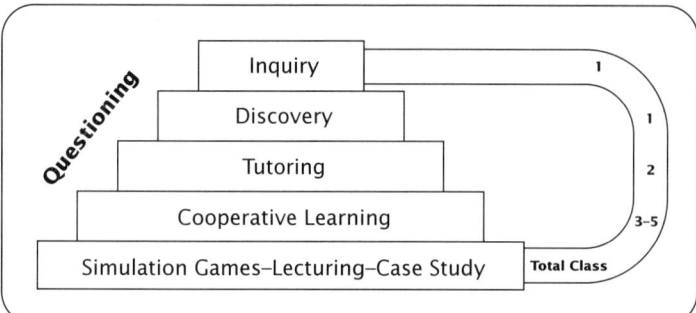

FIGURE 9.1 RELATIVE GROUP SIZE OF TEACHING METHODS

From Kenneth T. Henson, *Methods and Strategies for Teaching in Secondary and Middle Schools*, third edition. Published by Allyn and Bacon, Boston, MA. Copyright © 1996 by Pearson Education. Reprinted by permission of the publisher.

learning independently. Tutoring involves two students, and cooperative learning involves between three and five students. Questioning is used with all of these methods, so the class size may vary from one to everyone.

It is worth remembering that with all methods success depends on how the teacher implements them and whether the students' needs are met. For example, African American students' self-concepts, self-esteem, and academic confidence can be raised by publicly acknowledging their academic success (Garibaldi, 1992). Hispanic students value role models (Vasquez, 1990), and although most Asian American students are outstanding students, Yee (1992) warns that some Asian American youths are not outstanding, hard-working students.

> *Reflection*
>
> Review the wide variety of teaching strategies discussed in this chapter against the NMSA goals shown in Figure 1.1 and the Carnegie goals lists found in the Preface. Which of these strategies do you think lead to the attainment of the most of these goals?

Vignettes

You may have already begun to choose your own teaching strategies. The following vignettes will give you some opportunities to refine your ideas.

> ### Vignette One: A Methods Course Emphasizes Strategies
>
> Carole Harman had enjoyed her introductory course in education. She had also taken an exploratory course in education that provided interesting field experiences. These courses made her feel certain that she wanted to be a teacher.
>
> The next year Carole took two courses in her major (chemistry), two in math, and a general secondary methods course. But after only two weeks she felt lost in the education course. Her professor had begun talking about educational research and teaching strategies and the relationships between the two. Carole was uncomfortable because she had never taken a course in research methodology and did not have any background in teaching strategies.
>
> Almost from the start the professor began making such comments as "When selecting your strategies" or "You can apply your favorite strategy." Carole had never before thought about teaching strategies, which sounded like unnecessary educational jargon. She wondered whether other class members felt the same way, until one of them nearby mumbled, "How can you have a favorite strategy if you don't know what one is?"
>
> ### DISCUSSION
>
> 1. Why might an education professor assume that students in a general methods course have knowledge of teaching strategies? Teachers often get so close to their subjects that they expect their students to have more knowledge of and enthusiasm about the subject than they actually do. College professors are just as likely to make this mistake.

After all, educational strategies are this teacher's major subject.

2. Why is it important that teachers be familiar with many teaching strategies? Many teachers believe they need a good repertoire of methods to function in the classroom. What works with one group of students may not stimulate another group. The teacher who is familiar with various methods can shift quickly among them when the class's level of interest drops. (This is only one advantage of having a repertoire of methods. Perhaps you can think of others.)

3. What should the teacher know about each teaching strategy? To get the most benefit from each strategy, teachers must know the purposes that each method serves best, and the age levels for which it is most appropriate. Besides knowing how to use a strategy, teachers should recognize its strengths and limitations. What else will you want to know about methods that you might use? (You could consider their practicality, cost, and effects on other teachers.)

Vignette Two: Should Teaching in Secondary and Middle Schools Be Fun?

Louis Martinez was the most interesting math teacher ever to come to Jackson High. Before he arrived, three years ago, not enough students were interested in math to offer more than the very basic general mathematics, geometry, and first-year algebra. But when school opened this fall, Mr. Martinez had so many students requesting Algebra II that two sections were necessary. In addition, 27 students had signed up for trigonometry, and 15 others wanted a class in first-year calculus. For a school as small as Jackson High, this degree of interest in any single subject was incredible. Happy to see that so many of his students were sharing his enjoyment of mathematics, Mr. Martinez became even more enthusiastic, and his lessons became even more exciting.

The students enjoyed his classes for many different reasons. For one, they never knew what to expect from one day to the next; they just knew it would be different. Most of the lessons involved every student, and usually in a number of ways. Moreover, Mr. Martinez had a great collection of props, audio-visual materials, and games.

Then some of the other teachers began complaining about him. His classes were noisier than most, and although he had more equipment than most of his colleagues, his students were running all over the school borrowing other paraphernalia to use in math class. Basically, though, the other teachers' complaints stemmed from jealousy. Although they would never admit it, they would have tolerated the noise and other minor irritants if they could have their students become that enthusiastic about their classes.

Unfortunately, the complaints reached Mr. Martinez only after they had spread through the school and the community. The principal called him in to discuss the complaints and remind him how important it was not to alienate other teachers. Mr. Martinez was perplexed to learn that his successful teaching strategies had begun to cause trouble for him.

DISCUSSION

1. Is having a repertoire of teaching methods likely to get a teacher into trouble?
2. How might Mr. Martinez react to such an accusation?
3. How should Mr. Martinez deal with complaints from other teachers?

Summary

Today's teachers need a repertoire of teaching methods to meet the needs of individuals in their classes. Each method has strengths and weaknesses and should be selected and used accordingly. For example, the lecture is a poor motivator but an efficient way to build a framework around a topic. Therefore, lectures should be used sparingly and should be structured to involve students. Beginning each lesson with a few objectives can focus students' attention on the lesson. Moving at a brisk tempo can reduce boredom. Graphic organizers can enhance structure, and summaries can pull isolated facts together at points during the lesson and at the end of the lesson.

Case studies are motivating and offer students opportunity to sort out relevant information and make decisions. Tutoring can help both the tutor and the tutee, especially when teachers give clear directions and emphasize the value of learning to work with others. Inquiry learning and discovery learning are powerful methods because they use problem solving. Because they involve students, they are motivating. A major disadvantage of these methods is that they are not time efficient.

Simulations and games are great motivators. Students retain learning well when these methods are used. Homemade games are particularly effective. When using them, the teacher should keep the rules simple, keep the game shorter than a class period, and let chance play a part in determining success.

Story telling is a powerful teaching tool. All students love stories. Students should also be invited to invent and share their own stories.

Cooperative learning is effective when using small groups of no more than five students. Students should be encouraged to help other group members succeed. The most important teaching role when using cooperative learning is to resist the temptation to interfere with the group process.

Recap of Major Ideas

1. Use the lecture with highly motivated students who can take good notes. Most students do not have this ability.
2. The lecture is an effective means of introducing a unit, building a frame of reference, clarifying confusing issues, and summarizing major concepts in a lesson. It is not usually a good motivator, and it does not stimulate imagination and creativity.
3. Begin most lectures with a clear statement of objectives, keep them short and simple, and proceed briskly. A lecture should contain only a few major concepts and should provide activities that require students to apply the concepts.
4. Supplement lectures with audio-visual aids, gesturing, joking, and modeling.
5. Tutoring usually helps both the tutor and the tutee. It is more effective when used with other approaches, such as mastery learning.
6. Inquiry lessons offer students opportunities to cultivate their creative talents when they have freedom and flexibility. The absence of continuous feedback and frequent grades in inquiry learning makes self-motivated students anxious.
7. You enhance the effectiveness of questioning by giving students more time to respond, helping students provide acceptable answers, and encouraging students to ask questions.
8. Simulation games are good motivators and lead to increased retention. Used appropriately, they emphasize cooperation, not competition.
9. Cases enable students to study concepts in the context in which they occur.
10. Students learn more and develop their social skills during cooperative learning.
11. Most African American students' self-concepts are enhanced when their academic success is recognized publicly.

Activities

1. Make a list of your best teachers' best qualities. Review the effective schools research and the effective teachers research found in this book. Now, add the qualities found here to your own list.
2. Research the characteristics of several minority ethnic groups and make a list of these.

Looking Ahead

This chapter has introduced several methods and strategies you can use to help your students learn. The following chapter will help you improve your communication skills.

References

Alessi, S. M., & Trollip, S. R. (1991). *Computer-based instruction, methods, and development.* Englewood Cliffs, NJ: Prentice-Hall.

Alexander, W. M. (1995). The junior high school: A changing view. *Middle School Journal, 26*(3), 21–24.

Armstrong, D. G., Henson, K. T., & Savage, T. V. (2001). *Teaching today* (6th ed.). New York: Prentice-Hall.

Augustine, D. K., Gruber, K. D., & Hanson, L. R. (1989–1990, December/January). Cooperation works! *Educational Leadership, 47*(4), 411–516.

Barth, R. S. (1990). A personal vision of a good school. *Phi Delta Kappan, 71,* 512–516.

Berliner, D. C., & Gage, N. L. (1975). The psychology of teaching methods. In N. L. Gage (Ed.), *The psychology of teaching methods.* Chicago: National Society for the Study of Education.

Bernstrom, J. M., & O'Brien, L. A. (2001). Themes of discovery. *Educational Leadership, 58*(7), 29–33.

Bloom, B. S. (1984). The search for methods of group instruction as effective as one-to-one tutoring. *Educational Leadership, 41,* 4–17.

Bull, S. G., & Dizney, H. F. (1973). Epistemic—curiosity—arousing pre-questions: Their effect on long-term retention. *Journal of Educational Psychology, 65,* 45–49.

Campbell, J. (1967). *Colonel Francis Parker: The children's crusader.* New York: Columbia University Teachers' College Press.

Carnegie Council on Adolescent Development Staff (1995). *Great transitions: Preparing adolescents for a new century.* New York: Carnegie Foundation.

Cherniss, C. (1998). Social and emotional learning for leaders. *Educational Leadership, 55*(7), 28.

Cienkus, R. C., & Ornstein, A. (1997). Distance learning: Teaching by lecture/explanation. *High School Journal, 80,* 247–250.

Einstein, A., & Infield, L. P. (1938). *Evolution of physics: Growth of ideas from early concepts to relativity and quanta.* New York: Simon & Schuster.

Eisner, E. (2002). The kind of schools we need. *Phi Delta Kappan, 83*(8), 576–583.

Ellsworth, P. C., & Sindt, V. G. (1994). Helping "Aha" to happen: The contributions of Irving Sigel. *Educational Leadership, 51*(5), 40–44.

Farr, M. (1998). Nickerson High School physical science after-school tutoring program. *Journal of Critical Inquiry into Curriculum and Instruction,* 1(1), 41–47.

Garibaldi, A. M. (1992). Educating and motivating African American males to see. *Journal of Negro Education,* 61(1), 4–11.

Good, T. L., & Brophy, J. E. (2000). *Looking in classrooms.* (8th ed.). New York: Longman.

Goodlad, J. I. (1984). *A place called school.* New York: McGraw-Hill.

Gusky, T. R. (1990). Integrating innovations. *Educational Leadership,* 47 (Feb.), 11–15.

Harrison, C. J. (1990). Concepts, operational definitions, and case studies in instruction. *Education,* 110(4), 502–505.

Heckman, P. E., Confer, C. B., & Hakim, D. C. (1994). Planting seeds: Understanding through investigation. *Educational Leadership, 51*(5), 36–39.

Henson, K. T., & Eller, B. F. (1999). *Educational psychology for effective teaching.* Belmont, CA: Wadsworth.

Heyman, M. (1976). How to direct a simulation. *Phi Delta Kappan,* 16, 17–19.

Hock, M. F., Schumaker, J. B., & Deshner, D. D. (2001). The case for strategic tutoring. *Educational Leadership, 58*(7), 50–52.

Hostrop, R. W. (1972, Autumn). Simulation as stimulus to learning and retention. *Improving College and University Teaching,* 20, 283.

Hulten, B. H., & DeVries, D. L. (1976). *Team competition and group practice: Effects on students' achievement and attitudes.* (Report 212). Baltimore: Johns Hopkins University Center for Social Organization of Schools.

Jenkins, D. M., & Jenkins, K. D. (1991). The NMSA Delphi report: Roadmap to the future. *Middle School Journal,* 22(4), 27–36.

Johnson, D. W., & Johnson, R. (1989). *Cooperation and competition: Theory and research.* Edina, MN: Interaction Book Company.

Kagan, S. (1989–1990, December/January). The structural approach to cooperative learning. *Educational Leadership, 47*(4), 12–15.

King, A. (1990, November/December). Reciprocal questioning: A strategy for teaching students how to learn from lectures. *The Clearing House,* 64(2), 131–135.

Kowalski, T. J., Weaver, R. A., & Henson, K. T., (1990). *Case studies on teaching.* White Plains, NY: Longman.

Kowalski, T. J., Weaver, R. A., & Henson, K. T. (1994). *Case studies of beginning teachers.* White Plains, NY: Longman.

LeFrancois, G. R. (1999). *Psychology for teaching.* (10th ed.). Belmont, CA: Wadsworth.

Lemlech, J. K. (1999). *Classroom management.* (3rd ed.). Prospect Heights, IL: Waveland.

Lindblad, A. H., Jr. (1994). You can avoid the traps of cooperative learning. *The Clearing House, 67*(5), 291–293.

Lucas, L. A., Postma, C. H., & Thompson, J. C. (1975, July). Comparative study of cognitive retention used in simulation gaming as opposed to lecture: Discussion techniques. *Peabody Journal of Education, 52,* 261.

MacDonald, R. (1991, Fall). Tutoring: An effective teaching tool. *Kappa Delta Pi Record,* 28(1), 25–28.

Madden, N. A., & Slavin, R. E. (1983). Effects of cooperative learning on the social acceptance of main streamed academically handicapped students. *Journal of Special Education, 17,* 171–182.

Maddox, H., & Hoole, E. (1975). Performance decrement in the lecture. *Educational Review, 28,* 17–30.

Manning, M. L., & Lucking, R. (1991, January/February). The what, why, and how of cooperative learning. *The Clearing House,* 64(3), 152–156.

Martinez, M. E. (1998). What is problem solving? *Phi Delta Kappan,* 79(8), 605–609.

Moore, K. (1999). Middle and secondary school instructional methods. (2nd ed.). Boston: McGraw-Hill.

O'Neal, M., Earley, B., & Snider, M. (1991). Addressing the needs of at-risk students: A local school program that works. In Robert C. Morris (Ed.), *Youth at risk.* Lancaster, PA: Tecnomic, 122–125.

Paget, N. (1988, January). Using case methods effectively. *Journal of Education and Business, 63,* 175–180.

Parsons, J., & Jones, C. (1990, September/October). Not another test. *The Clearing House,* 64(1), 17–20.

Phillips, D. R., Phillips, D. G., Melton, G., & Moore, P. (1994). Beans, blocks, and buttons: Developing thinking. *Educational Leadership,* 51(5), 50–53.

Phillips, G. (1998, July 6). Making a difference in student behavior. South East/South Central Educational Cooperative. Lexington, KY: 1998 Principals' Academy Retreat.

Ramsey, I., Gabbard, C., Clawson, K., Lee, L., & Henson, K. T. (1990). Questioning: An effective teaching method. *The Clearing House,* 63(9), 420–422.

Reynolds, D., & Teddle, C. (2000). The processes of school effectiveness. In C. Tiddle & D. Reynolds (Eds.), *The international handbook of school effectiveness research,* pp. 134–159. New York: Falmer.

Rosenshine, B., & Stevens, R. (1986). Teaching functions. In M. C. Wittrock (Ed.), *Handbook of research on teaching* (3rd ed.). New York: Macmillan.

Rothstein, P. R. (1990). *Educational psychology.* New York: McGraw-Hill.

Rowe, M. B. (1974). Wait-time and rewards as instructional variable: Their influence on language, logic, and fate control, Part one. *Journal of Research in Science Teaching, 11,* 81–94.

Rowsey, R., & Mason, W. H. (1975). Immediate achievement and retention in audio tutorial vs. conventional lecture-laboratory instruction. *Journal of Research in Science Teaching, 12,* 393–397.

Sanders, J. R. (1973). Retention effects of adjunct questions in written and oral discourse. *Journal of Educational Psychology, 65,* 181–186.

Santiesleban, A. J. (1976). Teacher questioning performance and student affective outcomes. *Journal of Research and Science Teaching, 13,* 553–557.

Sawyer, D. M. (1992). The virtual computer: A new paradigm for educational computing. *Educational Technology,* 32(1), 7–14.

Shanahan, T. (1998). On the effectiveness and limitations of tutoring in reading. In P. D. Peterson & A. Iran-Nejad (Eds.), *Review of research in education, 23,* 217–234.

Shiman, D. A., & Mash, R. J. (1974). Questioning: Another view. *Peabody Journal of Education, 51,* 246–253.

Slavin, R. E. (1975). *Classroom reward structure: Effects on academic performance, social connectedness and peer norms.* Doctoral dissertation, Johns Hopkins University, Baltimore, MD.

Slavin, R. E. (1978). Student teams and comparison among equals: Effects on academic performance and student attitudes. *Journal of Educational Psychology, 70,* 532–538.

Slavin, R. E. (1995). *Cooperative learning* (2nd ed.). Boston: Allyn & Bacon.

Slavin, R. E., DeVries, D. L., & Hulten, B. H. (1975). *Individual vs. team competition: The interpersonal consequences of academic performance* (Report 188). Baltimore, MD: Johns Hopkins University Center for Social Organization of Schools.

Sobel, M. A. (1975, October). Junior high school mathematics: Motivation vs. monotony. *Mathematics Teacher, 68,* 479–485.

Special Study Panel on Education Indicators for the National Center for Education Statistics (1991, September). *Education Counts*. Washington, DC: U.S. Department of Education, p. 67.

Stefanich, G. P. (1990, November). Cycles of cognition. *Middle School Journal*, 22(2), 47–52.

Sund, R. B. (1971). Growing through sensitive listening and questioning. *Childhood Education*, 51, 68–71.

Taylor, A. J. R. (1976). Developing your own simulation for teaching. *The Clearing House*, 50, 104–107.

Titus, C. (1974, February). The uses of the lecture. *The Clearing House*, 383–384.

Vance, J. H. (1974, February). Mathematics laboratories—More than fun? *School Science and Mathematics*, 72, 617–623.

Vasquez, J. A. (1990). Teaching to the distinctive traits of minority students. *The Clearing House*, 63(7), 299–304.

Voth, R. (1975). On lecturing. *Social Studies*, 66, 247–248.

Weimer, R. C. (1975). An analysis of discovery. *Educational Technology*, 15, 45–48.

Williams, P. A., Alley, R. D., & Henson, K. T. (1999). Managing secondary classrooms. Boston: Allyn & Bacon.

Woods Hole Conference (1959). Woods Hole, MA.

Wylie, R. E. (1974). Simulation games for general mathematics. *Childhood Education*. 54, 307.

Yee, A. H. (1992). Asians as stereotypes and students: Misperceptions that persist. *Educational Psychology Review*, 4, 95–132.

10
Communications

We must learn to listen and listen to learn.

Erasmus

Objectives

- List three voice qualities that are important in teaching, and explain how to improve each one.
- Give one suggestion for helping a teacher improve the quality of classroom questions.
- Define set induction, and describe two techniques for establishing it in the classroom.
- Explain how teacher efficacy affects student achievement.
- Describe the difference in communication behavior of effective teachers and less effective teachers.
- Respond appropriately to an incorrect response, a correct confident response, and a correct doubtful response.
- Describe how to use review at the beginning and end of a lesson.
- Give an example of how the hidden curriculum can communicate positively (usefully) and an example of how it can communicate negatively.
- Plan one research study you can conduct in your classroom to address a major concern of yours.
- Give one suggestion to help teachers use computers to improve communications with parents.
- Give examples of ways the hidden curriculum can damage minority students.

COMMUNICATION

Need

Effective School Research

Messages
- Sense of Efficacy
- Sense of Meaning
- Expectations
- Emotions

Verbal Skills
- Voice Control
- Set Induction
- Examples
- Repetition
- Variety
- Questions
- Reinforcement
- Review

Nonverbal Skills
- Feedback
- Eye Contact
- Body Movement
- Using Silence
- The Hidden Curriculum

Connecting Statements	Agree	Disagree	Uncertain
1. Most beginning teachers talk too fast.			
2. Teachers should avoid using personal examples in their lessons.			
3. Students tend to emulate their teachers' behavior.			
4. Teachers tend to pause too long after asking a question, which bores many students.			
5. A teacher's nonverbal communication is more important than what the teacher says.			
6. Most student responses to higher-order questions are higher-order.			
7. Teachers should not direct questions to individual students because many students find this embarrassing.			

> *Tips for Teachers*
>
> During transescence, that awkward time between childhood and adolescence, young people are often confused. Just when they get it together, it comes apart. They may feel that nobody understands them. Too often, they cannot communicate their feelings effectively. This leads to further frustration, exacerbating the problems. When asked to do a chore at home and being later called to task for not completing the job satisfactorily, their common response is "Oh, I thought you meant. . . ."
>
> Teachers of this age group must clearly communicate what they expect of their students. Students of this age have no criteria to help them decide which concepts are academically important. When teachers explain how each activity fits into the lesson's goals or structure, students are no longer at a loss.
>
> Students often have teachers who fail to follow their own advice. If students are advised to behave one way and teachers behave differently, this further confuses these students. This chapter shows how verbal and nonverbal communication strategies can help in the classroom.

The Need for Communication Skills

The Lesson: Exciting or Boring?

Students are slow to arrive at Ms. Simms's history class. As the tardy bell rings, there are usually a few still coming in and walking casually to their desks. Equally predictable is the way Ms. Simms will present the lesson. She always begins by mumbling a few words about yesterday's lesson, even while the latecomers are ambling in. Early in the year these students got the impression that Ms. Simms did not really care whether they learned the subject. They still do not know if it is because her knowledge of history is inadequate or she is merely unable to communicate.

The scene in Miss Armstrong's class is different. There, students arrive quickly, find their seats, and open their books and notepads. The students recognize Miss Armstrong's expertise in her subject. She begins each lesson promptly and assertively. She presents many concepts, but she does this clearly, and it is obvious that she wants her students to understand. Furthermore, she seems to know when even one student is confused. Right away she gives an example that clarifies the matter. By the end of the period, she has given a clear picture of the subject under study; the personalities involved have come to life.

Why are some teachers confusing and boring while others are clear and interesting? The difference may be not how well teachers know their subjects but how well they communicate what they know. The teacher who communicates well can make a subject interesting and easy to learn; a poor communicator is apt to make lessons boring and confusing.

The importance of communications to teachers and learners cannot be overstated. In his dreams for an ideal school, Elliot Eisner (2002) said, "The kind of schools we need would encourage deep conversation in classrooms. They would help students learn how to participate in that subtle art, an art that requires learning how to listen as well as how to speak" (p. 582). Eisner was not talking about making polite conversation or the mere sharing of pleasantries, which itself is a worthy pursuit; he was talking about the need that teachers have, including the skills and opportunities, to have serious, in-depth discussions with students about the curriculum and about topics that students and teachers consider profoundly important. He went on to say that such discussions could convert schools into intellectual institutions.

This chapter will help you focus on your own communication skills. Before you read further, take a few minutes to list your own strengths in communicating, along with any limitations that may need attention. Consider such things as your voice, vocabulary, repertoire of examples and jokes, ability to ask questions, ability to listen to students, and ability to use expression and movements to show others how you feel. Include both verbal and nonverbal skills, because both are necessary for effective communication. Because teaching is a complex process, teachers must have good communication skills. In Chapter 1 we learned that in the past teachers have not made full use of research findings. Buckner and Bickel (1991) address the relationship between teachers' communication skills and their failure to use research: "A major barrier to bridging the gap between research and practice in most instructional settings has been communication" (p. 29).

Because teaching is a complex set of activities, teachers are expected to perform an increasing number of varied roles; their primary responsibility, however, is to ensure that students learn. This role—regardless of teaching techniques or strategies used—requires communicating. Today's teachers' many other roles also require communicating. Indeed, conversation affects students' thought processes and therefore what they learn (Cazden, 1986).

Your ability to teach your students depends on your ability to communicate. Teachers who are stimulating and exciting communicate more effectively than teachers who bore their students. Moreover, classroom communication is not merely a line between the teacher and student. Figure 10.1 shows the pattern of communication in the classroom. Although the figure may make your role seem complex, it is accurate. Effective teachers seem to develop a sixth sense that picks up and responds to students' many comments.

Teachers may engage in more than 1,000 interpersonal exchanges with students in a single day. Managing such complex processes requires teachers to be acutely alert to students. Teachers also learn to address a number of expressed (and even unexpressed) concerns simultaneously. In addition to talking, teachers learn to communicate nonverbally. As you read this chapter, see how many new verbal and nonverbal communication skills you can add to the list you made earlier.

Listening

Communication also involves listening. In fact, learning to really listen to students may be the most important skill teachers can develop, because it is an answer to meeting students' needs. Listen to young people rather them labeling them is the place to start to recognize their needs.

Perhaps the best place to begin communicating is by listening. Consider the student's perspective, which Hilliard (1999) says is very different from that of teachers: "Early adolescents are interested less in advice and more in getting their position heard" (p. 55). This shouldn't sound too strange; don't we teachers' have the same perspective?

Communicating in Multicultural Classrooms

The National Middle School Association recognized the need to make curricula and their teaching more relevant to all students, and listed this as a top-priority goal, " Both curriculum and instruction [should] become more relevant to the developing characteristics of middle-level students" (Jenkins & Jenkins, 1991). Multicultural classes often offer special challenges for overt and covert reasons. The high failure rate among minority students has recently been explained as the failure of teachers to communicate in ways that minority

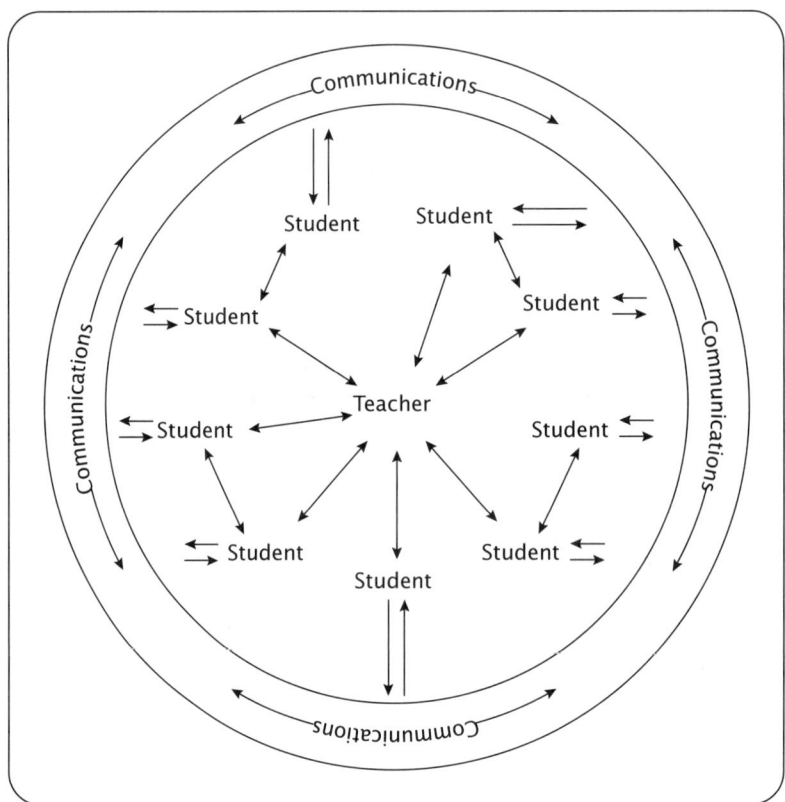

FIGURE 10.1 CLASSROOM COMMUNICATIONS

From Kenneth T. Henson, *Methods and Strategies for Teaching in Secondary and Middle Schools,* third edition. Published by Allyn and Bacon, Boston, MA. Copyright © 1996 by Pearson Education. Reprinted by permission of the publisher.

learners understand (Armstrong, Henson, & Savage, 2004). As noted by Henson and Eller (1999) "The traditional approach to multicultural education has been to give students information. Clearly, by itself this approach won't work" (p. 5). For example, in many classes, language barriers alone almost ensure misunderstanding. The same words often carry different meanings to students of different cultures. Gestures, hand signals, facial expressions, and other body language may carry very different meanings as well.

For example, the hand sign that North Americans use to ask someone to come closer means goodbye in Trinidad, and the bowed head that North Americans recognize as a sign of shame or even guilt is a sign of high respect in some cultures. The teacher who expects eye contact is expecting behavior that some students may consider insulting or disrespectful.

A good strategy for addressing prejudice is through conversation, yet, unfortunately many people are not ready to, nor can they successfully engage in such conversations (O'Neil, 1998). Information on holding conversations to reduce prejudice can be obtained by contacting Study Circles Resource Center, P.O. Box 203, 697 Pomfret, CT 06258; tel 203-928-2616; fax 203-928-3713.

Through group assignments, teachers can help students begin to understand their culturally different peers. You can provide special opportunities (activities) to help students learn more about other students' cultures. As you work to understand and help students learn about other cultures, remember to help minority students understand their mainstream classmates.

> **Teacher of the Year**
>
> Carefully, gradually bringing the rich diversity of students in my classes together in quartets, trios, and duets of writing discussion; problem solving; word processing; reporting, and a host of other interaction activities begins each student on a journey to the discovery of self and others—the journey that will bring them directly on route to the very global challenges of the twenty-first century.
>
> Former Pennsylvania Teacher of the Year Howard Selekman
> (Henson & Eller, 1999, p. 60).

You can enhance your ability to improve communication in the classroom by getting involved in the school's curriculum. For example, organize a cultural fair to celebrate the different cultures at your school. Any effort that helps students understand other cultures is likely to improve communication in the classroom.

Messages to Communicate

An unprecedented number of recent studies reveals several categories of messages that you must communicate for students to achieve maximum learning. Keep these in mind as you read the rest of this chapter. Think about ways to communicate these messages effectively.

A Sense of Efficacy

An important factor affecting learner achievement is teachers' confidence in their ability to cause students to learn (Raywid, 1998; Slavin, 1998). Fuller (1982) referred to this when he said, "**Efficacy**—the individual's perceived expectancy of obtaining valued outcomes through personal effort—appears to yield a variety of important effects in school organizations." Secondary and middle-level students must know that their teachers are able and determined to lead them to attain class goals. A sense of efficacy is empowering, and teachers need to be empowered. In fact, teacher empowerment is a goal set by the Carnegie Council on Adolescent Development Staff (1985).

But how do you achieve this confident image? By setting clear goals for the class, by asserting the leadership needed to get students on task quickly each period, and by managing all phases of the classroom environment toward these ends. Good and Brophy (1995) encourage teachers to uphold students' expectations for success:

Therefore, whatever their ability, the motivation of all students, even the most discouraged, can be reshaped by their teachers. Empty reassurances or a few words of encouragement will not do the job, but a combination of appropriately challenging demands with systematic socialization designed to make the student see that success can be achieved with reasonable effort should be effective. (p. 378)

Efficacy begins with an attitude—a positive belief in your students' ability and a belief in your ability to make students succeed. It also involves a determination that says if you do not succeed the first time, do not give up—we have just started. Teachers with efficacy are not timid. "The field of education is no place for cowards" (see Henson & Eller, 1999, p. 214; Lancaster, 1999). Teachers who display efficacy do not give excuses. If the necessary materials are not available, the efficacious teacher finds or makes other materials. Such teachers are invaluable to schools and to students. While getting the job done, they silently communicate to students that anything is possible if they believe in themselves.

Teachers can increase their levels of efficacy through several strategies. Leithwood, Menzies, and Jantzi (1994) explain:

Success raises one's appraisal of one's efficacy, although such appraisals are shaped by task difficulty, effort, effort expended, amount of help received, and other circumstances. Teachers who actually try out new practices in their classrooms, with sufficient on-site assistance to ensure success, will possess this kind of information. (p. 47)

Establishing a definite sequence for your own activities can contribute to a positive teacher image. Brooks (1985) examined videotapes of seventh-grade math classes on the first day of school and concluded that the sequence of activities on that day was a critical factor in communicating teacher competence. He recommends that teachers follow this sequence: call class to order, take roll, explain rules and procedures, introduce course content, solicit student information, talk about yourself, and preview tomorrow's lesson.

Classroom environment affects the types of communications that are appropriate and, consequently, the messages communicated. Green (1983) drew the following conclusions about communications:

1. Face-to-face interaction, between teacher and students and among students, is governed by context-specific rules.
2. Rules for participating in classroom activities are implicit and are learned through the action itself.
3. The meaning that results from communications is context-specific.
4. Over time, frames of reference are developed.
5. The diversity of classrooms makes communications complex and demanding for teachers and students.

A Sense of Meaning

Too often students go through the motions of learning without really understanding what they are doing and why they are doing it. The purpose of direct instruction is a search for meaning; direct instruction must never be an end in itself. All students need help in deciding what information is important. You should not assume that children have the necessary criteria to decide which are academically important concepts and which are unimportant. Your explanation of how each activity fits into the goals or structures of the lesson can help illuminate the lesson and make it meaningful to students. According to Fisher (1980), students "pay attention more when the teacher spends time discussing the goals or structure of the lesson and/or giving directions about what students are to do" (p. 26). But teachers seldom clearly explain what is expected of the students (Bruner, 1981).

Expectations

Several researchers have conducted studies to determine how teacher expectations affect students' learning. The expectation literature is consistently (although not unanimously) interpreted to show that teachers who communicate their goals for performance to their students have a powerful effect. Unfortunately, students and teachers may not appreciate the value of goals. Content goals often appear to have little salience for either students or teachers. Students do not think of themselves as mastering knowledge but rather as achieving what the teacher or test requires. As capsuled by Stake and Easley (1978), "Teachers are the key to what happens in the classroom" (p. 29). Maximum academic success also requires that teachers communicate clearly and frequently their behavioral expectations of students. Former Washington State Teacher of the Year Cynthia Lancaster (1999) says, "Standards for your class must be attainable and in effect from the time they are stated until the end of the term or until new standards are put in place" (p. 214).

The Role of Emotions

Since Aristotle, communication scholars have viewed communication as something one does to an audience; the message is something one transfers to the other (Gronbeck, McKerron, Ehninger, & Monroe, 1994). However, communications are more complex than a simple action between two individuals. Communication involves more than the physical exchange of ideas. Often our emotions affect our ability to receive a message. Gronbeck et al. (1994) stress the effect of emotions on communications:

> *Even when a message is completely clear and understandable, we often don't like it. Problems in "meaning" or "meaningfulness" often aren't a matter of comprehension but of reaction; of agreement; of shared concepts, belief, attitudes, values.* (p. 501)

Holm (2002) reminds teachers that an effective way to use emotions in the classroom is through the use of humor: "Humor is a unique communicative act. . . . The seeds planted by laughter can blossom into healthy classroom discussions, and isn't that what learning is all about?" (p. 6).

While communications can be fun, classroom communications are also complex. Communications experts who prepare communicators are among those who acknowledge the complexity of communications. Rudick (1994) says:

> *The premise that individual behavior is a part of a system rather than a characteristic of individuals provides an expanded view of the training process. . . . The trainee is seen as one system immersed in and inseparable from a larger ecological framework of systems . . . it is impossible to separate the client, the trainer, the setting, the community.*

Verbal Communication Skills

Teachers can develop and refine several technical skills to improve their ability to communicate with students.

Voice Control

Volume

Some teachers have such weak voices that most students cannot hear them. Their valuable planning is thus largely wasted. How can you ensure that everyone will hear you? The obvious answer is to speak loudly, but this may not be so easy. One way to increase your volume is to look at and talk to the students sitting across the room during the lesson. Even when you answer a question from a student in the front row, let students in the back row know that you are not ignoring them. Just because a student in the front row asks the question, do not assume that the rest of the class knows the answer.

A common mistake all teachers make is attempting to drown out talkative students. Grubaugh (1989) discusses an effective alternative: "For a teacher, it is best to time one's remarks at the trough of a wave of sound in the classroom so as to begin speaking in a softer voice to set a more quiet tone" (p. 38).

Another way to help yourself be heard is to reduce sound interference—for example, close the windows and doors to keep distracting sounds out. However, if your school does not have air conditioning, you will sometimes need to keep windows and doors open for ventilation. Traffic noises and other unavoidable interference will always require you to speak more loudly.

Tone

Once you have adequate volume, examine your voice to see if it is monotonous. Listen to yourself. When you do, you will feel obligated to speak louder, more clearly, and in a more interesting manner. If possible, have one of your lessons videotaped or make an audiotape of your classes. A videotape will help you improve your eye contact.

Clarity

An equally common voice problem is lack of clarity, frequently caused by speaking too quickly. Remember to speak slowly enough to give students time to absorb the message. Because of nervous tension, almost all beginning teachers talk too fast, leaving behind confused and discouraged students.

Pauses

At times you should pause for a minute, to give students time to think. When you introduce an important idea, stop for a minute, then continue. Also, after you ask a question, give students time to collect and organize their answers. Research shows that the most productive time lapse following a question is three seconds, but teachers usually are uncomfortable with silence and rush on after pausing for only one second (Rowe, 1978). Finally, if a student directs a question to you, pause for an instant to think before answering. A poor answer blurted out immediately is still a poor answer; a good answer is worth a moment's wait.

Even now, in your education courses, you may want to tape a short lesson given to a class of your peers. Try to have a minimum of ten or twelve students spaced throughout the room. Do not be ashamed to let others help you critique your lesson. You might ask one group to observe your voice and another to observe your eye contact.

Be aware of how you appear to students. Teachers who cannot speak in an interesting way cannot expect students to learn much. Take the time and make the effort to improve voice inflection. Finally, give students enough uninterrupted space to make errors. How can students discover or learn from mistakes if they aren't allowed to make mistakes? Borko and Elliott (1999) reported on a teacher who "often leaves the area when students are working independently because it's very difficult for her to remain there without providing assistance" (p. 398).

Set Induction

A major difference between the beginning teacher's and the experienced teacher's classes is often the amount of attention that students give the teacher at the start of the period. The experienced teacher may refuse to begin a lesson until all students give their undivided attention. You must get students to be quiet because you will generally begin a lesson with an explanation. This could describe what you have planned or be directions for the students. In either case, teachers prefer to give an introduction or directions one time only.

Teachers' strategies for getting students' attention on the lesson are collectively known as **set induction.** How do you get the whole class's attention? One approach is to face the class silently, looking at those whose attention you must capture. If you begin talking before the others are quiet, the noisy students usually get louder. Once things are quiet, you might say, "It took us a little while to get started. Is there a topic that we should discuss before we begin?" Frequently, there is, and a few minutes discussing it will be a good investment.

Another method for getting total class attention is to begin the lesson with a subject the group finds vital. It may not even be related to the day's lesson or to the subject. By listening to class conversation, you can determine what students' current interest is and begin the lesson with a discussion of that topic. Do not feel obligated to lead the discussion. Just remark, "Tom, you seem awfully interested in something. How about letting the rest of us in on it?"

Teachers have tricks for getting students' attention. Some teachers begin the period by talking very softly, then raise their voice to normal when the students become quiet. Students recognize the signal, and with some groups it is effective all year long.

There is merit in relating the attention getters to the cognitive aspects of the day's lesson. Studies have shown that by involving students cognitively, teachers can elevate students' achievement. In secondary school science classes, Riban (1976) found that having students define their own problems for investigation, discuss their problem with the teacher, and organize the collection of information, dividing responsibilities among themselves, resulted in increased student achievement that "exceeded any reasonable expectations" (p. 10).

A few days of experience will alert you to times when catching class attention will be difficult. For example, a drastic change in the weather from hot to cold or from rainy to fair, or vice versa, is an indicator of forthcoming boisterousness among middle-level students. An important high school event will often have this effect too. By keeping up with the local news, school news, and the weather, you can plan an appropriate entry into the day's lesson, for example, "Who went to the basketball game last night?" Or "Did you hear on the local news . . . ?" Once you let students express their opinions about the topic that holds their interest, they will become free to concentrate on other topics, and then you can introduce the day's planned lesson. Keep such set induction exercises brief.

Another effective method for achieving set induction is suspense. Begin the class by letting students guess what a diagram on the board represents, or begin by introducing a hypothetical case that will lead into the lesson. Perhaps you have a model that you can place so all can see it, or you may do a demonstration for the class. Such practices capture attention. You can increase effectiveness by using a few students, or perhaps the entire class, in the demonstration.

Using Examples

Examples can help clarify the lesson and make it a personal experience for each student, if the students can see how they relate to the lesson. Of course, the amount students learn depends on how clear the lesson is, but the influence of examples may be far greater than expected. One study of the effect of teacher clarity on learning found that this one variable accounted for 52 percent of the variance in mean class achievement (Hines, Cruickshank, & Kennedy, 1982).

Research shows that examples help achieve clarity. For example, effective mathematics teachers spend more time presenting new material and on guided practice than do less effective teachers (Evertson, Anderson, Anderson, & Brophy, 1980; Good & Grouws, 1979). According to Rosenshine (1986) "The effective teachers used this additional presentation time to give additional explanations and many examples" (p. 60) To be sure students understand the example, begin with simple examples and move to more complex ones.

Middle-level students tend to enjoy lessons that involve the teacher's previous experiences, especially when the examples involve activities that are most interesting to the specific age group. Ask students to give examples from time to time. By asking them for examples of the principle just introduced, you can determine how well they understand the lesson. Too often teachers follow information with the question, "Does everyone understand?" Students' admitting they do not understand is admitting a weakness that might be embarrassing. By asking an average achiever to give an example, you can gauge how clearly you have presented the lesson.

Using Repetition

Students admire and respect the teacher who takes the time and has enough patience to help those who have difficulty grasping a concept. This frequently requires repetitions. When and what should you repeat? Never refuse a serious request to repeat, but do not make the repetition verbatim. Explain the concept in different words. Saying the same thing, word for word, may elicit "I still don't get it."

Repetition is not only for the student who does not seem to understand. Full comprehension seldom comes when a concept is first introduced. All students benefit from repetition that varies from the introduction. Some classes have students who can restate what you have said well enough to help other students comprehend.

Because some students are reluctant to speak up when they are unsure, teachers may overlook the need for repetition. Because repeating everything would be boring, repeat only important points unless students request otherwise.

Providing Variety

Variety is a key element in good teaching. Every class session should contain several different experiences for each student. Do not lecture (teacher talk) or read to students for more than ten or fifteen minutes; invite students to contribute immediately afterward.

Variety is also needed from day to day. If most of today's lesson involves lecturing (heaven forbid), build tomorrow's lesson around group work, a field trip, a film, assignments at the chalkboard, or another totally different activity. Do not use a film or a group discussion for two consecutive days. Vary the activities daily or, better yet, within the period.

Using Questions

Students often become bored with lessons that are more teacher talk than student activities. Goodlad (1984) found that, on average, only 75 percent of class time is devoted to instruction, and most of that time the teacher is giving students information. Goodlad encourages teachers to teach the major principles and generalizations in their subject(s). Much of the information pertinent to any lesson is general and already known to students. To prevent monotony, intersperse questions with talking.

Do not ask only simple and basic questions, because questions can make students think. Good questions do not ask students to state a rule or quote a definition. Instead, they ask students to apply the rule. A good classroom question prompts students to use ideas rather than just remember them. Using this type of question is simple. You need only remember to ask the student for more information: "Why?" "How do you know that?" "How do you feel about that?" Direct questions to a particular student; otherwise the questions may go unanswered or the same few students may answer them all. When teachers use questions, they seldom use them in a way that promotes depth in understanding. Ellsworth and Sindt (1994) explain:

> *When many teachers question students, they often move from student to student, asking each one only one or two questions so as to involve as many students as possible. Sigel and Davis (1986) found that this practice results in very little distancing, and it is not, therefore, the best way to develop representational compliance.*

A better approach to achieving depth of understanding through questioning requires staying with a student with a succession of questions, requiring the student to explain, clarify, and justify the answer given.

Is it fair to embarrass students with direct questions? Suppose you direct a question to a student who cannot provide the correct answer. Once you direct a question to a student, you are obligated to help that student find an acceptable answer. This is not difficult if you remember to (1) pause to give time for organization of thoughts, (2) modify the answer until it is acceptable, and (3) provide hints for getting started. When used in this manner, questioning becomes a form of guided discovery. One former teacher recognizes that at times student answers will be incorrect or at best tangential and that in either case the teacher is obligated to protect the students' integrity (Mosston, 1972). He gives an example of how the teacher can respond effectively to an incorrect or tangential answer: "My question was not clear. Let me try this one. . . ."

Mosston, an expert on guided discovery, used diagrams (see Figure 10.2) to show how a series of carefully selected questions can guide students to discover relationships. Note that in Figure 10.2 the size of the steps of progress are not always equal, and neither are the sizes or frequencies of the reinforcements. To some extent the subject affects these variables, as does the learner's ability to follow a line of pursuit, and especially the teacher's skill to guide and reinforce students until they reach their goal. Mosston reminds us that in guided discovery the teacher, never the student, is the cause of failure.

When students respond correctly and confidently, you can simply ask another question or give a short statement of praise while maintaining the lesson's momentum (Rosenshine, 1986). However, if the student's response is correct but the student appears doubtful, give process feedback that explains the process used to derive the correct answer. For example, "Yes, Paul, you're correct because. . . ."

Classifying Questions

Teachers use questions to achieve very different types of objectives, so we do not rank them in higher and lower levels or from good to poor. Teachers who ask many higher-order questions (i.e., questions that seek to stimulate responses at the upper levels of the cognitive

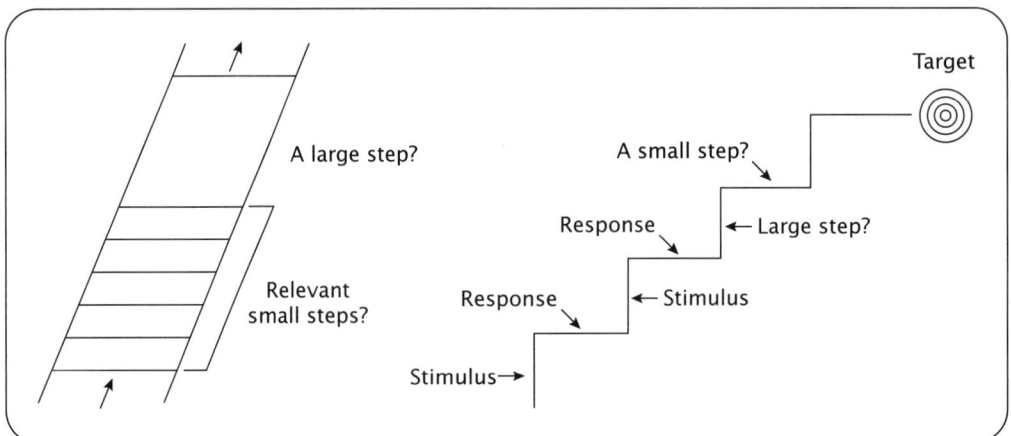

FIGURE 10.2 USING QUESTIONS TO GUIDE LEARNING This figure reminds the teacher that it is essential to remain alert to the size of the cognitive steps that are being dealt with. The size of the step determines the pace of the progress. Large steps may require large reinforcements with long intervals, whereas smaller steps may require reinforcements of less magnitude.

From *Teaching: From command to discovery* (p. 124) by M. Mosston, 1972. Belmont, CA: Wadsworth. Used with permission.

domain) have students whose attainment is higher than average (Redfield & Rousseau, 1981). Generally, however, teachers do not use higher-order questions well.

Considering the level of questions in the most widely used resource, the textbook, this is not surprising. By analyzing over 61,000 questions in textbooks, manuals, workbooks, and tests, Trachtenberg (1974) found that more than 95 percent of the questions were lower-order. Even when teachers do ask higher-order questions, their students seldom recognize that the questions are higher-order. In fact, Mills, Rice, Berliner, and Rousseau (1980) found that analysis, synthesis, and application questions elicit responses at these levels only 50 percent of the time. After reviewing the research of Mills and colleagues, Berliner (1990) concluded that "teachers need experience in learning to classify questions" (p. 64). In his book, *Strategic Questioning,* Ronald Hyman (1979) classifies questions according to cognitive process and other considerations.

We categorize questions to make them understandable. Because no one can design a system to improve the use of questions in the classroom by studying every imaginable question, we must reduce the number of elements under study by establishing categories of questions. However, the number of categories possible is also staggering, so we need to limit the number of categories. You could categorize questions according to number of words in a question or number of words required to answer a question, but such a system would be pointless. A more effective approach is to group questions according to the mental processes involved—that is, according to cognitive processes.

Cognitive Process Questions

Three main types of cognitive process questions are used regularly in classrooms: definitional questions, empirical questions, and evaluative questions. No one type is necessarily of a higher order than the others—that is, no hierarchy is implied.

THE CASE

From Empowerment to Leadership: Transforming a Problem into an Opportunity

Mary Ellen Krisko

Dr. Krisko is a former Wyoming state Teacher of the Year. She teaches at Worland Middle School in Worland, Wyoming.

Background

Empowerment affords teachers opportunities to actively participate in professional collegial relationships and to share knowledge and skills to initiate and implement pedagogical change in a professional learning community. Empowerment encourages teachers to participate in decision making with shared responsibility. Allowing teachers the opportunity to take ownership in the process encourages responsible risk taking, innovation, and creativity while sharing professional responsibilities and strengthening collegial relationships. Teachers are leaders in the classroom, but empowerment allows teachers to extend their leadership skills beyond the walls of the classroom.

Empowering a teacher with the responsibility of a position of leader puts student learning at the forefront of pedagogical change. Leadership is not a position of power or control; it is a position of responsibility. Teacher leadership has made significant advancements from traditional, formal managerial positions to leading and learning with others in a professional learning community. The impetus that has motivated schools to consider teachers for leadership positions is the paradigm shift in education reform. A leader in a restructured school facilitates the learning of others and creates strength within the school. When teachers connect through collaboration and collegiality, new forms of leadership emerge, affording teachers autonomy and active participation, and improving the school environment through continuous learning.

Leaders are learners, and teachers are at the center of student learning. As teachers lead, they develop a system-wide perspective of schooling through collaboration, communication, empowerment, collegiality, and learning. As the new emerging role of a teacher removes the teacher from isolation to active participation, new opportunities surface, student learning and performance increases, and teacher quality improves. The role of the principal changes when teachers are empowered to lead. Principals who assume a formative leadership role, partner with teachers through shared responsibility, school governance, collaboration, and collegial relationships and create a climate that allows schools to learn, grow, and change. With everyone involved, an atmosphere of commitment and excitement about learning permeates the school.

The Community

Worland is a ranching rural community in a Western state with a population of 7,000 residents. The majority of residents lives within the town but have a personal commitment to the open spaces of a Western atmosphere of ranching and farming on the plains and hunting and fishing in the nearby mountains. Students in the school district are of all economic levels, with approximately 25 percent on free or reduced-cost lunch. Although many students prepare for extending their education beyond high school in technical and college programs, many return to their hometown with little training for professional careers. Most ranching families raise cattle and horses as well as farm a portion of their land. The farming resources produce a healthy supply of sugar beets and barley for a local sugar beet processing plant and a distant beverage plant, respectively. There are a significant number of Hispanic residents located in the area, who maintain the beet fields during the growing season. A locally owned cola beverage plant employs the greatest number of residents and supports additional manufacturing companies to provide supplies and services. The business community provides a variety of products and services to support a comfortable lifestyle for semi-moderate-income families. Schooling is very important to the community, with the majority of parental support encouraging the improvement of both academic and athletic school-related activities.

The School

The middle school accommodates 356 students in grades 6, 7, and 8 and is located in the central part of the town. The school district provides bussing for all students in town as well as beyond the town limits. Twenty-four percent of the students attending are nonwhite; 26 percent are eligible for free or reduced-cost lunch; and 23 percent are identified with an Individual Educational Plan. The retention rate of students is less than 1 percent. Students have the opportunity to participate in extracurricular sports, student council, knowledge bowl, and yearbook.

When the State Department of Education developed guidelines for school improvement, the district administrators chose to approach the requirements at a superficial level, maintaining that status for a number of years. The standards and benchmarks were acquired by a nearby district that had contracted with consultants. With state dollars attached to the school improvement accreditation process, the district became uncomfortably aware of the consequences and ramifications of noncompliance with the guidelines, and time was running short regarding the deadline for validation of compliance. School improvement became a reality and a priority. The school district, under the direction of a new administration, empowered the principals of each school to comply with the guidelines of the State Department of Education.

The Leaders

The principal of the middle school assigned the task of school improvement to the grade-level and exploratory team leaders: Kent Gillette, Caroline Downs, Wendy Schmidt, and myself. We team leaders and newly appointed members of the School Improvement Steering Committee shouldered the responsibility of developing and implementing a school improvement plan and process, respectively. Kent was a former P.E. teacher who at the time taught eighth-grade science; Caroline, a certified science teacher, was teaching seventh-grade language arts; Wendy was the family and consumer science teacher with an elementary background; and I taught sixth-grade science. This core of teachers led the middle school staff members on a teacher-driven journey beyond anyone's expectations. For the process to be successful, the group of individuals chose to look at this task as empowerment rather than coercion, and as a challenge and an opportunity rather than a problem. Richard Schaal was hired as the new middle school principal and, respecting the responsibility of the steering committee, endorsed the accomplishments of our middle school staff.

Issues in Implementation

Six and a half years ago, four members of our middle school staff were placed in a rather uncomfortable position by my previous principal. We had to extend our skills beyond the walls of the classroom and to prepare our school for state accreditation within a seven-month period. Through collaborative efforts, our staff took advantage of an opportunity, which came as quickly as the "teachable moment." We turned a huge problem into an opportunity and that opportunity involved empowering the middle school staff in the school improvement process.

After attending a state accreditation meeting, our principal at that time called our school's grade-level and exploratory team leaders into his office. I was the sixth-grade team leader. In his office he mentioned that he needed someone to be responsible for organizing and coordinating the school improvement process for our school. There would be no compensation, and the work would be done on our own time. We looked at each other and decided that none of us wanted the job. After a bit of prompting, I was selected to take on this task. I was handed a large, black, State Department notebook and told, "This is what needs to be done." The grade-level team leaders were instructed to serve on a Steering Committee for guidance and support. They expressed their sympathies to me as they left the office, and I gave them the "Krisko Glare." I knew I couldn't do this. With a sophomore in college and a junior in high school, I was already exhausted trying to pick up a few extra dollars teaching a college biology night class. I tried to explain, but to no avail. So, I took the scary-looking black notebook and began to read. After a week of stewing and fussing, I was told that we would have three workdays during the rest of the school year to work on these projects and the State Department would be here in late October. I looked at my boss in disbelief. Years of work to do in seven months.

I am a task-driven person with a strong work ethic. I decided that the only way to pull off this horrendous task was to be positive and look upon this as an opportunity and a challenge. Our newly formed Steering Committee met and developed an action plan for school improvement accreditation. At the first staff meeting I explained what needed to be done. The staff just looked at me. I explained to them that we had an opportunity and a challenge. For years we have been coasting, doing our "own thing," yet at the same time, gathering valuable experience and developing ideas working with students. Our staff had written curriculum guides, discipline procedures, and course outlines, which continued to remain on the shelf gathering dust. For the first time our staff had an opportunity to use our pedagogical expertise and make things happen, allowing school improvement to be teacher-driven within the guidelines of the State Department. The staff kept looking at me. Not a word was said. I was confused, for I didn't hear the typical moans and groans. The "why reinvent the wheel" or "this too shall pass" statements were never mentioned.

I continued with the Steering Committee's plan, explaining the timeline for the project and the committees that needed to be formed. Still, they just looked at me. The Steering Committee members were strategically seated throughout the room, and Wendy, a member of the Steering Committee, stood up and asked if anyone in the room could state the mission statement of our school. No one could. She read it and asked what it meant. No one knew. Then Caroline and Kent quietly began to distribute sign-up sheets for the numerous committees we had planned to establish, and the staff began to respond. Committees were formed; each staff member was empowered with a specific responsibility, and a Steering Committee member would serve on the committee as a resource person. Clerical staff, custodians, cafeteria workers, counselors, administration, and teachers were involved. The question came up: "When are we supposed to do this?" I alluded to "now" and suggested guidelines for the committee structure. Select a chairman, seek solutions, and don't dwell on the problem. Consider a few options and propose it to the staff, which will be called the "Committee of the Whole" to arrive at a consensus. We began.

Within two weeks we had a mission statement with meaning, we had belief statements, and we had a good start on developing a student profile, which we had never done before. The Committee of the Whole met and a consensus was reached, accepting the first proposals. The excitement began. Within a month, skills, standards, assessments, community involvement, school climate, staff development, at-risk identification, facilities, and budget were addressed. Surveys were taken. Data were collected. During the third month standards were written, and the Steering Committee tried to keep a step ahead, providing models and samples to use. Every time the staff gathered, we fed them—cookies, popcorn, bowls of fruit, pop, donuts, etc.—to keep them going. The response was much more than ever expected. Whenever the Committee of the Whole achieved a consensus, we celebrated, and the enthusiasm became overwhelming. The reservoir of skills and knowledge from our colleagues overflowed.

Four months into the project, when thirty parents made a surprise visit at our school with a carry-in lunch, relieving us of our noontime duties to show their appreciation, we knew we were on the right track. Our staff was excited, for we had generated respect from the community and the community was becoming involved—a first for our school. By the end of the school year, standards and competencies were written, aligned with an appropriate core of skills, and a tremendous amount of data had been collected. Now, it was my turn to compile and organize everyone's work. It took the summer months to pull the work together, and out staff developed an incredibly awesome 149-page document.

During the summer, the Steering Committee met to discuss our next move. We had a new principal, Richard Schaal, and felt it necessary to "clue him in." He recognized our efforts and accomplishments and became as excited as we were, committing his total support. Our district secured the services of a consultant to help with the process. We learned how to develop goals from surveys and data collected refining our goals for our School Improvement plan.

When the new school year started in the fall, we continued at the same pace that was established the previous spring. The State Department was coming in late October, and we had a lot to do to polish our program. Goals became measurable. Flowcharts were developed. Each step generated more excitement, and we continued to celebrate. By mid-October, we realized that our school had developed a well-organized program. We had created an educational package that was compatible with our school and community. We did it; we did it well; we did it as a team; and we were very proud. I have never seen a staff so delighted with their accomplishments. We couldn't wait for the State Department to visit.

We took a problem and approached it as a challenge, which resulted in an opportunity. It took all of us—parents, community, students, and staff. Did the State Department approve? Mostly . . . we knew we had a weakness in assessments that needed work, which required more time. That was okay with us. What the State Department couldn't see was the tremendous cohesiveness established in our academic community and the dedication and commitment we made to our profession and to ourselves. We took the opportunity using our skills, knowledge, and experience. It was an awesome example of professionalism, empowering our middle school staff with the responsibility of the pedagogical process and creating a learning community with teachers as leaders participating in the decision-making process.

Further Reflection

1. How has education reform changed the role of today's middle-level teachers?
2. Why is it especially crucial for education reform in middle schools to be at the teacher level?
3. Dr. Krisko says that middle school teachers must be empowered. How can you increase your own power outside your classroom?
4. Why did the Steering Committee begin its work by writing a mission statement?
5. What was the Committee's reaction when it was told that the program had weaknesses, and how did it take this news?
6. This book emphasizes the importance of connections at the middle level. What role did connections play in this case study?
7. How does cooperative curriculum planning help teachers become life-long learners?
8. This case talks about a *learning community*. What is a learning community, and why are they important to middle schools?
9. How did this team solicit community involvement?

Definitional Questions

Definitional questions require students (or teachers) to define a word, term, or phrase. The following are examples of definitional questions:

1. What is a tornado?
2. Give an example of a verse in iambic pentameter.
3. What does it mean to play "piano"?

Notice that definitional questions search for exact answers or "true" feelings. In other words, you either know the correct answer or you don't.

Empirical Questions

Unlike definitional questions, which ask for a definite, specific answer, empirical questions give respondents an opportunity to express their perceptions of the world. These questions may ask for facts, generalizations, comparisons, explanations, conclusions, or inferences. For example:

1. Who wrote the play *Hamlet?* (Fact)
2. What generalizations can you make about the lifestyle in Great Britain? (Generalization)

3. How are American football and European football similar? Different? (Comparison)
4. What did the poet mean by the lines, "Oh, what tangled webs we weave when first we practice to deceive"? (Explanation)
5. What conclusions can you draw when you know that the number of lives lost in traffic accidents decreased by 50 percent following enactment of the 55-mph national speed law? (Conclusion)
6. On any day of the year, the number of drownings in the state of New York correlates significantly with the total sales of ice cream in the state. What do you infer from these data? (Inference)

Each of these empirical questions prompts us to observe the world around us to find answers and proof that our answers are correct.

Evaluative Questions

Evaluative questions ask students to express their opinions or values. They ask the respondent either to express an opinion or to justify one. For example:

1. Who is the greatest living fiction writer? (Opinion)
2. Why do you say that the Rolls Royce is the best car ever made? (Justification of opinion)

Now we will expand the three major types of cognitive process questions into a set of five categories:

1. Definitional
    a. Definitions
2. Empirical
    b. Facts
    c. Relationships of facts (generalizations, comparisons, explanations, conclusions, or inference)
3. Evaluative
    d. Opinions
    e. Justification of opinions

Using these five categories, write your categorizing number to the left of each question.

_____ 1. Which is worse—a tornado or a hurricane?
_____ 2. What is a sonnet?
_____ 3. You said that the Edsel was actually a very good car. How do you know this?
_____ 4. In what year did the Revolutionary War end?
_____ 5. What do you think is the major difference between the Democratic Party and the Republican Party?
_____ 6. Who was the greatest U.S. President of the twentieth century?
_____ 7. How fast does light travel?
_____ 8. What did Patrick Henry mean by "Give me liberty or give me death!"?
_____ 9. What is a decibel?
_____ 10. When did the stock market first crash?

Other Types of Questions

We have seen that questions used in the classroom can be effective when they are selected, analyzed, and grouped according to the cognitive processes they provoke. However, there are other considerations. For example, what demands does the question place on students? Does it require them to reproduce information given in class, or does it demand that they assemble information to produce their own answers? Another consideration might be the kind of mental activity or process the question requires. Except for rhetorical questions, which are not intended to draw a response, all questions must tell students what behavior is expected of them. A third consideration is the type of cue, if any, that the question gives to help clarify the expected answer.

Productive versus Reproductive Questions

A productive question asks students either to produce their own information (a productive question) or to reproduce an answer given earlier by another source, such as the textbook or teacher (a reproductive question). The context of the question determines whether it is productive or reproductive. For instance, if the question "Why did the issue of Soviet military forces in Cuba resurface in 1979?" had been discussed in class, or if you refer to a certain cause given by specific media, the question is reproductive. If the issue has not been discussed previously, students create their own explanations, making the question productive.

Information-Process Activity Questions

A second comparison is the information-process activity that you want the student to perform. There are three general ways you may expect students to perform: yes/no, selection, and construction. An example of a yes/no question is: "In the 1992 Presidential election, did President Clinton carry the state of New York?" Selection questions require the respondent to select from two or more given alternatives—for example, "Is *lonely* an adjective or an adverb?" Construction questions require students to construct their own response: "Explain your position on abortion."

Response-Clue Questions

There are five types of response-clue questions, which give clues to the type of response desired: *Wh*-words, parallel terms, cited terms, excluded terms, and questions that lead the respondent.

1. Questions with *Wh-words*, such as *when, why, what, who,* and *how,* may clue the student to answer in terms of time, reasons, things, people, and number.
2. Questions with *parallel terms* ask the student to provide more information about the same topic: "Can you give another reason?" "And then what happened?" "Who else was involved?"
3. Questions with *cited terms* offer a framework for the response—for example, "Which is the best college football team this year, in terms of cooperative teamwork?" "What were the major causes of the American Revolution, including social, economic, and political?"
4. Questions with *excluded terms* tell the respondent what not to include in answering—for example, "Other than its cost, why is electricity an undesirable source for heating homes?" "Besides earning good grades, why do you believe it is necessary to learn all you can?"

5. Questions that *lead or guide* the respondent to a yes or no response—for example, "Don't you agree?" "It's rather humid, isn't it?" "Most American cars aren't subcompacts, are they?"

The Questioning Grid

The questioning grid shown in Figure 10.3 can be used as an observation instrument in the classroom to record and classify questions as they are asked. For this purpose you may wish to record a T in the appropriate cells for all questions you ask and an S in the appropriate cells for each question students ask. Next to each question, list its type. Consider the following sample questions and their classifications:

Practice Questions	Question Type
1. To convert from centimeters to millimeters, do you divide?	Yes/no; reproduction
2. What is the symbol for silver—Ag or Si?	Selection: *Wh*-productive
3. What is the best gas to burn in a lawnmower?	Selection: *Wh*-reproductive
4. Is Athens the capital of Greece?	Construction-reproductive
5. If we exhaust our petroleum, will we turn to using coal?	Yes/no; productive
6. What are the basic differences between the Democratic and Republican parties?	Constructive: *Wh*-productive

			Production Type		**Information-Process Activity**			**Response-Clue**				
			Productive	**Reproductive**	**Yes/No**	**Selection**	**Construction**	***Wh*-Interrogative Words**	**Parallel Terms**	**Cited Terms**	**Excluded Terms**	**Leading the Respondent**
	Short Set	Expanded Set										
Cognitive Process	Definitional	Definitions										
Cognitive Process	Empirical	Facts										
Cognitive Process	Empirical	Relations between facts										
Cognitive Process	Evaluative	Opinions										
Cognitive Process	Evaluative	Justifications										

FIGURE 10.3 THE QUESTIONING GRID

From *Strategic Questioning* (p. 29) by Ronald Hyman, Englewood Cliffs, NJ: Prentice-Hall. Reprinted by permission.

Reinforcement

You frequently can elicit desired pupil behavior by using reinforcement. All students want to be able to answer questions and perform assigned classroom tasks; they also want to believe that the teacher looks on them favorably. Some students do not believe they can benefit from school because they feel incapable of "fitting in." Such special cases are discussed later. Here we will look at how a teacher can affect a student's attitude through reinforcement.

Too often the teacher responds to a student with "You're right, but that's not the answer I wanted," leaving the student confused and discouraged. Why not reverse this response, make the correction, and leave the student feeling correct? For example, "Your answer is not what I was looking for, but you are absolutely correct" or "That's interesting. I was expecting you to say . . . but you didn't. You gave an answer I had not even thought about."

To be effective, be sincere and address specific achievements. Former Alabama Teacher of the Year Susan Lloyd says, "Praise is a very effective way to encourage students. Simply notice when they do well, especially when they put forth special effort or when they've been creative and self-motivated. The only requirement is that the praise be sincere" (cited in Henson & Eller, 1999, p. 170). Too often teachers get into a rut and use the same reinforcement for every student. For example, they tend to overuse such general expressions as "good" and "okay," making the reward routine and ineffective. Other teachers overemphasize or overdramatize reward; sensing insincerity, students become skeptical of the teacher.

How can you judge how much emphasis to place on rewarding? The best guide is to consider the age group and give rewards only when students have earned them. Overpraising can easily embarrass students from middle-level age upward and produce negative results. The key is to allow each student to feel successful at least one time every day. For some students this will require teacher concentration, but with experience you will learn to create opportunities for students to experience success.

Review

Review is needed at least twice within each lesson—at the beginning and at the end. Between one day and the next, many things can intervene and distort students' memories of the previous lesson. By beginning each lesson with a brief review of the previous day's high points, you can tune students back into the topic under study.

According to Rosenshine (1986):

Effective teachers begin a lesson with a five to eight minute review of previous material, correction of homework, and review of relevant prior knowledge. To make sure that students possess the prerequisite skills for the day's lesson, the teacher can review concepts and necessary skills to do the next day's homework; have students correct each other's papers; ask about items where the students had difficulty or made errors; and review or provide additional practice on facts and skills that need reteaching. (p. 64)

Review at the end of the period can reemphasize the major points covered during the lesson, clarify the lesson, remove any misconceptions, and give students a feeling of accomplishment. Make a special effort to include material that will resurface at a later date. "Daily review is particularly important for teaching material that will be used in subsequent learning, for example, math facts, reading sight words, and grammar and skills such as math computation, math factoring, or solving chemical equations" (Rosenshine, 1986, pp. 64–65).

Teacher as Proactive Decision Maker

Classroom Situation

1. You will have in your classes several students who will welcome opportunities to demonstrate their knowledge and, in general, show off. Instead of trying to suppress this natural desire to let others know about their talents, provide a forum to let students communicate their special knowledge and skills.

Proactive Alternatives

1. Arrange for your class to be videotaped. You and your students may have to operate the camera. Let each student make a short two-minute presentation, giving students the option of working in groups.

2. Make videotaping a common activity in your classes. Tape each group presentation of assigned projects.

3. Many large schools have video communications of their own daily announcements piped into the classroom. Check with your principal. If your school has such equipment, schedule time for your students to become involved in these programs.

When reviewing, carefully select and clarify the major concepts developed during a period. Encourage students to ask questions about concepts they do not understand. This enables them to correct misconceptions and to process further the information they have gained. MacKenzie and White (1982) found that eighth- and ninth-grade students retained information gathered on a geography field trip when the trip was followed by such review activities as small-group discussions, sketching, and tasting leaves they had collected. Review also contributes to student achievement because it raises the level of students' interaction or involvement with the lesson. Used correctly, reviewing involves explicit instruction. During "explicit" instruction in well-structured areas, the teacher initially takes full responsibility for performing a task but, to increase students' alertness, gradually involves them in this part of the lesson.

Nonverbal Communication Skills

According to Galloway (1984) educators often overlook the relationship of setting and context to individual behavior and the influence of nonverbal expressions on teacher–student relationships. Students are turned on more by how we say things than by what we say. They watch constantly for excitement or enthusiasm in the teacher's expression. Even when you are not instructing verbally, students are getting information about how you feel. You communicate your attitudes, likes, dislikes, approval, and disapproval through facial expressions and other body language.

Whether they realize it or not, some teachers use their desks as walls for protection from their students; others use them as a symbol of authority. Thus the desk can become a nonverbal psychological barrier to good teacher–student communications. Until the teacher moves from behind it, true communication is not likely to occur.

The next time you are a classroom observer, take notes on the teacher's nonverbal communication. See how many different ways this teacher communicates nonverbally. If before you graduate you have an opportunity to peer-teach a lesson or to teach a lesson to public school students, near the end of the lesson you might ask your students what different ways they believed you were communicating nonverbally with them. Ask how they felt about what you did and about how you did it. Today's students tend to be honest and say what they feel, so you can learn much from them.

Feedback

While students receive nonverbal communication from you, you can simultaneously receive feedback from them. Alert teachers watch their students' movements and emotions and use what they see to adjust their teaching methods. For example, suppose several students begin yawning while you are teaching. You might open a window or lower the room thermostat. If the drowsiness continues, you might change your teaching style to include more inflection in your voice. Unless you are dealing with students who come from very poor homes—and therefore have poor nutrition and inadequate sleeping facilities—or with students who have night jobs, the yawning can probably be attributed to something you are or are not doing. Again, be aware of any clues students give you regarding a communication breakdown.

Another way to obtain feedback is to change the bulletin board to let students give their impressions of you. For example, at the end of each lesson or each day, middle-level students might be given a positive "thumbs-up tab" or a negative "purple-shaft tab" to attach to the board to show how the teacher left them feeling on that particular day. High-school teachers may prefer to use a closed suggestion box. You should use this information to improve your teaching style. For best results, let the students put the symbols on the board anonymously, lest some respond the way they think you want them to.

Eye Contact

An important nonverbal teaching skill is eye contact. Teaching should be a multichanneled dialogue. Beginning teachers, usually because of insecurity, avoid direct eye contact with students and instead look at their notes. To prevent this, try using fewer notes. A list of the major ideas—or at most a broad outline of the lesson—may work better than a detailed lesson plan. Focus on a few individuals in each conversation. Public school teaching is not lecturing. It is a multicommunicative process between teacher and students and among students.

We all know people who, when they talk to us, look over our shoulders, above us, or anywhere but directly at us. A little disconcerting, isn't it? We may become so distracted by this annoying behavior that we miss what they are saying. It's no different in the classroom. Without eye contact, teachers experience a communication breakdown and the learning environment becomes far from optimal.

Other Nonverbal Teacher Behaviors

Much of what a teacher does can be characterized as a combination of verbal and nonverbal behaviors. When you ask a student to settle down, you are communicating verbally. At the same time, however, you may be gesturing with your hands or giving a look that is actually more effective in getting your point across. Here are a few examples of such verbal and nonverbal communication (addressing mainly the nonverbal):

1. You have asked a question to which the student has responded incorrectly. Smiling, you indicate in a nice way that you were seeking a different answer. Your smile alone says, "That's all right. Nobody's perfect."

2. While you are talking, you see a student poking his pencil at a classmate. You pause, tilt your head downward, and look over the top of your glasses. The foolishness stops immediately.

These are examples of occasions when your nonverbal behavior can play an extremely important role in teacher–student relationships. With verbal reprimands only, these relationships would tend to weaken.

Body Movement

The time when teachers hid behind a desk is, we hope, long gone. You must circulate among your students so you can communicate with each one. Because talking to individual students often disturbs the others, much of the communication must be done nonverbally. Walk throughout the room, pause momentarily, or give a smile and nod your head to give your students confidence in you. Older students prefer nods, winks, and hand signals to excessive touching. Even more important, this type of individual recognition can help build self-confidence. Students feel good about themselves when they know their teacher is pleased with them.

Using Silence

Most teachers talk too much. After studying teachers for eight years, Goodlad (1984) reported that, on average, teachers talk 75 percent of each class period, leaving little opportunity for pupil participation. Good and Brophy (1997) say that "Teachers dominate classroom discussion, even sometimes they do not want to and are not aware of their behavior" (p. 25). Learning to remain quiet requires self-discipline. When advised by her supervisor that she talked too much, a first-year teacher made tapes of her classes and kept a daily log of her experiences. Over time she was able to analyze, record, and evaluate her progress. However, she did more. On her desk, she put a sign that said in Swedish, "Shut up." The teacher explained that she had a tendency to answer her own questions before the students could. She then noted, "The uncomfortable quiet can actually be a time for thinking . . . and if the teacher outwaits the students, one of the latter will begin speaking."

How much silence can you tolerate? How much can you refrain from talking? Instead of feeling obligated to respond to student comments, encourage other students to respond. Try to lead rather than dominate the discussions.

You will be asked many questions for which you will not have an answer. To bluff is pure folly, because it can misguide students and destroy your credibility. Do not feel obligated to know all the answers. Admitting your limitations will not show weakness if you show a willingness to seek the answers.

The Hidden Curriculum

The total process of communicating nonverbally, intentionally or not, has a considerable effect on students. Sometimes the effects are positive, and sometimes they are negative. Nonverbal communication is part of the hidden curriculum. Michael Radz (1978) states the significance of the hidden curriculum:

> One should not underestimate the knowledge, skills, and attitudes that are acquired through the informal culture of the school. Indeed, the hidden curriculum can reinforce classroom learning or make it a gross hypocrisy. It can promote the development of individual self-esteem or it can crush a fragile self-concept. It can make learning a meaningless experience in gamesmanship. (p. 6)

Teachers can use the hidden curriculum to communicate positive, constructive messages. For example, an orderly, task-oriented classroom routine can socialize students to the world of work (Doyle, 1986). The energy needed to communicate positive constructives can come from various sources, but it cannot come from nowhere. One possible energy source for helping at-risk students become more positive and self-confident is arts education. According to Sautter (1994):

> The arts promote the "hidden curriculum" of social behavior to improve self-discipline, self-motivation, self-esteem, and social interaction. These are all necessary characteristics contained within the spirit of the arts. (p. 436)

For further discussion on the significance of the hidden curriculum, see Henson (2001).

Detecting Boredom

Another group of nonverbal signals that teachers must learn to recognize are those that show boredom. Nierenberg's *How to Read a Person Like a Book* (1971) includes in this group: resting head in hands, giving a blank stare, and doodling. Other clear indicators of boredom are squirming (because it involves movement of the entire body as one shifts weight from hip to hip while simultaneously repositioning arms, legs, feet, and hands) and yawning, which adds the dimension of sound. Squirming might carry other messages, such as a need to use the restroom, and yawning may indicate a physical need for sleep, but what they probably mean is that communications are breaking down.

Students are also frequently seen resting their heads in their hands. They may or may not be aware that this gesture also symbolizes boredom. By the time they reach middle school, some know that such actions are not polite and have begun substituting more subtle expressions, such as giving a blank stare or silently doodling. A few highly creative individuals do express their creativity through doodling, and a few great thinkers are glassy-eyed

---

Proactive Exercise

Anticipated Situation

- You know that:

Some of your students will appear to be unmotivated. But the literature (Englander, 1999) tells us that everyone is motivated, although perhaps not toward academic matters. There are over thirty motivators that teachers can use in the classroom.

Proactive Alternative

- You can:

Focus on internal locus of control. Devise activities to enhance students' self-perceptions. You might begin by discovering student accomplishments and making these known in your classrooms.

Some of your students will have advanced computer skills. Ask these students to take on projects that involve helping classmates master new computer skills.

Encourage students to mentor classmates who are not as advanced in the topic under study. Prepare a reward system that gives credits to students whose help results in raising the performance level of the students they help.

when they engage in deep thought, but these are a minority and their wisdom can be detected by examining their drawings or pursuing their thoughts with questions. Sometimes students offer fake, hollow stares to trick the teacher, but most students today are quite open, both verbally and nonverbally.

Beyond the Curriculum

Half (52 percent) of all teachers believe that teachers should be involved with making changes in extracurricular activities. Three-fourths (76 percent) of all students believe that parents should be actively involved in changing the school's extracurricular activities. As shown in Table 10.1 students' support for parents' involvement is high; only one in five (19 percent) do not support parent involvement in extracurriculum decisions (MLS, 1998, p. 98).

The computer offers an unprecedented opportunity for parents to be connected to their children's academics around the clock. By setting up bulletin boards and list-serves, teachers can keep a continuous string of announcements to parents. Of particular value is the listing of due dates of assignments and dates of coming tests. No longer do parents need to ask their children what they learned in school today or what their teachers expect them to be doing.

Effective Schools Research

The effective schools research has provided additional insights that teachers can use to improve communications in the classroom. After reviewing approximately two decades of school effectiveness, Ornstein and Levine (1990) offer guidelines for implementing six multi-school projects to generate more effective elementary and secondary schools.

1. Enforce discipline; the school must be safe and orderly.
2. Establish remedial and tutoring programs.
3. Teachers must assign and properly check homework. Students must be held accountable for homework; teachers must explain and discuss homework.
4. Improvement goals must be sharply focused to avoid teacher and school overload.
5. Instructional teachers must avoid elaborate schemes to train all staff and must focus on a particular instructional technique.

TABLE 10.1 Students' Opinions on the Say Parents Should Have on Homework Assignments

QB8.2: How much of a say should parents have in decisions your school makes in the following areas: Homework assignments—how much and how often? Base: All students

| | | Sex | | Race/Ethnicity | | | |
| | | | | White | | Minority | |
	TOTAL	MALE	FEMALE	MALE	FEMALE	MALE	FEMALE
Base:	1,301	613	688	391	429	156	198
	%	%	%	%	%	%	%
A lot	19	21	18	17	16	30	21
Some	41	37	44	38	45	37	44
None	35	36	34	41	35	24	30
Don't know	5	6	5	4	4	9	5

6. Significant technical assistance must be available to faculty.
7. Effective school projects should be data-driven.
8. Effective schools must avoid reliance on bureaucratic implementation that stresses forms and checklists.
9. Effective schools should seek out and consider using materials, methods, and approaches that have been successful elsewhere.
10. The success of an effective school's project depends on a judicious mixture of autonomy among participating faculties and a mixture of autonomy among the faculties and directives from the central office, a kind of "directed autonomy."

Effective schools research also reports that academic achievement is highest at schools that become learning communities, where teachers plan and dialogue together. Former Utah Teacher of the Year Marilyn Grondel (1999) (quoted in Henson & Eller, 1999) echoed this when she said, "I believe that a successful teacher does not keep ideas and materials secret. A successful teacher becomes more successful by dialoguing with colleagues and sharing ideas and materials (p. 317)." Implied in this statement is that these teachers read professional journals daily, so as to have worthwhile ideas and materials to share. Flowers, Mertens, & Mulhall (2002) stress the importance of teacher dialogue: "We believe that providing teachers with opportunities to have structured discussions around improvement issues and best practices is also a very engaging and worthwhile professional development experience" (p. 58).

Vignettes

The following experiences give you an opportunity to see how important good communications are in instruction.

Vignette One: A Need for Tact in Questioning

Jack Cobb was a good biology teacher who planned thoroughly. Each day's lesson was highly content-oriented, but there was room for student participation. Jack claimed to be student-centered, but he was not very patient when he asked questions. In one particular class period he damaged the self-esteem of three students considered slow learners. In each case he had asked a question to which the student responded incorrectly. His response was "That's wrong. Who knows the answer?"

DISCUSSION

1. How can students be made to feel successful when responding incorrectly to a question? This chapter makes it clear that the teacher has both the opportunity and the responsibility for making a student feel successful. No matter how incorrect a response, a resourceful teacher can guide the student out of despair or embarrassment. Some techniques for doing this have been discussed, but here is another possibility:

   Jack Cobb did not realize, or did not care, that his remarks left students feeling inadequate. He could have said, "I don't believe you're totally correct. Would you like some help?" The student would surely have said yes. Then he could ask for volunteers. When the correct answer was given, Jack could go back to the original student and say, "Do you think that's right?"

   This type of response will let a student know that he or she was incorrect but will not exclude that student from the discussion. The student makes the decision to seek assistance and has the final comment, since the teacher returns to him or her for verification of the correct response.

2. Should slow learners be asked questions in class? All students should have an opportunity to respond to questions or to originate questions of

their own, but the teacher should be selective in matching questions to students. Unfortunately, too many questions require short answers of merely yes or no, but this may be the best type of question to ask a student with low achievement. Although shallow questions and responses result in little additional knowledge, they do give the student a chance to be successful.

However, slow students should not receive only low-level questions. When a student volunteers to respond to a question that appears too difficult, the student deserves a chance to try. If correct, the student will be pleased and so will you. The experience might provide the encouragement needed for accepting other challenges.

Vignette Two: Teaching Students, Not Subjects

When Sue began teaching in middle school, her students were amazed at how smart she was. She seemed to have the facts, names, and dates all memorized, and she could give from memory every detail of any war. But Sue never tried to show off. She was in fact a borderline introvert. When the beginning bell rang for each period, she seemed to lack the courage necessary to start the lesson. After calling the roll, she would mumble about the homework assignment for several minutes without looking up from her book. A typical lesson started like this:

[Looking down at her text]: All right, class, what did we learn yesterday? What did we say was the cause of World War II? What did we learn about Germany's economic status at the time? Why did the United States stay out of the war for so long?"

DISCUSSION

1. Why do you think Sue talked to her book instead of to her students?
2. How could Sue improve her questioning?

Summary

Teaching cannot occur without excellent communications. Effective teachers hold high but realistic expectations for all students; they know what they expect their students to gain from their classes and they know how to communicate these expectations clearly. For example, they begin their lessons with advance organizers to focus student attention on the important concepts, and when asking questions, effective teachers give students time to create good responses, even helping them when they falter. Effective teachers help their students succeed in many ways. One of the most important messages they communicate to their students is belief that all students in each class have the ability to succeed and the teacher has the ability to ensure that this happens.

Having good communications also requires a personal approach. Teachers must listen to their students. When using examples, they choose those that their students can easily relate to. Finally, effective teachers get involved with action research, working to improve the quality of daily learning in their classes.

Recap of Major Ideas

1. Teacher efficacy is essential for maximum learning and is established by setting clear goals and objectives, quickly getting all students on task, and keeping them on task until the goals and objectives are attained.
2. Teachers must communicate to students how each class activity relates to class goals. Otherwise, students will not know the purpose of the activities they are doing.
3. By communicating high but realistic levels of expectations to students, teachers can increase the amount of learning in each class.
4. Teacher educators have failed to impress on prospective teachers the importance of research for classroom teaching. As new information is discovered, teachers can use it to improve their teaching in ways that are currently unknown.
5. Teachers usually give students only one second to respond to questions. By giving them three seconds, they can significantly improve the learning process.

6. By listening to students, teachers can identify topics that prove to be excellent channels of communication.
7. Do not begin or continue a lesson without all students' attention.
8. Choose examples that relate to adolescent experiences rather than those that relate to your experiences.
9. When directing a question to a student, help the student respond favorably.
10. Nonverbal teacher behaviors communicate important messages to students. Improve your nonverbal communication skills by observing and critiquing yourself.
11. Get involved with research studies to improve your observational skills, instructional decision-making skills, and lesson-planning skills.

Activities

Good teaching requires good communication, but this does not always happen automatically. Some teachers depend mostly on verbal communications; others, who are less verbal, use more nonverbal strategies to communicate. Every teacher should combine verbal and nonverbal strategies to improve two-way communications in the classroom. The following activities may challenge you to relate these strategies to your own behavior style.

1. How much do you talk? When you are in a one-on-one conversation with a colleague, who dominates the discussion? Think about it. Do you tend to talk too much? Too little? Devise a plan for helping yourself reach a balance.
2. Now that you are aware of a number of effective nonverbal strategies for communicating, relate this knowledge to teaching. Consider your unique attributes and explain how you can use nonverbal communication techniques in your classroom.
3. From your own experience as a student, can you list any techniques not included in this book that could be effective for classroom application?
4. Check the library for additional recent books and articles on business and speech communications. Try to relate each to teaching, altering it to serve teachers better. Check for books that portray minority students very positively. Make a list of these books.

Looking Ahead

This chapter has suggested several ways you can improve your communications skills. The following chapter will continue this theme by helping you capture students' attention and hold that attention throughout each lesson.

References

Armstrong, D. G., Henson, K. T., & Savage, T. V. (2004). *Teaching today* (7th ed.). New York: Prentice-Hall.

Berliner, D. C. (1990, March). Creating the right environment for learning. *Instructor, 99,* 16–17.

Borko, H., & Elliott, R. (1999). Hands-on pedagogy vs. hands-off accountability. *Phi Delta Kappan, 80*(5), 394–400.

Brooks, D. M. (1985). Beginning the year in junior high: The first day of school. *Educational Leadership, 42,* 76–78.

Bruner, J. S. (1981). On instructability. Presented at the meeting of the American Psychological Association, Los Angeles.

Buckner, J. H., and Bickel, F. (1991, January). If you want to know effective teaching, why not ask your middle school kids? *Middle School Journal, 22*(3), 26–29.

Carnegie Council on Adolescent Development Staff (1995). *Great transitions: Preparing adolescents for a new century.* New York: Carnegie Foundation.

Cazden, C. (1986). Classroom discourse. In M. C. Wittrock (Ed.), *Handbook of research on teaching methods* (3rd ed.). New York: Macmillan.

Doyle, W. (1986). Classroom organization and management. In M. C. Wittrock (Ed.), *Handbook of research on teaching* (3rd ed.). New York: Macmillan.

Eisner, E. (2002). The kind of schools we need. *Phi Delta Kappan, 83*(8), 576–583.

Ellsworth, P. C., & Sindt, V. G. (1994). Helping "Aha" to happen: The contributions of Irving Sigel. *Educational Leadership, 51*(5), 40–44.

Evertson, C. C., Anderson, G., Anderson, L., & Brophy, J. (1980). Relationships between classroom behaviors and student outcomes in junior high mathematics and English classes. *American Educational Research Journal, 17,* 43–60.

Fisher, C. W. (1980). Teaching behavior, academic learning time, and student achievement: An overview. In C. Denham & A. Lieberman (Eds.), *Time to learn* (p. 26). Washington, DC: U.S. Department of Education, National Institute of Education.

Flowers, N. M., Mertens, S. B., & Mulhall, P. F. (2002). Research on middle school renewal. *Middle School Journal, 33*(5), 57–61.

Fuller, B. (1982). The organizational context of individual efficacy. *Review of Educational Research, 52*(1), 7–30.

Galloway, C. M. (Ed.) (1984). Nonverbal and teacher-student relationships: An intercultural perspective. *Theory into Practice, 16*(3), 129–133.

Good, T. L. (1984, August). Presented at the First Annual Conference for Relating Research and Practice, Michigan State University, East Lansing, MI.

Good, T. L., & Brophy, J. (1995). *Contemporary educational psychology* (5th ed). White Plains, NY: Longman.

Good, T. L., & Brophy, J. (1997). *Looking in classrooms* (7th ed.). White Plains, NY: Longman.

Good, T. L., & Grouws, D. A. (1979). The Missouri mathematics effectiveness project. *Journal of Educational Psychology, 71,* 143–155.

Goodlad, J. I. (1984). *A place called school.* New York: McGraw-Hill.

Green, J. L. (1983). A study of schooling: Some findings and hypotheses. *Phi Delta Kappan, 64,* 465–470.

Gronbeck, B. E., McKerron, R. E., Ehninger, R. D., & Monroe, A. H. (1994). *Principles and types of speech communication* (12th ed). New York: HarperCollins.

Grondel, M. (1999) A teacher's class. In K. T. Henson & B. F. Eller, *Educational psychology for effective teaching.* New York: McGraw-Hill.

Grubaugh, S. (1989). Nonverbal language techniques for better classroom management and discipline. *High School Journal, 73,* 34–40.

Henson, K. T. (2001). *Curriculum planning: Integrating multiculturalism, constructivism, and education reform* (2nd ed.). Belmont, CA: Wadsworth.

Henson, K. T., & Eller, B. F. (1999). *Educational psychology for effective teaching.* Belmont, CA: Wadsworth.

Hilliard, R. D. (1999). All I ever needed to know I learned in middle school. *SRATE Journal, 8*(1), 50–56.

Hines, C. V., Cruickshank, D. R., & Kennedy, J. J. (1982, March). Measures of teacher clarity and their relationships to student achievement and satisfaction. Presented at the annual meeting of the American Educational Research Association, New York.

Holm, T. (2002). Humor as a teaching tool: Careful you don't cut somebody. *The teaching professor, 16*(4), 6.

Hyman, R. T. (1979). *Strategic questioning.* Englewood Cliffs, NJ: Prentice-Hall.

Jenkins, D. M., & Jenkins, K. D. (1991). The NMSA Delphi report: Roadmap to the future. *Middle School Journal, 22*(4). 27–36.

Lancaster, (1999). A teacher's class. In K. T. Henson & B. F. Eller, *Educational psychology for effective teaching.* Belmont, CA: Wadsworth.

Leithwood, K., Menzies, T., and Jantzi, D. (1994). Earning teachers' commitment to curriculum reform. *Peabody Journal of Education, 69*(4), 38–61.

MacKenzie, A. A., & White, R. T. (1982). Fieldwork in geography and long-term memory structures. *American Educational Research Journal, 19,* 623–632.

Mills, S. R., Rice, C. T., Berliner, D. C., & Rousseau, E. W. (1980). The correspondence between teacher questions and student answers in classroom discourse. *Journal of Experiential Education, 48,* 194–209.

MLS (Metropolitan Life Insurance Company Survey) (1998). *The American teacher.* New York: Louis Harris and Associates.

Mosston, M. (1972). *From command to discovery.* Belmont, CA: Wadsworth.

Nirenberg, G. I. (1971). *How to read a person like a book.* New York: Pocket Books.

O'Neil, J. (1998). Why are all the black kids sitting together? *Educational Leadership, 55*(4), 12–17.

Ornstein, A. C., & Levine, D. U. (1990, November/December). School effectiveness and reform: Guidelines for action. *The Clearing House, 64*(2), 115–118.

Radz, M. A. (1978). Responsibility, education, and the early adolescent. In C. H. Sweat (Ed.), *Responsibility of education in the junior high middle school* (p. 6). Danville, IL: Interstate.

Raywid, M. A. (1998). Small schools: A reform that works. *Educational Leadership, 55*(4), 34–39.

Redfield, D. L., & Rousseau, E. W. (1981). A meta-analysis of experimental research on teacher questioning behavior. *Review of Educational Research, 51,* 237–245.

Riban, D. M. (1976). Examination of a model for field studies in science. *Science Education, 60,* 1–11.

Rosenshine, B. V. (1986). Synthesis of research on explicit teaching. *Educational Leadership, 43,* 60–69.

Rowe, M. B. (1978, March). Wait, wait, wait. *School Science and Mathematics, 78,* 207–216.

Rudick, K. L. (1994). Training and the transactional view. Unpublished manuscript, Eastern Kentucky University, Richmond, KY.

Sautter, R. C. (1994). An arts education school reform strategy. *Phi Delta Kappan, 75*(6), 432–437.

Siegel, M. A., & Davis, D. M. (1986). *Understanding computer-based education.* New York: Random House.

Slavin, R. E. (1998). Can education reduce social inequities? *Educational Leadership, 55*(4), 6–10.

Stake, R. E., & Easley, J. A. (Eds.) (1978). *Case studies in science education* (Vol. 1, p. 29). Urbana, IL: Center for Instructional Research and Curriculum Evaluation.

Trachtenberg, D. (1974). Student tasks in text material: What cognitive skills do they tap? *Peabody Journal of Education, 52,* 54–57.

11

Motivation

No man can reveal to you aught but that which already lies half asleep in the dawning of your knowledge.

Kahlil Gibran

Objectives

- List ten techniques for stimulating student interest.
- Explain how competition motivates students.
- Name two ways a teacher can solicit parents' cooperation.
- Explain Piaget's concept of "equilibrium."
- Role-play a teacher being confronted by an angry parent.
- State the relationship between self-concept and motivation.
- Describe the teacher's main responsibility in developing students' self-concepts.
- Explain the teacher's role in using humor in the classroom.
- Give three guidelines for using grade contracts.
- List five guidelines for using reinforcement in the classroom.
- Explain this statement: "Motivation is learning."
- Discuss the role that respect plays in classroom motivation.
- Give one guideline for using computers to motivate students.
- Explain the effect of differences in school experiences and home lives on minority students.

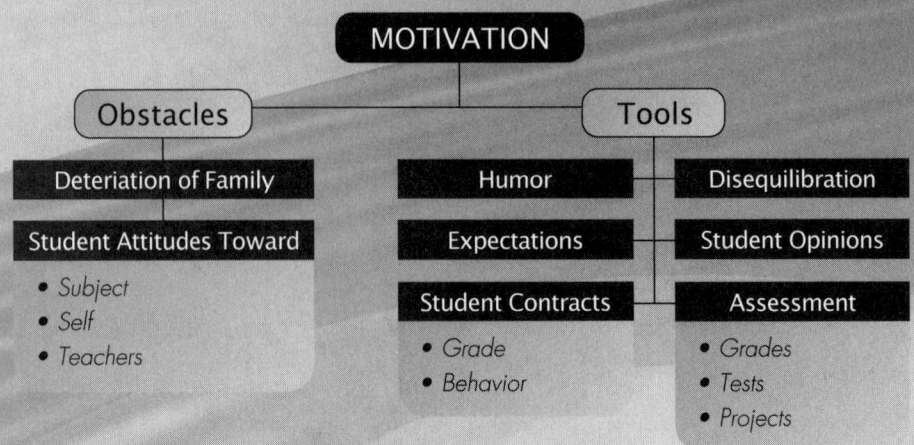

Connecting Statements	Agree	Disagree	Uncertain
1. The more reinforcement the better.			
2. Teacher enthusiasm cannot be planned.			
3. Effective motivation requires a variety of strategies.			
4. Teachers must tell students how to apply highly theoretical knowledge.			
5. The family is becoming less important in children's education.			
6. Humor in the classroom succeeds best when it is systematically planned to fit the lesson.			
7. Differences in cultural home environment and school experiences leave many minority students passive.			

> *Tips for Teachers*
>
> William Alexander, the father of the middle school, advised that the middle school should serve not just the intellect but the whole child. This chapter shows you how to relate better to the whole child. This is essential for motivating the transescent. For example, you will learn to use humor and enthusiasm to stimulate student interest. You will also learn how to protect students' self-concepts and nurture them toward positive growth.
>
> As you read this chapter, think about the relationship between the emotional self and cognitive development and how you can apply the understanding shared through Piaget's work to your own teaching career. Remember that although you cannot make your students succeed, you must create a climate that encourages and facilitates their achievement. This means that you must motivate your students.

Importance of Motivating

Today's world has many qualities that militate against students' progress in school. Earlier generations of teachers could always call Johnny's parents if his interest took a downward turn, but efforts to ensure student success today do not have such support. Even worse, the world is becoming an increasingly difficult place for young people. For several decades youths' attention spans have been decreasing. Short attention spans of youth are a definite characteristic of the twenty-first century. Today's teachers have adolescents' attention for approximately their age plus one minute (Hilliard, 1999).

Hootstein (1994) reported on a teacher who asked students what motivational strategies they would use if they could become the teacher. Their responses, in rank order of popularity, were

- Acting
- Watch videos and films
- Play games for review
- Give more sense of control

Although teachers recognize the need to motivate all students, obstacles often prevent them from doing so. Hootstein (1994) found that a main obstacle to motivation is a lack of time. Patterson (2003) shares this concern: "The advantages of longer blocks of time are numerous" (p. 572).

The family, as it was once thought of, no longer exists for most students. In 1989, when the Massachusetts Mutual Life Insurance Company asked 1,200 randomly selected adults to describe the word "family," only 22 percent picked the traditional definition of a group of people related by blood, marriage, or adoption; about 75 percent selected "a group of people who love and care for each other" (Seligmann, 1989).

Extrinsic versus Intrinsic Motivation

All motivators can be grouped into two types: extrinsic and intrinsic. Extrinsic motivators occur when students work for rewards such as candy or free time. Intrinsic motivators are stimuli that come from within; a student studies because she enjoys learning or she wants to improve herself. Of the two types, intrinsic motivators are the stronger, but intrinsic motivators take longer to achieve.

> **Teacher of the Year**
>
> Remember, a teacher wants to develop intrinsic motivation in her students and this can't be rushed or pushed. Give children a reason to learn and help them feel good about their own learning.
>
> Former Alabama Teacher of the Year Susan Lloyd (Henson & Eller, 1999)

This can be achieved by giving students opportunities to share their knowledge. For example, you can let students put on demonstrations or participate in shows or fairs.

Stefanich (1990) says that students' levels of motivation are often proportional to the degree to which they see relationships between their curricula and their outside lives:

> Soon after beginning school, many students that come from cultures which do not reflect the European traditions, make a decision that there is no relationship between what they learn at school and the world which exists outside the school. . . . It is not surprising that these students become passive in educational settings. (p. 48)

Motivating Students in Multicultural Classrooms

Although Stefanich cites members of cultural minority groups as being estranged from their curricula, mainstream ethnic group members may be estranged as well. Do not assume that students who are not interested in the lesson are not motivated. Borich (1988) defines motivation as what energizes or directs a learner's attention, emotions, and activities. According to this definition, all students are motivated by something. Englander (See Henson & Eller, 1999) agrees. Furthermore, he says that "Learners will work for some combination of over 30 different psychological motives such as curiosity, affiliation, achievement, power, exhibition, and activity (p. 385). The teacher must find ways to redirect the attention of those students who are not interested in the lesson.

Teachers daily face uninterested students who, skeptical of teachers' motives, feel that their time and energy could be spent more wisely elsewhere. You are largely responsible for changing these attitudes. Effective teachers exert much control over learning.

The prudent teacher is very aware that the classroom environment and the attitude of teachers, peers, and parents all affect the student's motivation to interact socially and succeed academically (Bandura, 1986). Peer pressure's negative effects on achievement are well known. The 1994 Gallup Poll (Elam, Rose, & Gallup, 1994) reported that 88 percent of the public consider negative attitudes of peers important and 63 percent consider the effects very important (p. 52). Brophy and Good (1986) say that measures of teacher control typically relate either positively or curvilinearly to achievement. Effective teachers use praise frequently, ask more questions, and move their classes at a brisk pace.

Having just spent four or five years studying a particular subject, you may assume, like other enthusiastic young teachers, that others share at least some of this interest. This assumption is dangerous. Instead, you will be wiser to analyze your students and identify any existing interests about the subject. Once you identify any, you may kindle a spark of interest into a more serious commitment.

Can a teacher really make all students like a particular subject and every lesson? This is an excellent question, the answer to which is no. Englander (1999) explains, "Everyone is motivatable but no one is motivated by everything" (p. 385). Motivation is a prerequisite to learning. To some, it is more: motivation is learning (Campbell, 1990). You can no more interest students against their will than you can force students to learn. Your best strategy is to entice students, but before you can do this successfully your students must have an appropriate mind-set toward the subject, toward themselves, and toward you, the teacher. "It is only when several strategies are carefully and systematically integrated that substantial improvements in learning become possible" (Guskey, 1990, p. 12).

The 26th Annual Phi Delta Kappa Gallup Poll of the public's attitudes toward the public schools (Elam et al., 1994) found that three-fourths of the public think that the schools should promote both a common cultural tradition and the diverse cultural traditions of the different population groups in the United States.

Farris (1990, p. 22) notes that "recognizing the needs of students and focusing on meeting those needs in the classroom are ways to generate solutions to motivation problems." The National Middle School Association listed as a priority goal the need for all middle-level teachers to increase their knowledge of the developing characteristics of the middle-level student: "Inservice/reeducation of existing middle-level and non-middle-level certified faculty is increased to implement and maintain knowledge of the middle-level child" (Jenkins & Jenkins, 1991).

Student Attitudes toward the Subject

Almost all content has the latent potential to fascinate students (Rinne, 1998). Although many students dislike studying, others are interested in learning. If members from both groups described the subjects they were taking in school, they would choose very different adjectives. This is true for every subject—some students actually love it, others hate it. Most who hate it find it boring, difficult, or both. The wellspring for motivation is the search for understanding, or attempting to comprehend why events happen (Weiner, 1979). However, as Rinne (1998, p. 621) testifies, almost any topic has latent intrinsic appeal and it is the teacher's job and responsibility to unlease this appeal to all students: "Almost all subject matter, no matter how dull, mundane, or prosaic it may seem at first, has latent intrinsic appeals that our most effective teachers have learned how to reveal to students" (p. 621). Let us look first at the students who find your subject boring and learn what you can do about it.

Hilliard (1999) reminds us of the psychological barrier that inhibits teachers' attempts to motivate adolescents. "Early adolescents are egocentric and have difficulty seeing events and intentions from another's viewpoint" (p. 54). Students are concerned with relevance. They are confronted with so much knowledge that they must be highly selective, choosing what they can use. Therefore teachers must show students how to apply what they are learning to practical problems, preferably in their own lives. For example, math ratios may bore some students until they learn to use them to determine their automobile's power and economy. One full-size station wagon retained the same size engine and relatively the same carburetor from one year to the next, but the manufacturer changed the ratio in the transmission, resulting in a gas-mileage loss of more than 33 percent. Other students may find ratios useless until they realize that they use them daily in cooking.

The wise teacher prepares a response to the age-old question, "Why do we have to study this stuff?" After all, it does seem unfair to force students to listen to something they perceive as useless. A textbook cannot provide this answer. It must come from you. You might begin by analyzing your own reasons for enjoying the subject. Take a moment now and list a few reasons why you majored in your subject. Now look at your list of reasons and determine how each can convince an uninterested student that this subject is worth studying. If your explanations seem ineffective, consider other ways you might convince students of your subject's worth. Try to recall your teachers' successful efforts. Perhaps they used demonstrations, anecdotes, or personal examples to awaken your interest. Can you think of a few techniques to stimulate your students? Imagine you are introducing a new unit of study. How might you use each of the following approaches to gain everyone's attention?

Demonstration	Questioning session
Problem	Debate
Personal experience	Joke
Group assignment	Discussion

Remember that students always see things in terms of their experiences, not yours (Hilliard, 1999). Can you alter each of your ideas to fit your class's age group?

Learning flourishes when students are involved vigorously. Involvement is a prerequisite for maximum learning. Wiske (1994) says that "understanding is . . . a capacity developed through the free exchange of ideas" (p. 19). Students need an opportunity to develop their own theories, which is unlikely to occur in classrooms in which students are passive. When students are not permitted to discuss their theories, they may harbor many misunderstandings. Heckman, Confer, and Hakim (1994) insist that students' theories are quite different than their teachers think they are. This is not to imply that the teacher's theories are always correct. All concepts are tentative (Gardner & Boix-Mansilla, 1994). For example, you could have students help with the demonstration. Remember, though, that involvement is a better motivator when it is meaningful. Also allow students to participate in the demonstration itself. With the problems approach, you might introduce a puzzle for everyone to work. When you use personal experiences, you can ask for volunteers to share their own experiences.

Were you able to think of ways to increase student involvement in the other areas? If not, give it another try. Once you begin to think of classrooms as places where students are always active, it becomes easier to plan meaningful experiences.

Student Attitudes toward Themselves

Motivation depends on self-perception. Each student comes to your room with a definite self-image as a person and as a student. A negative image is a strong barrier against learning. Minority students may have low self-esteem because the academic achievement level of their group is low. There is evidence that this low academic achievement level can be attributed not to the ethnic culture but to the family's low income level. When the academic performance levels of members of several families of different ethnic backgrounds were compared, the correlation with achievement was higher with income level than with ethnicity (Reich 1991; Henson & Eller, 1999).

Your job is to recognize these attitudes so that you can help the student change a negative self-concept. The task may seem monumental, but one of the greatest rewards of teaching is knowing that you will help some students find themselves and discover their own potential. Unfortunately, not all students have this experience—some drop out of school before making that discovery. Others just seem to putter along, somehow managing to get through high school or complete a high school equivalency program. Some of those who go to college come to realize that they can do more than even they ever believed.

You may hear a teacher say, "It's not my fault if they bring these attitudes to my class." This may be true. The fault may belong to previous teachers, parents, friends, or the student, but that is not the point. Teachers must know that they can become powerful negative motivators simply by the way they relate to students. Therefore, avoid making negative comments to the student or about the student, such as "You know him—he's a hopeless case" or "Her entire family is that way—dumb." Another common remark of teachers is "You can't make a sculpture out of mud." But remember that, at first, all clay looks a great deal like mud!

Teachers can and should help all students feel good about themselves. Schmoker (1990) explains the responsibility that effective teachers assume for ensuring that students earn the recognition that is so important in classroom motivation:

> *[Self-esteem] has become less a quality to be slowly earned than one quickly and easily given—not something wrought but spontaneously realized. The emphasis is more on creating good feelings than on connecting self-respect to effort and attainment. . . . There is something sadly comical about whole auditoriums full of students being told, indiscriminately, to feel good about themselves, even to stand up (I've seen this) and give testimonials on how much they like themselves. (p. 55)*

Jenkins (1994) also warns against using unearned compliments to improve self-esteem: "Don't make kids reinforcement junkies. . . . Real self-esteem comes not from hollow praise or little prizes given for effortless tasks, but from accomplishing something difficult" (p. 270).

Not everyone is an Einstein, and we cannot always mold people into the patterns we design, but that is not your role. Your role is to provide a climate in which students can see their own strengths, believe in themselves, and become what they want to become. They must perceive the possibility of success before they attempt something. Once they experience success repeatedly, they have a good chance of succeeding in any field of endeavor, school or otherwise. It is worth repeating: Students who perceive themselves as good students will work hard to protect that image, just as athletes with good reputations are willing to give it their very best. Never underestimate your power to affect students' self-images.

Teacher of the Year

I've come to the frightening conclusion that I am the decisive element in the classroom. It's my personal approach that creates the climate. It's my daily mood that creates the weather. As a teacher, I possess a tremendous power to make a child's life miserable or joyous. I can be a tool of torture or an instrument of inspiration. I can humiliate or humor.

Former Utah Teacher of the Year Marilyn Grondel
(Henson & Eller, 1999, p. 316)

The old cliche, "Success breeds success," is very true, but it does not explain how a teacher can help students who are not usually successful to succeed. Actually, no teacher can make anyone succeed. All you can do is create a climate conducive to learning, experimenting, or even failing. Some failure is inevitable and must be expected. What is important is how your students perceive and respond to failure, not the failure itself. If they see failure as defeat it can be devastating, but if you teach them to see failure as a stumbling block for growth, they can learn and grow from their mistakes.

Two other approaches that can help nurture the development of positive self-images are cooperative learning and service learning. Cooperative learning uses groups and requires all members of each group to help all other members. Service learning requires all participants to provide services to other members of the community. Cooperative learning and service learning, practices that encourage young adolescents to work well with others and contribute to their communities, are elements of a self-enhancing school.

Reflection

Abraham Maslow Speaks about Intrinsic Learning

Read the following paragraph and respond to the questions below.

> *To understand the breadth of the role of the teacher, a differentiation has to be made between extrinsic learning and intrinsic learning. Extrinsic learning is based on the goals of the teacher, not on the values of the learner. Intrinsic learning, on the other hand, is learning to be and to become a human being, and a particular human being. It is the learning that accompanies the profound personal experiences in our lives. . . . As I go back in my own life, I find my greatest education experiences, the ones I value most in retrospect, were highly personal, highly subjective, very poignant combinations of the emotional and the cognitive. Some insight was accompanied by all sorts of autonomic nervous system fireworks that felt very good at the time and which left as a residue the insight that has remained with me forever. (Maslow, 1973, p. 159)*

Such personal relationships with students affect the learning that occurs in classrooms. Brophy and Evertson (1976) found that more achievement occurs in classrooms where teachers involve students in planning and executing lessons. Solicit student suggestions about content selection and classroom activities, and use reasonable student-generated suggestions.

1. What does Maslow mean by intrinsic learning?
2. What is the teacher's role in promoting intrinsic learning?
3. How would you explain intrinsic learning in terms of the domains of the educational taxonomies? More exactly, which two of the domains does Maslow address? What does he say about the relationship between these two domains?

In the Reflection box, Abraham Maslow addresses the power of intrinsic motivators. Students who have high levels of self-confidence respond best to such motivators. Alvestad and Wingfield (1993) tested 240 fifth-graders and learned that students with high levels of self-confidence responded enthusiastically to computer assignments and achieved much more in the computer lab than students who felt less competent. The success rate for intrinsically motivated was highest when students were given more control of their own computer time (pp. 12–13).

A study conducted at Florida State University found that arts education, when integrated throughout the curriculum, can promote learning in various subjects. Although the research does not show firm cause–effect relationships, there is reason to believe that arts-integrated instruction can stimulate learning. Sautter (1994) explains:

> *Years of experience among arts educators and classroom teachers who use the arts to motivate and instruct students, thousands of successful artists-in-residence programs over the last 25 years, and a*

growing body of research in arts education all strongly suggest that education in and through the arts can play a significant role in changing the agenda, environment, methods, and effectiveness of ordinary elementary and secondary schools. (p. 433)

The arts-integrated curriculum can help students enrich their expression, enrich their knowledge in other subjects, give them another way of perceiving, and improve their performance in all their subjects. The College Entrance Examination Board found that students who took more than four years of music and art scored 34 points higher on the verbal sections of the Scholastic Aptitude Test (SAT) and 18 points higher on the math sections than students who took less than a year of these subjects (Sautter, 1994).

Student Attitudes toward the Teacher

What teacher qualities are important to you? Close your eyes for a moment and think of the best teacher you ever had. Can you remember and list the five most important qualities that made you like that teacher?

Now compare your list with the results of a survey taken to determine what teacher characteristics students prefer most. Did you include a statement that tells how the teacher felt about you? The students in the survey did. In fact, the most frequently mentioned quality was that the "favorite" teacher was concerned about the student—and in a very special way. The ideal teacher was determined to see that the student achieved in the subject and took whatever time necessary, in class or out, to explain the subject. An expert in the subject, this teacher knew how to get things across and was even willing to help students in areas other than academics.

The teacher's expertise in the subject also affects students' attitudes toward the teacher; however, the day has long since passed when students valued their teachers' knowledge more than their attitudes toward their students, if indeed this were ever true. As Fielding and Pearson noted (1994), "Recently, the process of allowing students to build, express, and defend their own interpretations has become a revalued goal of text discussion" (p. 66). Such practice reflects the nature of constructivism.

The profile of a good teacher is beginning to emerge, and this profile extends beyond knowledge and teaching skills—it includes how the teacher actually feels about the subject and the students. Few students will get excited about a subject if it appears to bore the teacher (Figure 11.1). A teacher who shows excitement or a serious love for the subject entices students to seek the reason for that excitement. Students develop positive attitudes toward teachers who are enthusiastic and task-oriented and present the material clearly (McConnell, 1977).

Teacher of the Year

Although training in the art of teaching is important, truly effective teachers must have an inherent love of the learning process.... My best advice to aspiring teachers is to get out there and experience life—have an adventure, and then translate that into your teaching."

Former Alabama Teacher of the Year Susan Lloyd
(Henson & Eller, 1999, p. 224)

FIGURE 11.1 AN EPITAPH FOR STUDENT VICTIMS

Another important teacher quality is humor. Educators are just beginning to learn about the role humor plays in motivation. Humor, sometimes, described as a social lubricant (Lemke, 1982), can relax the class in tense moments. For the prospective teacher, many questions quickly emerge: "How can I use humor when I can't even tell a joke? How much humor should I allow? And by encouraging humor, am I inviting discipline problems?"

One of the strongest messages is relayed to students by the teacher's willingness to take time to listen to students and hear their concerns. In a survey of personal qualities of excellent teachers, two-thirds of the students rated these instructors as those who "are willing to listen" (Buckner & Bickel, 1991, p. 26). In another survey of personal qualities of excellent teachers, two-thirds of the students rated these instructors as "those who are respectful toward students, accept students, are easy to talk with, demonstrate warmth and kindness, and are friendly" (Buckner & Bickel, 1991, p. 26). The personal teacher qualities that students rated highest are shown in Table 11.1. The top quality on this list—willingness to listen to students—can be understood by considering the following passage by Gardner and Boix-Mansilla (1994):

> The most important answers are those that individuals ultimately craft for themselves, based on their disciplinary understandings, their personal experiences, and their own feelings and values. (p. 18)

Personal accounts of school dropouts describe schools as places that are often large, bureaucratic, and impersonal. In contrast, good schools are described as having a human scale in which concern for the students and cooperation are highly valued. Even if [the school

TABLE 11.1 Rank order of "Very Important" Middle School Teacher Personal Characteristics (*N* = 394)

Excellent Teachers . . .	†f	%
1. Are willing to listen	325	82.5
2. Are respectful toward students	302	76.7
3. Accept students	291	73.9
4. Are easy to talk to	288	73.1
5. Demonstrate warmth and kindness	274	69.5
6. Are friendly	260	66.2
7. Are enthusiastic	232	58.9
8. Are optimistic	201	51.0
9. Are flexible	173	44.9
10. Are humorous	160	40.5
11. Are spontaneous	152	38.6
12. Look like they feel good about themselves	120	30.5

†Frequency of responses

Source: Buckner, J. H., & Bickel, F. (1991, January) If you want to know about effective teaching, why not ask your middle school kids? *Middle School Journal*, 22(3), 27. Reprinted by permission of National Middle School Association.

is] large, the ethic that "every student matters" is made real in the day-to-day life and interactions within the school. Teachers try to know and engage each student. Students believe that teachers are interested in them and care about their progress. Cooperation characterizes the relationships among adults as well. (p. 77) Teachers can raise student achievement in their classes by showing confidence in their student's abilities. Gilbert and Smith (2003, p. 83) explain, "When students feel valued by their teachers, they are more likely to work harder at assignments."

Teaching respect begins by giving respect. Former Nebraska Teacher of the Year Duane Obermeier echoes this message: "I firmly believe in treating students like fellow human beings who have feelings just like I do (Henson and Eller, 1999, p. 12)." Cynthia Lancaster, Former Washington State Teacher of the Year goes a step further and explains the effect of respect on learning: "Academic learning cannot and will not take place in a classroom that does not have an expectation and insistence on appropriate behavior" (Henson & Eller, 1999, p. 213).

The Role of Humor

According to Holm (2002), numerous empirical studies have found that the use of humor in the classroom engages students in active learning, motivates interests, and increases retention (p. 6). *Baughman's Handbook of Humor in Education* (Baughman, 1974) says that effective classroom humor is not always planned: humor is better described as an attitude or philosophy. In other words, the teacher's role is to accept humor. The students will provide the creativity and the delivery skills if you provide a climate for humor to develop. As Weber and Roff (1985) note, "[Humor] can be used to remove tension" (p. 38). It should be gentle, because "sarcasm endangers student–teacher relationships and student feelings of self-worth" (Weber & Roff, 1985, p. 39). Holm (2002) advises that you avoid making jokes too personal. Dialogueing with fellow teachers and daily reading the current literature will help you learn new ways to use humor in your classes.

The concern about discipline is justified. You do not want your classroom to turn into a circus. Achievement is higher where serious misbehavior is minimal (Evertson, Emmer, & Brophy, 1980). You can control the humor by establishing an understanding that it must be kept clean in content and vocabulary and that rudeness is not permitted. Sarcasm and ridicule endanger both the teacher–student relationship and students' feelings of self-worth (Charles, 1981; Gnagey, 1981). Short interruptions in a serious lesson might provide needed relaxation, because humor is psychologically relaxing, but you must keep such interruptions short.

Humor can also be planned into the lesson to increase retention of major ideas (Holm, 2002). For example, in one scenario the teacher introduces a science lesson by saying, "There are are three types of rocks: sedimentary, metamorphic, and ignorant . . . I mean, igneous." Of the three types, the chances are very good that the type of rock remembered best will be igneous.

It is easy to return to the lesson if the lesson is interesting and well structured. For this reason, a good lesson plan with clear objectives and adequate student involvement is indispensable to classroom motivation. The pace should be crisp, and students should remain challenged. For students to learn in an informal setting, however, you must have a well-structured lesson planned. A balance must be achieved. Do not become so enslaved to a lesson plan that you lose the students along the way.

How informal should a class be? A good rule of thumb is to make each class as informal as possible, retaining only enough structure to move through the lesson systematically, according to the plan. When the students become especially interested in a part of the lesson, allow time for discussing that part, but always return to the lesson plan.

> ## Reflection
>
> Reread John Steinbeck's speech at the beginning of Chapter 1. After you have reread this brief passage, respond to the following questions.
>
> 1. What techniques did Steinbeck's teacher use to motivate her students?
> 2. Steinbeck suggests that, in addition to her techniques for motivating students, this teacher had a special quality. Can you remember that quality? Can it be learned?
> 3. Defend or challenge Steinbeck's assertion that teaching is an art (as opposed to a science).
> 4. Identify the best teacher you have ever had. List four or five of this teacher's most important qualities.
> 5. Examine your list of teacher qualities in the preceding response. Does your favorite teacher meet Steinbeck's criteria for a "real" teacher?

Enthusiasm

You can talk at length about the importance of learning a particular subject or about certain information being essential to future learning, but unless you yourself appear to be interested in a lesson, your words will probably go unheard. On the other hand, if each day you are curious and excited about the lesson, students will wonder what you find so interesting. Teachers should have a desire for adventure.

To behave enthusiastically does not mean becoming overly emotional, yet you cannot afford to be nonchalant or just mildly interested. You need not compete with the entertainment world, because what you have to offer—useful knowledge and leadership—is better than entertainment. When you explain why the lesson is being pursued and how it can be applied, you want to be taken seriously.

Historically, gender has been considered a major determiner of academic success. As Latham (1998) has reported, "Several personal variables influence academic success more than gender affects academic success." According to Latham (1998), "Students' natural interests, skills and aspirations are likely to exert a far greater influence on their academic achievement than will their gender (p. 89)."

How can you appear both serious and excited? Think for a moment about the college courses you are taking now, and select a class you really enjoy. How would you describe the teacher? Does the teacher speak in a monotone? Does the teacher read a lecture to the class each day? Is the teacher afraid to let the class laugh a little when a humorous incident occurs? Does the teacher always sit behind a desk and require you to sit at your desk? Probably not. Most teachers we enjoy are neither foolishly funny nor extremely straightlaced, but they probably are intensely interested in the subject. For most teachers this is not a problem as long as their lesson has been well planned. Through mastering their subjects, teachers develop intellectual authority. Ironically, teachers must learn that their ownership of knowledge is always provisional. As Wiske (1994) explains, "Intellectual authority is provisional because truth is debatable" (p. 20). As noted by Fielding and Pearson (1994), "Recently the process of allowing students to build, express, and defend their own interpretations has become a revalued goal of text discussions" (p. 66).

THE CASE

The Role of Dispositions in Becoming an Effective Teacher

Adele Ducharme, Valdosta State University

Dr. Adele Ducharme *is the Department Head of Middle Grades and Secondary Education at Valdosta State University in Valdosta, Georgia. She received her B.S. in Elementary Education, her M.Ed. in Reading Education, and her Ed.D. in Elementary Education, all from Louisiana State University. Dr. Ducharme has twenty-five years of teaching experience, twelve as the head of the Department of Middle Grades Education. She has taught elementary school in Louisiana and was the Chair of Elementary Education at Troy State University in Montgomery, Alabama.*

Setting

Imagine yourself in South Georgia, a rural community with Interstate 75 running through it. The county has a population of 93,330, of whom 62.2 percent are white, 34.33 percent are black, 2.72 percent are of Hispanic origin, 1.49 percent are Asian and Pacific Islander, and 1.55 percent are other races. Average age of the population is 33.3. People's jobs in the county include executive and managerial, professional specialty, sales, administrative support, precision, production and craft, machine operator. The average per-capita income is $18,335 for the county. Middle school teachers' average salary is $37,600. Educational levels for the county are 11.33 percent elementary, 18.91 percent some high school, 31.70 percent high school graduates, 17.21 percent some college, 4.5 percent associate's degree, 9.83 percent bachelor's degree, and 6.52 percent graduate degree.

Education is a major employer. The community has a university and a military base. Two school systems (county and city) are the central focus of this community.

School

The middle school is located near the university campus. The building is old and was built for the junior high concept. The Southern Association of Colleges and Schools (SACS) and the Elementary/Middle Commission Accredited Georgia Accrediting Commission (GAC) accredit the school.

Student enrollment is 868, with 55.6 percent black, 39.3 percent white, 1.2 percent Hispanic, 2.9 percent Asian, and the remainder being members of other races. Gender composition of student population is 48.2 percent males and 51.8 percent females. About half of the students (52.3 percent) are eligible for free or reduced-price lunches. Last year's retention by race was 70.8 percent black, 20.8 percent white, 4.2 percent Hispanic, and 4.2 percent multiracial, with males being retained at a higher rate than females. Academic data from norm-referenced assessments (Stanford 9, for eighth grade) show students above state average in reading and social studies and below state average in mathematics, language, and science.

Student Teacher

Meet Rachel Advance, a tall blonde with a nice personality and a laid-back attitude. She is originally from a similar community in size and culture. She is involved in varsity athletics as a runner. Like many young people entering the teaching profession, Rachel has an unrealistic view of what it takes to become an effective teacher. Rachel began her preparation as a teacher in fall 1996, was admitted to Teacher Education in spring 1999, and began taking her major courses in fall 1999. She received B's in most of her major courses, graduating with a 3.13 GPA.

Rachel's content concentration areas were social studies and science. Her laissez-faire attitude was reflected in her lack of punctuality for class during her senior program. Rachel completed academic course assignments, meeting the expectations of her professors. She worked well with team members on group assignments.

Senior Program

The middle-grades program requires 900 hours of field experiences. Of the 900 hours, 750 hours are completed during a senior program that includes apprenticeship and student teaching. The senior program consists of Development/Education of Middle Grades Student Part 2, Humanities Methods for MGED, Science/Math Methods for MGED, Integrating Technology, and Apprenticeship of Middle Grades Teaching. Since four weeks of the semester are for apprenticeship and classes do not meet, courses are taught during the day with extended hours. Apprenticeship is four weeks of all-day work in the school. Apprentices follow the same hours as teachers. In fact, the apprenticeship can be considered the beginning of student teaching. Rachel was placed with a social studies mentor with whom she worked during apprenticeship and student teaching. Furthermore, candidates are placed in schools as a team and the team selects a team leader. Four candidates were placed at Rachel's school site, with the oldest member being selected as team leader.

Rachel began by observing and working with students one-on-one or in small groups. During the first four weeks, she gradually took over planning and teaching. The last week she was responsible for planning and teaching two consecutive classes for all five days.

During apprenticeship, behaviors were noticed that did not meet departmental standards principles. The Danielson Framework for Teaching rubric (Danielson, 1996) was used as the performance assessment instrument. She was rated unsatisfactory in the following areas:

1. Demonstrating knowledge of content and pedagogy
   - Knowledge of prerequisite relationships
2. Demonstrating knowledge of students
   - Knowledge of students' varied approaches to learning
   - Knowledge of students' skills and knowledge
3. Selecting instructional goals
   - Balance
4. Demonstrating knowledge of resources
   - Resources for students
5. Designing coherent instruction
   - Instructional materials and resources
   - Lesson and unit structure
6. Assessing student learning
   - Use for planning
7. Managing classroom procedures
   - Management of materials and supplies

As the faculty stated, "She was winging it." Her lack of planning was hindering her teaching and the students' learning.

When Rachel met with two faculty members for her semester reality check, she was informed of areas needing improvement: problems in organization, assertiveness, and assuming responsibility. Rachel was also given a copy of the scored rubric, with specific descriptions of behaviors she needed to demonstrate. Rachel also shared her vague view of apprenticeship. To ensure her student teaching accomplishment, she was placed on a five-week success plan, requiring her to work with the university counseling center for assistance with her organizational skills. Rachel appeared undaunted with the five-week plan idea.

The five-week plan required Rachel to address those concerns that the faculty and mentor had noted and discussed with her. The concerns would be remediated during the first five weeks of student teaching or Rachel would receive notification that she was unsuccessful in student teaching at this point. Rachel's remediation plan included:

- Completing all required paperwork on a daily basis, including changes and modifications of lesson plans and daily reflections.
- Submitting all of her weekly lesson plans to her mentor and university supervisor the Friday before teaching. If all lesson plans were not submitted and approved, she would not teach.
- Holding a daily conference with her mentor that included her planning and teaching, discussion of her strengths and weaknesses, and ways to improve.
- Being observed weekly by her university supervisor.
- Receiving satisfactory ratings over three or four weeks in order to continue with student teaching.

The first week of student teaching was renewal of students' attributes and school policy.

After the reality check, Rachel's peer team leader began working with her on organization and asking her to share how she completed her daily lesson plans. The peer continued to mentor Rachel during student teaching. The university supervisor met with the mentor and Rachel to review her contract for the five-week plan. The social studies mentor was very supportive, assuring Rachel that she would be successful. With a peer mentor, teacher mentor, and supervisor to support Rachel, she began self-examination of "Do I really want to teach, if so what do I need to do?" As spring semester began, Rachel's attitude was noticeably changing. She was open to advice and guidance, and she was seeking ideas from her peer team leader and other faculty members. Her behavior was shifting from "whatever happens is fine" to a "take-charge" demeanor.

At the end of five weeks, Rachel's detached attitude toward teaching had changed to an "I want to teach and make a difference" mind-set. As student teaching progressed, Rachel demonstrated strengths in preparation and teaching that had not been noted during apprenticeship. She identified students' needs and integrated technology into her lessons to meet these needs using a variety of approaches and materials appropriate to eighth-grade students. She was well prepared to teach each lesson. Most important, we noticed a change in her posture: she stood and walked erectly and she had a confident air about her. Her whole demeanor had changed. Rachel had decided she really wanted to teach. This was noted not only in her presentation, but also in her respect for the students, mentor, peers, and herself. She realized she had found what she wanted in a career, and she knew she could make a difference in students' lives. With gained confidence and her mentor's desire to acquire new skills, Rachel became a mentor to her mentor. Through demonstration and coaching, she taught her mentor how to integrate technology into the social studies curriculum.

At the end of each semester an outstanding middle-grades student teacher is selected. From the faculty and mentors' point of view, we have had many outstanding student teachers, but this was the first time that other student teachers nominated a peer as the outstanding student teacher. Rachel was selected as outstanding student teacher and made an impromptu dramatic talk at the awards ceremony. She had changed from an individual who did not know what she wanted out of life to a confident, outgoing, and dedicated educator, one with many characteristics of highly effective teachers. Rachel evolved into a teacher's teacher, respected by peers, students, and faculty.

Traits Rachel had at the end of student teaching that are observed in highly effective teachers were

- Mission-driven and passionate
- Positive and real
- Teacher-leader
- With-it-ness (somewhat)
- Own style of teaching

With experience, Rachel will improve in motivational expertise, instructional effectiveness, book learning, street smarts, and mental life. As a young teacher she needs more life experiences to complete the fullness of all ten traits of highly effective teachers (McEwan, 2002).

Further Reflection

1. If you looked into a mirror, what could you see in commitment to teaching and learning for a diverse population?
2. What would be your reaction if confronted with results of reality check like Rachel's?
3. Put yourself in Rachel's position after the reality-check meeting. Someone asks you what are your goals for student teaching. What would be your response?
4. If you were in Rachel's position, what strategies would you choose to use to succeed during student teaching or as a beginning teacher? What criteria would guide your choice of strategies?
5. In this case, Rachel's attitude toward teaching during apprenticeship was lax or was that only the surface view. What do you think could have caused Rachel's problems during apprenticeship? What is your attitude toward teaching, and how will this attitude affect your teaching? Give specific examples. What are other things that could cause you problems during student teaching or as a beginning teacher?
6. Outside influences may affect your behavior during student teaching. Think about how your own school experience may color your image of what should happen in the classroom. Consider your

personal life—how might this place demands on your time? What resources, people, finances, etc., do you have to assist you in managing your personal and professional life?

7. How are lesson plans important to the success of a teacher's instruction and students' learning? What would you do if a peer's lesson plans were lacking? What resources can you draw on to help the peer?
8. What is mentoring? What value does it have in student teaching and the first years of teaching? If a mentor is not assigned to you as a beginning teacher, how would you go about finding a mentor?
9. What behaviors should a mentor have to be effective in working with a student teacher or first-year teacher?
10. Rachel did not have any direct conflict with peers, mentor, or supervisor. She did have peers who worried about her. How would you deal with conflict, disagreements, or concerns that might occur between you and your mentor, supervisor, or peers?
11. What is the purpose of the five-week plan, and do you think this is the most appropriate means of supporting a student teacher or first-year teacher?
12. Does thorough lesson planning support flexibility of instruction?
13. What is the benefit of the student teacher mentoring the mentor in a field such as technology?
14. Do your dispositions make a difference in your ability to be a highly effective teacher?
15. What dispositions are essential for becoming an effective teacher?

Using Technology

Another approach to motivating students that most teachers today find effective is technology. The International Society for Technology in Education (ISTE) has produced a list of technology standards that are now required for all new teachers in many states (Armstrong, et al., 2004). Some states have developed their own technology standards for their teachers. ISTE standards have had major influence on these lists. While technology is a powerful tool for motivating students, its influence in your classroom will be determined by your skills and your willingness to use it. Some of the ways that contemporary teachers use technology in their classrooms include: (1) re-teaching and reinforcing content, (2) providing enrichment experiences for gifted students, (3) individualizing assignments, (4) promoting global perspectives, (5) using web sites, and (6) desktop publishing.

In general, it is accurate to say that most of today's teachers have embraced the use of computers. Perhaps more than any other reason for this change is the fact that computers have become prevalent in our schools and classrooms. Today, 99% of American schools have computers. As early as 2000, 84 percent of teachers had at least one computer in their classroom (National Center for Education Statistics, 2000). As you continue in this class and in your other classes, look for examples of effective use of technology in today's schools.

Using Space

Teachers are managers. Effective teachers continuously manage student behavior (See Chapter 12), lessons, content, and time. You can enhance effective use of all of these elements by careful use of classroom space. You might begin by placing your desk at the back of the room. This achieves some important goals. First, it prevents you from teaching behind a

Teacher as Proactive Decision Maker

Classroom Situation

1. Remember visiting Ms. Simms and Ms. Armstrong's classes at the beginning of this chapter. You know that you want your classes to resemble Ms. Armstrong's, each lesson getting off to a quick start, students remaining engaged from the beginning, with the lesson moving crisply throughout the period.

Proactive Alternatives

1. Establish a daily routine that ensures lively, focused lessons. For example your schedule may look like the following:
   - 8:00–8:10 Review yesterday's lesson.
   - 8:10–8:20 Call students' attention to the day's lesson objectives written *in advance* on the overhead projector or board.
   - 8:20–8:50 At intervals, refocus attention on the major concepts for the day.

---

major physical barrier. This will cause students to perceive you as being more friendly (Armstrong et al., 2004). It will also encourage you to move about throughout the room, enhancing your monitoring skills while also making you accessible to students who need help.

The location of student desks is equally important. Seats for small working groups should be placed so that there is space between groups. This will reduce the noise level. Each group should be in a location that is readily accessible to you and all class members. Providing space between groups will also reduce the level of distraction of students who are not group members.

Keeping Students Challenged

The most important type of behavior is internal. It often follows success. According to Jean Piaget, each individual strives to achieve and maintain a state of equilibrium (Evans, 1973). In other words, when students see inconsistency in information, they are internally motivated to remove that inconsistency. The process used to restore equilibrium is called equilibration (Henson & Eller, 1999, p. 44). Figure 11.2 shows how a student's learning progresses in steps or plateaus. The distance from A_1 to A_2 represents a quest for learning as it is being satisfied. When satisfaction is reached at A_2, the student is in a state of equilibrium and remains there until another contradiction arises at B_1 (Evans, 1973). Each time students satisfy the reason for an apparent inconsistency in information, they gain a higher plateau and reach a state of equilibrium in their thinking.

Do not allow students to become idle when they level off. Always be prepared to present students with further contradictions to their knowledge.

Does this suggest that your role is to introduce problems or contradictions purposely to puzzle students instead of helping students find answers? Piaget would answer yes. In simple terms, a contradiction occurs when students discover that understandings they hold contradict or appear to contradict each other. The teacher guides students to realize that they lack certain knowledge and then provides one or more learning experiences to help them gain necessary understanding. There is no force-feeding. Students must internally want to erase this contradiction. Once learning has occurred, those students are at peace, resting on a plateau. The teacher must then make them aware of another contradiction, and

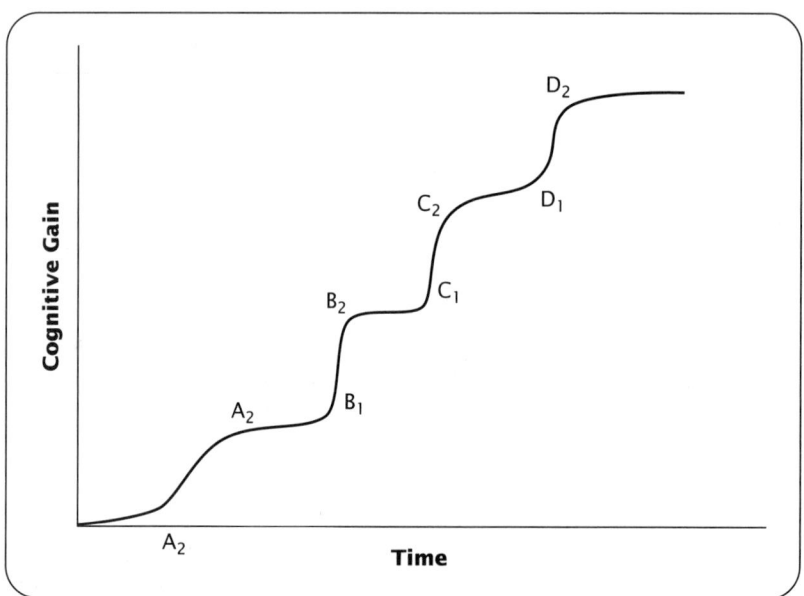

FIGURE 11.2 THE LEARNING PATTERN

From Kenneth T. Henson, *Methods and Strategies for Teaching in Secondary and Middle Schools*, third edition. Published by Allyn and Bacon, Boston, MA. Copyright © 1996 by Pearson Education. Reprinted by permission of the publisher.

the whole process repeats itself. This is motivation by keeping the student challenged—my interpretation of Piaget's theory of equilibrium.

Presenting too many contradictions at one time can have a nonmotivating effect. When faced with what seems to be an impossible task, students will tend to give up, feeling that they cannot succeed.

You can increase student interest dramatically simply by increasing the academic demands in the classroom: today's students want to be challenged more. Most teachers do not realize it, but many students are bored because teachers do not challenge them adequately (Frymier, 1979). A 1985 Gallup Poll supported this claim. Approximately half the teenagers contacted throughout the nation said that students do not have to work hard enough in school or on homework (Gallup, 1985). Even the learning materials in most schools are not interesting. According to Frymier (1979), 70 to 90 percent of the curricula are low in their ability to motivate, to stimulate creativity, and to challenge students' intellect. Therefore, the teacher must initiate the challenge by introducing more rigorous, yet relevant, knowledge and activities.

Teachers' self-expectations should include ensuring that students succeed. "Whether a school operates more as a bureaucracy or a community matters a great deal. It determines whether staff members see their job primarily as delivering services or whether they see it as succeeding in educating" (Raywid, 1998 p. 37).

Parents can play an important role in communicating high expectations to their children. Sometimes, however, parents need help in learning how to play this role. Many parents don't get any help from their schools regarding expectations. In fact, over one-third (35 percent) never get help. About half of all high school parents have not had any help.

Clarifying Goals and Procedures

As we saw in Chapters 2, 3, and 4, students will work more intensely when they know where they are headed and how to get there. Unfortunately, teachers and students do not talk much about content's meaning and purpose. In fact, teachers seldom give feedback, even when students make mistakes (Anderson, 1983). When students lose sight of the goals, they often lose interest. When they do not understand how to do assigned tasks, they become frustrated and discouraged. In both cases, poor work is usually the result.

Each task should begin with a clarification of the expected outcome. In other words, show your students how to recognize the answer, or concept or principle, when they find it. To be sure that students understand the proper procedures, you might begin each assignment by working a simple problem and then having the students work another problem collectively. Encourage questions and have students help one another with the sample problem.

Once you give the assignment, however, your job is far from over. Some students will still have questions about goals and procedures. Now you can help by circulating among the students and answering individual questions as they arise. Your availability and concern will motivate students who need help to ask questions.

Another way teachers can communicate their concern for students is by following up on each assignment. Such follow-ups increase the probability that students will complete the assignments (Phelps, 1991).

Using Students' Opinions

Make a special effort to seek students' opinions, letting them know that you value their suggestions, their likes and their dislikes, and above all their judgment. Giving them an opportunity to voice their ideas can help identify misconceptions. Until people have had an opportunity to express their opinions, they are not apt to consider others' opinions. In addition, just knowing that their questions and opinions are valued is great motivation. Consider one or more teachers you had who appeared to be intolerant of your questions or concerns. You probably soon lost the desire to ask about anything, and you probably also lost some respect for yourself and for those teachers.

Student Contracts as Motivators

Contracts were introduced in Chapter 7. Now let us examine their power to motivate. There are basically two kinds of student contracts: behavior contracts and grade contracts. Both are contingency contracts, and both affect behavior.

Behavior Contracts

A behavior contract is an agreement between the student and the teacher that if a student behaves in a specified manner the teacher will reward that behavior in a certain way. The reward for good behavior might range from a piece of candy for young children to free time for older students. Several authors have reported successful contingency contracting (Redmon & Farris, 1985; Salend, 1987).

Grade Contracts

Competition among students can have serious side effects—such as making the less capable feel inept, alienating students from their peers, and encouraging snobbishness in high achievers—but competition can be a strong motivator too. Americans are a competitive people, and the competitive attitude has been largely responsible for this nation's rapid development.

One way to retain the motivation and avoid the undesirable side effects is to encourage students to compete with themselves. Many of the best athletes do this. In fact, once golfers or bowlers become too interested in others' performance, their own performance often fails. Like bowling and golf, learning is in certain respects an individual activity in which learners compete with themselves. They are always challenged, yet they find that success is possible.

You can use student contracts to encourage students to compete with themselves. Unlike most teacher-made tests, which are norm-referenced and force students to compete with their classmates, student contracts are criterion-referenced and set the student only against the tasks at hand. Most contracts run for the duration of a grading period. Figure 11.3 is an example of a contract for a unit on art history.

To encourage students to be realistic in their expectations, you may stipulate that students can lower their expectations at any time, but the contract may contain a built-in penalty for any alterations. Most contracts do not permit students to raise their grade expectation, but in designing your contracts, try to fit them to your particular students' needs. The major disadvantage of using contracts is that you will need additional time to design, complete, and keep up with a large number of contracts. However, this disadvantage is offset by their empowering effect on students. As Hiller and Hietapelto (2001) have noted, contract grading "gives students a voice in their learning" (p. 661).

Grades, Tests, Projects

Many teachers believe that unannounced tests and threats of assigning low grades can be effective motivators, but research does not support this. When tests and threats are used in the traditional manner, the down-graded students continue to fail. Low test scores can also be discouraging, especially if the teacher does nothing to help the student acquire the missed

---

Grade Requirements
A   Meet the requirements for grade of B and visit a local art gallery. Sketch an example of a gothic painting. Visit a carpenter-gothic-style house and sketch the house. Show at least three similarities in the two products.
B   Meet the requirements for the grade of C and name and draw an example of each of the major classes of columns used in buildings.
C   Meet the requirements for the grade of D and submit a notebook record of the major development in art since 1900, naming at least six major painting styles and two authors of each style.
D   Attend class regularly and participate in all classroom activities.
I   _____ agree to work for the grade of _____ as described in this contract.

FIGURE 11.3 STUDENT CONTRACT FOR ART HISTORY

From Kenneth T. Henson, *Methods and Strategies for Teaching in Secondary and Middle Schools*, third edition. Published by Allyn and Bacon, Boston, MA. Copyright © 1996 by Pearson Education. Reprinted by permission of the publisher.

knowledge and skills. Unfortunately, teachers and students spend very little effort on reviewing and building skills that have not been learned (Chansky, 1962). Another study found that anxiety produced by grades actually lowered middle-ability students' grades (Phillips, 1962). So it appears that, although tests themselves can be sources of learning when time is spent going over the material covered (Stiggins, 1997), the use of tests or grades (or threats of either) to motivate is a serious misuse of tests that will not significantly increase students' motivational level.

Used correctly, however, tests can spark students' interest in content. Markle, Johnston, Geer, & Meichtry (1990) explain:

The power of tests and other evaluation procedures to shape students' perceptions of their teachers' expectations cannot be overestimated. Teachers can motivate students to strive for understanding by using evaluation procedures that determine how well new information can be related to other knowledge and how well students can use the newly taught information to solve novel problems. (p. 56)

Term Projects

Well planned individual or group term projects can be a highly motivating device in middle schools when used correctly. First, they must truly be term projects—lasting the entire term. This gives students time to select and research their chosen area of study. You can provide a list of topics to suggest ideas and boundaries, but you should let students choose their own particular project.

To increase motivation, find ways to display the projects. A science fair, art exhibit, or similar event is an excellent means of exposure. Parents and relatives can spur on the investigators and whet their enthusiasm.

Assignments for Extra Credit

Assignments for extra credit are common in many classrooms, yet they have limited power to stimulate interest. In fact, they often have the opposite effect. If extra-credit assignments are to motivate positively, the task must be meaningful and must be selected far in advance of the end of the term, preferably at the beginning of the term or study unit. Giving a student an opportunity to copy a 10,000-word report from an encyclopedia at the end of a semester is likely to produce a negative attitude toward learning rather than increase the student's motivation.

Extra Assignments for Corrective Measures

A major mistake that many teachers continue to make is assigning extra class work or homework in an attempt to correct misbehavior (e.g., assigning extra math problems or a written report to a student who becomes too loud or too active in class). This action causes students to associate school work with punishment; yet, it should be enjoyable and inviting.

Other Strategies

Parent Involvement

Parents can and should play a significant role in motivating their children. Where else could teachers learn more about the needs and interests of their students than from their parents? This was the attitude of the National Middle School Association when it listed as a priority goal for all middle schools that "Parents and schools form partnerships to meet the needs

> ### Teacher as Proactive Decision Maker
>
> **Classroom Situation**
>
> 1. You know that the majority of your class and you will find some of your future students disruptive and disrespectful. Many of these students do not have homes that show concern for others' feelings, and they would not know how to behave respectfully, even if they chose to.
>
> 2. You can anticipate that you will have students who, to say the least, lack motivation for your class. These students will need teachers who are themselves highly motivated. This is what former teacher of the year Ms. C. C. Lancaster (discussed in this chapter) meant when she said that teachers should have a desire for adventure.
>
> **Proactive Alternatives**
>
> 1. Make a list of expressions you can use to earn the respect of students through demonstrating your respect for them. Some examples might include:
>   - Start each directive with *please*: "John, please give me a moment...."
>   - Use students names in your examples: "Ann and Rosa, I want to thank you for always being ready when class begins."
>   - Stand at the door and welcome students as they enter your room.
>
> 2. Take a field trip of your own to learn more about your discipline. Plan a trip you know you will enjoy. Prepare a presentation of this trip for your class.

of the whole child" (Jenkins & Jenkins, 1991). Just over half (55 percent) of all high school teachers say that their schools have given parents information to help parents succeed in this role (MLS, 1998, p. 183), yet over one-third (38 percent) of teachers report that their schools never help teachers with their role in motivating their children. Middle schools give more help than high schools. Contrasting sharply with teachers' view of how little parents help motivate their children, 94 percent of students report that their parents encourage them to do well in school (See Table 11.2 and 11.3).

TABLE 11.2 School-Provided Information to Parents on How to Motivate Children

Q100C: Has your school provided parents with information on how to: Motivate their child, or not? Base: All teachers

	Total	Median Income of Community Where Most Students Live	
		$30,000 or Less	$30,001 or Over
Base:	1,035	595	416
	%	%	%
Has provided	55	51	59
Has not provided	38	43	32
Don't know	7	6	9

TABLE 11.3 Parental Encouragement to Do Well in School

QC1.1: Outside of school do your parents or guardians or other adults do any of the following thing with you, or not? Encourage you to do well in school.

Base: All students

	Total	Students' Grades		
		A/B Mostly	B/C Mostly	Worse Than C
Base:	1,301	805	367	109
	%	%	%	%
Yes, they do	94	97	93	77
No, they don't	4	2	4	19
Don't know	2	1	3	4

Reward and Reinforcement

Rewards can be an important motivator or stimulator of student interest. Substantial use of corrective feedback in the academic areas, praise for correct or proper behavior, and making use of students' ideas to let them know that their contributions are valued all have a positive relationship to achievement and attitudes (Gage & Berliner, 1984). Garibaldi (1992) reported that parent involvement is especially important to African American parents, who often need to be convinced that their children can succeed. Boutte & McCormick (1992) say that other community members should be brought in to serve as role models, especially for African American students. Some students work to please their teachers; others watch their teachers closely for feedback to assure themselves they are achieving at an acceptable rate. Your use of rewards can reinforce both types of students. Clark and Starr (1976) offer the following suggestions for teachers who want to improve their skills using rewards:

Techniques for Improving the Use of Rewards
1. Reward new [good] behavior every time it occurs.
2. Once a student becomes established, gradually reduce the frequency of reinforcement until the reinforcement comes at occasional and haphazard intervals.
3. At first, reward the behavior as soon as it occurs. Then, as students become more confident, delay the reward somewhat.
4. Select rewards that are suitable for the individual pupils.
5. With recalcitrant or resistive pupils, begin by giving small rewards.
6. Use contingency contracts. (p. 55)

Students need reinforcement on a regular basis. Phelps (1991) offers an example of daily use of a motivational strategy: "Teachers who 'shine the spotlight' on at least one student each day are more likely to see positive student behavior than teachers who merely recognize negative behaviors" (p. 241).

Behavior Modification

In education, behavior modification, like contingency contracts, is an agreement. Instead of earning grades, however, the student earns certain stated rewards for displaying specified types of behavior or for completing certain tasks. Behavior modification is more popular in middle schools; it is much more difficult to find adequate reinforcers for high school students (Warshaw, 1975). One reinforcer that has proved effective for secondary school classes is free time the student earns through certain specified performance. For example, in one English grammar class a 75 percent level of bad behavior was reduced to 15 percent by a contract that rewarded proper behavior by giving free time (Sapp, 1973).

In one program for a predominantly inner-city class of underachievers that provided the opportunity to earn free time, listen to records, read comic books, play games, receive candy bars and bubble gum, and participate in planning class activities, the average student grades rose from D to B and class attendance rose from 50 to 80 percent (Sapp, 1973). You should not expect such dramatic effects in every case, but these results are encouraging.

Summary of Strategies

Because any one technique for motivation is apt to produce different results with each application and each group of students, you will probably profit more if you concentrate less on specific techniques and more on general strategies for motivating students. Here is a summary of these strategies:

- Be honest with students. Don't pretend to know everything. It is far more important to be a teacher who is approachable than a teacher who is impeccable.
- Use the subject to motivate. Emphasize the areas of knowledge that have special appeal to each class's particular age group.
- Be pragmatic. Show students how they can use the knowledge in their daily lives.
- Use a variety of approaches. For each topic of study, select the approach(es) you believe will best stimulate student interest.
- Involve all students. Actively involve all students in each lesson. Remember that in a sense all individuals are motivated. The teacher's challenge is to provide meaningful activities for students to pursue—activities that lead to the discovery of knowledge and relationships pertinent to the lesson.
- Be positive. Students work harder and achieve more when they feel competent in what they are doing. Serious use of reinforcement can improve students' self-confidence.
- Be personal. Don't be afraid to relate to students on a personal basis. Teachers who remain formal at all times build barriers between themselves and their students.
- Use humor. Don't be afraid to enjoy your students. There's no time when student attention is more completely captured than when humor is occurring. Relax occasionally and let it happen.
- Be enthusiastic. Plan into the lesson events that you will enjoy. Enthusiasm is highly contagious.
- Challenge your students. Nothing is more boring than a lesson that fails to challenge the learners. Keep the pace brisk yet within students' reach.
- Use self-competition to motivate. Self-competition is challenging because all students can realistically compete with themselves. Grade contracts make expectations clear.
- Use rewards to reinforce positive behavior. Start rewarding all good behavior, then gradually decrease the frequency of the rewards.

Savage (1991) gives three general suggestions for applying motivation in the classroom. These guidelines provide a nice conclusion for this chapter:

Three factors of motivation can be helpful as teachers seek to apply motivation theory in the classroom: the needs and interest of the individual, the perception of the difficulty of the task, and the probability of success. If the teacher can relate school tasks to the interests and the needs of young-

sters, reduce the perception of effort required to an acceptable level, and increase the probability of success, the resultant increased attention to school tasks and decrease of discipline problems will help make teaching a very rewarding career. (p. 53)

The opportunities that teachers have to motivate their students are growing, and the future is exciting. For example, new microcomputer software offers exciting ways to motivate students. Magney (1990) explains: "Under the research microscope, the computer gaming curriculum comes off as clearly superior to conventional teaching on the affective dimension, both fostering higher levels of student interest and in promoting positive attitudes toward subject matter" (p. 56).

Motivation, however, is an illusive, ongoing challenge for all teachers. Just when you think you have developed the perfect system for motivating your students, you will get other students who will not be motivated by the same practices, or the students who formerly responded favorably to your system will change. Rinne (1998) explains: "What captures one student's attention might not affect another, and what appeals to one student today might miss the mark tomorrow (p. 621). Your best approach will be always to have on hand for each lesson a repertoire of high-interest activities.

Vignettes

You must include motivation strategies in each daily lesson plan. As you read the following vignettes, begin making a list of strategies that you will use each day and throughout the year to elevate your own enthusiasm level as well as your students'.

Vignette One: A Student Is Labeled a Failure

Mike Creswell was a quiet boy, although a bit mischievous at times. He often blushed and bowed his head whenever Jane, his teacher, spoke his name in the classroom. Jane's heart went out to Mike because he reminded her of an animal that had been kicked around so much it never knew when more punishment was coming. Mike appeared to distrust everyone, which probably explains why he had no close friends.

Jane met Mike's parents at a social affair and noticed that his father avoided mentioning that Mike was in her class. When she became convinced that he was not going to bring it up, Jane simply stated that she was pleased to have Mike in her class. Mr. Creswell immediately apologized for his son's inadequacies and then quickly changed the subject to another son, who was more academically inclined. Jane could see that Mr. Creswell was ashamed of Mike and that he did not really like the boy.

Through talking with other teachers, Jane learned that Mike's father constantly yelled at him at home, and some past incidents showed that Mike was actually beaten when he failed to live up to his father's expectations. Jane guessed that Mike preferred the beatings to the verbal downgrading, because the pain of physical punishment is temporary but the pain of being told you are unable to measure up never ends.

Some students never get over the damage their parents and teachers do by measuring them against a brother or sister who performed better in school. Most youths do not have the insight to see that what they can and do achieve is important, regardless of how much more or less someone else achieves. Unfortunately, many adults measure students against their parents.

Jane began encouraging Mike and rewarding him verbally for each task he performed successfully. By the end of the year, the quality of Mike's work had improved, and he had begun to relate better to her and to some of his classmates.

DISCUSSION

1. If a parent of one of your students seems ashamed of the child, how should you react? The parent who is ashamed of a son or daughter will

probably try to avoid discussing the child. Many teachers feel obligated to talk about the student at every opportunity without being obvious about it. The parent who reacts to an apparent weakness by ignoring the child is not behaving in an acceptable way. You can encourage discussion of the child's weakness with the parent if the weakness does exist. You can always offer to help the parent help the child correct it. You may be able to think of other approaches that suit your personality more.

2. How could the teacher make Mr. Creswell proud of his son? The teacher could initiate discussions about the areas in which Mike is most capable, which may or may not be academic. By checking Mike's cumulative records, standardized examination scores, and previous grades and by talking with other teachers, the teacher could identify Mike's strong areas. This would provide topics for discussion with Mr. Creswell.

3. How can you encourage other students to associate with a lonely child? By assigning the student tasks that the student can do, you allow the student to experience some success, and peers will begin to take notice. You can also assign group projects, making sure that the student can contribute to the group's assignment.

4. How can the teacher convince a parent not to compare one sibling with another? Emphasize that individuals excel in different areas. Furthermore, remind the parent that a child's failure to achieve does not always indicate lack of ability, but could indicate that the teacher or parents have failed to motivate the student.

A final note: Although state laws vary, Jane is responsible to report to the law any evidence that suggests a student is being physically abused. The school administrators and especially the counselor should become involved.

Vignette Two: A Student Teacher Uses Threats to Motivate

Bob Wright was eager to begin student teaching. On the first day that Ms. Lee, his supervisor, visited, Bob was presenting a well-organized lesson. He had a beautiful outline on the board and was discussing some interesting topics. However, the students were complacent and appeared to be unconcerned. The supervisor did not mention this to Bob, leaving him unaware of the students' response, or lack of it. During later observations, it was obvious that Bob had noticed something was wrong and was becoming upset with the students because they seemed so uninterested. Throughout the period he would remark, "You had better pay attention because this will be on our next test." Some of the few who initially were interested began to lose interest. Ms. Lee suggested to Bob that, instead of threatening to give a test, he try actually giving the test; each time he caught himself on the verge of saying "You had better . . . or else," he should go ahead and administer the "or else." By the end of the semester Bob's class was having healthy discussions. The students began listening to Bob and interacting with him.

DISCUSSION

1. Is the teacher justified in giving a pop quiz when students fail to complete homework assignments? Probably not, unless the teacher believes that the failure is the result of laziness and the quiz will motivate. The teacher's energy would be better spent improving lessons. Using pop quizzes can even lead to punishing students for what is really the teacher's inadequacy. An announced quiz set at a specific time each week would probably be a stronger motivator than an unannounced quiz. How do you feel about the use of pop quizzes to motivate? Can you defend your position?

2. How did Bob use the idea of a test? Bob used tests as a force to coerce students to study. His students' success probably occurred because he involved them in discussions and not because he gave unannounced tests. Students can be led to understand the worthwhile uses of test results. By using a test as a weapon against student misbehavior, the idea of testing becomes negative. Threatening students in any way is poor teaching practice.

> **Vignette Three: A Teacher Runs out of Material**
>
> The day had finally arrived for Mrs. King to begin teaching her own classes. It was exciting just to hear her describe the experience in the teacher's lounge later that morning. All had not gone well, however, and some teachers recalled similar experiences early in their own careers.
>
> Mrs. King's first class started well. She had a well-structured lesson that immediately captured the class's attention. When after a few moments she realized that the students were more interested in the lesson than in her, she felt relieved, and the first half of the hour went well. Time passed quickly and so did the lesson, and suddenly it was all over. The material was covered, but there were a good fifteen minutes left in the period. What could she do?
>
> Mrs. King did not have much experience, but she did not lack creativity. She immediately decided to review the lesson, but when this was accomplished in five minutes she was again at the point of panic. Then one student asked a question. From Mrs. King's report, the question was apparently answered thoroughly, since all ten remaining minutes were used in answering that one question. It was not an experience Mrs. King wanted to repeat. She began thinking of ways to avoid the task of stalling and ad-libbing to kill time.
>
> **DISCUSSION**
>
> 1. What can a teacher do to prevent running out of planned lesson material?
> 2. If there are no questions, how can a teacher fill the remainder of a class period?

Summary

Motivation is essential to learning. All students are motivated, but the teacher must find effective ways to channel their students' motivation toward the lessons. This can be done through helping them connect the curriculum to their personal lives, both in and outside of school. The challenge is accentuated in middle school because preadolescents are so egocentric.

You can increase your power to motivate by showing interest in your students' lives outside the classroom by attending sports events and student clubs, and by complimenting students. But compliments should always be sincere. You can also provide a threat-free climate by letting students know that you expect some failure and that you consider some failure as an essential prerequisite to success.

Above all, accept students for who they are, letting them know that you respect them. Be friendly and do not permit students to be rude to each other or to you. Let your students know that you have confidence in their ability to perform well in your class.

Students love suspense; so, give them mysteries to solve. Students also like high standards and clear directions. Make sure that the objectives for each lesson are clear. The arts can also be used to enhance students motivation because they welcome creativity and self-expression. Parents, too, can become partners if you remember to involve them with their children's academic program.

Recap of Major Ideas

1. You must convince students that the topics they study are worthwhile to them. This requires basing motivational efforts on students' perspectives, which may differ from yours.
2. Do not try to compete with the entertainment world. Teachers offer leadership, a quality that all middle school students need in their often unstructured lives.
3. You cannot force students to become interested in a lesson. At best, you can only spark student interest.
4. Application is an important avenue to motivation. Strive to show students how they can apply the material you teach to their daily lives.
5. Involving all students in lessons is a great motivation technique, yet teachers and students seldom discuss a lesson's purpose.
6. Positive student self-concepts are strong motivators, whereas negative concepts undermine your efforts to motivate.
7. Humor holds much potential for motivation. Successful use of humor does not require you to entertain students constantly. By relaxing the classroom atmosphere, you can allow natural humor to develop among the students.
8. Thorough planning and a well-structured lesson will enable you to be less formal. A controlled degree

of informality can contribute to students' motivational level.
9. Teacher enthusiasm is an indispensable element in motivation. You can ensure your own excitement by planning into each lesson activities that your students and you will enjoy.
10. Class tempo affects students' motivational level. Students tend to be more highly motivated when the lesson is fast enough to challenge them but not so fast that it confuses them.
11. Clarify goals. Students are more interested when they know what they are doing.
12. Give rewards and reinforcement only when students succeed. Therefore, assign tasks that students can perform well.
13. Space reinforcement at varying intervals.
14. Personal teacher–student relationships increase students' level of interest.
15. Use several strategies to achieve an effectively motivated classroom.
16. Parent involvement is needed, especially for African Americans, to convince them that their children can succeed.
17. Low academic achievement among minority students may be more attributable to level of income than to culture.
18. Curriculum experiences differ from the home lives of many minority students, making them passive at school.

Activities

The following activities will help you plan for a more stimulating climate in the classroom.
1. Examine your own personal traits. For each adjective you use to describe yourself, describe at least one way you can use this trait to make your class environment more interesting.
2. A degree of informality seems to be essential for maximum motivation in the classroom. Student teachers often ask, "How informal can I or should I be with my students without having them take advantage of my friendship?" Make a list of ways you can show your concern for your students. For each of these, explain how you can prepare to prevent their taking unfair advantage. It may be helpful if you decide at this time exactly where you will draw the line.
3. Make a list of teacher behaviors that can earn the respect of all students in a multicultural classroom.

Looking Ahead

This chapter has introduced several strategies you can use to enhance your students' interest level. The following and final chapter is provided to help you manage your classrooms in ways needed to provide a climate for optimal learning.

References

Alvestad, K. A., & Wingfield, A. L. (1993, January). A matter of motivation. *Executive Educator,* 1, 12–13.

Anderson, L. (1983, April). Achievement-related differences in students' responses to seatwork. Presented at the annual conference of the American Educational Research Association, Montreal.

Armstrong, D. G., Henson, K. T., & Savage, T. V. (2004). *Teaching today: An introduction to education* (7th ed.). Upper Saddle River, NJ: Merrill/Prentice-Hall.

Bandura, A. (1986). *Social foundations of thought and action.* Englewood Cliffs, NJ: Prentice-Hall.

Baughman, M. D. (1974). *Baughman's handbook of humor in education.* New York: Parker.

Borich, G. D. (1988). *Effective teaching methods.* Columbus, OH: Merrill.

Boutte, G. S., & McCormick, C. B. (1992). Educating and motivating African American males to succeed. *Journal of Negro Education,* 61(1), 4–11.

Brophy, J., & Good, T. L. (1986). Teacher behavior and student achievement. In Merlin C. Whittrock (Ed.), *Handbook of research on teaching* (3rd ed.) (p. 337). New York: Macmillan.

Buckner, J. H., & Bickel, F. (1991, January). If you want to know about effective teaching, why not ask your middle school kids? *Middle School Journal,* 22(3), 26–29.

Campbell, L. P. (1990, September–October). Philosophy = methodology = motivation = learning. *The Clearing House,* 64(1), 21–22.

Chansky, N. M. (1962). The X-ray of the school mark. *Educational Forum,* 12, 347–352.

Charles, C. (1981). *Building classroom discipline: From models to practice.* New York: Longman.

Clark, L. H., & Starr, I. S. (1976). *Secondary school teaching methods.* New York: Macmillan.

Danielson, C. (1996). *Enhancing professional practice, A framework for teaching*. Alexandria, VA: Association for Supervision and Curriculum Development.

Elam, S. M., Rose, L. C., & Gallup, A. M. (1994). The 26th annual Phi Delta Kappa Gallup poll of the public's attitudes toward the public schools. *Phi Delta Kappan*, 76(1), 41–56.

Englander, M. In K. T. Henson, & B. F. Eller (1999). *Educational psychology for effective teaching*. Belmont, CA: Wadsworth.

Evans, R. I. (1973). *Jean Piaget: The man and his ideas* (3rd ed.) (p. 141). New York: Dutton.

Evertson, C., Emmer, E., & Brophy, J. (1980). Predictors of effective teaching in junior high mathematics classrooms. *Journal for Research in Mathematics Education*, 11, 167–168.

Farris, R. A. (1990, November). Meeting their needs: Motivating middle level learners. *Middle School Journal*, 22, 22–26.

Fielding, L. G., & Pearson, P. D. (1994). Reading comprehension: What works. *Educational Leadership*, 51(5), 62–67.

Frymier, J. (1979, February). Keynote speech at Southwest Educational Research Association, Houston, TX.

Gage, N. L., & Berliner, D. C. (1984). *Educational psychology* (3rd ed.). Boston: Houghton Mifflin.

Gallup, A. M. (1985). The seventeenth annual Gallup poll of the public's attitude toward the public schools. *Phi Delta Kappan*, 67, 35–47.

Gardner, H., & Boix-Mansilla, V. (1994). Teaching for understanding within and across the disciplines. *Educational Leadership*, 51(5), 14–18.

Garibaldi, A. M. (1992). Educating and motivating African American Males. *Journal of Negro Education*, 61(1), 4–11.

Gilbert, S. L., & Smith, L. C. (2003). A bumpy road to action research. *Kappa Delta Pi Record*, 39(2), 80–83.

Gnagey, W. J. (1981). *Motivating classroom discipline*. New York: Longman.

Guskey, T. R. (1990, February). Integrating innovations. *Educational Leadership*, 47, 11–15.

Heckman, P. E., Confer, C. B., & Hakim, D. C. (1994). Planting seeds: Understanding through investigation. *Educational Leadership*, 51(5), 36–39.

Henson, K. T., & Eller, B. F. (1999). *Educational psychology for effective teaching*. Belmont, CA: Wadsworth.

Hiller, T. B., & Hietapelto, A. B. (2001, December). Contract grading promotes student responsibility, learning. *Journal of Management Education*, 25(6), 660–684.

Hilliard, R. D. (1999). All I ever needed to know about teaching, I learned in the middle school. *SRATE Journal*, 8(1), 50–56.

Holm, T. (2002). Humor as a teaching tool: Careful you don't cut somebody. *The Teaching Professor*, 16(4), 6.

Hootstein, E. W. (1994). Motivating students to learn. *The Clearing House*, 67(4), 213–216.

Jenkins, D. M., & Jenkins, K. D. (1991). The NMSA Delphi report: Roadmap to the future. *Middle School Journal*, 22(4), 27–36.

Jenkins, D. R. (1994). An eight step plan for teaching responsibility. *The Clearing House*, 67(5), 269–270.

Latham, A. S. (1998). Gender differences on assessments. *Educational Leadership*, 55(4), 88–89.

Lemke, J. L. (1982, April). *Classroom communication of science*. Final report to National Science Foundation/Rising to Individual Scholastic Excellence.

Magney, J. (1990). Game-based teaching. *Education Digest*, 60(5), 54–57.

Markle, G., Johnston, J. H., Geer, C., & Meichtry, Y. (1990, November). Teaching for understanding. *Middle School Journal*, 22(2), 53–57.

Maslow, A. (1973). What is a taoistic teacher? In L. J. Rubin (Ed.), *Facts and feelings in the classroom*. New York: Walker.

McConnell, J. (1977). *Relationships between selected teacher behaviors and attitudes/achievements of algebra classes*. Presented at the annual meeting of the American Educational Research Association.

McEwan, E. K. (2002). *10 traits of highly effective teachers*. Thousand Oaks, CA: Corwin Press.

MLS (1998). Metropolitan Life Insurance Survey. *The American teacher*. New York: Lewis Harris & Associates.

Patterson, W. (2003) Breaking out of our boxes. *Phi Delta Kappan*, 84(8), 569–574.

Phelps, P. H. (1991, March–April). Helping teachers excel as classroom teachers. *The Clearing House, 64*(4), 241–242.

Phillips, B. (1962). Sex, social class, and anxiety as sources of variation in school activity. *Journal of Educational Psychology, 53,* 361–362.

Raywid, M. A. (1998). Small schools: A reform that works. *Educational Leadership, 55*(4), 34–39.

Redmon, W. K., & Farris, H. E. (1985, January). Improving the academic productivity of high school students through behavior contracting: A model project. *Journal of Instructional Psychology, 12,* 46–58.

Reich, R. B. (1991). *The work of nations: Preparing ourselves for the 21st century capitalism.* New York: Knopf.

Rinne, C. H. (1998). Motivating students is a percentage game. *Phi Delta Kappan, 79*(8), 620–628.

Salend, S. J. (1987). Contingency management systems. *Academic Therapy, 22,* 245–253.

Sapp, G. L. (1973). Classroom management and student involvement. *High School Journal, 56,* 276–283.

Sautter, R. C. (1994). An arts education school reform strategy. *Phi Delta Kappan, 75*(6), 432–437.

Savage, T. V. (1991). *Discipline for self-control.* Englewood Cliffs, NJ: Prentice-Hall.

Schmoker, M. (1990). Sentimentalizing self-esteem. *The Education Digest, 60*(7), 55–56.

Seligmann, J. (1989, Winter/Spring). Variations on a theme. *Newsweek, 22*(2), 38–46.

Special Study Panel on Education Indicators for the National Center for Education Statistics (1991, September). *Education Counts.* Washington, DC: U.S. Department of Education.

Stefanich, G. P. (1990, November). Cycles of cognition. *Middle School Journal, 22*(2), 47–52.

Stiggins, R. J. (1997). *Student-centered classroom assessment* (2nd ed.). Columbus, OH: Merrill.

Warshaw, M. (1975, August). Behavior modification in secondary schools. *Educational Technology, 15*(8), 25–52.

Weber, W. A., & Roff, L. A. (1985). A review of the teacher education literature on classroom management. In W. A. Weber, L. A. Roff, J. Crawford, & C. Robinson (Eds.), *Classroom management: Reviews of the teacher education and research literature.* Princeton, NJ: Educational Testing Service.

Weiner, B. (1979). A theory of motivation for some classroom experiences. *Journal of Educational Psychology, 71,* 2–25.

Wiske, M. S. (1994). How teaching for understanding changes the rules in the classroom. *Educational Leadership, 51*(5), 19–21.

12
From Discipline to Self-Discipline

Good discipline is a by-product of interesting, exciting, and engaging instruction.

C. M. Evertson

Objectives

- Give two reasons why teachers must not rely on power and punishment for discipline.
- Contrast two different approaches to classroom discipline.
- Describe the public's attitude toward discipline in today's secondary and middle schools.
- Define discipline in terms of order and control.
- Explain the relationship between quietness and discipline.
- List three guidelines for conducting a private talk with a student who has misbehaved.
- Tell what is wrong with the adage, "Be tough at first and relax the rules as time passes."
- Describe at least one way that the teacher's role in discipline has changed.
- Explain the role of teacher efficacy in classroom discipline.
- Develop a set of guidelines to use to ensure positive behavior in the computer lab.

FROM DISCIPLINE TO SELF-DISCIPLINE

Preliminaries
- Definition
- Need
- Discipline and Instruction
- Teacher Efficacy
- Focus on Learning
- Cooperative Approach

Theories
- Faculty Psychology
- Stimulus–Response Approach
- Behavior Psychology
- Reality Theory
- Group Management Theory
- Assertive Discipline
- Corporal Punishment
- Maslow's Needs Hierarchy
- McGregor's Theories X & Y

Models
- Authoritarian
- Group Process
- Instructional
- Intimidation
- Training Model
- Behavior Modification
- Group Dynamics
- Cascade Model

Problems

Avoiding
- Use Names
- Use Enthusiasm
- Use Self-Respect
- Avoid Threats
- Public Reprimands
- Ridicule

Handling
- Anticipate and Prepare
- Ask Why
- Decelerate
- Private Talk
- Firmness and Consistency

Connecting Statements

	Agree	Disagree	Uncertain
1. Truly effective discipline and classroom management are inseparable terms.			
2. Discipline is the same as restraint.			
3. Physical punishment is sometimes the best approach to resolve a discipline problem.			
4. A quiet class is usually a well-disciplined one, and a noisy class is usually undisciplined.			
5. At the beginning of the year, the teacher should be strict, since it is easier to loosen the rules than to strengthen them.			
6. Discipline models should be consistent with accepted learning theories and with management theories in other fields.			
7. The ultimate goal should be to get students to discipline themselves.			

> ### Tips for Teachers
>
> Discipline presents a special challenge for the middle-level teacher. A recent survey shows that most middle-level teachers feel a strong need for more classroom management skills. The best approach is a preventive one. Use this chapter to learn how to prevent discipline problems. Avoid relying on your position of authority or, worse, corporal punishment to achieve discipline in your classes.
>
> Your position as teacher should get you through the first five minutes of your career. From then on, you will need the knowledge and skills offered in this chapter. To survive, you must master them. As the teacher, you must learn how to earn your students' respect and cooperation. Only then can you lead them to a state of self-discipline. Do not settle for anything less.

A Preview of Discipline

Following a brief period of secondary and middle school classroom observations for a seminar, a group of preservice college students gave the following reports.

Report 1. The eighth-grade English class was a farce. Chaos prevailed. At any one time it was impossible to tell who had the floor. Despite the teacher's efforts to gain control and focus the students' attention on the lesson, the discussion resembled a racquetball, forever bouncing in undetermined directions. The teacher's repeated reprimands and threats to the reluctant learners were evidence that the teacher did want to gain control of the situation, but each lesson was like all others—the teacher simply had no control. Each day students made little if any cognitive gain.

Report 2. The biology class was all business. When the teacher looked over his pair of narrow bifocals, a deadly silence fell over the room. Everyone knew who had control. When each daily lecture began, students sat upright and took notes. When seats were assigned, there were no disruptions, no discussion, and no questions. No one even thought about getting off task in this class. When the bell rang at the beginning of the period, it signaled the end of all social interaction. Even such nonverbal communications as smiles and nods of approval were seldom seen.

Report 3. Sixth grade was time for enjoying learning. Each day the students arrived alive with curiosity. Students brought with them truths captured as insects, rocks, leaves, and other treasures they often carried in their hands and pockets. When the class began, they always knew the daily objectives and how each activity led to one or more of those objectives. Almost every student felt capable of mastering the class's goals. But the classroom's organization and structure did not get in the way of learning or of enjoying each lesson. They also did not stay unnecessary quiet. In fact, this sixth-grade class was usually quite noisy. Somehow even private conversations seemed to focus at least to some degree on the topics being studied. Although a constant chattering and buzzing characterized the class, the teacher seemed able to get the students' attention.

A 1991 Gallup Poll (Elam, Rose, & Gallup, 1991) cited discipline and drugs as the public's two major concerns about U.S. schools. In fact, discipline and drugs have been the major concerns every year for the 23 years that this poll has been conducted. The public perceives the discipline problem in U.S. schools to be so great that Elam et al. (1991) drew the following conclusions.

The public is thoroughly consistent in its perceptions that (1) students in the public schools of the U.S. lack discipline and (2) improved discipline is the answer to many of the schools' problems. In the 1991 poll the general public ranked discipline second among the biggest problems with which public schools in their communities must deal, gave a disciplined environment (free of drugs and violence) the number-one ranking among the six national goals, ranked maintenance of student discipline second among factors important to parents in choosing a public school for their child, and rated firmer discipline first among suggestions for helping low-income and racial or ethnic minority students succeed in school (Elam et al., 1991).

These perceptions clash with the opinions of teachers, who usually perceive discipline problems to be much less serious than parents' lack of interest and support, lack of proper financial support, and pupils' lack of interest and truancy as major problems. Either the public has been misled, or the teachers are mistaken. Wherever the truth lies, this discrepancy in perceptions is a cause for serious concern.

The rapid deterioration of youth's behavior is reflected in the 1994 Gallup poll, which reported that "for the first time ever 'fighting,' 'violence' and 'gangs' shared the number one position with lack of discipline" (Elam, Rose, & Gallup, 1994, p. 42). Yet some of the concern results from the increased media attention this topic receives. This poll also reported that only a small percentage of teachers and students felt that violence has increased in the past year. Parents are concerned for their children's safety (Rose & Gallup, 1998). Students share this concern (Kenney & Watson, 1996).

By 1998, the Gallup poll (Rose & Gallup, 1998) saw lack of discipline drop to the number-two concern. Unfortunately, the concern that replaced it as the biggest problem facing the public schools was fighting, violence, and gangs. This change certainly does nothing to console the worries that beginning teachers have over their ability to maintain a productive climate in their classes. Shootings on school campuses in recent years, both in this country and abroad, have caused educators to become sensitive to bullying among students. For example, one study reported that from 1983 until 2000 the percentage of victimized students increased by 50 percent and the percent of students who were involved (both bulliers and victims) had increased by 65 percent (Olweus, 2003). By 2003, eleven states had written policy requiring schools to take steps to reduce bullying (Cooper & Snell, 2003). Remember from Chapter 4 that other approaches to reducing school violence include improving instruction to make lessons more interesting and engaging, and building a community in the classroom that expands throughout the school, overflowing and connecting to the local community. According to Schaps (2003, p. 31), "A growing body of research confirms the beliefs of building a sense of community in school. Students in schools with a strong sense of community are more likely to be academically motivated and to avoid violence and drugs." Schaps suggests the following as guidelines to set and assess the degree of community:

- My class is like a family
- Students in my class help one another learn
- I believe that I can talk to the teachers in this school about things that are bothering me
- Students in my class can get a rule changed if they think that it is unfair (p. 32)

Some schools elevate their spirit of community by using activities and symbols that celebrate learning and tie the current generation to future generations. Glickman (2003, p. 34) says, "Too few schools have symbols that will evoke the spirit of education in the future for students, teachers, staff, and parents. . . . Some schools, however, connect with the heart and soul of generations of students and continue to convey the promise of education for future generations" (p. 34). Some schools display quilts with symbols that tell their history. A school in Amherst, New Hampshire, has an annual event that pulls its faculty members together. The ritual is a Viking funeral held on the last day of school. All faculty members write last year's memories on notes, walk to the river together, and send the notes off in a cardboard Viking boat, releasing anger, sadness, and frustration. One school lets each student wear the school's original graduation robe, connecting the academic community from year to year.

A stronger sense of community helps students develop stronger positive self-identities—feelings of the self as learners and as human beings. Individual students need their own academic identities to prevent them from feeling alienated from the learning community. Jackson (2003) suggests that teachers build **identity education** programs to help all students and that each program should include metacognitive strategies to help students understand and improve their learning skills. The programs could include instruction on note taking, helping students identify and build on their strengths, and helping students learn how to benefit from study groups. Another area where students need help is with **pedagogical content knowledge.** Singham (2003, p. 590) explains, "In any subject, students arrive with preconceived knowledge that may conflict with what the instructor is trying to teach. This knowledge is often so deeply buried in the student's mind that he or she may not even be aware of it, but these discipline-specific learning obstacles drive learning nonetheless, and, if teachers do not take them into account, their best efforts can be nullified" (p. 590). Singham reminds us that such programs are good for all students and especially for those students who are currently falling behind.

Remember that Gilbert & Smith (2003) reminded us that most teachers haven't spent much time helping each other improve their teaching. Middle-level teachers have an especially strong need to collaborate because of the integrative quality of middle-level curricula. Wilms (2003) suggests that teachers use a process developed in Japan known as **lesson study.** In lesson study, "teachers work collaboratively as they develop lessons. Then they teach the lessons while observing one another to see how well their lessons worked. The feedback enables teachers to make a series of refinements" (p. 606).

Two important messages about lesson study are worth remembering. First, to work well, it must be reinvented by teachers, not administrators or "experts" and then given to teachers for implementation. Second, lesson study can help teachers connect standards with assessments and with curricula. Weissberg et al. (2003) say that good social and emotional programs go further; each is grounded in theory and research, teaches students to apply emotional skills and ethical values in daily life, builds connections between students and their school, provides developmentally and culturally appropriate instruction, addresses the affective and social dimensions of academic learning, involves families and communities as partners, and establishes successful organizational supports and policies.

A final reminder as you work to help your students build positive self-images; as mentioned earlier by Parsley & Corcoran (2003), it is imperative that teachers see value in each student and continuously search for opportunities to communicate that value to each student. By being a positive role model and showing respect for all students teachers can encourage students to help each other experience success (Osterman, 2003; Phelps, 2003). The goal here is to create an academic subculture in your room, which is essential for maximum growth of all students (Marzano, 1998). Taylor & Peterson (2003, p. 81) say that when adolescents know that they have the power to impact another's life by giving of themselves, they, too, can be changed forever. Further good news is that once adolescents become engaged in helping others, they enjoy being helpful. Referring to service learning programs, Phelps (2003, p. 5) says "Service learning can be a powerful attraction for adolescents, most of whom want to make a positive impact on the world."

Williams, Alley, and Henson (1999) have noted that beginning teachers are at a disadvantage because they are expected to begin their very first day of teaching with the same level of management skills that experienced teachers have. Wilson, Ireton, and Wood (1997) say that new teachers worry that they might not be able to meet the needs of students from diverse backgrounds (p. 36). The 2001 Gallup poll of the the public's attitudes toward the public schools (Rose & Gallup, 2001) found lack of discipline and lack of finances tied as the number-one problem of our schools, and fighting, violence, and gangs as major problems in the schools.

Novice teachers' inability to handle unruly classes is one of the most daunting responsibilities that contemporary teachers face (Williams, Alley, and Henson, 1999). When forty-one middle school teachers were asked to identify the most important skills for teachers, the highest-ranked skill was effective classroom management (Stokes, 2001). Interestingly, while one might assume that the level of this felt need might diminish with experience, the senior teachers (those with more than six years of experience) rated the need as critical as did their less experienced counterparts.

Discipline: A Definition

Discipline is defined in many ways. In the past, the term was associated with such concepts as punishment, restraint, and forced behavior, but many educators now reject such negative interpretations. A more contemporary view of discipline involves such concepts as order and control. Because order implies direction, discipline might be defined as a climate that is controlled to provide order. Even the manner in which teachers introduce control varies. The manner in which teachers give directives can affect whether students obey or ignore those directives. Hanny (1994) gives some practical advice: "Avoid making statements intended to change behavior by using the interrogatives" (p. 252). For example, instead of saying, "Will you sit down?," it is better to say, "Please sit down," giving the students no choice.

Reflection

Some, possibly most, contemporary educators reject the use of excessive force and constraint in the name of discipline. Yet some insist that force and even punishment are essential for disciplining certain students who, they maintain, do not understand anything else. These educators say that teachers are justified, even obligated, to use whatever measures are necessary to discipline their students. What is your position on this issue? Do you agree with either of these extremes?

Desirable Teacher Attitudes toward Discipline

Discipline Is a Must

Discipline, defined as order and control, is essential. Because each teacher must ensure that maximum learning occurs in the classroom, each teacher is responsible for maintaining the discipline necessary to meet this goal. "Effective schools maintain an orderly and safe climate that is conducive to learning and teaching" (Henson & Eller, 1999, p. 18). Following is one author's explanation of why all teachers must learn to manage their classes:

> *One of the most difficult challenges beginning teachers face is classroom management. If teachers do not succeed in this aspect of teaching, then their instructional efforts may fail as well. Many otherwise good teachers have left the profession because of their inability to manage the classroom effectively. (Phelps, 1991, p. 241)*

Hanny (1994) reinforces Phelps's assertion that all teachers must maintain an organized and controlled classroom climate: "You must have rules and the consequences of breaking them must be clear" (p. 252). McDaniel (1994) echoes the importance of having effective discipline and management skills: "The principles and practices of effective discipline and classroom management are among the most important professional concerns that practicing educators must deal with daily" (p. 247).

Beginning teachers are often threatened especially by multicultural classes because they know that they don't have the skills needed to work with students from diverse backgrounds (Wilson et al., 1997). A good place to start is by showing respect for all students, holding them to high but attainable expectations, and expressing confidence in your beliefs of their capabilities. When teachers instill pride in students, the students will often police themselves.

Discipline and Instruction

Deciding how to manage the classroom to prevent and control behavioral problems depends to a large degree on the type of instruction. Eighty percent of inappropriate behaviors result from ineffective teaching (Phillips, 1998). During a lecture—even a very short lecture—students must listen to the teacher or to classmates who are asking or answering questions. However, during a problem-solving lesson such as an inquiry lesson, a simulation game, or a case study, talking and sometimes moving around are not only tolerated but may even be required if the lesson is to succeed. Constructivist teachers recognize that students often require more activity to develop understanding, activity that may disrupt a lecture.

Attaining affective and psychomotor objectives may require even more interaction among students. Teachers who use an eclectic approach, choosing to lecture for part of a period and then using a student-centered approach such as small discussions for the rest of the period, should be more tolerant of productive noise and movement during the latter part of the period. To avoid sending a confusing message to students, explain why more noise and movement are permitted at one time than at another.

Some constants are vital during all types of lessons (e.g., a high level of respect for everyone and continuous focus on the lesson objectives). Student-centered lessons should not alter either of these goals; noise and movement should be productive, which can happen only in a climate of respect and focus. Focus is likely to be maintained only if the teacher begins the lesson, and indeed each part of the lesson, by reminding students of the objectives set for each teacher activity and each student activity.

Too often, students either listen passively or even participate in excellent activities without being aware of the lesson's major concepts. Near the end of each lesson, you should lead the students in reflecting on the major concepts addressed. After the lesson, at your first opportunity, reflect on the activities and whether they worked or not; vow to improve the lesson before teaching it again.

Use of Nonverbal Communications

Through their actions, teachers can communicate their attitudes and their expectations. Grubaugh (1989, p. 34) explains the importance of using nonverbal communications in classroom management and offers an example of how teachers can use this tool: the instructional setting and the teacher's nonverbal (body) language give students extremely strong impressions about a teacher's management and disciplinary intentions, tolerances, strengths, and weaknesses. In nearly all instances, the sound of people speaking rises and falls in patterns or waves. Time your remarks at the trough of a wave of sound in the classroom so that you can begin speaking in a softer voice to set a more quiet tone.

Some teachers already have a tremendous influence on their students' behavior, and all teachers can attain this influence. Thompson (1994) suggests the use of a nonintrusive approach to problem management: "There is no purpose in making a major crises out of every disciplinary situation" (p. 264). Teachers must realize they have this capacity. A desirable attitude is: As the teacher, I must and will establish and maintain in my classroom the climate necessary for maximum learning. Such an attitude makes students feel secure and is apt to earn more respect for a teacher than an attitude of doubt and insecurity.

Because discipline and instruction are inseparable, all good teachers are concerned with discipline. MacNaughton and Johns (1991) explain:

Good school and classroom discipline is not necessarily something that is attained once and for all. Schools, student body characteristics, and teacher backgrounds and personalities are all subject to change. This requires that you keep working at management and discipline much the same way as you would curriculum development. (p. 56)

Teachers must prepare to manage their classrooms. As Ban (1994) says, "Teaching school poses no more formidable challenge than managing student behavior" (p. 257).

Teacher Efficacy

Teacher efficacy, or teachers' belief in their ability to ensure their students' success, influences classroom behavior more than most people realized until recently. As noted in Chapter 10, a sense of efficacy is empowering, and in 1995 the Carnegie Council on Adolescent Development Staff (1995) set teacher empowerment as a major goal for all middle-level teachers. Many teachers believe that they cannot control their students, which they want to be able to do. In 1991 the National Center for Education Statistics reported the results of a 1988 study that found that about one-third of all high school teachers felt they had little or no disciplinary control over their students (Figure 12.1).

We have heard about individuals whose personalities seem so suited to teaching that they become referred to as "born teachers." When asked about any research that would support this claim, Emmer said, "I don't know of any research that backs up this impression, however, I have observed effective teachers with such varied personalities that I am dubious about the claims. What I have observed that is common among good managers is self-

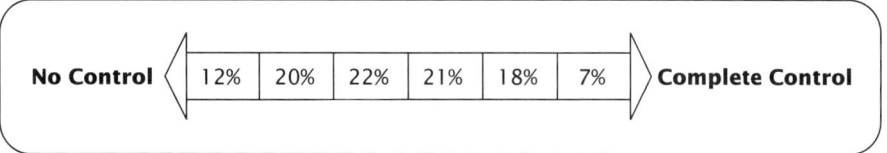

FIGURE 12.1 TEACHER DISCIPLINARY CONTROL OVER CLASSROOMS

Source: National Center for Education Statistics. (1991). *Education counts.* Washington, DC: U.S. Department of Education, p. 20.

confidence and assertiveness about enforcing reasonable rules and procedures" (Henson & Eller, 1999, p. 415).

The types of behaviors now considered serious show the extent of discipline problems in the schools (Table 12.1). However, there is more at stake than the teacher's survival that makes discipline a must for all teachers, and as Savage (1999) explains, teachers not only have the right to discipline students, they do not have the right not to. Savage says, "Teachers should not think that they have no rights, nor should misbehaving students interfere with their right to teach and the right of others to learn" (p. 204). Hanny (1994) shares this belief: "Those who want to learn have a right not to be disrupted by others" (p. 252).

Teachers must know and accept their responsibility to establish and maintain discipline, because that is a prerequisite to achieving good behavior in most classrooms. Good discipline does not just happen; it begins with certain teacher attitudes. Teachers must accept responsibility for classroom discipline, and "each teacher must find the discipline techniques

TABLE 12.1 The Top Problems Perceived in Schools in 1940 and 1982

1940	1982
1. Talking	1. Rape
2. Chewing gum	2. Robbery
3. Making noise	3. Assault
4. Running in the halls	4. Burglary
5. Getting out of turn in line	5. Arson
6. Wearing improper clothing	6. Bombings
7. Not putting paper in wastebaskets	7. Murder
	8. Suicide
	9. Absenteeism
	10. Vandalism
	11. Extortion
	12. Drug abuse
	13. Alcohol abuse
	14. Gang warfare
	15. Pregnancy
	16. Abortion
	17. Venereal disease

Source: Reprinted from *Harper's Magazine,* March 1985, and the Presidential Biblical Scoreboard with permission from the Biblical News Service, Costa Mesa, California. Taken from Johnston, W. J. (1985), *Education on Trial* (p. 20). San Francisco: ICS Press.

most congruent with his or her educational philosophy and individual student needs" (Bell & Stefanich, 1984, p. 134).

Furthermore, instruction in classroom management can diminish behavior problems and improve learning. Evertson (1989) studied these effects and reported that "this study supports the position that giving teachers opportunities to plan and develop academic and administrative routines that keep students productively engaged and keep inappropriate behavior to a minimum results in preserving instructional time" (p. 90).

A predictable pattern of how teachers view discipline occurs as teachers mature. Compare the difference in the way student teachers have been reported to view discipline with the assumptions that two experts use to describe discipline in their book. Preservice teachers tend to see problem behavior not as a result of the environment but rather as an intentional and controllable act by the student (Cunningham, 1988). In their book, *Comprehensive Classroom Management,* Jones and Jones (1986) present five key assumptions relative to effective classroom management:

1. Classroom management should be based on a solid understanding of students' personal, psychological, and learning needs.
2. Classroom management involves establishing positive teacher–student and peer relationships that help meet students' basic psychological needs.
3. Classroom management involves employing classroom organization and group management methods that maximize on-task student behavior.
4. Classroom management involves using instructional methods that facilitate optimal learning by responding to the academic needs of individual students and the classroom group.
5. Classroom management includes the ability to employ a wide range of counseling and behavioral methods that involve students in examining and correcting their inappropriate behavior. (p. 333)

These qualities (clear objectives, high expectations, regular homework, and careful monitoring) do not make the environment in effective schools rigid. Rather, these demands on students are balanced by a climate that reflects concern for all students. As Gathercoal (1990) explains: "Effective schools try to adapt to the child, not adapt the child to the school" (p. 23).

Educators' perception of the teacher's role in managing student behavior has changed over the years. Initially, the use of negative responses to misbehavior was stressed. Jones (1989) explains:

Historically teachers often depended on a loud voice, a paddle or some other form of intimidation to maintain control. Until very recently many teachers were presented with such oversimplified generalizations as don't smile until Christmas and don't grin until Thanksgiving. However, during the past two decades researchers have conducted both correlational and experimental studies the results of which suggest a variety of teacher behaviors that are associated with positive student behavior and student achievement gains. (p. 330)

However, the latter half of this century saw a shift from teachers' negative response to bad behavior to teachers' positive, preventive behavior. As Jones (1989) has said:

A new emphasis on classroom management was developed during the 1970s. This new direction emphasized not what teachers did in response to student misconduct, but rather how teachers prevented or contributed to students' misbehavior. This research, later labeled Teacher Effectiveness,

> has focused attention on three sets of teacher behaviors that influence students' behavior and learning: (1) Student–teacher relationships, (2) teachers' skill in organizing and managing classroom activities, and (3) teachers' instructional skills. (p. 331)

Too often teachers get a very narrow view of the causes of behavior problems. Others have noted this problem. Jones (1989) said: "Researchers, writers and trainers have presented various aspects of classroom management as isolated, often relatively simple solutions to a complex problem" (p. 333). McDaniel (1994) reminds educators that problems in the classroom often develop outside the classroom and are transported to the classroom: "The school is indeed a microcosm of the world outside" (p. 255). Oana (1993) says this more emphatically: "The problem is, today's schools, no matter how much they change, cannot cope with all the social ills its clients bring to their doors each day" (p. 5). Former Idaho Teacher of the Year Shirley Rau says that the reform reports have failed to help schools overcome society's illnesses: "There has been a lot of talk about education reform. We have an education president. Unfortunately, good intentions haven't been translated into any action" (Henson & Eller, 1999, p. 29).

A Focus on Learning

Historically, teachers have been reluctant to use student-centered discipline models. However, many students bring hurts with them, emotional wounds that interfere with their learning. Erb (1997) reminds us that we must not ignore the previous damages if indeed we are to help these students succeed. "Emotionally-barren homes, unsafe neighborhoods, and the deprivation of property can leave some children scared long before they enter a middle school" (p. 2). There have been some major shifts in the ways discipline has been defined over the years. Paramount among these is a recent tendency to substitute the term *classroom management* for discipline. The major difference is that classroom management is generally more positive. It connotes skills and leadership, but more important, it implies a specific purpose—to develop and maintain a classroom climate that maximizes learning.

This placing of learning as the basis for discipline is another important teacher attitude. Alabama Teacher of the Year Susan Lloyd says, "Disruptive behavior in my class is stopped not because it is against the rules, but because it reduces the amount of time they and the rest of the class have for learning" (Henson & Eller, 1999, p. 170). Teacher remedies for discipline problems today can be grouped into two categories: reactive and proactive. Proactive discipline is predicated on the necessity for forethought, anticipation, preparation, and consistency with regard to teacher behavior and the consequences occasioned by student behavior (Ban, 1994, p. 257).

Teaching and Discipline Are Inseparable

Many, perhaps most, discipline problems are the result of poor teaching. Whether a teacher uses the term *discipline* or *classroom management* does not matter, as long as the teacher realizes that these cannot be separated from the act of teaching. Nothing works better for establishing and maintaining discipline in a classroom than planning and executing a good lesson.

As explained by Evertson (1989), "Of course, good discipline is a by product of interesting, exciting, and engaging instruction" (p. 84). This idea was developed in Chapter 4 on planning daily lessons.

The Cooperative Approach

Thus far, we have described discipline as the teacher's sole responsibility. Teacher efficacy can contribute to establishing a desirable classroom climate. However, teachers should not be alone in their concern for maintaining a well-disciplined class. After all, if chaos prevails, the students suffer most. Therefore, many teachers choose to involve their students in maintaining discipline in their classrooms. This makes the job easier, and it also promotes a very important student attitude toward discipline. That attitude is self-discipline.

Data show that teachers can plan effective strategies for controlling classroom behavior. For example, Ban (1994) says, "teachers should ask students to identify common behavior problems in school" and "students should formulate a behavior statement of rule that deals with these identified misbehaviors" (p. 258). Students should be involved in setting some of the job classroom behavior rules. Ban (1994) explains: "In classrooms where students have had a part in shaping the rules of behavior, the power of peer pressure will work to ensure students' compliance with these rules" (p. 258).

Discipline: A Continuum of Views

FIGURE 12.2 DISCIPLINE CONTINUUM

The wide range of views about discipline can be seen by placing them on a continuum (Figure 12.2). Clearly, some teachers remain at the far left side of the continuum. Other teachers (such as the sixth-grade teacher at the beginning of the chapter) have moved to the opposite extreme. Teachers at the right side of the continuum often appear to have few or no discipline problems. In fact, they often seem to ignore the topic altogether, whereas teachers on the left side of the continuum may seem obsessed with the idea.

> *Reflection*
>
> Review the range of views of discipline shown in Figure 12.2 and make a list of objectives or statements to describe teachers who fall on the left side of the discipline continuum. Then make a list to describe teachers who belong on the right side. Perhaps you have already surmised that your net task will be to determine where you belong on this continuum. This may not be easy, but it is important because you must know where you stand concerning discipline so you can act accordingly.

Using Theories

Management Theories and Education

Teachers are not alone in their tendency to span the spectrum with their perceptions of discipline. Management practices should be consistent with our knowledge and theories of learning, and even these vary greatly. The following is a review of some major learning theories. As you recognize each of these from your earlier courses in educational psychology, see if you can place each theory accurately on the discipline continuum.

Faculty Psychology

Before the twentieth century there was little effort to understand the process of learning. The first collective beliefs that were actually written down and accepted by a significant number of psychologists (perhaps the vast majority) became known as *faculty psychology.*

Perceiving the brain as a muscle that had special capacities (faculties), these theorists believed that further development of the brain hinged on certain conditions. They believed that, like any muscle, the brain needed exercise to grow. This exercise should be difficult and boring, not enjoyable, and therefore lectures and recitation should be the major teaching methods.

Although faculty psychology seems absurd to many contemporary educators, this theory still plays a role in modern education. A visit to almost any school will reveal that faculty psychology continues to shape the climate in many classrooms. Some recent reports on education have given renewed life to these theories. Private schools designed and established according to the faculty psychology theory are growing in popularity and number.

Stimulus-Response Psychology

By the turn of the century, a new school of thought had become influential in shaping U.S. education. The *stimulus–response* (S–R) psychologists perceived all behavior as responses to stimuli. To effect learning, the teacher merely needed to change the classroom stimuli. This school of thought has some validity, because student behavior is indeed shaped to some degree by the total stimuli in the classroom environment. By removing undesirable stimuli, the teacher can remove much of the undesirable behavior. By adding other stimuli (rewards), new behavior could be added. However, recognizing that the degree to which a stimulus shapes behavior is determined somewhat by the individual (organism) who is responding, the S–R symbol that represented the stimulus–response theory was changed to S–O–R.

Behavioral Psychology

Some psychologists disagree with the stimulus–response psychologists, maintaining that only a small portion of human behaviors are responses to stimuli. *Behavioral* psychologists believe that most human behavior is overt—that is, purposive and self-initiated. They recognize that repetition, rewards, and reinforcements play important roles in shaping behavior. Some of the major education programs that emerged from this school of thought are programmed instruction, behavior modification, and computer-assisted instruction (CAI).

Phenomenology

By the middle of the twentieth century, some psychologists began paying more attention to the individual. Rogerian psychologists listened carefully to their clients and considered the individual's own perceptions. From this concern grew a new psychological theory called *phenomenology*. Unlike earlier psychologists, who focused their energy on finding more effective ways of forcing or persuading students to change their behavior, phenomenologists studied ways of getting students to change their own behavior. From this school of thought came the idea of the self-concept. These psychologists realized that students will work diligently to protect their self-image. By helping their students develop a positive image of themselves as competent students, a teacher could indirectly cause students to channel their own behavior in more positive directions.

> ### Reflection
> Now see where you would place each of the above learning theories on the discipline continuum. Clearly, they belong somewhere left of center, because each uses external stimuli. In effect, each perceives the teacher's role as combining repetition, rewards, reinforcements, and punishments to alter student behavior.

Reality Therapy

Reality therapy is an approach to behavior management that has been modified for classroom use by Dr. William Glasser, who contends that misbehavior results from a lack of involvement in the school process. Failure and lack of a sense of students' responsibility for the outcomes of their behavior causes misbehavior. Conversely, success begets success. According to this theory, teachers should (1) display strong positive emotional characters, (2) state rules clearly so they are understood, (3) spend some time each day with each student, (4) focus on present behavior and not refer to past behavior, and (5) require students to evaluate their own behavior. In addition, teacher and student(s) should (6) develop together a corrective plan that is simple, short, and success-oriented. It should have only a few rules, but they must be obeyed. Finally (7), the teacher should obtain a verbal or written commitment from the student(s) (Curwin & Mendler, 1984).

The philosophical basis for Glasser's theory is that society as a whole has shifted from socially sanctioned goals to personal goals—know yourself and know what you want. The result has been the emergence of an "identity society." For this reason, schools should shift from an external locus of control—do what the teacher says—to an internal locus of control, whereby students are involved in planning and directing the school activities. External locus of control is a major roadblock to at-risk students (Parsley & Corcoran, 2003).

Vars (1997) explains the significance of locus of control:

People with an external locus of control see their lives as controlled by other people or by "luck." They are unlikely to exert much effort on their own behalf. On the other hand, people with internal locus of control see themselves as having at least some influence over other events. Hence it is important to invite students to work with their teachers to make critical decisions at all stages of the learning enterprise, especially goal setting, establishing evaluation criteria, demonstrating learning, self-evaluation, and reporting. (p. 45)

According to Glasser, the major cause of classroom misbehavior is teachers' failure to involve students. Control theory is based on the belief that individuals are motivated internally, not externally, as Glasser contends many teachers think. More specifically, this internal motivation results from five basic needs: survival, love, power, fun, and freedom.

Control theory can best be thought of as self-control, since it refers to the student's being in control of his or her life. Unfortunately, according to this theory, the individual's genes know nothing about delayed gratification. A baby's needs are usually addressed immediately. By the time a child is old enough to enter school, the family usually has taught the child that the good feeling that good behavior brings is not immediate. In other words, the message is "work hard, succeed, and continue working hard; the reward will come later." Unfortunately, children without a supportive family find it hard to behave without immediate rewards.

Glasser warns that too many teachers believe that many students are getting support at home when actually they are not. The misconception occurs because most teachers come from supportive families. Another problem is that teachers mistake what they assume will bring good feelings to students. As explained in Chapter 11, by definition reinforcers must mean something to the student. Teachers have very few rewards at their disposal that most students find desirable.

In school as in the adult world, high achievers have an internal locus of control; they feel that they can control their behavior and, to a large extent, their lives. In contrast, low achievers usually have an external locus of control; they perceive their life circumstances as beyond their own control. For example, "Others are more successful because they have better luck than I have," or "I couldn't get to class on time because throughout the semester my alarm clock failed to ring." Reality therapy focuses on developing an internal locus of control.

Teachers who use reality therapy effectively demonstrate certain common behaviors. From the first day of school they work hard to create a warm, friendly, and totally noncoercive climate. They accept a certain amount of noise. They encourage students, yet remain realistic. For example, "Algebra will require hard work, but you can do it." They explain that grades themselves are meaningless and insignificant, yet because grades reflect behaviors that will empower students to fulfill real needs, grades are important.

Group Management Theory

In contrast to Glasser, who perceives discipline as a one-on-one cooperative endeavor between the teacher and each student, others believe that discipline problems are a product of group behavior and should be approached accordingly. As early as 300 BC, Plato warned about the negative influence that urbanization can have on a culture. In his *Republic,* Plato predicted that as cities grow, inhabitants' behavior changes, often for the worse. Nuby & Doebler (1999) have indicated that we are still failing to prepare new teachers for the challenge of teaching in urban settings. "Despite gains in many areas, little attention has been paid to meeting the challenge of equipping future teachers with the knowledge and skills needed to meet the social and emotional problems that exist in the urban setting, a site where teacher shortages often occur" (p. 41). The National Center for Education Statistics (1999) found that only 20 percent of today's teachers feel comfortable with students from diverse backgrounds.

One approach to meeting this challenge is by using groups. *Group management theory* recognizes that groups behave differently than individuals. Furthermore, as groups become larger, they also develop definite characteristics. Teachers must recognize groups' effects on the total classroom or on smaller groups within the classroom. The teacher can exert influence either directly or indirectly in two major directions. First, the teacher can give support to the group—for example, provide encouragement while standing ready to help the group achieve its goals. This requires guiding the class carefully toward the goals. Suppose one of the class's behavioral goals is for each student to remain at his or her desk. The teacher's role is to monitor the group and, when signs of restlessness appear, to alter the situation to provide for more movement. Or suppose near the end of the period students get off-target and wander—mentally if not physically. Recognizing the situation, the teacher introduces an assignment, summarizes the day's lesson, or uses a similar technique to pull the students back to the lesson.

Group management techniques are not concerned with blaming either the group or the individual for misbehaving. The perspective is more one of being alert at all times, managing the environment to reduce the number of problems and problem-causing elements, and helping the group and individuals overcome hurdles and reach their goals.

Group management is based on the philosophy that neither individuals nor groups want to misbehave, and that misbehavior is the result of barriers. When individuals or groups fail to make progress toward their goals, the goals are unclear, or too demanding, or environmental elements prevent their attainment—not because the individual or group wants to be difficult.

Should you choose to use punishment, use it only under certain conditions. Punishment should never be a teacher's first attempted solution to a problem, and when it is used, it should be administered objectively. The individual or groups being punished must clearly understand the reason, and the teacher must remain calm. Consider how much more appropriate it is to punish a student for breaking a window by having that student clean up the broken glass than to require the student to write "I will not break any more windows" a thousand times. By warning and rewarding students, teachers actually cultivate misbehavior.

You may learn that it is helpful to keep a written record of student misbehavior. The essential elements in records of misbehavior include the student, date, time, location, incident, description, corrective action, and follow-up. It is important to recognize that punishment can easily become a trap for teachers if they make it too harsh, get others to administer it, overuse it, or use it to make impossible demands of students. The ultimate goal of group management is, by helping students to analyze their own behavior, to lead them to a state of self-control—that is, self-discipline. Wasicsko and Ross (1994) provide further cautions and suggestions to guide the use of punishment in the classroom: "A major factor in creating classroom discipline problems is the overuse of punishments as an answer to misbehavior" (p. 249). They list several negative side effects that often accompany the use of punishment: bringing attention to those who misbehave, causing aggression, depression, anxiety, or embarrassment, bringing only a temporary halt to bad behavior, and disrupting the continuity of lessons.

Assertive Discipline

A popular management model that many educators do not support is *assertive discipline.* MacNaughton and Johns (1991) provide a summary discussion of this model:

> *A popular example of behavior management on one end of the continuum representing the degree of teacher power over students is assertive discipline. This strategy emphasizes systematic reinforcement and is more punishment-oriented than some of the other behavior management procedures. (p. 53)*

The basic theme of assertive discipline is that the assertive teacher clearly and firmly communicates requirements to the students and backs up words with appropriate actions that maximize compliance without violating students' best interests.

Assertive discipline requires teachers to take the following steps:

- Make clear that they will not tolerate anyone preventing them from teaching, stopping learning, or doing anything else that is not in the best interest of the class, the individual, or the teacher.
- Instruct students clearly and in specific terms about what behaviors are desired and what behaviors are not tolerated.
- Plan positive and negative consequences for predetermined acceptable or unacceptable behaviors.
- Plan positive reinforcement for compliance. Reinforcement includes verbal acknowledgement, notes, free time for talking, and, of course, tokens that can be exchanged for appropriate rewards.
- Plan a sequence of steps to punish noncompliance. These range from writing a youngster's name on the board to sending the student to the principal's office.
(MacNaughton & Jones, 1991, p. 53)

Corporal Punishment

Corporal punishment is technically defined as the infliction of physical pain upon the occurrence of a misbehavior (Vockell, 1991, p. 278). Although most educators oppose the use of corporal punishment in schools, some support its use. Johns and MacNaughton (1990) provide lists of arguments for and against the use of corporal punishment.

Pros and Cons of Corporal Punishment

Clearly, there are arguments for and against corporal punishment. Arguments in favor of retaining corporal punishment include the following.

- Corporal punishment is one procedure among many. As a consequence of rule infraction, it works with some students in some circumstances.
- Many parents support the practice. In such cases, use of corporal punishment is consistent support of home procedure.
- Corporal punishment is a considerably a less severe form of punishment than many other kinds. Administered judiciously and without rancor, it is far less harmful than suspension.
- Denying teachers the right to exercise judgment about the proper use of corporal punishment is to maintain that they are not fully capable of making professional decisions in the area of punishment.
- Use of corporal punishment in some aggravated situations and with some students reinforces the concept that a just society can deliver punishment where deemed appropriate.
- Corporal punishment is immediate, concrete, clears the air, and terminates the event. Aside from proper guidelines in its use, corporal punishment is simple and easily understood. Unlike many of the more complex models for promoting classroom management and discipline, corporal punishment does not require training and lengthy, time-consuming efforts to bring about changes in a pupil's behavior. (Jones & MacNaughton, 1991, pp. 390–391)

Arguments against corporal punishment include:

- There are many examples of the nonjudicious use of corporal punishment. Stories about the use of the paddle for minor offenses abound. Once paddling is institutionalized, it may well be used for every offense.
- The practice is discriminatory. It is used more on minorities and children of lower socioeconomic background, inner-city children, and nonconformists.
- It is ineffectual. To be at all effective, paddling of disruptive students would have to be repeated continuously and probably become more severe as the student got older and more accustomed to it.
- It is a dehumanizing practice, long outlawed in the U.S. military and in prisons in most Western nations. Schools are the only institution where striking another person is permitted. Corporal punishment is an aggressive, violent means of discipline that is antithetical to the purpose of U.S. education. It makes the teacher a poor model by promoting force as a means to settling arguments and establishing rights.
- The practice of corporal punishment causes psychological as well as physical harm. It can be the cause of posttraumatic stress disorders and school avoidance.

It is harmful to the self-esteem a school may be trying to encourage students to develop.
- Corporal punishment may be considered child abuse and even sexual abuse if its use is viewed as a violation of the body. In such a charged atmosphere, the use of corporal punishment is highly subject to lawsuits. (Jones & MacNaughton, 1990, pp. 390–391)

Recognizing the limitations and harmful effects of corporal punishment, most countries forbid its use in their public schools. Jambor (1988) identifies the few countries that permit its use: "Presently only a few developed countries still condone corporal punishment in their public schools: Australia, New Zealand, South Africa, and the United States" (p. 220).

Maslow's Hierarchy of Needs Revisited

Abraham Maslow (1954) developed a theory based on clinical observation and logic. According to Maslow, all human beings have some common needs, which fall into five clusters that can be arranged in the following hierarchy:

Needs	*Frequency*
	Low
Self-actualization needs	↑
Esteem needs	
Social needs	
Safety needs	↓
Physiological needs	
	High

Proactive Exercise

Anticipated Situation

- You know that:

    Parents of students who have special challenges often feel that they must be aggressive in defending the rights of their children. Some will accuse you of not wanting to help ensure their children's rights.

Proactive Alternative

- You can:

    Prepare a strategy to use to convince these parents that your number one concern is for the welfare of their children. Make a list of steps you can use to achieve this goal. You might begin by being a good listener. Always listen carefully to hear exactly what the parent is saying. Resist the temptation to defend yourself even against unfair and untrue accusations.

    Second. When negative comments are aimed at you or the school, refocus the conversation on the student.

    Third. Ask the parent for input or opinion. Parents do want to express their opinions; furthermore, they want you to value them. After all, they know this youngster a lot better than you do. By asking for their opinion, you show that you recognize their expertise.

THE CASE

Abandoned Adolescence and a Cry for Help

Pat Williams-Boyd, Eastern Michigan University

Dr. Pat Williams-Boyd is Associate Professor of Education at Eastern Michigan University. She received her Ph.D. in Curriculum and Instruction from University of Kansas and her Ph.D. in Ethnomusicology from Ball State University.

Jasmine was an outgoing eighth-grader who was a student in my English, honors music, and photography classes. She was moody, given to seeking more attention than most eighth-graders, but when I was close at hand, she laughed, talked freely, and interacted with the other students. When with her friends, she resorted to giving the appearance that she was taking excessive numbers of aspirins, not eating (although she was clearly overweight), and not going home in the evenings.

Jasmine lived in a suburban, university town. Despite the school board's self-praise for offering the same programs at both its middle schools, there was yet a decisive line between the school of haves and the school of have-nots. Jasmine went to the Title I school, socioeocnomically described as having 51 percent of its students receiving free or reduced-priced lunches. Although there was a small number of white middle-class families, the school neighborhood was predominantly low-socioeconomic black and white, with 10 percent of the population Hispanic and 15 percent First American. While the other middle school enjoyed air conditioning in its relatively new facility, when it rained our old building, proud though we were of it, was dotted with buckets and mops. While the other middle school students, from predominantly white, middle- to upper-class families, were researching and writing their papers on new computers, our school had bare wires protruding from exposed outlets.

The principal was strong and supportive, expecting "his" school to be what he called a "tight ship." I

> *Trust and care for your students as unique individual human personalities first and then see them as students, for the business of teaching and learning is about relationships, and all relationships are built on trust.*

created anything but calm waters. Because my classes, aside from English and social studies, were mostly elective classes, I enjoyed the distinct pleasure of working with over three-fourths of the school's students. Additionally, I coached volleyball, edited the school's literary anthology, and was the assistant drama director. From trips to Europe for which students saved for many years, to starting a parent involvement project—from creating a food panty and a clothes closet for those in need both within the school and eventually for the community, to all-night dance-a-thons to collect canned goods for the Salvation Army food banks—my students, their families, and I, along with two fellow teachers, created waves of enthusiasm, motivation, involvement, empowerment, and change. Jasmine was part of all of this.

As her eighth-grade year progressed, her grades began to drop dramatically, her attention in class grew fragmented at best, and her attendance and mood erratic. One cold winter morning as I arrived at school at 6:00 a.m., I saw Jasmine sitting and crying in my parking space. Saying nothing, I put my arms around her until she stopped crying. We walked into my office and the story of her family slowly unfolded, some of which I had already known.

When Jasmine was five, her father left home, telling her she was not the daughter he had hoped for. Jasmine's mother had taken a series of boyfriends through the years and had explicitly shared with Jasmine intimate details of their relationships. Marie

Winn (1983) contends that young adolescents like Jasmine have no childhood because there is an "end of secrecy." Things are discussed with children who are little prepared or mature enough to understand, things inappropriate for young adolescents whose moral conscience, sexual identity, and social responsibility have not been lovingly shaped and developed. When each relationship failed, Jasmine was told that particular boyfriend could not or did not want to have her in his household. During each relationship Jasmine became the babysitter, mother, and general caregiver for all the siblings who followed, while Jasmine's mother was playfully seeking a mate.

When Jasmine's older brother was sent to reform school, according to her mother, Jasmine was responsible. If she had only been what her biological father had wanted, he would never have left, and the older son would have "turned out" okay, and stayed at home. And last night? Even though underage, Jasmine drove down to the police station to pick up her mother who had been caught shoplifting at a local store in which she had finally gotten a job. As Jasmine left the house this particular morning, her mother's final words were, "If only you hadn't made your father leave, none of this would have happened."

As a young adolescent, Jasmine had been thrust into what psychologist David Elkind (1981) has referred to as responsibility and emotional overload. She had become the brunt of her parents' problems and, far more, it was up to her to work out the adult responsibilities that her mother's consequent behavior left in the wake. Exploited by her parents, Jasmine was robbed of her childhood, of her innocence, of the privileges of youth, of the joys and the heartaches of simply growing up. Rather, she had been jettisoned into the role of a parent, counseling her mother, caring for her siblings, accepting blame for a situation only by virtue of her existence within the family. It was a reversal of roles, a very real form of domestic abuse, often referred to as one of the seven deadly sins of childhood. Some researchers call it the parentification of the child.

Jasmine's mother became more of a personal companion, perhaps a trainer, but certainly not the cultural authority that would guide and direct her children. Jasmine was held responsible for her mother's and for the family's happiness. Rather than supporting Jasmine and assisting her through the developmental tasks that needed to be mastered during her young adolescent years and that would have a profound bearing on her adult relationships, her mother had her own parenting needs fulfilled by her daughter while destructively abandoning her responsibilities to Jasmine. Therefore, her daughter was left to create life on her own terms, often according to the vagaries of her friends, fluctuating, vacillating from day to day as adolescent friendships go. Loose footing, discrepant perspectives, opinions shaped by peer viewpoints rather than by the practical wisdom of the parent. Instead of her parents enabling her, quietly supporting her while she worked out her own completeness, Jasmine surveyed and made judgments of the world according to her own sense of reality.

Given that the three major tasks of adolescence are to develop identity, independence, and the capacity to form adult relationships, Jasmine's sense of herself and the fulfillment of these tasks were in grave jeopardy. Because of this role reversal, she felt used, exploited by her mother. She sensed she had lost her identity, the uniqueness of childhood without just cause, and because of her interactions with her mother and her mother's boyfriends, her trust in adult relationships was tenuous.

Jasmine's mother would call me and ask why Jasmine wasn't making better grades, why her moods were so unpredictable, why she couldn't come home from school sooner to do the laundry and clean the house. Why did Jasmine wear more makeup and dress a little less like a child with each of her mother's new boyfriends?

And what did the school do? They, too, hurried Jasmine along in proper fashion. The guidance counselor, a term loosely used, called Jasmine to her office. With a measure of anticipation tempered with distrust for adults, Jasmine nonetheless proceeded. And she was told, "If you have any hope of going to college, your grades must improve. Your schooling is important, Jasmine." Jasmine was living in the moment, just like most young adolescents. College was ethereal, only a word or the glimmer of an idea, certainly not anything connected to her sense of reality.

With little money in the family and even less love, Jasmine's hopes for the future were dim. She expressed her frustrations of hopelessness common to young adolescents in such situations, in the only ways she knew. Subconsciously she punished herself by overeating and gaining more and more weight while her friends dieted. More disturbing, she began to engage in self-destructive behavior—at first mildly cutting her arms with a razor and then making sure she changed clothes for gym class when her friends would notice the marks.

After school one Monday, while we were rehearsing with 135 kids for the spring play, a group of Jasmine's friends asked me to come with them into the back hallway. At a Friday slumber party, Jasmine told her friends she had taken a whole bottle of aspirins and then had fallen asleep, not to be awakened until late the following morning. Her friends were worried about what was happening and what might ensue. I quietly sat and listened, then quelled their fears that they had exposed a confidence, assured them they had exercised responsible behavior, and asked them if they would feel comfortable if I talked with Jasmine about what I had observed, not about what they had shared. Resilient though they are, young adolescents' confidence is often a fragile thing. Their trust is a gift earned through their perception of an adult's actions across time. In no way did I want to betray that trust; however, the situation was too serious to go unattended.

Jasmine was made to be an adult before she was ever a child. How many times I have seen this borne out in the lives of students from low-socioeconomic, single-parent families. "Whether a child acquires a healthy sense of autonomy or is burdened with excessive feelings of shame and doubt depends upon the skill with which parents match their demands to the child's competencies" (Elkind, 1981, p. 102), Jasmine had no founded sense of personal identity, no maternal authority figure who would provide her a sense of security either at home and or as she forged new peer relationships. So, with a distorted sense of power or lack of it, Jasmine could not rectify the discrepancy between the enormity of her responsibility at home and the paucity of her freedom. Is it any wonder that Jasmine seriously attempted suicide?

Yet her acting-out behavior was less an attempt to end her life than it was a cry for help—a cry that echoed across her deserted childhood, but was heard by her classroom teacher. There was one person Jasmine trusted, one place she felt safe, one place where she was "allowed" to be a child—with me. To paraphrase Frank Herbert, Jasmine was a child thrust into being a woman, and I feared that when she was a woman, she would seek in vain for the child that never was.

What did I do? While walking Jasmine home that evening after rehearsal, we talked, confided in each other, and put a daily plan into place that would connect and begin to ground her. Young adolescents do not have a backlog of experiences on which to draw. They are often unable to reason, "I have gotten through this situation before, I can do it again," for this is their "before." Sometimes it is possible to help them think through their options in a problem-solving format. However, because Jasmine was confronted with adult problems and responsibilities without the adult means to accomplish them, she felt helpless, hopeless, and powerless.

Teachers are not trained as mental health care providers, but when the ties of trust are forged, we may act as a bridge or a catalyst to a trained professional. When I asked Jasmine's permission to set up a time for both of us to talk with a social worker, she agreed. Teachers are not do-gooders with a plan for each of our student's lives. Neither are we schooled as counselors, psychologists, or social workers. But we are compassionate, caring educators dynamically engaged in the often messy but magical business of young adolescents and their growth. Returning to the school, I called the school nurse who had previously worked with Jasmine's family. Together we accessed the school case worker and the district school psychologist, to collaboratively construct a safety net for Jasmine and for her family.

In the vast number of cases like Jasmine's that I experienced across twenty-eight years in public education, I took the following basic steps:

- Take threats of suicide seriously.
- Talk openly and candidly with the student about her behavior and your concerns.
- Resist saying "I understand," for young adolescents feel they are the only one who has ever felt this way unless you actually have and are willing to disclose. Rather say, "If I hear you correctly I think you are saying . . . " or "I notice that you . . . ."
- Help the student think through possible options given the situation.
- Resist promising the student you will not share the situation with the parent. Ask if at an appropriate time it feels necessary to talk with the parent, the student will trust you to supportively share the situation and serve as an advocate.

- Share the information: with the school nurse, guidance counselor, principal, school psychologist, vice principal.
- Act as a liaison with a mental health provider.
- Continue to follow up with the student so she doesn't feel you have abandoned her to another adult; be willing to go with her to any counseling sessions.
- Set the minds of friends at ease by reassuring them they acted in a responsible fashion when they shared information about the student.

When I talked with Jasmine's mother, I exercised the following ideas:

- Seek the support of the building administrator.
- Share the situation with Jasmine's mother in a supportive rather than an accusatory fashion.
- Ask if the parent would be willing to meet with you and a mental health care provider in a place that is neutral and feels safe to the parent and at a time that fits the parent's schedule.
- Keep in touch with the parent, the case worker, and the school nurse in order to wisely support both the parent and the student.
- Follow up parental support with a Parent Project volunteer from the school if the parent agrees.

Just like all of my students, Jasmine taught me many lessons. Among them were:

1. Good things happen when people trust each other, work together, and keep the child at the center of all thinking and interactions.
2. Young adolescents watch their teacher closely and keenly sense those people whom they feel they can trust.
3. Each student represents a whole constellation of people as well as problems in the home.
4. A change in a young person's characteristic behavior is a signal or warning sign of a problem she feels incapable of addressing.
5. Signs of self-destructive behavior are usually a cry for help.
6. When we truly care about our teaching, we care about the whole child.
7. There is a vast array of professionals who are willing to help us with situations such as Jasmine's if we only ask.

Were there other signs of domestic abuse or indicators that would have alerted me to Jasmine's precarious position? Of course. Some of them might be:

- Unusual patterns of school attendance or arrival
- A change in relationships with peers, or a withdrawal from peers
- Inability to trust adults
- Eating disorders
- A sudden change in schoolwork or in grades
- Depression seen in nonparticipatory behavior, or overt withdrawal from school functions
- Sleep disturbances
- Excessive absence from home, or severe lack of desire to leave the school at the end of the day
- Inappropriate dress or poor hygiene
- Student makes indirect allusions such as Jasmine telling her friends she had ingested pills at the slumber party or perhaps even telling me she wished she could live with me
- Constant fatigue

This case study is not the plan of action for all the Jasmines of this world, for individual answers reside within each of us as we dare to become involved in the lives of our students. Apart from the counseling we accessed for Jasmine and eventually for her mother, alone I could not affect significant change at home. Yet it is within the school setting that we possess the incredible opportunity to impact kids' lives in ways which may touch them as they become their own person. Professional respect and trust in colleagues who also worked with Jasmine were a preclusion, a valued given in an enterprise which celebrates people and is constructed upon and around relationships. Schools must rethink and reshape evaluation systems that ignore the needs—developmental, emotional, physical, psychological, moral, and intellectual—which kids have and which may indeed not conform to the planned calendar on the counselor's desk.

Hurry kids? Why not, when we as a society are bent on the flutter of movement—to get there faster, sooner, before the other person, in more elegant fashion, with more trappings. It is as if we fear the moment and in our safe though deluded denial of its existence, we cloak it with the collective anticipation of the future. In our meandering across the galaxy of life, have we lost the power of who we are and who our students are in the now? In our haste have we excused away the silence of being for the noise of the anticipated? The Jasmines in our classroom are our constant reminders. It is from them that we continue to learn.

Further Reflection

1. How does a teacher win the trust of students?
2. How does a teacher approach a student about whom she is concerned?
3. How does a teacher decide when to intervene on behalf of a student?
4. To whom can a teacher turn for professional support of a student?
5. How should the family be approached when a teacher is concerned about a student like Jasmine?
6. What are the legal responsibilities and constraints to which teachers must respond when she receives information regarding a student like Jasmine?
7. Should teachers become involved in the lives of students apart from the academic success of the student? If so, to what extent? If not, why?

We experience the needs at the lower levels of the hierarchy more frequently. Furthermore, we must satisfy each level of needs before moving to the higher levels. Maslow's Hierarchy of Needs has been used extensively by management in business and industry for several decades.

McGregor's Theories X and Y

Douglas McGregor noticed that in a large national chain of department stores, some of the stores were highly successful while some were financial failures. On closer inspection he noted that the successful stores and the unsuccessful stores were managed under very different types of management. He named the successful management style Theory Y and the unsuccessful management style Theory X. The unsuccessful Theory X managers were the traditional type of managers. They all shared the following perceptions:

> Most people are inherently lazy.
> People must be closely supervised.
> People tend to shun responsibility.
> People like to be directed.
> Getting people to attain objectives requires the use of coercion, control, and threats of punishment.

In contrast, the highly successful Theory Y managers espoused the following beliefs:

> The expenditure of mental and physical effort is natural.
> If the conditions are right, people will not only accept responsibility but also seek it.
> If people become committed to objectives, they will exercise self-direction and self-control.
> Most people have a high degree of imagination, ingenuity, and creativity.

This more positive approach to management has become identified as modern management theory. However, some contemporary management theorists reject this theory as too idealistic. In all fairness, its accuracy depends on the particular environment.

THE CASE

Expecting the Unexpected

Robert Hilliard, State University of West Georgia

Robert Hilliard has been a middle-grades and high school classroom teacher. He has conducted workshops for middle-grade teachers and for parents of young adolescents in more than a hundred school districts. He presents at state, regional, and national conferences. His publications focus primarily on young adolescents and middle-grades classrooms. Robert has served on the Board of Directors for the Association of Teacher Educators and on the National Middle School Association committee that established the NCATE standards for Middle School Teacher Preparation in Colleges and Universities. His degrees are from Kansas, Missouri, and Arkansas. He is currently Coordinator of Middle Grades and Secondary Education at the State University of West Georgia.

Many teachers define parental support as parents who help their children with homework and/or support the school discipline plan. Star teachers, according to Haberman (1995), "describe parental support in terms of parents showing an interest in what their children do in school" (p. 10). In this instance, the best parental support comes with a caring stance and from an understanding of their child's developmental needs. Homework can be the source of a variety of problems. Meet Karen and Jill.

Best Friends Share

Karen and Jill were students in my eighth-grade class in earth science. Best friends, they maintained science grade averages at around a high "C" and a high "B," respectively. While grading science notebooks, I noticed that Karen's looked like it had already been graded. It appeared that Karen had erased someone's name, and written in her name on 4 of 12 papers. Holding the papers to the light, I could read the name of the previous owner, Jill. Our team policy, of giving both parties a zero, was given to students and parents at the beginning of the year and was restated before every test or quiz.

My first reaction was to give both girls a zero, but I was a first-year teacher and was shocked that these two students would be involved. I talked to my team leader, who suggested that I speak to each girl individually the following day when telling them about their zero grades. Before class, I informed Jill of my discovery and notified her of the zero for the notebook grade. Because the notebook was a test grade, her average dropped from 83 to a failing grade of 67. Jill said nothing and nodded her head. Karen said she knew what I was going to say and admitted to taking Jill's sheets and changing the name. She knew it meant receiving a zero.

When I told teammates about Jill receiving a failing grade because of the zero, the team leader advised me to change the grade to a 75. I immediately informed Jill. Two days later, I received a letter from Jill's mother:

> Jill informed us of the situation that occurred and we were expecting a call from you this evening. It is my understanding that Jill was asked by a classmate to use her notebook papers. Jill told her classmate no, but did agree when the classmate asked to just look

at the notebook. Jill came downstairs to get some sodas and did not think to check the notebook for any missing page. Jill did not realize, until you told her, that some papers were missing The classmate admitted to us that she had turned the notebook papers into you without Jill's knowledge. Jill told us that she explained the situation to you, yet you gave each a zero, which lowers Jill's grade to a 75. I would like to know why was Jill given a zero and told that she was also guilty of cheating when she had no idea that her classmate had taken her papers. Jill would not knowingly give her work papers to another classmate to turn in as their work. Giving Jill a zero for work she completed is not fair. Please reconsider the zero on this assignment.

I went to my team leader with the letter. Her advice was to call the mother and stand by my decision. Two other eighth-grade teachers suggested that I meet with the assistant principal. The assistant principal agreed to meet with both students. Karen said that Jill knew she had taken the papers. Jill said that Karen took the folder without her knowledge. There was no way to prove that either student was lying. Believing Jill, the assistant principal asked me to write up a disciplinary referral for Karen and to return Jill's grade to normal. She also asked me to call Jill's mother and thank her for making us aware that Jill was not aware of Karen's actions.

Before I could write the referral letter, I caught Karen copying answers for another homework assignment. Karen received two days in-school suspension. The girls remained friends and there were no other incidents of cheating by either student. (Based on Ruggeri, 2002.)

Questions and Observations

1. What is your view of the way in which the teacher handled the situation?
2. How would you have approached the situation?
3. What other alternatives could be used instead of a zero on notebook?
4. When should a parent be notified, and should this become part of the policy?
5. What is the role of the assistant principal?
6. How do you think the assistant principal should have handled the situation?
7. Did the assistant principal support the team's policy on cheating?
8. Was the letter to the teacher from the mother fair to Jill as a learner?
9. How will this case affect you when you begin teaching?

At the beginning of the second semester, I chose to discontinue giving grades for notebooks.

Concluding Reflections

Cheating is not uncommon, and knows no religious, racial or economic bounds. You will learn to really care about most of your students and will be hurt when you discover that they have cheated. They may not cheat in your class, but will often cheat when perceived need coincides with opportunity. You may have written policies and may believe you know how to handle the situation until it actually happens. When it happens, you realize that life is not clearly defined.

It is hard to know how to handle situations. You have to consider so many factors, including whether or not to bring it to an administrator. Once an administrator is informed, you must be willing to accept their analysis. In the above incident, because of discrepancies in the letter from the mother and a gut feeling, I believed that Jill was not telling the truth. That gut feeling was reinforced by *whispered* student remarks that I believe were intended to be overheard. Looking back, I think that it could have been handled differently, and I wished I had tried to find out why Karen was resorting to cheating and not doing her work. For that matter, why would Jill go along with it?

Best friends can sometimes be more accurately described as one best friend who will do anything to maintain the friendship. In this case, the girl was copying her homework for popular friends who agreed to let her tag along and not to beat her up. They even insisted that she imitate their style of writing.

Growing up is not easy. Adolescence is a turning point when we learn to take responsibility for our actions; however, the need to belong will usually supercede any sense of personal integrity. During this period of moral growth, parents, teachers, and students share responsibilities for mentoring, modeling, and setting realistic expectations.

You may hear *"We can't be all things to all students"* or *"We aren't their parents,"* but Haberman (1995) tells us that star teachers do share a sense of responsibility with parents. "They are more willing to call and to make home visits, even in unsafe neighborhoods" (p. 11). Hilliard (2002) relates a story of a young man about to be suspended from his middle school for chronic tardiness and excessive absences. Lazy and irresponsible? No. He was the oldest of three children whose single-parent mother worked two jobs. This child had the responsibility to get the younger children fed, dressed, and on the bus for school. Unfortunately, his bus came earlier than the bus for the two younger children.

A life of poverty often means living in dangerous neighborhoods. The young man would make sure they were on the bus and then run or hitch a ride to his school. He was usually late. The younger children were out of school earlier than he was, so he often cut his last class to be at the bus stop to walk his siblings home through the rough neighborhood. He had a keen sense of responsibility, but had limited verbal negotiation skills to explain his position. His mother was never able to make a parent conference and teachers did not know his circumstances. When teachers don't know, they can't make necessary adjustments or offer alternatives. The secret to good teaching is in the caring. Caring teachers make a point of knowing their students.

This chapter has not begun to touch on some of the more dramatic and tragic lives led by children labeled as at-risk. These children suffer more than low achievement scores and chronic absenteeism. These children have one or both parents who are incarcerated and are absent both physically and emotionally in their children's lives. These children have parents who abuse drugs, alcohol, and sometimes their own children. These parents put their child at risk by exposing them to child molesters, physical abuse, and chemical abuse. In June 2002, I met a 13-year-old girl whose father was chronically absent by doing drugs in the bathroom of his home. The daughter had been molested on a regular basis by the father's drug-addicted acquaintances since she was 10. She began smoking pot and drinking alcohol at age 9. At age 12, she moved in with her mother, also an addict and alcoholic, and continued to live in the same environment. When she wasn't out of school, she was in someone's classroom. There were no teacher referrals.

Every day, children face problems ranging from weight and body image to problems of alienation, bullying, lack of language skills, chronic medical problems, divorce and death of loved ones (including caretakers). They will be in your classrooms. These children are labeled at-risk. Pay more attention to the child than the label.

Reflection

Consider Maslow's Hierarchy of Needs, McGregor's Theory X, and McGregor's Theory Y. Where would you place each of these on the discipline continuum? Can you see a relationship between Maslow's Hierarchy of Needs and student behavior in the classroom? For example, can you name some physiological needs that must be met before students improve their self-esteem? Can you name any social needs that must be met before students can improve their self-image as competent students? Have you known teachers whom you would label Theory X managers? Theory Y managers? What traits did each exhibit?

Classroom Management (Discipline) Models

Being aware of learning theories and management theories from disciplines outside education will help us relate education discipline and management theories to the discipline continuum in Figure 12.2. Following are a few of the many discipline and management theories in use in education today. Weber, Roff, Crawford, and Robinson (1983) reviewed the literature on classroom management and grouped the strategies into the following eight categories: authoritarian, behavior modification, group process, instructional, intimidation, permissive, sociomotional climate, and cookbook. Because these groups are both numerous and self-descriptive, only selective examples will be given.

Authoritarian Strategies

The authoritarian approach to classroom management places the teacher in control from the very beginning. Using nonpunitive measures, the teacher establishes and enforces rules, issues commands, and uses mild desists (explains privately why the student is being asked to discontinue the behavior), proximity control (stays near the misbehaving student), and isolation. Jacob Kounin (1977) introduced the mild-desists strategy because he found that teachers seldom tell students why they consider certain behaviors bad. He further noticed that when teachers use strong reprimands they often do so publicly, making other students feel anxious.

Group Process Strategies

Group process strategies are based on a belief that classroom behavior occurs in a social or group context. The teacher's role is to set reasonable expectations, stay alert to the classroom group interactions (exhibit "with-it-ness"), foster group cohesiveness, involve students in decision making, and resolve conflicts through discussion, role playing, and negotiation.

Instructional Strategies

The instructional approach to classroom management uses the belief that the teacher's time is better spent preventing problems than solving them. Chapter 11 discusses this approach in detail. For decades, the most common approach to discipline has focused on ways of controlling student behavior by suppressing unwanted behavior. But as Kohn (2003, p. 28) suggests, perhaps our main focus should be on giving students a reason to want to behave positively: "Misbehavior may continue primarily because students resist instruction that emphasizes decontextualized skills or requires rote recall; activities intended to raise test scores rather than answer authentic questions, lessons they find neither relevant nor engaging—and that they had little or no role in designing." These teachers do not tolerate any foolishness. Classes managed by this style may or may not be characterized by a high degree of learning.

Models Developed Specifically for Education

The learning and management theories presented thus far in this chapter are adopted from other disciplines, and their relevance to the secondary and middle school classroom varies. This has prompted development of models designed specifically for classroom use. Following are descriptions of several popular ones. As you read about each model, see if you can place it on the discipline continuum (Figure 12.2).

Do not use the techniques presented thus far in this chapter in isolation; incorporate them into an overall consistent pattern. Several models showing examples of such structured approaches to discipline are available. In her book, *Classroom Discipline for Effective Teaching and Learning,* Laurel Tanner (1978) introduces the following models.

- Training model
- Behavior modification model
- Psychodynamic model
- Group dynamics model
- Personal-social growth model (p. 6)

Training Model

Discipline is always concerned with regulating or changing behavior. This may be achieved either externally or internally—that is, change can be effected by external stimuli, or it can be the result of the subject's own purposive behavior. The training model is concerned totally with the former category, since any training program for classroom behavior is almost certain to result from the teacher's effort rather than the students'.

Although the training model's effectiveness has been demonstrated by police officers, soldiers, and firefighters (to name only a few professions), who must learn to respond immediately and automatically to certain stimuli, most educators believe that this model is less desirable than the others for use with middle school and high school students. Their attitude is understandable, because school should prepare students to think for themselves rather than always to respond to others' desires or demands.

Even in the high school classroom, though, some degree of training is helpful. For example, students can learn to stop talking when the class is being addressed, to remain seated when they complete an assignment, or to raise their hands when they want to speak. Most of these patterns, though, are holdovers from the earlier grades. High school discipline programs should not overemphasize or overuse the training model.

Behavior Modification Model

Like the training model, behavior modification depends on external stimuli to effect the desired changes in behavior. But unlike the training model—which does not require its subjects to think, just respond automatically—behavior modification does require students to change their behavior to receive definite rewards.

Neither the training model nor the behavior modification model requires students to think through their behavior at a very high level; instead, students are conditioned to behave the way the teacher wants them to. Still, behavior modification strategies do work at the high school level. Behavior modification programs can reduce the amount of inappropriate behavior in secondary school classrooms by as much as 75 percent (Sapp, Clough, Pittman, & Toben, 1973). This method is used extensively with mentally and emotionally handicapped students.

Behavior modification is similar to assertive discipline. Palardy (1996) compares these models, giving their common weaknesses. "Like behavior modification, assertive discipline proposes a four-step sequence for dealing with students' maladaptive behavior. These include: (1) identifying the maladaptive behavior that needs to be changed, (2) identifying its opposite, i.e., the desired behavior, (3) rewarding the occupancies of the appropriate behavior, and (4) using extinction procedures (mainly negatives consequences) to help eliminate the maladaptive behavior" (p. 66).

Palardy (1996) identifies limitations of assertive discipline: (1) treating the symptom not the causes, (2) short-term benefits, (3) limited transfer value (may not work under different circumstances, and (4) devaluation of self-discipline (students need to learn to judge whether certain behaviors are appropriate and hold themselves responsible for behaving).

Psychodynamic Model

Unlike the training model and the behavior modification model, the psychodynamic model requires that the teacher know and understand each student. As an outgrowth of Freudian psychology, the model is based on the belief that knowing and understanding a student's behavior will lead to improvement in that behavior. This model is more advanced than the previous models in that it involves a search for the cause of misbehavior. Some educators criticize this model, however, because it does not offer suggestions to correct the behavior.

Group Dynamics Model

The group dynamics model recognizes that social interaction and social pressure affect students. Instead of focusing on an individual student, it looks at the individual in relation to the total group's behavior. The focus is on the teacher, and the goal is to design good working conditions for the total group. This model differs further from the models previously discussed in that it ties discipline to instruction. To avoid (or in response to) a behavior problem, the teacher would design a learning activity to divert students' attention from the problem to learning the lesson at hand. Use of this model requires an awareness of student behavior so that problems can be nipped in the bud as soon as they develop.

Like the psychodynamic model, this model recognizes that learning is a group activity, but it goes one important step further. Whereas the psychodynamic model depends solely on the teacher's understanding the students, this model requires the teacher to take action. In this sense it is far more practical.

Personal-Social Growth Model

Contemporary educators recognize that merely being able to regulate student behavior and suppress undesirable behavior is not enough. The title of this chapter reflects this concern. To become good citizens in a democratic society, students must ultimately learn to discipline themselves, to manage their own behavior. This requires experience—which means that you, the teacher, must be willing to share your power and responsibility for discipline with your students. Indeed, students must feel that they are in control. They must also understand the purpose(s) behind desired behavioral patterns. Ideally, they should see the class's desired goals and choose the ways to behave to attain these goals. This model is consistent with the school's responsibility for helping students become responsible citizens. As Chamberlin and Chambers (1994) attest, "Teaching students to be responsible should be viewed as an important and vital part of the total curriculum" (p. 204).

Trends in Discipline Today

The order of strategies and models just discussed reflects the chronological pattern of metamorphosis of discipline in U.S. education. At one time the school assumed total authority to define good discipline. Explains one educator, "With evangelic fervor . . . teachers have taught, indoctrinated, and compelled students to whom and what they were to comply with and become the ideal model that the school mystically judged as being desirable" (Hansen, 1974, p. 173).

Today, good discipline is not considered synonymous with total, blind conformity. Students are involved with deciding what type of discipline is best for doing the job in their particular setting. Educational psychologist Theodore Chandler (1990) says that the current trend of involving students in setting discipline strategies is an essential move:

> *Most discipline strategies are developed without student input and employ an external agent to identify, monitor, and remediate classroom disturbances. . . . Such an approach violates the tenants of at least four different cognitive-based theories and fails to address some psychological principles involved in the dynamics of change. (p. 124)*

The principles that Chandler says most discipline strategies violate are:

1. When people perceive that their freedom to act is hampered, they will act the opposite way.
2. Students (should be) at the center and (should have) nearly complete responsibility for their own fate.
3. Perceived inefficacy in coping with negative wants produces fearful expectations and avoidance behavior.
4. The way students perceive causes of their behavioral and academic performance determines whether they will take charge of a change or assume that change is external to them and out of their control. (p. 124)

Plymouth Junior High School's program for discipline reflects many current programs. It strives to put the responsibility on the student whenever possible, be consistent but flexible in enforcing the basic rules, and find alternatives for classroom activities, rewards, and consequences so that students do not force themselves into corners (Shook, 1975).

A school in Houston, Texas, developed a disciplinary system that reduced the frequency of corporal punishment to 7 percent and suspensions to 20 percent (Sanders & Yarbrough, 1976). The program's strategies were to provide a personal atmosphere, to help students clarify their values, to provide a crisis-intervention center for students with serious problems, and to provide an ever-changing set of objectives relating to students' real-life needs.

One reason that schools are turning to less authoritative means for disciplining is that teachers today realize that power does not bring student cooperation—on the contrary, it stimulates more resistance. A second and equally important reason is that it would be inconsistent to use force. The aim is to produce students who approach life's challenges courageously because they are able to relate to others, solve problems, and be responsible (Dinkmeyer & Dinkmeyer, 1976). Thompson (1994) addresses this current trend:

> *The ultimate goal of any disciplinary approach should be not merely to maintain an efficient learning environment but rather to develop within individual pupils a kind of self-discipline, the kind of self-discipline that arises out of risk-taking and coping with consequences. (p. 265)*

The Cascade Model for Classroom Discipline

Another modern classroom discipline model is the cascade model. This model presents a systematic plan for maintaining classroom discipline. Like a waterfall, it involves stages arranged in a particular sequence. By following the sequence, the teacher can approach classroom management logically. The early stages are preventive.

Preventive Discipline

Basic to the cascade model is a set of premises that includes certain attitudes. One premise holds that a good, positive climate will prevent discipline problems. This climate includes both the physical environment and a positive attitude toward students. Expectations are made clear to students. A major step in reducing discipline problems is to demonstrate positive expectations toward students.

The teacher is encouraged to involve students in developing rules at the beginning of each year. Even the rules are stated in positive terms: "If you need to say something, raise your hand" or "Have your homework completely finished, neat, and in on time." Consequences for violating the rules are also developed with student input. These consequences come in a certain order—for example, (1) warning, (2) detention, (3) time out, (4) in-school suspension, and (5) immediate removal from the classroom. If this sequence must be altered because of the nature of a particular student's history, explain the reason for the inconsistency to the student.

Plan early in the year. Evertson (1989) explains: "Thus, solving managerial and organizational problems at the beginning of the year is essential in laying the groundwork for quality learning opportunities for students" (p. 90). Dagley and Orso (1991) reinforce the need teachers have to communicate their expectations to their students early in the year: "Research on effective teachers strongly verifies the emphasis on getting the year off to a good start" (p. 52).

Good preventive discipline can occur only when students are relatively free. Another way of saying this is that good discipline cannot exist in classrooms where all students feel they are restricted unnecessarily. Thompson (1994) explains:

> *Preventive discipline is nothing other than the establishment of a positive learning environment that at once affords the pupils as much freedom of behavior as they can handle without infringing on the rights of others and minimizes the instances of challenge between teacher and pupils.* (p. 264)

Teachers who stop the class each time an infraction occurs actually promote problems. Figure 12.3 shows the distribution of several theories as related to imposed control and self-control. Moving from the left side toward the right side these theories contribute increasingly toward the development of self-discipline.

Parent Involvement

Remember that you don't always have to address student problems alone. On the contrary, the Carnegie Council on Adolescent Development staff (1995) was referring to teachers' need to develop positive cooperative relationships with parents and making them partners in education when it declared increased parent involvement a goal for all middle school

	LEARNING THEORIES				
	Faculty Psychology	Stimulus-Response Psychology	Behavioral Psychology	Phenomenology	
	NONEDUCATION MANAGEMENT THEORIES				Self-Controlled Discipline
Externally Imposed Discipline	McGregor X Theory	Maslow's Needs Theory		McGregor Y Theory	
	CLASSROOM MANAGEMENT THEORIES				
	Training Model	Behavior Modification Model	Psychodynamic Model	Group Dynamics Model	Personal-Social Growth Model
				Group Management Theory	Reality Therapy

FIGURE 12.3 DISCIPLINE CONTINUUM SHOWING GENERAL LOCATIONS OF MAJOR LEARNING THEORIES, MANAGEMENT THEORIES, AND DISCIPLINE THEORIES

teachers. The National Middle School Association had as a priority goal for all "Parents and schools to form partnerships to meet the needs of the whole child (Jenkins & Jenkins, 1991). Don't be afraid to involve parents. But you don't want every contact with parents to involve problems. Involve parents with goal setting. Get their physical support. Encourage your school to have a parents' day, when parents even assist with the lessons. According to Brown (1998), "The more parents are involved in classroom matters, the higher their expectations, and consequently, the better the student behavior." Williams et al. (1999) suggest using classroom management programs that involve parents and other community members. Site-based councils are an excellent means of achieving this goal. For example, they often revise the school's written discipline handbook. Involving parents in decisions to introduce new curriculum programs can have the same positive effects.

Supportive Discipline

Another premise involves supportive discipline, or reinforcing desired behaviors. These reinforcers may be verbal or nonverbal and written or nonwritten. Students are praised in specific terms and told why. Parents are often told about students' accomplishments and are encouraged to give praise at home for achievements at school.

Corrective Discipline

The next tier of steps in the cascade model is labeled corrective discipline. At this level the teacher approaches the students with the problem using the "I" approach—for example, "I can't start the class until the room is quieter. We waste several minutes at the beginning of each hour. Have you any suggestions how we might solve this problem?" Each suggestion is discussed, the students vote, and their choice is tried.

Adaptive Discipline

The fourth and final tier of the cascade model, adaptive discipline, is used when all else fails. Here, a private conference takes place. The teacher tries to remain positive to avoid damaging the student's self-image. Teacher and student identify a satisfactory or acceptable behavior and sign a contract. If the plan fails, they rework it until it succeeds. (For further references, see Rutter, Maughan, Mortimore, & Duston, 1979.)

Avoiding Discipline Problems

Control: Getting off to a Good Start

Rudeness begets rudeness, and sarcasm can spawn a climate of mistrust, dislike, and disrespect. Teachers can develop a climate of mutual respect by showing respect to all students at all times and by requiring that students treat their classmates and teachers with respect. Maximum learning requires a climate of respect and control.

Control is best achieved by cooperation between teacher and students, but it is your responsibility as teacher to have control from the first minute—before discussing a cooperative arrangement. Begin each year by setting rules that students understand. Make the rules specific, clear, and firm, being especially alert to "Teachers must use action not anger to control misbehavior" (McDaniel, 1994, p. 255). Continue the year being especially alert to students' needs and desires. In this context, "needs" refers not so much to present whims but to serious present and future needs. Some of these may be the adolescent's needs for approval, success, and independence and social needs. As students show that they can handle freedom, you can gradually remove restrictions. Each time you feel that the class has progressed beyond the need for a rule, suggest that it be removed. This lets students know that the class has earned the prerogative of canceling the rule if they so wish and that you are not just being inconsistent.

The firm teacher can become less strict more easily than the lenient teacher can become more strict, but there is danger in beginning the year with too many rules. Establish only essential rules and restrictions. In the 1950s a principal ruled that all boys must wear belts. This was in reaction to jeans worn so low on the hips that the navel showed through the often unbuttoned shirt. But the boys noticed that the principal did not define "belt." The rule was obeyed—the boys wore short ropes through belt loops, they wore ropes eight feet long (dragging on the floor), they wore string belts, they wore leather belts, but belts they did wear. The principal was also a learner, and he rescinded the rule promptly. One common mistake teachers make is to establish unnecessary and unenforceable rules.

Using Enthusiasm

The best single diversion from behavior problems is a well-planned and well-executed lesson that involves all students, especially if you are enthusiastic about the subject. Clear objectives and frequent feedback will contribute to a lesson's success. In addition to being clear, involving students, and giving frequent feedback, teachers can become more enthusiastic by including material and activities that both they and students will enjoy.

Using Names

The teacher who knows a student's name has more influence over that student, if that teacher uses the name appropriately. For example, suppose you are teaching a lesson on the first day of school and a boy sitting in the back row begins to distract other students while you are talking. It would be awkward to have to stop, look at the seating chart, and count seats to direct your reprimand to the right person. To say "You in the red-and-black-striped shirt" would get him the entire class's attention and encourage him to repeat the disruption to regain that attention. But to reprimand without designating the student might alienate other class members. Simply walking near the disruptive student is often all you must do to alleviate the problem. This technique is known as proximity control.

If you knew the boy's name, you could drop his name in the middle of a sentence as you presented the lesson, without even looking at him and without breaking the pace of the lesson. Such an action tells him and the rest of the class that you are very much aware of his attempts to disrupt the class but that the lesson is too important to be impeded by anyone's selfish attempt to gain attention.

Helping Students Learn Self-Respect

Students who perceive themselves as troublemakers make trouble. Those who perceive themselves as good students or good guys must live up to this image. Avoid saying and doing things that tend to downgrade students, and take any opportunity to say and do things to improve a student's self-image. Remember, in an earlier chapter, former Nebraska Teacher of the Year Duane Obermier said that students "respond to kindness, encouragement, a friendly tease, and a smile" (Henson & Eller, 1999, p. 12). This respect-focused relationship between teacher and students should be extended among all students. Students need to practice showing respect for others (Lemlech, 1999).

Avoiding Threats

Some teachers threaten groups of students and individuals, not realizing that the threatened person is challenged to misbehave. It is not uncommon for a teacher to remark "All right, class, I am not going to tell you again to be quiet," implying "I can make you wish you had behaved." Such a statement usually promotes misbehavior and diminishes learning. As Hart (1983) explains, the brain tends to "downshift" under threat. Avoid threats you never intend to carry out—better yet, avoid threats completely.

Avoiding Public Reprimand

Deal with any serious problem you have with a particular student privately. Reprimanding a student in the presence of peers will damage peer relationships, which are important to people of all ages, and it forces the student to rebut or concede. A rebuttal damages the student's relationship with you; a concession causes the student to lose face with peers. Public reprimand also threatens the rest of the class. Believing that they could receive the same treatment, students may lose confidence and trust in you. Your own behavior can set a tone for students to follow. McDaniel (1994) explains: "Teachers should employ the "soft reprimand" when a student's in-class behavior needs correcting" and "only after students have accepted their teachers as leaders can teachers begin refining and humanizing their techniques for discipline" (pp. 255–256).

Avoiding Ridicule

When students misbehave, try to change their future behavior patterns. That is all. Never ridicule a student, whether in public or in private. Ridicule is directed at a person, not at correcting behavior. Chamberlin and Chambers (1994) have recommended, "Praise in public, punish in private helps to create a trusting atmosphere" (p. 206).

Dealing with Problems

Be Prepared to Handle Problems When They Do Develop

The best way to avoid problems in the classroom is to be well prepared each day and to have interesting experiences for each class. However, even the most effective teachers have discipline problems, so it is good to be prepared and to think ahead to when a discipline problem might develop. What will you do?

Beginning teachers often ask for the best way to handle discipline problems. Any teacher's major goal should be to discover an approach to dealing with problems that leads students to discipline themselves. Savage (1991), who supports such an approach, explains how to achieve this goal:

> An important step for teachers who expect to work toward self-control in the classroom is the development of a hierarchy of consequences. The hierarchy should begin with relatively simply and unobtrusive responses and move progressively to more intrusive and serious ones. The development of this hierarchy can provide teachers with a plan of action and a sense of security when facing serious discipline problems. (p. 204)

Always Ask Yourself Why

As Thompson (1994) said, "All behavior is caused or purposive" (p. 261). Yet each teacher must determine his or her threshold of tolerance. Any classroom limitations or rules should exist to enhance student learning. "Preventive discipline is nothing other than the establishment of a positive learning environment that at once affords the pupils as much freedom of behavior as they can handle without infringing on the rights of others and minimizes the instances of challenge between teacher and pupil" (Thompson, 1994, p. 264).

No students want to misbehave, so why do they? There is a cause for all behavior. Classical psychologists say that all behavior is a reaction to a stimulus—that is, everything we do is in reaction to other people or other things. Phenomenologists believe that every misbehavior is an expression of a need and that therefore each time a student misbehaves we should ask ourselves, "What need is that student trying to satisfy?" The need may be for more attention or perhaps for peer approval if a student does not get adequate reinforcement from family and teachers. Hostile misbehavior may be an attempt to alleviate frustration because of some perceived injustice. Sometimes you cannot determine the need or the cause of the behavior. To ask misbehaving students what the need is will not help, because they probably do not know.

The creative teacher is often able to provide acceptable avenues for students to express themselves. When a student causes serious disruptions, study that student's cumulative record and discuss the problem with the school counselor. Learning more about the student may give you ideas about how to work more effectively with that student. Become more tolerant when you see that the student is attempting to improve previous unsatisfactory behavior.

Avoiding Confrontations

Because misbehavior is often an attempt to get attention or to express discontent, the person who misbehaves may seek to create a scene to confront the person who could draw the most attention to the disruption—the teacher.

Sometimes you may be tempted to engage in emotionally charged disputes with students. Remember, though, that an emotional person does not seek reasonable or rational answers but instead seeks to justify the behavior. Any argument will only make the student more defensive. You may be able to help students realize that their misbehavior is disruptive and provide opportunities for them to express their opinions, but you can do so only after they have calmed down.

Conflict Resolution

Problems between and among students are common in today's schools. Kenney and Watson (1996) warn that such common problems may be the most significant problems in schools and, therefore, must be attended to. First, the most significant problems in our schools may not be as we often imagine them. Gangs, drugs, and armed agitators may receive the most attention; however, most of the conflicts that surfaced during this project were related to everyday school reactions (p. 453).

- Students are interested in a safer, more orderly school environment (p. 453)
- Repression of feelings inhibits students' ability to relate to others or to feel empathy for others.
- "While a number of programs and strategies designed to address the issues of violence are being implemented in schools across the country, among the most successful means to intervene have been conflict resolution and cooperative learning strategies." (p. 527)

- "Nationwide, more than 2,000 schools conduct conflict resolution programs" (p. 527). Me-conflict programs focus on creative conflict resolution and alternatives to violence.
- "(Conflict resolution) is an important means of social interaction for young people."(p. 52)
- "The teachers listening and encouraging discussion of managing conflict helps not only the children who have been 'acting out,' but may be a critical opportunity to enable all at-risk youngsters to acknowledge their emotions and talk about them." (p. 527)

Left unattended, minor conflicts can become major causes of disruptions and often lead to violence. Strategy for dealing with conflicts among students is called **conflict resolution.** Currently, over 2,000 schools conduct conflict-resolution programs in which students are permitted to role-play their interpersonal problems (Houcke & Maxon, 1997). Such programs are often especially helpful to meet the needs of at-risk students.

The Private Talk

Avoiding a serious confrontation does not necessarily mean ignoring the student. If you do not ask a student to refrain from the undesirable behavior, that student and other class members may assume that you do not really care if rules are broken. The difference between noting a disruption and engaging in a confrontation is in the manner in which you take action. Be as quiet and uneventful as possible. If the student responds negatively, ignore the student, but if the disruption continues, ask the student to leave the room and wait outside

---

Teacher as Proactive Decision Maker

Classroom Situation

1. You know that on your first day some students will test you to see how much you will tolerate.

2. Regardless of how well you prepare to avoid disruption, it is possible that you will have one or more students who will not obey the established classroom procedures.

Proactive Alternatives

- Plan a discussion of classroom procedures. Emphasize the connection between expected classroom behavior and learning.
- Make a list of non-negotiable class rules. Discuss the need for each of these rules and invite the students to add any additional necessary rules. Keep this list short.
- Prepare a behavior contract to have on hand in the event that you have students who will not adjust to the expected class behavior.
- Prepare a private talk to have on hand to guide a meeting with each disruptive student. Include comments to ensure the student that

    You disapprove of the behavior, not the student.

    The problem belongs not just to you alone but to both of you.

until the end of the period, when you are free to arrange for a private talk. Private conferences can be effective if they place part of the responsibility for correcting the student's behavior on both the student and you, and if you look for the cause of the misbehavior.

If you ask a student to leave the classroom, you must have a private talk with the student before allowing him or her to reenter. Keep your emotions under cover during the private talk. You can express disappointment with the student's behavior, but make certain that the student does not interpret this as personal dislike. In an extreme case, when the student continues to misbehave after the private talk, call for the principal's assistance. Your mission, after all, is to provide a classroom environment conducive to learning; you cannot afford to allow one student to continue disrupting it.

Using Firmness and Consistency

All teachers should assert themselves. Apply whatever tactics you use to maintain discipline consistently with all students every day. Firmness does not imply harshness and constant sternness. If you are firm but calm, your students will appreciate it and your health will be better.

This chapter has provided several concrete suggestions to help you maintain a healthy, productive climate in your classroom. It has also attempted to shape your attitudes about discipline and cause you to think of this important part of your role as the complex phenomenon that it is. This chapter also attempts to help you base your own classroom management strategies on accepted models and on sound, accepted principles of adolescent psychology and learning theories. Avoid oversimplistic approaches that lack the support of research. Jones (1989) gives this advice:

> *Rather than providing teachers with a clear understanding of the breadth of research and practice in classroom management and encouraging teachers to be informal decision makers, many school districts and some universities present teachers with limited methods such as Assertive Discipline, ITIP, and Discipline With Love and Logic.* (p. 332)

As you continue in this class and throughout your teaching career, take every opportunity to learn all you can about students' highly complex behavior. As a teacher, you must maintain a classroom climate that encourages maximum learning, yet your relationship with your students will improve if you remember that every misbehavior has a cause. All students must discover behaviors that are acceptable to their peers and to their teachers.

In the Computer Lab

For several reasons the computer lab can, and often is, the area and time of day when a disproportionate number of behavioral problems occur. Why? First, students often perceive lab time as free time, when they are on their own to do whatever they choose to do. Second, the nature of the World Wide Web is a temptation to many students; after all, middle-level students are naturally curious and some do not require leadership to begin exploring. Furthermore, this may be the time of day when instructions are the most vague.

To adjust for these characteristics, start taking precautions at the beginning of the year, before the first visit to the computer lab. Talk to students about appropriate and inappropriate behavior in the lab. Be sure to have a clear assignment for the first visit and for each succeeding visit. For assignments that require new computer skills, carefully instruct students on the use of the computer and, once each lesson begins, supervise by circulating throughout the room to ensure that all students are keeping up. Don't forget the teacher's responsibility to serve as a role model. Let students see your excitement for the computer and share ways that you use the skills sought each day.

Royal Van Horn (1997) offers good advice and says it simply, "Don't let students do trivial things on computers" (p. 584). You can start by making sure that you purchase software that is not trivial. Choose only software that you know leads to the attainment of the course objectives.

Vignettes

Discipline is a problem in our schools. You must maintain discipline in the classroom. The following cases will help you develop the ability to discipline your future students. They show some of the real dilemmas in which teachers often find themselves. As you read each vignette, imagine yourself in the situation and decide how you would handle it.

Vignette One: A Principal Has Too Many Discipline Problems

Middletown School was divided into a middle and senior high, with the lower grades in one building, the upper grades in another, and the principal's office in a breezeway connecting the two buildings. The windows in Jan's classroom faced the breezeway. Jan had taught for only a few weeks at Middletown. Each time a discipline problem developed, she immediately referred the offender to the principal's office.

One day Jan was amused to see another teacher leading a student to the principal's office. Later that day she saw a replay of the event. After that, Jan began counting the number of times teachers marched offenders to the principal's office. The record for one day was nine trips; the record for one teacher in one day was three trips.

Jan began to realize that this principal was spending a large amount of time disciplining the students of teachers who could not or would not assume the responsibility. She resolved to handle all future discipline problems herself, except in an emergency.

DISCUSSION

1. How are the student's impressions of a teacher affected when the teacher takes discipline problems to the principal? The first time this occurs it may go unnoticed by the students, but if it is repeated again and again, the students will soon realize that the teacher is weak and unable to handle problems. Troubles in this teacher's class will increase.

2. Does the number of discipline problems reflect the quality of that teacher's teaching? Yes. The teacher who has planned an interesting lesson that involves the students will have fewer discipline problems than the teacher who is dull, boring, and poorly prepared.

Vignette Two: A First Telephone Call from a Parent

Don Harrader was a quiet member of the ninth-grade science class that John taught. In fact, it was difficult for John to think of Don as a member of the class, because Don was so withdrawn. Don was making above-average grades until a unit on simple machines began. He received an F at the end of the unit when an examination was administered. When John talked to Don about the grade, he replied that he just did not care for that part of the course.

The next day John was having lunch when the message arrived that Mr. Harrader had called and asked that he call back. John recalled Don's recent decline in grades and suspected this was why his father had called. John left the lunchroom and went directly to the telephone. Mr. Harrader immediately asked why Don had an F in John's class. Trying to be objective and honest, John answered that Don claimed to have no interest in simple machines. Don's father replied, "I understand, but I want to know if Don has been misbehaving in class." John assured him the answer was no, and the conversation ended.

In the days following, John did a lot of thinking about Don, Don's relationship with his father, and Don's lack of real friends among his peers. One weekend John parked by the tennis courts and was watching a match when Don walked by and saw him. He asked if John played tennis and would play a set with him. John agreed. He found that Don was certainly not the same boy he saw each day in science class. There was never a happier person. From that day on, John had no trouble stimulating Don's interest in class. When Don learned that his teacher was interested in rocks, he brought his rock collection to share with the rest of the class.

A simple telephone call had stimulated John's interest in Don. An unplanned tennis match had removed Don's apathy. Together these two events had resulted indirectly in motivating a shy student.

DISCUSSION

1. If an angry parent telephones, how should you respond? First, refrain from showing your emotions, so the parent can see that you are being objective regarding the student. This is the best way to show the irate parent that the parent is the one who is being unreasonable. Second, be honest with the parent. If the student is failing to do satisfactory work, say so. Frankness and honesty must prevail before the parent and you can begin working together to motivate the student, and you must initiate the honesty.

2. Parental neglect is the cause of many discipline problems at school. How can you provide attention for the neglected child? You can probably think of many ways to show interest in a student who is neglected at home. Most students have an area in which they have a strong interest, although they may never reveal it in the classroom. The teacher can often identify a student's interests by observing the student's activities outside the classroom. A teacher who shows an interest in a student's nonacademic activities may find that the student pays more attention to the teacher in class and to school assignments.

Summary

Traditionally, teachers have been taught strategies to force students to behave. A better approach is to plan to have students discipline themselves. Begin the year by clarifying your expectations for student behavior. Explain that the need for this type of behavior is to provide for learning. Learning cannot exist in a climate of chaos. Teachers have two major responsibilities for discipline: preventive and problem solving. Perhaps the most effective use of your time is to focus most of your energy on preventing misbehavior. Do this by providing a good lesson each period, a lesson with clear objectives and plenty of student activities. Monitor students to ensure that they understand the relationship between the activities and the lesson objectives. The several theories presented in this chapter are sequenced so that each theory is more self-discipline oriented than the preceding theory.

Regardless how good your classroom management skills are, occasional problems will surface, and you must be prepared to deal with them. Private conferences are effective. When they fail, you should consider having another conference and inviting the student and parents or guardians to that conference. During all conferences, focus on the behavior and on correcting it, not on placing blame. Give some of the responsibility for finding a solution to the student.

Recap of Major Ideas

1. All teachers experience discipline problems.
2. Good classroom discipline is essential for maximum learning. Because you are in charge of instruction, discipline is your responsibility.
3. Good discipline implies order and control. Quiet is important to facilitate order and control and for effective communication.
4. Begin each year by being firm yet friendly. Classroom humor is desirable, but it must not cause excessive disruption.

5. Too many rules can cause added problems. Tell students why each rule is necessary. Whenever feasible, involve students in setting classroom rules.
6. Be consistent and fair when establishing and maintaining good discipline.
7. The best deterrent to discipline problems is a well-planned and well-executed lesson, with clear goals, that involves all students. Your enthusiasm for the lesson helps motivate students.
8. Concentrate on preventing problems rather than trying to learn how to manage disasters. Although the latter skill may be helpful, few teachers feel they are experts in that area.
9. Avoid making threats and using sarcasm and public reprimands, because these tend to lower students' self-esteem and self-respect. Instead, look for opportunities to compliment students, thus helping them build a positive self-image.
10. When planned and executed correctly, private conferences can be an effective means of handling disruptive students. When private conferences fail, arrange a joint conference with the principal, counselor, and parents or guardians.

Activities

The following activities will help you deal with all these discipline concerns.

1. You have undoubtedly heard or read statements about school discipline that you do not agree with. Explain one way in which your idea of how students should behave differs from others' ideas.
2. Describe a problem that the schools in your community face. Explain how you would work to eliminate that problem if you were teaching in a local school.
3. Develop a discipline strategy building on one of your personal strengths.
4. What would you do if a student became enraged and refused to be quiet? The other students are waiting to see your reaction. How will you handle the situation?
5. Identify some student activities that can deter misbehavior.

References

Ban, J. R. (1994). A lesson plan approach for dealing with school discipline. *The Clearing House, 67*(5), 257–260.

Bell, L. C., & Stefanich, G. P. (1984). Building effective discipline using the Cascade Model. *The Clearing House, 58,* 134–137.

Carnegie Council on Adolescent Development Staff (1995). *Great transitions: Preparing adolescents for a new century.* New York: Carnegie Foundation.

Chamberlin, L. J., & Chambers, N. S. (1994). Developing responsibility in today's students. *The Clearing House, 67*(4), 204–206.

Chandler, T. A. (1990, November–December). Why discipline strategies are bound to fail. *The Clearing House,* 124–126.

Cooper, D., & Snell, J. L. (2003). Bullying: Not just a kid thing. *Educational Leadership, 60*(6), 22–25.

Cunningham, B. (1988). Preservice teachers' perceptions of children's problem behaviors. *Journal of Educational Research, 82*(1), 34–39.

Curwin, R. L., & Mendler, A. N. (1984, May). High standards for effective discipline. *Educational Leadership, 41,* 75–76.

Dagley, D. L., & Orso, S. K. (1991). Integrating summative and formative modes of evaluation. *NASSP Bulletin, 75,* 72–82.

Dinkmeyer, D., & Dinkmeyer, D., Jr. (1976). Logical consequences: A key to the reduction of disciplinary problems. *Phi Delta Kappan, 57,* 664–666.

Elam, S. M., Rose, L. C., & Gallup, A. M. (1991, September). The 23rd annual Gallup poll of the public's attitude toward the public schools. *Phi Delta Kappan, 73*(1), 41–56.

Elam, S. M., Rose, L. C., & Gallup, A. M. (1994). The 26th annual Phi Delta Kappan/Gallup poll of the public's attitude toward the public schools. *Phi Delta Kappan, 76*(1), 41–56.

Elkind, D. (1981). *The hurried child: Growing up too fast too soon.* Reading, MA: Addison-Wesley Publishing.

Emmer, E. (1999). A view from the field. In K. T. Henson & B. F. Eller, *Educational Psychology for Effective Teaching.* Belmont, CA: Wadsworth, pp. 414–415.

Erb, T. (1997). Student friendly classrooms in a not a very child-friendly world. *Middle School Journal, 28*(5), 24.

Evertson, C. M. (1989). Improving elementary classroom management: A school based training program for beginning the year. *Journal of Educational Research, 83,* 82–90.

Gathercoal, F. (1990, February). Judicious discipline. *Education Digest*, 20–24.

Gilbert, S. L., & Smith, L. C. (2003). A bumpy road to action research. *Kappa Delta Pi Record*, 39(2), 80–83.

Glickman, C. D. (2003). Symbols and celebrations that sustain education. *Educational Leadership*, 60(6), 34–39.

Grubaugh, S. (1989, October). Nonverbal language techniques for better classroom management and discipline. *High School Journal*, 73, 34–40.

Haberman, M. (1995). *Star teachers of children in poverty*. West Lafayette, IN: Kappa Delta Pi.

Hanny, R. J. (1994). Don't let them take you to the barn. *The Clearing House*, 67(5), 252–253.

Hansen, J. M. (1974). Discipline: A whole new bag. *High School Journal*, 57, 172–181.

Harper's Magazine. (1985, March). The top problems in schools in 1940 and 1982.

Hart, L. A. (1983). *Human brain and human learning*. New York: Longman.

Henson, K. T., & Eller, B. F. (1999). *Educational psychology for effective teaching*. Belmont, CA: Wadsworth.

Hilliard, R. (2002). *A parent's guide to young adolescents*. Atlanta, GA: Georgia Middle School Association.

Houcke, J. W., & Maxon, S. (1997). The role of teachers and the school in assuring children who live with violence. *Education*, 117(4), 522–529.

Jackson, D. B. (2003). Education reform as if student agency mattered. Academic microcultures and student identity. *Phi Delta Kappan*, 84(8), 579–585.

Jambor, T. (1988). Classroom management and discipline alternatives to corporal punishment: The Norwegian example. *Education*, 109(2), 220–225.

Johns, F. A., & MacNaughton, R. H. (1990). Spare the rod: A continuing controversy. *The Clearing House*, 63(9), 338–392.

Jones, V. F. (1989). Classroom management: Clarifying theory and improving practice. *Education*, 109, 330–339.

Jones, V. F., & Jones, L. S. (1986). *Comprehensive classroom management: Creating positive learning environments* (2nd ed.). Boston: Allyn & Bacon.

Kenney, D. J., & Watson, T. S. (1996). Reducing fear in the schools: Managing fear in the schools: Managing conflict through problem solving. *Education and Urban Society*, 28(4), 436–455.

Kounin, J. S. (1977). *Discipline and group management in classrooms*. Melbourne, FL: Krieger.

Lemlech, J. K. (1999). *Classroom management* (3rd ed.). Prospect Heights, IL: Waveland.

MacNaughton, R. H., & Johns, F. A. (1991, September). Developing a successful schoolwide discipline program. *NASSP Bulletin*, 75(536), 47–57.

Maslow, A. (1954). *Motivation and personality*. New York: Harper & Row.

McDaniel, T. R. (1994). How to be an effective authoritarian: A back-to-basics approach to classroom discipline. *The Clearing House*, 67(5), 25–256.

National Center for Education Statistics (1991). *Education counts*. Washington, DC: U.S. Department of Education.

National Center for Education Statistics (1999). *Teacher quality: A report on teacher preparation and qualifications of public school teachers*. Washington, DC: Department of Education.

Nuby, J., & Doebler, L. K. (1999). The impact of inner-city high school placement on teacher trainers: A qualitative analysis. *SRATE Journal*, 8(1), 41–45.

Oana, R. G. (1993). *Changes in teacher education: Reform, renewal, reorganization. A professional development leave report*. Bowling Green, OH: Bowling Green State University.

Olweus, D. (XXXX). A profile of bullying. *Educational Leadership*, 60(6), 6–11.

Orterman, K. F. (2003). Preventing school violence. *Phi Delta Kappan*, 84(8), 622–623.

Palardy, J. M. (1996, September). Taking another look at behavior modification and assertive discipline. *NASSP Bulletin*, 66–70.

Parsley, K., & Cocoran, C. A. (2003). The classroom teacher's role in preventing school failure. *Kappa Delta Pi Record*, 39(2), 84–87.

Penvy, B. (2002). *Through a glass, darkly*. Unpublished manuscript, University of West Georgia, Carrollton.

Phelps, P. H. (1991, March–April). Helping teachers excel as classroom managers. *The Clearing House*, 64, 241–242.

Phillips, G. (1998). Making a difference in student behavior. SouthEast South Central Educational Cooperative Principals' Academy Retreat, Lexington, KY.

Rose, L. C., & Gallup, A. M. (1998). The 30th annual Phi Delta Kappan/Gallup poll of the public's attitudes toward the public schools. *Phi Delta Kappan, 80*(1), 41–56.

Ruggeri, A. (2002). *Karen and Jill.* Unpublished manuscript, University of West Georgia, Carrollton.

Rutter, M., Maughan, B., Mortimore, P., & Duston, J. (1979). *Fifteen thousand hours.* Cambridge, MA: Harvard University Press.

Sanders, S. G., & Yarbrough, J. S. (1976). Achieving a learning environment with order. *The Clearing House, 50,* 100–102.

Sapp, G. L., Clough, J. D., Pittman, B., & Toben, C. (1973). Classroom management and student involvement. *High School Journal, 56,* 276–283.

Savage, T. V. (1999). *Discipline for self-control.* Englewood Cliffs, NJ: Prentice-Hall.

Schaps, E. (2003). Creating a school community. *Educational Leadership, 60*(6), 31–33.

Shook, J. (1975). Alternatives for managing disruptive classroom behaviors. *School and Community, 61,* 28–29.

Singham, M. (2003). The achievement gap: Myths and reality. *Phi Delta Kappan, 84*(8), 586–591.

Stokes, L. C. (2001). What middle school teachers perceive to be essential elements in preservice middle school teacher programs. *SRATE Journal,* 10(1), 28–32.

Thompson, G. (1994). Discipline and the high school teacher. *The Clearing House, 67*(5), 261–265.

Vars, G. F. (1997). Student concerns and standards too. *Middle School Journal, 28*(4), 44–49.

Vockell, E. L. (1991, March–April). Corporal punishment: The pros and cons. *The Clearing House, 64,* 279–283.

Van Horn, R. (1997) Improving standardized test scores. *Phi Delta Kappan, 78*(7), 584–585.

Wasicsko, M. M., & Ross, S. M. (1994). How to create discipline problems. *The Clearing House, 67*(5), 248–251.

Weber, W., Roff, L. A., Crawford, J., & Robinson, C. (1983). Classroom management. In W. A. Weber, L. A. Roff, J. Crawford, & C. Robinson (Eds.), *Classroom management: Reviews of the teacher education and research literature* (pp. 38–39). Princeton, NJ: Educational Testing Service.

Weissberg, R. P., Resnik, H., Payton, J., & O'Brein, M. O. (2003). Evaluating social and learning programs. *Educational Leadership, 60*(6), 40–45.

Williams, P. A., Alley, R., & Henson, K. T. (1999). *Managing secondary classrooms.* Boston: Allyn & Bacon.

Wilms, W. M. (2003). Altering the structure of American public schools. *Phi Delta Kappan, 84*(8), 606–615.

Wilson, B., Ireton, E., & Wood, J. A. (1997). Beginning teacher fears. *Education, 117*(3), 396–400.

Winn, M. (1983). *Children without childhood.* New York: Pantheon Books.

Name Index

A

Abraham, M. R., 95
Acheson, K. A., 88
Achilles, C. M., 89
Agne, K. J., 180, 211
Albrecht, C., 265–268
Alessi, S. M., 276
Alexander, J., 227, 230
Alexander, W. M., 283
Alfke, D., 283
Allan, K. K., 26
Allen, L. V. Z., 89, 131
Allen, J., 24
Alley, R., 107, 129, 216, 262, 376
Alvestad, K. A., 328
Anderson, G., 300
Anderson, J., 230
Anderson, L., 300, 339
Andrews, R. H., 189, 215
Applebee, A. N., 60
Arlin, M., 187
Armento, B. J., 90
Armstrong, D. G., 34, 64, 77, 118, 123, 143, 213, 256, 294, 336, 337
Astuto, T. A., 122

B

Badarack, G., 88
Bader, L. A., 208
Bainbridge, W. H., 33
Baines, C., 197
Baines, L., 197
Ban, J. R., 358, 361, 362
Bandura, A., 324
Banks, J. A., 227
Banks, R. S., 193
Barker, J., 275
Barnes, L. B., 242
Baron, M. A., 34
Barth, R. S., 257
Barton, J., 140
Baughman, M. D., 331
Beasley, M., 189
Beasley, W. W., 245
Beliveau, J., 155–158
Bell, L. C., 360
Benbow, C. P., 214
Bennett, C. K., 25, 26
Berliner, D. C., 64, 252, 302, 343
Bernauer, J. A., 10, 25
Berry, K., 107
Bickel, F., 293, 330
Bicouvaris, M., 280
Bishop, G. R., 241
Block, J. H., 119, 186
Bloom, B. S., 37, 38, 40, 43, 164, 186, 260, 261
Blumenthal, C., 193, 194
Blythe, T., 16, 62
Bohen, D. B., 34
Boix-Mansilla, V., 16, 326, 330
Boles, K., 101–104
Borich, G. D., 324
Boutte, G. S., 343
Bowen, A., 198–202
Boyer, E., 25
Bowen, A., 198–202
Bowles, K., 101–104
Bracey, G., 129
Bradley, D. F., 175, 202, 207
Brooks, D. M., 296
Brophy, J. E., 21, 23, 25, 91, 181, 252, 253, 269, 295, 300, 313, 324, 328, 331
Brown, C. L., 60
Brown, D. B., 214
Brownlie, F., 25
Bruner, J. S., 296
Buckner, J. H., 293, 330
Bull, S. G., 271

Bundy, E., 232
Bunny, S., 25
Burgess, G., 160
Burns, D. E., 213
Burns, R. B., 187
Buschee, F., 34
Busching, B., 24
Bush, G. H. W., 33
Butler, J. A., 194
Buttery, T. J., 59
Byrd, D. M., 24

C

Callan, R. J., 187
Campbell, J. K., 280, 284
Campbell, L. P., 325
Cameron, S., 7, 8, 13
Cardelle-Elawar, M., 26
Carnegie Council on Adolescent Development, 42, 59, 61, 76, 87, 89, 104, 120, 148, 175, 193, 252, 295, 358, 381
Carpenter, T. P., 88
Carroll, J. B., 186
Carruthers, M., 195
Carson, M. D., 88
Castaneda, A., 242
Cazden, C., 138, 293
Centra, J., 181
Chamberlin, L. J., 374, 384, 379, 384
Chambers, N. S., 379, 384
Chance, E. W., 88, 91
Chandler, P. M., 265–268
Chandler, T. A., 379
Chansky, N. M., 341
Charles, C. M., 331
Chattin-McNichols, J., 24, 25
Checkley, K., 176, 177
Cheney, C. D., 203
Cherniss, C., 258

393

Cheyney, A. B., 229
Chimes, M., 25, 227, 228, 231, 238
Chissom, B., 59
Christensen, C. R., 242
Christie, K., 91
Cienkus, R. C., 253
Ciscell, R. E., 93, 94
Clark, C. M., 87
Clark, D. C., 59
Clark, D. L., 122
Clark, L. H., 329, 343
Clark, S. N., 59
Clark-Thayer, S., 189
Clemens, S., 169
Cloonan, C., 35
Clough, J. D., 378
Cohen, A., 187
Cole, P., 198–202
Coleman, J. G., 195
Collins, A., 140
Combs, J., 24
Confer, C. B., 15, 283, 326
Consortium on Chicago School Research, 26
Cook, A., 10
Cooper, D, 354
Cooper, H., 100
Copenhaver, R. W., 24
Corcoran, C. A., 5, 243, 355, 364
Corey, S. M., 24
Coward, R., 10, 273
Cruickshank, D. R., 300
Cuban, L., 24
Cunningham, B., 360
Curts, J., 233–238

D

Dagley, D. L., 119, 121, 381
Dandridge, J. A., 231
Daniels, D. C., 8, 179
Darling-Hammond, L., 3, 24, 25, 232
Dauber, S. L., 214
Davis, H., 160
DeHann, R., 212

DeRoma, V. M., 145
Des Dixon, R. G., 76
Descamps, J., 121, 129
Deshner, D. D., 260
DeVries, D. L., 282
Dewey, J., 12, 13, 15, 23, 254
Dickenson, T. S., 91
Dicker, M., 25
Dinkmeyer D., 380
Dinkmeyer, D., Jr., 380
Dizney, H. F., 271
Doebler, L. K., 228, 365
Doll, R. C., 92
Donnell, P., 151
Doyle, W., 314
Druian, G., 194
Ducharme, D., 333–336
Duell, O. K., 151
Dugger, W. E., Jr., 20
Dunn, K., 187, 188, 190, 207, 215
Dunn, R. S., 187, 188, 190, 207, 215
Durr, W. K., 211
Duston, J., 382

E

Earle, K., 24, 89
Earley, B., 77, 256
Easley, J. A., 297
Economopoulos, M., 198–202
Edinger, M., 192
Education for All Handicapped Children Act, 195
Ehninger, R. D., 297
Einstein, A., 185, 262
Eisner, E., 64, 186, 272, 292
Elam, S. M., 42, 108, 120, 164, 231, 324, 325, 353, 354
Elkind, R., 194
Eller, B. F., 10, 75, 80, 140, 166, 180, 231, 243, 253, 257, 262, 273, 280, 294, 295, 296, 310, 316, 324, 326, 327, 329, 331, 337, 357, 358, 361, 383

Ellington, J., 15
Elliot, I., 178, 189
Elliott, R., 298
Ellsworth, P. C., 271, 301
Ellsworth, R. A., 151
Emig, V. B., 179
Emmer, E., 331, 358
Englander, M., 325
English, F. W., 139
Epstein, J. L., 130
Erasmus, C. C., 239
Erb, T., 361
Esgar, L. V., 217
Evans, R. I., 337
Evertson, C. M., 300, 328, 331, 351, 360, 361, 381

F

Faison, C. L., 59
Fantini, M. D., 231
Farr, M., 260
Farris, H. E., 339
Farris, R. A., 325
Federico, M. A., 202
Feldhusen, J. F., 212, 214
Felner, R. D., 87
Fielding, G., 139, 329, 332
Fielstein, L. L., 227
Finn, J. D., 76, 92
Fischer, R. L., 24
Fisher, C. W., 296
Fisher, J. F., 175, 202, 207
Flowers, N., 87, 316
Franklin, B., 12
Fried, R. L., 77
Friedman, R. S., 194
Froebel, F., 11
Frymier, J., 129, 193, 338
Fullan, M. G., 26, 230
Fulton, B. D., 89

G

Gage, N. L., 252, 343
Gall, M., 88
Gallagher, J. J., 93, 100, 129, 140, 142, 166, 211, 213

Galloway, C. M., 311
Gallup, A. M., 3, 33, 42, 108, 120, 123, 166, 231, 324, 338, 353, 354, 356
Gansneder, B., 193
Gardner, H., 16, 176–177, 326, 330
Garibaldi, A. M., 284
Garmston, R., 23, 32
Garrick-Duhaney, L., 202
Gates, S. L., 185, 187
Gathercoal, F., 360
Geer, C., 63, 90, 341
Gilbert, S. L., 331
Gibran, K., 1, 321
Gifford, S. P., 121, 140
Gilbert, S. L., 25, 203
Gilman, D. A., 88, 89, 175
Glasser, W., 364
Glatthorn, A. A., 232
Glickman, C., 355
Glover, J. A., 62
Gnagey, W. J., 331
Gomez, M. L., 227
Good, T. L., 21, 23, 25, 91, 180, 181, 252, 253, 269, 295, 300, 313, 324
Goodlad, J. I., 41, 275, 300, 313
Gordon, K., 230, 242
Gorman, B., 178, 179, 189
Grant, C. A., 243
Green, J. L., 296
Green, K., 195
Gregg, L., 59, 87
Griggs, S. A., 188, 189
Griswold, P. A., 166
Gronbeck, B. E., 297
Grondel, M., 70, 316, 327
Grouws, D. A., 180, 300
Grubaugh, S., 298, 358
Gruber, K. D., 281
Guernsey, M. A., 203
Guskey, T. R., 186, 187, 250, 325
Guyton, J. M., 227

H

Haberman, M., 129, 166, 227, 228
Hakim, D., 15, 287, 326
Halbach, A., 89
Hall, M., 24, 25
Hamilton, H., 91
Hanny, R. J., 356, 357, 359
Hansen, J. M., 379
Hanson, L. R., 281
Harman, A. E., 34
Harris, K. H., 166
Harrison, B. H., 282
Harrison, C. J., 62, 94
Hart, L. A., 76, 384
Hartley, S. H., 60
Havinghurst, R. J., 212
Hawke, L. M., 101–104
Hawke, M. F., 101–104
Heckman, P. E., 15, 283, 326
Hendricks, M., 24
Henry, M. A., 231, 245
Henson, K. T., 20, 34, 59, 62, 64, 75, 80, 92, 107, 118, 119, 129, 140, 143, 166, 180, 186, 216, 231, 242, 243, 253, 256, 257, 258, 259, 262, 273, 280, 294, 295, 296, 310, 314, 316, 323, 324, 326, 327, 329, 331, 337, 356, 358, 361, 383
Herbart, J., 11
Herrold, B., 202
Hewett, S. M., 265–268
Heyman, M., 279
Hibbard, K. M., 141
Hietapelto, A. B., 340
Hiller, T. B., 340
Hilliard, R., 24, 63, 176, 194, 195, 207, 227, 293, 323, 325, 326, 374–377
Hines, C. V., 300
Hock, M. F., 260, 261
Holm, T., 297, 331
Holmes, G. V., 193
Holloway, J. H., 202
Hoole, E., 253
Hootstein, E. W., 323
Hoover, J. J., 202
Hopping, L., 91
Hostrop, R. W., 277
Houche, J. W., 386
Hubbuch. S. M., 60
Hunter, M., 187
Hyman, J. S., 187
Hyman, R. T., 302, 309

I

Infield, L. P., 262
Ireton, E., 356, 357
Irvin, J. I., 59
Ives, B., 6

J

Jackson, B., 355
Jambor, T., 368
Janas, M., 9
Jantzi, D., 36, 296
Jefferies, B., 195
Jefferson, T., 211
Jenkins, D. M., 7, 24, 89, 108, 122, 141, 232, 280, 141, 142, 293, 325, 342
Jenkins, K. D., 7, 24, 89, 108, 122, 141, 232, 280, 141, 142, 293, 325, 342
Johns, F. A., 358, 366, 367
Johnson, B., 212
Johnson, D. M., 282
Johnson, D. W., 282
Johnson, H., 66–72
Johnston, C. A., 187
Johnston, J. H., 63, 90, 341
Johnston, J. M., 88, 96, 119
Johnston, W. J., 359
Jones, C., 118, 121, 256, 279
Jones, L. S., 360
Jones, V. F., 360, 361, 387
Julik, J. A., 180

K

Kagan, S., 281
Karweit, N., 194

Name Index

Kasa, K. D., 87
Keefe, J. W., 96, 140, 141, 142
Kendall, J. S., 123
Kennedy, J. J., 300
Kenny, D. J., 354, 355
Kiger, S., 88, 89, 175
King, A., 253
Klausmeier, H., 260
Kohlberg, L., 165
Kohn, A., 139, 186
Kopassi, R., 193
Kounin, J., 377
Kowalski, T. J., 62, 242, 258, 259
Krashen, S., 61
Krathwohl, D. R., 43, 164
Krisko, E., 303–306
Kryriacou, M., 190
Kyle, D. W., 232

L

Lacey, C., 74, 77
Lancaster, C., 297, 331
Langer, J. A., 60
Latham, A. S., 332
LeBlanc, P. R., 74, 77
LeFrancois, G. R., 252, 258
Leithwood, K., 36, 296
Lemke, J. L., 330
Lemlech, J. K., 256, 383
Lemmon, P., 189
Levine, D. U., 315
Levy, J., 76
Lewellen, J. R., 183
Lewis, C., 229
Lile, B., 195
Lile, G., 195
Lindblad, A. H., Jr., 121, 180, 281, 283
Little, D., 92
Lloyd, S., 130, 324, 329, 361
Locke, J., 254
Loeffler, M. H., 24, 25
Longstreet, W. S., 166
Lotan, R. A., 98
Louisell, R. D., 121, 129
Lowery, C. D., 24

Lucas, L. A., 272
Lucking, R., 229, 281

M

MacDonald, R., 260
MacIver, D. J., 130
MacKenzie, A. A., 311
MacNaughton, R. H., 358, 366, 367
Maddox, H., 253
Mager, R., 163
Magney, J., 192, 345
Manning, M. L., 229, 281
Markle, G., 63, 90, 119, 341
Marriott, V., 26
Marshall, C., 173
Martinez, M. E., 23, 276
Marx, R. W., 87
Marzano, R., 32, 60, 123
Mash, R. J., 270
Masia, B., 43, 164
Maslow, A. H., 178, 228
Mason, W. H., 257
Mather, C., 65, 148
Maughan, B., 382
Maxon, S., 386
Mayo, K. E., 47–52
McConnell, J., 329
McCormick, C. B., 343
McCormick, T. E., 228
McDaniel, E., 24
McDaniel, T. R., 357, 361, 382, 384
McEwin, C. K., 91
McGregor, D., 373
McIntyre, D. J., 24
McIntyre, L., 208
McKerron, R. E., 297
McLaughlin, H. J., 24, 25
McQueen, C., 91
Medford, L. F., 17–20
Meek, A., 3
Meichtry, Y., 63, 90, 119, 341
Meinich, S. L., 243
Menzies, T., 36, 296
Merrow, T., 33, 168

Mertens, J. B., 25, 316
Metropolitan Life Survey, 61, 104, 108, 315
Miller, M. S., 26
Miller, V., 24, 25
Miserando, M., 89
Miyagawa, R., 243
Molar, A., 89
Molyran, C. M., 180
Montessori, M., 276
Moore, K., 262, 274, 276
Moreno, R., 5
Morine, G., 74
Morris, R. C., 192
Mortimore, P., 382
Moser, A., 141, 142
Mosston, M., 301, 302
Mullis, I. V. S., 60
Mulhall, P., 25, 87, 316

N

Nash, P., 9, 24
National Center for Education Statistics, 145, 262, 336, 342, 358, 365
National Middle School Association, 76, 108, 122, 141, 180, 232, 280, 284, 382
Neilsen, L., 25, 26
Nelsen, M., 155–158
Nelson, W. W., 3, 9, 26, 123, 228
Nierenberg, G., II, 314
Noddings, N., 123
Norris, W. R., 24
Nuby, J., 228
Nye, B. A., 89

O

Oana, R., 361
Obermier, D., 5, 23, 383
O'Bryan, S., 25
Oddleifson, E., 59, 185
Oliva, P. F., 119
Olson, J., 189
Olson, M. W., 24
O'Neal, M., 77, 256

O'Neil, J., 294
Orlich, D. C., 41, 73
Ornstein, A. C., 253, 315
Orso, J. K., 119, 121, 381
Olweus, D., 354
Osterman, K. F., 356

P

Paget, N., 258
Palardy, M., 378
Parker, F., 12, 23, 254
Parsley, K., 5, 243, 355, 364
Parsons, J., 118, 121, 256, 279
Patterson, W., 33, 42, 60, 180, 228, 323
Payne, C., 238
Paznokas, L., 124–128
Pearson, P. D., 329, 332
Peik, W. E., 24
Perkins, D., 16, 62
Pernel, E., 208
Perrin, J., 185, 187, 190, 194, 215
Perrone, V., 141
Pestalozzi, J., 11
Peterson, P. L., 87
Phelps, P. H., 22, 107, 339, 343, 356, 357
Phillips, D. G., 137
Phillips, D. R., 137, 143
Phillips, G., 254, 357
Piaget, J., 338
Picasso, P., 40
Pittman, B., 378
Pitton, D. E., 175
Plato, 365
Popham, J., 139
Postma, C. H., 272
Postner, G., 141
Potter, D., 181, 195, 207
Pound, L., 193
Price, G. E., 188, 190
Public Agenda, 100

Q

Quinn, R., 189, 215

R

Radz, M., 313
Ramirez, M., 242
Rasch, B. W., 197
Rau, S., 80, 361
Raywid, M. A., 3, 295, 338
Redfield, D. L., 302
Redmon, W. K., 339
Reed, D. F., 227
Regnier, P., 63
Reich, R. B., 326
Reinstein, D., 61, 88
Renner, J. W., 95
Reyes, D. J., 184
Reys, B. J., 180
Reynolds, D., 3, 5, 278
Riban, D. M., 299
Rinne, C. H., 325, 345
Riven, H. N., 243
Robinson, C., 376
Roff, L. A., 331, 376
Romberg, T. A., 88
Rose, L. C., 3, 33, 42, 108, 120, 123, 166, 231, 324, 344, 353, 354, 356
Rosenshine, B. V., 269, 300, 301, 310
Ross, D. D., 232
Ross, S. M., 366
Rotheiser, C., 230
Rothstein, P. R., 254
Rousseau, E. W., 302
Rousseau, J. J., 11
Rowe, M. B., 269, 272, 298
Rowls, M., 24
Rowsey, R. E., 257
Rudick, K., 297
Rudnitsky, A. N., 141
Rutter, M., 382

S

Salend, S. J., 202, 339
Sanders, J. R., 271
Sanders, S. G., 380
Santa, C. M., 25
Santiestebau, A. J., 269

Sapp, G. L., 344, 378
Sautter, R. C., 314, 328, 329
Savage, T. V., 34, 64, 118, 143, 256, 344, 359, 384
Sawyer, D. M., 280
Schane, B., 36
Schaps, E., 354
Scheville, J., 64, 74, 88
Schmidt, P., 25, 227, 228, 231, 238
Schomoker, M., 32, 60, 327
Schumaker, J. B., 260
Selekman, H., 6, 8, 9, 90, 108, 231, 257, 295
Seligmann, J., 323
Sellers, V., 66–72
Seurat, G., 40
Shanahan, T., 260
Shaughnessy, J. M., 139
Shavelson, R. J., 181
Shiman, D. A., 270
Shook, J., 380
Shumsky, A., 24
Simmons, R., 143
Simpson, E. J., 45
Sindt, V. G., 271, 301
Singham, M., 239, 355
Slanton, D., 25
Slavin R., 5, 64, 187, 195, 228, 231, 281, 282, 295
Smelter, R. W., 197
Smith, G. A., 100
Smith, L. C., 25, 331, 355
Smith, M. W., 133
Smith, R. J., 227
Snell, J. L., 354
Snapp, J. C., 62
Snider, M., 77, 256
Sobel, M. A., 275
Socrates, 268
Solomon, S., 108
Spady, W., 230
Stake, R. E., 297
Stallworth, B. J., 109, 230
Starr, I. S., 343
Stefanich, G. P., 5, 65, 74, 119, 159, 255, 324, 360

Steinbeck, J., 3–5
Steinberg, L., 214
Stevens, K. B., 25
Stevens, V. R., 269
Stiggins, R. J., 140, 145, 146, 153, 341
Stokes, L. C., 91, 356
Stone, P., 177, 189
Sweeny, B., 123

T

Taba, H., 31, 74, 75
Tannebaum, M. D., 59
Tanner, L. N., 358–359, 377
Taylor, A. J. R., 278
Teddlie, C., 3, 5, 278
Tesconi, C. A., 232
Thomas, M. D., 33
Thompson, G., 358, 380, 381, 384, 385
Thompson, J. C., 272
Thompson, S., 59, 87, 186
Thrower, E. E., 162
Titus, C., 102, 256
Toben, C., 378
Tomei, L., 140
Tomlinson, C. A., 130
Torrance, E. P., 218
Towers, J. M., 34
Trachtenberg, D., 73, 302
Trollip, S. R., 276
Tsuchida, I., 229
Tuckman, B. W., 145
Tyler, R. W., 28, 32, 63
Tyson, H., 60
Tzv, L., 85

U

Unger, E., 34, 35
Vance, J. H., 274

V

Van Gulick, R. C., 63, 89, 185
Van Horn, R., 388
Van Tassel-Baska, J., 212–213
Vars, G. F., 76, 99, 364
Vasquez, J. A., 284
Venn, J., 202
Volkman, B., 162
Voltz, D. M., 228
Von Glasersfeld, E., 90
Voth R., 254
Vygotsky, L., 12, 16, 22–23

W

Wadsworth, D., 3
Waldron, K. A., 89, 131
Walker, V. N., 88, 91
Wallenhorst, M. P., 89
Walter, L. J., 32, 87, 95
Ward, M. W., 159
Warshaw, M., 344
Wasicsko, M. M., 366
Watson, C., 155–158
Watson, T. S., 354, 355
Weasmer, J., 11, 192
Weaver, R. A., 62, 242, 258, 259
Weber, W. A., 331, 376
Weimer, R. C., 273
Weiner, B., 325
Weisbourd, R., 355
Weissburg, R. P., 355
Weller, L. D., 60
Wellman, B., 23, 32
Wheeler, M., 24, 25
White, R. T., 311
Whitley, C., 47–52
Whitney, E., 144
Wiggins, G., 140, 142
Wilcox, B., 140, 230
Williams, P., 107, 129, 216, 262, 356, 382
Williams-Boyd, P., 369–373
Wilms, W. W., 355
Wilson, A. M., 193
Wilson, B., 356, 357
Wilson, S., 24
Wingfield, A. L., 328
Winton, J. J., 118, 120, 122, 130
Wiske, M. S., 326, 332
Wood, J. A., 356
Woods, A., 11, 192
Woods, R. K., 34
Woodward, A., 60
Wulf, K. M., 36
Wylie, R. E., 277

Y

Yarbough, J. S., 380
Yee, A. H., 284
Yudewitz, G. J., 197

Z

Zaharias, J., 89
Zahorik, J. A., 89
Zlatos, B., 34

Name Index

O'Neil, J., 294
Orlich, D. C., 41, 73
Ornstein, A. C., 253, 315
Orso, J. K., 119, 121, 381
Olweus, D., 354
Osterman, K. F., 356

P

Paget, N., 258
Palardy, M., 378
Parker, F., 12, 23, 254
Parsley, K., 5, 243, 355, 364
Parsons, J., 118, 121, 256, 279
Patterson, W., 33, 42, 60, 180, 228, 323
Payne, C., 238
Paznokas, L., 124–128
Pearson, P. D., 329, 332
Peik, W. E., 24
Perkins, D., 16, 62
Pernel, E., 208
Perrin, J., 185, 187, 190, 194, 215
Perrone, V., 141
Pestalozzi, J., 11
Peterson, P. L., 87
Phelps, P. H., 22, 107, 339, 343, 356, 357
Phillips, D. G., 137
Phillips, D. R., 137, 143
Phillips, G., 254, 357
Piaget, J., 338
Picasso, P., 40
Pittman, B., 378
Pitton, D. E., 175
Plato, 365
Popham, J., 139
Postma, C. H., 272
Postner, G., 141
Potter, D., 181, 195, 207
Pound, L., 193
Price, G. E., 188, 190
Public Agenda, 100

Q

Quinn, R., 189, 215

R

Radz, M., 313
Ramirez, M., 242
Rasch, B. W., 197
Rau, S., 80, 361
Raywid, M. A., 3, 295, 338
Redfield, D. L., 302
Redmon, W. K., 339
Reed, D. F., 227
Regnier, P., 63
Reich, R. B., 326
Reinstein, D., 61, 88
Renner, J. W., 95
Reyes, D. J., 184
Reys, B. J., 180
Reynolds, D., 3, 5, 278
Riban, D. M., 299
Rinne, C. H., 325, 345
Riven, H. N., 243
Robinson, C., 376
Roff, L. A., 331, 376
Romberg, T. A., 88
Rose, L. C., 3, 33, 42, 108, 120, 123, 166, 231, 324, 344, 353, 354, 356
Rosenshine, B. V., 269, 300, 301, 310
Ross, D. D., 232
Ross, S. M., 366
Rotheiser, C., 230
Rothstein, P. R., 254
Rousseau, E. W., 302
Rousseau, J. J., 11
Rowe, M. B., 269, 272, 298
Rowls, M., 24
Rowsey, R. E., 257
Rudick, K., 297
Rudnitsky, A. N., 141
Rutter, M., 382

S

Salend, S. J., 202, 339
Sanders, J. R., 271
Sanders, S. G., 380
Santa, C. M., 25
Santiestebau, A. J., 269

Sapp, G. L., 344, 378
Sautter, R. C., 314, 328, 329
Savage, T. V., 34, 64, 118, 143, 256, 344, 359, 384
Sawyer, D. M., 280
Schane, B., 36
Schaps, E., 354
Scheville, J., 64, 74, 88
Schmidt, P., 25, 227, 228, 231, 238
Schomoker, M., 32, 60, 327
Schumaker, J. B., 260
Selekman, H., 6, 8, 9, 90, 108, 231, 257, 295
Seligmann, J., 323
Sellers, V., 66–72
Seurat, G., 40
Shanahan, T., 260
Shaughnessy, J. M., 139
Shavelson, R. J., 181
Shiman, D. A., 270
Shook, J., 380
Shumsky, A., 24
Simmons, R., 143
Simpson, E. J., 45
Sindt, V. G., 271, 301
Singham, M., 239, 355
Slanton, D., 25
Slavin R., 5, 64, 187, 195, 228, 231, 281, 282, 295
Smelter, R. W., 197
Smith, G. A., 100
Smith, L. C., 25, 331, 355
Smith, M. W., 133
Smith, R. J., 227
Snell, J. L., 354
Snapp, J. C., 62
Snider, M., 77, 256
Sobel, M. A., 275
Socrates, 268
Solomon, S., 108
Spady, W., 230
Stake, R. E., 297
Stallworth, B. J., 109, 230
Starr, I. S., 343
Stefanich, G. P., 5, 65, 74, 119, 159, 255, 324, 360

Steinbeck, J., 3–5
Steinberg, L., 214
Stevens, K. B., 25
Stevens, V. R., 269
Stiggins, R. J., 140, 145, 146, 153, 341
Stokes, L. C., 91, 356
Stone, P., 177, 189
Sweeny, B., 123

T

Taba, H., 31, 74, 75
Tannebaum, M. D., 59
Tanner, L. N., 358–359, 377
Taylor, A. J. R., 278
Teddlie, C., 3, 5, 278
Tesconi, C. A., 232
Thomas, M. D., 33
Thompson, G., 358, 380, 381, 384, 385
Thompson, J. C., 272
Thompson, S., 59, 87, 186
Thrower, E. E., 162
Titus, C., 102, 256
Toben, C., 378
Tomei, L., 140
Tomlinson, C. A., 130
Torrance, E. P., 218
Towers, J. M., 34
Trachtenberg, D., 73, 302
Trollip, S. R., 276
Tsuchida, I., 229
Tuckman, B. W., 145
Tyler, R. W., 28, 32, 63
Tyson, H., 60
Tzv, L., 85

U

Unger, E., 34, 35
Vance, J. H., 274

V

Van Gulick, R. C., 63, 89, 185
Van Horn, R., 388
Van Tassel-Baska, J., 212–213
Vars, G. F., 76, 99, 364
Vasquez, J. A., 284
Venn, J., 202
Volkman, B., 162
Voltz, D. M., 228
Von Glasersfeld, E., 90
Voth R., 254
Vygotsky, L., 12, 16, 22–23

W

Wadsworth, D., 3
Waldron, K. A., 89, 131
Walker, V. N., 88, 91
Wallenhorst, M. P., 89
Walter, L. J., 32, 87, 95
Ward, M. W., 159
Warshaw, M., 344
Wasicsko, M. M., 366
Watson, C., 155–158
Watson, T. S., 354, 355
Weasmer, J., 11, 192
Weaver, R. A., 62, 242, 258, 259
Weber, W. A., 331, 376
Weimer, R. C., 273
Weiner, B., 325
Weisbourd, R., 355
Weissburg, R. P., 355
Weller, L. D., 60

Wellman, B., 23, 32
Wheeler, M., 24, 25
White, R. T., 311
Whitley, C., 47–52
Whitney, E., 144
Wiggins, G., 140, 142
Wilcox, B., 140, 230
Williams, P., 107, 129, 216, 262, 356, 382
Williams-Boyd, P., 369–373
Wilms, W. W., 355
Wilson, A. M., 193
Wilson, B., 356, 357
Wilson, S., 24
Wingfield, A. L., 328
Winton, J. J., 118, 120, 122, 130
Wiske, M. S., 326, 332
Wood, J. A., 356
Woods, A., 11, 192
Woods, R. K., 34
Woodward, A., 60
Wulf, K. M., 36
Wylie, R. E., 277

Y

Yarbough, J. S., 380
Yee, A. H., 284
Yudewitz, G. J., 197

Z

Zaharias, J., 89
Zahorik, J. A., 89
Zlatos, B., 34

Subject Index

A

Ability grouping, 168–171
   academic effects of, 168
   differential treatment, 181
      in-class, 181, 182
      interclass, 182–183
      precautions, 182
Accountability, teacher, 166
Accountability Basics Control Program, 17
Accreditation visit, preparation for, 304–306
Action research, 8, 24–26
Activities learner. *See* Involving students in planning
Adaptive discipline. *See* Discipline
Advance organizers, 185
Advance planning, 23–45, 66–94
Affective objectives, writing, 41–44
Aims, educational, 35
   at Hope High School, 141
Alignment. *See* Curriculum, alignment
All Children Can Learn, 33
Allocated time. *See* Time, allocated
Anatomy of learning unit, 77
Anxiety, 23
Art of teaching, 3–4
Arts education, 69, 215
Assertive discipline. *See* Discipline
Assessment, 116–172
Assignments. *See also* Homework
   for correcting behavior, 341
   for extra credit, 341
At-promise students, 195
At-risk students, 192–195
Attitudes of gifted and talented students, 213–214
Attitudes of parents. *See also* Gallup Poll of Public Attitudes toward the Schools
   of entitlement, 61
   toward children, 332–333
   toward tests, 121
Attitudes of public toward multicultural education, 316
Attitudes of students
   learning, 13, 130
   parent involvement in homework, 105–106
   sense of meaning or purpose of lessons, 296
   subjects, 325–326
   teachers, 329–331
   themselves, 326–329
Attitudes of student teachers, 333
Attitudes of teachers, 3–10
   covering textbooks, 60
   discipline, 357–361
   diversity, 227, 228
   efficacy, 295–296
   experimentation, 20
   Public Law 94-142, 208–209
   school involvement, 108
   students, 4–5
   testing, 139
   workload, 59
Attitudes of novice teachers toward ability to control student behavior, 356. *See also* Gallup Poll of Public Attitudes twoard the Schools
Attitudes toward schools. *See* Gallup Poll of Public Attitudes toward the Schools
Authentic tests, 139–143
Autonomy, teacher, 32

B

Behavior contracts, 339
Behavioral objectives. *See* Performance objectives
Behavior modification, 343–344
Bell curve. *See* Normal distribution curve
Benjamin Franklin Academy, 12
Body movement, 313
Bonus assignments. *See* Assignments, for extra credit
Boredom, preventing, 314–315. *See also* Motivation
Brainstorming, 76
Buffet metaphor, 69

C

California Instructional Video Clearinghouse, 296
California Test of Basic Skills, 189
Cardboard town, 124–128
Cardinal Principles of Secondary Education. *See* Seven Cardinal Principles of Secondary Education
Carnegie Council on Adolescent Development, 4, 42, 59, 76–77, 89, 104, 120, 141, 175, 358,
    staff, 59, 61
Cascade model. *See* Discipline models
Case studies
    Abandoned Adolescence and a Cry for Help, 369
    Assessment and Teaming: Meeting Everyone's Expectation, 155
    Classroom Microsociety, 124
    A Constructivist Approach to Teaching: How Polls Work, 233
    Doing What Makes Sense, 198
    Expecting the Unexpected, 374
    From Empowerment to Leadership: Transforming a Problem into an Opportunity, 303
    Making Connections, 265
    Planning for Student Engagement, 66
    Professional Learning Communities, 47
    The Role of Dispositions in Becoming an Effective Teacher, 333
    Sic Semper "Huh?," 101
    Substituting Involvement for Apathy, 47
Challenging students, 337–338. *See also* Homework
Character education, 164
Cheating, 374–376
Child-centered education. *See* Progressive education era
Citizenship. *See* Service learning programs
Class size, 69, 88–89
Classroom environment. *See* Creativity; Effective schools research; Hidden curriculum
Classroom management, 351–390
Classroom management discipline models. *See* Models
Cognitive domain, 38–41
    list of levels, 43

Cognitive mapping. *See* Concept mapping
Cognitive objectives, writing, 37–41
Collaboration in problem solving, 122, 141
Collateral learning, 15
Communication skills, 290–320
    complex nature of, 293
    diagram of classroom communications, 293
    listening, 293
    in multicultural classrooms, 225–249, 293–295
    need in classroom, 292–293
    number of teacher communications each day, 293
    nonverbal, 311–316
    set induction, 299
    use of examples, 299–300
    use of questions, 300–302, 306–309
    use of repetition, 145, 300
    variety, 300
    verbal skills, 297–311
    voice control, 297–298
Competitive evaluation, 121–123, 128–135
Complexity of teaching, 293
Computer labs, discipline in, 387–388
Computers
    axioms to guide use of, 301–303
    use to individualize, 192
Concept development, 62–64
    role of student in, 14
    role of teacher in, 62
Concept mapping, 64
Concepts. *See also* Constructivism
    role in learning, 16, 90
Confrontations, avoiding, 385–386
Connecticut, 34
Connections. *See also* Personal connections
    with former experiences, 11, 63
    with students' lives, 75, 80
    among subjects, 101–104
Consistency, teacher, 387
Constructivism, xiv. *See also* Constructivist teachers, role of
    definition, x
    history of, 20
Constructivist beliefs
    about learning, 14
    about motivation, 14

about purpose of learning, 13
about role of teachers, 16
Constructivist lesson on polls, 233–238
Constructivist teachers, role of, 15–16
Content. *See also* Concepts; Content generalizations
    guidelines for selecting, 64–65, 73–75
    importance in learning, 14
Content generalizations. *See* Concepts
Contracts, 339–340
    behavior contracts, 339
    contingency contracts, 339
    grade contracts, 340
    power to motivate, 339
    sample contract, 340
Control theory, 382
Cooperation versus competition, 12, 14
Cooperative learning, 16, 18, 20–21
    versus traditional grouping, 180
Cooperative planning, 33
Cooperative problem solving, 122, 141
Corporal punishment, 367–368
Corpuscular theory, 13
Creativity, 13, 14, 123, 213–214
Criterion-referenced tests, 186
Cultural dissonance, 232
Cultural diversity. *See* Multicultural education
Cultural expectations. *See* Cultural dissonance; Multicultural education
Curriculum
    alignment, 139–143
    coherence, 28, 65
    committees, involving parents, 61,
    components, 77–78
    definition, 92
    determiners, 59–61
    hidden, 314
Curriculum models. *See* Unit plan
Curriculum teaching, 139
    Taba's inverted model, 74–75

D

Daily lesson plans, 85–113
    appropriate length, 111
    characteristics of effective, 91
    need for structure, 91–92
    sample, 109–111
Daily planning, 76, 85–113
    traditional strategies, 87
    use of guidelines, 89
Demographics affecting education, 227–228
Desire to learn, 13. *See also* Lifelong learning
Developmental time. *See* Time, developmental
Dialogueing, 23, 60
Didactic teaching, 99
Differential treatment of students, unintential, 181
Discipline
    definition, 356
    need for, 357
    relation to instruction, 357–358
    trends in, 359
Discipline models and theories, 362
    adaptive discipline, 382
    assertive discipline model, 353–354, 366
    authoritarian strategies, 357, 377
    behavioral modification, 363, 378
    cascade model, 380
    continuum of views, 362
    cooperative approach, 362
    corporal punishment, 367–368
    corrective discipline, 382
    faculty psychology, 362–363
    focus on learning, 361
    group dynamics model, 379
    group management theory, 365–366
    group process strategies, 377
    instructional strategies, 377
    Maslow's hierarchy of needs, 368
    McGregor's Theories X and Y, 373–374
    personal social growth model, 379
    phenomenology, 363
    preventive, 380–381
    psychodynamic, 378–379
    reality therapy, 363–364
    stimulus–response psychology, 363
    training, 378,
    using, 362
Discipline
    in computer lab, 387–388
    trends in, 379–380
Discipline problems, handling, 384–388

Discovery learning, 273–276. *See also* Inquiry
        learning
    advantages, 274
    concept development, 275
    definition, 273
    disadvantages, 274–275
    teacher's role, 275
    use of, 276
Discussion, use of, 96–97, 185–186
Discussion tests. *See* Essay tests
Disequilibration theory, 324–325
Dispositions, 333–335
Diversions, using, 101–104
Diversity. *See* Multicultural education

E

Education reform, practices or elements of, 64
Effective schools research, 315–316
Efficacy, teacher. *See* Attitudes of teachers
Emotions
    effects on learning, 297
    empathizing, 23
Ends–means model, Tyler's, 87
Engaged time. *See* Time, engaged
Engaging students, 265
Enthusiasm, teacher, 332, 383
Equilibration theory, 337–338
Essay tests
    advantages, 143
    limitations, 143
    versus objective tests, 143
    scoring, 150
Ethics, teacher, 112
Evaluation, 116–136
Expectations, need to communicate, 33, 91, 339
Experiential education, 11
Explanation tests, 144
Extra credit, assignments for earning, 131
Extracurricular activities, 315
Extrinsic motivation, 14
Eye contact, 312

F

Faculty development, 47–52, 76–77, 303–306
Faculty psychology, 362–363
Fairness, 387

Father of child-centered education, 23
Father of progressive education, 23
Fear. *See* Anxiety; Threats
Feedback, 312
Field trips, 97–98
Follow-up. *See* Homework
Formative evaluation, 119–120, 341
Frame of reference, building, 254
Franklin Academy, 14
Free reading programs, 193
Freedom, of teacher. *See* Autonomy, teacher

G

Gallup Poll of Public Attitudes toward the Schools,
        42, 108, 120–121
Games. *See* Simulation games
Generalizing, example of, 159
Generalizations, content. *See* Concepts;
        Constructivism
Geographic isolation, 66–72
Gifted education, history of, 211–212
Gifted learners, 18, 211–215
    behavior, 18
    curriculum for, 212–215
    definitions, 212
    learning styles of, 190–191, 215
    opposition to programs for, 211
    projects for, 250–251, 213–214
    research on, 214–215
    techniques for teaching, 212–215
Goals, educational, 35–36
Grade contracts, 183, 340
Grading
    changing student's grade, 134
    systems, 131–132
    versus testing, 130
Group dynamics discipline model, 379
Grouping. *See* Ability grouping
Group management theory, 365–367
Guided discovery, 273. *See also* Inquiry learning
Guided education. *See* Mastery learning

H

Hidden curriculum, 313–314
Higher-order thinking levels, promoting, 73–74
High expectations for minorities, 243

High-stakes testing, 33
Homework, 104–111
    guidelines for assignments, 105–107
    need for follow-up, 107
    obstacles, 105
    parent involvement, 104–105
    to promote creativity, 106
Humor, 331–332

I

Identity education, 355
Imagination, developing. *See* Creativity
Inclusion, 197, 202
Index cards, use in planning, 111
Individualized Educational Programs (IEPs), 207–208
Individualizing education, 73–224
Individualizing instruction, 173–224
Information processing model, 183–186
Inquiry learning, 262–264. *See also* Discovery learning
Instructional models and theories, 183–192
Interclass ability grouping. *See* Ability grouping
Interdisciplinary team planning, 60
Internal motivation. *See* Intrinsic learning
Internet
    involving students, 95–100, 104–108
    power of, 11
    world education, 40
Internet web quests, 69
Intrinsic learning, 328
Involvement of parents. *See* Parent involvement
Involving students in planning, 65, 66–72

J

Jigsaw method, 21
Jigsaw II, 21

K

Kansas State Teachers Association, 3
Kindness, 3. *See also* Respect
Knowledge, nature of, 14
Knowledge base, 269

L

Learning community, 354
Learning cycle theory, 95
Learning-disabled students, 206–207
Learning for mastery, 186–187
Learning-style inventory, 177
Learning styles. *See* Matching learning and teaching styles
Learning styles model, 188
Learning theories. *See* Curriculum; Instructional models and theories
Learning unit. *See* Unit plan
Lecture, 253–258
    appropriate uses, 253–254
    implementation, 253–258
    improving, 255–258
    stimulus variation, 256
    strengths, 256
    structuring, 102–103
    tempo, 255–256
    vocabulary, 256–257
    weaknesses, 254
Lesson plans, daily. *See* Daily lesson plans; Daily planning
Lesson plans, sample, 109–111
Lesson study, 355
Lifelong learning, 8
Long-range planning. *See* Planning, long-range
Long-term memory, 185
Lounge lizards, 245
Low achievers. *See* Underachievers

M

Mainstreaming, 197, 202
Management, classroom, 351–392
Mapping, cognitive. *See* Concept mapping
Maslow's hierarchy of needs, 177–178
Mastery learning, 186–187
Matching learning and teaching styles, 187–192
McGregor's Theories X and Y, 373
Measurement, versus evaluation, 118–119
Mentally challenged students, 204–205. *See also* Trainable retarded students, teaching
Metacognition, 185
Metaphors, 69
Metropolitan Life Survey, 10, 61, 104, 108
Microcosm of society, school as, 22, 124–128

Middle-level education, priority of events, National Middle School Association Delphi Report, 7
Minorities, ethnic. *See* Multicultural education
Modeling, 71. *See also* Tutoring
Model of School Learning, A, 186
Models. *See also* Classroom management; Discipline models and theories
   behavior modification model, 378
   Block's learning for mastery model, 186–187
   Carroll's mastery learning model, 186–187
   information processing, 184
   instructional models and theories, 183–191
   learning cycle theory, 95
   matching learning and teaching styles, 176–181, 194–198
   personal-social growth model, 379
   psychodynamic model, 378–379
   Taba's inverted curriculum model, 74
   training model, 378
Montessori method, 276
Moral education. *See* Character education
Motivation, 321–350. *See also* Behavior modification
   definitions, 321–350
   extrinsic versus intrinsic, 323–324
   list of strategies, 330
   in multicultural classrooms, 324–325
   power of case studies to motivate, 258
   power of cooperative learning to motivate, 280–282
   power of discovery learning to motivate, 274
   power of grades, 341
   power of inquiry learning to motivate, 263
   power of lecture to motivate, 254
   power of questioning to motivate, 268, 272
   power of simulation games to motivate, 276–277
   power of tutoring to motivate, 260–261
   role of media, 271
Multicultural education, 225–249
   community link with, 244
   definition, 227
   dos and don'ts list, 213–215, 239–241
   necessity, 227
   number of concepts appropriate for multicultural classes, 70
   positive approach, need for, 228
   role of teacher, 238–239
   selecting materials, 241–242
   use of case studies, 242
   using process to praise diversity, 243
Multicultural textbooks, 71
Multiple-choice tests, 150
Multiple intelligences, 176–179
Multiple Intelligences Test Inventory, 179

N

Names of students, use of, 383
National Assessment of Educational Progress, 5
National Board Certified Early Adolescence/Generalist Teachers, 91
National Board for Professional Teaching Standards, 34
National Center for Education Statistics, 358
National certification, 34
National Council for Social Studies, 33, 35
National Council of Teachers of English, 33, 35
National Council of Teachers of Mathematics, 33, 35
National Education Summit, 33
National Middle School Association priority events, 5, 24, 33, 60, 89, 108, 122, 141, 180
   list of, 7
National Science Teachers Association, 33, 35
National standards, 33, 123
Naturalist philosophy, 11
Negotiating meaning, 12
New York State Regents Exam, 122
No Child Left Behind Act, 33, 53
Noncompetitive evaluation, 129–130. *See also* Criterion-referenced tests
Nonverbal communication, 358, 358
Normal distribution curve, 123, 127–128
Note cards. *See* Index cards

O

Objectives. *See* Performance objectives
Objective tests, 150
Ongoing assessment. *See* Progressive reporting

Oral reports, 98–99
Outcome-based teaching, 34

P

Parent involvement, 26, 61, 76–77, 104–111, 341–343, 381–382. *See also* Individualized Educational Programs
Parent-Teacher Organization (PTO), 18, 19
Parents, working with, 71, 133
Pauses. *See* Silence
Pedagogical content knowledge, 355
Perceptual screen, 185
Performance objectives, 30–56
   affective
   affective domain, 41–44
   cognitive domain, 37–41
   misuse of, 52–53
   psychomotor domain, 44–46
   use in content selection, 32–34
Performance terms, list of, 37
Personalizing teaching, 15, 33, 42
Personal connections, 90
Personal experiences, using, 70
Personal-social growth discipline model, 378
Perspectives, students'. *See* Attitudes of students
Phi Delta Kappa. *See* Gallup Poll of the American Public's Attitudes toward the Schools
Physically impaired students, 204
Place-based education, 100
Place Called School, A, 41
Planning
   daily, 85–113
   long-range, 57–84
   for multicultural classes. *See* Multicultural education
Pluralism, cultural. *See* Multicultural education
Portfolios, 140–143
Poverty, 61
Power
   and reform, 10
   sharing, 8
PowerPoint, 21, 89
Praise. *See* Reinforcement
Praxis, 25
Preadolescence, 6
Preventive discipline, 380

Priority of events for middle schools. *See* National Middle School Association priority events
Private talks, 386–387
Probability curve. *See* Normal distribution curve
Problem solving, 6, 23, 122, 141. *See* Discovery learning; Inquiry learning
Process evaluation, 78
Product evaluation, 78
Professional behavior, 245
Professional development. *See* Faculty development
Profession, teaching, 1–29
Programs (IEPs), in educating at-risk students. *See* At-risk students
Progressive education era, 12
Progressive reporting, 120–121
Psychodynamic discipline model, 378–379
Psychological disequilibrium, 16
Psychomotor domain objectives
   list of levels, 45
   writing, 45–46
Public Agenda 2000, 100
Public Law 94-142, 195–196, 208–209
Public Law 101-476, 196, 209–211
Public opinion. *See* Gallup Poll of Public Attitudes toward the School
Public reprimand, 365–366, 384
Punishment, use as a motivator, 33. *See also* Corporal punishment; Public reprimand; Ridicule, effects of; Threats, effects on learning
Purpose of schools, 12. *See also* Seven Cardinal Principles of Secondary Education
Purposes, statement of. *See* Aims, educational; Goals, educational; Performance objectives

Q

Questioning, 268. *See also* Wait time
   student-posed questions, 63
Questioning grid, 309
Questions, 161–165
   empirical, 306–307
   evaluative, 307
   information-process, 308
   need for specificity, 152
   productive, 308

Questions *(continued)*
    response-clue, 308–309
    reproductive, 308
Quilt metaphor, 69
Quizzes, 193

R

Reality therapy, 364
Reflection, xi, 9, 26
Regents Exam. *See* New York State Regents Exam
Reinforcement, 310. *See also* Behavior modification
Relationships. *See* Connections
Remediation. *See* Mastery learning
Reprimand, public. *See* Public reprimand
Research. *See* Action research
Respect, 5
Returning tests, 168
Review, 310–311
Rewards, use in teaching, 343
Ridicule, effects of, 384
Rite of Passage Experience, 140
Risk-free climate, 9, 23
Risk taking, 91
Role modeling, 356
Role of school. *See* Goals; Purpose of schools
Role of teachers in education reform, 25–26
Roll of Thunder, Hear My Cry, 72
Rural schools, teaching in, 66–72

S

Scholastic Aptitude Test, 5, 89
Secondary education, purpose of. *See* Seven Cardinal Principles of Secondary Education
Self-concepts of students, 122, 194, 355
Self-respect, teaching, 383
Sensory-deprived students, teaching, 205–206
Service learning, 21–23
Service learning programs, 100
Seven Cardinal Principles of Secondary Education, 35
Short-term memory, 185
Silence, 313
Silent curriculum. *See* Hidden curriculum; Nonverbal communication

Simulation games, 276
Slow learners. *See* Underachievers
Space, managing, 336–337
Special education, 195–220
    definition, 195
Special Study Panel on Education Indicators for the National Center for Education Statistics, 225
Standard error, 129
Standardized tests, 193. *See also* Scholastic Aptitude Test
Stanine scores, 128–129
Steinbeck, John, 3–4
Stimulus–response psychology, 363
Structure of knowledge, 15
Student attitudes. *See* Attitudes of students
Student-centered education. *See* Progressive education era
Student-initiated questions, 63
Student opinions, using, 339
Student-teaching, 198–202, 333–335
Study unit. *See* Unit plan
Styles, matching. *See* Matching learning and teaching styles
Summative evaluation, 121

T

Taba's inverted curriculum model, 74–75
Take-home tests, 121
Taxonomies, educational, 102
    affective domain, 163–164
    cognitive domain, 154, 158–163
Teachable moments, 303
Teacher autonomy. *See* Autonomy, teacher
Teacher efficacy. *See* Attitudes of teachers
Teacher perceptions. *See* Efficacy studies
Teacher qualities, 3–4
Teacher–student relationships, 265
Teachers, importance of, 3, 25
Teaching to the test, 142
Teaching strategies, 250–289
    case study, 258–259
    cooperative learning, 280–284
    discovery learning, 273–276
    inquiry learning, 262, 268
    lecture, 253–258

need for repertoire, 252
questioning, 268–272
simulation games, 276–280
story telling, 280
tutoring, 260–262
Tea kettle example of generalizing, 159
Team playing, 60, 91
Team teaching, 33, 91, 155–158
Teams–Games–Tournaments (TGT), 183
Technology, use to motivate, 336
Temporary nature of knowing, 15
Testing, 137–172
    administration, 165, 166–167
    alternatives, 151
    anxiety, 166
    authentic, 139
    construction, 141–149
    essay, 148–150,
    scoring, 150, 167–168
    sequencing test items, 139
    testing the test, 409
Test items. *See also* Essay tests
    fill-in-the-blank, 153
    matching, 153–154
    multiple-choice, 150–152
    objective, 144–145
    returning, 168
    scoring, 167
    take-home test, 121
Tests, types of, 143–145
    compare and contrast, 144
    essay, 143–144
    explanation, 144
    objective, 144–145
    situation, 144
Textbooks
    appropriate use in curriculum planning, 32, 95
    failure to cover concepts, 73–74, 88
    history of effect on curriculum, 88
    influence on curriculum, 95–96
    low cognitive level, 60
    overuse, 60, 65
    selection guidelines, 65
Texas Assessment of Academic Skills, 51
Threats, effects on learning, 384

Time
    allocated, 88, 93
    developmental, 88, 93
    engaged, 88, 93
    for teachers, 93–94
Time management strategies for teachers, 93
Trainable retarded students, teaching, 205
Training model for classroom discipline, 378
Transescence, 292
Tutoring, 260–262
    achievement, effects on, 260–261
    benefits of, 260–261
    developing tutoring lesson, 261
    multicultural considerations, 261
    using grouping, 260–261
Tyler's ends–means model, 32

U

Underachievers, 215–218
    characteristics of, 216–217
    helping, 216–217
    identifying, 216
    learning styles of, 216–217
Unintentional differential treatment of students of low expectations, 181
Unit plan 75–80
    components, 77
    sample unit plans, 78–79

V

Value, definition of, 43
Values education, 42–43
Verbs for performance objectives, 37
Videotaping, using, 66–72
Vision, role in curriculum planning, 60

W

Wait time, advantages of increasing, 269
Whole child, education for, 11, 32
Woodcock-Johnson achievement test, 189
Working memory, 185
Writing, 9

Z

Zone of proximal development, 12